PRINCIPLES
OF
MANAGEMENT
SCIENCE

With Applications
to
Executive Decisions

HARVEY M. WAGNER

School of Organization and Management
Yale University;
Consultant to the Firm
McKinsey & Company, Inc.

Second Edition

PRINCIPLES OF MANAGEMENT SCIENCE

With Applications to Executive Decisions

Prentice-Hall, Inc., Englewood Cliffs, New Jersey

Wagner, Harvey M.
   Principles of management science, 2nd ed.

   1. Management Science.   I Title
74-29417
ISBN: 0-13-709535-X

Current printing (last digit):

10   9   8   7   6   5   4   3

PRENTICE-HALL INTERNATIONAL, INC., *London*
PRENTICE-HALL OF AUSTRALIA, PTY., LTD., *Sydney*
PRENTICE-HALL OF CANADA, LTD., *Toronto*
PRENTICE-HALL OF INDIA PRIVATE LTD., *New Delhi*
PRENTICE-HALL OF JAPAN, INC., *Tokyo*

To Ruthie,
Whose Interest in Principles
Deserves Appreciating

Contents

Preface

This book is written primarily for college students who have no previous background in management science and who intend careers as administrators, executives, managers, or consultants in business, nonprofit enterprises, or government. The book is used in half-year or full-year introductory courses for undergraduates or graduates in business, economics, engineering, liberal arts, and public administration curricula.

The central goal of the book is to answer the question, "What are the *fundamental ideas* of management science?" The text does not presuppose any *advanced* training in business administration, industrial engineering, mathematics, statistics, probability theory, or economics. Therefore, the main ideas do not rely on the reader's being expert in these areas. The text does assume, however, that the reader is not entirely naive about such subjects.

PRINCIPAL OBJECTIVES

Beginning students frequently ask, "What must I learn about management science if I intend to become an executive rather than a specialist?" and "What must I learn about management science given that I want to apply it to real problems?" Regrettably, a single introductory management science course cannot completely answer either question. But such a course can better answer the first rather than the second question.

In the context of these two questions, the book's principal objectives are

- To introduce the important ideas in management science which are both fundamental and long lasting.
- To provide those students not going beyond a single introductory course with enough understanding and confidence to appreciate the strengths and inherent limitations of the management science approach.
- To prepare and motivate future specialists to continue in their study by having an insightful overview of management science.
- To demonstrate the cohesiveness of management science methodology.

Students who have been assigned this book as a text have increased their skills in formulating and building formal models of complex decision environments, in perceiving the critical issues to be resolved, and in isolating the basic phenomena that comprise the key elements of real situations. When faced with actual managerial problems, these students have learned from their grasp of the analytic fundamentals how to achieve sound and incisive evaluations of the important alternatives and how to attain the crucial insights.

COVERAGE AND EMPHASIS

Successful practitioners of management science are quick to point out that characterizing the subject by means of its component mathematical techniques can be highly misleading. Their reason is that real-life decisions do not arise with technical labels attached, such as *linear programming* or *risk analysis simulation*. A manager must be able to recognize what existing methods, if any, can yield worthwhile insights for taking appropriate courses of action. Granting the truth of these observations, we comment on why we organized the text by standard mathematical techniques rather than by various management problems.

Accumulated teaching experience of hundreds of instructors indicates that beginning students with only limited time for this subject better understand the model-building approach when they can *readily* discern the formal structure of the decision problem. Although realism is sacrificed in the classroom by adopting this pedagogic view, students so trained effectively bridge the gap between the techniques and their applications.

To warn students, however, of the trap of thinking that management science is synonymous with a collection of mathematical formulas, we take pains to *verbalize* the contribution that each model and technique make to decision-making. Students previously trained in science, engineering, or mathematics sometimes are surprised and even impatient that the text material is not written in a succinct mathematical style. But we suggest that thinking beyond the details of the formulas to the deeper significance of each approach, over the long pull, better prepares future managers and analysts to make successful applications.

Obviously, we had to exercise considerable judgment in selecting topics and in choosing the depth of treatment. In this regard, we were influenced considerably by more than 20 years of first-hand experience in applying management science to actual situations in business and government. The examples in the text often are scaled-down versions of real problems that we have encountered. The specific models that we chose, their complexity, and sequential development all reflect our observations of how most students come to appreciate and understand the pivotal concepts in management science.

Throughout, the book puts into focus the value of information derived from a management science solution and attempts to give an accurate representation of how a hypothetical example would be applied in a real situation. The text develops the student's skill in formulating and building models and, specifically, in translating a verbal description of a decision problem into an equivalent mathematical model. The book also explains the importance and the degree of severity of a model's assumptions, the connection between the starting assumptions and the derived results, and the seriousness of the assumptions for practical purposes. Finally, the text demonstrates by means of important examples the process and usefulness of constructing analogies, finding multiple interpretations of models, and deriving significant special cases from general models.

MATHEMATICS PREREQUISITES

The calculus is employed only in Chap. 15. Nevertheless, much of the text assumes a mathematical sophistication comparable to that acquired in standard college-level introductory calculus or a no-nonsense finite mathematics course. Elementary probability theory is first needed in Chap. 12.

SUGGESTIONS TO STUDENTS

If you have taken courses in both the calculus and elementary statistics or probability theory, you will recall that you could understand much of the calculus text without much help from the instructor whereas you needed the guidance of the instructor to fully understand the statistics or probability theory text. This is a very common occurrence among students. You will find management science to be more like statistics and probability theory than the calculus in that you can expect, as a matter of course, to rely on your instructor to amplify the ideas and techniques in this book. Since the concepts can be intricate, you may have to study several pages before comprehending the full idea. So be prepared for patient reading and some rereading. We have tried to avoid giving numerical examples that are so *misleadingly* simple that you are not sufficiently prepared for the exercises at the end of each chapter. As a result, you will find it advantageous to examine carefully the numerical illustrations in the chapters.

If your instructor assigns the exercises at the back of the chapters, do not wait until the last minute to begin the problems. The numerical exercises, although straightforward, can be fatiguing if attempted in a single evening session. Most students find that formulation problems require a "gestation period," so allow yourself a few days to ponder such exercises.

Surprisingly, it is difficult to write a *verbal* description of a management science problem that is completely unambiguous. More than once, thoughtful students have discovered vague wording in problems that we had assigned previously to other classes that experienced no difficulty in obtaining the intended solutions. Consequently, if you believe that an exercise displays a troublesome ambiguity, try to resolve it in a sensible way and make explicit on your paper the specific assumption that you adopted. The purpose of the exercises (namely, to give you practice in mathematical formulation) is well served by this procedure.

SUGGESTIONS TO INSTRUCTORS

The topic coverage has been purposely designed to give you considerable flexibility in choosing the subjects that you want to stress. The logical organization of the chapters is shown in Exhibit A.

In a one-term introductory course on mathematical programming models, you can include Chaps. 1 through 8, 10, 11, and 17, skipping all the starred (*) sections and optional material in smaller print. In a one-term introductory course on probabilistic models, you can include Chaps. 1, 12 through 17, also skipping optional and advanced material.

To assist you in selecting other combinations, the "Immediate Predecessors" of each chapter are shown in Exhibit B. In general, the chapters become progressively more difficult. Thus, although you could cover dynamic programming (Chaps. 8, 9, and 10) prior to linear programming, the reverse sequence ordinarily would be preferable, because the dynamic programming chapters assume the student already is somewhat familiar with multivariate constrained optimization models and solution techniques. *Any material designated by an asterisk or appearing between the symbols* ▶ *and* ◀ *and set in smaller print may be skipped without loss of continuity.*

The second edition has been written to make certain topics more accessible to beginning students and to update the coverage where a subject's fundamental ideas have changed. Specifically, the *major* revisions occur in Chaps. 6, 7, 10, 11, 12, and 16. The material on networks in Chaps. 6 and 7 is now organized so that each algorithm is presented in conjunction with the model's description and application. A slower-paced exposition of dynamic programming models is given in Chap. 10 the new material includes worked out numerical examples to clarify the approach. The explanation of models and methods for integer programming in Chap. 11 is extensively rewritten to reflect computational experience of recent years; approaches that have not worked well in practice are omitted. The material on stochastic programming in Chap. 12 is revised to be more suitable for assignment in an introductory course. Finally, the exposition of computer simulation in Chap. 16 is expanded and reorganized to give greater prominence to the model-building aspects of the approach.

The book contains more than 600 exercises, many of which have multiple parts. New exercises are added to most chapters in the second edition. The problems are grouped into three categories. The Review Exercises are keyed closely to the text and determine whether the student has understood the conceptual developments. The Formulation Exercises consist of "word problems" and test whether the student can translate a verbal statement into a precise mathematical model. The Computational Exercises provide practice problems for applying algorithms. There is "redundancy" in the multiple parts of many exercises, and consequently, you should examine the parts to ascertain which ones you want to assign.

This text does not treat the topics of deterministic and stochastic dynamic programming over an unbounded horizon, continuous nonlinear programming, transform methods and imbedded Markov chains for queuing models, and gives only a brief discussion of stochastic programming and network algorithms. An

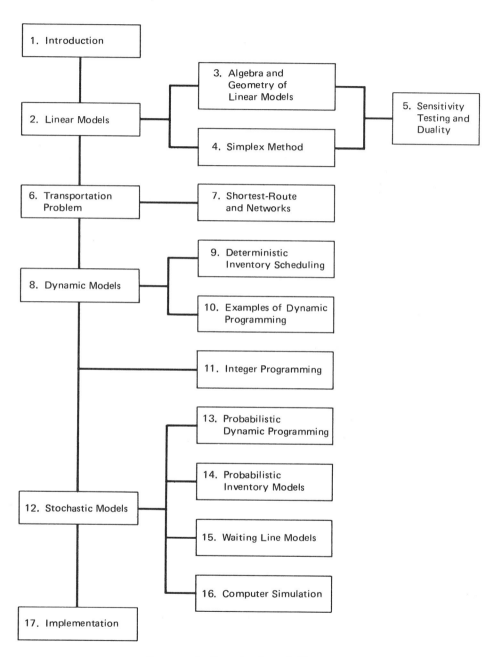

EXHIBIT A. Organization of Chapters.

	CHAPTER	Immediate Predecessors
2	Linear Models	1
3	Algebra and Geometry of Linear Models	2
4	Simplex Method	2
5	Sensitivity Testing and Duality	3, 4
6	Transportation Problem	2, 5
7	Shortest-Route and Other Network Models	6
8	Dynamic Models	1, (7)
9	Deterministic Inventory Schedule	8
10	Examples of Dynamic Programming	8
11	Integer Programming	7
12	Stochastic Models	5
13	Probabilistic Dynamic Programming	10, 12
14	Probabilistic Inventory Models	(9), 12
15	Waiting Line Models	12
16	Computer Simulation	12
17	Implementation	1

NOTE: Chaps. 12 through 16 require probability theory.
Chap. 15 requires differential and integral calculus.
( ) indicates desirable but not essential.

EXHIBIT B

extensive coverage of these topics at an introductory level can be found in my *Principles of Operations Research*, Prentice-Hall, 1975. Important replacement models are included in the dynamic programming chapters. Game theory has been omitted. In practicing operations research, we have found that game theory does not contribute any *managerial insights* to real competitive and cooperative decision-making behavior that are not *already* familiar to church-going poker players who regularly read the Wall Street Journal. (This is not to say, however, that the intricacies of real competitive economic behavior, such as price wars, advertising campaigns, mergers, and acquisitions, have yet become phenomena fully understood by management scientists.)

ACKNOWLEDGMENTS

Over the years since the first draft of this text was written, I have received many helpful suggestions from students and their instructors who have used the book. The list of persons who have provided sage counsel is now far too long to record here, but I must offer special thanks at least to Richard W. Cottle (Stanford), Eric V. Denardo (Yale), Hamilton Emmons (Case Western Reserve), Donald Erlenkotter (University of California, Los Angeles), Charles H. Falkner (University of Wisconsin), Arthur M. Geoffrion (University of California, Los Angeles), Richard B. Hoffman (Arthur Young & Co., Washington, D.C.), Charles L. Hubbard (Georgia State), Charles H. Kriebel (Carnegie Mellon), Rudolph P. Lamone (University of Maryland), Richard P. O'Neill (Louisiana State), Alan J. Rolfe (IDA, Arlington, VA), and Matthew J. Sobel (Yale). I am deeply indebted to Professor Robert E. Machol (Northwestern) whose friendly advice prompted many of the revisions in this new edition. And I again want to acknowledge Professor Arthur F. Veinott, Jr. (Stanford) who has continued to deeply influence my own thinking about the principles of management science.

In great measure, the managerial relevance of the book has been enhanced through my association since 1960 with McKinsey & Co., as a Consultant to the Firm, and particularly through the personal guidance of Dr. David B. Hertz, Douglas Watson, Warren M. Cannon, and D. Ronald Daniel.

A fine Instructor's Manual for the second edition was patiently prepared by Arthur S. Estey and Richard A. Ehrhardt (both of Yale), and a debt of gratitude remains to John Chamberlin, John M. Harrison, and Michael Saunders who wrote the previous Manual.

The secretarial skill and encouraging dispositions of Ms. Sheila Hill (Stanford) and Ms. Marcia Wheeler (Yale) triumphed admirably over the seemingly never-ending strain of typing redrafts and meeting deadlines for the first edition. The limited pleasures of struggling over rewrites for the second edition were shared by Ms. Wilma Golden, Ms. Sara Martin, and Ms. Ellen Mester (all of Yale), at last count. And we all can be thankful for the unsparingly, but deftly, employed red pencils of editors Mr. Will Harriss (RAND) and Mr. Kenneth Cashman (Prentice-Hall).

HARVEY M. WAGNER

New Haven, Connecticut

PRINCIPLES
OF
MANAGEMENT
SCIENCE

With Applications
to
Executive Decisions

CONTENTS

CHAPTER 1

The Art and Science
of Executive Decisions

1.1 ONCE UPON A TIME...

The goddess Athena sprang forth full-grown and in full armor from the brow
of Zeus. That is not quite the way *management science* made its debut on the con-
temporary scene, although there is a passing resemblence. Some of the subject's
central ideas trace as far back as the 18th and 19th centuries; but at that time
the prospects seemed dim that they would ever become practical tools for decision
makers. Other important principles were discovered early in this century. The
body of knowledge that is summarized in this text, however, by and large emerged
during and since World War II.

It is not coincidental that computer technology developed in a parallel fashion.
There would be negligible interest in management science beyond that generated
within the fraternity of applied mathematicians were it not for the staggering
analytic power made available by high-speed electronic computers. This augmentation of human intellect has turned theoretical findings into here-and-now
results. To illustrate, experienced management scientists do not hesitate anymore
to construct mathematical systems containing a 1000 simultaneous equations—
only a few decades ago, thinking of solving such large-scale systems was as "blue-
sky" as proposing to send men into outer space.

1.2 BY ANY OTHER NAME

Synonyms for the term *management science* are about as numerous and tenaciously
adhered to as dialects of English. A frequent American substitute is *operations
research*, and you will soon see that we use the two names interchangeably throughout this book. The British prefer *operational research*, and the subject used to be

1

called *operations analysis* at Yale. But there is no point in listing further designations, because, as a beginning student, your attention is better directed toward substantive matters.

For convenience, and with reasonable accuracy, you can simply define operations research as a scientific approach to problem-solving for executive management. An application of management science involves:

- Constructing mathematical, economic, and statistical descriptions or models of decision and control problems to treat situations of complexity and uncertainty.
- Analyzing the relationships that determine the probable future consequences of decision choices, and devising appropriate measures of effectiveness in order to evaluate the relative merit of alternative actions.

It is sometimes believed that operations research refers to the constant monitoring of an organization's ongoing activities—and, in fact, decision and control problems often do concern certain daily "operations" of the organization. Examples of this sort include production scheduling and inventory control, facility maintenance and repair, and staffing of service facilities, to name a few applications.

But many management science studies treat other kinds of decisions that bear on daily operations only indirectly. These studies usually have a planning orientation. Illustrations include determining the breadth of a firm's product line, developing a long-term program for plant expansion, designing a network of warehouses for a wholesale distribution system, and entering a new business by merger or acquisition.

Better decisions in a complex and uncertain environment. A preferable term to describe the subject of this book is *decision analysis*. An emphasis on making decisions or taking actions is central to all management science applications.

Decision analysis separates a large-scale problem into its subparts, each of which is simpler to manipulate and diagnose. After the separate elements are carefully examined, the results are synthesized to give insights into the original problem. You may wonder why such complex decision-making problems arise in the first place.

One reason is that in today's economy, technological, environmental, and competitive factors typically interact in a complicated fashion. For example, a factory production schedule has to take account of customer demand (tempered by the likelihood of a price-cut by competitors), requirements for raw materials and intermediate inventories, the capacities of equipment, the possibility of equipment failures, and manufacturing process restrictions. It is not easy to make up a schedule that is both realistic and economical.

Other reasons for complexity in real decision-making situations are that the organization (perhaps only half-knowingly) may be pursuing inconsistent goals, the responsibility and authority for making the required decisions may be greatly diffused within the organization, and the economic environment in which the company operates may be uncertain.

Distinguishing characteristics. There are many ways to approach management problems, and most of these ways are related. Certainly, there is no clear boundary line isolating the solutions derived by professional operations researchers from those derived by such people as industrial engineers, or economists specializing in economic planning, or accountants or financial analysts oriented toward management information systems. But most management science applications possess certain distinguishing characteristics. Specifically, a suggested approach to a particular problem must contain all the following qualities before we would call it a management science approach:

i. *A Primary Focus on Decision-Making.* The principal results of the analysis must have direct and unambiguous implications for executive action.

ii. *An Appraisal Resting on Economic Effectiveness Criteria.* A comparison of the various feasible actions must be based on measurable values that unequivocally reflect the future well-being of the organization. In a commercial firm, these measured quantities typically include variable costs, revenues, cash flow, and rate of return on incremental investment. A recommended solution must have evaluated the tradeoffs and have struck a suitable balance among these sometimes conflicting factors.

iii. *Reliance on a Formal Mathematical Model.* The procedures for manipulating the data should be so explicit that they can be described to another analyst, who in turn would derive the same results from the same data.

iv. *Dependence on an Electronic Computer.* This characteristic is not really a desideratum but rather a requirement necessitated by either the complexity of the mathematical model, the volume of data to be manipulated, or the magnitude of computations needed to implement the associated management operating and control systems.

In science we trust. To embrace operations research, a company must believe that applying the scientific method contributes to the analysis of managerial decisions. The adoption of management science calls for an act of faith in the potential benefits of a systematic approach to decision-making.

The legitimacy of the scientific method in the study of other subjects, such as physical phenomena, is hardly open to question. After hundreds of years of experience, chemists and physicists have developed efficacious laboratory techniques. But the virtue of applying scientific procedures to decision-making problems of significance is not so well-established; its recognition still calls for what the poet Coleridge described, in another context, as "the willing suspension of disbelief." Here is why.

Rarely, if ever, can a company perform what most people would regard as a bona fide "scientific" experiment to test the merit of an operations research solution. Consider a company that is contemplating using a mathematical model to arrive at its annual operating plan. Since the company's economic environment differs from year to year, it can never exactly repeat history, and therefore can never guarantee that the model solution will produce a realized improvement over the company's current planning approach.

Consider a second illustration. Suppose that an operations research model has been suggested for controlling a company's inventories. Again, testing whether the new system will definitely yield an improvement over the present approach is inherently limited. Although you could use historical data to compare how the suggested rule would have operated in the past, the comparison is not a truly scientific experiment with controlled variables. For one thing, you can only *assume* that historical data are indicative of what will happen in the future. For another, if the suggested rules improve service and customers recognize the improvement, then there may be an increase in customer demand. In other words, the very operation of the suggested policy can alter the environment.

Of course, before a manager accepts a specific operations research solution, he should perform various tests of reasonableness, including historical comparisons. But at some point after making such tests, even in an ideal situation, the manager will have to accept as axiomatic that a scientific approach has intrinsic merit. We make three amplifying observations before leaving this conclusion.

First, even though a company may be convinced about the worthiness of the scientific method to aid decision-making, it need not accept the results of a particular operations research study as being valid. After all, the specific project may have been ill conceived or poorly executed.

Second, a trust in science does not imply the abandonment of hunch and intuition. On the contrary, the history of science itself is studded with cases of important discoveries made through chance, hunch, serendipity—even dreams. Behavioral scientists have not yet developed ways to induce such flashes of brilliance consistently. But most executives who use their hunches well also seem to possess a high level of knowledge and understanding about their activities. So the question is not when to apply science and when to rely on intuition, but rather how to combine the two effectively.

Third, the inherent difficulty of demonstrating that a suggested solution is a sure-fire improvement is not unique to management science. Because of the inability to duplicate history, an act of faith is also required to accept any other proposed solution—including maintaining the status quo.

1.3 BOUNDARIES OF QUANTITATIVE ANALYSIS

Even when quantitative analysis is of central importance for a managerial decision process, a management-science-oriented system never supplies all the information required for action, no matter how sophisticated the system's design. Furthermore, a truly successful implementation of an operations research system must apply behavioral as well as mathematical science, because the resultant system must interact with human beings. And finally, the very process of constructing an operations research system involves the exercise of judgment in addition to the logical manipulation of symbols and data. We discuss below each of these boundaries on quantitative analysis.

Problems solved and unsolved. We have already mentioned that at the very inception of implementing an operations research system it is necessary for experienced executives to discern the relevance of the model. This alone is not enough, of course. Since the corporate owners hold these men responsible for wisely managing the firm, executives must continue to exercise their judgmental duty well beyond initial acceptance of the model. In one way or another, they must monitor the system to ensure that the underlying model remains valid, and in particular that it continues to be used properly to provide insights into the real decision-making problems of the company. (Managers must guard against thinking of the model as being reality, and hence of the accompanying answers as being sacrosanct.)

A newly implemented operations research system may well bring about a restructuring or an amplification of information. As a result, executives may act differently from how they might have acted without such information. There is no getting away from the fact, however, that an executive, not the model, takes the action.

In short, an operations research model is never sufficient unto itself; it cannot become entirely independent of judgment supplied by knowledgeable managers. This boundary on quantitative analysis is always manifest, because the number of questions that managers can pose is boundless, whereas the kinds of answers that a single model can provide are inherently limited.

Systems are for people. Clearly, there is more to a successful implementation of an operations research system than the mere design of a mathematically correct model. The system must operate in the larger context of managerial activity. The model must take account of the data sources, with respect both to quality of the data and to the goals and expertise of the people responsible for collecting the data. The system must also reflect the information requirements of the managers who review the analytic results, especially the needs for descriptive and interpretive commentary.

Most experienced practitioners of management science know how to solve these so-called problems of communication. But there is a more fundamental limitation on quantitative analysis: rarely, if ever, is a suggested operations research system in perfect harmony with previously existing managerial attitudes and predilections. To ignore this fact is to invite internal conflict, subterfuge, and sometimes downright sabotage of a new system.

For example, a corporate planning model may call for the development of *realistic sales forecasts*. You would expect that marketing executives should ordinarily be entrusted to provide these figures; but the traditional orientation of the marketing department may make it impossible for these personnel to articulate anything other than *sales goals*. If the motivational drive of the sales organization is to set up targets and then try to meet them, and if it is then called upon to enunciate both targets *and* realistic forecasts, severe organizational conflicts may break out.

The art of management science. The problem-solving ingenuity of professional operations researchers is still a limiting factor in the spread of quantitative analysis. Despite the enormous growth in the acceptance of management science models, there are preciously few "standard" applications. Even in areas of decision-making where the relevance of mathematical models has become well established, designing particular applications in specific companies requires significant skill on the part of the management scientist. Model formulations remain tailor-made to a large degree.

A considerable amount of "art" is still required for the successful practice of management science. This in turn means that whether you are a managerial user or a practitioner of operations research, you must have some facility with both the artistic and the scientific ingredients of the subject. A text-book, such as this one, can teach you many of the scientific aspects, and give you a modicum of practice in the art through the study of toy examples and the formulation and solution of small-scale problems. Unfortunately, however, it can do no more than make you aware of the artistic elements.

To help you understand this interplay between the art and the science of applying operations research, we offer an analogy with the fine arts. A knowledge of scientific principles, such as the chemistry of paint, the physiology of the eye, the physics of light, the psychology of color, and the laws of perspective, helps the artist master fully the craft of painting. Likewise, such knowledge also distinguishes the true connoisseur from the casual, albeit appreciative, Sunday museumgoer. By the same token, an understanding of the fundamentals of operations research is essential not only for the practitioner, but for the manager who wants to make truly effective use of the approach. If today's business world continues to become more complex, an executive will not be able to compete successfully in the role of a casual onlooker, or that very manager may end up as a museum exhibit.

1.4 IMPORTANCE OF MODEL-BUILDING

As you study this text, the most important skill that you can learn is gaining facility in formulating, manipulating, and analyzing mathematical models. This proficiency far transcends the mastering of specific mathematical techniques. *Model-building is the essence of the management science approach.*

Constructing a model helps you put the complexities and possible uncertainties attending a decision-making problem into a logical framework amenable to comprehensive analysis. Such a model clarifies the decision alternatives and their anticipated effects, indicates the data that are relevant for analyzing the alternatives, and leads to informative conclusions. In short, the model is a vehicle for arriving at a well-structured view of reality.

A mixed bag. The word "model" has several shades of meaning, all of which are relevant to management science. First, a "model" may be a substitute representation of reality, such as a small-scale model airplane or locomotive. Second, "model" may imply some sort of idealization, often embodying a simplification of details, such as a model plan for urban redevelopment. Finally, "model" may be used as a verb, meaning to exhibit the consequential characteristics of the idealized representation. This notion conjures up in the mind those television commercials dramatizing how love and happiness will result after a single application of the sponsor's product.

In management science, a model is almost always a mathematical, and necessarily an approximate, representation of reality. It must be formulated to capture the crux of the decision-making problem. At the same time, it must be sufficiently free of burdensome minor detail to lend itself to finding an improved solution that is capable of implementation. Striking a proper balance between reality and manageability is no mean trick in most applications, and for this reason model-building can be arduous.

You will find three pervasive and interrelated themes in operations research model-building. The first is an emphasis on measureable improvement. Concentrating on decisions that are optimal according to one or more specified criteria has been the forcing wedge for attaining *improved* decision-making. Typically, the optimization is constrained, in that the values of the decision variables maximizing the stated objective function are restricted so as to satisfy certain technological restraints. Often, the model includes restrictions that mirror the impact of dynamic phenomena.

The second theme is derivation of the analytic properties of a mathematical model, including the sensitivity of an optimal solution to the model's parameters, the structural form of an optimal solution, and the operating characteristics of the solution. To illustrate, if you have a mathematical model leading to an inventory replenishment policy, you will want to know how the rule depends on forecasts of customer demand, the specification of the rule (such as, "when down to n, order again"), and the long-run frequency of stockouts and the average inventory level.

The third theme is explicit recognition of system interactions. One of the difficult tasks in writing an elementary text is to convey how, in real applications, the model-building effort is oriented toward management system considerations. The results of an operations research analysis must be integrated into the management information, decision-making, and control systems fabric of the organization. Operations research applications cannot be undertaken in isolation from the surrounding managerial environment. For these reasons, an operations research project should be regarded, at least in part, as a systems effort.

In one easy lesson. We know that the notion of model-building, as described in a textbook, carries with it an aura of mystery. Regrettably, it is virtually impossible to provide you with a checklist for infallibly selecting and developing a

model. But rest assured, there is considerable evidence that most students who
have been trained in either business administration, engineering, economics,
mathematics, or the sciences have little trouble building models in practice, provided they are inclined to do so. And nowadays, rarely, if ever, will you be faced
with applying operations research unaided by an experienced practitioner. Therefore, you can count on being tutored at least the first time you use management
science.

1.5 PROCESS OF QUANTITATIVE ANALYSIS

We outline below the stages that are standard in applying quantitative analysis.
An experienced practitioner takes these steps almost instinctively, and frequently
does not attach formal labels to them. Actually, the components are not entirely
distinct, and at any point in time, several of the phases proceed in concert. As a
beginner, however, you will find it helpful to look over the entire process seriatim,
so that you can plan ahead accordingly.

A prelude to a quantitative analysis of a decision problem should be a thorough
qualitative analysis. This initial diagnostic phase aims at identifying what seem
to be the critical factors—of course, subsequent analysis may demonstrate that
some of these factors are not actually so significant as they first appear. In particular, it is important to attain a preliminary notion of what the principal decisions are, what the measures of effectiveness are among these choices, and what
sorts of tradeoffs among these measures are likely to ensue in a comparison of the
alternatives. There will be trouble ahead unless you get a good "feel" for the way
the problem is viewed by the responsible decision-makers. Without this appreciation, you may encounter considerable difficulty in gaining acceptance and implementing your findings. What is worse, your results could very well be erroneous
or beside the point.

Formulating the problem. The preceding diagnostic should yield a
statement of the problem's elements. These include the controllable or decision
variables, the uncontrollable variables, the restrictions or constraints on the variables, and the objectives for defining a good or improved solution.

In the formulation process, you must establish the confines of the analysis.
Managerial decision-making problems typically have multifold impacts, some of
them immediate and others remote (although perhaps equally significant).
Determining the limits of a particular analysis is mostly a matter of judgment.

Building the model. Here is where you get down to the fine detail. You
must decide on the proper data inputs and design the appropriate information
outputs. You have to identify both the static and dynamic structural elements,
and devise mathematical formulas to represent the interrelationships among these
elements. Some of these interdependencies may be posed in terms of constraints

or restrictions on the variables. Some may take the form of a probabilistic evolutionary system.

You also must choose a time horizon (possibly the "never-ending future") to evaluate the selected measures of effectiveness for the various decisions. The choice of this horizon in turn influences the nature of the constraints imposed, since, with a long enough horizon, it is usually possible to remove any short-run restrictions by an expenditure of resources.

Performing the analyses. Given the initial model, along with its parameters as specified by historical, technological, and judgmental data, you next calculate a mathematical solution. Frequently, a solution means values for the decision variables that optimize one of the objectives and give permissible levels of performance on any other of the objectives. The various mathematical techniques for arriving at solutions comprise much of the contents of this text.

As pointed out previously, if the formulation of the model is too complex and too detailed, then the computational task may surpass the capabilities of present-day computers. If the formulation is too simple, the solution may be patently unrealistic. Therefore, you can expect to redo some of the steps in the formulation, model-building, and analysis phases, until you obtain satisfactory results.

A major part of the analysis consists of determining the sensitivity of the solution to the model specifications, and in particular to the accuracy of the input data and structural assumptions. Because sensitivity testing is so essential a part of the validation process, you must be careful to build your model in such a way as to make this process computationally tractable.

Implementing the findings and updating the model. Unfortunately, most tyro management scientists fail to realize that implementation begins on the the very first day of an operations research project. There is no "moment of truth" when the analyst states, "Here are my results," and the manager replies, "Aha! Now I fully understand. Thanks for giving me complete assurance about the correct decision."

We consider the entire process of implementation in Chap. 17. But we mention here the importance of having those executives who must act on the findings participate on the team that analyzes the problem. Otherwise, the odds are heavy that the project will be judged only as a provocative, but inconclusive, exercise.

It is common for an operations research model to be used repeatedly in the analysis of decision problems. Each time, the model must be revised to take account of both the specifics of the problem and current data. A good practitioner of operations research realizes that his model may have a long life, and so documents its details as well as plans for its updating.

What's it all about? Having learned the basic components of the quantitative analysis process, you should step back to see what the entire approach accomplishes.

The major effort is constructing a mathematical representation of a complicated situation, along with gathering the required data. The model is essentially approximate—elaborate enough to capture the essentials, yet gross enough to yield computable solutions. The balance between detail and tractability is found by a trial and error process, involving considerable examination of preliminary findings and extensive sensitivity analysis.

When operations research is applied in a planning context, the solution usually consists of a most favorable set of values for the decision variables, with some information as to the cost of deviating from these values. When management science is used for developing an operating system, such as a means for controlling inventories, then the solution consists of a set of decision rules. Often, these rules are embodied in a computer program. For an inventory system, the computer routines analyze historical demand data, permit judgmental adjustments if specified, signal when replenishment is to take place, and calculate the reorder amount.

Only rarely does an operations research solution represent a precise forecast of what will happen in the future. Such an accurate prediction would be of interest; but the crux of the decision problem is to select among alternatives, not to forecast. A well-built model makes a valid comparison among the alternatives. In case this distinction between accurately predicting an outcome and legitimately comparing alternatives is puzzling, consider the following illustration.

A company is about to decide whether or not to open a new plant in Europe. An operations research model is constructed that contains forecasts of sales, costs, and revenues; the resultant solution probably indicates anticipated production levels. If the economic advantage of opening this new plant is relatively insensitive to a range of reasonable values for the forecasted figures, then the company can make the correct expansion decision. It does *not* need to commit itself, at the same time, to production levels; they would be determined subsequently when more accurate demand forecasts are available.

1.6 MANAGEMENT SCIENCE, LILLIPUTIAN STYLE

Before explaining how and why quantitative analyses have been valuable in aiding executive decision-making, we will examine a few highly simplified illustrations of operations research models. Since our only purpose is to show what mathematical decision models look like, we make no pretense about the realism of these formulations; you will find more practical versions in the subsequent chapters.

One-Potato, Two-Potato Problem. Mr. Dustin (nicknamed Dusty) Jacquette, is production manager of the Eye-to-I Brand frozen food company, which processes potatoes into packages of French fries, hash browns, and flakes (for mashed potatoes). At the beginning of the manufacturing process, the raw potatoes are sorted by length and quality, and then allocated to the separate product lines.

Dusty can purchase potatoes from two sources, which differ in their yields of various sizes and quality. These yield characteristics are displayed in Fig. 1.1. Observe that from Source 1, there is a 20% yield of French fries, a 20% yield of hash browns, and a 30% yield of flakes; the remaining 30% is unrecoverable waste. The figures for flakes and waste are also 30% for potatoes from Source 2, but the yield of French fries is relatively higher.

Product	Source 1	Source 2	Purchase Limitations
French fries	.2	.3	1.8
Hash browns	.2	.1	1.2
Flakes	.3	.3	2.4
Relative Profit	5	6	

FIGURE 1.1. Potato Yields and Profit.

How many tons of potatoes should Dusty purchase from each source? The answer depends, in part, on the profit contributions of the sources. These figures are calculated by adding the sales revenues associated with the yields per ton purchased for the separate products, and subtracting the costs of purchasing a ton of potatoes, which may differ between the two sources. Suppose the profit contribution per ton purchased is 5 for Source 1 and 6 for Source 2. Even though Source 2 is more profitable, it does not follow that the company should purchase all of its potatoes from Source 2.

The company also must recognize its sales potential. The market for the different frozen foods is limited. Dusty estimates upper limits on the tons of each product that can be sold; these values are indicated in Fig. 1.1. Storage costs are too high to permit manufacturing any product for inventory. Thus Dusty, in making his purchase decisions from the two sources, must be careful not to buy any tons of potatoes that would yield products in excess of 1.8 tons of French fries, 1.2 tons of hash browns, and 2.4 tons of flakes. These restrictions can be expressed mathematically as follows.

Let P_1 denote the amount (in tons) of potatoes that will be purchased from Source 1, and P_2 the amount from Source 2. Then the values for P_1 and P_2 are constrained by the linear inequalities

(1)

$$.2P_1 + .3P_2 \leq 1.8 \quad \text{for French fries}$$

$$.2P_1 + .1P_2 \leq 1.2 \quad \text{for hash browns}$$

$$.3P_1 + .3P_2 \leq 2.4 \quad \text{for flakes}$$

$$P_1 \geq 0 \quad \text{and} \quad P_2 \geq 0.$$

The nonnegativity restrictions $P_1 \geq 0$ and $P_2 \geq 0$ are imposed because a value such as $P_1 = -4$ would have no physical significance.

All values for P_1 and P_2 satisfying (1) are shown in the shaded region in Fig. 1.2.

Notice that each line in the diagram is represented by a restriction in (1) expressed as an equality. The arrow associated with each line shows the direction indicated by the inequality signs in (1). Observe that a pair of values for P_1 and P_2 that satisfies *both* the French fries and hash brown constraints will also satisfy the flakes constraint.

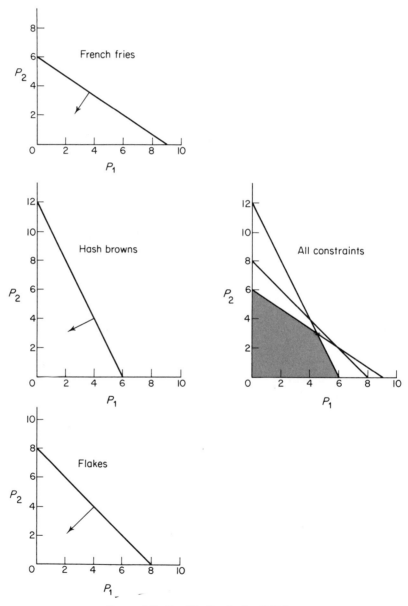

FIGURE 1.2. Feasible Purchasing Policies.

Optimal values for P_1 and P_2 are found by making the profit contribution as large as possible, consistent with the constraints. Therefore, the optimization problem is to

(2)
$$\text{maximize } (5P_1 + 6P_2)$$

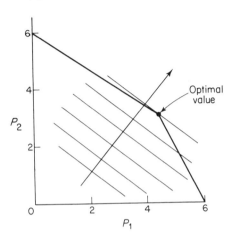

FIGURE 1.3. Maximum Profit.

subject to (1). In this simple problem, the solution can be exhibited graphically, as in Fig. 1.3.

Each of the parallel straight-line segments represents different combinations of P_1 and P_2 that give the same value for the linear objective function $5P_1 + 6P_2$. The highest segment still having a point in the feasible constraint region is the optimal value of the objective function, and such a point is an optimal solution. You can see in Fig. 1.3 that there is only one optimal solution in this example; it occurs at the intersection of the French fries and hash brown constraints. Consequently, you can calculate the optimal values by solving the associated simultaneous linear equations

(3)
$$.2P_1 + .3P_2 = 1.8 \quad \text{for French fries}$$
$$.2P_1 + .1P_2 = 1.2 \quad \text{for hash browns.}$$

The optimal answers are $P_1 = 4.5$ and $P_2 = 3$, as shown in Fig. 1.3, giving an objective-function value of 40.5.

This problem illustrates what is termed a *linear programming model*. Real applications of linear programming usually involve hundreds of constraints and thousands of variables. You will learn how to formulate and solve such models in Chaps. 2 through 7.

Secretary Problem. Ms. Kay Sera, the managing director of Watt, Willoughby, Willoughby, a consulting firm of economic analysts and forecasters, wishes to hire a new executive secretary, and is about to ask a placement service to send qualified persons for her to interview. She has found from past experience that she can determine from an interview whether a candidate, if hired, will turn out to be terrific, good, or just fair. She assigns a relative value of 3 to a terrific secretary, 2 to a good one, and 1 to a fair one. Her previous experience also leads her to believe that there is a .2 chance of interviewing a candidate who will be a terrific secretary, a .5 chance that the candidate will be a good one, and a .3 chance that the secretary will be a fair one.

She wishes to see only three candidates at most. Unfortunately, if she does not hire a secretary immediately after an interview, the person will take another job; hence, she has to decide right away.

If the first secretary she sees is terrific, she will hire the person immediately, of course. And if the candidate is fair, she has nothing to lose by interviewing a second candidate. But if the first candidate looks good, then she is not sure what to do. If she passes the person by, she may end up with only a fair secretary. Yet if she hires the secretary, she surrenders the chance of finding a terrific one. Similarly, if she chooses to see a second candidate, she will again face a difficult decision in the event that the interviewee turns out to be good.

The selection problem can be displayed conveniently by a so-called *decision tree*, shown in Fig. 1.4. The circled nodes represent the interviewed candidates, and the branches from these nodes show the chance events and their probabilities. The boxes indicate where a decision must be made, and the number at the end of a branch gives the relative value of stopping the decision process at that point.

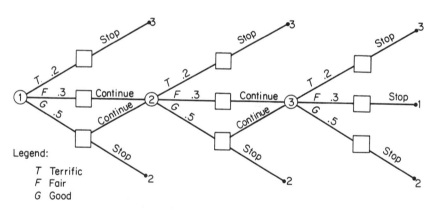

FIGURE 1.4. Decision Tree for Secretary Problem.

The problem of finding an optimal decision strategy can be solved by what is termed *dynamic programming*, and in particular, by a process known as *backward induction*. You will study dynamic programming models and solution techniques in Chaps. 8 through 10, and Chap. 13. The solution process is so simple in this example that you can compute the optimal hiring strategy very easily, as we have done below.

Suppose Ms. Sera does end up interviewing, and hence hiring, a third candidate. Then the expected value associated with the uncertain event is

(4) $3(.2) + 2(.5) + 1(.3) = 1.9.$

In other words, the average value of a secretary selected at random for an interview is 1.9. Assume that this expectation legitimately represents Ms. Sera's evaluation of the chancey event. Mark the number 1.9 above the circled Node 3 in Fig. 1.4.

Next consider what happens if Ms. Sera does interview a second candidate, who turns out to be good. If she decides to stop, then she obtains a value 2. But if she continues, then she can expect to receive only the value 1.9. So she should stop when the second candidate looks good. Put an × on the branch indicating "Continue" when the second secretary is good; this signifies not to take that action.

Now you are ready to determine the correct decision if the first secretary looks good. By stopping, Ms. Sera would obtain the value 2. But if she continues, then the expected value associated with the chancey outcome of the second interview, and possibly the third, is

$$(5) \qquad\qquad 3(.2) + 2(.5) + 1.9(.3) = 2.17.$$

The first term in (5) is for the event of seeing a terrific secretary, whom she hires; the second term is for the event of seeing a good secretary, whom she hires, as you already determined in the preceding paragraph; and the third term is for the event of seeing a fair secretary, and consequently continuing to the third chancey event that has a value of 1.9, given in (4). Since 2.17 is larger than 2, Ms. Sera should pass up the first secretary if the candidate turns out to be good. Mark 2.17 above the circled Node 2 in Fig. 1.4, and put an × on the branch indicating "Stop" when the first secretary is good.

To summarize, the optimal policy is to stop after the first interview only if the secretary is terrific, and to continue after the second interview only if the secretary is fair. The overall expected value of the interviewing process, given that Ms. Sera acts optimally, is

$$(6) \qquad\qquad 3(.2) + 2.17(.5) + 2.17(.3) = 2.336.$$

Mark this number above the circled Node 1 in Fig. 1.4. Since the quantity 1.9, calculated in (4), also represents the expected value if Ms. Sera interviews only a single secretary and hires the candidate, the difference $(2.336 - 1.9 = .436)$ is the incremental value from interviewing as many as two more persons.

Where-or-When Production Problem. The name of this problem arises from the observation that the associated mathematical model has several interpretations. One is in terms of deciding optimal production levels at each of several plants in a single time period; another is in terms of choosing optimal production levels at a single plant in each of several time periods. (The model also can be interpreted as a combination of the two problems, that is, as a where-*and*-when problem.)

O'Neil and Duprey Co., manufacturers of hymn books and religious articles, has N plants. The company's sales manager, Dolores Mae Shepherd, plans to manufacture a total of D units of a particular item during a stated time period. Hence, letting x_t denote the amount of production at Plant t, the levels $x_1, x_2, \ldots, x_N$ must satisfy the constraints

$$(7) \qquad\qquad x_1 + x_2 + \cdots + x_N = D \quad \text{and all} \quad x_t \geq 0.$$

Assume that the cost of producing x_t at Plant t is given by $(1/c_t)x_t^2$, where $c_t > 0$ is known from historical accounting information. Consequently, optimal values for the x_t are those that

(8) $$\text{minimize} \left(\frac{x_1^2}{c_1} + \frac{x_2^2}{c_2} + \cdots + \frac{x_N^2}{c_N} \right)$$

subject to (7).

This optimization problem can be solved by dynamic programming methods. The numerical answers can be easily computed from the insightful formula

(9) $$\text{optimal } x_t = \frac{c_t \cdot D}{c_1 + c_2 + \cdots + c_N} \quad \text{for } t = 1, 2, \ldots, N,$$

which yields the associated minimum cost

(10) $$\frac{D^2}{c_1 + c_2 + \cdots + c_N} \quad \text{(optimal policy)}.$$

For example, suppose that $N = 4$, $D = 500$, and

(11) $$\begin{aligned} c_1 &= 20 & c_2 &= 40 \\ c_3 &= 30 & c_4 &= 10, \end{aligned}$$

so that $c_1 + c_2 + c_3 + c_4 = 100$. Then (9) yields the optimal production levels

(12) $$\begin{aligned} x_1 &= \frac{20 \cdot 500}{100} = 100 & x_2 &= \frac{40 \cdot 500}{100} = 200 \\ x_3 &= \frac{30 \cdot 500}{100} = 150 & x_4 &= \frac{10 \cdot 500}{100} = 50, \end{aligned}$$

so that total cost from (10) is 2500 $(= 500^2/100)$.

Turning to the multiperiod version, suppose you interpret x_t as being the level of production in a single plant during Period t. Notice that in this version, all the costs are due to production, and no storage costs are incurred while the units are inventoried from Period 1 to the end of Period N, when the demand requirement D must be met. Given this view, you can state what would be the optimal value for x_t if the preceding levels $x_1, x_2, \ldots, x_{t-1}$ were already determined [not necessarily by (9)], namely,

(13) $$\text{optimal conditional } x_t = \frac{c_t \cdot (D - x_1 - x_2 - \cdots - x_{t-1})}{c_t + c_{t+1} + \cdots + c_N}$$

$$(x_1, x_2, \cdots, x_{t-1} \text{ are specified}).$$

Calculating $x_1, x_2, \ldots, x_N$ recursively (that is, successively, one by one, starting with x_1) from (13) yields the same values as computing each of them from (9).

In the above example, suppose instead of the values in (12), the company set $x_1 = 180$ and $x_2 = 196$, where here these are the production levels in Periods 1 and 2. Then given these nonoptimal previous choices, the optimal production levels for Periods 3 and 4 are

$$x_3 = \frac{30(500 - 180 - 196)}{30 + 10} = 93$$

(14)

$$x_4 = \frac{10(500 - 180 - 196 - 93)}{10} = 31$$

according to (13).

Economic Order Quantity Problem. In Chaps. 9 and 14, you will study a variety of inventory replenishment models that have proved successful in practice. The formulation below is perhaps the simplest such model. Its precise assumptions are only rarely satisfied in real life. Nevertheless, the resultant solution turns out to be sufficiently close to optimal for many practical situations as to make it a very useful approximation.

Sam Tulong, the owner of a downtown retail store selling men's and women's jeans, frequently has had difficulty in stocking short sizes of pants. He has decided to adopt a scientific approach to replenishing inventory, and thereby avoid getting caught with his pants down. Assume that he sells a particular size at the rate of, say, M units per week. For simplicity, suppose there is no uncertainty about this consumption. Hence, if the inventory level is kM units, then this stock is depleted in exactly k weeks. Further, suppose the rate M is unchanging over time, so that a replenishment order is regularly placed. The decision problem is to determine the most economical order quantity. (Assuming that the delivery time for an order is also known exactly, each replenishment action is initiated early enough so that the order arrives just when the inventory level falls to zero.)

Let the order quantity be denoted by Q. Then the level of inventory can be pictured by the sawtooth pattern shown in Fig. 1.5. Observe that each time a replenishment arrives, the inventory level shoots up by the order quantity Q. Then the level diminishes, as shown by the downward slope of the sawtooth, which equals $-M$.

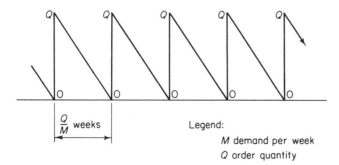

FIGURE 1.5. Pattern of Inventory Levels.

An optimal order quantity strikes a balance between the costs associated with replenishing and with holding inventory. Specifically, assume that a fixed setup cost K is incurred each time an order is placed, that a purchase cost c is paid for each item ordered, and that a holding cost h is assessed for each unit of inventory held per week. The setup cost is related to the effort expended in placing and receiving the order. The holding cost is associated with storage, insurance, and the capital tied up in inventory.

Let the economic criterion of effectiveness be measured as average cost per week. Then the contribution due to setup costs is $K(M/Q)$, since there are M/Q setups per week. The contribution due to purchase costs is cM, since M items are consumed per week. And the contribution due to holding costs is $h(Q/2)$, since $Q/2$ is the average level of inventory, as you can see in Fig. 1.5. Adding the components, you have

(15) $$\text{average cost per week} \equiv \text{AC} = \frac{KM}{Q} + cM + \frac{hQ}{2}.$$

The economic order quantity that minimizes AC is

(16) $$\text{optimal } Q = \sqrt{\frac{2KM}{h}},$$

which can be found by setting the derivative of AC with respect to Q equal to 0, and solving for Q. It follows from (16) that the optimal order quantity only doubles when the demand rate quadruples. Also note that the optimal quantity is determined by the *ratio* of setup to holding costs.

To illustrate, suppose that Sam Tulong sells 20 ($= M$) pairs of a particular jean each week, the weekly holding cost for this item is $.02 ($= h$), and the setup cost for reordering is $1.80. The wholesale cost of the jean is $5.00. Then according to (16), his optimal purchase quantity is

(17) $$Q = \sqrt{\frac{2(1.8)20}{.02}} = 60,$$

so that he reorders every three weeks. His average cost per week from (15) is $101.20 ($= $.60 + $100.00 + $.60$).

OR Airline Problem. The One-Ride Airline Company is opening a reservation service to be located in a suburban shopping center. A passenger making reservations will be able to telephone the office and state his request. The OR Airline Company wants to decide how many telephone lines to install for answering reservation calls. It can easily compute the telephone and personnel expenses that vary with the number of lines. But it also wishes to compare the level of service for several different numbers of lines. In particular, suppose the company seeks to determine the percentage of time all the lines will be busy and the average length of such busy periods.

This sort of analysis is classified as *queuing* or *waiting line theory*, and is explained in Chaps. 15 and 16. We could construct an explicit model and subject it to rigorous mathematical analysis, but instead, we explain here how the method of simulation can be used to determine the service figures. To keep the explanation easy, we present only a rudimentary technique, leaving to Chap. 16 a more detailed exposition of the simulation approach.

Suppose the company obtains data showing the statistical frequencies of minutes between successive incoming telephone calls. As a first approximation, assume that these successive interarrival times are completely independent (such independence does not hold precisely if, for example, a passenger calls up, finds the lines busy, and immediately redials the number). A convenient way to summarize this distribution is to use a pie diagram, such as the one in Fig. 1.6, where we assume for simplicity that the time between incoming calls never exceeds 5 minutes.

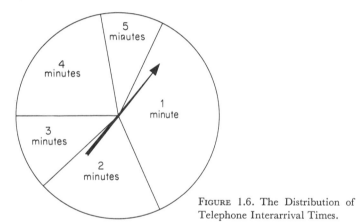

FIGURE 1.6. The Distribution of Telephone Interarrival Times.

Imagine a pointer, or spinner, affixed to the center of the pie diagram—the mechanism would look something like a wheel-of-chance at carnivals, or a device that is often included in a child's game to determine how many advances a player's piece may take at each turn. You can simulate the traffic of incoming calls by giving the pointer a succession of sharp spins, and jotting down the resultant sequence of interarrival times.

In addition, suppose the company has a frequency distribution of the number of minutes that incoming calls require. Assume that these service times are independent of each other and of the interarrival times. Then another pie diagram and spinner mechanism can be constructed for generating the service times.

You are now ready to simulate the system. To begin, suppose there is only a single telephone line. Then a simulated history may look like that in Fig. 1.7. The instants of incoming calls are recorded with ×'s on the time axis, and are determined by successive spins of the pointer mechanism for interarrival times. The telephone line becomes busy as soon as the first call arrives. The length of the busy period is determined by a spin of the pointer mechanism for service times. Notice that the calls arriving at the instants circled in Fig. 1.7 are not answered because the single telephone line is busy. You can obtain a good estimate of the percentage of time the line will be busy and the average length of a busy period by calculating the corresponding statistics for a fairly long simulated run.

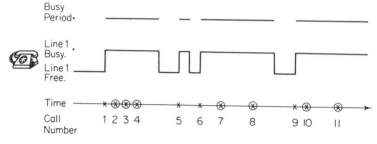

FIGURE 1.7. Simulated History for One Telephone Line.

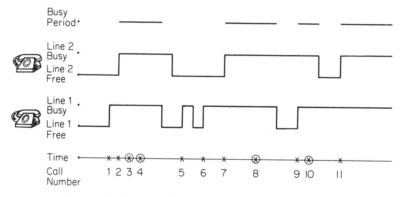

FIGURE 1.8. Simulated History for Two Telephone Lines.

Suppose next that there are two telephone lines. Then the same sequence of incoming calls can lead to a service history like that in Fig. 1.8. Observe that more incoming calls are answered. Here a busy period is defined to be a length of time during which both telephone lines are tied up. Note how these periods are shorter in Fig. 1.8 than in Fig. 1.7 for the particular history. As you can see, the same approach can be used to estimate service for any number of lines.

Commentary. As we stated at the beginning of this section, the above examples illustrate how mathematical models are constructed to analyze decision problems. We have made no attempt to be "realistic" in these examples. But as you continue reading this book, you will discover how to build practical models, and learn ways to solve problems with them.

1.7 AT THE END OF THE RAINBOW

Today, virtually every major corporation employs personnel who are responsible for applying management science. Usually, these people constitute a staff group at headquarters level. The group often reports to the controller, the chief financial officer, or the head of corporate planning; but with growing frequency, companies are also assigning operations researchers to report directly to line managers. In a parallel fashion, operations research activity has enjoyed a widespread growth within federal and local governments, as well as in other nonprofit organizations. This section tells why management science has succeeded so well.

Merits of a rational process. Obviously, executives must and do make decisions all the time. For a particular situation, an operations research model *may* yield the very same conclusion that an experienced manager would arrive at solely on intuitive grounds. Therefore, the benefits of using operations research have to be evaluated in terms of its long-run impact on the entire managerial process.

The proper comparison is well represented by the question, "If a company does not use operations research to guide the decision process, then what will it use, and will the answers be consistently as good?" Corporations that apply operations research—even when the approach does not meet all of the company's initial expectations—find that analyzing complicated managerial problems this way is a sounder method than traditional means. This assertion is amply borne out by the substantial support given to operations research in both the private and public sectors.

Qualities inherent in this particular rational approach make it a valuable method. These benefits include:

- Emphasis on assessing the system-wide interactions and ramifications of decision alternatives. Intrinsic in an operations research approach is the construction of a model that synthesizes the segments of an enterprise that are affected by a decision choice. Each individual part is constructed by personnel who are the most knowledgeable about the relevant data.
- Impetus to developing a full range of decision alternatives. The number of action possibilities that can be analyzed increases tremendously by the application of mathematics and computers.
- Focus on resolving the critical issues. The approach proceeds in the fashion of establishing implications of the form, "if Hypothesis H is true and Action A is taken, then Result R will occur." The method fosters interdepartmental communication. As a consequence, clashes of opinion within an organization can be sorted into disagreements over the probable truth of different hypotheses, and over the assumptions used in deriving the implications of different actions.

Important ancillary benefits emerge from the direction provided by the model for gathering data, quantifying the value of additional information, and documenting factual knowledge that may be required in subsequent decision analyses.

Having listed several of the important merits stemming from the rational analytic process of operations research, we hasten to point out that the advantages will occur to a greater or lesser degree, depending on the skill used in carrying out the study.

Managerial cutting edge. The preceding paragraphs dealt with *why* operations research is helpful in analyzing decision problems. Now we discuss *how* the approach is beneficial. We have classified the ways into four somewhat arbitrary and partially overlapping categories:

i. *Better decisions.* Frequently, management science models yield actions that do improve on intuitive decision-making. A situation may be so complex (because of intricate interrelationships among decisions, voluminous data pertinent to operations, and uncertainties of market activity) that the human mind can never hope to assimilate all the significant factors without the aid of operations-research-guided computer analysis.

Of course, in the past managers have made decisions in these situations without the aid of operations research. They had to. But the depth of their understanding and the quality of their decisions improve with the application of such models, as considerable experience has shown. Particular decisions may ultimately turn out to be wrong, but the improved decision-making process reduces the risk of making such erroneous decisions.

ii. *Better Coordination.* Sometimes operations research has been instrumental in bringing order out of chaos. The following example, drawn from an actual application, illustrates what can happen.

During special campaigns, a food manufacturer runs advertising that significantly increases sales volume. But manufacturing production facilities are limited, the supply of the foodstuff is limited, and the sales response is often erratic. In the past, consequently, the marketing and manufacturing divisions have been at opposite poles in terms of cooperative actions. An operations-research-oriented planning model becomes a vehicle for coordinating marketing decisions within the limitations imposed on manufacturing capabilities.

iii. *Better Control.* The managements of large organizations recognize that it is extremely costly to require continuous executive supervision over routine decisions. Operations research approaches combining historical experience with the scientific method have resulted in standardized and reliable procedures for handling everyday activities and for signaling dangerous trends. Executives have thereby gained new freedom to devote their attention to more pressing matters, except for those unusual circumstances which, when they arise, necessitate reviewing the course of everyday action. The most frequently adopted applications in this category deal with production scheduling and inventory replenishment.

iv. *Better Systems.* Often, a management science study is initiated to analyze a particular decision problem, such as whether to open a new warehouse. Afterwards, the approach is further developed into a system to be employed repeatedly. Thus the cost of undertaking the first application may produce benefits that are longer lasting than originally envisioned.

Where the action is. By this time, applications of operations research are so common in industry and government, and so diverse in the functional areas of decision-making, that we cannot hope to provide a complete survey. To give you some idea, however, we mention that there are numerous applications in industries such as aircraft, apparel, chemicals, cement, glass, computers, electronics, farm and industrial machinery, food, metal manufacturing and products, mining, motor vehicles, paper and wood products, petroleum refining, and pharmaceuticals, as well as in commercial banks, insurance companies, merchandising firms, public utilities, and transportation companies.

Depending on the industry, the applications pertain to extraction of natural resources, manufacturing, transportation and warehousing, plant size and location, inventory management, scheduling of workers and machines, forecasting, new product development, marketing, advertising, cash management and finance, portfolio management, mergers, and both short- and long-range corporate planning.

Most companies' early management science projects deal with monthly or quarterly scheduling, annual planning, inventory control, and other fairly well-defined areas of decision-making. After the operations research group demonstrates its capability in these areas, a company then applies its operations research talents to the study of high-level strategic problems, such as selecting new plant sites, entering new markets, acquiring overseas affiliates, and so forth.

Management science has provided a significant advance in the techniques of long-range strategic planning. Even senior executives have difficulty piecing together all the important considerations involved in a well-designed long-range plan. What is more, the operations research approach lends itself to the formulation of contingency plans, that is, a complete strategy indicating which courses of action are appropriate for various future events. In addition, the findings may include directions for obtaining and then utilizing critical information about such future events. In this way, the operations research model suggests the actions to be taken immediately and the ones to be postponed, and when to undertake a reassessment. For these reasons, more and more frequently, boards of directors of large corporations find strategic proposals being justified on the basis of extensive management science studies.

The growth of operations research in government and nonprofit corporations has been phenomenal. A long succession of military applications began during

World War II. Now governmental applications involve health, education, and welfare; air and highway traffic control; air and water pollution; police and fire protection; voter and school redistricting; and annual planning and budgeting by program, to name only a few.

Sometimes it is claimed that the lack of clear-cut objective functions to be optimized in nonprofit organizations raises a significant difference between applications in the private and public sectors. Industry most often measures improvement in terms of contribution to profit, but this criterion is by no means the only relevant one for decision-making. Businesses are always compromising among different objectives. Therefore, we feel that the absence of a profit measure is less important than it might seem at first glance.

Probably the most important difference between the public and private sectors concerns the exercise of decision-making responsibilities. The organizational structures of big corporations are complex, and the authority for taking actions may not always be precisely defined. But these structures are simple indeed in comparison with most governmental structures. The difference can be stated this way. In a commercial company, there is no one left to pass the buck to, once the necessity for making a decision reaches top management (or the board of directors). In an organization such as the Federal Government, even the President's decisions are subject to the review of—and thus become partly the responsibility of— Congressmen, who, along with the President, are publicly elected. Understand that diffuse responsibilities and authority only make it *difficult* to apply operations research outside of industry. As the record shows, plenty of applications are being made in governmental and nonprofit organizations.

1.8 IN THE BEGINNING . . .

Studying linear optimization models is an excellent way to begin learning about operations research. Hence, this subject is taken up in the next chapter and several to follow. As you read about linear and other models throughout the text, try to keep in mind the boundaries and the process of quantitative analysis (which we discussed in Secs. 1.3 and 1.4). By so doing, you will maintain a perspective on the strengths and limitations of management science.

REVIEW EXERCISES

1 Using the stages in the process of quantitative analysis as outlined in Sec. 1.5, explain how you would apply such an approach to the decision-making problems below. Also state what you think would be the merits of applying a rational process and what would be the associated managerial cutting edge (as discussed in Sec. 1.7).

(a) Exploring and drilling for crude oil.
(b) Harvesting of timber lands.

(c) Assigning customer orders to each of several steel rolling mills in a large steel corporation.
(d) Establishing field warehouses for the distribution of canned food.
(e) Locating and deciding the capacity of an ore reduction plant.
(f) Market-testing a new packaged soap product.
(g) Locating new sites for grocery stores.
(h) Establishing an advertising budget for the promotion of a soft drink.
(i) Determining the size of a bank balance for an aircraft company.
(j) Selecting a portfolio of securities in an insurance company.
(k) Deciding whether to merge two railroads.
(l) Planning for future growth in a computer manufacturing company.
(m) Deciding whether to automate a post office.
(n) Allocating funds to urban renewal projects.
(o) Selecting an intercontinental ballistic weapon system.
(p) Designing an effective national welfare program.
(q) Selecting a route for a superhighway.
(r) Establishing a single nationwide telephone number for emergency police services.
(s) Determining the number and location of fire stations in a city.
(t) Deciding whether to unify two separate school districts.
(u) Allocating funds among participating agencies in the United Fund.

One-Potato, Two-Potato Problem (Sec. 1.6). In exercises 2 through 5, draw a diagram showing the feasible purchasing policies and the optimal solution. Also calculate optimal values for P_1 and P_2 and the associated value of the objective function. Assume all the data as given in Fig. 1.1 except for the specific change indicated below in each separate part of the exercise.

2 (a) Sales limitation on French fries of 1.7. Of 1.9.
  (b) Sales limitation on hash browns of 1.1. Of 1.3.
  (c) Sales limitations on French fries of 1.7 and on hash browns of 1.1.
  (d) Sales limitations on French fries of 1.9 and on hash browns of 1.3.
  (e) Sales limitation on flakes of 2.5. Of 2.3. Of 2.1. Of 1.5.

3 (a) Profit of a ton from Source 2 of 7. Of 8.
  (b) Profit of a ton from Source 1 of 4.
  (c) Profit of a ton from Source 1 of 6 and from Source 2 of 2.
  (d) Profit of a ton from Source 1 of 6 and from Source 2 of 3.

4 (a) Yield of .25 French fries from a ton from Source 1.
  (b) Yield of .2 French fries from a ton from Source 2.
  (c) Yield of .3 hash browns from a ton from Source 1.
  (d) Yield of .15 hash browns from a ton from Source 2.

5 An additional restriction that
  (a) $P_1 \leq 3$.   (b) $P_2 \leq 2.5$.
  (c) $P_1 \leq 3$ and $P_2 \leq 2.5$.   (d) $P_1 \geq 5$.
  (e) $P_2 \geq 5$.   (f) $P_1 \geq 5$ and $P_2 \geq 5$.

Secretary Problem (Sec. 1.6). In exercises 6 through 10, draw a decision tree, and find an optimal interviewing policy. Assume all the data as given in Fig. 1.4 except for the specific change indicated below in each separate part of the exercise.

6 Kay Sera is willing to interview up to four candidates. What is the incremental value of interviewing as many as three *more* persons instead of only one? What is the incremental value of interviewing as many as four persons instead of a maximum of three?

7 Kay Sera is willing to interview up to five candidates. What is the incremental value of interviewing as many as four *more* persons instead of only one?

8 The relative value of a terrific secretary is 4. What is the incremental value of interviewing as many as two *more* persons instead of one?

9 (a) There is a .2 chance that an interviewee will be a good secretary, and a .6 chance that the person will be a fair one. What is the incremental value of interviewing as many as two *more* candidates instead of one?
  (b) There is a .1 chance that an interviewee will be a terrific secretary, a .4 chance that the person will be good, and a .5 chance that the person will be just fair. What is the incremental value of interviewing as many as two *more* candidates instead of one?

10 (a) There is a *cost* of .15 for each interview.
   (b) There is a *cost* of .15 for each interview and Kay Sera is willing to interview up to four persons.

Where-or-When Production Problem (Sec. 1.6). In exercises 11 through 15, assume the following data except for the specific change indicated below in each separate part of the exercise:

$$D = 100, \ N = 4, \ c_1 = 1, \ c_2 = 2, \ c_3 = 3, \ c_4 = 4.$$

Find the optimal value of each x_t and the associated minimum cost.

11 Assume the data as given above.

12 Let $D = 300$.

13 (a) Let $c_1 = 3$.
   (b) Let $c_4 = 2$.
   (c) Let $c_1 = 3$ and $c_4 = 2$.
   (d) Let $c_1 = c_2 = c_3 = c_4 = 2.5$.

14 (a) Let $N = 5$ and $c_5 = 5$.
   (b) Let $N = 5$ and $c_1 = c_2 = c_3 = c_4 = c_5 = 2$.

15 (a) Let $x_2 = 34$.
   (b) Let $x_2 = 6$.

Economic Order Quantity Problem (Sec. 1.6). In exercise 16, assume the following data except for the specific change indicated below in each separate part of the exercise: consumption rate $M = 5$, setup cost $K = 90$, and holding cost per unit $h = 4$. To simplify computations, let purchase cost $c = 0$.

16 Find the optimal economic order quantity, the associated average cost per week, and the corresponding number of weeks between successive orders.

    (a) Assume the data as given above. Then draw a graph of the average cost per week as a function of the order quantity Q. Indicate the optimal value for Q on your graph as well as the minimum average cost per week. Draw a graph of the sawtooth pattern of inventory levels for the optimal policy, analogous to that in Fig. 1.5.

    (b) Let $h = 16$.
    (c) Let $K = 360$.
    (d) Let $M = 20$.
    (e) Let $h = 16$ and $K = 360$.
    (f) Let $h = 16$ and $M = 20$.
    (g) Let $K = 360$ and $M = 20$.

OR Airline Problem (Sec. 1.6). Suppose you simulate the arrivals and service of telephone calls as follows. Toss four coins and assign an interarrival time between successive incoming calls of three minutes when there are four heads, two minutes when there are three heads, one minute when there are two heads, four minutes when there is one head, and five minutes when there are no heads (four tails). For each call determine an associated service time (which occurs if the caller does not find all the telephone lines busy) by tossing two coins and letting the service time be one minute when there are two heads, two minutes when there is one head, and three minutes when there are no heads (two tails).

17 In each experiment below, use the above method to simulate 20 calls. Calculate the average time between successive incoming calls, the average service time of those calls that are answered, the number of calls not answered (because all the lines are busy), the fraction of time that all the lines are busy, and the average length of time when all the lines are busy. In performing the calculations, assume that all the lines are free at the start, that the system shuts down two minutes after the twentieth call (regardless of whether or not it is answered), and that no more arrivals occur within this final two-minute interval. Also, draw a diagram (such as in Figs. 1.7 and 1.8) to display the simulated history. Let the number of telephone lines be

    (a) One.
    (b) Two.
    (c) Three.
    *(d) Calculate the theoretical average time between successive arrivals.
    *(e) Calculate the theoretical average service time, assuming that all calls are answered.

CONTENTS

CHAPTER 2

Formulation of Linear Optimization Models

2.1 INTRODUCTION

Unquestionably, linear optimization models are among the most commercially successful applications of operations research; in fact, there is considerable evidence that they rank highest in economic impact. This chapter initiates your study of linear models.

Qualitative analysis. To set the stage, suppose we consider the operations of a large firm in a process-oriented industry such as petroleum, chemicals, metal working, or wood products. Specifically, let us choose a major integrated oil company. As depicted in Fig. 2.1, the critical decisions in this type of firm relate to the processes of:

- Exploring for oil deposits
- Producing crude oil
- Exchanging proprietary crude oil for other companies' crudes at different locations
- Purchasing additional crude
- Shipping the crude to any of several refineries
- Cracking the crude into several blending stocks
- Combining the stocks into several dozen petroleum products
- Shipping the manufactured products from the refineries to marketing areas.

A decision to install a new cracking unit at a refinery, of course, affects the refinery's operating efficiency. But equally important, such a decision can and often does have a decided impact on all the other operations listed. The design characteristics of the new unit influence the selection and allocation of crudes, as well as

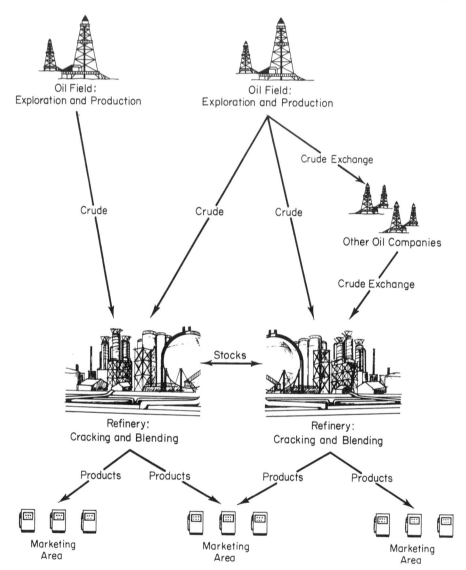

FIGURE 2.1. An Integrated Oil Company.

the relative composition and distribution of marketable products. Similarly, expanding the share of the market for gasoline products in a particular region has implications for setting refinery operating levels, for making crude-exchange agreements with other oil companies, and for deciding where to concentrate exploration activities.

For another illustration, we may look at a lumber manufacturing firm that owns raw timber resources, processes cut logs into various wood products, and distributes these commodities over a widespread geographical area, as shown in Fig. 2.2.

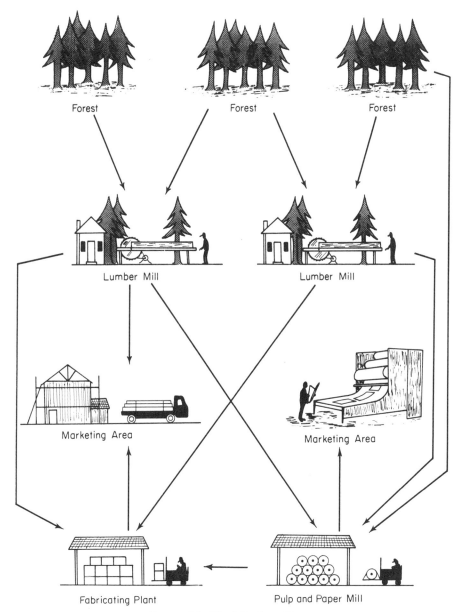

FIGURE 2.2. Wood Products Firm.

Just as with the petroleum firm, all strategic decisions must reflect the inherent constraint stemming from the nature of the raw material: any single log yields only a limited amount of each grade of sawn timber. To earn profits, the firm must carefully allocate these various grades to the different types of finished products. As a practical matter, then, the company must produce a slate of products that fully utilizes the material in the logs; but within this mode of operation there is still considerable discretion for deciding the particular composition of the final products slate.

Although both of these illustrations were simplified, the resource allocation decision problems posed have close counterparts in actual companies. The complexities to be found in real situations magnify the effort required to provide a scientific economic analysis of various decision consequences. Nevertheless, these very decision problems are now being solved in many major companies with the aid of linear optimization models, usually called **linear programming models.**

Profit potential. Why do successful companies bother to use such mathematical aids? Are not management experience, know-how, and intuition sufficient to ensure sound decisions? Executives with a profit-making outlook have long realized that the comprehensive planning of future operations is important to their company's success, and it is a rare manager who neglects such planning. In a large enterprise, however, merely recording the factual information required for analyzing significant decisions can entail a tremendous effort. Consequently, available staff time for testing the likely economic impact of a plan is a limiting factor for a company.

As you will see, linear programming provides a breakthrough in amplifying the analytic abilities of managers and their staff. The mathematical models you will study enable executives to evaluate a wider range of resource allocation plans than they would ever have thought possible. As we pointed out in Chap. 1, it is important to realize that the results of these tests are not meant to substitute for managers' experience and intuition. To the contrary, they provide the precise and comprehensive data required to apply their knowledge effectively.

The way it is. The purpose of this chapter is to introduce you to a variety of optimizing problems that lend themselves to a linear model formulation. In order not to detract from this purpose, the chapter will not deal with the numerical techniques for solving the models. That topic is treated in detail in Chap. 4.

If you want to learn how to apply linear programming, sooner or later you have to face up to the fact that real situations are much more complex than the One-Potato, Two-Potato Problem given in Chap. 1. Several other Lilliputian examples are in the Formulation Exercises at the end of the chapter; these will offer you an opportunity to refresh your abilities in writing and graphing linear relationships. But we think there is no point in our dillydallying with misleadingly simple toy problems. You need to become accustomed to models having more than two or three unknowns and restrictions, and the quicker, the better. Consequently, we have chosen to explain more typical-looking linear programming problems.

By the same token, you must learn to express decent-sized problems in algebraic terms, since, with plentiful data, graphical representations are out of the question. In a real application you will have to rely on employing an electronic calculator to find a numerical solution. Such computer routines require that you specify the model in an algebraic fashion. Therefore, you will need facility in translating verbal problem statements into mathematical symbols. In short, you are about to see linear programming like it is.

Study guide. In reading the examples below, ask yourself

1. What are the key decisions to be made? What problem is being solved?
2. What makes the real decision environment so complex as to require the use of a linear optimization model? What elements of this complexity are embodied in the model? What elements are ignored?
3. What distinguishes a practical decision from an unusable one in this environment? What distinguishes a good decision from a poor one?
4. If you were a manager, how would you employ the results of the analysis? What would be your interpretation of the answers? In what ways might you want or need to temper the results because of factors not explicitly considered in the models?

After presenting these examples, we will return to a discussion of the application of linear programming models in today's business firms.

2.2 PRODUCT-MIX SELECTION

In product-mix selection, the decision-maker wishes to determine the levels for a number of production activities during a specified period of time. These levels are constrained by technological or feasibility considerations, given in the form of linear equalities or inequalities. Subject to these restrictions, management seeks to optimize a particular objective function. In the instance below, the objective will be maximum profit. In the subsequent examples, you will see other objectives, such as minimum cost.

Suppose the Knox Mix Company has the option of using one or more of four different types of production processes. The first and second processes yield items of Product A, and the third and fourth yield items of Product B. The inputs for each process are labor measured in man-weeks, pounds of Material Y, and boxes of Material Z. Since each process varies in its input requirements, the profitabilities of the processes differ, even for processes producing the same item. The manufacturer, deciding on a week's production schedule, is limited in the range of possibilities by the available amounts of manpower and of both kinds of raw materials. The full technology and input restrictions are given in Fig. 2.3.

Linear axioms. We will make two crucial technological and economic assumptions about how the production processes operate:

i. *Divisibility*. For each activity, the total amounts of each input and the associated profit are strictly proportional to the level of output—that is, to the activity level. In other words, each activity is capable of continuous proportional expansion or reduction. To illustrate, the direct effect of doubling the inputs of any

Item	One Item of Product A		One Item of Product B		Total Availabilities
	Process 1	Process 2	Process 3	Process 4	
Man–weeks	1	1	1	1	≤ 15
Pounds of Material Y	7	5	3	2	≤ 120
Boxes of Material Z	3	5	10	15	≤ 100
Unit profit ($)	4	5	9	11	Maximize
Production level	x_1	x_2	x_3	x_4	

FIGURE 2.3. Knox Mix Product Selection.

process is the doubling of output and profits. In particular, to manufacture 10 units by Process 1 ($x_1 = 10$) requires 10 man-weeks, 70 pounds of Material Y, and 30 boxes of Material Z allocated to the activity, and the accrued profits are $40. The divisibility postulate further implies that the activity levels are permitted to assume fractional values as well as integer values. For example, we admit the technological possibility of $x_2 = 2.5$ or $x_4 = \frac{10}{3}$.

ii. *Additivity.* Given the activity levels for each of the decision variables x_j, the total amounts of each input and the associated profit are the sums of the inputs and profit for each individual process. To illustrate, in Fig. 2.3 1 unit of Process 1 ($x_1 = 1$) and 1 unit of Process 3 ($x_3 = 1$) require 2 man-weeks, 10 pounds of Material Y, and 13 boxes of Material Z, and yield $13 profit.

The assumptions of divisibility and additivity are equivalent to stating that the underlying mathematical model can be formulated in terms of linear relations. Strictly interpreted, the axioms imply constant returns to scale and preclude the possibility of economies or diseconomies of scale (in both the technology and profit aspects). Suitable mathematical devices of an advanced nature often make it possible to introduce economies and diseconomies into a modified linear model. In real situations the above two postulates may hold only approximately, but nevertheless well enough, to permit useful application of the linear approach. For all the examples in the remainder of this chapter, we assume the legitimacy of the two assumptions.

In the specific example there is one linear inequality relation for each labor and material restriction, and one linear relation expressing profitability:

(1)   maximize profit $\equiv$ maximize $(4x_1 + 5x_2 + 9x_3 + 11x_4)$,

subject to the constraints

$$1x_1 + 1x_2 + 1x_3 + 1x_4 \leq 15 \quad \text{(man-weeks)}$$

(2) $\qquad 7x_1 + 5x_2 + 3x_3 + 2x_4 \leq 120 \quad \text{(Material Y)}$

$$3x_1 + 5x_2 + 10x_3 + 15x_4 \leq 100 \quad \text{(Material Z)}.$$

There is no physical meaning to negative production levels, such as $x_1 = -4.2$, so we do not allow production to be "negative." We constrain each unknown production level to be either zero or positive, that is, to be **nonnegative,**

(3) $\qquad\qquad x_1 \geq 0 \qquad x_2 \geq 0 \qquad x_3 \geq 0 \qquad x_4 \geq 0.$

(A variable that is allowed *also* to assume negative values is said to be **unrestricted in sign.**)

Management's problem is to find values for all the unknown production levels x_j that satisfy the relations (2), (3), and also maximize profit (1). In general, such values need not be unique. There may exist **alternative optimal solutions.**

Rather than get side tracked at this juncture by discussing a method for calculating an optimal solution, the computational question will be postponed to Chap. 4. You will find it very helpful in reading Chaps. 4 and 5 to have a copy of Fig. 2.3, and we urge you to make one. Also, jot down now what you think may be an optimal solution to this example, so that you can check your guess against the answer given in Chap. 4.

We will demonstrate in Chap. 4 the remarkable fact that in linear programming problems having m restrictive relations (not including the nonnegativity constraints) and possessing finite optimal solutions, there is at least one best solution in which no more than m activity variables are employed at positive levels. Therefore in this example, there is an optimal solution using no more than three of the variables.

In addition to wanting optimal production values, management may also want to know how profit would be affected by increasing each input, by improving one of the technological processes, by a change in the cost of raw materials—and consequently a change in the profitability of the processes—or by some other resource used in the processes and heretofore not considered limited becoming scarce. In many real applications of linear programming models, these considerations are even more important than finding exact optimal production values. Techniques for such *sensitivity analysis* are presented in Chap. 5.

2.3 FEED-MIX SELECTION

The Hion Hog Farm Company may purchase and mix one or more of three types of grain, each containing different amounts of four nutritional elements; the data are given in Fig. 2.4. The production manager specifies that any feed mix for his livestock must meet at least minimal nutritional requirements, and he

Item	One Unit Weight of			Minimal Total Requirements Over Planning Horizon
	Grain 1	Grain 2	Grain 3	
Nutritional ingredient A	2	3	7	≥ 1250
Nutritional ingredient B	1	1	0	≥ 250
Nutritional ingredient C	5	3	0	≥ 900
Nutritional ingredient D	.6	.25	1	≥ 232.5
Cost per unit weight ($)	41	35	96	Minimize
Weight level	x_1	x_2	x_3	

FIGURE 2.4. Hion Hog Company Feed-Mix Selection.

seeks the least costly among all such mixes. Suppose his planning horizon is a two-week period, that is, he purchases enough to fill his needs for two weeks.

Assuming divisibility and additivity, we write the linear formulation as

(1) $$\text{minimize cost} \equiv \text{minimize } (41x_1 + 35x_2 + 96x_3),$$

subject to the constraints

(2)
$$2x_1 + 3x_2 + 7x_3 \geq 1250$$
$$1x_1 + 1x_2 \geq 250$$
$$5x_1 + 3x_2 \geq 900$$
$$.6x_1 + .25x_2 + 1x_3 \geq 232.5$$
$$x_j \geq 0, \quad \text{for } j = 1, 2, 3.$$

Note that in real applications of this model, as well as of the previous model, the number of activities can exceed the number of inequality restrictions. In the Product-Mix Selection Model, letting $x_j = 0$ for each variable is feasible in that all the constraints are satisfied; here the values $x_1 = 625$ and $x_2 = x_3 = 0$ provide one feasible solution. The optimal solution turns out to be $x_1 = 200, x_2 = 50,$ and $x_3 = 100$, so that the minimum cost is 19,550.

The production manager may want information other than merely values for each x_j, since the model may be an oversimplified version of the real problem. For example, he may want to know how much it will cost him to use a nonoptimal value for a specific x_j, how much excess over each minimal total nutritional requirement an optimal feed mix provides, how much he would save by reducing the minimal nutritional requirements, or how much the cost of a new feed component must drop, say Grain 4, before he seriously considers using this grain in his mix. These questions fall in the realm of sensitivity analysis.

2.4 FLUID-BLENDING SCHEDULE

Another variant of mixture models is the economic problem associated with blending fluids, such as crude oils, molten metals, and other chemicals, into saleable intermediate or finished products. Instead of using specific numerical values as we did in the previous examples, here we make use of a generalized notation.

Suppose the Twobridge Company, a firm that sells various chemical products, is planning to prepare amounts of three such blends. Each of the products may be blended from at least one of two chemical inputs, subject to certain availability and mixture constraints. Define the unknown activity levels as

x_{ij} = number of gallons of Chemical i to be used in the blend of Product j,

and we assume $x_{ij} \geq 0$. In the example, we have $i = 1, 2$, and $j = 1, 2, 3$.

The first pair of constraints limits the amount of input of each of the chemicals

(1)
$$x_{11} + x_{12} + x_{13} \leq 28$$
$$x_{21} + x_{22} + x_{23} \leq 25.$$

The top constraint in (1) indicates that the sum of the number of gallons of Chemical 1 used in Products 1, 2, and 3 cannot exceed the 28 gallons which are available during the planning horizon period. Similarly, the next constraint in (1) puts a limit of 25 gallons on the amount of Chemical 2 to be used.

The second set of constraints expresses the requirement that production must be scheduled to at least meet specific minimal levels of customer demand for each of the products:

(2)
$$x_{11} + x_{21} \geq 20$$
$$x_{12} + x_{22} \geq 10$$
$$x_{13} + x_{23} \geq 14.$$

Assume there is no volumetric loss when the two chemicals are blended. So the first constraint in (2) requires that amounts of Product 1 to be blended from both Chemicals 1 and 2 must be at least as large as the minimal level of demand 20.

The next restriction refers to a technological property to be satisfied by a mixture yielding Product 1. Suppose each input chemical contains a critical constituent. Specifically, a gallon of Chemical 1 has .1 gallon of this constituent, and a gallon of Chemical 2 has .2 gallon of this constituent. The constraint is that in the blend of Product 1, the proportional content of this constituent must be at least the fraction .15:

(3)
$$\frac{.1x_{11} + .2x_{21}}{x_{11} + x_{21}} \geq .15.$$

An analogous restriction may hold for Product 2:

(4)
$$\frac{.05x_{12} + .04x_{22}}{x_{12} + x_{22}} \leq .045;$$

here the fraction .045 is a maximal limit. After some algebraic manipulation both (3) and (4) may be rewritten in a standard *linear* form:

(5)
$$-.05x_{11} + .05x_{21} \geq 0$$
$$.005x_{12} - .005x_{22} \leq 0.$$

Finally, there may be a simple minimal ratio to be observed between the two chemical inputs in the Product 3 blend:

(6)
$$\frac{x_{13}}{x_{23}} \geq 3 \quad \text{or} \quad x_{13} - 3x_{23} \geq 0.$$

Letting p_{ij} be the profit associated with a unit of activity x_{ij}, we state the **objective function** as

(7)
$$\text{maximize profit} \equiv \text{maximize } p_{11}x_{11} + p_{12}x_{12} + p_{13}x_{13}$$
$$+ p_{21}x_{21} + p_{22}x_{22} + p_{23}x_{23}.$$

Examine how the model consisting of (1) through (7) is summarized in tabular form in Fig. 2.5. (From this point onward, we usually indicate zero coefficients of activities by blanks in the technology table.) *What questions would a manager want answered by this model?*

Item	One Gallon of						
	Chemical 1 in Product			Chemical 2 in Product			
	1	2	3	1	2	3	Restriction
Chemical 1 supply	1	1	1				≤ 28
Chemical 2 supply				1	1	1	≤ 25
Product 1 demand	1			1			≥ 20
Product 2 demand		1			1		≥ 10
Product 3 demand			1			1	≥ 14
Product 1 technology	−.05			.05			≥ 0
Product 2 technology		.005			−.005		≤ 0
Product 3 technology			1			−3	≥ 0
Unit profit ($)	p_{11}	p_{12}	p_{13}	p_{21}	p_{22}	p_{23}	Maximize
Activity level	x_{11}	x_{12}	x_{13}	x_{21}	x_{22}	x_{23}	

FIGURE 2.5. Twobridge Chemical Company Fluid-Blending Schedule.

2.5 DYNAMIC PLANNING—
INTEGRATED PRODUCTION PLANNING EXAMPLE

Each of the examples you have investigated so far has dealt with a single time period. But these planning problems can be expanded into decision models extending over several time periods. To illustrate, in the Product-Mix Selection Model, if raw material and manpower availabilities as well as unit profits change over time, and if it is possible to store excess raw materials and finished goods from one period to the next, then the optimization problem is truly dynamic. It does *not* factor completely into separate week-by-week optimization problems. Similar generalizations are possible in the feed-mix and blending models.

Common to all dynamic models is that current decisions have their effects both in the present and subsequent periods. Consequently, the important economic tradeoffs are not only those between activities within a single time period, but also those between activities in different time periods. Typically, such tradeoffs become significant when the decision-maker can invest, expand capacity, or train personnel with the effect of creating profit-making or cost-saving potentialities in future periods.

Qualitative analysis. The Out-of-Sink Appliance Company manufactures both dishwashers and washing machines. Its sales targets for the next year are shown in Fig. 2.6; the requirements are given in units and displayed for each of the four quarters during the year, a quarter being a three-month period. The **planning horizon** is thus said to be four periods. The activities in any period are to

- Utilize available workers to produce items for current and future demands
- Build inventories to meet subsequent requirements
- Alter the size of the work force.

The direct costs assignable to a production plan are those associated with manufacturing (in particular, the utilization of raw materials), with storing inventory (in particular, the cost of capital tied up in stocks), and with maintaining a labor force (in particular, the cost of wages). Each of these costs may change over the planning horizon. Specifically, the company anticipates fluctuations in raw materials costs because of cyclical supply and demand factors that occur during the year; the company's cost of capital will improve since its earnings are expected to increase during the coming year; and Out-of-Sink's current labor contract definitely calls for a wage increase at mid-year. As a result, it may save costs to produce some of the items earlier than required.

Although the variations in sales requirements and costs might make it desirable to vary production from one quarter to the next, Out-of-Sink cannot let the size of the work force fluctuate widely because it is difficult to hire skilled workers or lay off employees. Hence, leaving some of the work force idle during a quarter may prove to be economical. (In a real situation, the level of idleness would manifest itself in a slowdown or decrease in productivity.)

Time-staged formulation. Suppose that each dishwasher requires 1.5 labor hours and each washing machine 2 labor hours. At the final quarter of the previous year, the work force made available 5000 labor hours. Assume that Out-of-Sink management this year deems it unacceptable to let the size of the labor force fluctuate by more than 10% from one quarter to the next.

The five *nonnegative* decision variables in each Quarter t, where $t = 1, 2, 3, 4,$ are

d_t = number of dishwashers produced during Quarter t
w_t = number of washing machines produced during Quarter t
r_t = inventory of dishwashers on hand at the end of Quarter t in excess of the current sales target
s_t = inventory of washing machines on hand at the end of Quarter t in excess of the current sales target
h_t = available number of labor hours during Quarter t.

Let the quantities $r_0 = 75$ and $s_0 = 50$ be the inventories of dishwashers and washing machines at the beginning of the year.

Consider the constraints for the first quarter. The sales requirement for each product, given in Fig. 2.6, implies

(1)
$$d_1 + r_0 = 2000 + r_1 \quad \text{(dishwashers)}$$
$$w_1 + s_0 = 1200 + s_1 \quad \text{(washing machines),}$$

since production plus entering inventory must equal the first quarter's sales plus remaining inventory. It is convenient to rearrange the equations

(2)
$$d_1 + r_0 - r_1 = 2000 \quad \text{(dishwashers)}$$
$$w_1 + s_0 - s_1 = 1200 \quad \text{(washing machines).}$$

The labor hours constraint is written simply as

(3) $1.5d_1 + 2w_1 \leq h_1$ or equivalently $1.5d_1 + 2w_1 - h_1 \leq 0.$

Finally, since the available number of labor hours during the first quarter must be within 10% of 5000, the number of labor hours available at the final quarter of the previous year, you impose the two constraints

(4) $h_1 \geq .9(5000) = 4500$ and $h_1 \leq 1.1(5000) = 5500.$

For any other Quarter t, the analogous five linear constraints are

(5)
$$d_t + r_{t-1} - r_t = E_t$$
$$w_t + s_{t-1} - s_t = M_t$$
$$1.5d_t + 2w_t - h_t \leq 0$$
$$h_t \geq .9h_{t-1} \quad \text{and} \quad h_t \leq 1.1h_{t-1},$$

where E_t and M_t are the sales targets for dishwashers and washing machines in Quarter t, as given by Fig. 2.6.

Product	Symbol	Sales Targets			
		1st Quarter	2nd Quarter	3rd Quarter	4th Quarter
Dishwashers	E_t	2000	1300	3000	1000
Washing machines	M_t	1200	1500	1000	1400

FIGURE 2.6. Out-of-Sink Appliance Company Sales Targets.

Let c_t be the cost of each dishwasher and v_t the cost of each washing machine manufactured in Quarter t. Similarly, let j_t and k_t be the inventory holding cost per unit for period-end stocks of dishwashers and washing machines, respectively. And finally, let p_t be the wage cost per labor-hour available in Quarter t. Illustrative values are given in Fig. 2.7. Then the objective form, comprised of total direct costs, can be written as

$$\text{minimize} \quad [(c_1 d_1 + v_1 w_1 + j_1 r_1 + k_1 s_1 + p_1 h_1)$$
$$+ (c_2 d_2 + v_2 w_2 + j_2 r_2 + k_2 s_2 + p_2 h_2)$$
(6)
$$+ (c_3 d_3 + v_3 w_3 + j_3 r_3 + k_3 s_3 + p_3 h_3)$$
$$+ (c_4 d_4 + v_4 w_4 + j_4 r_4 + k_4 s_4 + p_4 h_4)].$$

The entire model is summarized in Fig. 2.8. Study the complexities that arise in determining a dynamic plan. For example, notice that a decision to increase the available number of labor hours within a quarter has an immediate impact on the costs of that period. But such a decision also may influence the number of dishwashers and washing machines that can be produced that quarter, the size of the labor force in subsequent periods, and hence production in later quarters. A decision to produce more dishwashers during a quarter may require cutting back

Decision Variable	Cost Symbol	Unit Costs			
		1st Quarter	2nd Quarter	3rd Quarter	4th Quarter
Dishwasher	c_t	125	130	125	126
Washing machine	v_t	90	100	95	95
Dishwasher inventory	j_t	5.0	4.5	4.5	4.0
Washing machine inventory	k_t	4.3	3.8	3.8	3.3
Labor hour	p_t	6.0	6.0	6.8	6.8

FIGURE 2.7. Out-of-Sink Appliance Company Unit Costs.

the production of washing machines in that quarter, as well as inducing changes in the production levels and inventories in both earlier and later quarters. *In what ways do you think that a manager would find such a planning model useful?*

d_1	w_1	r_1	s_1	h_1	d_2	w_2	r_2	s_2	h_2	d_3	w_3	r_3	s_3	h_3	d_4	w_4	r_4	s_4	h_4	
1	-1																			$= 2000 - r_0$
	1	-1																		$= 1200 - s_0$
1.5	2		-1																	≤ 0
			1																	≥ 4500
				1																≤ 5500
		1			1	-1														$= 1300$
			1			1	-1													$= 1500$
					1.5	2		-1												≤ 0
				-.9				1												≥ 0
				-1.1					1											≤ 0
							1			1	-1									$= 3000$
								1			1	-1								$= 1000$
										1.5	2		-1							≤ 0
									-.9				1							≥ 0
									-1.1					1						≤ 0
												1			1	-1				$= 1000$
													1			1	-1			$= 1400$
															1.5	2		-1		≤ 0
														-.9				1		≥ 0
														-1.1					1	≤ 0
125	90	5.0	4.3	6.0	130	100	4.5	3.8	6.0	125	95	4.5	3.8	6.8	126	95	4.0	3.3	6.8	Minimize

FIGURE 2.8. Out-of-Sink Appliance Company Dynamic Model.

▶ Observe in Fig. 2.8 the repeating pattern of coefficients. This format frequently occurs in dynamic linear programming models, although in more general situations, some of the coefficient values may change from one time period to the next. Also note that there are only a relatively few nonzero coefficients in the table. This low density of nonzero elements is typical in dynamic linear programming models. ◀

2.6 PRODUCT ALLOCATION THROUGH A TRANSPORTATION NETWORK

Many important linear programming models have what is termed a **network structure,** which yields a very simple kind of technology table. We provide a typical example below, and subsequently explain why it is equivalent to a network problem. But first let us mention what this special technology looks like, so you will know it when you see it.

For any activity variable in a network structure, the entire set of constraints contains no more than two nonzero entries, these coefficients being either $+1$ or -1. When there *are* two coefficients for an activity, then one is $+1$ and the other -1. When the technology of the model has this form, it is usually possible to interpret the optimization problem in terms of routing the flow of a single commodity through a network. Sometimes it is necessary to manipulate the equations of the model in order to establish the network structure of the problem. In Chap. 6 you will study network models in detail.

In case you forgot. Employing the $\sum$ (sigma) summation symbol considerably reduces the amount of writing to express lengthy expressions. You will see this claim borne out in the model below. If you have never taken a statistics course, or did so long ago, you may need a brush up on the rules for using the $\sum$ symbol. By means of examples, we present such a review next. (If you don't need this review, skip directly to the model.)

1. Consider the summation

$$c_1 x_1 + c_2 x_2 + c_3 x_3 + c_4 x_4 + \cdots + c_n x_n.$$

In $\sum$ notation, this sum is written as

$$\sum_{j=1}^{n} c_j x_j,$$

where the so-called *index of summation*, in this case j, may be any conveniently chosen letter. Any other index would serve as well, such as

$$\sum_{t=1}^{n} c_t x_t.$$

2. The expression

$$c_1 x_1 + d_1 y_1 + c_2 x_2 + d_2 y_2 + c_3 x_3 + d_3 y_3 + \cdots + c_n x_n + d_n y_n$$

can be written in several ways, two of which are

$$\sum_{t=1}^{n} (c_t x_t + d_t y_t) \quad \text{and} \quad \sum_{t=1}^{n} c_t x_t + \sum_{t=1}^{n} d_t y_t.$$

3. Suppose that all the c_j in the above expressions are equal; for example, suppose every $c_j = 5$. Then

$$5x_1 + 5x_2 + 5x_3 + \cdots + 5x_n$$

can be written simply as

$$5 \sum_{j=1}^{n} x_j.$$

4. Consider the expression

$$a_{i1} x_1 + a_{i2} x_2 + a_{i3} x_3 + \cdots + a_{in} x_n.$$

Here the coefficient of each x_j is a_{ij}, where i is a fixed, but unspecified, number. This expression is written as

$$\sum_{j=1}^{n} a_{ij}x_j.$$

5. Suppose the summation involves two subscripts:

$$c_{11}x_{11} + c_{12}x_{12} + c_{21}x_{21} + c_{22}x_{22} + c_{31}x_{31} + c_{32}x_{32}.$$

Notice that the first subscript takes the values 1, 2, and 3, and the second subscript takes the values 1 and 2; also, every combination of values for the first and second subscripts appears. This so-called *double summation* can be abbreviated as

$$\sum_{i=1}^{3} \sum_{j=1}^{2} c_{ij}x_{ij}.$$

The above examples cover almost all the applications of the $\sum$ notation we use in this book.

Example. A large dairy firm, the Saur Milk Company, has m plants located throughout a state. Daily milk production at Plant i can supply at most S_i gallons, for $i = 1, 2, \ldots, m$. By daybreak, the firm must furnish its n distributing warehouses with at least D_j fresh gallons, for $j = 1, 2, \ldots, n$, to meet demand requirements. The economic problem facing the distribution manager, Dawn Shirley Light, is to designate which plants are to furnish which warehouses so that total transportation costs are a minimum.

Let x_{ij} be the number of gallons shipped from Plant i to Warehouse j, and c_{ij} be the associated shipping cost per gallon. A mathematical specification of Ms. Light's model is

(1)   minimize $\displaystyle\sum_{i=1}^{m} \sum_{j=1}^{n} c_{ij}x_{ij}$

subject to the restrictions

(2) $\displaystyle\sum_{j=1}^{n} x_{ij} \leq S_i,$ for $i = 1, 2, \ldots, m$ (supply restrictions)

(3) $\displaystyle\sum_{i=1}^{m} x_{ij} \geq D_j,$ for $j = 1, 2, \ldots, n$ (demand requirements)

(4)   each $x_{ij} \geq 0.$

Figure 2.9 is a convenient tabular summary of the situation. If $\sum_{i=1}^{m} S_i \geq \sum_{j=1}^{n} D_j$, so that total supply is at least as large as total demand, it is always possible to find a *feasible* transportation schedule in which no more than $(m + n - 1)$ routes are utilized. As shown in Chap. 6, an *optimal* solution also exists in which no more than $(m + n - 1)$ routes are employed.

Plant \ Warehouse	1	2	3	⋯	n	Supplies
1	c_{11} x_{11}	c_{12} x_{12}	c_{13} x_{13}	⋯	c_{1n} x_{1n}	S_1
2	c_{21} x_{21}	c_{22} x_{22}	c_{23} x_{23}	⋯	c_{2n} x_{2n}	S_2
3	c_{31} x_{31}	c_{32} x_{32}	c_{33} x_{33}	⋯	c_{3n} x_{3n}	S_3
⋮	⋮	⋮	⋮	⋱	⋮	⋮
m	c_{m1} x_{m1}	c_{m2} x_{m2}	c_{m3} x_{m3}	⋯	c_{mn} x_{mn}	S_m
Demands	D_1	D_2	D_3	⋯	D_n	

FIGURE 2.9. Transportation Table.

▶ To construct one such feasible schedule with at most $(m + n - 1)$ routes, start at the upper-left corner, or, as it sometimes is called, the *northwest corner*, and allocate the available production S_1 to each demand requirement, beginning with D_1, until the production is exhausted. Then continue the process with S_2, and so forth. Figure 2.10 illustrates the procedure with an example. Needless to say, this trial routing may be, and often is, far from optimal. ◀

Network equivalence. Suppose we multiply by -1 each warehouse demand-requirement relation in (3). Multiplication by a negative number reverses the sense of the inequalities. Then the technology can be written as in Fig. 2.11.

Observe that in the column for each x_{ij} there are only two nonzero coefficients, $+1$ and -1, the former indicating an output at Plant i and the latter an input at Warehouse j. You can visualize the plants and warehouses as a set of points in space or, using network terminology, as a set of nodes. Each x_{ij} variable then corresponds to a flow along a directed link or arc between the Nodes i and j, and c_{ij} corresponds to the associated cost of a unit of flow. We draw the network for this example as Fig. 2.12. To complete the network specification, we show each plant's supply and each warehouse's demand requirement. As a network flow problem,

Plant \ Warehouse	1	2	3	4	Supplies
1	c_{11} 2	c_{12} 8	c_{13}	c_{14}	10
2	c_{21}	c_{22} 1	c_{23} 3	c_{24} 2	6
3	c_{31}	c_{32}	c_{33}	c_{34} 15	15
Demands	2	9	3	17	

FIGURE 2.10. Initial Feasible Solution.

the task is to allocate the amounts at the positive nodes along the various arcs so as to meet the negative nodes' requirements at a minimum cost. In management science literature, this model is often referred to as the *Hitchcock-Koopmans Transportation Problem*.

It is a remarkable property of the network problem, described by (1) through (4), that if the model has a feasible solution, an optimal solution exists for which all the x_{ij} have integer values (provided S_i and D_j are integers).

Shipping Activities

		x_{11}	x_{12}	x_{13}	...	x_{1n}	x_{21}	x_{22}	x_{23}	...	x_{2n}	...	x_{m1}	x_{m2}	x_{m3}	...	x_{mn}	
Plant Supplies	1	1	1	1	...	1												$\leq S_1$
	2						1	1	1	...	1							$\leq S_2$
	⋮											...						⋮
	m												1	1	1	...	1	$\leq S_m$
Warehouse Demands	1	−1					−1						−1					$\leq -D_1$
	2		−1					−1						−1				$\leq -D_2$
	3			−1					−1						−1			$\leq -D_3$
	⋮				⋱					⋱		...				⋱		⋮
	n					−1					−1						−1	$\leq -D_n$
		c_{11}	c_{12}	c_{13}	...	c_{1n}	c_{21}	c_{22}	c_{23}	...	c_{2n}	...	c_{m1}	c_{m2}	c_{m3}	...	c_{mn}	Minimize

FIGURE 2.11. Transportation Network Example.

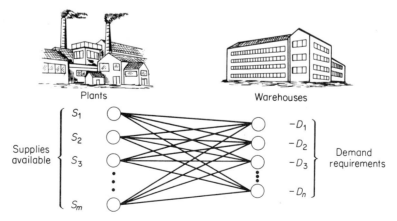

FIGURE 2.12. Transportation Network Schematic.

2.7 INDUSTRIAL IMPORTANCE
OF LINEAR OPTIMIZATION MODELS

The beginning of this chapter briefly discussed actual industrial applications of linear programming. Now that you have studied several small-scale models, you are ready to proceed with this topic in more detail.

We start again with the example of a major integrated oil company. This industry's use of linear optimization models deserves special attention for two important reasons. First, oil companies throughout the world have the best overall record of success in early and continued application of linear programming. Their experience amply demonstrates that it is practical and profitable to use mathematical models for planning purposes. Second, the oil companies, encouraged by their initial success, have pioneered the application of linear optimization methods to a wide variety of decision areas, and thus have demonstrated techniques for making this scientific approach workable in a competitive business environment.

Look back at Fig. 2.1 (p. 30) to review how the *flow* of material starts with the activity of pumping crude from the earth and ends with the activity of marketing gasoline at service stations. Linear programming models have been formulated and tested to aid in decision-making at every major point in this stream. Specifically, models have been developed to:

- Schedule production from a series of underground oil reservoirs so as to maximize profit, subject to equipment-capacity limitations and constraints imposed by physical pumping phenomena
- Determine the net profitability of exchanging a proprietary crude for another company's crude, given the configuration of refineries and the associated economics of processing the exchanged crude
- Calculate the incremental cost of increasing the amount of a product for a spot sale (for example, manufacturing a specified amount of jet fuel for a government contract), given the targeted quantities of other products to be manufactured
- Plan weekly minimum-cost schedules for refinery unit operations and product-blending, taking into account crude availabilities, throughput constraints on the refining units, performance characteristics of each product (such as octane rating), and the pre-established shipping requirements for the products
- Establish the return on investment of a proposed new refinery unit, realizing its full impact on existing units
- Route products from several refineries to a number of marketing areas along least-cost transportation paths, recognizing factors of differential costs of manufactured products at the separate refineries, relative shipping charges, and seasonal variations in customer demand
- Construct an annual plan to integrate the major decisions of the entire company.

By no means have we exhausted all the linear programming applications, or even all the important ones within an oil company. But the list is long enough to convey the wide applicability of the approach.

Since each oil company has its peculiar characteristics, such as refinery location and age configuration, marketing districts, crude-oil reserves, and so forth, firms differ in their use of linear programming models. Some find it convenient to have one or two comprehensive models that can be repeatedly employed to make several of the analyses described above. Other companies have constructed separate models for each specific purpose, with differing degrees of complexity and detail.

Certain patterns of use are well established, however, and these can guide you to an understanding of how linear programming is presently being employed in the oil industry. Many refineries calculate optimal operating schedules on a weekly or a monthly basis. A number of oil companies apply a linear programming analysis whenever they are considering a major agreement for the exchange of crude or other products. More and more, oil firms are periodically analyzing their distribution patterns to discover transportation cost savings and profit potentials for new or expanded markets. The leading firms are using linear optimization models to test different strategies for long-term growth (e.g., five years). In the dozen largest oil companies in the world, you will typically find 25 to 35 people—and often two or three times that many—whose prime responsibility is to apply linear programming to the analysis of important decisions.

Similar trends exist in other major industries, including chemicals, iron and steel, aluminum, wood products, food processing, and banking. The applications include production planning, allocating customer orders to different manufacturing plants, establishing cash flow requirements, scheduling work force levels and composition, purchasing raw materials, and deciding whether to make or buy a product. Some firms use linear programming as a performance-control device to establish variable cost budgets for a plant with significantly fluctuating output levels, and to compare actual cost performance with scientifically determined standards. Frequently, a linear optimization analysis is undertaken as a special study. For example, companies have used linear programming to establish the number and location of warehouses and new plants, the profitability of a particular line of business, and the appropriate capacity dimensions of a new piece of heavy equipment.

Improving profit. It is no easy task, of course, to apply a linear optimization model to a real business problem; use of the model must be justified on the basis of its potential, direct or indirect, contribution to the company's profits. The principal costs incurred by utilizing this approach are associated with the tasks below.

1. *Establishing the Appropriate Framework of Analysis.* It is a rare manager who immediately recognizes that solving his decision-making problem is tantamount to solving a linear programming model. Even the executive thoroughly trained in

the *techniques* of linear optimization models finds it difficult to conclude at first glance that such methods will pay off. The reason is simply that a certain amount of skillful trial and error is usually required to determine whether the essence of a complex decision problem can be captured in a linear model. To illustrate, the analyst must consider thoroughly the proper selection of a criterion function to be optimized. In some instances he may test **multiple criteria,** that is, apply several different (perhaps incommensurable) objective functions, to see if they point toward significantly different strategies. He must also exercise care in depicting the relevant constraints to be imposed on the optimization. The dangers here are twofold: he must not overlook any significant constraining factor, but on the other hand, he must not impose so many restrictions that optimization becomes impossible. The latter danger has proved the more difficult to avoid. In fact, model formulation entails about a third of the effort required in applying linear programming.

2. *Obtaining the Required Data.* Applications of linear optimization to actual planning problems typically involve 100 to 200 constraints, with two to three times as many unknowns. And models with 500 to 1000 constraints are steadily becoming more common. These large-scale applications arise when a plan is to integrate several manufacturing plants, each represented by a medium-scale model, and when a firm wants to develop a long-term program of growth. Obtaining the necessary data for a model is by far the largest of all the tasks listed here. It can easily represent half the work required.

3. *Calculating and Analyzing the Trial Answer.* Once the model has been constructed with actual data, it is necessary to calculate an optimal result. Without high-speed electronic computers, it would be virtually impossible to solve realistic industrial linear programming models. However, in minutes, these devices perform operations that would consume the equivalent of decades or even centuries of manual computing. The cost of computing a linear programming solution is now the smallest portion of the entire expense involved.

4. *Testing the Validity and Sensitivity of the Answer. Modifying the Trial Model as Necessary.* Any mathematical model of a management decision problem is inherently an abstraction. Consequently, there is no guarantee that the first trial model will produce an answer that is practical, given the myriad considerations not *explicitly* taken into account in the analysis. The solution must be examined carefully for its soundness. Further, the answer must undergo sensitivity tests to determine whether it depends critically on the exact values of particular data. If it does, the analyst may need to improve the accuracy of his data before he can rely on the validity of the model's result. Chapter 5 discusses sensitivity analysis in detail.

By studying the examples in this chapter and answering the exercises below, you will gain considerable experience in translating the essence of a complex situation into the form of a linear optimization model. In the chapters to follow, you will be introduced to additional examples that will highlight certain problems with special structures.

REVIEW EXERCISES

1 Four study-guide questions are posed at the end of Sec. 2.1. Discuss the answers to these questions in the context of each example treated in the chapter:

(a) Knox Mix Company (Sec. 2.2).
(b) Hion Hog Farm Company (Sec. 2.3).
(c) Twobridge Chemical Company (Sec. 2.4).
(d) Out-of-Sink Appliance Company (Sec. 2.5).
(e) Saur Milk Company (Sec. 2.6).

2 One reason that the models treated in this chapter are approximations to reality is that the axioms of divisibility and additivity rarely hold exactly. How good do you think these approximations are when applied to situations such as the

(a) Knox Mix Company (Sec. 2.2).
(b) Hion Hog Farm Company (Sec. 2.3).
(c) Twobridge Chemical Company (Sec. 2.4).
(d) Out-of-Sink Appliance Company (Sec. 2.5).
(e) Saur Milk Company (Sec. 2.6).

3 *Knox Mix Company* (Sec. 2.2). Using a diagram like Fig. 1.3 for the One-Potato, Two-Potato Problem discussed in Chap. 1, draw the feasible production policies, indicate an optimal policy, and calculate the associated value of the objective function *assuming* you can utilize only

(a) Process 1 and Process 3 (so that $x_2 = x_4 = 0$).
(b) Process 1 and Process 4 (so that $x_2 = x_3 = 0$).
(c) Process 2 and Process 3 (so that $x_1 = x_4 = 0$).
(d) Process 2 and Process 4 (so that $x_1 = x_3 = 0$).

4 *Knox Mix Company* (Sec. 2.2)

(a) Suppose you let $x_2 = x_3 = x_4 = 2$. What is the best value for x_1?
(b) Suppose you let $x_1 = x_2 = x_3 = 2$. What is the best value for x_4?
(c) Suppose you let $x_1 = x_3$ and $x_2 = x_4 = 0$. What is the best value for x_1 (and x_3)?
(d) Suppose you let $x_2 = x_4$ and $x_1 = x_3 = 0$. What is the best value for x_2 (and x_4)?
(e) Suppose you let $x_1 = x_2 = x_3 = x_4$. What is the best value for x_1 (and each other x_j)?

5 *Hion Hog Company* (Sec. 2.3). Using a diagram like Fig. 1.3 for the One-Potato, Two-Potato Problem discussed in Chap. 1, draw the feasible purchase policies, indicate an optimal policy, and calculate the associated value of the objective function *assuming* you can utilize

(a) Grain 1 and Grain 2 but not Grain 3 (so that $x_3 = 0$).
(b) Grain 1 and Grain 3 but not Grain 2 (so that $x_2 = 0$).
(c) Grain 2 and Grain 3 but not Grain 1 (so that $x_1 = 0$).

(d) Grain 1 and Grain 2, after setting $x_3 = 120$ for Grain 3.
(e) Grain 1 and Grain 3, after setting $x_2 = 100$ for Grain 2.
(f) Grain 2 and Grain 3, after setting $x_1 = 150$ for Grain 1.

6 *Hion Hog Company* (Sec. 2.3)

(a) Suppose you let $x_2 = x_3 = 100$. What is the best value for x_1?
(b) Suppose you let $x_1 = x_2 = 150$. What is the best value for x_3?
(c) Suppose you let $x_1 = x_2$ and $x_3 = 0$. What is the best value for x_1 (and x_2)?
(d) Suppose you let $x_1 = x_3$ and $x_2 = 0$. What is the best value for x_1 (and x_3)?
(e) Suppose you let $x_2 = x_3$ and $x_1 = 0$. What is the best value for x_2 (and x_3)?
(f) Suppose you let $x_1 = x_2 = x_3$. What is the best value for x_1 (and x_2 and x_3)?

7 *Hion Hog Company* (Sec. 2.3). Given that the optimal solution is $x_1 = 200$, $x_2 = 50$, and $x_3 = 100$, can the minimal total requirement for any of the ingredients be raised without also raising total cost? Justify your answer.

8 *Twobridge Chemical Company* (Sec. 2.4). Either indicate a feasible solution or demonstrate that no feasible solution exists if

(a) $x_{11} = 10$, $x_{12} = 5$, $x_{13} = 10.5$.   (b) $x_{21} = 5$.
(c) $x_{13} = 15$.   (d) $x_{23} = 5$.

9 *Out-of-Sink Appliance Company* (Sec. 2.5). In what ways do you think a manager would find such a planning model useful?

10 *Out-of-Sink Appliance Company* (Sec. 2.5). Find a feasible solution for each part.

(a) Assume that every period inventory is kept at a minimum.
(b) Assume that every period the size of the work force is kept to a minimum.

11 *Out-of-Sink Appliance Company* (Sec. 2.5). State how to alter the formulation for each stated assumption.

(a) No dishwashers can be produced in Quarter 4.
(b) The labor force can be increased by 12%, but cannot be decreased by more than 5%.
(c) The combined inventory of dishwashers and washing machines cannot exceed 600 in any quarter.
(d) At the end of Quarter 4, inventory must be at least 200 dishwashers and 120 washing machines.

12 *Transportation Network* (Sec. 2.6). Write all the linear restrictions (2) and (3) and the complete objective function (1) for a transportation problem in which

(a) $m = 2$ and $n = 3$.   (b) $m = 3$ and $n = 2$.
(c) $m = n = 3$.   (d) $m = 3$ and $n = 4$.

13 Explain your understanding of the following terms:

linear programming model
divisibility
additivity
nonnegative variable
variable unrestricted in sign
feasible solution
objective function
optimal solution

alternative optimal
    solutions
multiple criteria
sensitivity analysis
time-staged problem
planning horizon
network.

FORMULATION EXERCISES

14 The president, Chip Monk, of the Tim Burr Company wants to best utilize the wood resources in one of its forest regions. Within this region, there is a sawmill and a plywood mill; thus timber can be converted to lumber or plywood.

Producing a marketable mix of 1000 board feet of lumber products requires 1000 board feet of spruce and 4000 board feet of Douglas fir. Producing 1000 square feet of plywood requires 2000 board feet of spruce and 4000 board feet of Douglas fir. This region has available 32,000 board feet of spruce and 72,000 board feet of Douglas fir.

Sales commitments require that at least 5000 board feet of lumber and 12,000 square feet of plywood be produced during the planning period. The profit contributions are $45 per 1000 board feet of lumber products and $60 per 1000 square feet of plywood. Let L be the amount (in 1000 board feet) of lumber produced and P be the amount (in 1000 square feet) of plywood produced.

(a) Express the problem as a linear programming model.
(b) Employing a diagram like Fig. 1.3 for the One-Potato, Two-Potato Problem in Chap. 1, exhibit the feasible product mixes and indicate an optimal solution.

15 The plant manager, Rollin K. Old, of the Jericho Steel Company must decide how many pounds of pure steel x_1 and how many pounds of scrap metal x_2 to use in manufacturing an alloy casting for one of its customers. Assume that the cost per pound of pure steel is 3 and the cost per pound of scrap metal is 6 (which is larger because the impurities must be skimmed off). The customer's order is expressed as a demand for at least five pounds and the customer is willing to accept a greater amount if Jericho requires a larger production run.

Assume that the supply of pure steel is limited to four pounds and of scrap metal to seven pounds. The ratio of scrap to pure steel cannot exceed 7/8. The manufacturing facility has only 18 hours of melting and casting time available; a pound of pure steel requires three hours whereas a pound of scrap requires only two hours to process through the facility.

(a) Express the entire problem as a linear programming model.
(b) Employing a diagram like Fig. 1.3 for the One-Potato, Two-Potato Problem in Chap. 1, exhibit the feasible mixes of pure steel and scrap metal, and indicate an optimal solution.

Type of Pollutant	Pounds of Pollutant Emitted	
	Per 1000 Gallons of Product 1	Per 1000 Gallons of Product 2
Gas CM	24	36
Gas SD	8	12
Particulates	100	50

FIGURE 2.13

16 The Fowlayer Chemical Company has been ordered by its state government to install and employ antipollution devices. The corporation makes two products; for each of these products, the manufacturing process yields excessive amounts of irritant gases and particulates (airborne solids). Figure 2.13 shows the daily emission, in pounds, of each pollutant for every 1000 gallons of product manufactured. The company is prohibited from emitting more than G_1, G_2, and P_1 pounds of Gas CM, Gas SD, and Particulates, respectively. The profit for each thousand gallons of Products 1 and 2 manufactured per day is p_1 and p_2, respectively.

The production manager, Jose Ken Uzi, has approved the installation of two anti-pollution devices. The first device removes .75 of Gas CM, .5 of Gas SD, and .9 of the Particulates, regardless of the product made. The second device removes .33 of Gas CM, none of Gas SD, and .8 of the Particulates for Product 1, and .25 of Gas CM, none of Gas SD, and .6 of the Particulates for Product 2. The first device reduces profit per thousand gallons manufactured daily by c_1, regardless of the product; similarly, the second device reduces profit by c_2 per thousand gallons manufactured daily, regardless of the product. Sales commitments dictate that at least R_1 thousand gallons of Product 1 be produced per day, and R_2 thousand gallons of Product 2. Let the decision variables be

$$x_1 \equiv \left(\begin{array}{l}\text{thousands of gallons of Product 1 made per day}\\ \text{without using any pollution control device}\end{array}\right)$$

$$x_{11} \equiv \left(\begin{array}{l}\text{thousands of gallons of Product 1 made per day}\\ \text{using the first control device}\end{array}\right)$$

$$x_{12} \equiv \left(\begin{array}{l}\text{thousands of gallons of Product 1 made per day}\\ \text{using the second control device.}\end{array}\right).$$

Let the variables y_1, y_{11}, and y_{12} be defined similarly for Product 2.
Formulate the appropriate optimization model.

17 An account executive, Lotta Billings, of the Flagg-Poole Advertising Company has announced that she can optimally allocate her client's advertising dollars by means of linear programming. Her approach is to identify the various audiences the client wants addressed—such as teenagers, young married couples, the geriatric group, etc. Let the index i represent the ith audience. The client must specify a desired level of exposure E_i for each audience i. Then each advertising vehicle (such as *Readers' Digest*, a prime-time television spot commercial, a color ad in a Sunday newspaper, etc.) is

scored for its effectiveness in each of the identified audience categories. Let the index j represent the jth advertising vehicle, and a_{ij} the scored effectiveness for the ith audience of allocating a dollar to the jth vehicle.

Each decision variable is designated as x_j, which represents the total amount of dollars allocated to the jth advertising vehicle during a promotion campaign. Her client's objective is to minimize its total advertising expenditure while still meeting its desired levels of product exposure.

(a) Assume that there are four audiences and five advertising vehicles. Write the linear programming model implied by the above description.

(b) Discuss whether you think this linear programming model is an appropriate approach for choosing an optimal allocation of advertising dollars.

18 The Best Tasties Corporation makes four different kinds of breakfast cereals: Noisies, Soggies, Bursties, and Reposies. Each of these is a composite of ingredients (grains, vitamins, sugar, and preservatives). Let the index i represent Ingredient i, where $i = 1, 2, \ldots, I$. Let a_{Ni} be the amount of Ingredient i in a pound of Noisies, and similarly a_{Si}, a_{Bi}, and a_{Ri} be the amounts for the other three cereals. Assume that M_i is the maximum amount of Ingredient i available during the next month for making all of these breakfast cereals.

The profit contribution of a pound of Noisies is represented by p_N, and similarly, the profit contributions for the other cereals are represented by p_S, p_B, and p_R. Let x_N, x_S, x_B, and x_R represent the number of pounds of each breakfast cereal manufactured during the next month. At least 105,000 pounds of Noisies must be manufactured, as well as at least 130,000 pounds of Soggies, 45,000 pounds of Bursties, and 600,000 pounds of Reposies.

Show how an optimal production schedule can be obtained by a linear programming formulation.

19 The Turned-On Transistor Radio Company manufactures Models A, B, and C which have profit contributions of 16, 30, and 50, respectively. The weekly minimum production requirements are 20 for Model A, 120 for Model B, and 60 for Model C.

Each type of radio requires a certain amount of time for the manufacturing of component parts, for assembling, and for packaging. Specifically, a dozen units of Model A require three hours for manufacturing, four hours for assembling, and one hour for packaging. The corresponding figures for a dozen units of Model B are 3.5, 5, and 1.5, and for a dozen units of Model C are 5, 8, and 3. During the forthcoming week, the company has available 120 hours of manufacturing, 160 hours of assembling, and 48 hours of packaging time.

Formulate the production scheduling problem as a linear programming model.

20 Prior to the end of each harvest season, the Fickle Pickle Co. must contract for the purchase of cucumbers from each of N growers. This produce is then shipped to M processing plants to be converted into pickles. The Manager of Agricultural Purchases, Bumper Krupp, has collected historical data on the cucumbers grown by different farmers and has determined the variation in cucumber size to expect from each purchasing source. There are D classes of cucumbers (measured in terms of diameter size).

Plant i required R_{ik} bushels of cucumbers of Diameter k, where $i = 1, 2, \ldots, M$ and $k = 1, 2, \ldots, D$.

Let x_j be the number of bushels purchased from Grower j, and let U_j be the maximum number of bushels available from Grower j. Let p_{jk} be the fraction for a bushel purchased from Grower j that has cucumbers of Diameter k. (For example, if $p_{34} = .5$, then one-half of each bushel purchased from Grower 3 falls into the Diameter 4 size class.) Thus

$$p_{jk} \geq 0 \quad \text{and} \quad \sum_{k=1}^{D} p_{jk} = 1.$$

The cost per bushel of purchasing cucumbers from Grower j is c_j and the cost per bushel of shipping cucumbers from Grower j to Plant i is c_{ji}.

Note that, typically, a purchase plan causes the company to have more of certain size cucumbers than they actually require. Assume that after purchase, the cucumbers are sorted by size at the grower's location, and bushels of any size cucumbers that are found to be in excess supply relative to requirements are destroyed without additional cost at the grower's site.

Formulate an appropriate optimization model that indicates how many bushels to purchase from each grower, and which size cucumbers to ship to each plant.

21 The manager, Polly Wannacracker, of the Boilen Oil Company wishes to find the optimal mix of two possible blending processes. For Process 1, an input of one barrel of Crude Oil A and three barrels of Crude Oil B produces an output of 50 gallons of Gasoline X and 20 gallons of Gasoline Y. For Process 2, an input of four barrels of Crude Oil A and two barrels of Crude Oil B produces an output of 30 gallons of Gasoline X and 80 gallons of Gasoline Y. Let x_1 and x_2 be the number of barrels Wannacracker decides to use of Process 1 and Process 2, respectively.

The maximum amount of Crude Oil A available is 120 barrels and of Crude Oil B, 180 barrels. Sales commitments require that at least 2800 gallons of Gasoline X and 2200 gallons of Gasoline Y are produced. The unit profits of Process 1 and Process 2 are p_1 and p_2, respectively.

Formulate the blending problem as a linear programming model.

22 The dispatcher, Helen Copter, of High Tail Airfreight Company, which operates out of a central terminal, has 8 aircraft of Type 1, 15 aircraft of Type 2, and 11 aircraft of Type 3 available for today's flights. The tonnage capacities (in thousands of tons) are 45 for Type 1, 7 for Type 2, and 5 for Type 3.

Ms. Copter must dispatch planes to Cities A and B. Tonnage requirements (in thousands of tons) are 20 at City A and 28 at City B; excess tonnage capacity supplied to a city has no value. A plane can fly only once during the day.

The cost of sending a plane from the terminal to each city is given by the following table.

	Type 1	Type 2	Type 3
City A	23	15	1.4
City B	58	20	3.8

Let x_1, x_2, and x_3 denote the number of planes of each type sent to City A, and similarly, y_1, y_2, and y_3 the number sent to City B.

(a) Formulate a linear programming model of this routing problem.
(b) Discuss whether an answer so derived would represent an optimal solution to the actual routing problem.

23 The Glassey-Staire Television Network wants to establish competitive but profitable prices for advertising time. The following is a simplified version of its pricing problem. Assume there are three classifications of network advertising time: prime-evening, weekday, and Saturday/Sunday afternoon (before 6 p.m.). Let p_1, p_2, and p_3 be the price per minute for each of these time slots, respectively.

The network sells large blocks of time to K major advertisers who have a significant effect on the determination of the prices. The network knows that Advertiser k wants to purchase a package consisting of a_{1k}, a_{2k}, and a_{3k} minutes in the three time slots and is willing to pay up to A_k dollars for this package. The network also sells time to many smaller advertisers and figures that *in toto* it can sell M_1, M_2, and M_3 minutes of prime, weekday, and weekend time, respectively, provided that its prices are suitable with regard to the K major advertisers.

(a) Formulate the pricing problem as a linear programming model.
(b) Suppose Glassey-Staire wonders whether it should consider satisfying all but one of its major advertisers. How would you analyze this possibility?

24 The city of Shlepping, Mass. is comprised of three public school districts, each of which has a different proportion of resident black and white students. The city's Board of Education wants to devise a busing plan that will, to the greatest extent feasible, give the three districts the same racial proportions within their schools. Among alternative busing plans that meet the stated goal, the BOE will choose one that economizes total transportation costs.

The BOE has hired a consultant, Farah S. Canby, to draw up a plan, and has stated that the proportion (or fraction) of white students in each district should not differ by more than .1 from the proportion of white students in the entire city. (For example, if the proportion of white students in the entire city is .73, then the proportion of white students in each district must be between .63 and .83.) From published statistics, Canby learned that the numbers of black and white school-age residents in Districts 1, 2, and 3 are b_1, w_1; b_2, w_2; and b_3, w_3; respectively. The maximum number of students that can be accommodated in Districts 1, 2, and 3 are N_1, N_2, and N_3, respectively. The cost per student of transporting a pupil from District i to District j is c_{ij}.

Let the decision variables be x_{ij} and y_{ij} $(i \neq j)$, representing the number of black and white students, respectively, bused from District i to District j. Formulate an appropriate optimization model to assist Canby in devising an acceptable plan.

25 *Trim Problem.* A mill of the Fine-Webb Paper Company produces so-called liner board in jumbo reels having a standard width of 68 inches. (Each reel has a fixed length.) The company's customers, however, order reels having smaller widths (and the same fixed length as the larger reel). Today's orders are for 110 reels of 22-inch width, 120 reels of 20-inch width, and 80 reels of 12-inch width. These smaller widths are to be cut from the larger standard size reel.

For example, the company can decide to slit a jumbo into two reels each 22 inches wide, and one reel 20 inches wide; this leaves 4 inches of trim waste from the 68-inch jumbo. The production scheduler, Manny Blanks, wants to manufacture today's orders so as to minimize total trim waste.

(a) Find every possible way to slit a 68-inch jumbo reel into combinations of 22-inch, 20-inch, and 12-inch width reels. One such combination was already illustrated in the example. Calculate the trim waste for each combination. Label the combinations $1, 2, 3, \ldots$, and let x_i be the number of jumbo reels cut into Combination i.

(b) Formulate the problem as a linear programming model. (Note that if any smaller reels in excess of the customer requirements are produced, these too must be counted as waste.)

(c) Show that the objective function also can be written as

$$\text{minimize } 68(x_1 + x_2 + \cdots).$$

26 *Trim Problem.* Answer the questions in exercise 25 assuming that the width of the jumbo roll is 100 inches, and that today's orders are for 110 reels of 25-inch width, 120 reels of 30-inch width, and 80 reels of 35-inch width. [Note that the coefficient in part (c) is no longer 68.]

27 *Trim Problem.* Answer the questions posed in exercise 25 assuming that the width of the jumbo roll is 200 inches, and that today's orders are for 110 reels of 30-inch width, 120 reels of 55-inch width, and 80 reels of 65-inch width. [Note that the coefficient in part (c) is no longer 68.]

28 The purchasing agent, Lola Bayh, of the Fly-by-Night Airline must decide on the amounts of jet fuel to buy from three possible vendors. The airline refuels its aircraft regularly at the four airports it serves.

The oil companies have said that they can furnish up to the following amounts of fuel during the coming month: 275,000 gallons for Oil Company 1; 550,000 gallons for Oil Company 2; and 660,000 gallons for Oil Company 3. The required amount of jet fuel is 110,000 gallons at Airport 1; 220,000 gallons at Airport 2; 330,000 gallons at Airport 3; and 440,000 gallons at Airport 4.

When transportation costs are added to the bid price per gallon supplied, the combined cost per gallon for jet fuel from each vendor furnishing a specific airport is shown in the table.

	Company 1	Company 2	Company 3
Airport 1	10	7	8
Airport 2	10	11	14
Airport 3	9	12	4
Airport 4	11	13	9

(a) Formulate the decision problem as a linear programming model.
(b) Is the model equivalent to a transportation or a network problem? Explain.

29 The Seymour Hayes Manufacturing Company produces a small component for an industrial product and distributes it to five wholesalers at a fixed *delivered* price of $2.50 per unit. Sales forecasts indicate that monthly deliveries will be 2700 units to Wholesaler 1; 2700 units to Wholesaler 2; 9000 units to Wholesaler 3; 4500 units to Wholesaler 4; and 3600 units to Wholesaler 5.

   The monthly production capacities are 4500 at Plant 1; 9000 at Plant 2; and 11,250 at Plant 3. The direct costs of producing each unit are $2.00 at Plant 1, $1.00 at Plant 2, and $1.80 at Plant 3.

   The transportation costs of shipping a unit from a plant to a wholesaler are given below.

	Whlslr. 1	Whlslr. 2	Whlslr. 3	Whlslr. 4	Whlslr. 5
Plant 1	$.05	$.07	$.11	$.15	$.16
Plant 2	.08	.06	.10	.12	.15
Plant 3	.10	.09	.09	.10	.16

   Formulate a linear programming model to indicate optimal production amounts at each plant, and to show how many components each plant supplies each wholesaler.

30 The Faye Stout Rayon Company has introduced a new synthetic acetate fiber that it expects will replace much of its current sales of staple rayon. The resultant large demand for the synthetic coupled with production difficulties at the plant make it necessary for the Stout Co. to ship substitutions, when permitted, to some of its customers. Thus, a customer ordering acetate Fiber 3 may actually be shipped some of Fiber 5 if Fiber 3 is in short supply and the switch is allowed by the customer. Even with such substitutions, not all customer demand for certain fiber types can be satisfied. For each of the acetate types in short supply, the company wants to fill the same proportion of every customer's order. (In other words, if the total orders for Fiber k are 150,000 pounds and only 100,000 pounds of these orders can be supplied, some of the supply possibly being substitute product, then each customer who ordered Fiber k receives a shipment of $\frac{2}{3}$ of the quantity ordered, the shipment being comprised of Fiber k and permitted substitutes.) Further, in case of short supply, the company also tries to ship each customer its fair share of the actual fiber it ordered. (For example, if 150,000 pounds of Fiber k were ordered and only 50,000 pounds of Fiber k are available, then each customer receives *about* $\frac{1}{3}$ of its ordered quantity of Fiber k. The remaining $\frac{2}{3}$ of its ordered quantity may be satisfied with permitted substitute product shipped by Stout Co.)

   Let 10 be the total number of fibers manufactured and 70 the total number of customers. Let x_{ijk} be the pounds of Fiber k that are shipped to Customer i to satisfy its order q_{ij} for Fiber j, where $i = 1, 2, \ldots, 70$, and $j = 1, 2, \ldots, 10$, and $k = 1, 2, \ldots, 10$. When $j \neq k$, a substitute product is being shipped. The amount of Fiber j available for shipment is A_j pounds. The cost per pound of shipping Fiber k to Customer i who ordered Fiber j is c_{ijk} (this cost may include a penalty for substitution; if substitution of Fiber k for Fiber j in Customer i's order is not permitted, this cost can be set arbitrarily large). Let x_j be the fraction of each customer's order for Fiber j that is actually filled (with Fiber j and permitted substitutes). For each Customer i, let d_{ij} be the penalty cost per pound of Fiber j ordered but not filled (with Fiber j and permitted substitutes). Finally, require that every customer receives at least 95% but no more than 105% of its fair share of each fiber ordered that is in short supply. Formulate an appropriate optimization model.

31 The Kleen City Police Department has the following minimal *daily* requirements for policemen and policewomen:

Time of Day (24-Hour Clock)	Period	Minimal Number of Police Required During Period
2–6	1	22
6–10	2	55
10–14	3	88
14–18	4	110
18–22	5	44
22–2	6	33

Note, consider Period 1 as following immediately after Period 6.

Each person works eight consecutive hours. Let x_t denote the number of persons starting work in Period t every day. The Police Department has retained the consulting services of a European expert, Herr Kohm D'Phuz, to obtain a daily schedule that employs the least number of policemen and policewomen, provided that each of the above requirements are met.

Formulate a linear programming model to find an optimal schedule.

32 Around 435 B.C., Sparta decided to draft reserve troops to supplement its regular army. New warriors could be enlisted for 1, 2, 3, or 4 years. Let x_{1t}, x_{2t}, x_{3t}, and x_{4t} be the number of warriors enlisted in Year t for 1, 2, 3, and 4 years, respectively. The associated unit costs are c_{1t}, c_{2t}, c_{3t}, and c_{4t}. In each Year t, the minimal total reserve warrior strength was set at R_t; R_t varied from year to year.

As a Spartan general, you could find an optimal enlistment policy for the ensuing 10 years by solving the problem as a linear programming model. For simplicity, let $t = 1$ denote the year 435 B.C.

Formulate a linear programming model to find an optimal policy.

33 The Haut Dam Water System is comprised of several dams, reservoirs, and river tributaries. One of these, the Gaul Dam Reservoir, is used for recreation (swimming, water skiing, canoeing). It is important to keep the average depth of this reservoir within prescribed limits, which vary from one month to the next. Rhoda Boate is the Section Chief in the state's Waterways Department. She is responsible for monthly decisions on how much water to release from the Haut Dam into the Gaul Dam. The engineers in her department have estimated a rapid rate of seepage and evaporation at Gaul Dam; since rainfall is negligible, Gaul Dam must be maintained by spillage from Haut Dam.

Suppose that Boate's department plans ahead for 20 months. During Month t, let x_t denote the average depth of the reservoir prior to augmenting with Haut Dam water; $x_1 = 25$ for Month 1. Let y_t be the number of feet Boate decides to *add* to the average depth in Month t—that is, a positive value for y_t indicates a decision to augment the reservoir with dam water. Let L_t and U_t represent the lower and upper prescribed limits, respectively, of the average reservoir depth after augmentation of dam water in Month t. Assume that x_{t+1} is .75 of the average reservoir depth in Month t after augmentation.

(a) Suppose that the cost of augmenting the reservoir is c_t per foot in Month t. Formulate an appropriate optimization model.

*(b) Suppose that the cost of augmenting the reservoir is c_t per foot in Month t, provided that the augmentation amount does not exceed 5 feet. Any augmentation in excess of 5 feet incurs a cost of d_t per foot in Month t. Revise your answer in part (a) to reflect this cost structure.

34 The personnel director, Ona Tripp, of the Feedem-Speedem Airline Company must decide how many new stewardesses to hire and train over the next six months. The requirements expressed as the number of stewardess-flight-hours needed are 8000 in January; 9000 in February; 7000 in March; 10,000 in April; 9000 in May; and 11,000 in June.

It takes one month of training before a stewardess can be put on a regular flight; so a girl must be hired at least a month before she is actually needed. Each trainee requires 100 hours of supervision by experienced stewardesses during the month of training so that 100 less hours are available for flight service by regular stewardesses.

Each experienced stewardess can work up to 150 hours in a month, and Feedem-Speedem has 60 regular stewardesses available at the beginning of January. If the maximum time available from experienced stewardesses exceeds a month's flying and training requirements, the regular girls work fewer than 150 hours, and none are laid off. By the end of each month, approximately 10% of the experienced stewardesses quit their jobs to be married or for other reasons.

An experienced stewardess costs the company $850 and a trainee $450 a month in salary and other benefits.

(a) Formulate the hiring-and-training problem as a linear programming model. Let x_t be the number of stewardesses that begin training in Month t, where $x_0 = 60$. Define any additional symbols that you need to express the decision variables.

(b) The above statement of the problem assumes a six-month planning horizon. Suppose you add July's requirements to the model. Would the previous solution necessarily change? Explain.

35 *Knox Mix Company* (Sec. 2.2). Suppose that by using overtime production, the company has available an additional 5 man-weeks. The unit profit from overtime production is .9 of the unit profits displayed in Fig. 2.3. Formulate the product-mix selection problem by adding the decision possibilities of utilizing the production processes on overtime. Assume that the technological coefficients in Fig. 2.3 remain unchanged for overtime production.

36 *Knox Mix Company* (Sec. 2.2). Assume that the technological data shown in Fig. 2.3 are valid for each of four consecutive time periods. Suppose you can store *excess* (or *unused*) Material Y and Material Z from one period to the next at a holding cost per unit per period of h_Y and h_Z, respectively. Formulate the product-mix selection problem as a dynamic planning problem. Be sure to define new symbols that indicate the time period for each production variable, and to specify the storage activities.

37 *Twobridge Chemical Company* (Sec. 2.4). Assume that the data in Fig. 2.5 are valid in each of six consecutive periods, except that the available supplies of chemicals, the demands for the products, and the profits of each activity vary from period to period. State how you would modify the model to permit excess supplies of Chemicals 1 and 2 in one period to be inventoried for possible use in succeeding periods, and to allow for Products 1, 2, and 3 made in one period to be stored for meeting demands in subsequent periods. Be sure to define new symbols that indicate the time period for each production variable and to specify the storage activities.

38 The Monty Zooma Company has announced the introduction of an exciting new perfume Revenge. The product manager, Tuffon de Butts, wants to draw up a production and employment plan for the next 18 months. Assume that each worker can produce 300 bottles of perfume per month. Perfume can be stored from one month to the next, but due to spoilage and pilferage, there is a 5% loss (in other words, for each 100 bottles stored in Month t, only 95 are available in Month t + 1). The initial level of employment is 50 workers; each month, additional workers may be hired if needed, released if not needed, or kept on the payroll but left idle. Workers left idle have a tendency to quit, and the attrition rate is 10%. Hence for each 10 workers left idle in Month t, only 9 choose to remain on the work force at Month t + 1. There is only a 1% monthly attrition rate for workers engaged in production.

For each Month t, let e_t be the number of workers engaged in perfume production, s_t the inventory of bottles at the end of the month, x_t and y_t the increase and decrease, respectively, in the work force at the beginning of the month, and d_t the number of workers left idle. Let the corresponding unit costs be c_t, i_t, h_t, f_t, and n_t, respectively. In Month t, de Butts expects to sell S_t bottles of perfume, and hence wants to find a minimum cost employment and production plan that is capable of meeting these sales requirements. Assume that at the start of Month 19, inventory of bottles must be at least I, and the work force must be at least W. Formulate an appropriate optimization model.

39 The president, DeWitt Quigley, of the Expando Manufacturing Company, which produces a single type of item, wishes to enlarge its capacity over the next six periods (a period is three months). The company's objective is to have its production capacity as large as possible by the beginning of the seventh period.

Each item produced in a period requires 100 dollars (for the purchase of raw materials and the payment of wages), and one unit of plant capacity; it yields 140 dollars of sales revenue at the beginning of the *next* period.

In each period, the company can use either or both of two construction techniques to expand its plant. Each requires cash in the period the expansion is initiated, and one takes more time than the other. Specifically, building a unit of capacity by Expansion Method 1 requires 20,000 dollars when the construction activity is started and yields the added capacity by the beginning of the following period. Building a unit of capacity by Expansion Method 2 requires 15,000 dollars when the construction activity is started and yields the added capacity by the beginning of the period *after* the following one.

The company has 250,000 dollars to finance production and expansion in Period 1, but requires that the subsequent production and expansion activities be self-funding

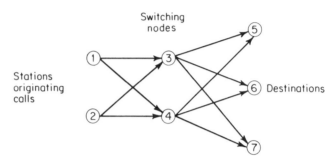

FIGURE 2.14

that is, no supply of cash will be forthcoming from *outside* sources after the first period). In Period 7 production must be feasible at full capacity. The plant capacity at the start of Period 1 is 800.

For each Period t, let x_t denote the production level; u_t and v_t the levels of capacity expansion using Methods 1 and 2, respectively; w_t unused cash at the end of the period; and z_t unused plant capacity.

Show how the problem can be solved by a linear programming formulation.

40 A renowned money market trader, Perspa Cassidy, often finds profitable arbitrage transactions in foreign currencies. Suppose that Cassidy faces possible trades in seven different currencies (U.S. dollar, British pound sterling, French franc, German deutsche mark, Italian lira, Swiss franc, and Japanese yen). Let x_{ij} be the amount of Currency i that Cassidy sells in exchange for Currency j, and let r_{ij} be the exchange rate. For example, $r_{12} = .43$ indicates that for each U.S. dollar that Cassidy sells, she can obtain .43 pound sterling.

Assume that with rapid communications, Cassidy knows the current values of all r_{ij} at any moment, and that she can execute virtually simultaneous exchange agreements. The only requirement on Cassidy is that she is not short on any currency. In other words, Cassidy must at least be able to cover the total sales of each currency with the proceeds coming from any of the other exchanges that yield that currency.

Cassidy seeks a set of currency exchanges that yield a profit measured in U.S. dollars.

(a) Formulate an appropriate optimization model.
(b) What are the possible optimal values for the objective function?

41 The Babylon Corporation finds its internal telephone communication network is failing to meet peak-load requirements because of limited transmission capacities and has asked a communications consultant, Wanda Rapp, for advice. Two stations originate calls, and three stations receive the calls; more than one call can be sent or received by any station. The calls are transmitted through links and two switching nodes. Figure 2.14 illustrates the situation.

The decision problem facing Ms. Rapp is to increase the transmission capacity of the network in an economic manner. Increasing the capacities to handle the entire peak-load requirements may be too expensive, but some improvement in service is required.

Let a_{ij} be the daily peak-load requirements of messages originating at Station i and destined for Station j, where $i = 1$ and 2 and $j = 5$, 6, and 7. Let C_{kj} be the present link-transmission capacity between Switching Node k and Destination j, where $k = 3$ and 4, and $j = 5$, 6, and 7. Let S_k be the present transmission capacity for messages flowing through Switching Node k.

Define

$$x_{ikj} = \begin{pmatrix} \text{the number of calls originating at Station i, destined for Station j,} \\ \text{and passing through Switching Node k} \end{pmatrix}$$

$$c_{kj} = \begin{pmatrix} \text{new transmission capacity along the link between} \\ \text{Switching Node k and Destination j} \end{pmatrix}$$

$$s_k = \begin{pmatrix} \text{new transmission capacity through} \\ \text{Switching Node k} \end{pmatrix}.$$

The constraints to be satisfied are

(i) The total number of calls from each originating station to each destination cannot exceed the peak-load requirement for such calls.

(ii) The total number of calls passing along the link between a switching node and a destination cannot exceed the corresponding link-transmission capacity.

(iii) The total number of calls passing through any switching node cannot exceed the corresponding transmission capacity.

(iv) The new link and node capacities must be at least as large as at present.

The service-level requirement is specified as follows. The routing of calls must satisfy the restriction that the ratio of the *total* number of calls that are actually transmitted to the sum of all the peak-load requirements must be at least f (where $f < 1$).

The cost of increasing link-transmission capacity by one unit between Switching Node k and Destination j is d_{kj}, and of increasing node-transmission capacity at Switching Node k by one unit is d_k.

Show how a linear programming formulation can be used to find a minimum-cost plan for increasing link and node capacities, subject to the above-mentioned constraints.

CONTENTS

CHAPTER 3

Algebraic and Geometric Representations of Linear Optimization Models

3.1 INTRODUCTION

Chapter 2 scanned a wide assortment of linear optimization models. For the most part, the constraints were written as immediate translations of a verbal description. The chapter gave scant notice to the possible connections among different formulations, nor did it elaborate on how much flexibility you have in specifying a model. We provide this information here.

In the initial sections below, you will study how to manipulate linear constraints into different-appearing but mathematically equivalent statements. The techniques presented are helpful for two reasons. First, they enable you to prepare any particular problem you may have for numerical solution by the techniques discussed in Chaps. 4 and 5. Second, they permit you to formulate the model in a way that will subsequently enable you to see how to apply powerful mathematical analysis.

The remainder of the chapter deals with geometric representations of a linear optimization model. Of course, two- and three-dimensional geometric constructions are not sufficient for solving actual large-scale applications; however, these pictorial interpretations do aid you in developing intuition about the workings of a linear programming model.

In all honesty, though, if you are impatient to learn how to find numerical solutions to linear programming models, go ahead and read Chap. 4. You can come back later to read the material in this chapter.

3.2 GENERAL ALGEBRAIC FORMULATION

We can summarize the mathematical representations of the several models you studied in Chap. 2 in the following way. Letting x_j be the level of Activity j, for $j = 1, 2, \ldots, n$, you want to select a value for each x_j such that

$$p_1 x_1 + p_2 x_2 + \cdots + p_n x_n$$

is maximized, or minimized, depending on the context of the problem. The x_j are constrained by a number of relations, each of which is one of the following types:

$$a_1 x_1 + a_2 x_2 + \cdots + a_n x_n \geq a$$
$$b_1 x_1 + b_2 x_2 + \cdots + b_n x_n = b$$
$$c_1 x_1 + c_2 x_2 + \cdots + c_n x_n \leq c.$$

The first relation includes the possible restriction $x_j \geq 0$.
Such a constrained optimization problem may have

(i) no feasible solution, that is, there may be no values of all the x_j, for $j = 1, 2, \ldots, n$, that satisfy every constraint;
(ii) a unique optimal feasible solution;
(iii) more than one optimal feasible solution; or
(iv) a feasible solution such that the objective function is unbounded; that is, the value of the function can be made as large as desired in a maximization problem, or as small in a minimization problem, by selecting an appropriate feasible solution.

In a few instances, Chap. 2 indicated how there can be more than one explicit way to represent the linear relations characterizing a linear optimization model. For example, in the dairy company model of Sec. 2.7, the sense of the demand-requirements inequalities (3) was reversed by changing the sign of all the constants.

Changing the sense of the optimization. Any linear maximization model can be viewed as an equivalent linear minimization model, and vice versa, by accompanying the change in the optimization sense with a change in the signs of the objective function coefficients. Specifically,

$$\text{maximize } \sum_{j=1}^{n} c_j x_j \quad \text{can be treated as} \quad \text{minimize } \sum_{j=1}^{n} (-c_j) x_j$$

and vice versa. Of course, if V is the optimal value of the right-hand expression above, then $-V$ is the optimal value of the left-hand expression.

Changing the sense of an inequality. All inequalities in a linear programming model can be represented with the same directed inequality since

(1) $$\sum_{j=1}^{n} a_j x_j \leq b \quad \text{can be written as} \quad \sum_{j=1}^{n} (-a_j) x_j \geq -b,$$

and vice versa. To illustrate, the following two inequalities are equivalent:

$$1x_1 - 1x_2 \leq -4 \qquad -1x_1 + 1x_2 \geq 4.$$

Converting an inequality to an equality. Any inequality in a linear model can be represented as an equality by introducing a nonnegative variable as follows:

(2) $\quad \sum_{j=1}^{n} a_j x_j \leq b \quad$ can be written as $\quad \sum_{j=1}^{n} a_j x_j + 1s = b \quad$ where $s \geq 0$

(3) $\quad \sum_{j=1}^{n} a_j x_j \geq b \quad$ can be written as $\quad \sum_{j=1}^{n} a_j x_j - 1t = b \quad$ where $t \geq 0$.

It is common to refer to a variable such as s in (2) as a **slack variable,** and t in (3) as a **surplus variable.**

To illustrate, in the Product-Mix Selection Example of Sec. 2.2, the constraint on the availability of pounds of Material Y was

$$7x_1 + 5x_2 + 3x_3 + 2x_4 \leq 120.$$

An equivalent way of viewing this restriction is

$$7x_1 + 5x_2 + 3x_3 + 2x_4 + 1y = 120 \quad \text{where} \quad y \geq 0,$$

where y in interpreted as left-over or unused pounds of Material Y. Here y is a slack variable.

Similarly, in the Feed-Mix Selection Example of Sec. 2.3, you can write the constraint on Nutritional Ingredient A as

$$2x_1 + 3x_2 + 7x_3 - 1a = 1250 \quad \text{where} \quad a \geq 0,$$

where a is viewed as the overfulfillment of the requirement for Ingredient A. Thus a is a surplus variable.

*Converting equalities to inequalities. Any linear equality or set of linear equalities can be represented as a set of like-directioned linear inequalities by imposing one additional constraint. To motivate the idea, note that $x = 8$ is equivalent to the combination $x \leq 8$ and $x \geq 8$, which in turn can be written as the pair $x \leq 8$ and $-x \leq -8$. As you should check graphically, the equations $x = 1$ and $y = 2$ are equivalent to the combination $x \leq 1, y \leq 2$, and $x + y \geq 3$, which in turn can be expressed as $x \leq 1, y \leq 2$, and $-x - y \leq -3$. The idea generalizes as follows:

(4) $\qquad \sum_{j=1}^{n} a_{ij} x_j = b_i \quad$ for $i = 1, 2, \ldots, m \quad$ can be written as

(5) $$\sum_{j=1}^{n} a_{ij}x_j \le b_i \quad \text{for } i = 1, 2, \ldots, m \quad \text{and} \quad \sum_{j=1}^{n} \alpha_j x_j \le \beta$$

where

(6) $$\alpha_j = -\sum_{i=1}^{m} a_{ij} \quad \text{and} \quad \beta = -\sum_{i=1}^{m} b_i.$$

Thus for $m = 1$, (5) is simply

(7) $$\sum_{j=1}^{n} a_{1j}x_j \le b_1 \quad \text{and} \quad -\sum_{j=1}^{n} a_{1j}x_j \le -b_1.$$

For an illustration, consider the system

$$1x_1 + 1x_2 \qquad\quad = 1$$

$$2x_1 \qquad - 4x_3 = -5.$$

Apply (5) and (6) to verify that this system is equivalent to the system below:

$$1x_1 + 1x_2 \qquad\quad \le 1$$

$$2x_1 \qquad - 4x_3 \le -5$$

$$-3x_1 - 1x_2 + 4x_3 \le 4.$$

*Converting variables unconstrained in sign to nonnegative variables. When for some j, x_j is unconstrained in sign in a linear model, two transformations are helpful in finding a numerical solution. The first is to select a constraining *equality* containing x_j. This can always be done, possibly after converting an inequality to an equality. Then, using this relation as a *definition* for x_j, substitute for x_j in all the other linear relations, including the objective function, and simplify by collecting terms.

For example, if x_1 is unconstrained in sign and appears in relation 1, which is stated as an equality, write

(8) $$x_1 = \frac{1}{a_{11}}\left(b_1 - \sum_{j=2}^{n} a_{1j}x_j\right).$$

Then the right-hand side of (8) is substituted wherever x_1 appears in the model. As is easily seen, the resultant relations are still linear in the remaining variables.

During the optimizing computational process, the definitional relation for x_j may be completely ignored. *After* a solution for the remaining variables is obtained, x_j can be computed from its definitional relation.

The second transformation converts x_j into the difference between two nonnegative variables and substitutes this difference for x_j wherever x_j appears. Specifically,

(9) $$x_j \equiv x'_j - x''_j \quad \text{where } x'_j \geq 0 \quad \text{and} \quad x''_j \geq 0.$$

Thus this transformation expands the number of variables in the model, and preserves linearity of the original relations. The legitimacy of the substitution of (9) requires an argument, but the idea is simple enough and you may want to justify it for yourself.

▶ A third transformation, closely allied to the idea used in relations (4), (5), and (6), is to add only a single new nonnegative variable z and make the conversion

(i) $$x_j \equiv x'_j - z \quad \text{where } x'_j \geq 0 \quad \text{and} \quad z \geq 0$$

for each x_j unconstrained in sign.

Suppose x_j, for $j = 1, 2, \ldots, k \leq n$, is unconstrained in sign. Then the constraints

(ii) $$\sum_{j=1}^{n} a_{ij} x_j = b_i \quad \text{for } i = 1, 2, \ldots, m$$

become

(iii) $$\sum_{j=1}^{k} a_{ij} x'_j + \sum_{j=k+1}^{n} a_{ij} x_j - \alpha_i z = b_i \quad \text{for } i = 1, 2, \ldots, m,$$

where

(iv) $$\alpha_i = \sum_{j=1}^{k} a_{ij} \quad \text{for } i = 1, 2, \ldots, m. \qquad ◀$$

*Converting lower-bounded variables to nonnegative variables. When an x_j is bounded below by $b_j \neq 0$, it is possible to convert the model into one with a nonnegative variable (that is, where b_j is replaced with 0) by employing the relation

(10) $$x_j \equiv b_j + x'_j \quad \text{where} \quad x'_j \geq 0.$$

Thus the right-hand side of (10) is substituted for x_j wherever x_j appears.

3.3 CANONICAL FORMS FOR
LINEAR OPTIMIZATION MODELS

As you will see in later chapters, it is convenient to be able to write *any* linear optimization model in a compact and unambiguous form. The various transformations above allow you to meet this objective, although it is now apparent that there is considerable latitude in the selection of a particular canonical form to employ. We illustrate two such representations here.

Any linear optimization model can be viewed as

(1)
$$\text{maximize } \sum_{j=1}^{n} c_j x_j$$

subject to

(2)
$$\sum_{j=1}^{n} a_{ij} x_j \leq b_i \quad \text{for } i = 1, 2, \ldots, m$$

(3)
$$x_j \geq 0 \quad \text{for } j = 1, 2, \ldots, n.$$

Similarly, any linear optimization model can be written as

(4)
$$\text{minimize } \sum_{j=1}^{n} c_j x_j$$

subject to

(5)
$$\sum_{j=1}^{n} a_{ij} x_j = b_i \quad \text{for } i = 1, 2, \ldots, m \quad (b_i \geq 0)$$

(6)
$$x_j \geq 0 \quad \text{for } j = 1, 2, \ldots, n.$$

It is typical, although not required, that $n > m$ in (5).

3.4 GEOMETRIC INTERPRETATION

In undertaking the solution and mathematical analysis of linear optimization models in Chaps. 4 and 5, you will see that a grasp of the *algebraic* nature of this type of model is required. Your comprehension of the algebraic properties may be enhanced, however, through a geometric interpretation of the ideas. Accordingly, in order to deepen your understanding of the properties of linear optimization models, we turn to description of the geometry of these problems. So that you do not misconstrue the intent here, we emphasize that a geometric viewpoint usually affords very little help in obtaining numerical solutions to *actual* linear optimization models.

Solution space representation—two dimensions (variables). You have already seen this representation in the One-Potato, Two-Potato Problem of Chap. 1. You may want to skim over the example to refresh your memory. Here we proceed directly to the consideration of a numerical example:

(1)
$$\text{maximize } \quad 12x_1 + 15x_2$$

subject to

(2)
$$4x_1 + 3x_2 \leq 12$$

(3)
$$2x_1 + 5x_2 \leq 10$$

(4)
$$x_1 \geq 0 \quad \text{and} \quad x_2 \geq 0.$$

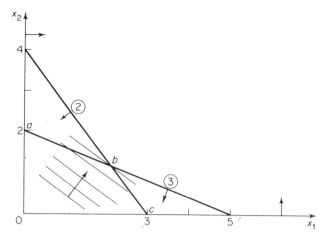

FIGURE 3.1. Solution Space.

The problem is graphed in Fig. 3.1. Observe that both (2) and (3) are drawn as equations. Then each inequality is indicated by an arrow on the side of the line representing permissible values of x_1 and x_2. Since the two variables must be non-negative, the region of permissible values is bounded also by the two coordinate axes.

Accordingly, the polygon $\overline{oabc}$ represents the region of values for x_1 and x_2 that satisfy all the constraints. This polygon is called the **solution set.** The set of points described by the polygon is **convex,** meaning that if any two points of the polygon are selected arbitrarily, then a straight-line segment joining the two points contains only points of the polygon. The vertices o, a, b, and c are referred to as the **extreme points** of the polygon in that they are not on the interior of any line segment connecting two distinct points of the polygon.

The parallel lines in the figure represent various values of the objective function. The arrow points in the direction of increasing values of the objective function. The optimal solution is at the extreme point b, where $x_1 = \frac{15}{7}$, $x_2 = \frac{8}{7}$, and $12x_1 + 15x_2 = \frac{300}{7}$.

Alternative optimal solutions. If the coefficients of the objective function are changed so as to alter the direction of the parallel lines in Fig. 3.1, it is clear that the optimal solution point may change, but in any case there is *always* an extreme-point optimal solution. Consider, in Fig. 3.2, a problem for one specific rotation of the parallel lines:

(5)   maximize $4x_1 + 10x_2$

again subject to the same constraints (2), (3), and (4).

Now, all the points (an infinite number) on the segment $\overline{ab}$ are optimal. Thus

$x_1 = \frac{15}{7}$ and $x_2 = \frac{8}{7}$ are still optimal. But so are $x_1 = 0$ and $x_2 = 2$, as well as any positive-weighted average of these two optimal solutions. The optimal value of the objective function is 20.

Unbounded optimal solutions. The third illustration, shown in Fig. 3.3, is based on the model

(6)   maximize $-2x_1 + 6x_2$

subject to

(7) $-1x_1 - 1x_2 \leq -2$

(8) $-1x_1 + 1x_2 \leq 1$

(9) $x_1 \geq 0$ and $x_2 \geq 0.$

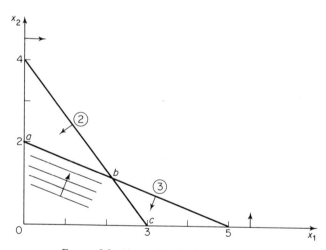

FIGURE 3.2. Alternative Optimal Solutions.

The solution set for this problem is *unbounded*. Check that it is convex, and verify that a and b are the only extreme points. The objective function for the problem can be made arbitrarily large. Given any value for the objective function, there always is a solution point having an even greater objective function value. And there always is such a point satisfying (8) with equality.

Infeasible problem. The fourth illustration, shown in Fig. 3.4, is based on the problem

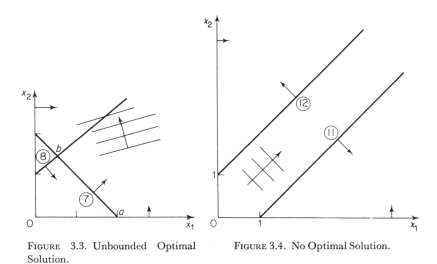

FIGURE 3.3. Unbounded Optimal Solution.   FIGURE 3.4. No Optimal Solution.

$$\text{(10)} \qquad\qquad \text{maximize} \quad 1x_1 + 1x_2$$

subject to

$$\text{(11)} \qquad\qquad -1x_1 + 1x_2 \leq -1$$

$$\text{(12)} \qquad\qquad 1x_1 - 1x_2 \leq -1$$

$$\text{(13)} \qquad\qquad x_1 \geq 0 \quad \text{and} \quad x_2 \geq 0.$$

Figure 3.4 illustrates that the problem does not have a feasible solution.

Conclusion. We will summarize the results of the several geometric illustrations you have studied.

   (i) If the solution set is nonempty, it is convex and may be either bounded or unbounded.

  (ii) If the solution set is nonempty, the optimal value of the objective function may be finite or unbounded. If finite, then an optimal solution exists at an extreme point.

REVIEW AND COMPUTATIONAL EXERCISES

1 Explain your understanding of the following terms:

sense of optimization	*lower-bounded	solution set
sense of an inequality	variable	convex set
slack variable	canonical form	extreme-point solution.
surplus variable	solution space	

In Secs. 3.2 and 3.3, you read that any linear programming model can be transformed into certain specified canonical forms. Two such representations are

$$\text{maximize} \sum_{j=1}^{n} c_j x_j$$

subject to   (Form 1)

$$\sum_{j=1}^{n} a_{ij} x_j \leq b_i \quad \text{for } i = 1, 2, \ldots, m$$

$$x_j \geq 0 \quad \text{for } j = 1, 2, \ldots, n,$$

and

$$\text{minimize} \sum_{j=1}^{n} c_j x_j$$

subject to   (Form 2)

$$\sum_{j=1}^{n} a_{ij} x_j = b_i \quad \text{for } i = 1, 2, \ldots, m, \quad \text{and where} \quad b_i \geq 0$$

$$x_j \geq 0 \quad \text{for } j = 1, 2, \ldots, n.$$

In exercises 2 through 5, transform each problem into Form 1 and Form 2.

2 Consider

$$\text{minimize} \quad 3x_1 - 4x_2 + 1x_3$$

subject to

$$-1x_1 \qquad + 5x_3 \leq 50$$

$$2x_1 - 3x_2 \qquad \geq 12.$$

(a) Assume every $x_j \geq 0$.

*(b) Assume the first constraint is an equality and every $x_j \geq 0$.

*(c) Assume $x_1 \geq 4$, $x_2 \geq 0$, and $x_3 \geq 0$.

*(d) Assume $x_1 \geq 0$, $x_2 \geq -5$, and $x_3 \geq 0$.

3 Consider

$$\text{maximize} \quad 1x_1 - 2x_2 + 3x_3$$

subject to

$$1x_1 + 1x_2 + 1x_3 \leq 7$$

$$1x_1 - 1x_2 + 1x_3 \leq -2$$

$$3x_1 \qquad + 2x_3 \geq 5$$

$$1x_2 - 1x_3 \geq 1.$$

(a) Assume every $x_j \geq 0$.

(b) Assume $x_1 \geq 0$, $x_2 \geq 0$, and $x_3 \leq 0$.

*(c) Assume the last constraint is an equality and every $x_j \geq 0$.

*(d) Assume $x_1 \geq 0$, $x_2 \geq 2$, and $x_3 \geq 0$.

*(e) Assume $x_1 \geq 0$, $x_2 \geq 0$, and x_3 is unconstrained in sign.

*(f) Assume $x_1 \geq 0$, $x_2 \geq 0$, and $x_3 \geq -4$.

4 Consider

$$\text{minimize} \quad -2x_1 + 5x_2 - x_3 + 6x_4$$

subject to

$$4x_1 \qquad - 2x_3 + x_4 \leq 2$$

$$2x_1 + x_2 + 4x_3 - x_4 \geq 12$$

$$-3x_1 + 2x_2 \qquad - 8x_4 \geq -31$$

$$x_1 + x_2 + x_3 + x_4 \leq 12.$$

(a) Assume every $x_j \geq 0$.

(b) Assume $x_4 \leq 0$ and every other $x_j \geq 0$.

*(c) Assume the first and third constraints are equalities and every $x_j \geq 0$.

*(d) Assume $x_4 \geq 2$ and every other $x_j \geq 0$.

*(e) Assume $x_4 \geq -2$ and every other $x_j \geq 0$.

*(f) Assume x_4 is unconstrained in sign and every other $x_j \geq 0$.

*(g) Assume $x_1 \geq 0$, $x_2 \geq -6$, $x_3 \geq 0$, and $x_4 \geq -2$.

*(h) Assume $x_1 \geq 0$, $x_3 \geq 0$, and x_2 and x_4 are unconstrained in sign.

5 Consider

$$\text{maximize} \quad -x_1 + 5x_2 + 5x_3 - 2x_4$$

subject to

$$-5x_1 + 3x_2 - 4x_3 + x_4 \geq -10$$

$$3x_1 + 6x_2 - 2x_3 - x_4 \leq 7$$

$$x_1 + 4x_2 + 4x_3 + 3x_4 \geq 15$$

$$2x_1 + x_2 + 2x_3 - 6x_4 \leq -11.$$

(a) Assume every $x_j \geq 0$.

(b) Assume $x_1 \leq 0$ and every other $x_j \geq 0$.

*(c) Assume the second and fourth constraints are equalities and every $x_j \geq 0$.

*(d) Assume $x_1 \geq 2$ and every other $x_j \geq 0$.

*(e) Assume $x_1 \geq -2$ and every other $x_j \geq 0$.

*(f) Assume x_1 is unconstrained in sign and every other $x_j \geq 0$.

*(g) Assume $x_1 \geq -2$, $x_2 \geq 0$, $x_3 \geq 0$, and $x_4 \geq -3$.

*(h) Assume $x_2 \geq 0$, $x_3 \geq 0$. and x_1 and x_4 are unconstrained in sign.

In exercises 6 through 20, draw the solution space representation. Identify all the extreme points. In each of the parts, indicate an optimal solution. State whether it is unique, and if it is not, give two more optimal solutions. Be sure you calculate optimal values for x_1 and x_2 and find the associated value of the objective function.

6 Consider the constraints

$$-x_1 + x_2 \leq 2$$

$$6x_1 + 4x_2 \geq 24$$

$$x_1 \geq 0 \quad \text{and} \quad x_2 \geq 1.$$

(a) Minimize x_1.   (b) Minimize x_2.
(c) Maximize x_1.   (d) Maximize x_2.
(e) Minimize $x_1 + x_2$.   (f) Maximize $x_1 + x_2$.
(g) Maximize $-x_1 + 2x_2$.   (h) Maximize $x_1 - 2x_2$.
(i) Maximize $-3x_1 - 2x_2$.

7 Answer the questions in exercise 6 assuming also that $x_1 \leq 5$.

8 Answer the questions in exercise 6 assuming also that $x_2 \leq 4$.

9 Answer the questions in exercise 6 assuming also that $x_1 \leq 5$ and $x_2 \leq 4$.

10 Consider the constraints

$$-10x_1 - 15x_2 \geq -150$$

$$5x_1 + 11x_2 \geq 55$$

$$x_1 - x_2 \geq 0$$

$$x_1 \geq 4 \quad \text{and} \quad x_2 \geq 0.$$

(a) Maximize x_1.   (b) Minimize x_1.
(c) Maximize x_2.   (d) Minimize x_2.
(e) Maximize $x_1 + x_2$.   (f) Minimize $x_1 + x_2$.
(g) Maximize $x_1 + 3x_2$.   (h) Maximize $-2x_1 + x_2$.
(i) Maximize $-x_1 - 3x_2$.   (j) Maximize $-x_1 - 2x_2$.

11 Answer the questions in exercise 10 assuming the lower bound $x_1 \geq 6$.

12 Answer the questions in exercise 10 assuming the lower bound $x_1 \geq 15$.

13 Answer the questions in exercise 10 assuming the lower bound $x_1 \geq 20$.

14 Answer the questions in exercise 10 assuming the additional constraint $x_2 \leq 5$.

15 Answer the questions in exercise 10 assuming the additional constraint $x_2 \geq 6$.

16 Answer the questions in exercise 10 assuming the additional constraint $x_2 \geq 8$.

17 Consider the constraints

$$x_1 + x_2 \geq 5$$
$$-7x_1 + 8x_2 \leq 8$$
$$3x_1 + 2x_2 \leq 18$$
$$0 \leq x_1 \leq 4 \quad \text{and} \quad 0 \leq x_2 \leq 6.$$

(a) Maximize x_1.   (b) Minimize x_1.
(c) Maximize x_2.   (d) Minimize x_2.
(e) Maximize $x_1 + x_2$.   (f) Minimize $x_1 + x_2$.
(g) Maximize $3x_1 + 5x_2$.   (h) Minimize $3x_1 + 5x_2$.
(i) Maximize $-2x_1 - x_2$.   (j) Maximize $-x_1 - 2x_2$.
(k) Minimize $x_1 - 2x_2$.   (l) Minimize $2x_1 - x_2$.

18 Answer the questions in exercise 17 assuming the first constraint is $x_1 + x_2 \geq 6$.

19 Answer the questions in exercise 17 assuming the first constraint is $x_1 + x_2 \geq 4$.

20 Answer the questions in exercise 17 assuming the new bounds $0 \leq x_1 \leq 4.5$ and $0 \leq x_2 \leq 3$.

FORMULATION EXERCISES

21 Show how to transform the constraint

$$\left| \sum_{j=1}^{n} a_j x_j \right| \leq b$$

so that it can be encompassed in a linear programming model.

*22 Consider an optimization model with linear constraints such as those in Sec. 3.3. Suppose that the objective function is

$$\text{maximize} \quad \left[\text{minimum} \left(\sum_{j=1}^{n} c_j x_j, \sum_{j=1}^{n} d_j x_j \right) \right].$$

Show how this criterion can be encompassed in a linear programming model.

CONTENTS

CHAPTER 4

Simplex Method
of Solution

4.1 THEORY IN PERSPECTIVE

You will probably never have to calculate manually the solution of a linear programming model in a real application, since an electronic computer will do the work for you. You may legitimately ask, then, "Why do I need to know the underlying *theory* of linear optimization models? Isn't it enough merely to have the skill to formulate them?" It is difficult to answer these questions convincingly for a student who has not *already* learned the fundamentals of linear optimization theory; but in the light of considerable experience in applying linear programming to industrial problems, we are persuaded that an executive must understand the principles explained here in order to make truly effective and sustained use of this management tool.

The following analogy may help win you over to our point of view. In learning to drive a car, it strains the intellect only mildly to learn to speed up, slow down, go forward or backward, turn, and so forth—in short, to master the skill of driving. To qualify as a topnotch driver, however, you need to know more. You should have an idea of how to care for the battery; otherwise you may make the mistake of playing the radio for a long time with the ignition off. If you drive on icy highways, a knowledge of the braking mechanism should help you control your car when it skids. If your engine overheats suddenly, an understanding of the radiator's function may suggest the correct remedy. Summing up, to be a good driver you must know more than how to handle your auto under ideal conditions. You must know enough about its mechanism to be able to skirt danger when possible. On the other hand, you can obviously be an excellent driver without the training of an automobile mechanic.

By the same token, the manager who resolutely avoids familiarizing himself with the basic mechanism of his operations research application is flirting with trouble. If he really wants to maintain control, he must nurture his insight to the approach. Only a modest effort is required to reach the appropriate level of knowledge; it does not entail your becoming an expert theoretician.

You may ask another serious question concerning the value of studying linear optimization theory: "Do I have any assurance that the methods I learn now will remain relevant in a few years, given the rapidity of new advances in technology?" Of course, we can only speculate about the future, but history offers guidance. Again, the automobile analogy is helpful in framing an answer. If you glance at a typical early-model car, you recognize at once that it *is* an auto. Despite the vast technological improvements in automobile design, much of the basic structure has remained unchanged.

The advances in methods for solving linear optimization models show a similar pattern. Each decade of development has brought substantial modifications in computer methods for solving linear programming problems. Nevertheless, certain fundamental ideas have withstood the test of time, and still provide the basic structure of all approaches. These are the principles you will learn next.

4.2 ASSESSMENT OF THE OBJECTIVE

In this chapter, you will examine a computational method—an **algorithm** —for deriving numerical solutions to linear programming models. The task goes beyond merely specifying steps that eventually lead to a solution. The goal is to discover a systematic method that permits you to analyze and fully understand a model and its complex interrelations. Such a goal is essential, for in actual applications of linear programming you always want more than a mere numerical answer. Usually, you want to know precisely how the answer depends on the input specifications, that is, how sensitive the solution is to the original data. The importance of sensitivity analysis is apparent since often the technological specifications are based on estimates and the constraints included may only be approximate. Further, a number of real constraints may be provisionally left absent from the model. And the objective function may not completely exhaust the factors of relevance in evaluating a solution.

An equally important objective is perceiving the basic structure of optimizing algorithms. By concentrating in this chapter on what is known as the *simplex technique*, you will become familiar with the algorithmic method. As a result, you will gain the insights needed for a sound understanding of approaches to other optimization models studied in subsequent chapters.

Rather than start with a full-blown statement of the simplex algorithm, we begin slowly with some simplifying assumptions. Otherwise, you might easily get bogged down in detail, and lose sight of the central ideas, which are very intuitive. Rest assured, by the time you finish this chapter, you will have learned all the details necessary to apply the algorithm to *any* linear programming model.

Preliminary analysis. Before exploring the simplex algorithm, we briefly examine a small linear programming model so as to appreciate the hurdles to be encompassed by a technique of solution. Consider the problem

(1) $$\text{maximize} \quad 2x_1 + 3x_2 + 7x_3 + 9x_4$$

subject to

(2) $$1x_1 + 1x_2 + 1x_3 + 1x_4 + 1x_5 \qquad\qquad = 9$$

(3) $$1x_1 + 2x_2 + 4x_3 + 8x_4 \qquad + 1x_6 = 24$$

$$x_j \geq 0 \quad \text{for } j = 1, 2, \ldots, 6.$$

As a start toward solution, try the maximal amount of x_4, the variable having the largest coefficient in the objective function. Check that this trial amount is $\frac{24}{8} = 3$ and is determined by the coefficients in (3). The associated objective function value is $9(3) = 27$. If you try instead the maximal amount of x_3, which you can verify to be $\frac{24}{4} = 6$, then the associated objective function value is the larger amount $7(6) = 42$. Thus, because of the constraining relations, it is not always best to use only a variable with the largest payoff per unit.

Check that letting $x_3 = 6$ implies that $x_5 = 3$. Since the latter variable does not contribute to the value of the objective function, we ask next whether we can improve the solution further by combining several other economic variables. Even in a problem as small as this, it would be wearisome to test various combinations unless some simple rules were available that allowed us to skip over clearly inferior solutions.

Suppose you guess next that an optimal solution contains x_2 and x_3 at positive levels, and all the other variables at zero levels. It is easy to verify whether this conjecture is valid. You need only be able to manipulate (2) and (3) by the usual method in elementary algebra for solving two simultaneous linear equations. In mathematics literature, the approach often is called **Gaussian elimination.**

As a preliminary, bring x_1, x_4, x_5, and x_6 to the right-hand side of the equality signs:

(4) $$1x_2 + 1x_3 = 9 - 1x_1 - 1x_4 - 1x_5$$

(5) $$2x_2 + 4x_3 = 24 - 1x_1 - 8x_4 \qquad - 1x_6.$$

Then eliminate x_2 from (5) by multiplying (4) by 2 and subtracting the result from (5) to obtain (7):

(6) $$1x_2 + 1x_3 = 9 - 1x_1 - 1x_4 - 1x_5$$

(7) $$2x_3 = 6 + 1x_1 - 6x_4 + 2x_5 - 1x_6.$$

Next *normalize* the coefficient of x_3 in (7) by dividing by 2, yielding (9):

(8) $$1x_2 + 1x_3 = 9 - 1x_1 - 1x_4 - 1x_5$$

(9) $$1x_3 = 3 + \tfrac{1}{2}x_1 - 3x_4 + 1x_5 - \tfrac{1}{2}x_6.$$

Finally, you should *eliminate* x_3 from (8) by subtracting (9) from (8), giving the pair of equations

(10) $x_2 = 6 - \frac{3}{2}x_1 + 2x_4 - 2x_5 + \frac{1}{2}x_6$

(11) $x_3 = 3 + \frac{1}{2}x_1 - 3x_4 + 1x_5 - \frac{1}{2}x_6.$

The combined normalizing and eliminating operation is sometimes called **pivoting.**

The present hypothesis is that $x_1 = x_4 = x_5 = x_6 = 0$. Then from (10) and (11) you can conclude that $x_2 = 6$ and $x_3 = 3$. [Check that these values satisfy (2) and (3).] For this solution, the value of the objective function (1) is $3(6) + 7(3) = 39$. Since you previously examined a solution ($x_3 = 6$) that gave an objective function value of 42, you know the current guess is not optimal. However, we are seeking a simple way to discover whether the current guess is optimal without referring to any *previous* trials.

To proceed in this pursuit, substitute the relations for x_2 and x_3 as given in (10) and (11) into the objective function:

$$2x_1 + 3(6 - \frac{3}{2}x_1 + 2x_4 - 2x_5 + \frac{1}{2}x_6)$$
$$(12) \quad + 7(3 + \frac{1}{2}x_1 - 3x_4 + 1x_5 - \frac{1}{2}x_6) + 9x_4$$
$$= 39 + 1x_1 - 6x_4 + 1x_5 - 2x_6.$$

It is evident from (12) that raising the value of either x_1 or x_5 from zero will increase the objective function beyond 39. In fact, according to the coefficients of x_1 and x_5 in (12), for each unit you introduce of either of these variables, the objective function goes up by 1.

Suppose you decide to increase x_1. How large can you make it? Looking at (10) and (11), which are merely rearranged versions of (2) and (3), you can check that if you increase x_1 and leave $x_4 = x_5 = x_6 = 0$, then x_2 will decrease by $\frac{3}{2}$ and x_3 will increase by $\frac{1}{2}$ for each unit of x_1 added. But for a feasible solution all $x_j \geq 0$. Therefore, x_1 can be made only as large as 4, at which point x_2 becomes 0. Further, according to (12), the corresponding value of the objective function is $39 + 1 \cdot 4 = 43$.

You are now ready to try your newest guess at an optimal solution, namely that x_1 and x_3 are positive and all the rest of the variables are zero. Check your understanding of the way we progressed from the pair (2) and (3) to the pair (10) and (11) by carrying out the analogous computations to solve for x_1 and x_3. You should obtain

(13) $x_1 = 4 - \frac{2}{3}x_2 + \frac{4}{3}x_4 - \frac{4}{3}x_5 + \frac{1}{3}x_6$

(14) $x_3 = 5 - \frac{1}{3}x_2 - \frac{7}{3}x_4 + \frac{1}{3}x_5 - \frac{1}{3}x_6.$

If you set $x_2 = x_4 = x_5 = x_6 = 0$, then $x_1 = 4$ and $x_3 = 5$. The value of the objective function is $2(4) + 7(5) = 43$. Notice the objective function equals

$39 + 1(4) = 43$, as predicted by (12), and is an improvement on the previous guess.

To test for optimality, you can substitute as before the relations for the solution variables (13) and (14) into the objective function. Verify that this gives

(15) $$43 - \tfrac{2}{3}x_2 - \tfrac{14}{3}x_4 - \tfrac{1}{3}x_5 - \tfrac{5}{3}x_6.$$

Now you can see that if the variables x_2, x_4, x_5, or x_6 are utilized at *any* level above zero, the objective function must decrease from its current value 43. Thus the present solution is indeed optimal.

*4.3 THE ALGORITHMIC METHOD

You will study several types of algorithms throughout this book. By far, the type used most often is an iterative approach: at each trial solution, starting with the first, the instructions specify whether to stop the computations or to proceed to a new trial solution. It is essential to know when a suggested computational scheme is a bona fide algorithm for solving a problem.

Consider, for example, the process we used to solve the small problem above. Whenever we wanted to test the optimality for a specified pair of variables, we had no trouble in finding unique values for this pair that satisfied all the constraints. Was this only luck? We devised a simple procedure for testing whether a trial solution could be improved by introducing another variable. Does this approach always work? We found that bringing one variable into a trial solution caused only one other variable to leave the solution. Is this sort of uniquely determined substitution inevitable? We discovered an optimal solution rather rapidly. Is such speed typical?

You will find it helpful for understanding both the simplex method and other algorithms in subsequent chapters to have a general framework for viewing computational techniques. Specifically, to evaluate such algorithms, you should examine four interrelated characteristics.

1. **Completeness.** Are the algorithm's rules unambiguous? Is there a practical method for always obtaining a first trial solution to initiate the algorithm? Is the method described in terms of rules so well specified that they can be performed by a person or an electronic calculator having only the ability to read and follow the rules without exercising further judgment?

2. **Domain of applicability.** What mathematical problems does the algorithm purport to solve? How easy is it to determine whether a specific problem falls within this domain of applicability? When the calculations terminate, does the final-trial answer invariably provide an exact solution to the problem? If not, is there an indication of the existence and cause of failure?

3. **Convergence properties.** Does the algorithm always converge? If so, does it unfailingly converge to a correct solution? Will the method terminate in a finite number of iterations? For actual problems, how many iterations occur until convergence? Do the trial solutions progressively improve the objective function value? If the calculations are stopped short of obtaining an optimal solution, is the final-trial answer usable?

4. **Computational requirements.** How severe is the computational burden needed to obtain a solution? How much numerical accuracy is required to ensure the method operates satisfactorily?

Establishing the answers to many of these questions is often a routine exercise for an operations researcher. But the most subtle category of questions is that relating to determining the convergence properties of an algorithm. Although the topic of convergence in algorithmic methods involves a number of intricacies, the ideas essential for the purposes here can be demonstrated simply. For the sake of illustration, suppose you are trying to maximize the value of an objective function, provided the solution satisfies certain constraints. This would be so if you were solving a linear programming model. The cases in Fig. 4.1 show how the value of the objective function might vary from one iteration to the next for a specific algorithm.

Case 1. At each iteration you observe a strict improvement in the objective function. Convergence to an optimal solution occurs after a finite number of iterations. In the example, the optimum is reached at iteration 7.

Case 2. At each iteration you observe a strict improvement in the objective function. However, convergence to an optimal solution does *not* occur in a finite number of iterations. At each trial, the solution gets a little bit better, but the improvements get progressively smaller.

Case 3. At each iteration you observe a strict improvement in the objective function. And, as in the preceding case, convergence does not occur in a finite number of iterations. But the objective function is tending to a limiting value that is *below* the true optimum!

Case 4. Convergence to an optimal solution occurs in a finite number of iterations, and each solution is at least as good as the preceding one. But at some iterations the objective function does not show a *strict* improvement. In the example, the objective function stalls at iterations 3, 7, and 8.

Case 5. Prior to convergence, the value of the objective function decreases for several iterations. In the illustration (*Case 5* of Fig. 4.1), this phenomenon occurs at iterations 4 and 5.

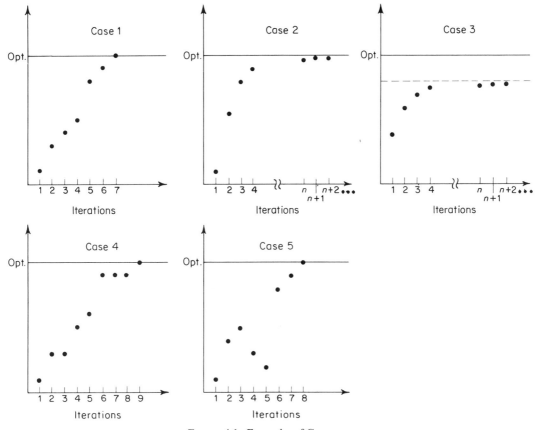

FIGURE 4.1. Examples of Convergence.

Thus the objective function in an algorithm may or may not converge to a limiting value in a finite number of iterations. If it does converge, the limiting value may or may not be the truly optimal value. And, in any case, the objective function may or may not show a strict improvement during the course of the iterations.

4.4 INTRODUCTION TO
THE SIMPLEX ALGORITHM

Many different algorithms have been proposed to solve linear programming problems, but the one below has proved to be the most effective in general. Recognize, however, that if you are able to assume more about the form of the problem— such as that it has a network flow structure—then even better algorithms can be applied. We discuss these methods for special models in Chaps. 6 and 7.

Let us verbalize the reasoning process used in Sec. 4.2 to solve the illustrative example. In that case, there were two equations. You examined trial solutions having two unknowns at positive levels and the remaining variables at zero levels. If the approach is to generalize, it is reasonable to suppose that in an m-equation model, you would choose m variables to have positive levels, and let the remaining variables equal zero. Assume for the time being that a feasible solution exists and the optimal value of the objective function is finite. We remove these restrictive assumptions later. Then the procedure appears to be the following.

Step 1. Select a set of m variables that yields a feasible starting trial solution. Eliminate the selected m variables from the objective function.

Step 2. Check the objective function to see whether there is a variable that is equal to zero in the trial solution but would improve the objective function if made positive. If such a variable exists, go to *Step 3*. Otherwise, stop.

Step 3. Determine how large the variable found in the previous step can be made until one of the m variables in the trial solution becomes zero. Eliminate the latter variable and let the next trial set contain the newly found variable instead.

Step 4. Solve for these m variables, and set the remaining variables equal to zero in the next trial solution. Return to *Step 2*.

Interestingly, after tidying up the language of these steps to remove certain ambiguities, the resulting algorithm in fact does find an optimal solution to a general linear programming model in a finite number of iterations. Often this method is termed *Dantzig's simplex algorithm*, in honor of the mathematician who devised the approach.

We first examine a "well-behaved" problem and explain the **simplex method** by means of this example. Afterwards we complete the presentation of the details.

Example. Consider the model

$$\text{maximize}\quad 4x_1 + 5x_2 + 9x_3 + 11x_4$$

subject to

$$1x_1 + 1x_2 + 1x_3 + 1x_4 \le 15$$

$$7x_1 + 5x_2 + 3x_3 + 2x_4 \le 120$$

$$3x_1 + 5x_2 + 10x_3 + 15x_4 \le 100$$

$$x_1 \ge 0 \quad x_2 \ge 0 \quad x_3 \ge 0 \quad x_4 \ge 0.$$

You may recall that this is the Product-Mix Selection Example in Sec. 2.2. Did you jot down your guess of the optimal solution?

Let x_0 be the value of the objective function and add slack variables. Then write the system as

$$
\text{(1)} \quad
\begin{aligned}
1x_0 - 4x_1 - 5x_2 - 9x_3 - 11x_4 &= 0 && \text{Row 0} \\
1x_1 + 1x_2 + 1x_3 + 1x_4 + 1x_5 &= 15 && \text{Row 1} \\
7x_1 + 5x_2 + 3x_3 + 2x_4 \qquad + 1x_6 &= 120 && \text{Row 2} \\
3x_1 + 5x_2 + 10x_3 + 15x_4 \qquad + 1x_7 &= 100 && \text{Row 3,}
\end{aligned}
$$

where *all* the variables must be nonnegative. Notice how the introduction of the variable x_0 in Row 0 permits us to express the objective function in equation form.

The task of *Step 1* is to find a starting feasible solution to (1). There are a large number of such solutions, but it is certainly most convenient to begin with $x_0 = 0$, $x_5 = 15$, $x_6 = 120$, $x_7 = 100$, and all other variables equal to 0. In other words, start with an all-slack solution. We term this an *initial feasible basic solution,* and x_0, x_5, x_6, and x_7 are known as the **basic variables,** sometimes shortened to **the basis.** The remaining variables we call **nonbasic.**

The word *basic* stems from the mathematical property that the solution is represented by four variables, "four" being the number of linear relations, and that the values of these four variables are uniquely determined (and dependent on the constants on the right-hand side of the equations). As you will discover, the simplex method employs only trial *basic* solutions. Despite the restriction to this class of solutions, the simplex method nevertheless determines an optimal solution, provided one exists.

If you interpret x_0 as profits, then the current solution is certainly not very profitable. Undoubtedly you can improve it. A moment's reflection leads to examining the coefficients in Row 0 of those variables currently not in the basis. Specifically, look at the coefficients of x_1, x_2, x_3, and x_4. Each negative coefficient represents how much x_0 will increase if you let the corresponding variable equal 1. This conclusion about the interpretation of the coefficients in Row 0 remains valid throughout the trial calculations, and we record the general principle here.

INTERPRETATION OF COEFFICIENTS IN Row 0. Each coefficient represents the increase (for negative coefficients) or decrease (for positive coefficients) in x_0 with a unit increase of the associated nonbasic variable.

For *Step 2* the simplex method adopts the following easy-to-apply rule for deciding the variable to enter the next trial basis.

SIMPLEX CRITERION I (MAXIMIZATION). If there are nonbasic variables having a negative coefficient in Row 0, select one such variable with the most negative coefficient, that is, the best per-unit potential gain (say x_j). If all nonbasic variables have positive or zero coefficients in Row 0, an optimal solution has been obtained.

According to *Criterion I*, you should introduce x_4. Each unit of x_4 added brings about an increase of 11 in x_0. Clearly, the larger you make x_4, the more you increase x_0. But examine the constraints (1). Notice that as you increase x_4, you must decrease every current basic variable corresponding to a row wherein x_4 has a positive coefficient. Specifically, if x_4 is increased to the level 1, then verify in (1) that

  (i) x_5 must be decreased by 1 so that the Row 1 constraint remains satisfied,
  (ii) x_6 must be decreased by 2 so that the Row 2 constraint remains satisfied,
  (iii) x_7 must be decreased by 15 so that the Row 3 constraint remains satisfied.

How big can x_4 become before one of the current basic variables reaches its lower bound 0? Check that this number is $x_4 = \frac{100}{15} = 6.66$, at which value you find $x_7 = 0$. Such being the case, introduce x_4 into the basis and remove x_7.

We summarize the preceding discussion by the following rule for *Step 3*.

SIMPLEX CRITERION II. (a) Take the ratios of the current right-hand side to the coefficients of the entering variable x_j (ignore ratios with zero or negative numbers in the denominator). (b) Select the minimum ratio—that ratio will equal the value of x_j in the next trial solution. The minimum ratio occurs for a variable x_k in the present solution; set $x_k = 0$ in the new solution.

The calculations indicated by *Criterion II* are performed in Fig. 4.2.

Basic Variables	Current Solution	÷ Coeffs. of x_4	= Ratios	Min.	Next Solution
x_0	0	−11	−−		
x_5	15	1	15		
x_6	120	2	60		
x_7	100	15	6.66	6.66	$x_4 = 6.66,\ x_7 = 0$

FIGURE 4.2. *Iteration 1: Criterion II* for x_4 *Entering Basis.*

Now that you know x_4 is to replace x_7 in a trial basis, you perform *Step 4*. Rewrite the relations (1) so that x_4 has a coefficient of 1 in Row 3 and coefficients of 0 in Rows 0, 1, and 2, just as x_7 does in (1). The process by which this is achieved is known as a **change-of-basis** calculation, or a **pivot operation**. First divide Row 3 by 15, the coefficient of x_4,

$$
\begin{array}{lll}
1x_0 - 4x_1 - 5x_2 - 9x_3 - 11x_4 & = 0 & \text{Row 0} \\
1x_1 + 1x_2 + 1x_3 + 1x_4 + 1x_5 & = 15 & \text{Row 1} \\
7x_1 + 5x_2 + 3x_3 + 2x_4 \qquad + 1x_6 & = 120 & \text{Row 2} \\
\tfrac{1}{5}x_1 + \tfrac{1}{3}x_2 + \tfrac{2}{3}x_3 + 1x_4 \qquad\qquad + \tfrac{1}{15}x_7 & = \tfrac{20}{3} & \text{Row 3.}
\end{array}
$$

(2)

By pivoting on 15, you have created the coefficient of 1 for x_4 in Row 3. Note that the mathematical manipulation is legitimate, for all you have done is divide equals by equals (both sides of Row 3 by 15). Create coefficients equal to 0 in Rows 0, 1, and 2 as follows:

- Row 0: multiply Row 3 by 11 and add to Row 0,
- Row 1: multiply Row 3 by -1 and add to Row 1,
- Row 2: multiply Row 3 by -2 and add to Row 2.

The result is

(3)

$$1x_0 - \tfrac{9}{5}x_1 - \tfrac{4}{3}x_2 - \tfrac{5}{3}x_3 \qquad\qquad + \tfrac{11}{15}x_7 = \tfrac{220}{3} \quad \text{Row 0}$$

$$\tfrac{4}{5}x_1 + \tfrac{2}{3}x_2 + \tfrac{1}{3}x_3 \quad + 1x_5 \qquad - \tfrac{1}{15}x_7 = \tfrac{25}{3} \quad \text{Row 1}$$

$$\tfrac{33}{5}x_1 + \tfrac{13}{3}x_2 + \tfrac{5}{3}x_3 \qquad + 1x_6 - \tfrac{2}{15}x_7 = \tfrac{320}{3} \quad \text{Row 2}$$

$$\tfrac{1}{5}x_1 + \tfrac{1}{3}x_2 + \tfrac{2}{3}x_3 + 1x_4 \qquad + \tfrac{1}{15}x_7 = \tfrac{20}{3} \quad \text{Row 3.}$$

As before, the mathematical manipulations are legitimate, for all you have done is multiply equals by equals (both sides of each row by a constant) and then add equals to equals (one row to another row). Consequently, the relations (3), although appearing to be in different form from (1), are equivalent to (1). The usefulness of the form of (3) is that by letting $x_1 = x_2 = x_3 = x_7 = 0$, you see immediately the values for the new trial-basic solution, Fig. 4.3.

As a check of your understanding, observe that the new basic solution has profit $x_0 = \tfrac{220}{3}$, which can be calculated from the relation

x_0	$\tfrac{220}{3}$
x_5	$\tfrac{25}{3}$
x_6	$\tfrac{320}{3}$
x_4	$\tfrac{20}{3}$

FIGURE 4.3. Second Trial Basic Solution.

$$\begin{pmatrix}\text{new}\\\text{profit}\end{pmatrix} = \begin{pmatrix}\text{profit from}\\\text{previous}\\\text{solution}\end{pmatrix} + \begin{pmatrix}\text{number of units}\\\text{of new}\\\text{basic variable}\end{pmatrix} \times \begin{pmatrix}\text{per-unit potential gain}\\\text{from new basic variable}\\\text{as was given by the}\\\text{previous coefficient in Row 0}\end{pmatrix}$$

$$\tfrac{220}{3} = 0 + \tfrac{20}{3}(11).$$

You are now better able to interpret *Criterion II*. If x_5 (or x_6) is eliminated instead of x_7, then in finding new values for x_4, x_7, and x_6 (or x_5), you would obtain negative numbers, contrary to the nonnegativity constraints. Try to eliminate x_5 instead of x_7 for a second-trial solution and thereby verify these remarks.

Iteration 2. At this point the first iteration of the simplex method has been completed. On returning to *Step 2*, you are ready to determine whether an optimal solution has been obtained or if another simplex iteration is required. *Criterion I*, which examines the nonbasic variables, indicates that a still better solution seems to exist. You might profitably enter into the basis either x_1, or x_2, or x_3. *Criterion I* selects x_1, since it promises the greatest gain per unit increase. Next perform the *Step 3* calculations, using *Criterion II* as shown in Fig. 4.4.

Basic Variables	Current Solution ÷ Coeffs. of x_1		= Ratios	Min.	Next Solution
x_0	$\frac{220}{3}$	$-\frac{9}{5}$	--		
x_5	$\frac{25}{3}$	$\frac{4}{5}$	$\frac{125}{12}$	$\frac{125}{12}$	$x_1 = \frac{125}{12}$, $x_5 = 0$
x_6	$\frac{320}{3}$	$\frac{33}{5}$	$\frac{1600}{99}$		
x_4	$\frac{20}{3}$	$\frac{1}{5}$	$\frac{100}{3}$		

FIGURE 4.4. *Iteration 2: Criterion II* for x_1 Entering Basis.

From Fig. 4.4 notice that x_1 will replace x_5 in the next trial solution. You must rewrite (3) to reflect the substitution. To make the change-of-basis calculation in *Step 4*, first divide by the pivot $\frac{4}{5}$ in Row 1, causing the coefficient of 1 to be removed from x_5 and to appear for x_1:

(4)

$$1x_0 - \tfrac{9}{5}x_1 - \tfrac{4}{3}x_2 - \tfrac{5}{3}x_3 \qquad\qquad + \tfrac{11}{15}x_7 = \tfrac{220}{3} \quad \text{Row 0}$$

$$1x_1 + \tfrac{5}{6}x_2 + \tfrac{5}{12}x_3 \qquad + \tfrac{5}{4}x_5 \qquad - \tfrac{1}{12}x_7 = \tfrac{125}{12} \quad \text{Row 1}$$

$$\tfrac{33}{5}x_1 + \tfrac{13}{3}x_2 + \tfrac{5}{3}x_3 \qquad\qquad + 1x_6 - \tfrac{2}{15}x_7 = \tfrac{320}{3} \quad \text{Row 2}$$

$$\tfrac{1}{5}x_1 + \tfrac{1}{3}x_2 + \tfrac{2}{3}x_3 + 1x_4 \qquad\qquad + \tfrac{1}{15}x_7 = \tfrac{3}{20} \quad \text{Row 3.}$$

Then to complete the pivot operation, create coefficients equal to 0 for x_1 in Rows 0, 2, and 3 as follows:

· Row 0: multiply Row 1 by $\frac{9}{5}$ and add to Row 0,
· Row 2: multiply Row 1 by $-\frac{33}{5}$ and add to Row 2,
· Row 3: multiply Row 1 by $-\frac{1}{5}$ and add to Row 3.

The result is

(5)

$$1x_0 \qquad + \tfrac{1}{6}x_2 - \tfrac{11}{12}x_3 \qquad + \tfrac{9}{4}x_5 \qquad + \tfrac{7}{12}x_7 = \tfrac{1105}{12} \quad \text{Row 0}$$

$$1x_1 + \tfrac{5}{6}x_2 + \tfrac{5}{12}x_3 \qquad + \tfrac{5}{4}x_5 \qquad - \tfrac{1}{12}x_7 = \tfrac{125}{12} \quad \text{Row 1}$$

$$- \tfrac{7}{6}x_2 - \tfrac{13}{12}x_3 \qquad - \tfrac{33}{4}x_5 + 1x_6 + \tfrac{7}{12}x_7 = \tfrac{455}{12} \quad \text{Row 2}$$

$$\tfrac{1}{6}x_2 + \tfrac{7}{12}x_3 + 1x_4 - \tfrac{1}{4}x_5 \qquad + \tfrac{1}{12}x_7 = \tfrac{55}{12} \quad \text{Row 3.}$$

The third trial-basic solution appears in Fig. 4.5. Notice that at each iteration, the coefficients of any variable not in the trial solution have the interpretation that if a unit of this variable is introduced, the current basis variables will be changed by these amounts. In (3), for example, introducing each unit of x_1 will decrease x_5 by $\frac{4}{5}$, x_6 by $\frac{33}{5}$, and x_4 by $\frac{1}{5}$. Corroborate this statement with the values you have derived for the third solution, in which $\frac{125}{12}$ units of x_1 were actually introduced.

Also observe that prior to introducing x_1 into the basis, x_2 looked attractive in (3). Entering x_1 caused x_2 to change its indication in the present iteration (5).

Iteration 3. Having completed the second simplex iteration, once more examine the coefficients in Row 0 to ascertain whether you have discovered an optimal solution. It now appears favorable to enter x_3. The calculations to determine which variable leaves the basis are given in Fig. 4.6. You will find from these calculations that x_4, which entered at the first iteration, is now to be removed from the basis. Frequently in applications of the simplex method, a variable enters the solution at one iteration and is removed at a later iteration. It is this possibility that prohibits stating a *helpful*

x_0	$\frac{1105}{12}$
x_1	$\frac{125}{12}$
x_6	$\frac{455}{12}$
x_4	$\frac{55}{12}$

FIGURE 4.5. The Third Trial Basic Solution.

upper bound on the number of simplex iterations necessary to solve any linear programming problem.

As with the preceding iterations, create a coefficient of 1 for the entering variable x_3 in Row 3 by dividing Row 3 by $\frac{7}{12}$. This gives

$$
\begin{aligned}
&1x_0 && + \tfrac{1}{6}x_2 - \tfrac{11}{12}x_3 && + \tfrac{9}{4}x_5 && + \tfrac{7}{12}x_7 = \tfrac{1105}{12} && \text{Row 0}\\
&1x_1 + \tfrac{5}{6}x_2 + \tfrac{5}{12}x_3 && + \tfrac{5}{4}x_5 && - \tfrac{1}{12}x_7 = \tfrac{125}{12} && \text{Row 1}\\
&\quad -\tfrac{7}{6}x_2 - \tfrac{13}{12}x_3 && -\tfrac{33}{4}x_5 + 1x_6 + \tfrac{5}{12}x_7 = \tfrac{455}{12} && \text{Row 2}\\
&\quad \tfrac{2}{7}x_2 + 1x_3 + \tfrac{12}{7}x_4 - \tfrac{3}{7}x_5 && + \tfrac{1}{7}x_7 = \tfrac{55}{7} && \text{Row 3.}
\end{aligned}
$$

(6)

Now create coefficients equal to 0 for x_3 in the remaining rows as follows:

· Row 0: multiply Row 3 by $\frac{11}{12}$ and add to Row 0,
· Row 1: multiply Row 3 by $-\frac{5}{12}$ and add to Row 1,
· Row 2: multiply Row 3 by $\frac{13}{12}$ and add to Row 2.

Basic Variables	Current Solution	÷ Coeffs of x_3	= Ratios	Min.	Next Solution
x_0	$\frac{1105}{12}$	$-\frac{11}{12}$	--		
x_1	$\frac{125}{12}$	$\frac{5}{12}$	25		
x_6	$\frac{455}{12}$	$-\frac{13}{12}$	--		
x_4	$\frac{55}{12}$	$\frac{7}{12}$	$\frac{55}{7}$	$\frac{55}{7}$	$x_3 = \frac{55}{7}$, $x_4 = 0$

FIGURE 4.6. *Iteration 3: Criterion II for x_3 Entering Basis.*

The result is

$$
\begin{aligned}
1x_0 \quad + \tfrac{3}{7}x_2 \qquad\quad + \tfrac{11}{7}x_4 + \tfrac{13}{7}x_5 \qquad\quad + \tfrac{5}{7}x_7 &= \tfrac{695}{7} \qquad \text{Row 0} \\
1x_1 + \tfrac{5}{7}x_2 \qquad\quad - \tfrac{5}{7}x_4 + \tfrac{10}{7}x_5 \qquad\quad - \tfrac{1}{7}x_7 &= \tfrac{50}{7} \qquad \text{Row 1} \\
- \tfrac{6}{7}x_2 \qquad\quad + \tfrac{13}{7}x_4 - \tfrac{61}{7}x_5 + 1x_6 + \tfrac{4}{7}x_7 &= \tfrac{325}{7} \qquad \text{Row 2} \\
\tfrac{2}{7}x_2 + 1x_3 + \tfrac{12}{7}x_4 - \tfrac{3}{7}x_5 \qquad\quad + \tfrac{1}{7}x_7 &= \tfrac{55}{7} \qquad \text{Row 3.}
\end{aligned}
$$

(7)

At this iteration you have just seen another aspect to the computational rule in *Criterion II*. Had you attempted to eliminate a variable where a negative ratio occurred in Fig. 4.6—this would be x_6—then x_3 would have become negative. Since such a condition is not permitted, the negative coefficient causes the basic variable for the associated row to increase in value as the new variable is introduced into the solution. If you ever tried to eliminate a basic variable in a row where 0 occurs as the coefficient of the entering variable, you would not be able to carry out the prescribed pivoting manipulations. The very first operation would call for a division by 0, which is not permissible.

To sum up, *Criterion II* ensures that each new basic solution results only in zero or positive values for the trial values of the basis. Consequently, the solution remains feasible at *every* iteration.

Iteration 4. All the coefficients in Row 0 of (7) are nonnegative, and consequently *Criterion I* asserts you have found an optimal solution (Fig. 4.7). Thus the calculations are terminated in *Step 2*. Check that the values in Fig. 4.7 do indeed satisfy (1).

x_0	$\dfrac{695}{7}$
x_1	$\dfrac{50}{7}$
x_6	$\dfrac{325}{7}$
x_3	$\dfrac{55}{7}$

FIGURE 4.7. Fourth Trial and Optimal Basic Solution.

Summary. In brief the simplex method consists of

Step 1. Select an initial basis.

Step 2. Apply *Simplex Criterion I*. If the current-trial solution is not optimal, proceed to *Step 3*. Otherwise, stop.

Step 3. Apply *Simplex Criterion II*.

Step 4. Make a change of basis, and return to *Step 2*.

Optimality. It is a simple matter to demonstrate that you have in fact found an optimal solution. Since you have derived the final formulation (7) from the original equations (1) only by elementary operations, such as multiplying equals by equals and adding equals to equals, the two formulations are merely different-appearing views of the *same* problem. Suppose you had started with (7). Rearranging Row 0 slightly, you can write the objective function as

$$(8) \qquad \text{maximize} \quad x_0 = \tfrac{695}{7} - \tfrac{3}{7}x_2 - \tfrac{11}{7}x_4 - \tfrac{13}{7}x_5 - \tfrac{5}{7}x_7.$$

If the nonbasic variables x_2, x_4, x_5, or x_7 have *any* feasible value other than zero, then the above relation shows that x_0 will be less than its present value of $\tfrac{695}{7}$.

The final Row 0 coefficients of the original variables are sometimes referred to as **relative** or **shadow costs.** They represent the decrease in the optimal value of the objective function resulting from a unit increase in a nonbasic variable, assuming the final basis remains feasible. (The final Row 0 coefficients of the slack variables are sometimes called **shadow prices,** and their interpretation is discussed at length in the next chapter.)

For example, suppose you decided to set $x_2 = 1$; then the value of x_0 would decrease by $\tfrac{3}{7}$. The values of the basic variables would also change, and you could examine this effect in the same way you used for x_0. Consider the basic variable x_1 in Row 1 of (7):

$$(9) \qquad\qquad x_1 = \tfrac{50}{7} - \tfrac{5}{7}x_2 + \tfrac{5}{7}x_4 - \tfrac{10}{7}x_5 + \tfrac{1}{7}x_7.$$

By letting $x_2 = 1$, you decrease the value of x_1 by the amount $\tfrac{5}{7}$.

Alternative optima. You saw in Chap. 3 (Fig. 3.2) that a linear programming problem may have more than one optimal solution. The two-dimensional diagrammatics show that if more than one optimal solution exists, then an infinite number exist. The corresponding generalization to larger problems is valid.

To illustrate how this situation occurs, suppose that instead of x_2, the initial formulation (1) contains the variable x_8 having different coefficients

$$(10) \quad
\begin{aligned}
1x_0 - 4x_1 - 2x_8 - 9x_3 - 11x_4 \qquad\qquad\qquad &= 0 && \text{Row 0} \\
1x_1 + 1x_8 + 1x_3 + 1x_4 + 1x_5 \qquad\qquad &= 15 && \text{Row 1} \\
7x_1 + 9x_8 + 3x_3 + 2x_4 \qquad + 1x_6 \qquad &= 120 && \text{Row 2} \\
3x_1 + .2x_8 + 10x_3 + 15x_4 \qquad\qquad + 1x_7 &= 100 && \text{Row 3.}
\end{aligned}$$

It is straightforward to check that the final iteration (7) would appear as

$$1x_0 \qquad\qquad + \frac{11}{7}x_4 + \frac{13}{7}x_5 \qquad + \frac{5}{7}x_7 = \frac{695}{7} \quad \text{Row 0}$$

$$1x_1 + \frac{9.8}{7}x_8 \qquad - \frac{5}{7}x_4 + \frac{10}{7}x_5 \qquad - \frac{1}{7}x_7 = \frac{50}{7} \quad \text{Row 1}$$

(11)
$$- \frac{2.8}{7}x_8 \qquad + \frac{13}{7}x_4 - \frac{61}{7}x_5 + 1x_6 + \frac{4}{7}x_7 = \frac{325}{7} \quad \text{Row 2}$$

$$- \frac{2.8}{7}x_8 + 1x_3 + \frac{12}{7}x_4 - \frac{3}{7}x_5 \qquad + \frac{1}{7}x_7 = \frac{55}{7} \quad \text{Row 3.}$$

If you introduce x_8, then x_1 leaves the basis according to *Criterion II*, and the alternative basic optimal solution is

(12)
$$x_0 = \frac{695}{7} \qquad\qquad x_8 = \frac{50}{9.8} = 5.10$$

$$x_6 = \frac{3045}{7(9.8)} = 44.39 \qquad x_3 = \frac{679}{7(9.8)} = 9.90,$$

where $x_1 = x_4 = x_5 = x_7 = 0$. It is easy to show that any **positive-weighted average** of these two basic optimal solutions also yields an alternative optimal (feasible) solution:

(13)
$$x_0 = \frac{695}{7}$$

$$x_1 = w(\tfrac{50}{7}) + (1 - w)0$$

$$x_3 = w(\tfrac{55}{7}) + (1 - w)9.90$$

$$x_6 = w(\tfrac{325}{7}) + (1 - w)44.39$$

$$x_8 = w(0) + (1 - w)5.10,$$

where w is the **weighting factor** such that $0 < w < 1$. [Try $w = .5$ in (13) and calculate x_1, x_3, x_6, and x_8. Check that these values satisfy the original constraints and yield an objective function value of $\frac{695}{7}$.]

Conclusion. It is fair to say that the optimal solution to even the small problem in this section was not obvious from the start. In larger models, the importance of being able to approach an optimal solution in a systematic fashion is manifest. We turn next to an evaluation of the simplex algorithm in terms of the four characteristics discussed in Sec. 4.3; if you skipped that section, go back and read it now.

*4.5 TABULAR REPRESENTATION

In preceding from one trial solution to the next, it is both cumbersome and unnecessary to write $x_1, x_2, \ldots, x_n$ as we have in the previous section. Only the *coefficients* of the variables are needed in the computations. Once you have understood the straightforward logic of the simplex iterations, you can save yourself considerable writing effort by organizing the computations in a convenient tabular form called a **simplex tableau.**

Figure 4.8 depicts the approach for the example in Sec. 4.4.

Iteration	Basis	Current Values	x_1	x_2	x_3	x_4	Row
1	x_0	0	−4	−5	−9	−11	0
	x_5	15	1	1	1	1	1
	x_6	120	7	5	3	2	2
	x_7	100	3	5	10	$\boxed{15}$	3
			x_1	x_2	x_3	x_7	
2	x_0	$\frac{220}{3}$	$-\frac{9}{5}$	$-\frac{4}{3}$	$-\frac{5}{3}$	$\frac{11}{15}$	0
	x_5	$\frac{25}{3}$	$\boxed{\frac{4}{5}}$	$\frac{2}{3}$	$\frac{1}{3}$	$-\frac{1}{15}$	1
	x_6	$\frac{320}{3}$	$\frac{33}{5}$	$\frac{13}{3}$	$\frac{5}{3}$	$-\frac{2}{15}$	2
	x_4	$\frac{20}{3}$	$\frac{1}{5}$	$\frac{1}{3}$	$\frac{2}{3}$	$\frac{1}{15}$	3
			x_5	x_2	x_3	x_7	
3	x_0	$\frac{1105}{12}$	$\frac{9}{4}$	$\frac{1}{6}$	$-\frac{11}{12}$	$\frac{7}{12}$	0
	x_1	$\frac{125}{12}$	$\frac{5}{4}$	$\frac{5}{6}$	$\frac{5}{12}$	$-\frac{1}{12}$	1
	x_6	$\frac{455}{12}$	$-\frac{33}{4}$	$-\frac{7}{6}$	$-\frac{13}{12}$	$\frac{5}{12}$	2
	x_4	$\frac{55}{12}$	$-\frac{1}{4}$	$\frac{1}{6}$	$\boxed{\frac{7}{12}}$	$\frac{1}{12}$	3
			x_5	x_2	x_4	x_7	
4	x_0	$\frac{695}{7}$	$\frac{13}{7}$	$\frac{3}{7}$	$\frac{11}{7}$	$\frac{5}{7}$	0
	x_1	$\frac{50}{7}$	$\frac{10}{7}$	$\frac{5}{7}$	$-\frac{5}{7}$	$-\frac{1}{7}$	1
	x_6	$\frac{325}{7}$	$-\frac{61}{7}$	$-\frac{6}{7}$	$\frac{13}{7}$	$\frac{4}{7}$	2
	x_3	$\frac{55}{7}$	$-\frac{3}{7}$	$\frac{2}{7}$	$\frac{12}{7}$	$\frac{1}{7}$	3

FIGURE 4.8. Condensed Simplex Tableau for Product-Mix Selection Problem.

4.6 Completeness and Domain of Applicability

At some iterations, the operations stated in *Criteria I* and *II* of the simplex algorithm may be ambiguous as to the variable to introduce into or to remove from the basis. In *Criterion I*, when two or more variables appear equally promising, as indicated by the values of their coefficients in Row 0, an arbitrary rule may be adopted for selecting one of these. For example, use the lowest-numbered variable, or one suspected to be in the final basis.

In *Criterion II*, when two or more variables in the current basis are to fall simultaneously to the level zero upon introducing the new variable, only one of these is to be removed from the basis. The others remain in the basis at zero level. The resultant basis is termed **degenerate.** As we discuss in Sec. 4.8 below, a delicate question of theory is involved in the selection of a tie-breaking rule. Unless some care is given to the method of deciding which variable is to be removed from the basis, you cannot *prove* the method always converges. However, long experience with simplex computations has led to the conclusion that for all *practical* purposes, the selection can be arbitrary and the associated danger of nonconvergence is negligible.

If you find at some iteration in applying *Criterion II* that there is no positive coefficient in any row for the entering variable, then there exists an unbounded optimal solution. In this event, the entering variable can be made arbitrarily large, the value of x_0 thereby increases without bound, and the current basis variables remain nonnegative. Thus we now may drop the earlier assumption that the optimal value of the objective function is finite. The simplex algorithm provides an indication of when an unbounded optimal solution occurs. *Criterion II* is easily reworded to cover this case.

Starting basis. Here we turn to the selection of an initial basis to begin the algorithm. Because each constraint in the example of the preceding section was of the form

$$(1) \qquad \sum_{j=1}^{n} a_{ij}x_j \leq b_i \quad \text{where } b_i \geq 0,$$

adding a slack variable to each relation and starting with an all-slack basic solution provided a simple way of initiating the simplex algorithm. As you recall from Chap. 2, relation (1) does not encompass all the constraints that may be found in a linear optimization model. But the discussion in Chap. 3 enabled us to assert that the constraints in any linear programming model can be written as

$$(2) \qquad \sum_{j=1}^{n} a_{ij}x_j = b_i \quad \text{for } i = 1, 2, \ldots, m \quad \text{where } b_i \geq 0.$$

In this form, if a variable appears only in constraining relation i and has a coefficient of 1, as would be the case for a slack variable, it can be used as part of the initial basis. But relation i may not have such a variable. (This would occur, for example, if the ith equation were linearly dependent on one or more of the other equations, such as being a sum of two equations.) Then we may employ the following approach.

Write the constraints as

$$(3) \qquad \sum_{j=1}^{n} a_{ij}x_j + 1y_i = b_i \quad \text{for } i = 1, 2, \ldots, m \quad \text{where } b_i \geq 0,$$

and where $y_i \geq 0$; then use y_i as the basic variable for relation i. (We have assumed, for simplicity, that every constraint requires the addition of a y_i.) The name **artificial variable** is given to y_i because it is added as an artifice in order to obtain an initial-trial solution. Is this approach legitimate? The answer is yes, provided you satisfy *Condition A*.

> CONDITION A. To ensure that the final solution is meaningful, every y_i must equal 0 at the terminal iteration of the simplex method.

If the constraints admit of no feasible solution, it will be impossible to satisfy *Condition A*. At the final iteration of the simplex algorithm, at least one y_i will be in the solution at a positive level, indicating the infeasibility condition. Thus you can remove the assumption made in Sec. 4.4 that a feasible solution exists. If one does not, the simplex algorithm will tell you so.

We can state at last that the instructions for carrying out the rules of the simplex method are complete. They can be, and, of course, have been, programmed for operation on every large-scale electronic computer.

The Big M Method. There are a number of computational techniques for guaranteeing *Condition A*. Since they are of interest principally to operations-research specialists, however, we do not delve into them here except to mention a simple but somewhat inelegant approach.

Add to the maximizing objective function each y_i with a large **penalty-cost coefficient:**

$$(4) \qquad x_0 - \sum_{j=1}^{n} c_j x_j + \sum_{i=1}^{m} M y_i = 0,$$

where M is relatively large. Thus each y_i variable is very costly as compared to any of the x_j variables. To initiate the algorithm, you first eliminate each y_i from (4) by using (3). This gives

$$(5) \qquad x_0 - \sum_{j=1}^{n} c_j x_j - M \sum_{i=1}^{m} \sum_{j=1}^{n} a_{ij} x_j = -M \sum_{i=1}^{m} b_i,$$

which simplifies to

$$(6) \qquad x_0 - \sum_{j=1}^{n} (c_j + M \sum_{i=1}^{m} a_{ij}) x_j = -M \sum_{i=1}^{m} b_i.$$

Because the y_i variables are so expensive, the very technique of optimizing drives the y_i variables to zero, *provided* there exists a feasible solution. (Incidentally, whenever a y_i drops from a basis at some iteration, you need never consider using it again, and can eliminate it from further computations.)

An example will clarify the approach. Consider the problem

(7)·   maximize $-3x_1 - 2x_2$

subject to

(8) $1x_1 + 1x_2 = 10$

(9) $1x_1 \geq 4$

(10) $x_1 \geq 0 \quad x_2 \geq 0.$

Then, after adding a surplus variable x_3 in (9), you can write the model as

(11)
$$\begin{aligned}
x_0 + 3x_1 + 2x_2 & = 0 \quad \text{Row 0} \\
1x_1 + 1x_2 & = 10 \quad \text{Row 1} \\
1x_1 \qquad - 1x_3 & = 4 \quad \text{Row 2.}
\end{aligned}$$

Next, introduce artificial variables y_1 and y_2, and let $M = 10$, giving

(12)
$$\begin{aligned}
x_0 + 3x_1 + 2x_2 \quad + 10y_1 + 10y_2 & = 0 \quad \text{Row 0} \\
1x_1 + 1x_2 \qquad + 1y_1 \qquad & = 10 \quad \text{Row 1} \\
1x_1 \qquad - 1x_3 \qquad + 1y_2 & = 4 \quad \text{Row 2.}
\end{aligned}$$

To initiate the algorithm, you have to subtract $(M = 10)$ times Row 1 and $(M = 10)$ times Row 2 from Row 0 to eliminate y_1 and y_2:

(13)
$$\begin{aligned}
x_0 - 17x_1 - 8x_2 + 10x_3 \qquad\qquad & = -140 \quad \text{Row 0} \\
1x_1 + 1x_2 \qquad + 1y_1 \qquad & = 10 \quad \text{Row 1} \\
1x_1 \qquad - 1x_3 \qquad + 1y_2 & = 4 \quad \text{Row 2.}
\end{aligned}$$

Verify that $x_1 = 4$ and $x_2 = 6$ are optimal.

Minimization. Many linear programming models have, as their objective, minimizing a linear function. They can be solved by changing the signs of the coefficients in the objective function, as was pointed out in Sec. 3.2. Then *Criterion I* (Maximization) is applied to the revised form. But we find it convenient to record here, for future purposes, a restatement of *Criterion I* when minimization is called for and the objective function is left in its original form.

SIMPLEX CRITERION I (MINIMIZATION). If there are nonbasic variables having a plus coefficient in Row 0, select one such variable with the most positive coefficient (say x_j). If all nonbasic variables have minus or zero coefficients in Row 0, an optimal solution has been obtained.

An example will clarify the procedure. Consider the trivial linear programming problem

$$(14) \qquad\qquad \text{minimize} \quad -2x_1 + 3x_2$$

subject to

$$(15) \qquad\qquad 0 \le x_1 \le 6 \quad \text{and} \quad 0 \le x_2 \le 10.$$

We could proceed to solve the problem by first changing both the signs of the coefficients in (1) and the sense of optimization:

$$(16) \qquad\qquad \text{maximize} \quad 2x_1 - 3x_2.$$

This transformation will give the same optimal values for x_1 and x_2. Then if we use the simplex algorithm format in the preceding section, we would start the iterations with the model

$$(17) \quad
\begin{aligned}
x_0 - 2x_1 + 3x_2 \qquad\qquad &= 0 \quad \text{Row 0} \\
1x_1 \qquad + 1x_3 \qquad &= 6 \quad \text{Row 1} \\
1x_2 \qquad + 1x_4 &= 10 \quad \text{Row 2,}
\end{aligned}$$

and enter x_1 into the basis according to *Criterion I* (Maximization).

But we can instead employ (1) directly by defining the variable x_0 equal to the objective function in (1), and setting up the initial formulation as

$$(18) \quad
\begin{aligned}
x_0 + 2x_1 - 3x_2 \qquad\qquad &= 0 \quad \text{Row 0} \\
1x_1 \qquad + 1x_3 \qquad &= 6 \quad \text{Row 1} \\
1x_2 \qquad + 1x_4 &= 10 \quad \text{Row 2.}
\end{aligned}$$

Here we would apply *Criterion I* (Minimization), so that at the first iteration we select x_1 to enter the basis, since its coefficient is $+2$ in Row 0.

In a minimization problem, no revision in *Criterion II* is needed, because this second rule is aimed only at keeping each basic solution feasible.

Summary. So far you have learned that

(i) The simplex algorithm applies to *all* linear optimization models.
(ii) At the final iteration, the terminal answer *is* an exact solution to the problem.

4.7 IMPORTANT PROPERTY OF AN OPTIMAL SOLUTION

We have *not* yet established that the simplex algorithm terminates for all linear programming models. We discuss this point in the next section. But assuming that convergence can be established, you have discovered a remarkable proposition:

> THEOREM OF THE BASIS. If a linear optimization model has a finite optimal solution, then there exists an optimal *basic* solution.

Recall that in a linear model with m constraints, a basis is a set of m variables having *unique* values that satisfy the constraints when all the other variables are assigned 0 value.

To see the full impact of this theorem, suppose you want to solve a linear programming model with 50 (linearly independent) constraints and 300 unknowns. If the hypothesis of the theorem holds, there is an optimal solution containing at most 50 variables at a positive level. Adding more variables may improve the optimal value of the objective function, but it will not increase the number of variables required for an optimal solution beyond 50. Notice that adding more linearly independent constraints to a model enlarges the size of the set of basic variables. Therefore, an optimal solution to the augmented model usually requires more variables to be at a positive level.

How do you know the Theorem of the Basis is correct? You know because when the hypothesis is true, the simplex method actually *constructs* such an optimal basic solution.

*4.8 CONVERGENCE PROPERTIES

Establishing convergence is usually the hardest single task in the development of an algorithm. You will see why.

You know by the way *Simplex Criteria I* and *II* operate that each successive trial solution is feasible and the value of the objective function is no worse than at the previous solution. Suppose, for the moment, that at each iteration the objective function to be maximized actually increases. This information alone is not enough to establish convergence in a finite number of iterations. The objective function may improve by smaller and smaller amounts, as you saw in *Case 2* of Fig. 4.1 (p. 97). What is worse, the value of the objective function may not be approaching the optimum, as you saw occur in *Case 3* of Fig. 4.1.

But you can make use of more information about the algorithm. The simplex method proceeds from one *basic* solution to another. Since the values for any set of basic variables are uniquely determined, it is not possible to return to any previous basic solution, given the assumption that the objective function improves at each trial. There are only a finite number of basis sets—certainly no more than the combination of n things taken m at a time, $\binom{n}{m} = n!/[m! \, (n - m)!]$, for an

m-equation and n-variable problem. Therefore only a finite number of iterations can occur, and we already have argued that *when* termination takes place, the final solution *is* optimal.

Now has convergence been established? Unfortunately, no. The argument in the preceding paragraphs *assumed* that the objective function increases at each iteration. However, in many linear optimization problems, the objective function actually *stalls* for several iterations. This occurs in the following way.

At some iteration, when *Criterion II* is applied the minimum ratio is zero. (Such an event can arise when, on the previous iteration, more than one variable in the basis is driven to zero as the new variable enters. Thus at the present iteration, one or more *basic* variables are at zero level, so that the basic solution is degenerate.) Therefore the new variable enters the basis at zero level, and all the remaining variables as well as the objective function remain unchanged. The change-of-basis calculation in *Step 4* does cause the Row 0 coefficients to be modified, and hopefully at the next iteration the new variable selected leads to a minimum ratio that is strictly positive. But it is conceivable that the objective function stalls again. This condition could persist for several iterations, until eventually a previous basis might reappear! Then the cycle would start all over again, and convergence would not occur.

To sum up, we almost have a finite convergence proof, and would have one if we could force the objective function to make a strict increase at each iteration. To put your mind at ease, we hasten to mention that a finite convergence proof can be devised. Using slightly more advanced mathematical analysis than is employed in this book, it is possible to demonstrate that the simplex method can be made to cause a strict increase in the objective function. In order to provide the proof, *Criterion II* must be revised slightly to eliminate the ambiguity over which variable to remove from the basis when a tie occurs, and the notion of a "strict increase in the objective function" has to be suitably defined.

In practice, degeneracy has not caused the number of iterations required until convergence to be a real problem. Considerable empirical evidence suggests that most actual applications are solved within the range of $1.5m$ to $3m$ iterations, where m is the number of constraints and the starting basis is comprised only of slack, surplus, and artificial variables.

▶ In the example of Sec. 4.4, you saw that a variable, namely x_4, entered and later left the basis. It is this phenomenon that causes the number of iterations to exceed the number of equations. The following example will startle your intuition about what can happen in the course of iterations:

(i)   maximize $1y$

subject to

$$3x - 2y + 4z + 1u = -2$$

$$3x \qquad - 8z + 1v = \quad 6$$

(ii)
$$15x + 6y - 12z + 1w = 222$$

$$1x \quad\quad + 4z + 1t = 12$$

$$x \geq 0 \quad y \geq 0 \quad z \geq 0 \quad u \geq 0 \quad v \geq 0 \quad w \geq 0 \quad t \geq 0.$$

Figure 4.9 shows the succession of trial solutions. Observe that in proceeding from the initial to the second solution, variable z replaces the variable t. Then in going from

Current Solution	Values of						
	x	y	z	u	v	w	t
Initial		1			6	216	12
2		7	3		30	216	
3	6	13	1.5			72	
4	6	25	1.5	24			
5	2	32		56			10
6		37		72	6		12
7		43	3	72	30		

FIGURE 4.9. An Example of Slow Convergence.

Note: Objective function = $1y$

the fourth to the fifth solution, t replaces z. Finally, in progressing from the sixth to the seventh solution, z replaces t again. The variable z starts outside the basis, later enters, then leaves, and finally enters again. The variable t starts in the basis, leaves, enters, and then leaves again. Notice also that variable x replaces v at the third solution, and later v replaces x at the sixth solution. All in all, the simplex method requires examining seven solutions to obtain convergence. (Note that the objective function, $1y$, does improve at each iteration.)

When we tried to establish finite convergence of the simplex method, recall we only stated that **cycling** is conceivable. We did not demonstrate that an example exists where cycling *does* occur if an arbitrary rule is used to break ties when degeneracy arises. Here is such an illustration. (It was discovered by sheer ingenuity.)

The example assumes the following arbitrary tie-breaking rule for *Criterion II*: If two variables are candidates to leave the basis, the variable with the smaller subscript is chosen. The model is

(iii)
$$\text{maximize} \quad \tfrac{3}{4}x_1 - 150x_2 + \tfrac{1}{50}x_3 - 6x_4$$

subject to

$$\tfrac{1}{4}x_1 - 60x_2 - \tfrac{1}{25}x_3 + 9x_4 + x_5 \quad\quad\quad = 0$$

(iv)
$$\tfrac{1}{2}x_1 - 90x_2 - \tfrac{1}{50}x_3 + 3x_4 \quad + x_6 \quad = 0$$

$$1x_3 \quad\quad\quad\quad + x_7 = 1$$

$$x_j \geq 0 \quad \text{for} \quad j = 1, 2, \ldots, 7.$$

The sequence of trial solutions is shown in Fig. 4.10. At each iteration, there is no ambiguity in the application of *Criterion I*. Thus, for the initial solution, the variable x_1 is chosen to enter. Because of degeneracy, either variable x_5 or x_6 can be dropped from

Current Solution	Row O Coefficients of							Basic Variables Having Values $0\ \ \ 0\ \ \ 0$			Objective Function Value
	x_1	x_2	x_3	x_4	x_5	x_6	x_7				
Initial	$-\frac{3}{4}$	150	$-\frac{1}{50}$	6	0	0	0	x_5	x_6	x_7	0
2	0	-30	$-\frac{7}{50}$	33	3	0	0	x_1	x_6	x_7	0
3	0	0	$-\frac{2}{25}$	18	1	1	0	x_1	x_2	x_7	0
4	$\frac{1}{4}$	0	0	-3	-2	3	0	x_3	x_2	x_7	0
5	$-\frac{1}{2}$	120	0	0	-1	1	0	x_3	x_4	x_7	0
6	$-\frac{7}{4}$	330	$\frac{1}{50}$	0	0	-2	0	x_5	x_4	x_7	0
7	$-\frac{3}{4}$	150	$-\frac{1}{50}$	6	0	0	0	x_5	x_6	x_7	0

Note: Optimal solution is $x_1 = \frac{1}{25}$, $x_3 = 1$, $x_5 = \frac{3}{100}$, and objective function $= \frac{1}{20}$

FIGURE 4.10. Example of Cycling.

the basis. The tie-breaking rule for *Criterion II* as enunciated above selects x_5. Observe that the seventh solution is identical with the initial solution, and consequently cycling ensues. Also note that the objective function is stalled at the value 0, whereas the optimal value of the objective function is $\frac{1}{20}$. The cycling is eliminated as soon as a mathematically sound tie-breaking rule is used.   ◀

*4.9 COMPUTATIONAL REQUIREMENTS

Most real applications of linear programming involve at least several dozen and quite often several hundred constraints. Therefore the computational burden of the simplex method must be discussed in the context of employing a high-speed electronic calculator. The total number of calculations required by the simplex method to solve a particular problem usually depends heavily on the computer program employed. For practical applications, several million arithmetic operations are usual. Considerable experience suggests that, as a *rough* approximation, the computational burden increases as the cube of the number of constraints. Thus a 200-equation problem is likely to require 8 times as many calculations as a comparable 100-equation model.

REVIEW EXERCISES

1 (a) Solve for x_1 and x_3 in (2) and (3) of Sec. 4.2, and verify the result in (13) and (14).
  (b) Substitute in the objective function the expressions for x_1 and x_3 from part (a) and verify the result in (15) of Sec. 4.2.

Exercises 2, 3, and 4 refer to the numerical example in Sec. 4.4 with certain specified changes in the data.

2 What variable do you enter into the basis at iteration 1 of the simplex method if the objective function to be maximized is

(a) $14x_1 + 5x_2 + 9x_3 + 11x_4$? (b) $4x_1 + 5x_2 + 9x_3 + 8x_4$?
(c) $4x_1 + 5x_2 - 9x_3 + 11x_4$? (d) $-4x_1 - 5x_2 - 9x_3 - 11x_4$?

3 Given that you enter variable x_4 into the basis at iteration 1 of the simplex method, what variable do you remove from the basis and what will the new value of x_4 be if

(a) The coefficient on the right-hand side of Row 2 is 24? Is 10?
(b) The coefficient on the right-hand side of Row 3 is 330? Is 75?
(c) The coefficient of x_4 in Row 3 is 25? Is 10? Is -25?
(d) The coefficient of x_4 in Row 2 is 30?
(e) The coefficients on the right-hand sides of Rows 1, 2, and 3 are 44, 66, and 22, respectively, and the coefficients of x_4 in these rows are -5, 10, and 2, respectively?
(f) The coefficients on the right-hand sides of Rows 1, 2, and 3 are 20, 90, and 150, respectively, and the coefficients of x_4 in these rows are 2, -9, and 15, respectively.
(g) The coefficients on the right-hand sides of Rows 1, 2, and 3 are 10, 100, and 200, and the coefficients of x_4 in these rows are -1, 0, and -20, respectively.

4 Assume that you enter variable x_4 into the basis at iteration 1. What are the new values of the basic variables if

(a) You remove variable x_5 instead of x_7?
(b) You remove variable x_6 instead of x_7?
(c) Are the values in parts (a) and (b) feasible? Explain.

Exercises 5 through 14 refer to the numerical example in Sec. 4.4. In each part of an exercise, certain coefficients are altered. Find an optimal solution and the associated value of the objective function. Think carefully about each problem, because you may find that it is not necessary to redo all the arithmetic. It may be possible to "salvage" many of the previous computations in Sec. 4.4.

5 Assume that the objective function to be maximized is

(a) $4x_1 + \frac{33}{7}x_2 + 9x_3 + 10x_4$.
(b) $5x_1 + 5x_2 + 9x_3 + 11x_4$.
(c) $5x_1 + \frac{33}{7}x_2 + 9x_3 + 10x_4$.

6 Assume that the coefficient on the right-hand side of

(a) Row 2 is 145.
(b) Row 2 is 65.
(c) Row 1 is 12.
(d) Row 1 is 8.
(e) Row 1 is 24.

7 Assume that the objective function to be maximized is $5x_1 + 5x_2 + 9x_3 + 11x_4$ and the coefficient on the right-hand side of Row 1 is 20.

8 Assume that the first constraint, prior to adding a slack variable, is stated as

$$2x_1 + 2x_2 + 2x_3 + 2x_4 \leq 30.$$

9 Assume that the coefficient of

(a) x_2 in Row 3 is 8.
(b) x_4 in Row 3 is 18.
(c) x_2 in Row 2 is 4.
(d) x_4 in Row 2 is 1.
(e) x_1 in Row 2 is 9.
(f) x_3 in Row 2 is 8.

10 Assume that the coefficients in Rows 0, 1, 2, and 3 of

(a) x_1 are 40, 10, 70, and 30, respectively.
(b) x_2 are 20, 4, 20, and 20, respectively.
(c) x_3 are 45, 5, 15, and 50, respectively.

11 Suppose you require $x_4 = 3$.

12 (a) Consider the variable x_8 defined in (10) of Sec. 4.4. Calculate the coefficients of x_8 at each of the simplex iterations, that is, in (2) through (7) of Sec. 4.4.

(b) Verify that if you enter x_8 into the basis found at iteration 4, the solution is given by (12) of Sec. 4.4.
(c) Let $w = .4$ in (13) of Sec. 4.4 and calculate optimal values for x_1, x_3, x_6, and x_8. Check that these values satisfy the original constraints and yield an objective-function value of $\frac{695}{7}$.

13 Consider the variable x_8 defined in (10) of Sec. 4.4. Determine whether entering x_8 into the basis found at iteration 4 improves the solution if the coefficient of x_8 in

(a) Row 2 is 7, instead of 9.
(b) Row 2 is 10, instead of 9.
(c) Row 3 is 1.2, instead of .2.
(d) Row 3 is .1, instead of .2.

14 Suppose another variable z is added to the example in Sec. 4.4, and at iteration 4, the coefficients of z in (7) are -1 in Rows 0 through 4. What is an optimal solution? Exhibit a solution having an objective-function value 150.

15 Consider the example (7) through (10) in Sec. 4.6. In each part below, apply the Big M Method, with $M = 20$, and derive a starting set of equations analogous to those in (13).

(a) Add the constraint $x_2 \geq 3$.
(b) Let the first constraint be $5x_1 + 6x_2 = 56$, instead of (8).
(c) Let the first constraint be $-5x_1 + 6x_2 = 16$, instead of (8).

16 For a given set of constraints, suppose an all-slack-variable basis provides a feasible initial solution. What variable do you enter into the basis at iteration 1 of the simplex method given that the objective function to be minimized is

  (a) $4x_1 + 5x_2 - 9x_3 + 11x_4$.
  (b) $-4x_1 + 5x_2 - 9x_3 + 11x_4$.
  (c) $-4x_1 - 5x_2 - 9x_3 - 11x_4$.
  (d) $4x_1 + 5x_2 + 9x_3 + 11x_4$.
  (e) Given your answers in each of the preceding parts and that the constraints of the problem are Rows 1, 2, and 3 in (1) of Sec. 4.4, state what slack variable drops from the basis.

17 Explain your understanding of the following terms:

algorithm   shadow prices
Gaussian elimination   positive-weighted average
algorithmic convergence   weighting factor
basis and basic solution   degenerate basic solution
basic and nonbasic variable   artificial variable
change of basis   penalty-cost coefficient
pivot operation (or pivoting)   *simplex tableau
relative (or shadow) costs   *cycling.

COMPUTATIONAL EXERCISES

18 *One-Potato, Two-Potato Problem* (Sec. 1.6). Apply the simplex method to solve

$$\text{maximize} \quad 5P_1 + 6P_2$$

subject to

$$.2P_1 + .3P_2 \le 1.8$$

$$.2P_1 + .1P_2 \le 1.2$$

$$.3P_1 + .3P_2 \le 2.4$$

$$P_1 \ge 0 \quad \text{and} \quad P_2 \ge 0.$$

19 Apply the simplex method to solve

$$\text{maximize} \quad 15x_1 + 6x_2 + 9x_3 + 2x_4$$

subject to

$$2x_1 + x_2 + 5x_3 + .6x_4 \le 20$$

$$3x_1 + x_2 + 3x_3 + .25x_4 \le 24$$

$$7x_1 \qquad\qquad + \quad x_4 \le 70$$

$$\text{every } x_j \ge 0.$$

(*Hint:* you should find an optimal solution in no more than three iterations.)

20 Solve exercise 19 where you minimize $-15x_1 - 6x_2 - 9x_3 - 2x_4$.

21 (a) Apply the simplex method to solve

$$\text{maximize} \quad 30x_1 + 23x_2 + 29x_3$$

subject to

$$6x_1 + 5x_2 + 3x_3 \le 52$$

$$4x_1 + 2x_2 + 5x_3 \le 14$$

$$\text{every } x_j \ge 0.$$

   (*Hint:* you should find an optimal solution in no more than three iterations.)
   (b) Solve part (a), assuming that the two right-hand side coefficients are 62, instead of 52, and 40, instead of 14. (*Hint:* you should find an optimal solution in no more than four iterations.)

*22 Solve exercise 21 where you minimize $-30x_1 - 23x_2 - 29x_3$.

23 Apply the simplex method to solve

$$\text{maximize} \quad 60x_1 + 26x_2 + 15x_3 + 4.75x_4$$

subject to

$$20x_1 + 9x_2 + 6x_3 + 1x_4 \le 40$$

$$10x_1 + 4x_2 + 2x_3 + 1x_4 \le 20$$

$$\text{every } x_j \ge 0.$$

   (*Hint:* you should find an optimal solution in no more than five iterations.) Does the objective function increase at every iteration? Is there a unique optimal solution?

24 *Alternative Optimal Solutions*

   (a) Apply the simplex method to solve

$$\text{maximize} \quad 1x_1 + 1x_2$$

subject to

$$1x_1 + 1x_2 \le 15$$

$$1x_1 \qquad \le 10$$

$$1x_2 \le 10$$

$$x_1 \ge 0 \quad \text{and} \quad x_2 \ge 0.$$

   (b) Alter the coefficients of x_1 to be 10, instead of 1, in both the objective function and constraints. Apply the simplex method to solve.   (*Continued on page 108.*)

(c) Alter the coefficients of x_2 to be 10, instead of 1, in both the objective function and constraints. Apply the simplex method to solve.

(d) In each of the above parts, indicate how you know at the final iteration that there are alternative optimal solutions. Using formulas analogous to those in (13) of Sec. 4.4, characterize *all* the optimal solutions.

25 *Unbounded Optimal Solution.* Consider the constraints

$$x_1 - x_2 \leq 1$$

$$-x_1 + x_2 \leq 1$$

$$x_1 \geq 0 \quad \text{and} \quad x_2 \geq 0.$$

Apply the simplex method and assume that the objective function is

(a) Maximize x_1.

(b) Maximize x_2.

(c) Maximize $x_1 + x_2$.

(d) In each of the above parts, indicate a solution having objective-function value 100.

26 Consider the constraints graphed in exercise 10 of Chap. 3:

$$-10x_1 - 15x_2 \geq -150$$

$$5x_1 + 11x_2 \geq 55$$

$$x_1 - x_2 \geq 0$$

$$x_1 \geq 0 \quad \text{and} \quad x_2 \geq 0.$$

(We have eliminated the explicit constraint $x_1 \geq 4$ which was shown in exercise 10 of Chap. 3.)

Use the Big M Method, with $M = 10$, to find an initial basis. (*Hint:* do *not* add an artificial variable for the first constraint.) Solve for an optimal solution by the simplex method and assume that the objective function is

(a) Maximize $x_1 + x_2$.   (b) Minimize $x_1 + x_2$.

(c) Maximize $x_1 + 3x_2$.   (d) Maximize $-2x_1 + x_2$.

(e) Maximize $-x_1 - 3x_2$.   (f) Maximize $-x_1 - 2x_2$.

(g) State in each of the above parts whether there is a *unique* optimal solution, and if there is not, calculate an alternative optimal solution. (*Hint:* do *not* add an artificial variable for the first constraint.)

27 Consider the constraints graphed in exercise 6 of Chap. 3:

$$-x_1 + x_2 \leq 2$$

$$6x_1 + 4x_2 \geq 24$$

$$x_1 \geq 0 \quad \text{and} \quad x_2 \geq 1.$$

Use the Big M Method, with $M = 10$, to find an initial basis. Obtain an optimal solution by the simplex method and assume that the objective function is

(a) Minimize x_1.   (b) Minimize $x_1 + x_2$.

(c) Maximize $x_1 + x_2$.   (d) Maximize $-x_1 + 2x_2$.

(e) Maximize $x_1 - 2x_2$.   (f) Maximize $-3x_1 - 2x_2$.

(g) State in each of the above parts whether there is a *unique* optimal solution, and if there is not, calculate an alternative optimal solution.

28 Answer the questions in exercise 27 assuming that $x_1 \leq 5$.

29 Answer the questions in exercise 27 assuming that $x_2 \leq 4$.

30 *No Feasible Solution.* In Sec. 3.4, you saw a simple example that had no feasible solution:

$$\text{maximize} \quad x_1 + x_2$$

subject to

$$-x_1 + x_2 \leq -1$$

$$x_1 - x_2 \leq -1$$

$$x_1 \geq 0 \quad \text{and} \quad x_2 \geq 0.$$

Apply the Big M Method to see what happens in this case. (Show that *Condition A* in Sec. 4.6 cannot be satisfied, regardless of how large a value you assign M.)

31 *Redundancy and Degeneracy.* Consider the problem

$$\text{maximize} \quad 2x_1 - 10x_3$$

subject to

$$5x_1 + 3x_2 + 10x_3 = 40$$

$$x_1 + x_2 + 40x_3 = 10$$

$$\text{every } x_j \geq 0.$$

Use the Big M Method to derive an optimal solution when the model is augmented by the constraint

(a) $6x_1 + 4x_2 + 50x_3 = 50$.

(b) $6x_1 + 4x_2 + 10x_3 = 50$.

CONTENTS

CHAPTER 5

Sensitivity Testing
and Duality

5.1 POSTOPTIMALITY ANALYSIS

In Chap. 4 you studied the mechanics of obtaining an optimal solution to a linear programming model. As a result you learned the important considerations for understanding the algorithmic approach and acquired an initial insight into the mathematical structure of a linear model—discovering, for example, that if a linear optimization model has a finite optimal solution, there exists an optimal *basic* solution.

But recall that the stated goal has been to provide systematic methods by which you can fully analyze and comprehend the complex interrelations in a linear programming application. We pursue this objective here.

The experienced user of a linear programming model rarely confines his interest to the numerical values of an optimal solution, unless he has already applied the model so many times that he fully understands the range of validity of the answer. Typically, he wants to know how far the input parameter values can vary without causing violent changes in a compound optimal solution or the composition of a basis set. Such an investigation is termed a **sensitivity** or **postoptimality analysis.**

Many important postoptimality questions are easily answered, given the numerical information at the final simplex iteration. Three illustrative examples are, "If the profit contribution of a particular basic activity decreases, does the current solution remain optimal? What happens if resource availability is curtailed? What happens if a new activity is added?" Other sensitivity questions can be sufficiently complex to require an electronic computer for the analysis, but even then, most electronic computer codes make considerable use of the previous optimal solution, and do *not* solve the revised model from scratch.

In the sections to follow, we explore the fundamental ideas that underlie sensitivity analysis in linear programming. The methods we present relate to the model

(1)
$$\text{maximize} \sum_{j=1}^{n} c_j x_j$$

subject to

(2)
$$\sum_{j=1}^{n} a_{ij} x_j \le b_i \quad \text{for } i = 1, 2, \ldots, m$$

(3)
$$x_j \ge 0 \quad \text{for } j = 1, 2, \ldots, n.$$

The mechanics of sensitivity testing are straightforward, and rather than confuse the presentation with frightening-looking formulas, we explain the ideas in terms of the Product-Mix Selection Example that was solved in Sec. 4.4. We repeat here both the initial and final systems of equations, labeling them (I) and (F):

(I)
$$
\begin{array}{llll}
1x_0 - 4x_1 - 5x_2 - 9x_3 - 11x_4 & = 0 & \text{Row 0} \\
\quad 1x_1 + 1x_2 + 1x_3 + 1x_4 + 1x_5 & = 15 & \text{Row 1} \\
\quad 7x_1 + 5x_2 + 3x_3 + 2x_4 + 1x_6 & = 120 & \text{Row 2} \\
\quad 3x_1 + 5x_2 + 10x_3 + 15x_4 \quad\quad 1x_7 & = 100 & \text{Row 3,}
\end{array}
$$

and

(F)
$$
\begin{array}{llll}
1x_0 + \tfrac{3}{7}x_2 + \tfrac{11}{7}x_4 + \tfrac{13}{7}x_5 + \tfrac{5}{7}x_7 & = \tfrac{695}{7} & \text{Row 0} \\
1x_1 + \tfrac{5}{7}x_2 - \tfrac{5}{7}x_4 + \tfrac{10}{7}x_5 - \tfrac{1}{7}x_7 & = \tfrac{50}{7} & \text{Row 1} \\
- \tfrac{6}{7}x_2 + \tfrac{13}{7}x_4 - \tfrac{61}{7}x_5 + 1x_6 + \tfrac{4}{7}x_7 & = \tfrac{325}{7} & \text{Row 2} \\
\tfrac{2}{7}x_2 + 1x_3 + \tfrac{12}{7}x_4 - \tfrac{3}{7}x_5 + \tfrac{1}{7}x_7 & = \tfrac{55}{7} & \text{Row 3,}
\end{array}
$$

where x_0 is being maximized.

We ask you to copy (I) and (F) on a sheet of notepaper to keep before you as you read the text below.

5.2 OBJECTIVE FUNCTION

First we investigate whether a previously optimal feasible solution remains optimal if the coefficients in the objective function are altered. Such alterations do not affect the feasibility of the previous solution; therefore, whenever an improved solution is possible, you need only reinitiate the simplex method computations, starting at the previous final iteration.

Consider the coefficients of the nonbasic variables x_2 and x_4 in Row 0 of (I). It is intuitive that if they are made less profitable, the current solution remains optimal. If you sufficiently increased their profitability, however, you could eventually improve on the current solution. At what level of unit profit for x does the present solution become nonoptimal?

Suppose the unit-profit coefficient of x_2 is $(5 + p_2)$, where p_2 is nonnegative. Then Row 0 in (I) would be written:

(1) $1x_0 - 4x_1 - (5 + p_2)x_2 - 9x_3 - 11x_4 = 0$ Row 0.

In performing each simplex iteration, you added a multiple of a row to Row 0. Consequently at the final iteration, Row 0 of (F) must be

(2) $1x_0 + (\frac{3}{7} - p_2)x_2 + \frac{11}{7}x_4 + \frac{13}{7}x_5 + \frac{5}{7}x_7 = \frac{695}{7}$ Row 0,

as you should verify. Thus, subtracting p_2x_2 in (1) causes p_2x_2 to be subtracted in all subsequent Row 0 equations.

You can see that if p_2 is greater than $\frac{3}{7}$, the coefficient of x_2 in (2) is negative. Then x_2 would enter the next basic solution, according to *Simplex Criterion I* (Maximization). Similarly, if the coefficient of x_4 were increased by more than $\frac{11}{7}$, the current basic solution would no longer be optimal.

Thus, the final Row 0 coefficients of the nonbasic variables represent the largest positive increments to the original objective function coefficients that leave the current solution optimal.

Suppose you substantially reduce the profitability of x_1 or x_3, which are in the basis. It is plausible that the current basic solution might not remain optimal. It is not so intuitive that if you *increased* one of these unit-profit coefficients, the current solution could become nonoptimal. Within what range can the profitability of x_1 vary before the present solution can be improved?

To answer this question, you proceed as before. Row 0 in (I) becomes

(3) $1x_0 - (4 + p_1)x_1 - 5x_2 - 9x_3 - 11x_4 = 0$ Row 0,

and in (F) correspondingly becomes

(4) $1x_0 - p_1x_1 + \frac{3}{7}x_2 + \frac{11}{7}x_4 + \frac{13}{7}x_5 + \frac{5}{7}x_7 = \frac{695}{7}$.

To draw any conclusions about a critical range for p_1, you first must recreate a coefficient equal to 0 for x_1 in Row 0. This is achieved in the usual fashion. Multiply Row 1 of (F) by p_1 and add it to (4) to give

(5) $1x_0 + (\frac{3}{7} + \frac{5}{7}p_1)x_2 + (\frac{11}{7} - \frac{5}{7}p_1)x_4 + (\frac{13}{7} + \frac{10}{7}p_1)x_5 + (\frac{5}{7} - \frac{1}{7}p_1)x_7$

$= \frac{695}{7} + (\frac{50}{7})p_1$ Row 0.

Look carefully at (5), and check that for

(6) $-\dfrac{3}{5} \leq p_1 \leq \dfrac{11}{5},$

the current solution remains optimal. If p_1 is less than $-\frac{3}{5}$, the coefficient of x_2 becomes negative. If p_1 exceeds $\frac{11}{5}$, the coefficient of x_4 becomes negative. Consequently, as soon as p_1 falls outside the range in (6), the present basis is no longer optimal.

5.3 RIGHT-HAND-SIDE CONSTANTS

Now we investigate whether a previously optimal basis remains feasible if a constant on the right-hand side is altered. When the basis remains feasible, the new solution is optimal, because the coefficients in Row 0 are unchanged.

Consider the constant on the right-hand side of Row 2 of (I). Suppose you change it to $(120 + 1Y)$. Observe in (F) that the slack x_6 for this row is in the final basis, and so x_6 will change by the amount Y. Consequently from Row 2 of (F), the present solution remains feasible so long as $Y \geq -\frac{325}{7}$. (The value of $x_6 = 0$ if $Y = -\frac{325}{7}$.)

Next consider the constant on the right-hand side of Row 1 of (I). Suppose you alter it to $(15 + 1M)$. Over what range of M does the current solution remain feasible?

You can determine the answer if, while performing the simplex arithmetic, you carry along the quantity $1M$ on the right-hand side of the equations. Notice, however, that row for row the quantity $1M$ added on the right of (I) is just like the quantity $1x_5$ already appearing on the left of (I). It follows that at any iteration, the coefficients of M will be the same row by row as the coefficients of x_5. Hence at the final iteration you must have

$$\text{(1)}\quad \begin{array}{llllll}
1x_0 & +\frac{3}{7}x_2 & +\frac{11}{7}x_4 + \frac{13}{7}x_5 & +\frac{5}{7}x_7 = \frac{695}{7} + \frac{13}{7}M & \text{Row 0} \\
& 1x_1 + \frac{5}{7}x_2 & -\frac{5}{7}x_4 + \frac{10}{7}x_5 & -\frac{1}{7}x_7 = \frac{50}{7} + \frac{10}{7}M & \text{Row 1} \\
& -\frac{6}{7}x_2 & +\frac{13}{7}x_4 - \frac{61}{7}x_5 + 1x_6 & +\frac{4}{7}x_7 = \frac{325}{7} - \frac{61}{7}M & \text{Row 2} \\
& \frac{2}{7}x_2 + 1x_3 + \frac{12}{7}x_4 & -\frac{3}{7}x_5 & +\frac{1}{7}x_7 = \frac{55}{7} - \frac{3}{7}M & \text{Row 3.}
\end{array}$$

As always, setting the nonbasic variables x_2, x_4, x_5, and x_7 to zero yields the values for the basic variables, which are now expressed in terms of M. For feasibility, all the constants on the right-hand side of (1) must be nonnegative; therefore, the current solution remains feasible for

$$\text{(2)}\quad -\frac{50}{10} \leq M \leq \frac{325}{61},$$

as you should verify. If $M < -\frac{50}{10}$, the basic variable x_1 becomes negative, and if $M > \frac{325}{61}$, the basic variable x_6 becomes negative.

Suppose $M = 1$, which can be interpreted as augmenting the scarce resource man-weeks in Row 1 by one unit. Then the value of the objective function increases by $\frac{13}{7}$, as you can see in Row 0 of (1), and all the basic variables remain nonnegative. In other words, $\frac{13}{7}$ is the incremental value of another man-week at an optimal solution.

5.4 DUALITY

The techniques you have learned so far in answering questions about the sensitivity of an optimal solution may have seemed logical but ad hoc. In the same way, we could continue to develop methods for testing the sensitivity to the technological coefficients a_{ij}, for deciding whether it would be beneficial to enter into the basis a newly added variable, and for altering the solution when new constraints are imposed.

But there *is* a unifying concept, namely, **duality,** that establishes the interconnections for all of the sensitivity analysis techniques. If you are like most beginning students, you will first think of duality as being an abstract idea and, consequently, somewhat puzzling and remote. The reaction of most beginners when they read the Dual Theorem below is, "That's nice. So what?" At this point in your understanding, the only reply we can give is, "Keep the faith, baby." If ever the maxim applies that "there is nothing more practical than a good theory," this is it. We would be less than honest if we did not admit that many effective practitioners of linear programming have managed to avoid understanding duality. The most successful, however, know it cold.

We begin with a statement of the duality relationships and give a few immediate implications. Then in the subsequent sections we show how to employ duality for sensitivity testing.

Primal and dual problems. Consider the pair of linear programming models:

$$(1) \qquad \text{maximize} \sum_{j=1}^{n} c_j x_j$$

subject to

$$(2) \qquad \sum_{j=1}^{n} a_{ij} x_j \leq b_i \quad \text{for } i = 1, 2, \ldots, m$$

$$(3) \qquad x_j \geq 0 \quad \text{for } j = 1, 2, \ldots, n.$$

and

$$(4) \qquad \text{minimize} \sum_{i=1}^{m} b_i y_i$$

subject to

$$(5) \qquad \sum_{i=1}^{m} a_{ij} y_i \geq c_j \quad \text{for } j = 1, 2, \ldots, n$$

$$(6) \qquad y_i \geq 0 \quad \text{for } i = 1, 2, \ldots, m.$$

For the sake of definiteness, we arbitrarily call (1), (2), and (3) the **primal problem** and (4), (5), and (6) its **dual problem.**

As an illustration, consider the following pair of problems:

(7)   maximize $4x_1 + 5x_2 + 9x_3$

subject to

$$1x_1 + 1x_2 + 2x_3 \leq 16$$
(8) $7x_1 + 5x_2 + 3x_3 \leq 25$

$$x_1 \geq 0 \qquad x_2 \geq 0 \qquad x_3 \geq 0 \qquad \text{Primal;}$$

and

(9)   minimize $16y_1 + 25y_2$

subject to

$$1y_1 + 7y_2 \geq 4$$
(10) $1y_1 + 5y_2 \geq 5$

$$2y_1 + 3y_2 \geq 9$$

$$y_1 \geq 0 \qquad y_2 \geq 0 \qquad \text{Dual.}$$

Loosely put, the dual problem can be viewed as the primal model flipped on its side:

(i) The jth column of coefficients in the primal is the same as the jth row of coefficients in the dual.

(ii) The row of coefficients of the primal objective function is the same as the column of constants on the right-hand side of the dual.

(iii) The column of constants on the right-hand side of the primal is the same as the row of coefficients of the dual objective function.

(iv) The direction of the inequalities and sense of optimization are reversed in the pair of problems.

The proposition of significance is the following:

DUAL THEOREM. (a) In the event that both the primal and dual problems possess feasible solutions, then the primal problem has an optimal solution x_j^*, for $j = 1, 2, \ldots, n$, the dual problem has an optimal solution y_i^*, for $i = 1, 2, \ldots, m$, and

(11) $$\sum_{j=1}^{n} c_j x_j^* = \sum_{i=1}^{m} b_i y_i^*.$$

(b) If either the primal or dual problem possesses a feasible solution with a finite optimal objective-function value, then the other problem possesses a feasible solution with the same optimal objective-function value.

To start demonstrating the ramifications of duality, we show that *any* feasible solution to one problem provides a bound on the optimal value of the objective function for the other problem.

Let x_j actually satisfy the primal constraints, and y_i similarly satisfy the dual constraints. Multiply the ith constraint in the primal by y_i. Likewise multiply the jth constraint in the dual by x_j. Since $y_i \geq 0$ and $x_j \geq 0$, the directions of the inequalities are unchanged by the multiplication. Add all the resultant constraints from the primal to give

$$(12) \qquad \sum_{i=1}^{m} y_i \left(\sum_{j=1}^{n} a_{ij} x_j \right) \leq \sum_{i=1}^{m} b_i y_i,$$

and add all the resultant constraints from the dual to give

$$(13) \qquad \sum_{j=1}^{n} x_j \left(\sum_{i=1}^{m} a_{ij} y_i \right) \geq \sum_{j=1}^{n} c_j x_j.$$

Note that adding like-directed inequalities preserves the inequality direction.

The calculated quantities on the left-hand sides of (12) and (13) are the same; therefore,

$$(14) \qquad \sum_{j=1}^{n} c_j x_j \leq \sum_{i=1}^{m} b_i y_i.$$

Consequently, the value of the objective function for a feasible solution to one of the problems bounds the objective-function value in the other problem for *any* feasible solution, including an optimal one.

For the example of the primal problem stated in (7) and (8), and its dual in (9) and (10), we can write (14) as

$$(15) \qquad 4x_1 + 5x_2 + 9x_3 \leq 16y_1 + 25y_2,$$

for any *feasible* primal and dual solutions. A feasible solution to the primal problem is $x_1 = x_2 = 0$ and $x_3 = 8$, which has an objective-function value of 72. A feasible solution to the dual problem is $y_1 = 5$ and $y_2 = 0$, which has an objective-function value of 80. Therefore, the optimal objective-function value for *both* primal and dual problems lies within the range of 72 to 80.

If one problem has an unbounded optimal solution, then the other problem cannot have a feasible solution. For example, suppose for any value of the primal objective function, *no matter how large*, there exists a feasible solution yielding this value. Then the dual problem can have no feasible solution. If it did, a contradiction would arise. By (14), the dual solution would provide an upper bound on the value of the primal objective function for *any* feasible primal solution. But we assumed that the primal objective can be made arbitrarily large.

We also point out that the Dual Theorem indicates the fundamental test for optimality of a trial feasible solution to the primal problem. If there is a corresponding feasible solution to the dual problem such that the values of both objective functions are equal, then the two solutions must be optimal in their respective problems. To illustrate, you can verify that in examples (7) through (10) the solution $x_1 = 0$, $x_2 = \frac{2}{7}$, and $x_3 = \frac{55}{7}$ is feasible in the primal problem, and the solution $y_1 = \frac{30}{7}$ and $y_2 = \frac{1}{7}$ is feasible in the dual problem. Both solutions have the same objective-function value $\frac{505}{7}$, and hence they are optimal.

▶An interesting corollary of the Dual Theorem is the following:

THEOREM OF COMPLEMENTARY SLACKNESS. Let x_j^*, for $j = 1, 2, \ldots, n$, and y_i^*, for $i = 1, 2, \ldots, m$, be corresponding feasible solutions to the primal and dual problems, respectively. Then both are optimal if and only if

$$y_i^* \cdot \left(\sum_{j=1}^{n} a_{ij}x_j^* - b_i \right) = 0 \quad \text{for} \quad i = 1, 2, \ldots, m$$

$$x_j^* \cdot \left(\sum_{i=1}^{m} a_{ij}y_i^* - c_j \right) = 0 \quad \text{for} \quad j = 1, 2, \ldots, n.$$

This implies that whenever a constraint in one of the problems holds with strict inequality, so that there is slack in the constraint, the corresponding variable in the other problem equals 0.   ◄

Variations. You know from previous chapters that not all linear programming models are formulated as either (1), (2), and (3), or as (4), (5), and (6). For example, consider the problem

(16)   minimize $12u_1 + 60u_2 + 93u_3$

subject to

$$8u_1 - 1u_2 - 3u_3 = 2$$
(17) $$2u_1 + 5u_2 + 9u_3 = 33$$

$$u_1 \geq 0 \qquad u_2 \geq 0 \qquad u_3 \geq 0.$$

It differs from (5) in that the linear constraints in (17) are equalities. You can, of course, apply the methods of Chap. 3 to transform these equalities into inequalities, and then find the corresponding maximization problem. Let's see what happens when you make the necessary transformation.

Specifically, you express the first equality restriction in (17) as the pair of inequalities

$$8u_1 - 1u_2 - 3u_3 \geq 2$$
(18)
$$8u_1 - 1u_2 - 3u_3 \leq 2,$$

or equivalently,

$$8u_1 - 1u_2 - 3u_3 \geq 2$$
(19)
$$-8u_1 + 1u_2 + 3u_3 \geq -2.$$

You treat the second equation in (17) similarly. As a result, you have an enlarged transformed model comprised of the objective function (16), four inequalities, two of which are shown in (19), and the three nonnegativity conditions in (17). This resultant model is of the form (4), (5), and (6), with $m = 3$ and $n = 4$.

You now can write the corresponding maximization problem (1), (2), and (3) as

(20)   maximize $2z_1 - 2z_2 + 33z_3 - 33z_4$

subject to

$$8z_1 - 8z_2 + 2z_3 - 2z_4 \leq 12$$

$$-1z_1 + 1z_2 + 5z_3 - 5z_4 \leq 60$$

(21)

$$-3z_1 + 3z_2 + 9z_3 - 9z_4 \leq 93$$

$$z_1 \geq 0 \qquad z_2 \geq 0 \qquad z_3 \geq 0 \qquad z_4 \geq 0.$$

Note the special pattern of coefficients in (20) and (21), namely, the coefficients of z_1 and z_2 differ only in sign, as do the coefficients of z_3 and z_4. This suggests a further simplification. Define the variables r_1 and r_2 as

(22) $r_1 = z_1 - z_2$ and $r_2 = z_3 - z_4.$

Then (20) and (21) can be rewritten more simply as

(23)   maximize $2r_1 + 33r_2$

subject to

$$8r_1 + 2r_2 \leq 12$$

(24) $$-1r_1 + 5r_2 \leq 60$$

$$-3r_1 + 9r_2 \leq 93$$

$$r_1 \quad \text{and} \quad r_2 \quad \text{unrestricted in sign.}$$

Note that r_1 and r_2 may be negative, since each represents the difference of two nonnegative numbers in (22).

You may check that $u_1 = \frac{3}{2}$, $u_2 = 0$, and $u_3 = \frac{10}{3}$ satisfy the restrictions in (17) and give an objective-function value of 328 in (16); the values $r_1 = -1$ and $r_2 = 10$ satisfy (24) and give an objective-function value of 328 in (23). [Correspondingly, you can let $z_2 = 1$, $z_3 = 10$, and $z_1 = z_4 = 0$; these values are feasible in (21) and give an objective function value of 328 in (20).] Hence, you have feasible solutions to the minimizing and maximizing problems yielding the same objective-function values, and so they must be optimal.

Observe that problem (23) and (24) differs from the model (1), (2), and (3) only in the restriction on the sign of the variables; the equalities in (17) imply the variables in (24) are unrestricted in sign. This relationship generalizes, thereby giving another dual pair of linear programming models:

(25)   minimize $\sum_{i=1}^{m} b_i y_i$

subject to

(26)
$$\sum_{i=1}^{m} a_{ij} y_i = c_j \quad \text{for } j = 1, 2, \ldots, n$$

(27)
$$y_i \geq 0 \quad \text{for } i = 1, 2, \ldots, m,$$

and

(28)
$$\text{maximize } \sum_{j=1}^{n} c_j x_j$$

subject to

(29)
$$\sum_{j=1}^{n} a_{ij} x_j \leq b_i \qquad \text{for } i = 1, 2, \ldots, m$$

(30)
$$x_j \quad \text{unrestricted in sign} \quad \text{for } j = 1, 2, \ldots, n.$$

Further generalizations are given in the special material below.

▶   Consider the following pair of canonical linear programming problems:

(i)
$$\text{maximize } \sum_{j=1}^{n} c_j x_j$$

subject to

(ii)
$$\sum_{j=1}^{n} a_{ij} x_j \leq b_i \quad \text{for } i = 1, 2, \ldots, h \leq m$$

(iii)
$$\sum_{j=1}^{n} a_{ij} x_j = b_i \quad \text{for } i = h + 1, h + 2, \ldots, m$$

(iv)
$$x_j \geq 0 \quad \text{for } j = 1, 2, \ldots, k \leq n$$

(v)
$$x_j \text{ unrestricted in sign} \quad \text{for } j = k + 1, k + 2, \ldots, n,$$

and

(i')
$$\text{minimize } \sum_{i=1}^{m} b_i y_i$$

subject to

(ii')
$$\sum_{i=1}^{m} a_{ij} y_i \geq c_j \quad \text{for } j = 1, 2, \ldots, k$$

(iii')
$$\sum_{i=1}^{m} a_{ij} y_i = c_j \quad \text{for } j = k + 1, k + 2, \ldots, n$$

(iv')
$$y_i \geq 0 \quad \text{for } i = 1, 2, \ldots, h$$

(v')
$$y_i \text{ unrestricted in sign} \quad \text{for } i = h + 1, h + 2, \ldots, m.$$

The Dual Theorem is valid for the above pair of problems.

Test your facility with the idea of duality by this exercise. Take as correct the relationships (1) through (6). Then derive the correspondence between (iii) and (v′) by employing the devices in Chap. 3. The duality relationships can be summarized as follows:

Primal (Maximize)	Dual (Minimize)
Objective function	Right-hand side
Right-hand side	Objective function
jth column of coefficients	jth row of coefficients
ith row of coefficients	ith column of coefficients
jth variable nonnegative	jth relation an inequality ($\geq$)
jth variable unrestricted in sign	jth relation an equality
ith relation an inequality ($\leq$)	ith variable nonnegative
ith relation an equality	ith variable unrestricted in sign. ◀

5.5 SOLUTION TO THE DUAL PROBLEM

By now, you must be wondering how to *calculate* a solution to the dual problem. But like the character in Molière who is delighted to hear he has been speaking prose all his life without knowing it, you have already calculated dual solutions without knowing it.

OPTIMAL VALUES OF DUAL VARIABLES. (a) The coefficients of the slack variables in Row 0 of the final simplex iteration of a maximizing problem are the optimal values of the dual variables. (b) The coefficient of variable x_j in Row 0 of the final simplex iteration represents the difference between the left- and right-hand sides of the jth dual constraint for the associated optimal dual solution.

To illustrate, consider the Product-Mix Selection Example originally written as

$$\text{maximize} \quad 4x_1 + 5x_2 + 9x_3 + 11x_4$$

subject to

$$1x_1 + 1x_2 + 1x_3 + 1x_4 \leq 15$$

$$7x_1 + 5x_2 + 3x_3 + 2x_4 \leq 120$$

$$3x_1 + 5x_2 + 10x_3 + 15x_4 \leq 100$$

$$x_j \geq 0 \quad \text{for } j = 1, 2, 3, 4.$$

Verify that the dual problem is

(1)   minimize $15y_1 + 120y_2 + 100y_3$

subject to

$$1y_1 + 7y_2 + 3y_3 \geq 4$$

$$1y_1 + 5y_2 + 5y_3 \geq 5$$

(2) $$1y_1 + 3y_2 + 10y_3 \geq 9$$

$$1y_1 + 2y_2 + 15y_3 \geq 11$$

$$y_1 \geq 0 \quad y_2 \geq 0 \quad y_3 \geq 0.$$

Look at the coefficients of the three slack variables in Row 0 of the final iteration, which we have been referring to as (F), given in Sec. 5.1. You can conclude
from (a) above that the optimal values of the dual variables are

(3) $$y_1^* = \frac{13}{7} \quad y_2^* = 0 \quad y_3^* = \frac{5}{7}.$$

Copy these values as you will want to refer to them below.
    First verify that the constraints in (2) are satisfied:

(4) $1(\frac{13}{7}) + 3(\frac{5}{7}) = \frac{28}{7} \geq 4 \qquad 1(\frac{13}{7}) + 10(\frac{5}{7}) = \frac{63}{7} \geq 9$

          $1(\frac{13}{7}) + 5(\frac{5}{7}) = \frac{38}{7} \geq 5 \qquad 1(\frac{13}{7}) + 15(\frac{5}{7}) = \frac{88}{7} \geq 11.$

    Second, check that the value of the dual objective function is the same as the
value of the primal objective function:

(5) $15(\frac{13}{7}) + 120(0) + 100(\frac{5}{7}) = \frac{695}{7}.$

    The values in (3) must be optimal, since they satisfy all the dual constraints and
yield an objective-function value equal to the optimal primal value.
    Finally, calculate the differences between the left- and right-hand sides of (4).
For example, the second and third constraints give

(6) $$\frac{38}{7} - 5 = \frac{3}{7} \qquad \frac{63}{7} - 9 = 0.$$

These are the coefficients of x_2 and x_3, respectively, in Row 0 of (F), as claimed in
(b) above.
    By reference to the notion of duality, you now can deepen your understanding
of what is really happening in the simplex method. Interpret the coefficients of
the slack variables in Row 0 of the primal problem at each iteration as trial values
of the dual variables. Likewise view the other coefficients in Row 0 as the difference between the left- and right-hand sides of (2), using these trial values for the
dual variables. *Then the simplex method can be seen as an approach that seeks feasibility
for the dual problem while maintaining feasibility in the primal problem.* As soon as feasible
solutions to *both* problems are obtained, the iterations terminate.

5.6 MORE POSTOPTIMALITY ANALYSIS

We promised that if you studied the Dual Theorem, you then would be better able to understand and do sensitivity analysis. Now we make good on our word. To start, we review what you have already learned at the beginning of the chapter, this time making clear where duality enters the picture. Afterwards, we answer some new sensitivity questions.

Objective function. Recall in the Product-Mix Selection Example that the dual restriction corresponding to the primal variable x_2 is

$$(1) \qquad\qquad 1y_1 + 5y_2 + 5y_3 \geq 5.$$

If the objective function coefficient of x_2 becomes $(5 + p_2)$, then $(5 + p_2)$ appears on the right-hand side of (1). Substituting the optimal values of the dual variables into (1), where $(5 + p_2)$ is used, yields

$$(2) \qquad\qquad 1(\tfrac{13}{7}) + 5(0) + 5(\tfrac{5}{7}) \geq 5 + p_2,$$

or

$$(3) \qquad\qquad \frac{3}{7} \geq p_2.$$

Thus the current dual solution remains feasible provided p_2 does not exceed $\tfrac{3}{7}$. If p_2 is made larger than this fraction, the dual solution is no longer feasible, and consequently the primal solution is no longer optimal. This conclusion agrees with what we found in Sec. 5.2.

Right-hand-side constants. In Sec. 5.3, we derived in an ad hoc fashion that the coefficient of a slack variable in Row 0 of an optimal solution represents the incremental value of another unit of the resource associated with that variable. And in the preceding section we stated that the optimal value of a dual variable is the very same coefficient. Putting the two statements together, we have the following:

INTERPRETATION OF THE DUAL VARIABLES. The optimal value of a dual variable indicates how much the objective function changes with a unit change in the associated right-hand-side constant, *provided* the current optimal basis remains feasible.

This interpretation accords with the fundamental equality relation (11) of the Dual Theorem in Sec. 5.4, which states:

$$(4) \qquad \begin{aligned} &\text{optimal value of } x_0 \\ &= \sum (\text{right-hand-side constants}) \times (\text{optimal dual variables}). \end{aligned}$$

The optimal values of the dual variables are often called **shadow prices.**

When the right-hand-side constants represent quantities of scarce resources, the shadow price indicates the unit worth of each resource as predicated on an optimal solution to the primal problem. For the Product-Mix Selection Example, the value $\frac{13}{7}$ is the shadow price for the first constraint (man-weeks), and similarly 0 holds for the second constraint (pounds of Material Y), and $\frac{5}{7}$ for the third constraint (pounds of Material Z). Therefore, an additional man-week increases the profit level by $\frac{13}{7}$; an additional pound of Material Z increases the profit level by $\frac{5}{7}$; but an additional pound of Material Y does not improve the profit level. Why? Because Material Y is already in excess supply, as evidenced by the slack variable x_6 being in the optimal basis.

   In general, a resource in excess supply is indicated by the slack variable for that resource appearing in the final basis at a positive level. You would expect the corresponding shadow price to be zero, because *additional* excess supply is of no value. This is precisely what occurs. Since the slack is in the basis, its final Row 0 coefficient is zero.

   Interpreting the values of the dual variables as shadow prices leads to an insightful view into the meaning of the dual problem. In the context of the Product-Mix Selection Example, think of each dual variable as representing the true marginal value of its associated resource, assuming that the company is acting optimally. Then (4) indicates that total profit is the same as evaluating the total worth of all the resources in scarce supply. Interpret each coefficient a_{ij} as the consumption of the ith resource by the jth activity. The summation $\sum_{i=1}^{m} a_{ij} y_i$ represents the underlying economic cost of using the jth activity, evaluated according to the shadow prices. The constraints of the dual problem ensure that at an optimal solution, the profit of an activity can never exceed its true economic worth. What is more, you will never employ an activity if its profit is less than its economic worth.

▶ The following example shows why the above interpretation of the dual variables has to be qualified with the proviso that the current basis remains feasible. Consider

(i)   maximize $-x_1 - x_2$

subject to

$$2x_1 - x_2 \leq 2$$

(ii) $-x_1 + 2x_2 \leq 0$

$$x_1 \geq 0 \qquad x_2 \geq 0.$$

The solution $x_1 = x_2 = 0$ is clearly feasible and thus is optimum. [You may find it helpful to draw a two-dimensional diagram of the solution space implied by (ii) and single out the unique optimum.]

   Add slack variables x_3 and x_4 to the inequalities in (ii). Then if you choose x_3 and x_4 to be basic variables, after pivoting, you will find that $x_3 = 2$, $x_4 = 0$, which is a degenerate solution. The corresponding dual variables are $y_1 = y_2 = 0$. Further, the associated Row 0 relation will be $x_0 + x_1 + x_2 = 0$, so that both nonbasic variables have strictly positive coefficients. If, instead, you choose x_1 and x_3 to be the basic variables, then after pivoting, you will find that $x_1 = 0$, $x_3 = 2$, and the corresponding variables are $y_1 = 0$, $y_2 = 1$. Further, the Row 0 relation will be $x_0 + 3x_2 + 1x_4 = 0$, so that both nonbasic variables have strictly positive coefficients. Thus, because the optimal solution leads to a degenerate basis, you have found different optimal values for (y_1, y_2), each set corresponding to one of the optimal bases. Suppose now the second constraint is

(iii) $$-x_1 + 2x_2 \leq d_2.$$

For d_2 nearly zero, which value for y_2 indicates how the objective function will change? If $d_2 > 0$, then $x_1 = x_2 = 0$ is still optimal, and so $y_2 = 0$ is correct. The basis with x_1 and x_3 is not feasible for $d_2 > 0$ (x_1 has a negative value). If $d_2 < 0$, then $y_2 = 1$ is correct, for then you must have $x_1 > 0$ for feasibility.   ◀

Technological coefficients. To begin consideration of sensitivity tests on the a_{ij}, suppose an entirely new activity is added to the model. Is it advantageous to enter it into the basis? The easiest test is to check whether the associated dual constraint is satisfied by the current values of the dual variables. If not, the new activity should be introduced.

Consider the Product-Mix Selection Example, as given by (I) in Sec. 5.1. Suppose you add another variable:

(5)

$$+ \quad 1x_8 \quad \underline{\text{Row 1}}$$

$$+ \quad \tfrac{2}{7}x_8 \quad \underline{\text{Row 2}}$$

$$+ \quad 17x_8 \quad \underline{\text{Row 3.}}$$

Let the profit coefficient of x_8 in the objective function be c_8. At what value of c_8 is it attractive to enter x_8? The associated dual relation is

(6) $$1y_1 + \tfrac{2}{7}y_2 + 17y_3 \geq c_8.$$

Substitute the current optimal values of the dual variables in (6) to obtain

(7) $$1(\tfrac{13}{7}) + \tfrac{2}{7}(0) + 17(\tfrac{5}{7}) \geq c_8,$$

or

(8) $$14 \geq c_8.$$

Therefore, if c_8 exceeds 14, you should enter x_8 into the basis.

If x_j is a nonbasic variable, you can study the effect of changing its technological coefficients a_{ij} in exactly the same fashion. To illustrate, x_4 is nonbasic in the optimal solution of the Product-Mix Selection Example. Consider the possibility that its coefficient in Row 3 is altered by A. Then the associated dual restriction is

(9) $$1y_1 + 2y_2 + (15 + A)y_3 \geq 11.$$

Substitute the current optimal values of the dual variables in (9) to obtain

(10) $1(\frac{13}{7}) + 2(0) + (15 + A)(\frac{5}{7}) \geq 11$

or

(11) $A \geq -\frac{11}{5}.$

Therefore, if A is smaller than $-\frac{11}{5}$, you should enter x_4 into the basis.

If x_j is a basic variable, analyzing the effect of changing a technological co-efficient is more complex. The analysis involves a simultaneous consideration of both the primal and dual problems. The derivation goes beyond the scope of this text, but can be found in several advanced books on linear programming.

5.7 SUMMARY

In Secs. 5.1 to 5.6, you have seen how to probe the sensitivity of an optimal solution of a linear programming problem to changes in the model formulation. In particular you studied how to

(i) Find the range of variation in each objective-function coefficient and right-hand-side constant over which the current basis remains optimal, provided the basis remains feasible.
(ii) Evaluate the economic impact of specific changes in the model's data.
(iii) Revise a previously optimal solution after adding new variables.

The mechanics for all these postoptimality analyses are straightforward extensions of the simplex-method arithmetic. But duality is the key idea that ensures the mechanics are correct.

Every linear optimization model has a dual formulation. In solving one of these problems, you automatically solve the other. As you progress in learning the fundamentals of operations research, you will find the notion of duality frequently reappearing.

REVIEW EXERCISES

The problems in exercises 1 through 7 refer to the Product-Mix Selection Example in Sec. 4.4, with the initial system of equations being given by (I) and the final system by (F), as shown at the beginning of Sec. 5.1. Think carefully about each problem, because in many of the exercises you do *not* need to repeat *all* the computations of the simplex algorithm to obtain the answer.

1 (a) Assume the coefficient of x_2 in the original objective function is $4\frac{6}{7}$, instead of 5. Calculate the coefficients of x_2 in Row 0 at each iteration of the simplex method, and verify that at the final iteration the coefficient is $\frac{4}{7}$ $(= \frac{3}{7} + \frac{1}{7})$.

(b) Answer part (a) for a coefficient of $5\frac{2}{7}$, instead of 5.

(c) Assume the coefficient of x_4 in the original objective function is 10, instead of 11. Calculate the coefficients of x_4 in Row 0 at each iteration of the simplex method, and verify that at the final iteration the coefficient is $\frac{18}{7}$ ($= \frac{11}{7} + 1$).

(d) Answer part (c) for a coefficient of 12, instead of 11.

(e) Assume the coefficient of x_3 in the original objective function is $(9 + p_3)$. Over what interval for p_3 does the basic solution in (F) remain optimal? What variable do you enter into the solution when p_3 lies below the interval? When p_3 lies above this interval?

(f) Assume the slack variable x_6 has a coefficient p_6 in the original objective function. Answer the questions posed in part (e) for p_6 instead of p_3.

2 Is the basic solution in (F) still optimal if the original objective function is to maximize

(a) $6x_1 + 5x_2 + 9x_3 + 12x_4$?
(b) $3\frac{3}{4}x_1 + 5\frac{2}{7}x_2 + 9x_3 + 12\frac{3}{4}x_4$?
(c) $3\frac{1}{2}x_1 + 5x_2 + 9x_3 + 12x_4$?
(d) $6\frac{1}{2}x_1 + 5\frac{2}{7}x_2 + 9x_3 + 11x_4$?
(e) $4x_1 + 5\frac{2}{7}x_2 + 8x_3 + 12\frac{3}{4}x_4$?
(f) $4x_1 + 5x_2 + 7\frac{1}{2}x_3 + 12x_4$?
(g) $4x_1 + 5x_2 + 13\frac{1}{2}x_3 + 12x_4$?
(h) $4x_1 + 5\frac{2}{7}x_2 + 13x_3 + 12x_4$?
(i) In each case above, if the basic solution in (F) is not optimal, state which variable you enter into the next basis.

3 Is the basic solution in (F) still optimal if the original objective function is to maximize

(a) $7x_1 + 8x_2 + 14x_3 + 18x_4$?
(b) $8x_1 + 9x_2 + 15x_3 + 21x_4$?
(c) $11x_1 + 16x_2 + 32x_3 + 46x_4$?
(d) $12x_1 + 17x_2 + 33x_3 + 45x_4$?
(e) $33x_1 + 50x_2 + 103x_3 + 163x_4$?
(f) In each case above, if the basic solution in (F) is not optimal, state which variable you enter into the next basis.

*4 Assume the coefficient of x_1 in the original objective function is $(4 + A_1)$ and, similarly, the coefficient of x_3 is $(9 + A_3)$.

(a) Using a manner analogous to the derivation of (5) and the resultant inequalities in (6), in Sec. 5.2, derive a set of inequalities for the pair (A_1, A_3) such that the basic solution in (F) remains optimal provided the pair satisfies all these inequalities.

(b) Draw a graph of the region implied by the set of inequalities in part (a).

(c) Assume the coefficient of x_1 in the original objective function is c_1, and similarly the coefficient of x_3 is c_3. Analogous to part (b), draw a graph of the region for (c_1, c_3) such that the basic solution in (F) remains optimal provided this pair of coefficients lies within the displayed region.

5 (a) Assume that the right-hand-side constant in Row 2 of (I) is 100, instead of 120. Calculate the right-hand-side constants in all the rows at each iteration of the simplex method, and verify that at the final iteration the constant in Row 2 is $\frac{185}{7}$ ($= \frac{325}{7} - 20$).

(b) Answer part (a) for a constant ($120 - \frac{325}{7}$), instead of 120.

(c) Assume that the right-hand-side constant in Row 1 of (I) is 11, instead of 15. Calculate the right-hand-side constants in all the rows at each iteration of the simplex method, and verify that the basic solution in (F) is still optimal.

(d) Answer part (c) for a constant of 20, instead of 15.

(e) Assume that the right-hand-side constant in Row 1 of (I) is ($15 + M$). Verify the assertion in (2) of Sec. 5.3 that the basic solution in (F) remains feasible provided M satisfies $-\frac{50}{10} \le M \le \frac{325}{61}$.

(f) Assume that the right-hand-side constant in Row 3 of (I) is ($100 + Z$). Over what interval for Z does the basic solution in (F) remain feasible?

6 Does the basic solution in (F) remain feasible if the right-hand-side constants in Rows 1, 2, and 3 are, respectively,

(a) 20, 110, and 130?

(b) 25, 75, and 215?

(c) 15, 30, and 185?

(d) 18, 150, and 40?

(e) 22, 150, and 80?

(f) In each case above, indicate the optimal values of each variable and the objective-function value if the basic solution in (F) remains feasible. Otherwise, indicate the infeasibility.

*7 Assume that the right-hand-side constant in Row 1 is ($15 + M$) and in Row 3 is ($100 + Z$).

(a) Derive a set of inequalities for the pair (M, Z) such that the basic solution in (F) remains feasible provided the pair satisfies all these inequalities.

(b) Draw a graph of the region implied by the set of inequalities in part (a).

(c) Assume the right-hand-side constant in Row 1 is b_1, and, similarly, that the constant in Row 3 is b_3. Analogous to part (b), draw a graph of the region for (b_1, b_3) such that the basic solution in (F) remains feasible provided this pair of constants lies within the displayed region.

(d) How do your answers to the preceding parts change if the right-hand-side constant in Row 2 is 121? Is 119?

The problems in exercises 8 through 11 below refer to the Product-Mix Selection Example in Sec. 4.4, which is repeated at the beginning of Sec. 5.5.

8 In parts (a)-(h), modify the example as indicated and write the dual problem.

(a) The primal objective function to be maximized is $7x_1 + 8x_2 + 7x_3 + 13x_4$.

(b) The right-hand-side constants in Rows 1, 2, and 3 are 30, 80, and 155, respectively.

(c) The coefficients of x_3 in Rows 1, 2, and 3 are 1, 4, and 9, respectively.

(d) The coefficients of x_2 in Rows 1, 2, and 3 are 1, 6, and -9, respectively, and the objective-function coefficient is -3, instead of 5.

(e) There is an additional variable z having coefficients in Rows 1, 2, and 3 of 1, 1, and 18, respectively, and an objective-function coefficient of 13.

(f) There is an additional constraint $4x_1 + 7x_2 - 5x_3 - 6x_4 \le 50$.

(g) All the modifications in the above parts are in effect.

(h) Examine the dual problem as given by (1) and (2) in Sec. 5.5. Specify two feasible solutions and the corresponding values of the objective function.

*9 Review the iterations of the simplex algorithm, as given in Sec. 4.4. At each iteration,

(a) What are the trial values for the dual variables?

(b) What are the associated infeasibilities in the dual problem, and the corresponding value of the dual objective function?

*10 Find optimal values for the dual variables, assuming that the basic solution in (F) of Sec. 5.1 is optimal and the objective-function coefficients of x_1 and x_3 are, respectively,

(a) 7 and 14.

(b) 8 and 15.

(c) 11 and 32.

(d) 12 and 33.

(e) 33 and 103.

11 (a) Assume the coefficient of x_4 in the objective function is $(11 + p_4)$. Use the dual constraint associated with x_4 to derive the largest value for p_4 that leaves the basic solution in (F) optimal.

(b) Find the optimal value of the primal objective function if the right-hand-side constants in Rows 1, 2, and 3 are, respectively,

16, 120, and 100	15, 120, and 101	16, 120, and 101	14, 121, and 101
14, 120, and 100	15, 120, and 99	14, 120, and 99	16, 119, and 99.

*(c) Assume the right-hand-side constant in Row 1 is $(15 + M)$. Will the objective function increase by more or less than $\frac{13}{7}M$ for $M > \frac{325}{61}$? For $M < -\frac{50}{10}$? Give an economic justification of your answers using the context of the Product-Mix Selection Example.

(d) Suppose the coefficient of x_2 in Row 3 is $(5 + A_3)$. How small can A_3 be such that the basic solution in (F) remains optimal?

(e) Suppose the coefficient of x_2 in Row 1 is $(1 + A_1)$. How small can A_1 be such that the basic solution in (F) remains optimal?

(f) Suppose you add a variable z having coefficients in Rows 1, 2, and 3 of 1, 1, and 18, respectively. What is the largest coefficient for z in the objective function such that the final basic solution in (F) remains optimal?

(g) Answer part (f) assuming the coefficient of z in Row 3 is 16.

*(h) What are the coefficients for z in Rows 1, 2, and 3 of (F), given the coefficients for z stated in part (f)? Answer the same question using the data in part (g).

12 Explain your understanding of the following terms:

postoptimality analysis
sensitivity analysis
duality
primal and dual programs
shadow prices.

COMPUTATIONAL EXERCISES

13 Consider the following problem

$$\text{maximize} \quad -2x_1 - 1x_2 + 3x_3 - 2x_4$$

subject to

$$1x_1 + 3x_2 - 1x_3 + 2x_4 \leq 7 \quad \text{Resource A}$$

$$-1x_1 - 2x_2 + 4x_3 \qquad \leq 12 \quad \text{Resource B}$$

$$-1x_1 - 4x_2 + 3x_3 + 8x_4 \leq 10 \quad \text{Resource C}$$

$$\text{every } x_j \geq 0.$$

If you add x_5, x_6, and x_7 as slack variables, you have at the final iteration of the simplex method

$$x_0 + \tfrac{7}{5}x_1 \qquad\qquad + \tfrac{12}{5}x_4 + \tfrac{1}{5}x_5 + \tfrac{4}{5}x_6 \qquad\qquad = 11 \quad \underline{\text{Row 0}}$$

$$\tfrac{3}{10}x_1 + 1x_2 \qquad + \tfrac{4}{5}x_4 + \tfrac{2}{5}x_5 + \tfrac{1}{10}x_6 \qquad = 4 \quad \underline{\text{Row 1}}$$

$$-\tfrac{1}{10}x_1 \qquad + 1x_3 + \tfrac{2}{5}x_4 + \tfrac{1}{5}x_5 + \tfrac{3}{10}x_6 \qquad = 5 \quad \underline{\text{Row 2}}$$

$$\tfrac{1}{2}x_1 \qquad\qquad\qquad + 10x_4 + 1x_5 - \tfrac{1}{2}x_6 + 1x_7 = 11 \quad \underline{\text{Row 3.}}$$

(a) State optimal values for each x_j and the objective function. Is the optimal solution unique?
(b) For each nonbasic variable, give an interval for its objective-function coefficient such that the basic solution in part (a) remains optimal.
(c) Answer part (b) for each basic variable.
*(d) Assume the coefficient of x_2 in the objective function is $(-1 + p_2)$, and similarly, the coefficient of x_3 is $(3 + p_3)$. Derive a set of inequalities for the pair (p_2, p_3) such that the basic solution in part (a) remains optimal provided the pair satisfies all these inequalities. Draw a graph of the region implied by this set of inequalities.
(e) Give an interval for each right-hand-side constant such that the basic solution in part (a) remains optimal.
*(f) Assume that the right-hand-side constant for Resource A constraint is $(7 + A)$ and for Resource B constraint is $(12 + B)$. Derive a set of inequalities for the

pair (A, B) such that the solution in part (a) remains feasible provided the pair satisfies all these inequalities. Draw a graph of the region implied by this set of inequalities.

(g) Write the dual problem. Indicate optimal values for the dual variables and *calculate* the associated value of the dual objective function.

(h) Write an economic interpretation of each dual variable and illustrate your interpretation with numerical examples.

(i) For each nonbasic variable, use the associated dual restriction to derive an interval for its objective-function coefficient such that the solution in part (a) remains optimal.

(j) Suppose two new variables x_8 and x_9 are added to the model. Assume the coefficients for x_8 in the constraints for Resources A, B, and C are 5, -3, and 1, respectively, and the objective-function coefficient is 2. Assume that the coefficients for x_9 in the constraints are -2, 10, and 12, and the objective-function coefficient is -4. Can the solution in part (a) be improved? If so, show how. If not, indicate what happens if x_9 is introduced into the basis.

*(k) Find the coefficients for x_8 and x_9 appropriate to the equations for Rows 0, 1, 2, and 3 shown above.

(l) Suppose the coefficient of x_1 in the Resource A constraint is $(1 + a_1)$. How small can a_1 be such that the solution in part (a) remains optimal? How large?

(m) Suppose the coefficient of x_1 in the Resource B constraint is $(-1 + a_2)$. How small can a_2 be such that the solution in part (a) remains optimal? How large?

(n) Answer the questions in parts (l) and (m) for the coefficients of x_4.

14 In each of the parts below, state optimal values for the decision variables and the objective function. For each variable, give an interval for its objective-function coefficient such that the basic solution at the final iteration of the simplex method remains optimal. Give an interval for each right-hand-side constant such that the basic solution at the final iteration remains optimal. Write the dual problem. Indicate optimal values for the dual variables and *calculate* the associated value of the dual objective function. For each nonbasic variable, use the associated dual restriction to derive an interval for its objective-function coefficient such that the final solution remains optimal.

(a) The One-Potato, Two-Potato Problem in Sec. 1.6 and exercise 18 of Chap. 4.

(b) The problem in exercise 19 of Chap. 4.

(c) The problem in exercise 21, part (a), of Chap. 4.

(d) The problem in exercise 21, part (b), of Chap. 4.

(e) The problem in exercise 23 of Chap. 4.

15 Suppose at some iteration in solving a linear programming model, you arrive at the relations shown in parts (a) and (b). Note that x_0 is being maximized and the variables x_4, x_5, and x_6 are the slacks in the constraints for Resources A, B, and C, respectively. Find an optimal solution and indicate whether it is unique. State how much an additional unit of each resource is worth. Give optimal values for the dual variables. Interpret the meaning of the dual variables, and illustrate your interpretation with numerical examples.

(a)

$$x_0 \quad - 4x_2 \qquad\qquad - 1x_4 \qquad\qquad - 2x_6 = 150 \quad \text{Objective function}$$

$$- 1x_2 \qquad + 6x_4 + 1x_5 + 3x_6 = 12 \quad \text{Resource A}$$

$$1x_1 + 5x_2 \qquad + 10x_4 \qquad\quad + 6x_6 = 15 \quad \text{Resource B}$$

$$+ 1x_2 + 1x_3 + 1x_4 \qquad\quad + 10x_6 = 10 \quad \text{Resource C}$$

(b)

$$x_0 - 2x_1 + 5x_2 \qquad\qquad - 1x_5 \qquad = 38 \quad \text{Objective function}$$

$$2x_1 - 2x_2 \qquad + 1x_4 + 4x_5 \qquad = 4 \quad \text{Resource A}$$

$$2x_1 \qquad + 1x_3 \qquad + 4x_5 \qquad = 12 \quad \text{Resource B}$$

$$4x_1 + 4x_2 \qquad\qquad - 6x_5 + 1x_6 = 18 \quad \text{Resource C}$$

16 Consider the problem

$$\text{maximize} \quad -30x_1 + 24x_2 + 20x_3 + 20x_4 + 25x_5$$

subject to

$$-3x_1 + 1x_2 + 2x_3 + 3x_4 + 5x_5 \le 19$$

$$-3x_1 + 4x_2 + 3x_3 + 2x_4 + 1x_5 \le 57$$

$$\text{every } x_j \ge 0.$$

(a) Write the dual problem and verify that a feasible solution is $y_1 = 4$ and $y_2 = 5$.
(b) Use the information in part (a) to derive an optimal solution to both the primal and dual problems.

17 Consider the problem

$$\text{maximize} \quad -1x_1 + 7x_2 - 5x_3 + 14x_4$$

subject to

$$3x_1 + 4x_2 + 5x_3 + 5x_4 \le 60$$

$$-1x_1 + 1x_2 - 2x_3 + 2x_4 \le 10$$

$$\text{every } x_j \ge 0.$$

(a) Write the dual problem and verify that a feasible solution is $y_1 = 1$ and $y_2 = 4$.
(b) Use the information in part (a) to derive an optimal solution to both the primal and dual problems.

18 Each part below refers to an example in Sec. 3.4. Write the dual problem, and draw a solution space representation. Indicate a solution to the dual problem on the graph and calculate the corresponding values for the dual variables and the dual objective function.

(a) Relations (1) through (4).   (b) Relations (5), and (2) through (4).
(c) Relations (6) through (9).   (d) Relations (10) through (13).

*19 In parts (a) and (b), assume that x_1 and x_2 yield an optimal basic solution. State the dual problem and optimal values for the dual variables. Find the largest values for c_3 and c_4 that allow the assumption that x_1 and x_2 comprise an optimal basis.

(a) Maximize $-1x_1 + 18x_2 + c_3x_3 + c_4x_4$ subject to

$$1x_1 + 2x_2 + 3x_3 + 4x_4 \leq 15$$

$$-3x_1 + 4x_2 - 5x_3 - 6x_4 \leq 5$$

$$\text{every } x_j \geq 0.$$

(b) Maximize $-13x_1 + 24x_2 + c_3x_3 + c_4x_4$ subject to the same constraints as in part (a).

20 Consider the following problem

$$\text{minimize } \sum_{t=1}^{T} y_t$$

subject to

$$y_T + y_1 \geq r_1$$

$$y_{t-1} + y_t \geq r_t \quad \text{for } t = 2, 3, \ldots, T$$

$$\text{every } y_t \geq 0.$$

An example of this model is the Kleen City Police Department Problem, stated in exercise 31 of Chap. 2.

(a) Display the model in full for $T = 5$, where $r_1 = 8$, $r_2 = 7$, $r_3 = 10$, $r_4 = 10$, and $r_5 = 2$.

(b) Calling the above problem the dual, write the associated primal problem.

(c) Solve the primal by the simplex algorithm and indicate the associated dual solution. (*Hint:* you need no more than five iterations.)

(d) Find optimal primal and dual solutions when $r_1 = 9$, instead of 8.

CONTENTS

CHAPTER **6**

The Transportation Problem

6.1 SIGNIFICANCE OF NETWORK MODELS

Chapters 6 and 7 explore several important special cases of linear programming models. In this chapter you will concentrate on transportation problems, and in the next chapter you will study other network optimization models, the most important of which involves the finding of the shortest (or least-cost) routes in a network. Such network problems have a twofold importance. They often pertain to problems of product distribution. Consequently, they are economically significant for many commercial enterprises that operate several plants and hold inventory in local warehouses. In addition, networks have a mathematical structure identical to that of other operations research models that seem unrelated at first glance. But these two reasons alone do not warrant your singling out network models to study in *greater* detail.

The key justification is that the mathematical characteristics of network models are so special that by exploiting these structural properties you can obtain major efficiencies in finding optimal solutions. In actual industrial applications, network models often contain thousands of activities and hundreds of constraints, so that using a streamlined algorithm is not only worthwhile but sometimes a practical necessity. By investigating networks, you also benefit from seeing how a variety of apparently disparate operations research models are amenable to an insightful unifying mode of analysis.

6.2 CLASSICAL TRANSPORTATION PROBLEM

The **transportation** (or **distribution**) **problem** was an early example of linear network optimization and is now a standard application for industrial firms having several manufacturing plants, warehouses, sales territories, and distribution outlets. The model's primary usefulness is for planning. In this instance, the strategic decisions involve selecting transportation routes so as to allocate the production of various plants to several warehouses or terminal points. You already saw an example of this sort in the Saur Milk Company Problem of Sec. 2.6. Some companies find it necessary to review their distribution decisions as often as every month, especially if their order mix is subject to considerable variation. But typically a firm draws up such a distribution plan yearly.

In the standard interpretation of the model, there are m supply points with items available to be shipped to the n demand points. Specifically, Plant i can ship at most S_i items, and Demand Point j requires at least D_j items. The S_i and D_j are fixed in reference to a stated time interval or *planning horizon*. The cost of shipping each unit from Plant i to Demand Point j is c_{ij}. The objective is to select, for the duration of the horizon, a routing plan that minimizes total transportation costs.

The mathematical description of the classical transportation problem is

$$\text{(1)} \qquad\qquad \text{minimize} \sum_{i=1}^{m} \sum_{j=1}^{n} c_{ij} x_{ij}$$

subject to

$$\text{(2)} \qquad\qquad \sum_{j=1}^{n} x_{ij} \leq S_i \quad \text{for } i = 1, 2, \ldots, m \quad \text{(supply)}$$

$$\text{(3)} \qquad\qquad \sum_{i=1}^{m} x_{ij} \geq D_j \quad \text{for } j = 1, 2, \ldots, n \quad \text{(demand)}$$

$$\text{(4)} \qquad\qquad x_{ij} \geq 0 \quad \text{for all } i \text{ and } j.$$

The network and technology tables for this model are shown in Figs. 6.1 and 6.2. (You may find it helpful to review Sec. 2.6, where we first introduced this model.)

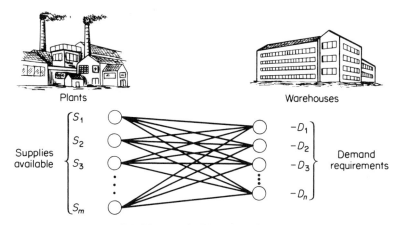

FIGURE 6.1. Network for Transportation Problem.

Warehouse

Plant	1	2	3	$\cdots$	n	Supply:
1	c_{11} x_{11}	c_{12} x_{12}	c_{13} x_{13}	$\cdots$	c_{1n} x_{1n}	S_1
2	c_{21} x_{21}	c_{22} x_{22}	c_{23} x_{23}	$\cdots$	c_{2n} x_{2n}	S_2
3	c_{31} x_{31}	c_{32} x_{32}	c_{33} x_{33}	$\cdots$	c_{3n} x_{3n}	S_3
$\vdots$	$\vdots$	$\vdots$	$\vdots$	$\ddots$	$\vdots$	$\vdots$
m	c_{m1} x_{m1}	c_{m2} x_{m2}	c_{m3} x_{m3}	$\cdots$	c_{mn} x_{mn}	S_m
Demand:	D_1	D_2	D_3	$\cdots$	D_n	

(a) Transportation Table.

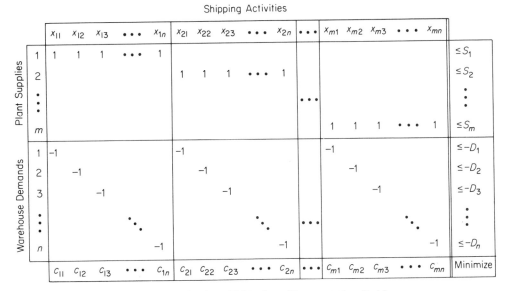

(b) Technology Table for a Transportation Problem.

FIGURE 6.2

In the mathematical description (1) through (4), the nonnegative quantity x_{ij} represents the amount of goods shipped from Plant i to Demand Point j. Observe in (2) that the sum of the shipments from Plant i to *all* the Demand Points cannot exceed the available supply S_i. Similarly, in (3) the sum of the shipments to Demand Point j from *all* the Plants must be at least the demand requirement D_j. In a network representation such as Fig. 6.1, it is convenient to distinguish available supplies from demand requirements by letting the supplies be positive numbers and the requirements be negative numbers. Hence, we may find it convenient to rewrite (3) into an equivalent formulation by multiplying both sides by minus one, thereby altering the direction of the inequality, to yield

$$(3') \qquad -\sum_{i=1}^{m} x_{ij} \leq -D_j \quad \text{for } j = 1, 2, \ldots, n \quad \text{(demand)}.$$

The technology table in Fig. 6.2 displays the model using (3') instead of (3). The objective function (1) sums the costs associated with all the individual shipments.

A key result in network theory is that among all the optimal solutions to the model (1) through (4), there is at least one in which each x_{ij} is integer-valued, provided the S_i and D_j are all positive integers, which we assume from here on. Therefore, strengthening (4) to

$$(5) \qquad x_{ij} = 0, 1, 2, \ldots$$

does not adversely affect the value of (1). What is more, the simplex method will find such an optimal solution. These results are demonstrated in Sec. 6.7.

If the unit cost of producing an item differs from plant to plant, then this cost is included in the determination of c_{ij}. If for physical or economic reasons a certain plant is inaccessible to a particular demand point, then the associated x_{ij} is eliminated or, if more convenient, the corresponding c_{ij} is defined to be arbitrarily large. To simplify the discussion, assume $c_{ij} \geq 0$. Then (3) can be rewritten with equalities.

For the model to possess a feasible solution, it certainly is necessary that total supply is at least as large as total demand, $\sum_{i=1}^{m} S_i \geq \sum_{j=1}^{n} D_j$. There are a number of applications in which you would expect to find the total supply in excess of the total demand requirements. For example, S_i sometimes represents the production *capacity* of Plant i during the planning horizon, rather than an amount of the commodity actually manufactured for distribution at the start of the period. In analyzing a standard transportation model and devising an optimizing algorithm, however, it is convenient to assume that total supply equals total demand:

$$(6) \qquad \sum_{i=1}^{m} S_i = \sum_{j=1}^{n} D_j.$$

Employing a simple-minded formal device permits you to assert (6) without any loss of generality: create a fictitious destination with a requirement of $\sum_i S_i - \sum_j D_j$. Then let this fictitious destination be labeled the nth. Let $c_{in} = 0$ so that the interpretation of x_{in} is "slack capacity at Plant i." The sum of the capacities now equals the sum of the requirements. Consequently, with this device the relations (2) can just as well be written as equalities. Therefore, *unless stated otherwise, hereafter assume* (6) *holds and* (2) *and* (3) *are equalities*, so the model is

(7)
$$\text{minimize} \sum_{i=1}^{m} \sum_{j=1}^{n} c_{ij} x_{ij}$$

subject to

(8)
$$\sum_{j=1}^{n} x_{ij} = S_i \qquad \text{for } i = 1, 2, \ldots, m \quad \text{(supply)}$$

(9)
$$\sum_{i=1}^{m} x_{ij} = D_j \qquad \text{for } j = 1, 2, \ldots, n \quad \text{(demand)}$$

(10) $\qquad x_{ij} = 0, 1, 2, \ldots$ for all i and j,

where all the S_i and D_j are positive integers satisfying (6).

Example. The Peason Earth Company, a large construction contractor, must supply dirt fill to four sites at which it is building large factories. The company has three land sources at which it will remove dirt fill with a steam shovel and then load the fill onto trucks for transport to the construction sites. The cost of removing each thousand cubic feet of fill from Land Source i and trucking it to Factory Site j is c_{ij}. Land Sources 1, 2, and 3 have available 9, 4, and 3 thousands of cubic feet of fill, respectively; Factory Sites 1, 2, 3, and 4 require 2, 5, 1, and 6 thousands of cubic feet of fill, respectively. Observe that the total fill available at all three land sources, namely 16 thousand cubic feet, exceeds the total fill requirements at all four plant sites, which is, namely, 14 thousand. Hence, create a fictitious fifth site with the requirement 2 thousand cubic feet ($= 16 - 14$). You can interpret the shipment of fill from any Land Source i to Site 5 as the amount of fill left unused at Source i, and its unit shipping cost is $c_{i5} = 0$. The appropriate transportation table then appears as Fig. 6.3.

The mathematical model (7) through (10) for this example contains 15 ($= 3 \times 5$) shipment variables, three supply restrictions, and five demand restrictions. To illustrate, the supply restriction (8) for Land Source 2 is simply

(11) $\qquad\qquad x_{21} + x_{22} + x_{23} + x_{24} + x_{25} = 4$

and the demand restriction for Site 3 is

(12) $\qquad\qquad x_{13} + x_{23} + x_{33} = 1.$

Applying the model. Implicit in the mathematical description of the model (7) through (10) is the assumption that only a single type of commodity is being shipped. Why? Because in meeting the demand *requirements*, the model does not distinguish among the sources of supply. All the supply arriving at Demand Point j is commingled insofar as satisfying the demand constraint is concerned. In the above example, the single-commodity assumption appears reasonable

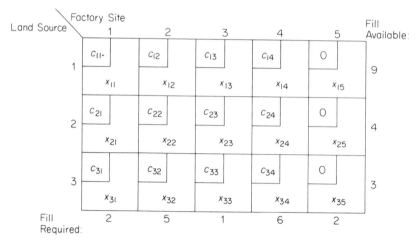

FIGURE 6.3. Peason Earth Company Transportation Table.

provided that there is little to distinguish the quality of the dirt fill from among the different land sources.

But in applications dealing with the shipment of manufactured products from several plants, the single-commodity assumption would seem to restrict the application of the model. After all, how many multiplant firms distribute only one product? Occasionally, a multiplant, multiproduct company can establish a separate routing pattern for each of its major commodities; but usually there is a decided economic advantage to restricting the number of plants that serve a warehouse or sales district. Therefore, most firms determine a complete distribution system by taking *explicit* account of the entire product line. As you can imagine, you have to use ingenuity to fit an actual distribution problem into the mold of a standard transportation model. It is impossible to catalog here all the devices that have proved successful for this purpose in actual practice. One approach is sketched below to illustrate the basic notions.

Establish the product mix required over the planning horizon at each Demand Point j. Designate the total amount D_j of all products in some convenient and meaningful common unit of measurement, such as tons. Analogously, specify S_i in the same units. To calculate c_{ij} *assume* that if Plant i ships a ton to Demand Point j, the ton is comprised of the precise product mix required at Demand Point j.

How usable and good will the resultant numerical solution be? To answer sensibly, you must keep two factors in mind. First, the essence of the solution is a *plan* for product distribution during a specified time interval. That is, the model provides an assignment of plants to demand destination points. The numerical values of the x_{ij} are inherently approximate, since in most real applications the values of D_j are only *forecasts* of requirements during the planning horizon. Therefore, the x_{ij} solution values do not represent amounts actually transported, but merely estimate the order of magnitude of future shipments. Second, the plan's relative merit must be judged against whatever practical alternatives the firm can devise, including, of course, the current routing. In line with these points, many companies have improved their profits significantly by adopting a distribution *plan* based on a standard transportation model solution.

What's in a name. We conclude with a word about the nomenclature of network models. All the network models discussed in this and the following chapters are examples of linear programming problems. With the exception of the two models at the end of the next chapter, by an appropriate definition of symbols, all the problems can be shown to be examples of the model formulated above as (7) through (10). Therefore, in a formal mathematical sense, these are all illustrations of the classical transportation problem, even though they may have nothing to do with shipping a commodity. However, the category of transportation problems itself can be subdivided to give prominence to certain significant models in which additional assumptions are made. To illustrate, when $n = m$ and $S_i = D_j = 1$ for all i and j, the model is termed an *assignment problem*, for reasons made clear in Sec. 6.4. The assignment problem in turn encompasses an important subclass of so-called shortest- (or longest-) route models. These are illustrated in Secs. 7.2 and 7.5. To keep matters straight as you read, ask yourself what the additional structural assumptions are in each transportation model that make it convenient to narrow the problem's designation with a special term.

▶**Seasonal variation.** The transportation model has been described as a method of finding a plan for a single time period, such as a span of 12 months. In certain instances, a company may want to shift its distribution routing plan at different times of the year to reflect seasonal variation in the pattern of demand requirements or supply availabilities. If commodity items available in one month cannot be inventoried to satisfy the requirements of subsequent months, then the firm only need solve 12 separate transportation problems, one for each month. Most companies facing serious seasonal variations, however, do have the opportunity to hold inventories in anticipation of demand. Considerations of optimal seasonal inventory buildups can be accommodated by a straightforward reinterpretation of the symbols in the transportation model.

To illustrate, suppose a firm with two plants and three demand points desires to establish an inventory distribution plan for January, February, . . . , December. Assume that company policy is to have no seasonal inventory on hand at the beginning of the year. Then let S_i, for $i = 1, 2, \ldots, 12$, denote the availability of the product for the first plant for the 12 months, and similarly, S_i, for $i = 13, 14, \ldots, 24$, refer to the second plant. By an analogous convention, let D_j, for $j = 1, 2, \ldots, 12$, refer to the first destination's requirements; for $j = 13, 14, \ldots, 24$, to the second's; and for $j = 25, 26, \ldots, 36$ to the third's. Assume $\sum_{i=1}^{24} S_i - \sum_{j=1}^{36} D_j$. (This restriction can be weakened, if necessary.)

Certain x_{ij} must be eliminated to prevent the supply in midyear being used to meet the requirements at the start of the year. For example, you must remove $x_{6,25}$, which would represent shipping items available at the first plant in June to meet the January requirements at the third destination. In determining c_{ij} for the remaining x_{ij}, you may want to include an inventory holding cost. This figure would reflect expenses directly associated with an inventory buildup, such as warehouse rental or interest charged on short-term borrowings if bank financing is used.   ◀

6.3 TRANSSHIPMENT MODEL

It is important to extend the classical transportation model to include cases in which a location can act as a point of transshipment. For example, transshipment often occurs in the distribution system of national department store chains. Such companies typically have regional warehouses that ship to smaller district warehouses, which in turn ship to the retail stores. In this illustration, the district warehouses are the transshipment points. The transshipment model is a useful tool for a company deciding on the optimal number and location of its warehouses, since the network analysis yields a minimum-cost routing plan for any specific configuration of warehouses. An additional reason for studying the model is that other operations research models which turn out to be mathematically equivalent to network problems have the transshipment form.

The model is illustrated here by means of a commercial example which, although hypothetical, is suggested by a real application arising out of the operations of military logistics systems.

The Raycov Discount Store Problem. This company has eight large major appliance discount stores located in several states. The Marketing Manager, Upham Price, has decided to close out a certain costly item in order to liquidate the stock now on hand. Before launching the advertising campaign, management wants to position its current inventory among the eight stores according to its sales expectations at each location. To do this, it is necessary to redistribute some of the stock.

Figure 6.4 is a diagrammatic map; the numbered nodes, or points, represent the eight stores. A positive value next to a node signifies the amount of inventory to be redistributed to the rest of the system. A negative value indicates the additional amount of stock required for the sale. Thus Stores 1 and 4 have excess stock of ten and two items, respectively. Stores 3, 6, and 8 require three, one, and

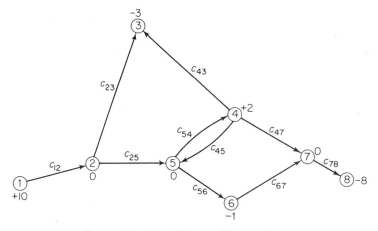

FIGURE 6.4. Map of Raycov Discount Stores.

eight more items, respectively. The inventory positions of Stores 2, 5, and 7 are to remain unchanged.

Observe that an appliance may be shipped through Stores 2, 4, 5, 6, and 7. Consequently, these locations are termed **transshipment** (or **intermediate**) **points.** Each *remaining* store is termed a **source** if it has excess inventory, and a **sink** if it needs stock. Consequently Store 1 is a source, and Stores 3 and 8 are sinks.

The value $c_{ij} \geq 0$ refers to the cost of shipping each of these items along the indicated route. To transport an appliance from Store 1 to Store 6, the total shipping cost is $c_{12} + c_{25} + c_{56}$. The shipping route from Store 1 to Store 6 uses 2 and 5 as transshipment points. The model allows for a shipment between 4 and 5 in either direction. Assume in this situation that $c_{45} \neq c_{54}$, for the following reason. At the time the shipment must be made the company has space available in its own truck only on the route from 4 to 5. It has to incur a higher cost in the reverse direction because it must hire a common carrier. After carefully inspecting the figure, you will realize that you cannot rule out either one of the routes between 4 and 5 until the entire problem has been analyzed. In this example, the company's objective is to redistribute its inventory at the lowest total transportation cost.

Equivalence to a transportation problem. We describe two ways to convert the transshipment problem to a standard transportation problem. Such conversions are of practical significance because they permit you to use readily available computer programs written to solve standard transportation problems. You need only supply the computer the data for the transshipment model in one of the formats below. Another reason for interest in the equivalence is that it ensures there is no difficulty in finding an optimal solution with integer-valued variables.

In the first approach, you start by finding the *least-cost* ways to send one item each from Store 1, which has an excess supply, to Stores 3, 6, and 8, which require more items. Denote the associated minimum costs by the symbols c_{13}, c_{16}, and c_{18}. In an example such as this, these least-cost ways usually can be found by inspection. For example, using real data you would expect that $c_{13} = c_{12} + c_{23}$; in unusual examples, it could occur that $c_{13} = c_{12} + c_{25} + c_{54} + c_{43} < c_{12} + c_{23}$. Similarly, $c_{16} = c_{12} + c_{25} + c_{56}$, and c_{18} equals the smaller of

$$c_{12} + c_{25} + c_{56} + c_{67} + c_{78} \quad \text{and} \quad c_{12} + c_{25} + c_{54} + c_{47} + c_{78}.$$

In larger and more complex examples, where the inspection process is unwieldy, you would either derive empirical formulas for these least-costs or resort to the shortest-route algorithms described in Chap. 7. Turning to Store 4, which has an excess supply, you continue similarly by finding c_{43}, c_{46}, and c_{48}.

Then you can proceed by using a standard transportation problem table, as illustrated by the trial solution in Fig. 6.5. Note that in this condensed table there is one row for each store with an excess supply, and one column for each store with a demand requirement. The transshipment points are not shown explicitly.

But if, say, a least-cost way to ship a unit from Store 4 to Store 8 is via Store 7, then the trial level of $x_{48} = 2$ indicates that there are two units that are transshipped from Store 4 through Store 7 destined for Store 8.

The alternative approach, presented next, often has certain advantages over the first method in actual large-scale applications. Specifically, the alternative does not entail what might be a considerable computational effort to calculate all the least-cost routes required by the first approach. In addition, it may have fewer variables in the resultant standard transportation problem. And, finally, it can more easily handle capacity constraints on each route.

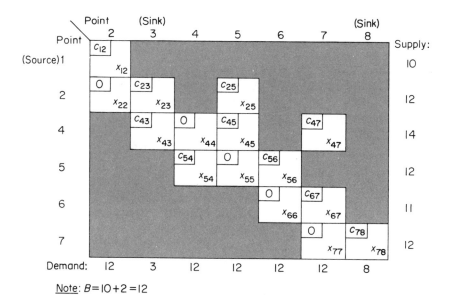

Note: c_{ij} is the least cost of shipping a unit from Point i to Point j.

FIGURE 6.5. Condensed Transshipment Table.

To see the idea of the second alternative, study Fig. 6.6, which is constructed from the network in Fig. 6.4. Observe that the *source* Point 1 appears in the table only in the first row—the reason is that it is the only point that unequivocally

FIGURE 6.6. Expanded Transshipment Table.

ships out items. Analogously, the *sink* Points 3 and 8 appear in the table only among the columns—the reason is that of the points that receive items, they are the only ones that never ship them out. Each of the other transshipment points appears as both a row and a column, since the other points may both receive and ship out items in an optimal routing.

All existing connections between pairs of points, such as those between Points 1 and 2, Points 5 and 6, Points 4 and 3, are indicated by a permissible shipment quantity in the table. Nonexistent connections between pairs of points, such as between Points 1 and 6, are shaded in the table. Note that possible shipments are indicated at the intersection of the row and column associated with each of the transshipment points—namely, x_{22}, x_{44}, x_{55}, x_{66}, and x_{77}. The associated unit transportation costs equal 0. As you will see, these are fictitious shipments from each point to itself, and they facilitate modeling the transshipment network as a standard transportation problem. We provide an explanation of these shipment quantities below.

Check in Fig. 6.6 that the supply quantity for the *source* Point 1, and the demand quantities for *sink* Points 3 and 8, agree with the original quantities shown in the network of Fig. 6.4. The supply and demand quantities used for the transshipment points are not so immediate. Note in Fig. 6.6 that for each transshipment point, the net difference between the amount supplied and the amount demanded is the same as that quantity appearing in the network of Fig. 6.4. For example, look at Point 4—the amount supplied is 14, the amount demanded is 12, and the net difference is 2 ($= 14 - 12$). Similarly, for Point 6, the net difference is -1 ($= 11 - 12$). For Points 2, 5, and 7, the net difference is 0 between the amount supplied and the amount demanded in Fig. 6.6. By now you may have discovered that all of the original quantities representing the amounts supplied and demanded at the transshipment points have been increased by the number 12. This quantity is designated as a fictitious **buffer stock.** Any sufficiently large number will work, and the number that we selected is the sum of all the quantities available for shipment out, which, in the example, comprises the 10 units at Point 1 and the 2 units at Point 4. For some unit-cost values, an optimal routing transships all these 12 units at Points 1 and 4 through Point 5. More specifically, such a shipment schedule is $x_{12} = 10$, $x_{23} = 3$, $x_{25} = 7$, $x_{45} = 2$, $x_{56} = 9$, $x_{67} = x_{78} = 8$, and all other shipments $x_{ij} = 0$. Pencil in these shipment quantities on both Figs. 6.4 and 6.5. You will see that all the requirements are met in Fig. 6.4, and the quantities transshipped are 10 units through Point 2, 9 units through Point 5, and 8 units through Point 6.

Correspondingly, in the table of Fig. 6.5, you also must calculate the values for the fictitious shipments associated with the transshipment points. These quantities are $x_{22} = 2$, $x_{44} = 12$, $x_{55} = 3$, $x_{66} = 3$, and $x_{77} = 4$. All the other fictitious shipments $x_{kk} = 0$. Observe that, for each *transshipment* point that has a nonnegative quantity to be supplied—namely, Points 2, 4, 5, and 7—the net difference between the amount demanded and the fictitious shipment in Fig. 6.6 represents the transshipment quantity. For example, the net difference 10 ($= 12 - 2$) gives the number of units transshipped through Point 2; the net difference 0 ($= 12 - 12$)

gives the number of units transshipped through Point 4. For each *transshipment* point that has a negative quantity, indicating the number of units that are demanded—Point 6 in the example—the net difference between the amount supplied and the fictitious shipment in Fig. 6.6 represents the transshipment quantity. Thus, the net difference 8 ($= 11 - 3$) gives the number of units transshipped through Point 6. Since the fictitious shipment variables x_{kk} have a unit transportation cost $c_{kk} = 0$, their levels do not contribute to the total cost of a shipment schedule in Fig. 6.6. Finally, note that if we set the fictitious buffer amount larger than 12, then no harm is done—it causes each x_{kk} to increase but at no extra cost. If you set the buffer amount less than 9, however, then the illustrative solution is ruled out. We have suggested a safe approach of setting the buffer equal to the total amount available for shipping out of all the points.

As further practice in interpreting the expanded version of the transshipment model, consider the illustrative feasible routing in Fig. 6.7. Study the table carefully.

Begin with the first row of the table, representing the supply available at Source Point 1. Note that the 10 units available are shipped to Point 2. Next look at the row and column for Point 2. Observe that $S_2 = D_2 = B = 12$, because Point 2 is a transshipment point without any supply or demand. Since the solution already has $x_{12} = 10$, you must have $x_{22} = 2$ in order that the demand requirement

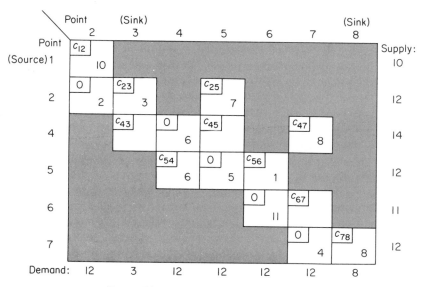

FIGURE 6.7. Illustrative Feasible Routing.

$D_2 = 12$ be satisfied. This in turn means that the other 10 units of S_2 can be shipped out, and are shown going to Point 3, which is a sink, and Point 5, which is a transshipment point. In other words, the 10 units from Point 1 are transshipped through Point 2 to Points 3 and 5.

Skipping down to the fourth row for Point 5, you can see that the seven units entering are then shipped out to Points 4 and 6. In particular, one unit enters Point 6 from Point 5.

Now look at the row and column for Point 6. Observe that $S_6 = 11$ whereas $D_6 = 12$, in keeping with the requirement for one unit at Point 6. Since $x_{56} = 1$ and $D_6 = 12$, you must have $x_{66} = 11$; so the unit entering Point 6 is not shipped out.

Continue your investigation, and verify that Store 1 ships three units to Store 3 via Point 2, one unit to Store 6 via Points 2 and 5, and six units to Store 8 via Points 2, 5, 4, and 7. Store 4 ships its two units to Store 8 via Point 7.

To assist you in converting any transshipment problem into an expanded form such as in Fig. 6.6, we summarize in general terms the conversion procedure that we applied. Recall that a node that is *not* a transshipment point is designated as a source if it has supply to be shipped and as a sink if it has demand to be filled.

(i) Designate a row for each *source*. Its S_i value is the stock supplied.

(ii) Designate a column for each *sink*. Its D_j value is the amount of stock demanded.

(iii) Designate a row *and* a column for each *transshipment point*. Let T_k be the point's net stock position. If stock is supplied, T_k is a positive number. If stock is demanded, T_k is a negative number. Then for Point k, let $S_k = T_k + B$ and $D_k = B$, where B is the sum of the stock available at *all* points.

(iv) Permit x_{ij}, for $i \neq j$, only for arcs existing in the original network. For a transshipment Point k, also permit x_{kk} with $c_{kk} = 0$.

Thus Rule (i) pertains to Store 1 and Rule (ii) to Stores 3 and 8. With $B = 12$, Rule (iii) states, for example, that $D_4 = 12$ and $S_4 = 2 + 12 = 14$; $D_5 = 12$ and $S_5 = 0 + 12 = 12$; and $D_6 = 12$ and $S_6 = -1 + 12 = 11$.

To achieve the second conversion to a standard transportation model, B has been introduced in the role of a fictitious buffer stock at each transshipment point. If k is such a point, B has been included in both S_k and D_k. Therefore the sum of *all* the S_i remains equal to the sum of *all* the D_j. The value of S_k must be sufficiently large to accommodate any transshipment amount that is optimal. One simple way to achieve this condition is to let B be the sum of the stock available at *all* points. The *total* amount of stock transshipped through Point k is $B - x_{kk}$ if $T_k \geq 0$, and is $T_k + B - x_{kk}$ if $T_k < 0$.

Mathematical model. To complete your understanding of the transshipment model, you should now turn to a precise mathematical description of the problem. This formal characterization is conveniently shown by the technology in Fig. 6.8. Observe there is one equation for each store, or node, of the network. There is also one variable x_{ij} for each arc to represent the amount to be shipped from Point i to Point j. A positive value on the right of an equality sign designates stock available for redistribution. A negative value indicates a requirement at that store. In summary, the linear programming technology in Fig. 6.8 is an immediate translation of the network diagram in Fig. 6.4.

Shipping Activities

Points	x_{12}	x_{23}	x_{25}	x_{43}	x_{45}	x_{47}	x_{54}	x_{56}	x_{67}	x_{78}	
1	1										= 10
2	-1	1	1								= 0
3		-1		-1							= -3
4				1	1	1	-1				= 2
5			-1		-1		1	1			= 0
6								-1	1		= -1
7						-1			-1	1	= 0
8										-1	= -8
	c_{12}	c_{23}	c_{25}	c_{43}	c_{45}	c_{47}	c_{54}	c_{56}	c_{67}	c_{78}	Minimize

FIGURE 6.8. Transshipment Example.

Observe that whereas there are only 8 equations and 10 variables in the technology table of Fig. 6.8, there are 13 row and column restrictions and 15 variables shown in the expanded transshipment table of Fig. 6.6. The increase of five in each of these dimensions of the problem is due to the presence of the five transshipment points. But this increase in size has a negligible computational impact because the transshipment variables x_{kk} are always in a solution.

6.4 ASSIGNMENT MODEL

The assignment problem can be posed succinctly as follows: each of n tasks can be performed by any one of n agents. The cost of Task i being accomplished by Agent j is c_{ij}. Assign one agent to each task to minimize the total cost.

Why should this problem interest you? As usual, one reason is that the model can be applied—admittedly not very often in this case—to consequential business situations. An example is provided in the next paragraph. A more compelling reason is that this problem provides a vital link between linear programming problems and so-called combinatorial problems. The latter include those situations in which the unknown activity levels *must* be integer-valued. Such problems are studied in more detail in Chaps. 8, 10, and 11.

The Short Circuitry Company Problem. This manufacturer of complex electronic equipment has an order for several thousand units of a newly designed product, which is assembled from component modules. The company's chief engineer, Annette Werk, has decided to subcontract for n of the components, and has selected n outside subcontractors who have demonstrated high-quality performance capability on previous occasions. Each job is sizable enough to prevent a subcontractor from accepting more than one task. Every subcontractor is required to submit to Ms. Werk a bid on each of the modules, and thereby specify the total cost for which it would bill the electronics company for producing the separate components. A few individual bids are far out of line, indicating that some of the subcontractors really do not want to accept a particular job assignment. With this information, the electronic equipment firm lets out the n contracts for the n components so that the total cost incurred is minimal.

Mathematical model. To formulate the **assignment problem** in mathematical programming terms, define the activity variables as

(1)
$$x_{ij} = \begin{cases} 1 & \text{if Task i is performed by Agent j} \\ 0 & \text{otherwise} \end{cases}$$

$$\text{for } i = 1, 2, \ldots, n \quad \text{and} \quad j = 1, 2, \ldots, n,$$

and let c_{ij} be the corresponding cost. In the Short Circuitry Company illustration, the index i refers to the component number and the index j to the subcontractor. Then the optimization model is

(2)
$$\text{minimize } \sum_{i=1}^{n} \sum_{j=1}^{n} c_{ij} x_{ij}$$

subject to

(3)
$$\sum_{j=1}^{n} x_{ij} = 1 \qquad \text{for } i = 1, 2, \ldots, n$$

(4)
$$\sum_{i=1}^{n} x_{ij} = 1 \qquad \text{for } j = 1, 2, \ldots, n$$

(5)
$$x_{ij} = 0 \text{ or } 1 \quad \text{for all } i \text{ and } j.$$

Notice that the assignment model (2) through (5) is a special case of the standard transportation model, where $m = n$ and $S_i = D_j = 1$ [in (7) through (10) of Sec. 6.2]. It is now accepted terminology to refer to any standard transportation problem where $m = n$ and $S_i = D_j = 1$ as an assignment problem. Observe, however, that the above illustration as well as most applications of the assignment model do not pertain to the optimization of transportation or shipping activities.

6.5 DUALITY IN
THE TRANSPORTATION PROBLEM

The size of transportation problems in actual applications is so large that a naive application of the simplex method would be grossly inefficient and in some instances not even possible, given the capabilities of available computer programs. It is possible to exploit the special structure of a network technology so that the required computational effort becomes reasonable. The key notion is to take full advantage of the duality relationships in a transportation problem. To begin, we repeat the mathematical formulation of the transportation problem:

x_{11}	x_{12}	x_{13}	x_{14}	x_{21}	x_{22}	x_{23}	x_{24}	x_{31}	x_{32}	x_{33}	x_{34}	
1	1	1	1									$= S_1$
				1	1	1	1					$= S_2$
								1	1	1	1	$= S_3$
1				1				1				$= D_1$
	1				1				1			$= D_2$
		1				1				1		$= D_3$
			1				1				1	$= D_4$
c_{11}	c_{12}	c_{13}	c_{14}	c_{21}	c_{22}	c_{23}	c_{24}	c_{31}	c_{32}	c_{33}	c_{34}	Minimize

FIGURE 6.9. Technology Table for Transportation Problem ($m = 3$ and $n = 4$).

(1)
$$\text{minimize} \sum_{i=1}^{m} \sum_{j=1}^{n} c_{ij}x_{ij}$$

subject to

(2)
$$\sum_{j=1}^{n} x_{ij} = S_i \quad \text{for } i = 1, 2, \ldots, m \quad \text{(supply)}$$

(3)
$$\sum_{i=1}^{m} x_{ij} = D_j \quad \text{for } j = 1, 2, \ldots, n \quad \text{(demand)}$$

(4)
$$x_{ij} \geq 0 \quad \text{for all } i \text{ and } j,$$

where all the S_i and D_j are positive integers satisfying

(5)
$$\sum_{i=1}^{m} S_i = \sum_{j=1}^{n} D_j \quad \text{(total supply = total demand)}.$$

The technology table for this model is illustrated in Fig. 6.9 for the cases $m = 3$ and $n = 4$.

Because of the equality between total supply and total demand in (5), and the structure of the supply and demand equations (2) and (3), the model contains a redundancy, in that if any $m + n - 1$ of the restrictions in (2) and (3) are satisfied, then the remaining restriction is satisfied too. [This fact can be demonstrated mathematically by multiplying each restriction in (3) by -1; by then adding any selection of $m + n - 1$ of the restrictions, and by using (5) to simplify the constant on the right-hand side. The resulting composite equation will be identical to the remaining restriction.] Consequently, any one of the supply and demand equations in (2) and (3) can be dropped without harm. The resultant model then consists of $m + n - 1$ *independent* restrictions, and so any basic solution contains this number of variables.

In Fig. 6.9, the table is partitioned into an upper section pertaining to the supply constraints and a lower section pertaining to the demand constraints. The dual linear programming model corresponding to Fig. 6.9 is displayed in Fig. 6.10. Observe that, for convenience, we have designated two symbolic letters, v and w, for the dual variables, matching the supply and demand partitioning in Fig. 6.9.

v_1	v_2	v_3	w_1	w_2	w_3	w_4	
1			1				$\leq c_{11}$
1				1			$\leq c_{12}$
1					1		$\leq c_{13}$
1						1	$\leq c_{14}$
	1		1				$\leq c_{21}$
	1			1			$\leq c_{22}$
	1				1		$\leq c_{23}$
	1					1	$\leq c_{24}$
		1	1				$\leq c_{31}$
		1		1			$\leq c_{32}$
		1			1		$\leq c_{33}$
		1				1	$\leq c_{34}$
S_1	S_2	S_3	D_1	D_2	D_3	D_4	Maximize

FIGURE 6.10. Dual Technology of the Transportation Problem ($m = 3$ and $n = 4$).

Thus we have associated the three dual variables v_1, v_2, and v_3 with the three supply constraints in the transportation problem, and the four dual variables w_1, w_2, w_3, and w_4 with the four demand constraints. You may wish to glance back at Sec. 5.4 to check the correspondences with the groups of problems (25) through (27) and (28) through (30). The objective function and constraints in Fig. 6.10 correspond to (28) through (30) in Sec. 5.4. The objective function and nonnegativity conditions on the x_{ij} in Fig. 6.9 correspond to (25) through (27) in Sec. 5.4. Because the constraints (2) and (3) of the transportation problem are equalities instead of ($\geq$) inequalities, the associated variables in the maximization problem are unrestricted in sign.

The illustration of the dual model in Fig. 6.10 generalizes appropriately. Specifically, the dual linear programming problem that corresponds to the general transportation model of (1) through (4) can be written as

$$(6) \qquad \text{maximize} \quad \sum_{i=1}^{m} S_i v_i + \sum_{j=1}^{n} D_j w_j$$

subject to

$$(7) \qquad v_i + w_j \leq c_{ij} \quad \text{for all } (i, j),$$

where the v_i and w_j are unrestricted in sign.

In the next section, you will see how to put the dual relationships to good advantage in applying the simplex algorithm to solve transportation problems.

6.6 SIMPLEX TECHNIQUE
FOR TRANSPORTATION PROBLEMS

Here we apply the simplex method to solve the transportation model. We demonstrate that the special structure of the transportation model substantially reduces the computational burden of the algorithm. This section motivates the method with a brief review of certain essentials from Chaps. 4 and 5, formulates the computational rules, and illustrates them with an example. Then Sec. 6.7 fills in several of the missing details on how to apply the method.

Simplex steps. The standard simplex method instructions are paraphrased below as a starting point of the discussion:

Step 1. Select a set of $m + n - 1$ routes that provides an initial basic feasible solution.

Step 2. Check whether the solution is improved by introducing a nonbasic variable. If so, go to *Step 3*; otherwise stop.

Step 3. Determine which route leaves the basis when the variable that you selected in *Step 2* enters.

Step 4. Adjust the flows of the other basic routes. Return to *Step 2*.

As you will see in the illustration below, all four steps are very easily performed for a transportation problem. Assume the model has been put in a classical transportation problem format and is arrayed in a standard $m \times n$ table, such as Fig. 6.11. The ensuing discussion refers to this table. We begin with a verbal description of the algorithm. Do not be concerned if you find certain details unclear, since the intent here is only to motivate the overall logic of the approach. A careful description of the steps is given afterwards.

Suppose you have a trial basic-feasible solution, which consists of shipments or flows on $m + n - 1$ basic routes. If a new unit of flow is introduced on a nonbasic route, then to maintain feasibility in both the corresponding row and column of Fig. 6.11, a unit must be withdrawn from a basic route in the same row, and similarly in the same column. But these two alterations in turn lead to *unit* changes in the flows of other basic variables. For reasons that will be apparent shortly, each nonbasic variable gives rise to a unique *pattern* of alterations of the basic variables.

Therefore you can evaluate the resultant change as follows: take the total increase in cost from adding a unit of flow to both the new route and the appro-

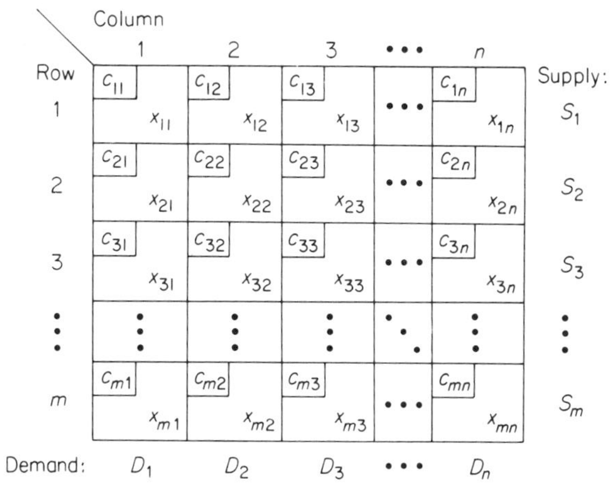

FIGURE 6.11. Transportation Tableau.

priate basic routes, and deduct the total decrease in cost from removing a unit of flow on the other basic routes in the associated unique pattern of alterations. If the net amount shows an improvement and the new route is selected to enter the solution, then the pattern of alterations also indicates how many units of flow can be placed on the new route. Specifically, the various flows are increased and decreased according to the pattern until that level is reached where a basic variable is reduced to zero and thereby dropped from the basis.

If the procedure for testing whether a nonbasic route should enter a trial solution were really as tedious as the above description suggests, this approach would be a marginal improvement at best on the way the simplex algorithm was applied in Chap. 4. You can evaluate a nonbasic route much more simply, however, by employing an insight from duality and exploiting the structure of the network.

You learned in Sec. 5.5, which discussed the solution of the dual problem, that for a given basic solution, the value from introducing a unit of a nonbasic variable is the difference between the left- and right-hand sides of the dual restriction for this variable. Thus the key idea is to solve the $m + n - 1$ dual restrictions corresponding to the current basis:

(1) $v_i + w_j = c_{ij}$ for each basic variable x_{ij},

and then with these values to evaluate

(2) $v_i + w_j - c_{ij}$ for x_{ij}, a nonbasic variable.

The quantities in (2) correspond to the coefficients in Row 0 of the simplex method. When (2) is positive, the nonbasic variable x_{ij} is a candidate to enter the next basis. If all such quantities are nonpositive, implying dual as well as primal feasibility, the current basic solution is optimal.

Algorithm illustrated. Consider the transportation problem shown in Fig. 6.12. (Jot down on a piece of paper your guess of an optimal solution; calculate its objective-function value.)

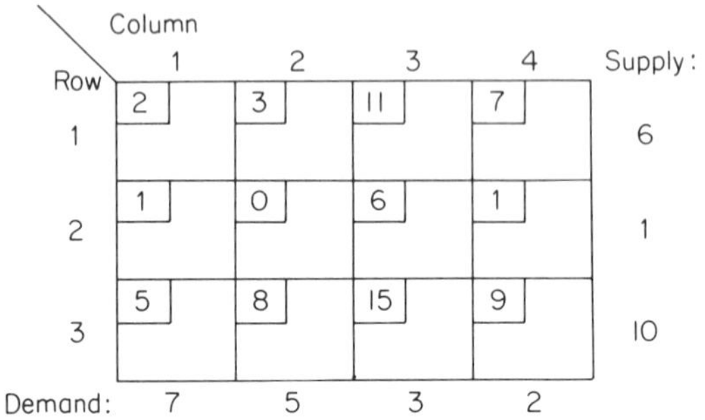

FIGURE 6.12. Transportation Example.

Step 1 of the algorithm asks for a starting trial basic solution, which contains $m + n - 1 = 3 + 4 - 1 = 6$ active routes. Suppose you allocate the supply of 6 units available in Row 1 to the cheapest route $(1, 1)$. This exhausts the supply and leaves one more unit of demand to be filled in Column 1. Similarly, allocate the supply of 1 unit in Row 2 to the cheapest route $(2, 2)$. The supply of 10 in Row 3 is then routed to meet all the remaining unfilled demand. The result, displayed in Fig. 6.13, has an objective-function value of 112. (Was your guessed solution any better? The advanced material below discusses a method for selecting a good initial solution.)

Step 2 calls for an evaluation of each unused route to see whether a unit of flow on the route improves the objective function. Consider route $(1, 2)$. As you can see from Fig. 6.13, one unit allocated to this route *must* be withdrawn from the flow on route $(1, 1)$. Then to meet the demand requirement in Column 1, another unit must be shipped on route $(3, 1)$, and this unit may be removed from route $(3, 2)$. The pattern of alterations is shown in Fig. 6.14.

Will introducing a unit of flow on $(1, 2)$ reduce the value of the objective func-

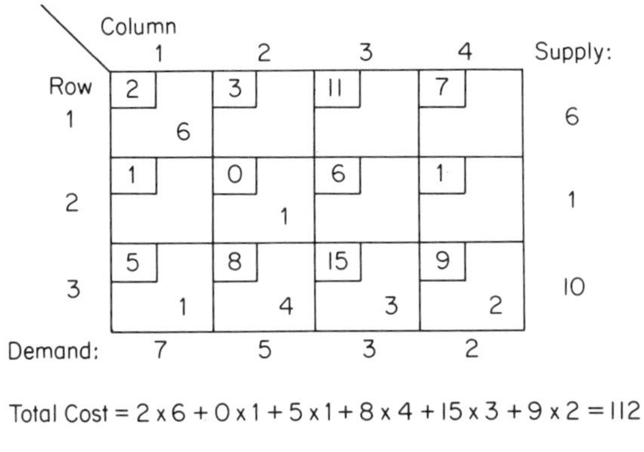

FIGURE 6.13. Initial Basic Solution.

Total Cost = $2 \times 6 + 0 \times 1 + 5 \times 1 + 8 \times 4 + 15 \times 3 + 9 \times 2 = 112$

tion? A saving of 10 (= 2 + 8) results from reducing a unit of flow on routes (1, 1) and (3, 2). However, there is a partially offsetting increase in cost of 8 (= 3 + 5) due to adding a unit of flow on routes (1, 2) and (3, 1). The net improvement is 2 (= 10 − 8).

Row \ Column	1	2	3	4	Supply:
1	[2] 6−1	[3] +1	[11]	[7]	6
2	[1]	[0] 1	[6]	[1]	1
3	[5] 1+1	[8] 4−1	[15] 3	[9] 2	10
Demand:	7	5	3	2	

Improvement Potential = Total Decrease − Total Increase
= (2 + 8) − (3 + 5) = 2 per unit

FIGURE 6.14. Pattern of Alterations for One Unit of Flow on Route (1, 2).

By a similar analysis, you can obtain the improvement potentials for the other nonbasic routes, as summarized in Fig. 6.15. Each of these is the value that would appear as the coefficient of the associated x_{ij} in Row 0 of the simplex method.

Row \ Column	1	2	3	4
1	[2] $\underline{O}$	[3] 2	[11] 1	[7] −1
2	[1] −4	[0] $\underline{O}$	[6] 1	[1] 0
3	[5] $\underline{O}$	[8] $\underline{O}$	[15] $\underline{O}$	[9] $\underline{O}$

Note: The symbol $\underline{O}$ appears for current basic routes.

FIGURE 6.15. Improvement Potentials for Nonbasic Routes—Initial Solution.

Now you will see that it is unnecessary to obtain the specific pattern of alterations for each nonbasic route in order to find its improvement potential. You can arrive quickly at the same result by evaluating the dual variables, and then by looking at the difference between the left- and right-hand sides of the dual constraints associated with the nonbasic routes. The network structure makes this process easy. A short-cut method that uses *only* an $m \times n$ table containing c_{ij} (such as Fig. 6.15) will be described. But in order to clarify what is actually going on, the mathematical relations involved in the short-cut will be explained first.

The system of linear equalities that yields trial values for the dual variables was shown in (1) above. Applied to the initial solution, Fig. 6.13, the six dual equalities for the basic routes are

$$
\begin{array}{lll}
v_1 \quad\;\; + w_1 & = 2 & \text{route } (1,\, 1) \\[4pt]
v_2 \qquad\;\; + w_2 & = 0 & \text{route } (2,\, 2) \\[4pt]
v_3 + w_1 & = 5 & \text{route } (3,\, 1) \\[4pt]
v_3 \qquad + w_2 & = 8 & \text{route } (3,\, 2) \\[4pt]
v_3 \qquad\qquad + w_3 & = 15 & \text{route } (3,\, 3) \\[4pt]
v_3 \qquad\qquad\qquad + w_4 = 9 & & \text{route } (3,\, 4).
\end{array}
$$

(3)

Observe that in (3) there are six equations and seven unknowns. To obtain a solution, one of the variables must be selected and given an arbitrary value. You are at liberty to choose any variable and assign it any convenient value. Choose v_3 since it appears in four of the relations, and let $v_3 = 0$ for convenience. The reason (3) has an "extra" variable is the redundancy in the $m + n = 7$ supply-and-demand restrictions. Giving an arbitrary value to v_3 is equivalent to dropping the Row 3 supply equation in order to remove the redundancy in the $m + n$ relations.

With $v_3 = 0$, notice how remarkably simple it is to solve for the remaining variables. You can proceed as follows:

(4)

$$
\begin{aligned}
v_3 &= 0 \quad \text{(arbitrary)} \\[4pt]
w_4 &= 9 - v_3 = 9 \\[4pt]
w_3 &= 15 - v_3 = 15 \\[4pt]
w_2 &= 8 - v_3 = 8 \\[4pt]
w_1 &= 5 - v_3 = 5 \\[4pt]
v_2 &= 0 - w_2 = 0 - (8 - v_3) = -8 \\[4pt]
v_1 &= 2 - w_1 = 2 - (5 - v_3) = -3.
\end{aligned}
$$

Thus, by knowing only the values of the previously found variables, you can obtain each dual variable one by one. *In a network technology, you will always be able to proceed in such a sequential fashion.*

The mathematical term **triangularity** is used to describe a structure that admits this sequential approach of finding solution values. You can appreciate the appropriateness of the term by looking at the structure of (3). When v_3 vanishes (that is, equals 0), the array has a triangular appearance. We say that a system of m linear equations in m unknowns has a **triangular structure** if, possibly after rearranging the order of the variables and the equations, the variable that appears first in equation k is also the kth unknown, and it does not appear in any equation beyond the kth.

The triangularity property holds for the system of dual equations (3) after you select *any* dual variable and assign it an arbitrary value. However, to *see at a glance* that the system is triangular, you would have to rearrange the sequence of variables and equations. For example, if you choose to let v_1 vanish, then the variables can be arranged in the sequence $v_2, w_2, w_3, w_4, v_3, w_1$, and the routes in the sequence $(2, 2), (3, 2), (3, 3), (3, 4), (3, 1)$, and $(1, 1)$ to *exhibit* the triangular structure.

Also note in (4) that if v_3 is set at a value other than 0, then each v_i increases and each w_j decreases by this amount. Thus any sum $(v_i + w_j)$ remains unchanged as does the test quantity $v_i + w_j - c_{ij}$.

You would suspect from your knowledge about duality that a similar triangularity property also holds for the equations that determine values of the basic x_{ij}. To see this, write the conservation of flow constraints, omitting all nonbasic routes and dropping the redundant supply equation for Row 3 (corresponding to the selection of v_3):

(5)
$$
\begin{array}{llll}
x_{11} & & = 6 & \text{Row 1} \\
& x_{22} & = 1 & \text{Row 2} \\
x_{11} & + x_{31} & = 7 & \text{Column 1} \\
& x_{22} + x_{32} & = 5 & \text{Column 2} \\
& x_{33} & = 3 & \text{Column 3} \\
& x_{34} & = 2 & \text{Column 4.}
\end{array}
$$

Notice that the row of coefficients in the kth equation of (5) are the column of coefficients for the kth variable in (3) (not counting v_3). Whereas (3) is *upper* triangular in shape, the system (5) is *lower* triangular and can be solved quickly starting with variable x_{11}.

You are now ready to determine the improvement potential for each *nonbasic* route from the formula

(6)
$$ v_i + w_j - c_{ij}. $$

Using the values for the dual variables that you found in (4), you can obtain

(7)
$$
\begin{array}{ll}
-3 + 8 - 3 = 2 & \text{route } (1, 2) \\
-3 + 15 - 11 = 1 & \text{route } (1, 3) \\
-3 + 9 - 7 = -1 & \text{route } (1, 4) \\
-8 + 5 - 1 = -4 & \text{route } (2, 1) \\
-8 + 15 - 6 = 1 & \text{route } (2, 3) \\
-8 + 9 - 1 = 0 & \text{route } (2, 4).
\end{array}
$$

Each *positive* number signifies a possibility for reducing the value of the objective function. Thus three routes offer an improvement, and you should select route (1, 2) because it is the one with the greatest potential. [This is the same rule as *Simplex Criterion I* (Minimization).]

Step 3 involves the determination of how much flow to allocate to route (1, 2). The pattern of alterations of the basic variables in the initial solution was already established for this route in Fig. 6.14. Recall that the flows on routes (1, 1) and (3, 2) decrease, and these amounts are presently 6 and 4. Consequently, the largest possible increase of flow on route (1, 2) is 4, causing route (3, 2) to be dropped from the new basis. This calculation is the same as *Simplex Criterion II*.

Step 4 performs the implied rerouting of flow, giving the second-trial basic solution in Fig. 6.16, with an objective-function value of 104.

	Column 1	2	3	4	Supply:
Row 1	2	4			6
2		1			1
3	5		3	2	10
Demand:	7	5	3	2	

FIGURE 6.16. Second Basic Solution.

Total Cost = Previous Total Cost − Total Improvement
= 112 − 2(4) = 104

Iteration 2. Next return to *Step 2* to check whether this solution is optimal or whether a further improvement is possible. The dual equalities for the new basis are

$$v_2 + w_2 \qquad\qquad\qquad\qquad = 0 \qquad \text{route (2, 2)}$$

$$w_2 + v_1 \qquad\qquad\qquad = 3 \qquad \text{route (1, 2)}$$

$$v_1 + w_1 \qquad\qquad = 2 \qquad \text{route (1, 1)}$$

(8)

$$w_1 \qquad + v_3 = 5 \qquad \text{route (3, 1)}$$

$$w_3 \quad + v_3 = 15 \qquad \text{route (3, 3)}$$

$$w_4 + v_3 = 9 \qquad \text{route (3, 4).}$$

The variables and equations in (8) have been sequenced so that the triangularity of the system is apparent when you let $v_3 = 0$. The solution values are

$$v_3 = 0$$
$$w_4 = 9$$
$$w_3 = 15$$
(9) $$\qquad w_1 = 5$$
$$v_1 = 2 - w_1 = -3$$
$$w_2 = 3 - v_1 = 6$$
$$v_2 = 0 - w_2 = -6,$$

and the improvement potentials are

(10)
$$
\begin{aligned}
-3 + 15 - 11 &= 1 &\quad \text{route } (1, 3) \\
-3 + 9 - 7 &= -1 &\quad \text{route } (1, 4) \\
-6 + 5 - 1 &= -2 &\quad \text{route } (2, 1) \\
-6 + 15 - 6 &= 3 &\quad \text{route } (2, 3) \\
-6 + 9 - 1 &= 2 &\quad \text{route } (2, 4) \\
0 + 6 - 8 &= -2 &\quad \text{route } (3, 2).
\end{aligned}
$$

Consequently, route (2, 3) enters the next solution. The corresponding pattern of alterations is shown in Fig. 6.17. Notice that all but one of the previous basic routes are altered. (It is possible to have a case in which every basic route is revised.) Flow decreases on routes (2, 2), (1, 1), and (3, 3). Route (2, 2) drops from the basis first, when the total change is one unit of flow. In this instance, therefore, the quantities in Fig. 6.17 also represent the flows for the third-trial basis.

Row \ Column	1	2	3	4	Supply:
1	2 − 1	4 + 1			6
2		1 − 1	+ 1		1
3	5 + 1		3 − 1	2	10
Demand:	7	5	3	2	

Total Cost = 104 − 1(3) = 101

FIGURE 6.17. Pattern of Alterations for One Unit of Flow on Route (2, 3)—Third Solution.

Iteration 3. A simplified procedure. Now that you have seen the method to develop the improvement potentials in *Step 2* of the algorithm, it is no longer necessary to write the full dual equations for the basic variables. A short-cut is to fill in an $m \times n$ table with the potentials. Start by drawing a table with the structure appearing in Fig. 6.18. Insert all the c_{ij} in the small upper left boxes and the symbol $\underline{0}$ for each basic route in the current solution. Leave blank all the other table entries, including the v_i and w_j.

	Column 1	Column 2	Column 3	Column 4	v_i
Row 1	2 / $\underline{0}$	3 / $\underline{0}$	11 / 1	7 / −1	−3
Row 2	1 / −5	0 / −3	6 / $\underline{0}$	1 / −1	−9
Row 3	5 / $\underline{0}$	8 / −2	15 / $\underline{0}$	9 / $\underline{0}$	0
w_j	5	6	15	9	

FIGURE 6.18. Improvement Potentials for Nonbasic Routes—Third Solution.

Next select any v_i or w_j and give it an arbitrary value. Suppose, as previously, you let $v_3 = 0$. Then enter the selected value at the edge of the corresponding row or column (Row 3 in the example). Look across the row or column for basic routes. In Row 3, the routes $(3, 4)$, $(3, 3)$, and $(3, 1)$ qualify. The dual equation for each of these routes permits you to determine another dual variable. For the example, $w_4 = 9$, $w_3 = 15$, and $w_1 = 5$. Write these values along the edge of the table.

Continue until all dual variables are evaluated. For the illustration, you can proceed in the sequence $v_2 = -9$, $v_1 = -3$, and $w_2 = 6$.

Lastly, for each nonbasic route calculate $(v_i + w_j - c_{ij})$ and enter the result in the table. The final array appears as Fig. 6.18, where you can see that only route $(1, 3)$ shows a potential improvement.

To test your understanding of the steps, develop the pattern of alterations when route $(1, 3)$ is introduced. Verify that the largest amount of possible flow on route $(1, 3)$ is one unit, and the new flows are those in Fig. 6.19.

	Column 1	Column 2	Column 3	Column 4	Supply:
Row 1		5	1		6
Row 2			1		1
Row 3	7		1	2	10
Demand:	7	5	3	2	

FIGURE 6.19. Fourth and Optimal Basic Solution.

Total Cost $= 101 - 1(1) = 100$

Iteration 4. Perform the calculations to test for optimality of the solution, and check your answers with the results in Fig. 6.20. How close to optimal was the solution you guessed at the beginning of the illustration?

Row \ Column	1	2	3	4	v_j
1	2 / -1	3 / $\underline{0}$	4 / $\underline{0}$	7 / -2	-4
2	1 / -5	0 / -2	6 / $\underline{0}$	1 / -1	-9
3	5 / $\underline{0}$	8 / -1	15 / $\underline{0}$	9 / $\underline{0}$	0
w_j	5	7	15	9	

FIGURE 6.20. Improvement Potentials for Optimal Solution.

▶ If the original problem in fact is a transshipment model, then the resultant expanded transshipment tables have both a Row i_k and Column j_k for each transshipment Node k. Accordingly, there will be two dual variables v_{i_k} and w_{j_k}. Since the buffer amount B is sufficiently large, each $x_{i_k j_k}$ is in every trial basis. Consequently $v_{i_k} + w_{j_k} = 0$, so that v_{i_k} and w_{j_k} will differ only in sign for these rows and columns. ◀

6.7 FURTHER COMMENTS ON THE SIMPLEX METHOD

A few supplementary remarks are appropriate to conclude the description of the simplex method as applied to transportation problems.

Although we have referred to the algorithm as "the simplex method applied to transportation problems" and have used terminology that is accordingly consistent, we really have not explicitly demonstrated the equivalence. We suggest that you take our word for it, unless you have a burning interest in this technical question. In that case, you can read the discussion in the advanced material below.

Special structure. The text has mentioned repeatedly that transportation problems have a special structure to be exploited. The important proposition is the theorem below.

TRIANGULARITY THEOREM. After dropping any one of the equations in the redundant system of restrictions for the transportation problem, every basis has the triangularity property. Hence, since all the coefficients in the constraints are 1, no multiplication or division is needed to sequentially determine the values of any set of basic variables; only addition and subtraction are required.

Thus when the simplex method is applied to a transportation problem, no division or multiplication is required for *Steps 3* and *4*. The technique was explained in a way that recognized and consequently exploited this fact.

Optimality. The following line of reasoning demonstrates that when the algorithm terminates, an optimal solution in fact has been obtained.

First, observe that since a solution for a transportation model must allocate the *entire* supply S_i among the routes in Row i, you can subtract the *same* constant from each c_{ij} in that row without affecting which solutions are optimal. Similarly, you can diminish each c_{ij} in Column j. In this subtraction process, let the final value of v_i be the constant used for Row i and the final value of w_j the constant for Column j. Then suppose you replace the original objective-function values c_{ij} by the *new* values $[c_{ij} - (v_i + w_j)]$. As we have reasoned, the model with the original c_{ij} and the model with the *new* coefficients have the very same optimal solutions.

Second, recall that, at termination of the simplex algorithm,

$$(1) \qquad\qquad 0 \le c_{ij} - (v_i + w_j) \quad \text{for all } (i, j) \text{ in network,}$$

since the quantities in (1) are merely the negative of the entries in the final improvement potential tables. Therefore, the minimum value of the *new* objective function cannot be smaller than 0, because the new objective-function coefficients are all nonnegative.

Finally, notice that since *equality* holds in (1) for the basic routes, the terminating solution uses only routes where the *new* cost coefficients are 0. Consequently no better solution can exist.

If the improvement potential for a nonbasic route has zero value, then an alternative optimal solution can be found by introducing the route into the basis according to *Steps 3* and *4.*

Integrality. Several times previously, we emphasized that if the transportation model is further restricted by the condition that the variables must be integers,

$$(2) \qquad\qquad \text{every } x_{ij} = 0, 1, 2, \ldots,$$

the optimal value of objective function is not increased. The following terse argument demonstrates the assertion: the simplex algorithm always finds an optimal solution to a linear programming model, and when the technique is applied to a *transportation* problem, the method looks *only* at solutions satisfying (2).

The underpinnings of the above argument are

   (i) There exists an optimal basic solution, since the transportation model has a finite optimal solution.
   (ii) Every basis is triangular.
   (iii) Each technological coefficient is either 1 or -1.

The combined effect of these three points is that only additions and subtractions of integers occur in the sequential determination of each basic x_{ij}.

Completeness. In *Step 2*, if more than one route shows the greatest potential improvement, you can select one arbitrarily. In *Step 3*, if the flow on more than one basic route becomes zero when the new route enters, then the new basis will be degenerate. Only one route should be dropped, and the others should remain in the new basis at zero level. For practical purposes, a particular "tie-breaking" rule to select the route that drops is of no consequence. However, as you already saw in Chap. 4, the degeneracy condition must be dealt with to prove that the method always terminates in a finite number of trials. (The advanced material below suggests a method of rescaling a problem so that degeneracy never arises and the objective function strictly improves at each iteration.)

An example will help to clarify the procedure for applying *Step 3* when degeneracy arises. Suppose the example in Fig. 6.15 is modified so that $c_{21} = -6$, thereby making the shipment x_{21} profitable (instead of costly) to use. As a result, the improvement potential for x_{21} in Fig. 6.17 is no longer -4; instead it is 3, and hence route (2, 1) should be introduced in the next solution. The associated pattern of alterations is displayed in Fig. 6.21. Observe that the flows in both routes (2, 2) and (3, 1) drop to level zero. As the above paragraph suggests, one of these two routes arbitrarily can be selected to leave the basic solution, and the

Row \ Column	1	2	3	4	Supply:
1	6				6
2	+1	1−1			1
3	1−1	4+1	3	2	10
Demand:	7	5	3	2	

FIGURE 6.21. Pattern of Alterations for One Unit of Flow on Route (2, 1).

other will remain in the basic solution at zero level. Suppose you drop the route (3, 1).

You are now ready to test whether the trial solution in Fig. 6.21 is optimal. The corresponding table of improvement potentials is shown in Fig. 6.22. Observe that route (2, 2) is treated as being in the basic solution, even though its flow level is zero. You can see in Fig. 6.22 that (1, 2) is the next route to introduce into a

Row \ Column	1	2	3	4	v_i
1	2 / 0	3 / 5	11 / 4	7 / 2	0
2	−6 / 0	0 / 0	6 / 1	1 / 0	−8
3	5 / −3	8 / 0	15 / 0	9 / 0	0
w_j	2	8	15	9	

FIGURE 6.22. Improvement Potentials for Nonbasic Routes.

trial solution, since it has the largest improvement potential. In determining the associated pattern of alterations, you will find that the flow increases occur on routes (1, 2) and (2, 1), and the flow decreases on routes (1, 1) and (2, 2). Since the flow level on (2, 2) is already zero, no actual alterations in flow take place. But you still apply *Step 3* because you drop route (2, 2) from the current solution and introduce route (1, 2), which enters at zero level. The new trial solution is displayed in Fig. 6.23, and the associated improvement potentials are calculated in Fig. 6.24. Observe that even though the actual flows remained unchanged, introducing route (1, 2) and dropping route (2, 2) altered the improvement potentials.

From Fig. 6.24, you select route (3, 1) to introduce into the next trial solution. At this iteration, the pattern of alterations indicates that flow increases on routes (3, 1) and (1, 2) and decreases on routes (1, 1) and (3, 2); the level of change here is five units, thus causing route (3, 2) to leave the basic solution. The resultant set of shipments is shown in Fig. 6.25. The associated improvements potentials are given in Fig. 6.26 and indicate that the current trial solution is optimal. In this

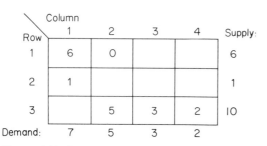

FIGURE 6.23. Degenerate Trial Solution.

Row \ Column	1	2	3	4	Supply
1	6	0			6
2	1				1
3		5	3	2	10
Demand	7	5	3	2	

FIGURE 6.24. Improvement Potentials for Degenerate Trial Solution.

Row \ Column	1	2	3	4	v_i
1	2 / 0	3 / 0	11 / -1	7 / -3	-5
2	-6 / 0	0 / -5	6 / -4	1 / -5	-13
3	5 / 2	8 / 0	15 / 0	9 / 0	0
w_j	7	8	15	9	

FIGURE 6.25. Final Solution.

Row \ Column	1	2	3	4	Supply
1	1	5			6
2	1				1
3	5		3	2	10
Demand	7	5	3	2	

FIGURE 6.26. Improvement Potentials for Final Solution.

Row \ Column	1	2	3	4	v_i
1	2 / 0	3 / 0	11 / -1	7 / -1	-3
2	-6 / 0	0 / -11	6 / -2	1 / -3	-11
3	5 / 0	8 / -8	15 / 0	9 / 0	0
w_j	5	0	15	9	

example, the final solution has positive shipment levels on all the basic routes, but it is possible for an optimal solution to be degenerate.

Domain of applicability. The method applies to all network problems that can be converted to a transportation model format. Notice that the c_{ij} do not have to be nonnegative to perform the steps.

▶ **Convergence.** By the very nature of the transportation problem, an optimal solution must have a finite objective-function value. If the trial solutions make a strict improvement at each iteration, then the method must converge, since the objective function is reduced by at least one unit each time. But when degeneracy occurs, the objective function can stall for several iterations, and the possibility of cycling arises.

It is always possible to rescale the units and slightly perturb the supplies and demands, so that degeneracy never arises during the calculations. The following scheme can be shown to achieve this result. Let the new available supplies be nS_i, for $i = 1, 2, \ldots, m - 1$, and $nS_m + n$, and the new requirements be $nD_j + 1$, for $j = 1, 2, \ldots, n$. Then the objective function will improve at every iteration. The final 'answer is scaled back to the original units by dividing each x_{ij} by n and rounding so as to preserve the supply and demand restrictions, which always can be done. Since the rounded answer is feasible and uses the same basic routes, it remains optimal.

Relation to the standard simplex method. Figure 6.27 depicts a simplex tableau tracing the iterations. It employs the condensed format introduced in Fig. 4.8 on p. 95. The redundancy has been removed.

Notice at every iteration that each coefficient in Rows 1 through 6 is either $+1$ or -1, a condition that arises because of the network structure. The pattern of coefficients in each column corresponds to the pattern of alterations occurring when the nonbasic route is introduced. You can see that pivoting requires only additions and subtractions for this structure.

Initial basic solution. In selecting a starting solution for *Step 1*, you must be careful to pick a basis, that is, $m + n - 1$ routes with flows *uniquely* determined by the S_i and D_j. It is usually worthwhile to perform a preliminary analysis of the c_{ij} to assist in selecting a good initial basis.

In the discussion of optimality, you learned that a constant may be subtracted from every c_{ij} in a row or in a column without affecting the selection of an optimal solution. Furthermore, when the optimal dual variables v_i and w_j are the constants for Row i and Column j, the revised costs are nonnegative and flow occurs only on zero-cost routes. These observations motivate the suggestion:

(i) Subtract the smallest c_{ij} in Row i from every cost coefficient in that row so as to form a new array.

(ii) Subtract the smallest of the numbers in Column j of the new array from every other entry in that column so as to yield a **relative cost** table.

(iii) Select an initial basis with reference to the relative costs.

The procedure is illustrated for the example in Figs. 6.28 and 6.29. To ensure that you pick a basis, follow the procedure:

(i) Select route (i, j) from those permitted and let the flow x_{ij} be the smaller of the amounts available, $a_i \geq 0$, and required, $r_j \geq 0$. For the first route chosen, $a_i = S_i$ and $r_j = D_j$.

(ii) If $a_i < r_j$, check off Row i and permit no more routes to be selected in Row i. Decrease by x_{ij} the amount required in Column j, and let r_j now be this new amount. Return to *Instruction (i)*.

(iii) If $a_i > r_j$, check off Column j and permit no more routes to be selected in Column j. Decrease by x_{ij} the amount available in Row i, and let a_i now be this new amount. Return to *Instruction (i)*.

Iteration	Basis	Values	x_{12}	x_{13}	x_{14}	x_{21}	x_{23}	x_{24}	Row
	x_0	112	2	1	−1	−4	1		0
	x_{11}	6	1	1	1				1
	x_{22}	1				1	1	1	2
1	x_{31}	1	−1	−1	−1	1			3
	x_{32}	4	[1]				−1	−1	−1 at x24, 4
	x_{33}	3		1			1		5
	x_{34}	2			1			1	6

Iteration	Basis	Values	x_{32}	x_{13}	x_{14}	x_{21}	x_{23}	x_{24}	Row
	x_0	104	−2	1	−1	−2	3	2	0
	x_{11}	2	−1	1	1	1	1	1	1
	x_{22}	1				1	[1]	1	2
2	x_{31}	5	1	−1	−1		−1	−1	3
	x_{12}	4	1			−1	−1	−1	4
	x_{33}	3		1			1		5
	x_{34}	2			1			1	6

Iteration	Basis	Values	x_{32}	x_{13}	x_{14}	x_{21}	x_{22}	x_{24}	Row
	x_0	101	−2	1	−1	−5	−3	−1	0
	x_{11}	1	−1	[1]	1		−1		1
	x_{23}	1				1	1	1	2
3	x_{31}	6	1	−1	−1	1	1		3
	x_{12}	5	1				1		4
	x_{33}	2		1		−1	−1	−1	5
	x_{34}	2			1			1	6

Iteration	Basis	Values	x_{32}	x_{11}	x_{14}	x_{21}	x_{22}	x_{24}	Row
	x_0	100	−1	−1	−2	−5	−2	−1	0
	x_{13}	1	−1	1	1		−1		1
	x_{23}	1				1	1	1	2
4	x_{31}	7		1		1			3
	x_{12}	5	1				1		4
	x_{33}	1	1	−1	−1	−1		−1	5
	x_{34}	2			1			1	6

FIGURE 6.27. Simplex Tableau.

FIGURE 6.28. Row Reduction Calculation.

Row \ Column	1	2	3	4	Subtract
1	0	1	9	5	$2 (= c_{11})$
2	1	0	6	1	$0 (= c_{22})$
3	0	3	10	4	$5 (= c_{31})$

FIGURE 6.29. Column Reduction Calculation and Relative Costs.

Row \ Column	1	2	3	4
1	0	1	3	4
2	1	0	0	0
3	0	3	4	3
Subtract	0	0	6	1

(iv) If $a_i = r_j$, stop if $m + n - 1$ routes have been selected. Otherwise, perform either *Instruction (ii)* or *(iii)*, but not both. However, if *only* Row i remains, perform *Instruction (iii)*, or if *only* Column j remains, perform *Instruction (ii)*. The initial solution will be degenerate.

The procedure is illustrated in Figs. 6.30 and 6.31 by an example having a degenerate initial solution. To check your understanding, perform the operations indicated in Fig. 6.30 on the table in Fig. 6.31.   ◀

6.8 SENSITIVITY TESTING

You found in Chap. 5 that the notion of duality is central in examining how a change in model formulation affects an optimal solution. We review a few of

Instruction	Calculation
i	Pick $x_{11} = r_1 = D_1 = 1$
iii	Check Column 1. Set $a_1 = 7 - 1 = 6$
i	Pick $x_{12} = a_1 = r_1 = 6$
iv (ii)	Check Row 1. Set $r_2 = 6 - 6 = 0$
i	Pick $x_{23} = a_2 = r_3 = 2$
iv (ii)	Check Row 2. Set $r_3 = 2 - 2 = 0$
i	Pick $x_{32} = r_2 = 0$
iv (iii)	Check Column 2. Set $a_3 = 3 - 0 = 3$
i	Pick $x_{34} = a_3 = r_4 = 3$
iv (iii)	Check Column 4. Set $a_3 = 3 - 3 = 0$
i	Pick $x_{33} = a_3 = 0$
iv	Stop ($p - 1 = 3 + 4 - 1 = 6$ routes)

FIGURE 6.30. Selection of an Initial Basis.

Row \ Column	1	2	3	4	Supply:
1	1	6			7
2			2		2
3		0	0	3	3
Demand:	1	6	2	3	

FIGURE 6.31. Initial Basis.

these ideas here in the context of the transportation problem. We make use of the numerical example in Sec. 6.6. You will find it helpful to copy the optimal basic solution exhibited in Fig. 6.21 and the corresponding improvement potentials in Fig. 6.22.

Objective function. The simplex algorithm terminates when the values of the dual variables v_i and w_j are such that all the test quantities $(v_i + w_j - c_{ij})$ are nonpositive. To illustrate, for route (1, 4) in Fig. 6.22, the test quantity equals -2 $(= -4 + 9 - 7)$, where $c_{14} = 7$. This test quantity remains nonpositive for any larger value of c_{14}. If the unit shipment cost is reduced by 2, which is the magnitude of the test quantity, so that $c_{14} = 5$, then the test quantity becomes 0; any further reduction in c_{14} implies that the current solution in Fig. 6.21 is no longer optimal. Similarly, the test quantity for the nonbasic route (3, 2) is -1, where $c_{32} = 8$. Hence, the current solution remains optimal provided that $c_{32} \geq 7 = 8 - 1$.

Sensitivity testing for a c_{ij} that corresponds to a basic route in an optimal solution is more complicated, but the same general idea applies. The current solution remains optimal provided that all the test quantities stay nonpositive. To illustrate, suppose that the unit cost of route (1, 3) is $11 + p_{13}$. In Fig. 6.22, the value of p_{13} is 0. In Fig. 6.32, we have constructed an analogous table where p_{13} appears explicitly.

Row \ Column	1	2	3	4	v_i
1	2 $-1 + p_{13}$	3 0	$11 + p_{13}$ 0	7 $-2 + p_{13}$	$-4 + p_{13}$
2	1 -5	0 $-2 - p_{13}$	6 0	1 -1	-9
3	5 0	8 $-1 - p_{13}$	15 0	9 0	0
w_j	5	$7 - p_{13}$	15	9	

FIGURE 6.32. Sensitivity Analysis for Unit Cost of (1, 3).

The entries in Fig. 6.32 are found as before. For example, arbitrarily set $v_3 = 0$. Then find w_3 from the dual restriction associated with the basic route (3, 3)

(1) $w_3 = 15 - v_3 = 15.$

Similarly, determine v_1 by the dual restriction associated with the basic route $(1, 3)$,

(2) $v_1 = 11 + p_{13} - w_3 = -4 + p_{13},$

and w_2 by the dual restriction associated with route $(1, 2)$,

(3) $w_2 = 3 - v_1 = 7 - p_{13}.$

The other v_i and w_j are calculated analogously.

The test quantities also are found as before. For example, the test quantity for the nonbasic route $(1, 1)$ is

(4) $v_1 + w_1 - c_{11} = -4 + p_{13} + 5 - 2 = -1 + p_{13}.$

In order for the current shipment schedule in Fig. 6.21 to remain optimal, the value of p_{13} must be such that all the test quantities are nonpositive.

(5)
$$-1 + p_{13} \leq 0 \qquad -2 + p_{13} \leq 0$$
$$-2 - p_{13} \leq 0 \qquad -1 - p_{13} \leq 0.$$

The restrictions in (5) imply that if

(6) $-1 \leq p_{13} \leq 1,$

or, equivalently, if

(7) $10 \leq c_{13} + p_{13} \leq 12,$

the current solution remains optimal.

Supplies and demands. In the discussion to follow, assume that you have obtained a nondegenerate optimal solution, that is, assume that every basic route has at least one unit of flow. This condition is satisfied by the solution in Fig. 6.21.

Suppose that both supply S_i and demand D_j are increased by a unit so that the new amounts are $S_i + 1$ and $D_j + 1$, which indicates that an additional unit of supply is available and an additional unit of demand is required. A glance at the objective function for the dual problem (6) in Sec. 6.5 suggests that this alteration will add $v_i + w_j$ to the optimal value of the objective function.

For example, suppose the data in Fig. 6.21 are altered so· that $S_2 = 2$ and $D_1 = 8$. Then the objective function becomes $[100 + (-9 + 5) = 96]$. At first it seems surprising and paradoxical that *adding* one more unit of flow to a transportation schedule can actually *reduce* total cost. You are shipping more for less. But the cost reduction occurs because the extra flow allows the shipments on routes $(3, 1)$ and $(2, 3)$ to increase by a unit, and the shipment on route $(3, 3)$ to decrease by a unit, thereby resulting in -4 $(= c_{31} + c_{23} - c_{33} = 5 + 6 - 15)$ as the net reduction in cost. The appropriate alterations in the previous optimal solution are determined by the following approach.

Tentatively, let the nonbasic shipment $x_{21} = 1$ account for the additional supply and demand. Since you want to maintain the same basic set of routes, you must reduce this tentative shipment x_{21} back to zero level. The necessary pattern of alterations is similar to that which you would have found had you wanted to increase flow on the nonbasic route $(2, 1)$; the pattern is displayed in Fig. 6.33.

If supply S_i and demand D_j are increased by a unit and x_{ij} is a basic variable in the current optimal solution, then you increase x_{ij} by a unit, and the new optimal value of the objective function increases by c_{ij} $(= v_i + w_j$, since x_{ij} is basic).

Row \ Column	1	2	3	4	Supply:
1		5	1		6
2	1−1		1+1		2
3	7+1		1−1	2	10
Demand:	8	5	3	2	

FIGURE 6.33. Pattern of Alterations for One Unit of Flow Removed from Route $(2, 1)$.

Finally, suppose that only a single supply S_p is increased by a unit, whereas all the demands are left unchanged; thus an oversupply is created. For example, suppose $S_1 = 7$ in Fig. 6.21. You can view the situation as one in which there is an appended fictitious demand point with demand $D_5 = 1$, x_{15} represents excess supply at Source i, and all the associated unit costs $c_{15} = c_{25} = c_{35} = 0$. Temporarily, let $x_{15} = 1$. The improvement potentials associated with this enlarged model and trial solution are displayed in Fig. 6.34. Observe that all the

Row \ Column	1	2	3	4	5	v_i
1	2 / −1	3 / 0	11 / 0	7 / −2	0 / 0	−4
2	1 / −5	0 / −2	6 / 0	1 / −1	0 / −5	−9
3	5 / 0	8 / −1	15 / 0	9 / 0	0 / 4	0
w_j	5	7	15	9	4	

FIGURE 6.34. Improvement Potentials when $S_1 = 7$ with Previous Optimal Solution and $\overset{\bullet}{x}_{15} = 0$.

dual variables in Fig. 6.34 are the same as those in Fig. 6.22, and w_5 is determined by the dual equation for x_{15}

$$(8) \qquad\qquad w_5 = 0 - v_1 = 4.$$

Similarly, all the test quantities in Fig. 6.34 are the same as those in Fig. 6.22, except the quantities in the new fifth column. Note that the test quantity for route (3, 5) is positive, indicating that further improvement is possible by adding flow along this route. The associated pattern of alterations is given in Fig. 6.35. The

Row \ Column	1	2	3	4	5	Supply:
1		5	1+1		1−1	7
2			1			1
3	7		1−1	2	+1	10
Demand:	7	5	3	2	1	

FIGURE 6.35. Pattern of Alterations for Assigning Excess Supply to Source 3.

altered solution removes the unit of excess supply from Source 1 and locates it at Source 3. The improvement potentials for this altered solution are shown in Fig. 6.36 and indicate optimality. The value of the objective function becomes $[100 + 11 - 15 = 96]$, or alternatively, using the dual variables in Fig. 6.22 $[100 + (v_1 + w_3) - (v_3 + w_3) = 100 + v_1 - v_3]$.

Row \ Column	1	2	3	4	5	v_i
1	2 / −1	3 / 0	11 / 0	7 / −2	0 / −4	−4
2	1 / −5	0 / −2	6 / 0	1 / −1	0 / −9	9
3	5 / 0	8 / −1	15 / 0	9 / 0	0 / 0	0
w_j	5	7	15	9	0	

FIGURE 6.36. Improvement Potentials for Assigning Excess Supply to Source 3.

Actually, the above analysis can be summarized simply. Given that the supply S_p is increased by a unit, the new optimal allocation assigns the *excess* unit of supply to that source k that has $v_k = $ maximum (v_i), and the quantity $[v_p - v_k] \le 0$ is thereby added to the objective function.

REVIEW EXERCISES

1 Consider the transportation problem (1) through (4) in Sec. 6.2. Let the number of supply points $m = 5$ and the number of demand points $n = 4$.

  (a) Write the model in full detail (that is, display the objective function and the constraints without using the summation symbol).

  (b) Draw the corresponding network in Fig. 6.1, and construct the two tables in Fig. 6.2.

  (c) Write in full detail the corresponding dual problem; use the notation in Sec. 6.5.

2 *Excess Supply.* Consider a transportation problem in which

$$S_1 = 6 \quad S_2 = 7 \quad S_3 = 8 \quad \text{and} \quad D_1 = 3 \quad D_2 = 4 \quad D_3 = 5.$$

Create a fictitious destination and construct a table like that in Fig. 6.2a in which total supply equals total demand. Be sure you indicate the cost coefficients c_{ij} for the fictitious destination and its D_j.

3 Write the full equations for a standard transportation model with $m = 2$ and $n = 3$, where total supply equals total demand [use the notation in (8), (9), and (10) of Sec. 6.2]. Show that if you add the supply constraints in (8) for $i = 1, 2$, and from this sum subtract the demand constraints in (9) for $j = 1, 2$, you obtain the demand constraint for $j = 3$. Indicate where you use the assumption that total supply equals total demand.

*4 *Seasonal Variation.* Suppose a firm having two plants and three demand points is planning a production schedule for four periods. Assume over Periods 1, 2, 3, and 4 that Plant 1 has available supplies of 5, 6, 7, and 8, respectively, and similarly Plant 2 has available supplies of 9, 10, 11, and 12, respectively. Assume over Periods 1, 2, 3, and 4 that Demand Point 1 has demands 4, 4, 11, and 11, respectively; similarly, Demand Point 2 has demands 5, 3, 7, and 7, respectively; and Demand Point 3 has demands 3, 7, 5, and 5, respectively. Let c_{ij} be the cost of shipping a unit from Plant i to Demand Point j in any period.

(a) Display the optimization problem in a table like that in Fig. 6.2a. Be sure you indicate which x_{ij} must be eliminated.

(b) Is there a feasible solution to this numerical example? Justify your conclusion. Give a general rule for discerning whether such a problem has a feasible solution.

(c) Explain how to modify the formulation when the total supply exceeds total demand.

(d) Suppose each unit of inventory held at the end of a period incurs the cost h. Will adding this cost change the optimal solution in part (a)? Will it change the optimal solution in part (c)?

Exercises 5 through 10 refer to the case of the Raycov Discount Store, displayed in Fig. 6.4.

5 In each part below, state which stores are transshipment (or intermediate) points, which are sources, and which are sinks. Also state whether the resulting map has a feasible shipping pattern that meets the demand requirements. Assume the removal of the route from

(a) Store 4 to Store 5.   (b) Store 5 to Store 4.
(c) Store 6 to Store 7.   (d) Store 2 to Store 5.
(e) Store 4 to Store 7.   (f) Store 4 to Store 3.

6 In each part below, state which stores are transshipment (or intermediate) points, which are sources, and which are sinks. Assume a route is added from

(a) Store 7 to Store 4.   (b) Store 6 to Store 8.
(c) Store 8 to Store 6.   (d) Store 3 to Store 4.
(e) Store 1 to Store 3.   (f) Store 3 to Store 1.

7 In each part below, construct a condensed transshipment table like that in Fig. 6.5. Show a feasible solution, and indicate whether or not your solution implies a unique routing from the supply point to the demand point. Construct an expanded transshipment table like that in Fig. 6.6; indicate the sources and sinks.

(a) Stock of 11 available at Store 1, and stocks of 2 and 9 required at Stores 3 and 8, respectively. No stock available or required at any other store.

(b) Stocks of 10 and 5 available at Stores 1 and 5, respectively, and stocks of 4, 2, 1, and 8 required at Stores 3, 4, 6, and 8, respectively. No stock available or required at any other store.

(c) Stocks of 10, 1, 3, and 6 available at Stores 1, 2, 6, and 7, respectively, and stocks of 3, 2, 7, and 8 required at Stores 3, 4, 5, and 8, respectively.

(d) Answer the above parts when the route from Store 6 to Store 7 is removed. Also state whether there is a feasible solution.

8 (a) Consider the routing in Fig. 6.7. Explain in detail how this routing implies that Store 1 ships three units to Store 3 via Point 2; one unit to Store 6 via Points 2 and 5; and six units to Store 8 via Points 2, 5, 4, and 7; and that Store 4 ships its two units to Store 8 via Point 7. Display this routing on a map like that in Fig. 6.3.

(b) Show how Fig. 6.7 is altered if Store 1 ships six units to Store 8 via Points 2, 5, 6, and 7.

(c) Show how Fig. 6.7 is altered if Store 1 ships eight, instead of six, units to Store 8, and Store 4 ships two units to Store 3, instead of to Store 8.

(d) Explain in detail the routing implied in Fig. 6.7 by letting

$$x_{12} = 10 \quad x_{22} = 2 \quad x_{25} = 10 \quad x_{43} = 3 \quad x_{44} = 11$$

$$x_{54} = 1 \quad x_{55} = 2 \quad x_{56} = 9 \quad x_{66} = 3 \quad x_{67} = 8 \quad x_{77} = 4 \quad x_{78} = 8.$$

Display this routing on a map like that in Fig. 6.4.

9 Add routes from Store 3 to Store 2; Store 3 to Store 4; Store 5 to Store 3; Store 7 to Store 6; and Store 3 to Store 8. Construct a technological table like that in Fig. 6.8 for the stocks available and required in the specified part of exercise 7.

(a) Part (a).

(b) Part (b).

(c) Part (c).

10 Suppose there is one unit of stock available at Stores 1, 4, and 5, and a requirement of one unit of stock at Stores 3, 7, and 8. No stock is available or required at Stores 2 and 6.

(a) Construct a condensed transshipment table like that in Fig. 6.5. Indicate whether the table yields an assignment problem.

(b) Construct an expanded transshipment table like that in Fig. 6.6. Indicate whether the table yields an assignment problem.

11 Explain how a standard transportation problem can be converted into a (large) assignment problem. Illustrate your technique using an example with two supply points having stocks $S_1 = 3$ and $S_2 = 2$, and two demand points having requirements $D_1 = 4$ and $D_2 = 1$.

12 Arrange the dual variables and dual equalities (3) in Sec. 6.6 to display at a glance the triangularity property when you set equal to zero the dual variable indicated in each part below.

(a) w_4.
(b) w_1.
(c) v_2.
(d) Arrange the shipment variables and equalities (5) in Sec. 6.6 to display at a glance the upper triangularity property.
(e) Do the same where the equality for Row 3 is made explicit and the equality for Column 4 is dropped as the redundant relation.
(f) Do the same where the equality for Row 3 is made explicit and the equality for Column 1 is dropped as the redundant relation.
(g) Do the same where the equality in Row 3 is made explicit and the equality for Row 2 is dropped as the redundant relation.

13 In each part below, find the pattern of alterations, like that in Fig. 6.14, when the indicated nonbasic route is selected in Fig. 6.13. Also calculate the associated improvement potential and verify your answer in Fig. 6.15. Finally, show the values for the new basic solution if the route indicated is selected.

(a) Route (1, 3).   (b) Route (1, 4).
(c) Route (2, 1).   (d) Route (2, 3).
(e) Route (2, 4).

14 In each part below, solve the dual equalities (3) in Sec. 6.6 using the indicated value for the selected dual variable.

(a) $v_3 = 1$.   (b) $v_3 = -1$.
(c) $w_4 = 0$.   (d) $w_4 = 1$.
(e) $w_1 = 0$.   (f) $w_1 = -1$.
(g) Verify that $v_i + w_j$, for every i and j, has the same value in each part above. Explain why.

15 *Northwest Corner Rule.* In Sec. 2.6, the following rule was described for finding an initial solution to a transportation model: start at the upper-left corner, or, as it is sometimes called, the *northwest corner*. Allocate the available supply S_1 to each demand requirement, beginning with D_1, until the supply is exhausted. Then continue the process with S_2 and the remaining unfilled demand requirements. Etc.

(a) Consider the example in Fig. 6.12. Let $S_2 = 2$ and $D_2 = 6$. Apply the northwest corner rule to obtain an initial solution. Calculate the associated trial value for the objective function.
(b) Revise the trial solution in part (a) for the case $S_2 = 1$ and $D_2 = 5$, which are the values in Fig. 6.12. Be sure to maintain a basic solution having $m + n - 1$ routes.
(c) Indicate how to amend the above statement of the northwest corner rule to ensure that the process yields a basic solution containing $m + n - 1$ routes.
(d) In Fig. 6.12, let $S_1 = 7$, $S_2 = 5$, and $D_4 = 7$. Is a feasible solution using routes

x_{11}, x_{13}, x_{22}, x_{31}, x_{33}, and x_{34} a basic solution? If not, explain why, and apply your answer to part (c). (*Hint:* ascertain whether feasible values for the x_{ij} are *uniquely* determined.)

16 In each part below, find the pattern of alterations, like that in Fig. 6.17, when the indicated nonbasic route in Fig. 6.16 is selected. Also, calculate the associated improvement potential and compare your answer to (10) in Sec. 6.6. Finally, show the values for the new basic solution when the route indicated is actually selected.

   (a) Route (3, 2).
   (b) Route (1, 4).
   (c) Route (2, 4).

*17 Construct a basic solution for a transportation problem with $m > 2$ and $n > 2$ such that *every* basic route is revised when a particular nonbasic route is introduced. (*Hint:* let $m = n$, and let the basic solution be found by using the northwest corner rule in exercise 16.)

18 In each part below, assume that the indicated nonbasic route is selected in Fig. 6.16 at iteration 3. Continue the transportation simplex process to find the optimal solution. Use the tabular method, like that in Fig. 6.18, to calculate the improvement potentials.

   (a) Route (1, 3).
   (b) Route (2, 4).

19 (a) Explain why subtracting the same constant from each c_{ij} in a specified Row i of Fig. 6.2(a) yields a new problem that has the same optimal solutions as the original problem.
   (b) Consider the transportation model applied to the distribution of an item that is manufactured at m plants. Let p_i be the production cost of each item at Plant i and t_{ij} the cost of transporting each item from Plant i to Warehouse j. Suppose total potential production at all the plants equals total demand at all the warehouses. Given your answer in part (a), explain why the actual values for the p_i do not influence an optimal distribution plan. Would your explanation be modified if total potential production exceeded total demand? If so, how?

20 In each part below, determine whether an alternative optimal solution would be indicated in Fig. 6.24, and if it would, find such a basic solution.

   (a) $c_{11} = 3$.   (b) $c_{11} = 1$.
   (c) $c_{32} = 8$.   (d) $c_{32} = 9$.
   (e) $c_{32} = 7$.

*21 *Degeneracy.* In each part below, apply the transportation simplex method to find an optimal solution and use the starting solution given in exercise 16.

   (a) Part (a).
   (b) Part (b).
   (c) Part (d).

*22 *Degeneracy.* In each part below, apply the rescaling procedure suggested in the special material of Sec. 6.7 for removing degeneracy. Solve the perturbed model by the transportation simplex method, and indicate how to find the optimal solution in the original problem. Use the data and starting solution in exercise 16.

(a) Part (a).
(b) Part (b).
(c) Part (d).

23 Consider the example in Fig. 6.12. Apply the transportation simplex method to find the optimal solution starting with the basis:

$$x_{11} = 2 \quad x_{12} = 4 \quad x_{22} = 1 \quad x_{31} = 5 \quad x_{33} = 3 \quad x_{34} = 2.$$

*24 Solve the problem in exercise 23 using the ordinary simplex method as presented in Chap. 4. (If you prefer, use either of the tabular formats presented in Sec. 4.5.) Check that at every iteration each variable corresponds to the pattern of alterations occurring when the associated nonbasic route is introduced. (*Suggestion:* to get the calculations started, eliminate any one of the equations as the redundant relation, and solve for the basic x_{ij} indicated in exercise 23.)

25 Let the initial basic solution in Fig. 6.13 employ the route (2, 3), instead of (2, 2). Find the optimal solution using the transportation simplex method. (Note that this initial starting basis is suggested by an analysis of the relative costs in Fig. 6.31.)

*26 (a) Consider the technique in Sec. 6.7 for deriving the relative costs displayed in Fig. 6.31. Apply the technique where you first perform the column calculations (ii) and then the row calculations (i). Are your answers the same as those in Fig. 6.31.
(b) Show that the solution in Fig. 6.19 is optimal for a problem having c_{ij} as indicated in Fig. 6.31. Show the relation between the value of the optimal solution in Fig. 6.19 and the process generating the c_{ij} in Fig. 6.31.
(c) Show that the solution in Fig. 6.19 is optimal for a problem having c_{ij} as indicated in your answer to part (a).

*27 *Initial Basic Solution*

(a) Perform the operations indicated in Fig. 6.32 on the table in Fig. 6.33.
(b) Use the same selection sequence of x_{ij} shown in Fig. 6.32 to find an initial basis for the supplies and demands:

$$S_1 = 3 \quad S_2 = 4 \quad S_3 = 5 \quad D_1 = 3 \quad D_2 = 1 \quad D_3 = 4 \quad D_4 = 4.$$

28 Consider the problem in Fig. 6.12. In each part below, calculate how small the indicated objective-function coefficient can be (leave the other costs unchanged) such that the solution in Fig. 6.19 remains optimal.

(a) c_{12}.   (b) c_{13}.
(c) c_{23}.   (d) c_{31}.
(e) c_{33}.   (f) c_{34}.

*29 Suppose you have an optimal solution in which every basic route has at least one unit of flow, as in Fig. 6.19. Suppose S_p is increased by a unit, so that an oversupply is created. Show that the new optimal allocation will assign the *excess* to that source k with $v_k = $ maximum v_i, and that $[v_p - v_k]$ will be added to the objective function.

30 Consider the example in Sec. 6.6. Suppose $S_2 = 2$. Find a new optimal solution (using sensitivity analysis on the previous optimal solution), and verify that total cost is reduced by $v_2 = -9$.

31 Consider the optimal solution shown in Fig. 6.19. In each part below, use sensitivity analysis to find a revised optimal solution and the associated value of the objective function

(a) $S_1 = 7, D_1 = 8$.   (b) $S_1 = 7, D_4 = 3$.
(c) $S_2 = 2, D_2 = 6$.   (d) $S_2 = 2, D_4 = 3$.
(e) $S_3 = 10, D_2 = 6$.

32 Consider the solution in Fig. 6.19. In each part below, suppose the supply at Point i is $S_i - g$ and the demand at Point j is $D_j - g$. State how large g can be such that the basis in Fig. 6.19 remains optimal. Also, indicate an optimal solution for this value of g.

(a) $S_1 - g$ and $D_2 - g$.   (b) $S_1 - g$ and $D_3 - g$.
(c) $S_2 - g$ and $D_3 - g$.   (d) $S_3 - g$ and $D_1 - g$.
(e) $S_3 - g$ and $D_3 - g$.   (f) $S_3 - g$ and $D_4 - g$.

33 Answer questions in exercise 32 for each part below. [*Hint*: the pattern of alterations for the basic variables is the same as if you were going to add a unit of flow on route (i, j).]

(a) $S_1 - g$ and $D_1 - g$.   (b) $S_1 - g$ and $D_4 - g$.
(c) $S_2 - g$ and $D_1 - g$.   (d) $S_3 - g$ and $D_2 - g$.

34 Explain your understanding of the following terms:

transportation (or distribution) problem	sink point
	buffer stock
transshipment (or intermediate) point	assignment problem
	triangularity
source point	relative cost.

FORMULATION EXERCISES

35 The Nick U. Moore Razor Blade Company has announced a revolutionary product development, and the sales response to the company's advertising program has been gratifying. The company has two manufacturing plants and three distributing warehouses located in different parts of the United States. The company ships its razor blades to the warehouses by rail in carload lots. (*Continued on page 178.*)

This month's supply at Plants 1 and 2 are $S_1 = 150$ and $S_2 = 250$, respectively. The sales potentials at Warehouses 1, 2, and 3 are $D_1 = 175$, $D_2 = 225$, and $D_3 = 300$, respectively. As you can see, potential demand vastly exceeds available supply, and consequently some demand will go unsatisfied.

Assume the cost of shipping a carload from Plant i to Warehouse j is t_{ij}, and that the sales revenue per carload at Warehouse j is p_j. (The company is able to charge different prices for its razor blades in different parts of the country.)

(a) Formulate a transportation model to obtain a profit maximizing solution. Be sure to indicate how you would compute each objective-function coefficient c_{ij}.

(b) Construct the associated table like that in Fig. 6.2a. Be sure to indicate the values for each S_i and D_j, as well as each c_{ij}.

36 The Hugh Otto Bean Pitchers Company must meet demand commitments for $D_1, D_2, \ldots, D_N$ units of its product in Periods 1, 2, ..., N, respectively. The company's production capacity in Period t is m_t units, assuming that its work force is employed for one shift a day. The associated direct cost of each unit is p_t. By using overtime, the company also can produce e_t more units at a direct cost of q_t, where $q_t > p_t$. Because the demand commitments fluctuate considerably, the company expects that it may have to build inventory in some periods to meet demand in subsequent periods. Each unit of inventory at the end of Period t incurs a holding charge h_t.

(a) Assuming D_t, m_t, and e_t are integer-valued, formulate a transportation model that will find a cost-minimizing production and inventory plan. Be sure to indicate how to compute each objective-function coefficient.

(b) Using your answer in part (a), construct a table like that in Fig. 6.2a for the data ($N = 4$).

$$D_1 = 12 \qquad D_2 = 9 \qquad D_3 = 18 \qquad D_4 = 22$$

$$m_1 = 10 \qquad m_2 = 8 \qquad m_3 = 10 \qquad m_4 = 12$$

$$e_1 = 8 \qquad e_2 = 6 \qquad e_3 = 5 \qquad e_4 = 4$$

$$p_t = 14 \qquad q_t = 21 \quad \text{and} \quad h_t = 1 \quad \text{for all } t.$$

*(c) Suggest an easy-to-apply rule for finding an optimal plan for such a model, in which p_t, q_t, and h_t may differ from period to period. Then employ your suggestion to solve part (b).

37 The Sinbad Steamship Company operates a freighter schedule between Ports X and Y and Ports A, B, and C. The schedule for the next 15 days is shown in the first table.

Dates	Port of Origin	Port of Destination	Dates	Port of Origin	Port of Destination
3	X	A	10	X	A
4	Y	A	10	X	C
6	X	C	10	Y	B
6	Y	A	13	Y	B
9	X	B	15	Y	B
9	Y	A	15	Y	C

After a freighter goes from a port of origin to a port of destination, it may return to either port of origin. The *total* time (in days) to sail from port to port, in either direction, is shown in the second table.

	A	B	C
X	2	3	2
Y	1	2	1

Suppose three freighters are at Port X and three at Port Y on Day 1. Let the expense of returning a freighter to Port X from Ports A, B, and C be p_A, p_B, and p_C, respectively, and similarly let the cost of returning a freighter to Port Y be q_A, q_B, and q_C, respectively.

The Sinbad Company wants to find a routing for ships from Ports A, B, and C back to Ports X and Y that minimizes total cost. Show how this problem can be solved by a transportation model.

Let a supply point correspond to (Date t, Port of Destination i), which specifies that at Date t, one or more freighters (depending on the schedule requirements above) arrive at the Port of Destination i (either Port A, B, or C), and are ready to be returned to a port of origin (either Port X or Y). For example, since on Date 6 a freighter must leave Port X and go to Port C, taking two days of travel time, there is at least one freighter available at Supply Point (6 + 2, C).

Let a demand point correspond to (Date t, Port of Origin j), which specifies that on Date t one or more freighters (depending on the schedule requirements above) sail from Port of Origin j (either Port X or Y). For example, a demand point is (9, X).

Note that the shipping times make it impossible to send a freighter from some of the supply points in sufficient time to meet the requirements at some of the demand points. For example, Supply Point (6 + 2, C) cannot meet the requirement at Demand Point (9, X), because it takes two days to go from Port C to Port X.

Construct a transportation table that indicates the structure of the model. Be sure to indicate the appropriate S_i, D_j, and every c_{ij}. Display a feasible solution in the table, and interpret your solution in terms of an actual schedule for the six freighters.

38 Consider the case of the Sinbad Steamship Company in exercise 37. Suppose the company wants to find the *minimum* number of freighters required to meet the schedule, regardless of shipping costs. Show how to solve this problem by a transportation model. Construct a transportation table that indicates the structure of the model. Be sure to indicate the appropriate S_i, D_j, and every c_{ij}.

Try to determine a feasible solution in the table for five freighters, and interpret your solution in terms of an actual schedule. Try to do the same for four freighters.

(*Hint:* add a fictitious supply point having a large number of freighters available that can be used to meet *any* requirement, and a fictitious demand point for any excess supply of freighters. Verify that the objective is to minimize the number of freighters that meet requirements from the fictitious supply point.)

39 The Marcus Metal Company mines ore at Locations 1 and 2, transports it to processing mills at Locations 3 and 4, and ships the final product to Locations 5, 6, and 7, where it is sold. A schematic map of the locations and product flow is given in Fig. 6.37.

Let S_1 and S_2 represent the maximum supply available at Locations 1 and 2, respectively, and D_5, D_6, and D_7 the demand requirements that must be met at Locations 5, 6, and 7, respectively. The total maximum supply exceeds the total demand requirements.

Assume m_i is the cost of a unit of supply at Mine i ($i = 1, 2$), p_j is the processing cost of unit of supply at Mill j ($j = 3, 4$), s_{ij} is the shipping cost of a unit of supply from Mine i to Mill j ($i = 1, 2$ and $j = 3, 4$), and t_{jk} is the shipping cost of a unit of supply from Mill j to Location k ($j = 3, 4$, and $k = 5, 6, 7$).

(a) Construct a condensed transshipment table like that in Fig. 6.5. Be sure to indicate in detail how to calculate each objective-function coefficient c_{ij}.
(b) Construct an expanded transshipment table like that in Fig. 6.6. Be sure to indicate how to calculate each objective-function coefficient.
(c) Construct a technology representation like that in Fig. 6.8. Use inequalities where appropriate to indicate that total supply exceeds total demand.

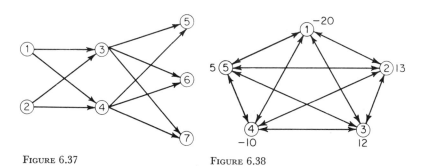

FIGURE 6.37   FIGURE 6.38

40 Consider the transshipment network in Fig. 6.38, where a positive number at a node or point indicates a supply and a negative number a requirement. Note there are two arcs, one in each direction, between every pair of nodes. The unit cost of shipping each item from Node i to Node j is c_{ij}; c_{ij} need not equal c_{ji}.

(a) Construct a condensed transshipment table like that in Fig. 6.5.
(b) Construct an expanded transshipment table like that in Fig. 6.6. Be sure to indicate the values for the supplies and demands.
(c) In the table of part (b), indicate the following shipment plan: five units from Node 5 to Node 4 via Node 3; five units from Node 2 to Node 4 via Nodes 5 and 3; eight units from Node 2 to Node 1 via Node 5; and 12 units from Node 3 directly to Node 1.
(d) Give another routing having the same cost as that in part (c).
(e) Construct a technology representation like that in Fig. 6.8.
*(f) Formulate the technology in part (e) so that the supply constraints are "less-than-or-equal" inequalities, and the demand constraints are "greater-than-or-equal" inequalities. Then write the associated dual *maximizing* problem.

41 Consider the transshipment network in Fig. 6.39, where a positive number at a node (or point) indicates a supply and a negative number a requirement; nodes with 0

indicate there is neither a supply nor a demand. Note there are two arcs, one in each direction, between connected nodes. The unit cost of shipping each item from Node i to Node j is c_{ij}; c_{ij} need not equal c_{ji}.

(a) Construct a condensed transshipment table like that in Fig. 6.5. Show a feasible solution, and indicate whether your solution implies a unique routing.

(b) Construct an expanded transshipment table like that in Fig. 6.6. Are there any sources or sinks? Be sure to indicate in your table the values for the supplies and demands.

(c) In the table of part (b) indicate the following shipment plan: two units from Node 3 to Node 1 via Nodes 2 and 4; two units from Node 6 to Node 1 via Node 4; four units from Node 6 to Node 5 via Node 4; two units from Node 8 to Node 5

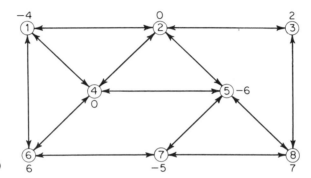

FIGURE 6.39

via Nodes 3, 2, and 4; and five units from Node 8 to Node 7 via Nodes 3, 2, 4, and 5.

(d) Construct a technology representation like that in Fig. 6.8.

42 The McReady Company operates a machine shop. Today's order file consists of n jobs, each of which can be manufactured on any of n different machines. Let t_{ij} be the amount of time (make-ready or setup plus manufacturing) to complete Job i on Machine j. Formulate an optimization model to get all the orders completed with a minimum *total* expenditure of time. How do you modify the formulation if the objective is to complete all jobs as soon as possible?

43 Joe Friendly, the Associate Dean of a large business school, must make a class assignment schedule for the faculty. Specifically, he must assign n professors to teach n classes. In the past, the students have filled out teacher-effectiveness rating questionnaires, so the Associate Dean has information as to how well the students liked the professors when they have taught these several classes. (In some cases, a professor has never taught a particular class, so the Associate Dean must guess at a rating. In other cases, the professor does not wish, or is not prepared, to teach a particular class, and so the Associate Dean must rule out this assignment.)

(a) Explain how the Associate Dean might use a mathematical model to maximize student happiness.

(b) In your opinion, is this any way to run a business school?

44 A young married couple, Eve and Steven, want to divide the household chores between them so that both have the same number of tasks and so that the time spent

per week on household duties is kept to a minimum. (Fortunately, there are an even number of tasks: marketing, cooking, dishwashing, laundering, cleaning floors, bed-making, dusting, and maintaining the car.) The time that Eve and Steven need to perform these tasks is given in Fig. 6.40.

Time for Weekly Chores (hours)

	Marketing	Cooking	Dish-washing	Laundering	Cleaning	Bed Making	Dusting	Maintaining the Car
Eve	1	6	2	1.5	.75	1	1	1
Steven	1.5	5.5	1.5	1.5	1	.75	.5	1.5

FIGURE 6.40

(a) Formulate the appropriate optimization model assigning chores to Eve and Steven.
(b) Can you improve this marital arrangement?

45 The Lieberman Supply Company stocks an item that deteriorates with time as measured in weekly periods. Suppose that Lieberman has on hand four such items, indexed $i = 1, 2, 3$, and 4, the present age of each being denoted by A_i. He has contracted to sell his stock as follows: he must deliver one item t_1 weeks from now, one item t_2 weeks from now, one item t_3 weeks from now, and one item t_4 weeks from now. The revenue he receives for each item is a function of its age at the time of delivery; this function is denoted as $R(A)$, A being the relevant age.

Formulate an optimization model that can enable Lieberman to determine which item he should supply at each delivery date so that he can maximize his total revenue.

COMPUTATIONAL EXERCISES

46 Consider a transportation problem with $m = 3$ and $n = 3$, where

$$c_{11} = 5 \qquad c_{12} = 3 \qquad c_{13} = 8$$
$$c_{21} = 14 \qquad c_{22} = 4 \qquad c_{23} = 5$$
$$c_{31} = 4 \qquad c_{32} = 2 \qquad c_{33} = 8.$$

(a) Suppose $S_1 = 4$, $S_2 = 4$, and $S_3 = 8$; and $D_1 = 2$, $D_2 = 4$, and $D_3 = 10$. Apply the transportation simplex method to find an optimal solution.
(b) Use sensitivity analysis to determine how your solution in part (a) changes if $S_1 = 5$ and $D_1 = 3$. What is the new value of the objective function?
(c) Answer the questions in part (b) for $S_2 = 5$ and $D_2 = 5$.
(d) What is the smallest value of c_{22} that will allow your solution in part (a) to remain optimal? Similarly, how small can c_{12} be?   (Continued on p. 183.)

(e) Give a range of values for c_{23} that allows the solution in part (a) to remain optimal. Do the same for c_{33}. Do the same for c_{32}.

47 Consider a transportation problem with $m = 4$ and $n = 4$, where

$$c_{11} = 7 \quad c_{12} = 9 \quad c_{13} = 1 \quad c_{14} = 10$$
$$c_{21} = 22 \quad c_{22} = 25 \quad c_{23} = 16 \quad c_{24} = 26$$
$$c_{31} = 28 \quad c_{32} = 32 \quad c_{33} = 24 \quad c_{34} = 32$$
$$c_{41} = 12 \quad c_{42} = 14 \quad c_{43} = 6 \quad c_{44} = 16.$$

(a) Suppose $S_1 = 7, S_2 = 3, S_3 = 7$, and $S_4 = 8$; and $D_1 = 5, D_2 = 5, D_3 = 7$, and $D_4 = 8$. Apply the transportation simplex method to find an optimal solution.
(b) Use sensitivity analysis to determine how your solution in part (a) changes if $S_2 = 4$ and $D_4 = 9$. What is the new value of the objective function?
(c) Rework part (b) for $S_3 = 8$ and $D_3 = 8$. (*Exercise continued on p. 218.*)
(d) What is the smallest value of c_{11} that will allow the solution in part (a) to remain optimal? Similarly, what is the smallest value of c_{21}? Similarly, how small can c_{31} be?
(e) Give a range of values for c_{23} such that the solution in part (a) remains optimal. Do the same for c_{43}. Do the same for c_{42}.

48 Consider a transportation problem with $m = 4$ and $n = 4$, where

$$c_{11} = 5 \quad c_{12} = 5 \quad c_{13} = 7 \quad c_{14} = 13$$
$$c_{21} = 4 \quad c_{22} = 3 \quad c_{23} = 8 \quad c_{24} = 16$$
$$c_{31} = 13 \quad c_{32} = 13 \quad c_{33} = 14 \quad c_{34} = 24$$
$$c_{41} = 18 \quad c_{42} = 18 \quad c_{43} = 24 \quad c_{44} = 34.$$

(a) Suppose $S_1 = 3, S_2 = 4, S_3 = 9$, and $S_4 = 18$; and $D_1 = 15, D_2 = 5, D_3 = 7$, and $D_4 = 7$. Apply the transportation simplex method to find an optimal solution.
(b) Use sensitivity analysis to determine how your solution in part (a) changes if $S_1 = 4$ and $D_1 = 16$. What is the new value of the objective function?
(c) Rework part (b) for $S_2 = 5$ and $D_1 = 16$.
(d) Rework part (b) for $S_1 = 4$ and $D_2 = 6$.
(e) What is the smallest value of c_{44} that will allow the solution in part (a) to remain optimal?
(f) Give a range of values for c_{33} such that the solution in part (a) remains optimal. Do the same for c_{23}. Do the same for c_{34}.

49 *Fly-by-Night Airline*

(a) Solve the case given in exercise 28 of Chap. 2.
(b) What is the optimal value of the objective function and what are the revisions to the purchase plan in part (a) if one more gallon is required at Airport 1? At Airport 2? At Airport 3? At Airport 4? (*Continued on p. 184.*)

(c) What is the optimal value of the objective function and what are the revisions to the purchase plan in part (a) if one more gallon is offered by Oil Company 1? By Oil Company 2? By Oil Company 3?

(d) What is the optimal value of the objective function and what are the revisions to the purchase plan in part (a) if one more gallon is offered by Company 1 and required at Airport 1? At Airport 2? At Airport 3? At Airport 4?

50 *Hayes Manufacturing Company*

(a) Solve the case given in exercise 29 of Chap. 2.
(b) What is the value of an extra unit of capacity at each plant?
(c) What is the cost associated with an extra unit of demand by each wholesaler?
(d) Give a range for the direct cost of production at each plant such that the solution in part (a) remains optimal.

51 *Hugh Otto Bean Pitchers Company*

(a) Apply the transportation simplex algorithm to solve the case in exercise 36. Be sure to indicate the amount produced in each period and the level of inventory at the end of each period.

*(b) Did you obtain the same solution as you did in exercise 36, part (c). If not, do the two solutions have the same total cost?

52 *Sinbad Steamship Company.* Apply the transportation simplex method to solve the case in exercise 37, where

$$p_A = 1 \qquad p_B = 2 \qquad p_C = 4$$

$$q_A = 4 \qquad q_B = 2 \qquad q_C = 1.$$

Be sure to indicate an optimal routing for each ship.

53 *Sinbad Steamship Company.* Apply the transportation simplex method to solve the case in exercise 38. Be sure to indicate an optimal routing for each ship.

54 Consider the network in exercise 40, where $c_{ij} = c_{ji}$ and

$$c_{12} = 14 \qquad c_{13} = 4 \qquad c_{14} = 1 \qquad c_{15} = 6$$
$$c_{23} = 10 \qquad c_{24} = 13 \qquad c_{25} = 5$$
$$c_{34} = 3 \qquad c_{35} = 2$$
$$c_{45} = 8.$$

(a) Find an optimal solution by applying the transportation simplex method to the appropriate condensed transshipment table, like that in Fig. 6.5. Be sure to indicate an optimal routing and state whether it is unique.

(b) Answer part (a) using an expanded transshipment table, like that in Fig. 6.6.

(c) What is the smallest value for c_{45} such that the current solution remains optimal? For c_{24}? For c_{34}? For c_{35}?

55 *Raycov Discount Store Example.* Consider the network in Fig. 6.4. Assume that

$$c_{12} = 1 \qquad c_{23} = 7 \qquad c_{25} = 3 \qquad c_{43} = 1 \qquad c_{45} = 3 \qquad c_{47} = 4$$

$$c_{54} = 2 \qquad c_{56} = 5 \qquad c_{67} = 3 \qquad c_{78} = 1 .$$

(a) Apply the transportation simplex method to a condensed transshipment table, like that in Fig. 6.5. Be sure to indicate the implied optimal routing.

(b) Apply the transportation simplex method to an expanded transshipment table, like that in Fig. 6.6. Be sure to indicate the implied optimal routing.

(c) Does your solution change if the route from Store 6 to Store 7 is removed? If so, how?

(d) Suppose you add a route from Store 1 directly to Store 3. How small can the associated value c_{13} be such that the solution in part (a) remains optimal? Similarly, for a direct route from Store 2 to Store 7, what is the smallest possible value of c_{27}?

56 Rework exercise 55 using the supply and demand data given in exercise 7, part (a).

57 Rework exercise 55 using the supply and demand data given in exercise 7, part (b).

58 Rework exercise 55 using the supply and demand data given in exercise 7, part (c).

59 *Marcus Metal Company.* Consider the case in exercise 39, where

$$S_1 = 10 \qquad S_2 = 15 \qquad D_5 = 8 \qquad D_6 = 10 \qquad D_7 = 2$$

$$m_1 = 1 \qquad m_2 = 2 \qquad p_3 = 3 \qquad p_4 = 5$$

$$s_{13} = 1 \qquad s_{14} = 1 \qquad s_{23} = 6 \qquad s_{24} = 3$$

$$t_{35} = 1 \qquad t_{36} = 2 \qquad t_{37} = 3 \qquad t_{45} = 3 \qquad t_{46} = 2 \qquad t_{47} = 1.$$

(a) Find an optimal solution by applying the transportation simplex method to the appropriate condensed transshipment table, like that in Fig. 6.5. Be sure to indicate the optimal routing and flow of goods.

(b) Rework part (a) using an expanded transshipment table, like that in Fig. 6.6.

(c) What is the optimal value of the objective function and what are the revisions in the solution if $S_1 = 11$? If $S_1 = 9$? If $S_2 = 16$? If $S_2 = 14$? If $D_5 = 9$? If $D_6 = 11$? If $D_7 - 3$? If $S_1 = 11$ and $D_7 = 3$? If $S_2 = 16$ and $D_5 = 9$?

(d) How large can m_1 be such that the solution in part (a) remains optimal? Similarly, how large can m_2 be? Similarly, how large can p_3 be? Similarly, how large can p_4 be?

(e) Suppose it is possible to transship the product through any of the Locations 5, 6, and 7 to any other of these locations at the cost c_{kh}. How small can each value of c_{kh} be (where k and h equal 5, 6, and 7, and $k \neq h$), such that the solution in part (a) remains optimal?

60 Consider the network in exercise 41, where $c_{ij} = c_{ji}$ and

$$c_{12} = 15 \quad c_{14} = 8 \quad c_{16} = 55 \quad c_{23} = 28$$

$$c_{24} = 5 \quad c_{25} = 12 \quad c_{38} = 6 \quad c_{45} = 48$$

$$c_{46} = 48 \quad c_{57} = 20 \quad c_{58} = 7 \quad c_{67} = 12 \quad c_{78} = 10.$$

(a) Find an optimal solution by applying the transportation simplex method to the appropriate condensed transshipment table, like that in Fig. 6.5. Be sure to indicate the optimal routings.

(b) Rework part (a) using an expanded transshipment table, like that in Fig. 6.6.

(c) What is the smallest cost for the arc between Nodes 1 and 6 such that the solution in part (a) remains optimal? For the arc between Nodes 4 and 6?

(d) Suppose you add a direct route between Nodes 1 and 3. How small can the value be for $c_{13} = c_{31}$ such that the solution in part (a) remains optimal? Similarly, for a route between Nodes 4 and 7, what is the smallest possible value for $c_{47} = c_{74}$?

*61 Review the case of the Kleen City Police Department in exercise 31 of Chap. 2 and the general formulation in exercise 20 of Chap. 5.

(a) Show that when the number of periods, T, is an even number, the model is equivalent to a network problem. Display the network for the Kleen City case.

(b) Explain why the model is not equivalent to a network problem when the number of periods, T, is an odd number.

*62 *Bottleneck Production Line Assignment Problem.* Suppose each of n persons is to be assigned to performing one of n jobs on a single production line. Person i assigned to Job j can produce a_{ij} items per unit of time, where $a_{ij} \geq 0$. The problem is to assign the persons to maximize the *rate* of production for the *entire* line. The bottleneck is whatever person in the assignment produces at the slowest rate. Hence, the optimization problem is to pick an assignment that makes the bottleneck rate as large as possible.

(a) Verify that a solution to such a problem does not depend on the actual magnitudes of the a_{ij}, but only on their ordering (or ranking).

(b) Consider any feasible assignment and let $a*$ be the slowest rate for this assignment. Suppose that you solve a standard assignment problem in Sec. 6.4 with $c_{ij} = 0$ if $a_{ij} > a*$ and $c_{ij} = M$ otherwise, where M is arbitrarily large. Verify that any feasible solution with total cost equal to zero provides an improved bottleneck assignment. On the basis of this observation, suggest a complete algorithm for finding an optimal bottleneck assignment.

*(c) Given the validity of part (a), rank the a_{ij}, and calculate the associated amount $b_{ij} = 1 - 2^{-m}$, where m is the rank order of a_{ij}. For simplicity of exposition, assume all the a_{ij} are distinct. Thus, the largest a_{ij} yields a corresponding $b_{ij} = 1 - 2^{-1}$; the next largest a_{ij} yields a corresponding $b_{ij} = 1 - 2^{-2}$; and the smallest a_{ij} yields a corresponding $b_{ij} = 1 - 2^{-n^2}$.

Show that an optimal solution to the assignment problem using the b_{ij} also solves the bottleneck problem.

*63 Consider the classical transportation problem in Sec. 6.2. In each part below, further constraints are added. Suggest a way to reformulate the model to yield an enlarged transportation problem in standard format (like that in Fig. 6.2a).

(a) Each activity has a capacity restriction $x_{ij} \leq u_{ij}$.

(b) $\sum\limits_{i=1}^{2} \sum\limits_{j=1}^{n} x_{ij} \leq u.$

(c) $x_{11} + x_{12} + x_{13} \leq u$ where $n > 3$.

*64 Consider a capacitated transshipment problem where each $x_{ij} \leq u_{ij}$. Suggest a way to reformulate the model to yield an enlarged transportation problem in a standard format (like that in Fig. 6.2a).

*65 *Capacitated Transportation Problem.* Consider the model (7) through (10) in Sec. 6.2, and assume that each shipment variable is constrained by an upper bound, that is, each $x_{ij} \leq u_{ij}$, where u_{ij} is an integer. The steps of the simplex method in Sec. 6.6 are modified easily to handle such bounds as follow.

In *Step 3*, suppose flow on a nonbasic route is to be increased. Then to determine the largest amount of flow possible, take into consideration the capacity constraints on the new route and those current basic routes with *increased* flow. If any one of these bounds is reached *before* the flow on some other basic route becomes zero, then put the associated flow at its capacity level and let it be the variable left out of the basis in the next trial solution.

In *Step 2*, also consider each nonbasic route with flow at its capacity level. If the improvement potential is negative, then the route is a candidate for *reduced* flow. If it is selected, the procedure in *Step 3* is reversed to reflect a diminution of flow. A trial solution is optimal when every nonbasic route is at zero flow if it has a nonpositive improvement potential and at capacity flow if it has a positive improvement potential.

Solve each part below using this modification of the simplex algorithm.

(a) The problem in exercise 46 with $u_{ij} = 3$ for all i and j.
(b) The problem in exercise 47 with $u_{ij} = 3$ for all i and j.
(c) The problem in exercise 48 with $u_{ij} = 5$ for all i and j.

CONTENTS

CHAPTER 7

Shortest-Route and Other Network Models

7.1 TOPICS IN FOCUS

One of the simplest, yet very important, examples of a network optimization model is the problem of finding shortest routes. Sections 7.2 through 7.4 illustrate applications of the model and show how to compute the shortest routes. As you will see in the next few chapters, the shortest-route model is intimately related to dynamic and multistage models having deterministic linkage. Hence, it is critical that you understand the logic underlying the methods for determining optimal solutions as a step toward analyzing models in which dynamic elements play a central role.

The second part of this chapter deals with special cases of network optimization problems. The managerial applications treated are critical path scheduling and employment scheduling.

7.2 SHORTEST-ROUTE MODEL

The **shortest-route problem** can be explained simply: given a network in which each arc has an associated length, find a shortest path to a specified node from any of the other nodes. This problem actually encompasses a broad range of important operations research applications, including replacing equipment and scheduling complex projects. Because these specific illustrations are so diverse, it is helpful at the start to fix in mind the basic ideas of the model in general terms.

General description. Consider a network comprised of a set of **nodes,** certain pairs of which are connected by **directed** (that is, direction-oriented)

arcs. For example, look at the network in Fig. 7.1. Usually, one node is distinguished as the **terminal.** Then the problem is to find a shortest path to the terminal from at least one other designated point, and sometimes from every other point. The amount c_{ij} represents the length associated with traversing the arc that starts at Node i and ends at Node j.

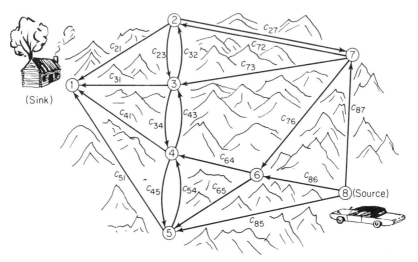

FIGURE 7.1. Example of Shortest-Route Model.

In applications of the model, the c_{ij} actually may be measured in units other than distance. To illustrate, c_{ij} may denote the cost of going from Node i to Node j. In that case, the problem is to find a **least-cost** path. Or c_{ij} may represent the time to travel between the nodes. Then the objective is to find a **minimum-duration** path.

Frequently in these applications, c_{ij} does not equal c_{ji}. Further, some nodes may not be connected directly, which can be indicated by letting the corresponding $c_{ij} = \infty$, and sometimes the so-called **triangle inequality** $c_{ij} \leq c_{ik} + c_{kj}$ does not hold for all possible i, j, and k.

A network like the one in Fig. 7.1 may contain paths that are **cycles.** This means that for two or more nodes it is possible to find a path leading out of a node and eventually back again. In Fig. 7.1, there are many cycles, one such being from Node 2 to Node 7 to Node 3 and back again to Node 2. If the total length of a path around a cycle is negative, then by repeatedly traversing this cycle, the objective function can be made arbitrarily small. Therefore, without imposing any further restrictions on the problem as stated, an unbounded solution can occur. Such a possibility will now be ruled out by assuming that *if a network contains cycles, the total length of every cycle path is nonnegative.* This condition is innocuous for the typical operations research application, where often all $c_{ij} \geq 0$.

From source to sink. Suppose the problem is to find a best path to the terminal from a single origin point. The model is easily shown to be *mathematically* equivalent to an assignment problem. To demonstrate this equivalence for the network in Fig. 7.1, designate Node 1 as the terminal and Node 8 as the origin. Then consider the ordinary transshipment problem in which a unit of stock is available at Node 8 (a source) and is required at Node 1 (a sink). All other nodes of the network are treated as transshipment points.

This view leads to the formulation in Fig. 7.2, which corresponds to an assignment model with the buffer stock $B = 1$. Notice that the shortest-route problem is a special case of the assignment model in which the objective coefficients $c_{kk} = 0$ appear in the so-called subdiagonal of the table.

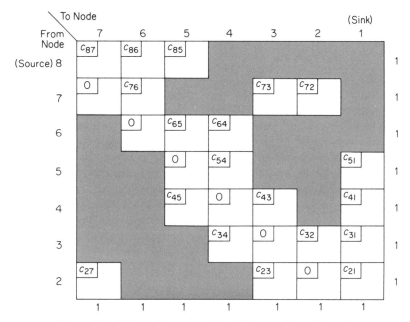

FIGURE 7.2. Tabular Representation of Shortest-Route Example.

A mathematical description of the shortest-route problem is

(1) $$\text{minimize} \sum_{\substack{(i, j) \text{ in} \\ \text{network}}} c_{ij} x_{ij}$$

subject to

(2) $$\sum_{\substack{(k, j) \text{ in} \\ \text{network}}} x_{kj} - \sum_{\substack{(i, k) \text{ in} \\ \text{network}}} x_{ik} = \begin{cases} 1 & \text{for } k = s \quad \text{(source)} \\ 0 & \text{for all other } k \\ -1 & \text{for } k = r \quad \text{(sink)} \end{cases}$$

(3) $$x_{ij} \geq 0 \quad \text{for all } (i, j) \text{ in network.}$$

In the linear programming technology table corresponding to (1), (2), and (3) for the example in Fig. 7.1, there will be one equation for each node and one variable for each arc. To illustrate, for $k = s = 8$, (2) indicates

(4) $$x_{85} + x_{86} + x_{87} = 1 \quad \text{(Source Node 8)}$$

and for $k = 7$, (2) states

(5) $$x_{72} + x_{73} + x_{76} - x_{27} - x_{87} = 0 \quad \text{(Node 7)}.$$

It is much easier to solve a shortest-route problem than to solve a general assignment model.

There are countless seemingly different applications of the shortest-route problem. Remember the one in the Raycov Discount Store Problem in Sec. 6.3? There you learned that the transshipment model can be approached by finding first a least-cost route from each node having available stock to every node requiring additional stock, and then an optimal solution to a standard transportation model using these minimum-cost paths. Here is another application.

Equipment replacement. The Rhode-Bloch Trucking Company is preparing a leasing plan for transportation equipment extending over five years. The company can meet its requirements by leasing a new piece of equipment at the *beginning* of Year 1 and keeping it until the *beginning* of Year $j \leq 6$. If $j < 6$, then the company replaces the equipment at the beginning of Year j and keeps it until the beginning of Year k (≤ 6), etc. The cost figure c_{ij} (for $1 \leq i < j \leq 6$) embodies the rental fee plus the expected running and maintenance costs of equipment leased at the start of Year i and replaced at the start of Year j. The network for the problem is shown in Fig. 7.3. In this characterization, a unit of stock is made available at Node 1 and routed to Node 6. Each transshipment node appearing in an optimal solution indicates the year a replacement is to occur.

Notice that there are no cycles in the network in Fig. 7.3; consequently it is called **acyclic.**

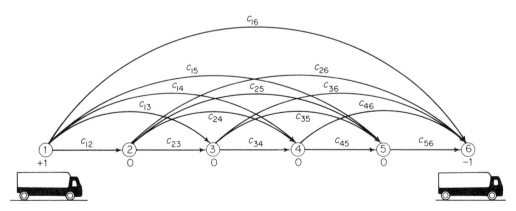

FIGURE 7.3. Rhode-Bloch Trucking Company Equipment Replacement Network.

7.3 SHORTEST-ROUTE ALGORITHM
IN A GENERAL NETWORK

In Sec. 7.2 you saw examples of optimization models that proved equivalent to finding a shortest route in a network. Here you will study a method of solution which, like the simplex algorithm, relies heavily on duality.

Suppose that a network contains several routes from the Source Node s to the Sink Node r, and suppose that you want to obtain a shortest one. For example, in Fig. 7.4, suppose that you want to find the shortest route from Source Node 5

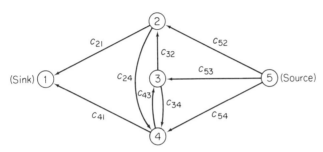

FIGURE 7.4. Shortest-Route Illustration.

to the Sink Node 1. As you learned in Sec. 7.2, you can view the problem as a linear programming model, where the technology table for the example is given in Fig. 7.5. Let y_k be the dual variable associated with Node k, so that the dual problem corresponding to the model in Fig. 7.5 is

(1)   maximize $-y_1 + y_5$

subject to

$$y_5 - y_4 \leq c_{54} \qquad y_5 - y_3 \leq c_{53} \qquad y_5 - y_2 \leq c_{52}$$

(2) $$y_4 - y_3 \leq c_{43} \qquad y_4 - y_1 \leq c_{41} \qquad y_3 - y_4 \leq c_{34}$$

$$y_3 - y_2 \leq c_{32} \qquad y_2 - y_4 \leq c_{24} \qquad y_2 - y_1 \leq c_{21},$$

(3)   each y_k unrestricted in sign.

The justification for (3) is that the linear restrictions in the primal model of Fig. 7.5 are all equalities. Observe in (2) that there is a restriction for each arc in the network.

In general, then, given that you wish to find a shortest route in a network

Shipping Activities

	x_{54}	x_{53}	x_{52}	x_{43}	x_{41}	x_{34}	x_{32}	x_{24}	x_{21}	
5	1	1	1							= 1
4	-1			1	1	-1		-1		= 0
3		-1		-1		1	1			= 0
2			-1				-1	1	1	= 0
1					-1				-1	= -1
	c_{54}	c_{53}	c_{52}	c_{43}	c_{41}	c_{34}	c_{32}	c_{24}	c_{21}	Minimize

(Leftmost label: Nodes:)

FIGURE 7.5. Technology Table for Shortest-Route Illustration.

starting at Source Node s and terminating at Sink Node r, the associated dual linear programming problem is

$$(4) \qquad \text{maximize} \quad -y_r + y_s$$

subject to

$$(5) \qquad y_i - y_j \le c_{ij} \quad \text{for all } (i, j) \text{ in network,}$$

where each y_k is unrestricted in sign.

Method. The algorithm proceeds to solve for the dual variables:

(i) Start by letting $y_r = 0$, and all other $y_k = \infty$.
(ii) If there continues to be any arc (i, j) such that $y_i > c_{ij} + y_j$, then change the corresponding value of y_i to $c_{ij} + y_j$. Otherwise stop.

Thus the values of y_k are successively decreased until (5) holds for *all* arcs. The technique will converge in a finite number of calculations, provided that the sum of c_{ij} around every loop of the network is nonnegative. [The speed of convergence can be accelerated by using a systematic approach in applying Instruction (ii), as is explained in the advanced material below.]

The method actually obtains a shortest route to the Terminal Node r from every other node. Specifically, to find the path for *any* Node s, determine the arc (s, t) for which $y_s - y_t = c_{st}$. The algorithm guarantees there is at least one such arc. Similarly, at Node t find the arc (t, u) such that $y_t - y_u = c_{tu}$. Continue in the same fashion to trace a route that eventually leads to Node r. Notice that the value of y_k is the length of a shortest route from Node k to Node r. Although each y_k is unique, there can be more than one shortest path from Node k.

Example. The technique is illustrated for the example in Fig. 7.6, which is the same network structure as Fig. 7.1. You seek the shortest paths to Node 1 from every other node. The procedure is best followed by making the calculations directly on the network diagram. Copy Fig. 7.6 on a piece of paper, or write lightly with pencil on the page.

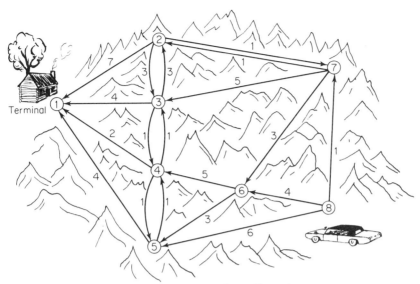

FIGURE 7.6. Shortest-Route Example.

Start by putting a 0 adjacent to Node 1 and the symbol ∞ next to all the other nodes. There are many ways to proceed—here is one:

$$
\begin{aligned}
c_{41} + y_1 = 2 + 0 &< \infty = y_4, & \text{therefore let } y_4 = 2 \\
c_{34} + y_4 = 1 + 2 &< \infty = y_3, & \text{therefore let } y_3 = 3 \\
c_{64} + y_4 = 5 + 2 &< \infty = y_6, & \text{therefore let } y_6 = 7 \\
c_{54} + y_4 = 1 + 2 &< \infty = y_5, & \text{therefore let } y_5 = 3 \\
c_{65} + y_5 = 3 + 3 &< 7 = y_6, & \text{therefore let } y_6 = 6 \\
c_{85} + y_5 = 6 + 3 &< \infty = y_8, & \text{therefore let } y_8 = 9 \\
c_{23} + y_3 = 3 + 3 &< \infty = y_2, & \text{therefore let } y_2 = 6 \\
c_{73} + y_3 = 5 + 3 &< \infty = y_7, & \text{therefore let } y_7 = 8 \\
c_{72} + y_2 = 1 + 6 &< 8 = y_7, & \text{therefore let } y_7 = 7 \\
c_{87} + y_7 = 1 + 7 &< 9 = y_8, & \text{therefore let } y_8 = 8.
\end{aligned}
$$

(6)

As soon as the new value is calculated in (6) for each y_k, be sure to put it next to Node k in your diagram. At this point

(7)
$$
\begin{aligned}
y_1 = 0 \quad y_2 = 6 \quad y_3 = 3 \quad y_4 = 2 \\
y_5 = 3 \quad y_6 = 6 \quad y_7 = 7 \quad y_8 = 8.
\end{aligned}
$$

The values in (7) now satisfy (5) for *all* the arcs in the figure, so the calculations terminate.

In Fig. 7.7, the values for y_k appear next to each node, and the arcs in the short-est paths have been drawn with heavier lines. The value of $y_8 = 8$ represents the length of the shortest route from Node 8 to Node 1. The route consists of Node 8 to Node 7 to Node 2 to Node 3 to Node 4 to Node 1; as a check, observe that the length of this route is $[8 = c_{87} + c_{72} + c_{23} + c_{34} + c_{41}]$. If the shortest-route problem were posed as a linear programming model, analogous to that in

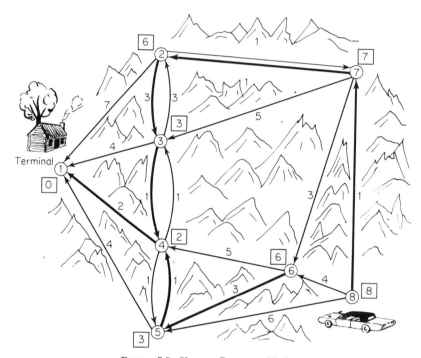

FIGURE 7.7. Shortest Routes to Node 1.

Fig. 7.5, then the associated feasible solution would be $x_{87} = x_{72} = x_{23} = x_{34} = x_{41} = 1$ and all other $x_{ij} = 0$; the primal objective-function value would equal 8. Since you have found values for the y_k in (7) that are feasible in the corresponding dual problem, and the dual objective-function value also is 8 $(= -y_1 + y_8)$, the routing must be optimal according to the Dual Theorem.

▶A succinct mathematical statement of the conditions the y_i must satisfy is

(i) $$y_i = \underset{\substack{(i, j) \text{ in} \\ \text{network}}}{\text{minimum}} (c_{ij} + y_j) \quad \text{for all } i \neq r,$$

where $y_r \equiv 0$.

As the text remarked, if you are inauspicious in your application of Instruction (ii) of the algorithm, you may have to perform many more calculations than necessary. An efficient approach for the case of all $c_{ij} \geq 0$ is the following: Assume the network contains p nodes. Begin with Instruction (i), and then apply Instruction (ii) to all arcs (i, r) in the network. Call the resultant value for each y_k ($k \neq r$) the tentative label for Node k. Determine the smallest value of the $p - 1$ tentative labels, and designate that value permanent. Suppose it is y_t for Node t. Then y_t will equal the length of the shortest path from Node t to Node r. (If several nodes tie for the smallest value, designate as permanent the value for the smallest numbered node among the ties.) Next, apply Instruction (ii) to all arcs (i, t) in the network ($i \neq r$), once more possibly yielding some revised tentative labels. Determine the smallest value of the remaining $p - 2$ tentative labels, and designate that value as permanent. Suppose it is y_q for Node q, selecting among ties as before. Continue in the same fashion, this time applying Instruction (ii) to all arcs (i, q), provided that Node i does not have a permanent label. Thus after each application of Instruction (ii), you find another node with its shortest distance to Node r. After $p - 1$ applications, you will have found *all* the permanent values for the y_k. If you seek a particular y_s, you may find its permanent value in less than $p - 1$ applications of the steps. In the example of Fig. 7.6, the permanent values of the y_k are found in the sequence $y_1 = 0, y_4 = 2, y_3 = 3, y_5 = 3, y_2 = 6, y_6 = 6, y_7 = 7$, and $y_8 = 8$.

Sometimes you may want to calculate the shortest routes between *every* pair of nodes. The following approach is an efficient way of doing so. Define

(ii) $$c_{ij} = \begin{cases} \text{length of arc } (i, j) \text{ if } (i, j) \text{ is in network,} \\ \infty \text{ if } (i, j) \text{ is not in network and } i \neq j, \\ 0 \text{ if } i = j. \end{cases}$$

Consider the network comprised of only Nodes $1, 2, \ldots, q - 1$ ($< p$) and for this abbreviated network, let

(iii) $$d_{ij} = \begin{pmatrix} \text{shortest distance between Nodes i and j, when} \\ \text{only Nodes } 1, 2, \ldots, q - 1 \text{ are in the network} \end{pmatrix}.$$

Similarly, let

(iv) $$d_{ij}^* = \begin{pmatrix} \text{shortest distance between Nodes i and j, when} \\ \text{Nodes } 1, 2, \ldots, q \text{ are in the network} \end{pmatrix}.$$

Then

(v) $$d_{qj}^* = \underset{k=1,2,\ldots,q-1}{\text{minimum}} (c_{qk} + d_{kj}) \quad \text{for } j = 1, 2, \ldots, q - 1$$

(vi) $$d_{iq}^* = \underset{k=1,2,\ldots,q-1}{\text{minimum}} (d_{ik} + c_{kq}) \quad \text{for } i = 1, 2, \ldots, q - 1$$

(vii) $$d_{qq}^* = 0$$

(viii) $$d_{ij}^* = \text{minimum} (d_{ij}, d_{iq}^* + d_{qj}^*) \quad \text{for } i, j = 1, 2, \ldots, q - 1.$$

Therefore, starting with $q = 2$, and proceeding to successively larger values of q up to $q = p$, you apply, in turn, (v) through (viii). (For $q = 2$, $d_{ij}^* = c_{ij}$, for $i, j, = 1, 2$.) The algorithm involves a total of $p(p - 1)(p - 2)$ additions.   ◀

7.4 SHORTEST-ROUTE ALGORITHM
IN AN ACYCLIC NETWORK

The shortest-route algorithm can be made even simpler when the network is acyclic, for then the dual variables y_k can be determined recursively, that is, sequentially.

As a preliminary step, number the nodes from 1 to p such that if the network contains an arc (i, j), then $i > j$. To do this, designate the sink or terminal as Node 1, which has only inward-pointing arcs. Check off this node *and* all its arcs, and consider these arcs no further in the labeling process. Look for *any* other node that has *only inward*-pointing arcs. Designate it as Node 2. Check off this node *and* all its arcs, and consider these arcs no further in the labeling process. Continue in the same manner until all nodes have been numbered. The y_i will be determined in the same order as the nodes are numbered.

The algorithm is

(1) $$y_1 = 0 \qquad\qquad\qquad \text{(terminal)}$$

(2) $$y_i = \underset{\substack{(i, j) \text{ in} \\ \text{network}}}{\text{minimum}} (c_{ij} + y_j) \quad \text{for } i = 2, 3, \ldots, p.$$

To see how the recursion (2) works, consider the network in Fig. 7.8, where the c_{ij} are indicated next to each arc. The algorithm proceeds as follows:

(3)
$$y_1 = 0$$
$$y_2 = \text{minimum } (c_{21} + y_1) = (1 + 0) = 1$$
$$y_3 = \text{minimum } (c_{31} + y_1, c_{32} + y_2) = \text{minimum } (4 + 0, 1 + 1) = 2$$
$$y_4 = \text{minimum } (c_{41} + y_1, c_{43} + y_3) = \text{minimum } (4 + 0, 1 + 2) = 3$$
$$y_5 = \text{minimum } (c_{51} + y_1, c_{54} + y_4) = \text{minimum } (6 + 0, 2 + 3) = 5$$
$$y_6 = \text{minimum } (c_{64} + y_4, c_{65} + y_5) = \text{minimum } (3 + 3, 2 + 5) = 6$$
$$y_7 = \text{minimum } (c_{72} + y_2, c_{73} + y_3, c_{76} + y_6)$$
$$\quad = \text{minimum } (8 + 1, 6 + 2, 1 + 6) = 7$$
$$y_8 = \text{minimum } (c_{85} + y_5, c_{86} + y_6, c_{87} + y_7)$$
$$\quad = \text{minimum } (6 + 5, 4 + 6, 1 + 7) = 8.$$

As in the preceding section, the calculations may be done on the diagram itself. The routes are determined as before, and the solution here is shown in Fig. 7.9.

In an *acyclic* network, you can find the longest route as easily. Simply substitute "maximum" for "minimum" in (2). You will find this observation helpful in the dynamic programming chapters in which some models deal with maximum profit, rather than minimum cost, optimal solutions.

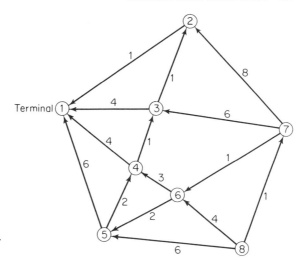

FIGURE 7.8. Acyclic Network Example.

*7.5 CRITICAL PATH SCHEDULING

This version of the **longest-path problem** is frequently applied to schedule major projects, such as the construction of a multistory office building, a maintenance overhaul of large-scale equipment, a research and development program for a new weapon system, and the market introduction of a new product. Critical path scheduling is also designated by a variety of acronyms and other names, such as CPS, CPM, and PERT. The approach has been developed to such an extent that adequate coverage of all its nuances would require an entire chapter and take you too far afield from the topic of the present chapter. However, you will find it instructive to see how the longest-route model can be applied to this sort of scheduling. The description to follow contains a number of simplifications, but the structural essentials are retained.

The Swift Building Company Example. This firm must complete a construction project comprised of n tasks. Management has estimated the time

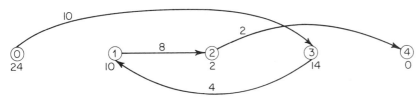

FIGURE 7.9. Shortest Routes in Acyclic Network.

needed for completing each task, and has established a precedence-ordering among the tasks to indicate which must be finished before each particular task can commence. As you will see in the illustration below, it is necessary to specify only the jobs that *immediately* precede a task to determine such an ordering. The company wants to calculate the earliest possible completion date for the entire project.

Suppose the project consists of five jobs, A, B, C, D, and E. It is convenient terminology to add a fictitious Job F that is to start when the entire project is finished. The precedence-ordering among the tasks is exhibited in Fig. 7.10 along with the completion times for each task. Thus Job C cannot start until Job A is finished, and Job E cannot begin until *both* Jobs B and D are finished. The entire project is finished as soon as both Jobs C and E have ended.

To formulate the corresponding mathematical optimization model, let the variables represent the starting time for each of the projects. Introduce *only* those variables essential to the analysis. Note that Jobs A and B can be considered as beginning at time 0, because they have no predecessors. Similarly Job C can be considered as starting at the same time as Job D, since both have the same immediate predecessor, namely Job A. Therefore, you need to include only the variables

$$y_{CD} = \text{starting time of Jobs C and D}$$
$$y_E = \text{starting time of Job E}$$
$$y_F = \text{starting time of Job F.}$$

Recall that y_F in fact is the time at which the entire project is finished.

The appropriate linear programming model is

(1) $$\text{minimize} \quad y_F$$

subject to

(2) $$y_{CD} \geq t_A$$

(3) $$y_E \geq t_B$$

(4) $$y_E \geq t_D + y_{CD}$$

(5) $$y_F \geq t_C + y_{CD}$$

(6) $$y_F \geq t_E + y_E.$$

Relations (2) through (6) are mathematical translations of the precedence relations in Fig. 7.10, and use the completion times given there. To illustrate, (3) and (4) require that Job E does not start until both Jobs B and D are completed. The completion time of Job B is merely t_B, and of Job D is its own starting time plus completion time. Notice restrictions (2) through (6) make is *unnecessary* to impose an *explicit* constraint that the variables be nonnegative. Consequently, from a formal point of view, the variables are unconstrained in sign.

The technology of the model is summarized in Fig. 7.11. At first glance it does not seem to have a network structure, but further study reveals that its dual comes

Job	Immediate Predecessors	Completion Time
A	--	t_A
B	--	t_B
C	A	t_C
D	A	t_D
E	B,D	t_E
"F"	C,E	--

FIGURE 7.10. Swift Building Company Example: Precedence Ordering.

y_{CD}	y_E	y_F	
1			$\geq t_A$
	1		$\geq t_B$
-1	1		$\geq t_D$
-1		1	$\geq t_C$
	-1	1	$\geq t_E$
		1	Minimize

FIGURE 7.11. Critical Path Tableau of Swift Building Company.

close to the desired format. With the few simple manipulations, given in the special material below, you can show the dual is a longest-path problem. The longest route itself is termed the **critical path,** since if the completion time of any job on this route increases, the finish date is delayed accordingly. (A critical path is not necessarily unique.)

In actual applications of critical path scheduling, which often encompass several hundred jobs, the analyst uses information such as that given in Fig. 7.10 and immediately draws a corresponding network. However, the algorithm that finds the longest path in the constructed acyclic network really solves the problem expressed in terms comparable to (1) through (6).

More sophisticated versions of critical path scheduling treat the job completion times as variables subject to a constrained optimization. In such cases, the analysis determines the tradeoff possibilities for reducing total project duration by increasing expedite costs.

▶ Take the three dual relations implied by Fig. 7.11 and sum them to form a redundant fourth equation. Recall that the dual relations are equalities, since the three variables in Fig. 7.11 are unconstrained in sign. Second, take each of the same three relations and multiply both sides by (-1) to change the signs of the coefficients.

The resultant model is shown in Fig. 7.12, with the redundant equation appearing in

x_{01}	x_{02}	x_{12}	x_{13}	x_{23}	
1	1				= 1
-1		1	1		= 0
	-1	-1		1	= 0
			-1	-1	= -1
t_A	t_B	t_D	t_C	t_E	Maximize

FIGURE 7.12. Swift Building Company: Tableau of Dual Problem.

Restriction: $x_{ij} \geq 0$

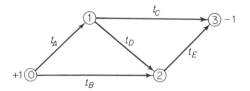

FIGURE 7.13. Swift Building Company: Network of Dual Problem.

the top row. The associated network is drawn in Fig. 7.13. The problem is to find the longest route in an acyclic network; the problem is structurally equivalent to a shortest-path model.   ◀

*7.6 EMPLOYMENT SCHEDULING

The next application of network analysis demonstrates how it is sometimes necessary to manipulate the original formulation of a model in order to discover that the problem has a network equivalent.

The Spitzen-Pollish Company is a contract maintenance firm that provides and supervises semiskilled workers for major overhauls of chemical processing equipment. A standard job frequently requires a thousand or more workers and may extend from one or two weeks to a few months. Since the client's plant often is not located in a major metropolitan area, the maintenance company may have to transport the workers for several hundred miles. The firm's operating expenses include the costs of transportation, food, and on-site housing, as well as the workers' wages.

For a routine assignment, the firm can estimate fairly accurately the number of crews required on a day-to-day basis for the duration of the job. The daily requirements fluctuate enough to impel the company to vary the number of crews on site during the overhaul period, in an effort to keep operating costs at a minimum. However, there are costs that do not depend on how long a crew remains on site: costs associated with recruiting, transporting, and then briefing a new crew. The firm sometimes finds it economical, therefore, to retain crews in excess of requirements if the workers will be needed a few days later. Thus for each contract, the firm seeks a work force schedule that minimizes total labor expenses.

To construct the mathematical model that produces an optimal schedule, assume that the overhaul begins at the start of Period 1 and ends at the *start* of Period n. Let

$$x_{ij} = \text{number of crews beginning work at the start of Period i and}$$
$$\text{terminating at the start of Period j (for } 1 \le i < j \le n),$$

and let $c_{ij} \ge 0$ be the associated total operating cost of such a crew. Assume c_{ij} increases if the interval of employment increases; that is;

(1) $$c_{ij} \le c_{hk} \quad \text{for } h \le i < j \le k.$$

Finally, let R_k be the number of crews actually needed during Period k, for $k = 1, 2, \ldots, n - 1$.

Then the constraints of the problem are

(2) $$\sum_{j=2}^{n} x_{1j} = R_1$$

(3) $$\sum_{i=1}^{k} \sum_{j=k+1}^{n} x_{ij} \geq R_k \quad \text{for } k = 2, 3, \ldots, n-2$$

(4) $$\sum_{i=1}^{n-1} x_{in} = R_{n-1}$$

(5) $$\text{every } x_{ij} = 0, 1, 2, \ldots,$$

and the objective function is

(6) $$\text{minimize} \sum_{i=1}^{n-1} \sum_{j=i+1}^{n} c_{ij} x_{ij}.$$

Relation (2) states that the total number of crews starting work in Period 1 equals that period's requirements. Because of (1), it is not economical to have excess crews at the start. By the same token, relation (4) specifies that there are no excess crews in the final work period, $(n-1)$. At intermediate periods, Spitzen-Pollish may find it desirable to have more crews on site than are essential, which is permitted by the inequality in (3).

The model is displayed in its entirety in Fig. 7.14, where $n = 6$. Nonnegative surplus variables s_k, $k = 2, 3, 4$, have been added to convert (3) to equalities.

x_{12} x_{13} x_{14} x_{15} x_{16}	x_{23} x_{24} x_{25} x_{26}	x_{34} x_{35} x_{36}	x_{45} x_{46}	x_{56}	s_2 s_3 s_4		Row
1 1 1 1 1						$= R_1$	1
1 1 1 1	1 1 1 1				-1	$= R_2$	2
1 1 1	1 1 1	1 1 1			-1	$= R_3$	3
1 1	1 1	1 1	1 1		-1	$= R_4$	4
1	1	1	1	1		$= R_5$	5
c_{12} c_{13} c_{14} c_{15} c_{16}	c_{23} c_{24} c_{25} c_{26}	c_{34} c_{35} c_{36}	c_{45} c_{46}	c_{56}	0 0 0	Minimize	

FIGURE 7.14. Spitzen-Pollish Company Employment-Scheduling Model.

Any connection between the technology in Fig. 7.14 and that of a network model is not obvious; but educated intuition suggests that further insight might be developed by transforming the technology into another equivalent format. The triangular appearance of the coefficients in successive sets of columns provides the clue for the transformations on the rows of Fig. 7.14.

Take Row 4 and subtract it from Row 5. Similarly, subtract Row 3 from Row 4, Row 2 from Row 3, and Row 1 from Row 2. The results are shown in Rows 5', 4', 3', and 2' of Fig.7.15. Then multiply Row 5 by (-1), thereby changing the

x_{12}	x_{13}	x_{14}	x_{15}	x_{16}	x_{23}	x_{24}	x_{25}	x_{26}	x_{34}	x_{35}	x_{36}	x_{45}	x_{46}	x_{56}	s_2	s_3	s_4		Row
1	1	1	1	1														$= R_1$	$1' = 1$
-1					1	1	1	1							-1			$= R_2 - R_1$	$2' = 2 - 1$
	-1				-1				1	1	1				1	-1		$= R_3 - R_2$	$3' = 3 - 2$
		-1				-1			-1			1	1			1	-1	$= R_4 - R_3$	$4' = 4 - 3$
			-1				-1			-1		-1		1			1	$= R_5 - R_4$	$5' = 5 - 4$
				-1				-1			-1		-1	-1				$= -R_5$	$6' = -5$
c_{12}	c_{13}	c_{14}	c_{15}	c_{16}	c_{23}	c_{24}	c_{25}	c_{26}	c_{34}	c_{35}	c_{36}	c_{45}	c_{46}	c_{56}	0	0	0		Minimize

FIGURE 7.15. Spitzen-Pollish Equivalent Network Formulation.

signs of the coefficients on the right-hand side, and add this redundant relation as Row 6' in Fig. 7.15.

Now the problem has the form of a transshipment model. As a consequence, the integrality stipulation in (5) causes no added difficulty in finding a solution. The network for the model is given in Fig. 7.16, where Node 1 is the source and Node 6

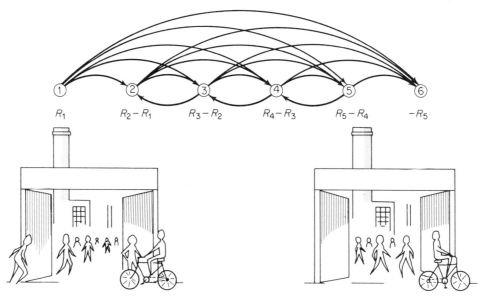

FIGURE 7.16. Network Representation of Spitzen-Pollish Employment-Scheduling Model.

is the sink. The other nodes are transshipment points. The corresponding trans-shipment array appears in Fig. 7.17. The buffer stock quantity can be set at

$$(7) \qquad B = .5 \left[R_1 + \sum_{k=2}^{5} |R_k - R_{k-1}| + R_5 \right].$$

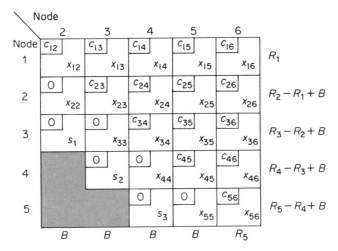

FIGURE 7.17. Tabular Form of Spitzen-Pollish Employment-Scheduling Model.

Notice that without any further assumptions about the R_k, the model is *not* a shortest-route problem, and the activities s_k appear below the subdiagonal of the transportation table in Fig. 7.17. However, if $R_k = 1$, for $k = 1, 2, \ldots, 5$, then you can eliminate the s_k because no cost would be saved in routing a unit from Node j to Node k if $k < j$. Furthermore, $B = 1$ in (7). Thus, in this case, the model does simplify to a shortest-route problem in an acyclic network. What is more, the network is identical to that for the equipment replacement problem considered in Sec. 7.2 and illustrated by the network diagram in Fig. 7.3.

REVIEW EXERCISES

1 (a) Display the technology table corresponding to (1), (2), and (3) in Sec. 7.2 for the shortest-route example in Fig. 7.1.

  (b) Assume every $c_{ij} \geq 0$. Verify that the constraints in (2) can just as well be written as "greater-than-or-equal" inequalities. Then display the associated dual maximization problem.

2 Consider the shortest-route example in Fig. 7.1. Add arcs from Node 4 to Node 7 and from Node 6 to Nodes 3 and 7; delete arcs from Node 4 to Node 3, from Node 6 to Node 5, and from Node 7 to Node 2.

  (a) Draw the revised network, and construct the corresponding tabular representation like that in Fig. 7.2.

  (b) For part (a), display the technology table corresponding to (1), (2), and (3) in Sec. 7.2. (*Continued on p. 206.*)

*(c) Assume every $c_{ij} \geq 0$. Verify that the constraints in (2) can just as well be written as "greater-than-or-equal" inequalities. Then display the associated dual maximization problem.

3 Consider the shortest-route example in Fig. 7.1. Add arcs from Node 1 to Nodes 3 and 4, and from Nodes 5 and 6 to Node 8.

   (a) Construct a tabular representation like that in Fig. 7.2 where the sink is Node 2 and the source is Node 7.
   (b) For part (a), display the technology table corresponding to (1), (2), and (3) in Sec. 7.2.
   *(c) Assume every $c_{ij} \geq 0$. Verify that the constraints in (2) can just as well be written as "greater-than-or-equal" inequalities. Then display the associated dual maximization problem.

4 *Equipment Replacement.* Consider the example of the Rhode-Bloch Trucking Company, displayed in Fig. 7.3.

   (a) Show a routing through the network corresponding to replacing equipment in Years 3 and 5. In Years 2 and 5. In Years 3 and 4. In Year 3 only. In Year 4 only. Indicate the corresponding costs incurred over the horizon.
   (b) Construct a tabular representation of the problem like that in Fig. 7.2.
   (c) Describe a technology table corresponding to (1), (2), and (3) in Sec. 7.2.
   (d) Suppose that the cost of running and maintaining the equipment for one, two, three, four, and five consecutive periods is 1, 3, 6, 10, and 15, respectively. Suppose that if a rental at the start of Period 1 extends over one, two, three, four, or five consecutive periods, the rental cost is 5, 9, 13, 16, or 19, respectively. These rental costs increase by one each period; for example, if a rental at the start of Period 3 extends over one, two, or three consecutive periods, the costs are 7, 11, or 15, respectively. Calculate each c_{ij} from these data.
   (e) Assume every $c_{ij} \geq 0$. Verify that the constraints in (2) can just as well be written as "greater-than-or-equal" inequalities. Then display the associated dual maximization problem.

5 *Equipment Replacement.* Consider the example of the Rhode-Bloch Trucking Company, displayed in Fig. 7.3. Revise the network for the case where $n = 8$, and each piece of equipment must be kept at least three years.

6 Consider the network in Fig. 7.6. Delete the arcs from Node 4 to Node 3, from Node 6 to Node 5, and from Node 7 to Node 2. Add arcs corresponding to $c_{47} = 1$, $c_{63} = 3$, and $c_{67} = 1$.

   (a) Apply the algorithm in Sec. 7.3 to find the shortest routes to Node 1 from every other node, and indicate their corresponding lengths.
   (b) How small can c_{64} be such that your answer in part (a) remains optimal?
   (c) How large can c_{34} be such that your answer in part (a) remains optimal?
   (d) How large can c_{41} be such that your answer in part (a) remains optimal?

7 Consider the network in Fig. 7.6. Delete the arc from Node 5 to Node 4. Add arcs corresponding to $c_{13} = 1$, $c_{14} = 2$, $c_{56} = 3$, and let $c_{72} = 4$.

   (a) Apply the algorithm in Sec. 7.3 to find the shortest routes to Node 2 from every other node, and indicate their corresponding lengths. If there are several optimal solutions, indicate the alternatives.

   (b) Suppose you add an arc from Node 8 to Node 3. What is the smallest value of c_{83} that will allow your answer in part (a) to remain optimal?

   (c) Suppose you add an arc from Node 8 to Node 1. What is the smallest value of c_{81} that will allow your answer in part (a) to remain optimal?

   (d) Suppose you add an arc from Node 5 to Node 2. What is the smallest value of c_{52} that will allow your answer in part (a) to remain optimal?

8 Carry out the node-numbering process given at the beginning of Sec. 7.4 to verify that the labels for the network shown in Fig. 7.8 have been correctly assigned.

9 Consider the network in Fig. 7.8. Delete arcs c_{32} and c_{76}. Add an arc corresponding to $c_{74} = 5$.

   (a) Apply the algorithm in Sec. 7.4 to find the shortest routes, and their respective lengths, from each node to Node 1. If there are several optimal solutions, indicate the alternatives.

   (b) What is the smallest value of c_{86} that will allow your answer in part (a) to remain optimal?

   (c) Suppose you add an arc from Node 8 to Node 3. What is the smallest value of c_{83} that will allow your answer in part (a) to remain optimal?

   (d) Suppose you add an arc from Node 8 to Node 2. What is the smallest value of c_{82} that will allow your answer in part (a) to remain optimal?

*10 *Critical Path Scheduling.* Consider the case of the Swift Building Company, as shown in Fig. 7.10. Suppose the immediate predecessors for Job C are Jobs A and D; for Job D is Job B, instead of Job A; and for Job E is only Job B.

   (a) Reformulate the linear programming model appropriate to the new restrictions.

   (b) Display the corresponding critical path tableau, as in Fig. 7.11.

   *(c) Display the corresponding dual problem, as in Fig. 7.12, and construct the associated network, as in Fig. 7.13.

*11 *Critical Path Scheduling.* A network representation for the Swift Building Company case is shown in Fig. 7.10. An alternative network representation can be constructed as follows. Let Node S represent the starting point; all arcs out of Node S have 0 length. Let Node T represent the terminating point. In addition, there is a node for each job. There is an arc from Node i to Node j if Job i is an immediate predecessor of Job j; the length of the arc is t_i, the time to complete Job i. Any jobs that can start immediately have S as an immediate predecessor. Any job not followed by other jobs has an arc into Node T. Node T serves the same purpose as Job F in Fig. 7.10, and so Job F can be replaced by T.

   (a) Draw this alternative network for the case in Fig. 7.10.   (*Continued on p. 208.*)

(b) Compare Fig. 7.10 with the above network representation.

(c) Draw the network for the case in exercise 10.

*12 *Employment Scheduling.* Consider the case of the Spitzen-Pollish Company discussed in Sec. 7.6. Let $n = 8$, and assume that a crew must be kept for at least two periods.

(a) Display the technology as in Figs. 7.14 and 7.15.

(b) Draw the associated network as in Fig. 7.16.

(c) Construct the associated tabular form as in Fig. 7.17.

*13 *Employment Scheduling.* Consider the case of the Spitzen-Pollish Company discussed in Sec. 7.6. Let $n = 9$, and assume that a crew must be kept for at least one period but not longer than four periods. Answer the questions in exercise 12.

*14 *Employment Scheduling.* Suppose $n = 6$ in the model of Sec. 7.6. Let the wage cost per crew in Period k be designated as w_k, where

$$w_1 = 100 \qquad w_2 = 150 \qquad w_3 = 180 \qquad w_4 = 200 \qquad w_5 = 120.$$

A crew hired to start in Period k incurs the hiring cost g_k, where

$$g_1 = 1 \qquad g_2 = 2 \qquad g_3 = 3 \qquad g_4 = 2 \qquad g_5 = 1.$$

A crew released at the end of Period k incurs the severence cost f_k, where

$$f_1 = .3 \qquad f_2 = .5 \qquad f_3 = .7 \qquad f_4 = .4 \qquad f_5 = .1.$$

If a crew works t consecutive periods, the resultant transportation, housing, recreation, and related expenses are h_t, where

$$h_1 = 12 \qquad h_2 = 13 \qquad h_3 = 14 \qquad h_4 = 18 \qquad h_5 = 25.$$

Calculate the appropriate values for all the objective-function coefficients c_{ij}.

15 Explain your understanding of the following terms:

shortest-route problem
node
directed arc
terminal
cycle.

FORMULATION EXERCISES

16 Consider the network in Fig. 7.18. The problem is to find a shortest route from Node 11 to Node 1. Let c_{ij} be the length of arc (i, j).

(a) Construct a tabular representation like that in Fig. 7.2.

(b) For part (a), display the technology table corresponding to (1), (2), and (3) in Sec. 7.2.

17 Consider the network in exercise 20. Add an arc from Node 2 to Node 11. Suppose the problem is to find a shortest route from Node 9 to Node 3. Answer the questions posed in exercise 16.

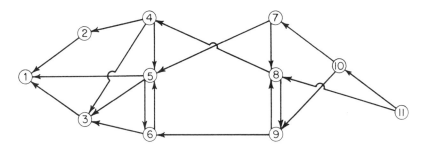

FIGURE 7.18

18 *Equipment Replacement.* The Goode-O'Toole Company runs a machine shop containing an expensive drill press that must be replaced periodically as it wears out. The Vice-President of Manufacturing has just authorized installing a new model, but has asked the foreman to devise an optimal replacement plan for the next seven years, after which the drill press will no longer be needed.

Let p_t be the cost of a new model in Period t, where

$$p_1 = 100 \qquad p_2 = 105 \qquad p_3 = 110 \qquad p_4 = 115$$

$$p_5 = 120 \qquad p_6 = 125 \qquad p_7 = 130,$$

so that the currently authorized installation incurs the cost 100. Let v_k be the salvage value of a press that is sold at the end of k periods of use, where

$$v_1 = 50 \qquad v_2 = 25 \qquad v_3 = 10 \qquad v_4 = 5 \qquad v_5 = 2 \qquad v_6 = 1 \qquad v_7 = 0.$$

Thus, if the new press is sold at the end of the first period, Goode-O'Toole realizes a revenue of 50; if it is sold at the end of Period 2, the revenue is 25; if it is sold at the end of Period 7, the revenue is 0.

Let r_k be the operating cost of a piece of equipment during its kth consecutive period of use, where

$$r_1 = 30 \qquad r_2 = 40 \qquad r_3 = r_4 = 50 \qquad r_5 = 60 \qquad r_6 = 70 \qquad r_7 = 100.$$

(a) Formulate a shortest-route problem to find an optimal replacement policy.
(b) Construct a tabular representation of the problem like that in Fig. 7.2. Be sure to calculate every c_{ij}.
(c) Display a technology table corresponding to (1), (2), and (3).

19 The chief field engineer, Oscar Veight, of the Doug D. Pitt Mines must provide a plan for removing ore from a new mining area. A cross section of the area is shown in Fig. 7.19. An excavation plan can be characterized by a continuous path (comprised of line segments shown in Fig. 7.19), starting at Node 1 and ending at Node 15. The expected net profit for a path depends on the depth of the excavation as well as the expected amount of recoverable ore. For example, if the line segment (5, 6) is part of the excavation plan, then the associated net profit can be calculated by estimating the

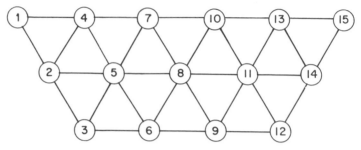

Figure 7.19

recoverable ore in the earth above $(5, 6)$—that is, the recoverable ore between this segment and the surface—and subtracting the cost of removing this earth. Let p_{ij} be the net profit associated with segment (i, j); not all p_{ij} are positive. Show how to find an optimal excavation plan.

20 A British transportation magnate, Sir Q. Layshen, operates a charter air freight business between five major airports in Western Europe. Each morning, Sir Q. receives data on the air cargo available for him to transport from one city to another. He also knows the net revenue associated with his chartering a plane between each pair of cities given the cargo load implied by the shipment data. For example, if he can ship a plane load of commodities from City i to City j, then he earns the net revenue (shipping charges less chartering cost) r_{ij}. Let n_{ij} (integer) be the maximum number of plane loads between City i and City j that he can handle for the day, where $0 \leq n_{ij} < \infty$. Assume that there are a sufficient number of planes available for charter at each city.

Sir Q. may route a charter plane among any number of cities provided that the route terminates at the city where the flight originated; in other words, he must return each airplane to its home base. This round-trip requirement implies that Sir Q. may have to fly an empty plane between some cities; the associated cost d_{ij} represents the chartering fee for an aircraft flying "deadheaded." Flight times are sufficiently short that even if a plane is routed to all five cities, it can return to its home base by the end of the day.

Formulate an optimization model that maximizes Sir Q.'s profits. (*Hint:* Let x_{ij} represent the number of chartered planes carrying cargo between City i and City j and z_{ij} the number of chartered planes flying deadheaded between City i and City j.)

21 A midwest grain cooperative, Vaults of the Flours, Inc., has contracted to ship 3000 tons of barley and 6000 tons of oats to Eastern Europe. This tonnage of grain is stored in 5 silo locations, and must be sent by rail car to 4 ports on the Great Lakes for loading onto ships. In order to meet the terms of the contract, the cooperative must send the grain from the silos over the next seven days, and the cooperative's dispatcher, Wheaton Dawks, must determine the port destination of this grain and how much is to be loaded onto rail cars each day. The rail shipping costs vary with the distance from a silo to a port and with the type of grain, so that Dawks wants a least-cost allocation and routing.

Assume that the shipping time from any silo location to any port is two days; hence grain arriving on Day t must be shipped on Day $t - 2$. Let R_{jt} and S_{jt} be the tonnage of barley and oats, respectively, that must be loaded onto ships at Port j on

Day t, starting with Day 3. Grain may be stored overnight without charge at the port provided that the tonnage does not exceed T_{jt} at Port j on Day t. The maximum combined tonnage of both grains that can be loaded on freight cars at Silo Location i on Day t is M_{it}, and B_i and A_i are the tons of barley and oats, respectively, stored at Silo Location i and available for shipment during the next seven days. The cost per ton of shipping barley from Silo Location i to Port j is c_{ij}; similarly, d_{ij} is the shipping cost for oats. Let x_{ijt} and y_{ijt} be the tons of barley and oats, respectively, sent from Silo Location i to Port j on Day t.

(a) Formulate the appropriate optimization problem.
(b) Show how to alter your formulation if the cost of overnight storage at Port j is e_j per ton.
*(c) Reformulate your model in part (a) assuming that the rail transport time from Silo Location 1 is only one day (the other transportation times are still two days).

22 May Kway, the mayor of a major industrial city, Chocloggo, wishes to assess the maximum amount of vehicular traffic per hour that can leave downtown Chocloggo and arrive at the city's principal suburb Owdda Town. The road network traveled by motor vehicles is shown in Fig. 7.20. The arcs represent large roadways, the figures

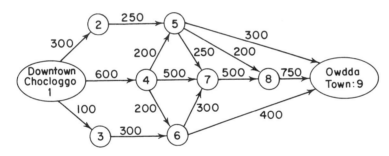

FIGURE 7.20

adjacent to the arcs are the maximum number of vehicles per hour (measured in hundreds of vehicles) that can flow along the roads, and the nodes are intersections. Formulate an optimization model that answers Ms. Kway's question.

23 Consider the vehicular flow problem for the city of Chocloggo in exercise 22. Suppose that mayor May Kway wants to recommend to the state legislature that a budget of K million dollars be appropriated to improve the roadways so as to increase the maximum hourly flow from the downtown area. Assume that the maximum flow capacity on each arc (i, j) in Fig. 7.22 can be increased by y_{ij} at the cost of $c_{ij}y_{ij}$ million dollars, where the expansion level $y_{ij} \geq 0$ is to be determined by the city's planning agency. [For example, the flow along arc $(2, 5)$ can be increased from its current level 250 to $250 + y_{25}$ at the cost of $c_{25}y_{25}$.] A practical upper limit on the traffic flow along arc (i, j) is u_{ij}.
   Show how to formulate a model to provide the city with a road capacity expansion

plan that maximizes the potential vehicular flow and stays within the proposed capital budget.

24 Aretha Holly, the owner of extensive woodlands in Canada, each November draws up a territorial plan for cutting several hundred thousand Christmas trees that are shipped to several market locations. Specifically, trees may be harvested from any one of 5 forest tracts and shipped to any one of 3 markets. The cost of cutting each thousand trees at Tract i is h_i, and the revenue from selling each thousand trees at Market j is r_j. The cost of shipping each thousand trees from Tract i to Market j is c_{ij}.

This year Ms. Holly intends to cut a *total* of 50 thousand trees. Figure 7.21 shows the upper and lower bounds on the trees to be cut at each of the forest tracts, and minimum and maximum shipment quantities that must be satisfied at each market location. Formulate a profit optimization model that indicates the number of trees to be cut on each tract and the market destination of these trees.

*25 Utopian Construction Company wants to apply critical path scheduling to two projects. For each, formulate the appropriate linear programming model. Display the corresponding critical path tableau, as done in Fig. 7.11. Construct a network like that in Fig. 7.13. Throughout, let t_j denote the completion time for Job j.

(a)

Job	Immediate Predecessors
A	–
B	–
C	A
D	A
E	B, C
F	B, C
G	D, E
H	F

(b)

Job	Immediate Predecessors
A	–
B	–
C	A
D	A
E	B
F	B
G	D
H	C, F

*26 In exercise 11, an alternative technique was outlined for constructing a network representation for a critical path project. Apply this method to the designated part of exercise 25.

(a) Part (a).
(b) Part (b).

Tract	Harvest Quantities	
	Lower Bound	Upper Bound
1	5	15
2	10	20
3	5	5
4	6	18
5	4	12

Market	Shipment Quantities	
	Minimum	Maximum
1	10	20
2	5	15
3	24	30

FIGURE 7.21

*27 After finding the critical path in the project in part (a) of exercise 25, the Utopian Company realizes that it *must* schedule overtime labor in order to fulfill its contractual obligation to complete the project by time T.

The network representation of the project has six nodes, indexed $i = 1, 2, \ldots, 6$, where Node 1 denotes the start of the project and Node 6 designates that all the tasks are complete. Let

$$d_{ij} = \begin{pmatrix} \text{shortest possible interval of time required to} \\ \text{complete the task associated with arc } (i, j) \end{pmatrix} ;$$

each d_{ij} is a known constant, and typically involves utilizing overtime to the fullest extent possible.

Let the decision variables be

$$y_{ij} = \begin{pmatrix} \text{the interval of time } \textit{exceeding } d_{ij} \text{ to complete} \\ \text{the task associated with arc } (i, j) \end{pmatrix} ,$$

$$t_i = \begin{pmatrix} \text{the } \textit{earliest} \text{ point in time to start} \\ \text{any task leading out from Node } i \end{pmatrix} .$$

The y_{ij} and t_i are the unknowns in the optimization problem. These values must satisfy the constraints

$$t_i + d_{ij} + y_{ij} \leq t_j \quad \text{for every arc } (i, j).$$

In addition, $t_6 \leq T$ to meet the contractual commitment.

If full overtime is not used on the task associated with arc (i, j), then $y_{ij} > 0$; assume the associated cost *savings* is $s_{ij} y_{ij}$.

(a) Write a linear programming formulation of the optimizing problem. Show all the constraints and the entire objective function.

*(b) Write the corresponding dual problem. Is it a network problem? If so, explain its structural components.

*28 *Caterer Problem.* The Cole Food Company, a catering firm, requires r_j fresh napkins at the start of Day j, where $j = 1, 2, \ldots, T$. Normal laundering takes one full day at B cents a napkin; rapid laundering takes overnight at C cents a napkin. New napkins may be purchased at A cents a napkin. The caterer wants a plan for purchasing and laundering napkins to minimize total costs, subject to meeting all the fresh-napkin requirements.

Let x_j be the number of napkins purchased for use on the jth day; v_j the number of clean napkins left over (at the end of the day); y_j the number sent for normal laundry service (at the end of the day); z_j the number sent for rapid laundry service (at the end of the day); and s_j the number of soiled napkins on hand and not sent to the laundry (at the end of the day). The technology matrix is summarized in Fig. 7.22.

(a) Write in full the model for $T = 5$.
(b) Draw the associated network. (*Hint*: add a redundant restriction corresponding to a fictitious node.)

	x_j	v_j	y_j	z_j	s_j
Allocation of clean napkins in Day j	−1	1			
Allocation of soiled napkins in Day j			1	1	1
Allocation of clean napkins in Day j+1		−1		−1	
Allocation of soiled napkins in Day j+1					−1
Allocation of clean napkins in Day j+2			−1		
Allocation of soiled napkins in Day j+2					
Costs	A	0	B	C	0

FIGURE 7.22

COMPUTATIONAL EXERCISES

29 Consider the network in Fig. 7.23. The number on each arc represents the distance between the nodes, and $c_{ij} = c_{ji}$.

(a) Find the shortest routes, and their lengths, from each node to Node 1.
(b) Find the shortest routes, and their lengths, from each node to Node 2.

30 Consider the network in Fig. 7.24. The number on each arc represents the distance between the nodes, and $c_{ij} = c_{ji}$.

(a) Find the shortest routes, and their lengths, from each node to Node 1.
(b) Find the shortest routes, and their lengths, from each node to Node 3.

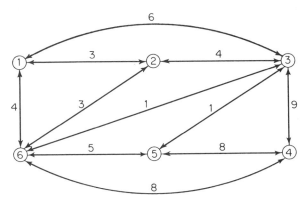

FIGURE 7.23

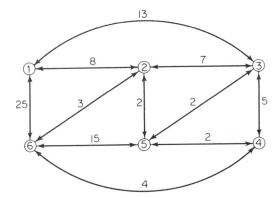

FIGURE 7.24

31 Consider the network in Fig. 7.25. The number on each arc represents the distance between the nodes, and $c_{ij} = c_{ji}$.

(a) Find the shortest routes, and their lengths, from each node to Node 1.
(b) Find the shortest routes, and their lengths, from each node to Node 3.

32 Consider a network consisting of six nodes. Assume $c_{ij} = c_{ji}$ and that there are arcs in each direction corresponding to

$$c_{12} = 15 \qquad c_{13} = 5 \qquad c_{14} = 8 \qquad c_{15} = 3$$

$$c_{16} = 10 \qquad c_{26} = 3 \qquad c_{36} = 5 \qquad c_{46} = 2$$

$$c_{23} = 9 \qquad c_{34} = 3 \qquad c_{45} = 4 \qquad c_{56} = 7.$$

(a) Find the shortest routes, and their lengths, from each node to Node 1.
(b) Find the shortest routes, and their lengths, from each node to Node 2.

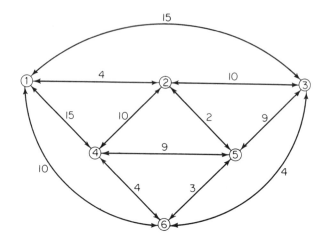

FIGURE 7.25

*33 In each part below, use the algorithm in the advanced material of Sec. 7.3 to find the
shortest routes from every node to every other node and indicate the corresponding
distances.

(a) Network in exercise 29.
(b) Network in exercise 30.
(c) Network in exercise 31.
(d) Network in exercise 32.

34 Consider the network in Fig. 7.26. The number on each arc represents the associated
length c_{ij}. Where an arrow head appears on both ends of an arc, the length shown
applies to each of the two directions.

(a) Find the shortest routes, and their lengths, from each node to Node 1.
*(b) Discuss the problem of finding the longest routes.

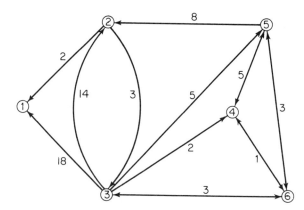

FIGURE 7.26

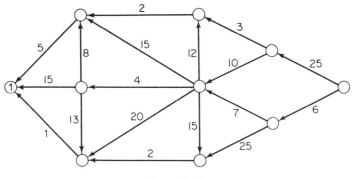

FIGURE 7.27

35 Consider an acyclic network with five nodes and an arc from each Node i ($i = 2, 3, 4,$ 5) to every Node j, where $j < i$. Let $c_{ij} = i + (i - j)^2$. Find the shortest routes, and their lengths, from each Node i to Node 1.

36 Consider the acyclic network in Fig. 7.27. The number on each arc is the associated length c_{ij}.

   (a) Label the nodes by the technique given at the beginning of Sec. 7.4.
   (b) Find the shortest routes from each node to Node 1 and indicate their lengths.
   (c) Find the longest routes from each node to Node 1 and indicate their lengths.

37 *Equipment Replacement.* Apply the shortest-route algorithm in Sec. 7.4 to solve the Rhode-Bloch Trucking Company case in exercise 4.

38 *Equipment Replacement.* Consider the Goode-O'Toole Company case in exercise 18.

   (a) Apply the shortest-route algorithm in Sec. 7.4 to find an optimal replacement policy.
   (b) Determine a range for p_2, the cost of a new model in Period 2, such that the policy in part (a) remains optimal. Do the same for p_3. For p_4. For p_5.
   (c) Determine a range for r_2, the cost of operating a piece of equipment during its second consecutive period of use, such that the policy in part (a) remains optimal. Do the same for r_3. For r_4. For r_5.

*39 *Equipment Replacement.* Consider the network in Fig. 7.3. Interpret the amounts that are sequentially calculated by the shortest-route algorithm (1) and (2) in Sec. 7.4 in the context of this network.

*40 *Employment Scheduling.* Consider the example in Fig. 7.6, with the cost data as given in exercise 14. Let $R_1 = 10$, $R_2 = 15$, $R_3 = 9$, $R_4 = 20$, $R_5 = 12$.

   (a) Apply the transportation simplex method to the tabular form in Fig. 7.17. Be sure to indicate how many crews start each period in an optimal plan.
   (b) What is the optimal value of the objective function, and what are the revisions in the plan from part (a) if $R_1 = 11$? If $R_2 = 14$? If $R_1 = 11$ and $R_2 = 14$? If $R_3 = 8$? If $R_4 = 21$? If $R_3 = 8$ and $R_4 = 21$?

CONTENTS

CHAPTER 8

Introduction to Dynamic Optimization Models

8.1 ANALYSIS OF DYNAMIC PHENOMENA

Dynamic elements—time considerations—were foremost in several of the operations research applications you examined in previous chapters, such as the integrated production planning example in Sec. 2.5. But the emphasis so far has been on presenting algorithmic techniques for coming to grips with a host of simultaneous constraints. You saw, for example, the way the simplex method provides a feasible solution to all the restrictions at each iteration. You undertook sensitivity analysis of linear programming solutions in the same context. Chapters 6 and 7 explored the special structure of network models, and focused on efficient methods for obtaining numerical solutions to large-scale problems. One important departure from this orientation is the solution method for the shortest-route problem in an acyclic network, Sec. 7.4. In that method you took advantage of the "one-way" characteristic of the network. You should carefully review that material, pp. 198–199, before starting the next section.

In Chaps. 8 through 10, the simultaneity aspect still remains crucial, but the stress will now shift to dynamic relationships in optimization models. These chapters provide only deterministic examples, in that each decision leads to a *uniquely* determined outcome. Models with probabilistic outcomes are left for Chap. 13. You will find, however, that the analytic solution to most of the probabilistic problems are direct generalizations of the concepts you will learn in Chaps. 8 through 10.

Here you will concentrate on the form and properties of optimal solutions. You will study the conditions that must be satisfied by an optimal time-staged decision process, and discover how to exploit these conditions to determine the best action. Frequently, the term *dynamic programming* is applied to this sort of analysis.

219

The main topic explored in Chap. 8 is sensitivity analysis on time as a variable. For example, you will see how lengthening the span of a planning horizon can profoundly affect your choice of a correct immediate decision. A related subject studied is the influence of starting conditions, such as the level of resources on hand, and of constraints, such as capacity limitations.

So that you keep the proper perspective, we emphasize that numerical solutions to all the models in Chaps. 8 through 10 can be obtained by applying algorithms you have previously studied (in particular, the method of obtaining a shortest route in an acyclic network). The salient goal is learning how to characterize the models in such a way as to clarify their dynamic properties. Part of this task is accomplished merely by augmenting your operations research vocabulary with new terms, and introducing you to a helpful mathematical notation. But, as you will come to appreciate, there are no simple rules that can be applied mechanically to all problems so as to expose their dynamic properties. Experience *is* the best teacher, and therefore the text contains a wide variety of examples. Many specific optimization problems can be formulated in several apparently different ways, with each formulation highlighting a certain structural relationship, as you will see.

Importance of dynamic programming. These introductory comments are meant to help you make a transition from the point of view of the previous chapters. But nothing has been said about the practical importance of the models you are to study next. Are such problems of major economic consequence?

Whereas most industrial applications of the linear programming models you have seen are oriented to planning decisions in the face of large-scale complex situations, dynamic programming models are typically applied to much smaller-scale phenomena. The following illustrations typify dynamic programming decision models:

- Inventory reordering rules indicating when to replenish an item and by what amount
- Production-scheduling and employment-smoothing doctrines applicable to an environment with fluctuating demand requirements
- Spare-parts level determination to guarantee high-efficiency utilization of expensive equipment
- Capital-budgeting procedures for allocating scarce resources to new ventures
- Selection of advertising media to promote wide public exposure to a company's product
- Systematic plan or search to discover the whereabouts of a valuable resource
- Scheduling methods for routine and major overhauls on complex machinery
- Long-range strategy for replacing depreciating assets.

Most of these applications are treated in detail in this chapter and the chapters to follow, and so no further explanation is supplied here.

Frequently, the decision processes embraced by several of the above models may themselves be *micro*. But many real operating systems call for thousands of such decisions each week. These models are valuable, then, because they make it possible to take a myriad of actions through a routine (often computerized) approach with a modicum of human intervention. Needless to say, even if these decisions are inconsequential taken singly, in aggregate they can exert a major effect on a business's profits. A reduction of 25% or more in maintenance costs or in aggregate dollar inventory levels, with no degradation of service, has been the solid reward for many companies employing dynamic programming models.

A word of guidance. The common characteristic of all dynamic programming models is expressing the decision problem by means of a recursive formulation. If you have never applied this type of formal reasoning to solve a problem, then you will probably find the associated mathematical notation strange, and perhaps even puzzling. The advice below is aimed at helping you overcome these difficulties.

Plan to read the sections at least twice. First concentrate on getting a feeling for the decision problem and on becoming familiar with the symbols. Then, on the second reading, pay more attention to the details of the presentation, including the nature of the mathematical expressions. Carefully follow the numerical examples, and check the calculations. Finally, be patient and give yourself plenty of time to study the sections. Reading about dynamic programming can be slow going, even if you have previously studied recursive relations. Rest assured, if you proceed as suggested, that after mastering a few examples you will suddenly find it much easier to understand subsequent recursive formulations—this threshold effect in learning is what psychologists refer to as the "aha!" phenomenon.

8.2 STAGECOACH PROBLEM: AN ALLEGORY

An allegorical example will explain several important concepts in dynamic programming and establish a symbolic way to view time-oriented models. There will be nothing new to you in the nature of the problem—you are simply to find a shortest route through an acyclic network. However, the particular illustration will contain more contextual structure than that appearing in Sec. 7.4, where you learned the shortest-route algorithm.

The scenario. Once upon a time there lived a Mr. Mark Off who decided to seek his fortune in San Francisco. In his day, the stagecoach was the only means of public transportation from the East, where he lived, to the West. His travel agent showed him a United States map, Fig. 8.1, depicting the various stagecoach routes then available. Each block on the map represents a state; each state is numbered for convenience. Notice that the entire trip from East to West requires Mark Off to take four stages, regardless of the particular routing.

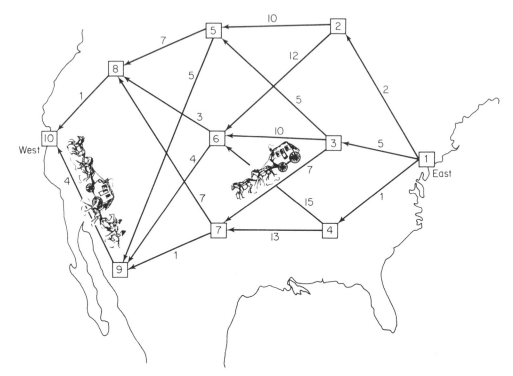

FIGURE 8.1. Stagecoach Problem.

Since the traveler knew the trip presented serious hazards to life and limb, he decided to take out an insurance policy before leaving. The cost of the policy depended on which routes he selected, since the greater the danger, the higher the cost. Let c_{ij} denote the policy cost of traveling from State i to State j. Illustrative values of c_{ij} appear in Fig. 8.1. Mark Off's objective was to pick a route from East to West that minimized the total policy cost. (See if you can find an optimal route.)

Mark Off analyzed the problem as follows. He perceived as significant the following principle.

PRINCIPLE OF OPTIMALITY. An optimal policy must have the property that regardless of the route taken to enter a particular state, the remaining decisions must constitute an optimal policy for leaving that state.

Thus he knew that an optimal routing out of State 6, say, did not depend on the particular routing that resulted in his entering State 6. (How would you calculate an optimal routing from State 6?) Pressing his logic further, he reasoned that if he knew optimal routings out of States 5, 6, and 7, then he could fairly easily determine an optimal route out of State 3, in case he decided to enter there.

Why? Because he need only compare the immediate cost when he leaves State 3—either c_{35}, c_{36}, or c_{37}—*plus* the known costs of optimal routes out of States 5, 6, and 7, respectively, and then pick a state giving the minimum combined cost. By the same token, as soon as he has found optimal policies for States 2, 3, and 4, he could find an optimal routing from State 1.

With the principle of optimality and its computational implications in mind, he defined the symbols

$$f_n(s) = \text{minimum policy cost when he is in State s}$$
$$\text{with } n \text{ more stages to go to his final destination,}$$

$$j_n(s) = \text{a decision yielding } f_n(s).$$

Most beginning students are driven up the wall by this sort of notation, which is always used in specifying dynamic programming models. It looks even more complicated than the formulas employed in statistics texts, and those are bad enough. But like it or not, each of the letters is essential to the meaning. The letter f signals to you that the number being represented is a value for the objective *function*. The letter s tells you that the objective-function value actually depends on the *state* of the system. And the subscript n gives you the dynamic information that there are n stages left to go when the system is in State s. By the same token, the Decision j also depends on both the Stage n and the State s and signifies his journey.

As you read this and other dynamic programming examples, you may find it helpful to repeat to yourself the definition of the symbols, just as if you were learning a new language. The reason we did not need such horrendous notation to explain linear programming models is that those problems are solved in one fell swoop. But here we creep up on a solution by stages. Hopefully, we have managed at least to *ease* your anxiety by this justification.

Returning to Mark Off's problem, he realized that when he arrives at State 10 with no more stages to go, he has no more policy cost to pay and he terminates his journey. In terms of the symbols previously defined, this means that

(1) $f_0(10) = 0$ for $j_0(10) = $ stop.

But then Mark Off saw that with hardly any effort he could also calculate $f_1(8)$ and $f_1(9)$, because they were simply $f_0(10)$ plus $c_{8,10}$, and $c_{9,10}$, respectively. Heady with success, he examined how he could compute $f_2(6)$, the minimum policy cost when he is in State 6 with two more stages to go to his final destination. He noticed that he had only two ways to leave State 6, should he decide to enter there. One way is to go to State 8; the associated policy cost is $c_{6,8}$ plus $f_1(8)$, which he already has computed. The other is to go to State 9; the associated policy cost is $c_{6,9}$ plus $f_1(9)$, which he also has computed. Aha! The value of $f_2(6)$ must be the smaller of these two sums. (Is this how you calculated an optimal routing from State 6?)

Mark Off suspected that there must be a method in his madness, and, of course, he was right. The method—or madness—can be succinctly stated by a so-called dynamic recursive relationship:

$$(2) \qquad f_n(s) = \underset{\substack{(s,\,j)\text{ in}\\ \text{network}}}{\text{minimum}} [c_{sj} + f_{n-1}(j)] \quad \text{for } n = 1, 2, 3, 4.$$

This formula, expressed in words, states the fact that Mark Off should compare each possible sum of the policy cost for the immediate stage, going from State s to State j, and the *optimal* policy cost when he arrives at State j with only $n - 1$ more stages to go to his final destination. He should decide on a j that gives the smallest value of these sums. Mark Off's reasoning was to apply (2) by calculating first of all the values for $f_1(s)$, namely, $f_1(8)$ and $f_1(9)$; then, in turn, for $n = 2$, he would calculate the values for $f_2(5), f_2(6), f_2(7)$, followed by the values for $f_3(2)$, $f_3(3)$, and $f_3(4)$. His entire problem was solved once he found the value of $f_4(1)$, because this put him at the beginning of his journey, starting at the initial State 1 with four stages to go.

The above approach for solving the problem might almost be termed a method of lifting yourself by your own bootstraps. First you perform a small, even trivial, computation. You use that result to perform a subsequent computation, and you continue in the same fashion. In symbolic terms, the computation in (2) states that you can find the values of $f_1(s)$ when you know the values of $f_0(s)$. You then can find the values of $f_2(s)$, having calculated the values of $f_1(s)$, and so on. This sort of procedure is referred to as a **recursive algorithm,** and the formula is known as a **recursion.**

Computational process. We review the idea of employing a recursive algorithm by doing the actual calculations for the numerical values of c_{ij} appearing in Fig. 8.1.

For $n = 1$, the calculations implied by (2) and (1) are trivial:

$$(3) \qquad \begin{aligned} f_1(8) &= c_{8,10} + 0 = 1 \quad \text{for } j_1(8) = 10 \quad (s = 8) \\ f_1(9) &= c_{9,10} + 0 = 4 \quad \text{for } j_1(9) = 10 \quad (s = 9). \end{aligned}$$

To keep the rest of the calculations straight, use the tables shown in Figs. 8.2 through 8.5.

There is one table for each possible Stage n, namely, $n = 1, 2, 3$, and 4. The format for a table is to have a row for each possible entering stage, given that there are n stages to go, and a column for each possible state at the next stage. Thus for $n = 1$, shown in Fig. 8.2, there are two rows for States 8 and 9, because Mark Off may choose to enter either of these states. But there is only one column for State 10, since that is the only destination from both States 8 and 9. For $n = 2$, shown in Fig. 8.3, Mark Off may choose to enter either State 5, 6, or 7, and so three rows are needed; he then may travel to either State 8 or 9, and so two columns are required.

The entries in a table are the sum of the immediate cost c_{sj} to go from State s to State j and the subsequent policy cost $f_{n-1}(j)$ associated with an optimal route

$n = 1$
$c_{sj} + f_0(j)$

	Decision:		
s	10	$j_1(s)$	$f_1(s)$
Entering State: 8	1 + 0	10	1
9	4 + 0	10	4

FIGURE 8.2. Stagecoach Problem.

$n = 2$
$c_{sj} + f_1(j)$

Decision:

	8	9	$j_2(s)$	$f_2(s)$
5	7 + 1	5 + 4	8	8
Entering State: 6	3 + 1	4 + 4	8	4
7	7 + 1	1 + 4	9	5

FIGURE 8.3. Stagecoach Problem.

out of State j. In each row, you examine these sums to find the smallest. That minimum is labeled $f_n(s)$ and an associated optimal decision is designated as $j_n(s)$; both are shown on the right of each table.

The computations for $n = 1$ are repeated in Fig. 8.2. In this particular example, when $n = 1$, the only feasible action is $j = 10$. Therefore, $j_1(8) = j_1(9) = 10$, as you already saw in (3).

When $n = 2$, recall j can be either 8 or 9. To complete the calculations when there are two more stages to go, it is necessary to have the c_{ij} and *only* the values $f_1(j)$. The computations are shown in Fig. 8.3. Observe that $f_1(8) = 1$ is added to each c_{s8} in the $j = 8$ column and $f_1(9) = 4$ is added to each c_{s9} in the $j = 9$ column. The table shows that with two stages left it is optimal to go to State 8 from States 5 and 6, and to State 9 from State 7.

The analysis for $n = 3$ appears in Fig. 8.4. Notice here that two entries are blanked out, since it is not possible to go from State 2 to State 7 or from State 4 to State 5. Once again observe that the *only* data required from the previous Fig. 8.3 are the values of $f_2(j)$. This is a key point in all dynamic programming applications: *the value of an optimal policy with* n *stages left to go depends on the economic consequence of the immediate action and the corresponding* value *of an optimal policy with* n − 1 *stages remaining.*

$n = 3$
$c_{sj} + f_2(j)$

Decision:

	5	6	7	$j_3(s)$	$f_3(s)$
2	10 + 8	12 + 4		6	16
Entering State: 3	5 + 8	10 + 4	7 + 5	7	12
4		15 + 4	13 + 5	7	18

FIGURE 8.4. Stagecoach Problem.

The computations terminate in Fig. 8.5 with $n = 4$. There you see that the minimum policy cost is

$$(4) \qquad\qquad f_4(1) = 17 \quad \text{for } j_4(1) = 3.$$

What is the corresponding optimal policy? To answer this question, you must trace through the tables in the following fashion. Starting with the table for $n = 4$, shown in Fig. 8.5, you find that an optimal decision is to go from State 1 to State 3. Progressing to the table for $n = 3$, shown in Fig. 8.4, you see that when Mark Off enters State 3 (third row of table), an optimal decision is to go to State 7. Continuing to the table for $n = 2$, shown in Fig. 8.3, you find that when he enters State 7, an optimal decision is to go to State 9. And from State 9 he ends up at State 10. In summary, an optimal policy is the route from State 1 to 3 to 7 to 9 to 10, which as $f_4(1)$ indicates, has a policy cost of $5 + 7 + 1 + 4 = 17$.

You should understand that the dynamic programming method is more efficient than enumerating and evaluating every possible policy. In this particular problem, there are 14 distinct routes from East to West. To evaluate the policy cost of any route, it is necessary to add the four (one for each stage) appropriate c_{ij}. Therefore, a naive enumeration approach would have required 42 $(= 14 \times 3)$ additions, as compared to a total of 16 additions in Figs. 8.3 through 8.5. The relative advantage of the recursive method is overwhelming in typical applications, where complete enumeration is usually out of the question.

$$n = 4$$
$$c_{sj} + f_3(j)$$

	Decision:				
s ╲ j	2	3	4	$j_4(s)$	$f_4(s)$
Entering State: 1	2 + 16	5 + 12	1 + 18	3	17

FIGURE 8.5. Stagecoach Problem.

A study questionnaire. The stagecoach allegory contains several concepts and approaches that recur in subsequent applications. To master these ideas, when you study each new model ask yourself:

(i) What are the policy or decision variables?

(ii) What is the criterion or objective function for determining an optimal policy?

(iii) How is the problem characterized and then analyzed in terms of stages?

(iv) What characterizes the state of the problem at each stage?

(v) How do the constraints influence the states of the problem and the feasible values of the policy variables?

Once you are able to formulate a model in multistage terms, you have taken the first step toward analyzing the problem's dynamic characteristics.

8.3 ELEMENTARY INVENTORY MODEL

Inventory decisions included in previous planning models—for example, the integrated production planning model in Sec. 2.5—were imbedded in a large and complex system of constraints. Now the scope is narrowed considerably so as to concentrate on several essentials of dynamic inventory decision processes. The model you are about to study plays the same role in the field of operations research as do Newton's elementary laws in the field of physics—well, *nearly* the same role. Although the situation considered by the model is idealized, it encompasses many important considerations for choosing an inventory policy.

Keep in mind that the primary purpose of the discussion below is to examine the dynamic phenomena of inventory processes. For this reason, the description of the model does not comment on the severity or realism of the assumptions; these are taken up in Sec. 8.5. For the same reason, the economic concepts introduced are only described in brief. They will be elaborated in Chap. 14 which is devoted entirely to inventory models.

By way of encouragement and motivation, however, let it be said that manufacturing firms have implemented versions of this model with demonstrable economic benefits. As you would imagine, in such instances all the calculations involved have been computerized.

Dependable Manufacturing Company Example. This firm wishes to establish a production schedule for an item during the next N time periods. Assume the company has an accurate forecast of the amount it requires to meet demand for each of the N periods.

The manufacturing time to produce a batch of these items is negligible, so that production in Period t can be used to fill, entirely or partially, the demand in that period. Since the demand requirements do vary from one period to another and there are certain economies of batch production, it is often economical for the firm to produce more than is needed in one period and store the excess until it is required later. However, there is a cost of holding the resultant inventory. Depending on the circumstances, this expense is attributable to such factors as interest on capital borrowed for financing the inventory buildup, storage rental fees, insurance, and maintenance. Such inventory holding cost must be taken into account in determining a production schedule.

The objective of the Dependable Manufacturing Company is to devise a schedule that minimizes the total production and inventory holding costs subject to the restriction that it meets all the demand requirements on time. (Would you believe that the company uses the slogan "Dependable is dependable"?) We begin the analysis by translating this qualitative statement of the problem into a mathematical model.

Model formulation. Define the policy variables

$$x_t = \text{production quantity in Period t}$$
$$i_t = \text{inventory at the } end \text{ of Period t.}$$

Assume that D_t is the demand requirement in Period t, where each D_t is a non-negative integer known at the beginning of the planning horizon.

Suppose that in each Period t the cost incurred depends only on the production quantity x_t and the ending inventory level i_t, and possibly on Period t itself. Let this cost relationship for Period t be designated by the function $C_t(x_t, i_t)$. [For example, the cost function may have the form $C_t(x_t, i_t) = 3x_t^2 + 1.5i_t$.] Then the objective function can be written as

$$(1) \qquad \text{minimize} \sum_{t=1}^{N} C_t(x_t, i_t).$$

Several constraints are imposed on the policy variables x_t and i_t. We restrict production to be integer-valued

(2) $x_t = 0, 1, 2, 3, \ldots$ for each Period t   (integer-valued production levels).

We assume that the management desires a policy in which the inventory level is zero at the end of Period N:

$$(3) \qquad\qquad i_N = 0 \quad \text{(no ending inventory)}.$$

Finally, we stipulate that each period's demand must be entirely satisfied on time. This condition can be imposed by means of two constraints. The first might be called an "accounting identity" since it states that

$$\begin{pmatrix} \text{inventory at the end} \\ \text{of Period t} \end{pmatrix} \equiv \begin{matrix} \text{inventory entering Period t} \\ \textit{plus} \\ \text{production in Period t} \\ \textit{less} \\ \text{demand in Period t,} \end{matrix}$$

or, symbolically,

$$i_t = i_{t-1} + x_t - D_t.$$

We find it more convenient to rearrange the terms in this relationship, and express the constraint as

(4) $i_{t-1} + x_t - i_t = D_t$ at each Period t, for $t = 1, 2, \ldots, N,$

where i_0 is a specified level of initial inventory at the beginning of the planning horizon.

The second constraint we impose to ensure that Dependable meets its requirements on time is that each period's entering inventory and production must always be large enough to make ending inventory a nonnegative quantity. Actually, we also want to restrict inventory levels to be integer-valued (which is a harmless assumption given that demands and production levels are integer-valued).

Thus, we require

(5) $i_t = 0, 1, 2, 3, \ldots$ at each Period t, for $t = 1, 2, \ldots, N - 1$.

Restricting ending inventory to be nonnegative, given the relationship (4), ensures that entering inventory plus production in each Period t is sufficient to meet demand in Period t.

Observe that (4) is a linear restriction. If each cost function $C_t(x_t, i_t)$ is linear, then the model is equivalent to a network problem and is easily solved by the methods in the preceding chapter. But in most actual applications of production models, the cost functions are nonlinear. For example, a costly setup may be required to produce a batch of items, so that the cost of producing the first unit is greater than the *incremental* cost of producing subsequent units. And when production exceeds the normal capacity level during a period, then the incremental cost may again increase due to the use of overtime.

To cope with such nonlinearities in each $C_t(x_t, i_t)$, we turn to a dynamic programming version of the problem.

Dynamic characterization. Recall in the stagecoach problem that the computational idea was to start at the end (no more stages to go) and work back to the beginning. We use the same approach for this problem. Here, the end is when there is only one period left in the planning horizon, and the beginning is when there are N periods to go.

In writing the mathematical formulas, we will find it convenient to use an indexing system in which the subscript 1 denotes the *end* of the horizon and the subscript N the *beginning*. Specifically, we define

$$d_n = \begin{pmatrix} \text{the demand requirement in that period} \\ \text{when there are } n \text{ more periods to go} \end{pmatrix},$$

$$c_n(x, j) = \begin{pmatrix} \text{cost of producing } x \text{ and having } j \text{ items of } \textit{ending} \text{ inventory} \\ \text{in that period when there are } n \text{ more periods to go} \end{pmatrix}.$$

In this notation, $d_1 \equiv D_N$ and $d_N \equiv D_1$. Similarly, $c_1(x, j) \equiv C_N(x, j)$.

For example, if the periods are months, $N = 4$, and the beginning of the horizon is January, then D_1 is January's demand and D_4 is April's. In the formulas, we want to use the reverse numbering system so that d_4 is January's demand and d_1 is April's. Thus d_2, the demand when there are two months to go until the end of the horizon, refers to March's requirements.

Can you guess what determines the state of the production system at the start of any period? The answer is entering inventory. Knowing the earlier demands and production decisions that led to this inventory level has no relevance to your current production decision. With this in mind, define

$$f_n(i) = \text{minimum policy cost when entering inventory}$$
$$\text{is at level } i \text{ with } n \text{ more periods to go,}$$

$$x_n(i) = \text{a production level yielding } f_n(i).$$

Since inventory at the end of the horizon is 0, according to (3), you can write

$$(6) \qquad f_0(0) = 0 \quad (n = 0).$$

Next look at $n = 1$. Entering inventory, i, can be any integer amount between the limits of 0 and d_1; but regardless of the specific level, the production amount must be $d_1 - i$ so that all of the final period's demand is met. It follows then that

$$(7) \qquad f_1(i) = c_1(d_1 - i, 0) \quad \text{for } i = 0, 1, \ldots, d_1.$$

Going on to $n = 2$, observe that if entering inventory is designated by i and the production level by x, then the associated cost is

$$c_2(x, i + x - d_2) + f_1(i + x - d_2),$$

assuming that you act optimally for $n = 1$. Note that the quantity $i + x - d_2$ is simply inventory at the *end* of the period. The value for i can be any integer amount between 0 and $d_1 + d_2$; if i exceeds $d_1 + d_2$, then (3) is not satisfied, since end-of-horizon inventory will be positive. Given i, the integer value of x must be at least as large as $d_2 - i$ in order to meet the period's demand requirement, but no larger than $d_1 + d_2 - i$ because ending inventory must be 0. An optimal x is one that minimizes the above sum. This analysis of $n = 2$ can be summarized by the computation

$$f_2(i) = \underset{x}{\text{minimum}} \; [c_2(x, i + x - d_2) + f_1(i + x - d_2)],$$

where $i = 0, 1, \ldots, d_1 + d_2$ and the minimization is over only nonnegative integer values of x in the range $d_2 - i \le x \le d_1 + d_2 - i$.

As in the stagecoach problem, once you know the values for $f_2(i)$, you can find the values for $f_3(i)$, and so on, until you eventually calculate $f_N(i_0)$, where i_0 is initial inventory, as before. The general recursion is written as

$$(8) \qquad f_n(i) = \underset{x}{\text{minimum}} \; [c_n(x, i + x - d_n) + f_{n-1}(i + x - d_n)]$$

$$\text{for } n = 1, 2, \ldots, N,$$

where $i = 0, 1, \ldots, d_1 + \cdots + d_n$ and the minimization is over only nonnegative integer values of x in the range $d_n - i \le x \le d_1 + d_2 + \cdots + d_n - i$.

Observe that by letting entering inventory, i, be the state variable, the only independent decision variable in the recursion (8) is x, for ending inventory is merely $(i + x - d_n)$. Note that since $f_0(0)$ and $f_1(i)$ are easily computed in (6) and (7), it is straightforward to calculate, in turn, $f_2(0), f_2(1), \ldots, f_2(d_1 + d_2)$, then $f_3(0), f_3(1), \ldots, f_3(d_1 + d_2 + d_3)$, continuing, for successively larger values of n, eventually to $f_{N-1}(0), f_{N-1}(1), \ldots, f_{N-1}(d_1 + d_2 + \cdots + d_{N-1})$, and finally to $f_N(i_0)$.

To find an optimal schedule, you then check what production level $x_N(i_0)$ yielded the value for $f_N(i_0)$; this is an optimal decision at the start of the horizon. At the next stage, the entering inventory level will be $i_0 + x_N(i_0) - d_N$. Find a production level that yields the value for $f_{N-1}(i_0 + x_N(i_0) - d_N)$, and so on. The process will be clear when you study the example in the next section.

You should pause here to make certain you understand what has been done to characterize the model in dynamic programming terms. The problem is being viewed in stages, where n denotes the number of stages (here periods) until the end of the final period. To illustrate, suppose again that $N = 4$ and the periods are January, February, March, and April, so that $n = 1$ refers to April and $n = 4$ to January. The January requirements are denoted by d_4 in the dynamic programming recursion (8). Similar notation is used for the cost functions. There is nothing really subtle so far.

What *is* novel is letting the level of entering inventory describe the state when there are n periods left to go. Continuing with the four-month illustration, observe that given the amount of inventory at the beginning of April and that month's demand requirement, you must produce exactly the difference between these two amounts. This fact is recognized in (7). Thus the optimization in April is trivial, given entering inventory.

By the same token, given the amount of inventory at the beginning of March and that month's demand requirement, you must produce *at least* the difference between these two amounts.

Your production decision x in March, in turn, affects the amount of entering inventory in April. Specifically, what enters April is $(i + x - d_2)$. Given this amount, you act optimally in April. But you already completed April's optimization analysis at the previous stage. Therefore, in deciding the optimal March production, you need compare only March costs plus the corresponding costs of acting *optimally* after March. The entirety of these considerations is expressed by the right-hand side of the dynamic programming recursion (8). The same line of reasoning can then be repeated for February, and finally for January.

▶ The recursion (8) is equivalent to the method of finding a shortest route in an acyclic network. You might wonder, "What does such a network look like for this model?" A diagrammatic network equivalent of (8) for an actual problem can be dense with nodes and arcs. The underlying structure can be illustrated adequately, however, by the following simple case:

(i) $d_n = 1$ for $n = 1, 2, 3, 4$ (stationary demand)

(ii) $x = 0, 1, 2$ (restricted production levels).

The network is pictured in Fig. 8.6. Each node, designated by the symbol (i, n), corresponds to a possible level of the state variable i when there are n periods remaining. The five nodes on the left designate the different possibilities for initial inventory $i_0 = 0, 1, 2, 3, 4$. The single node on the right reflects the restriction that ending inventory is 0.

Consider an arc between (i, n) and $(j, n - 1)$. Since $j = i + x - d_n$, then $x = j - i + d_n$ at the period when there are n periods to go. One arc appears for each feasible action. The associated cost $c_n(x, j)$ appears with the abbreviated symbol "nxj"; for example, $c_4(0, 1)$ is indicated by 401.

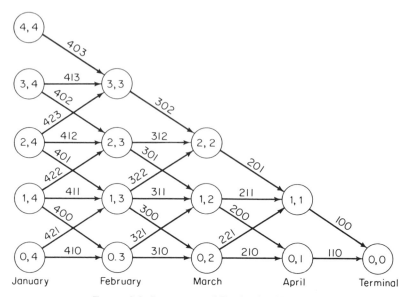

FIGURE 8.6. Inventory and Production Network.
Node Designation: (entering inventory, periods remaining) = (i, n).
Arc Cost Designation: $c_n(x, j) = nxj$.

Given a starting level of inventory for January, the least-cost path to the terminal node provides an optimal production policy. For example, one unit of inventory is on hand at the start of January; then you seek a least-cost route from node $(1, 4)$ to node $(0, 0)$. ◀

8.4 NUMERICAL SOLUTION

Now that you have a formulation of the inventory model, you are ready to solve the Dependable Manufacturing Company's specific problem. We perform the numerical calculations in this section. In subsequent sections, we analyze the effect on an optimal policy of lengthening the time horizon N, and show how an optimal policy can be drastically influenced by the imposition of a constraint. This example will demonstrate just how perplexing so-called combinatorial problems can be, even when they are small scale.

In fairness we must explain that the particular numbers below have been carefully chosen to produce the dynamic phenomena we wanted to exhibit; you should not conclude that the dynamic behavior illustrated is typical of inventory processes. You also should realize, however, that it would have been difficult to forecast the exact nature of the results *prior* to the dynamic programming analysis. This means that in a real situation you may not be able to judge beforehand whether an optimal policy is extremely sensitive to the length of the planning horizon.

To keep the analysis simple, we assume stationarity over time in the demand requirements and the cost functions. Specifically, let

(1) $D_t = 3$ for all periods   (stationary demand).

Assume that the cost function is simply the sum of a term due to production and a linear inventory holding cost:

(2) $$C_t(x_t, i_t) = C(x_t) + hi_t \quad \text{for all periods,}$$

where

(3)
$$\begin{aligned}
C(0) &= 0 & C(1) &= 15 & C(2) &= 17 \\
C(3) &= 19 & C(4) &= 21 & C(5) &= 23
\end{aligned}$$

(4) $$h = 1.$$

Thus production cost can be viewed as consisting of a setup cost of 13 plus a variable unit cost of 2 per item produced; succinctly, $C(x_t) = 13 + 2x_t$ for $x_t > 0$. Holding cost is just 1 times the level of ending inventory.

An added complication is that the Dependable Manufacturing Company has limited production capacity and storage space. In particular, it cannot produce more than five units in a period and hold more than four units at the end of the period:

(5) $$x_t = 0, 1, \ldots, 5 \quad \text{and} \quad i_t = 0, 1, \ldots, 4 \quad \text{for all periods.}$$

Notice that because the setup cost is high relative to the other costs, an optimal schedule will attempt to avoid frequent production. But since production x_t cannot exceed 5 and demand is 3, a schedule cannot increase inventory by more than 2 each period. Thus if initial inventory is 0, two setups are required in the first two periods. It is not at all obvious what is the best schedule of setups and production for longer time horizons. The dynamic programming analysis will provide the answers.

Dynamic formulation. Given the above data for the Dependable Manufacturing Company, you can write the appropriate dynamic recursion to reflect the specifics of the problem. Remember that

$$f_n(i) = \text{minimum policy cost when } i \text{ is the entering inventory} \\ \text{level with } n \text{ more periods to go,}$$

$$x_n(i) = \text{a production level yielding } f_n(i).$$

For $n = 1$,

(6)
$$\left.\begin{aligned}
f_1(i) &= C(3 - i) \\
x_1(i) &= 3 - i
\end{aligned}\right\} \quad \text{for } i = 0, 1, 2, 3,$$

to ensure that demand is met and the level of inventory at the end of the horizon is 0. The general recursion is

(7) $$f_n(i) = \underset{x}{\text{minimum}} \, [C(x) + 1(i + x - 3) + f_{n-1}(i + x - 3)]$$

$$\text{for } n = 2, 3, \ldots,$$

where $i = 0, 1, 2, 3, 4$ and the minimization is over only nonnegative integer values in the range $3 - i \leq x \leq$ minimum $(5, 7 - i)$. The production constraint in (5) keeps x from exceeding 5; and the *end* of period inventory constraint in (5) keeps x from exceeding $7 - i$. (Note that $x \leq$ minimum $(5, 6 - i)$ for $n = 2$.)

In order to perform the analyses of interest, it is necessary to have the values of $f_n(i)$ available; therefore this task is completed next. The format of the numerical solution tables is very similar to that used in the stagecoach problem. There is one table for each Stage n. A row in a table corresponds to a value of entering inventory i, and a column to a production level x. Because demand has to be met each period and the inventory at the end of a period cannot exceed 4, certain entries in the tables are eliminated from consideration—they represent infeasible combinations. The entries appearing in the body of a table are the sum of costs for the immediate period and cost of an optimal policy in the subsequent periods. For each row, the minimum of these sums is shown at the right under the column designated by $f_n(i)$ along with an associated optimal production level $x_n(i)$.

$$f_1(i) = C(3-i)$$

i	$x_1(i)$	$f_1(i)$
0	3	19
Entering Inventory: 1	2	17
2	1	15
3	0	0

FIGURE 8.7. The Dependable Manufacturing Company Model ($n = 1$).

The $f_1(i)$, given by (6), are tabled in Fig. 8.7. The function $f_2(i)$ is computed in Fig. 8.8. Note the detailed construction of the table. There are five rows, one for each feasible value of i. Several of the possibilities are blocked out. For example, if $i = 1$, then $x \geq 2$ in order that all demand be met. If $i = 4$, then $x \leq 2$ in order that inventory at the end of the horizon is zero. The first entry in each column x is the value $C(x)$ from (3). The second entry is the holding cost $h = 1$ times the level of ending inventory. For example, if $i = 3$ and $x = 0$, then ending inventory is 0, and 0 appears as the second term in the sum for this case. If $i = 3$ and $x = 1$, then ending inventory is 1, so 1 appears as the second term in the sum for this case. And so forth along the $i = 3$ row. Finally, the third term is the value of $f_1(i + x - 3)$ calculated previously in Fig. 8.7.

Given a level i, $f_2(i)$ is the minimum sum in the body of the table for that row, and $x_2(i)$ is a corresponding production level. Thus if $i = 1$ with two periods left to go, the best production level is 5, which yields a cost of 26 for these two periods. Any other value for x is more costly.

The calculations yielding $f_3(i)$ are shown in Fig. 8.9. Here $C(x) + 1(i + x - 3)$ is the first term, and $f_2(i + x - 3)$ from Fig. 8.8 is the second. The remaining values of $f_n(i)$, for $n = 4, 5, 6$, are summarized in Fig. 8.10. You should test your understanding of the dynamic programming recursive calculations by constructing a complete table, laid out like Fig. 8.9, to produce $f_4(i)$. Compare your results with those in Fig. 8.10. Observe that the production levels, 3 and 4, are optimal when $n = 4$.

Network formulation. Despite the heavy notation and the elaborate tables for calculating optimal dynamic production schedules using the recursive

$C(x) + 1(i + x - 3) + f_1(i + x - 3)$

Production:

Entering Inventory: i \ x	0	1	2	3	4	5	$x_2(i)$	$f_2(i)$
0				19 + 0 + 19	21 + 1 + 17	23 + 2 + 15	3	38
1			17 + 0 + 19	19 + 1 + 17	21 + 2 + 15	23 + 3 + 0	5	26
2		15 + 0 + 19	17 + 1 + 17	19 + 2 + 15	21 + 3 + 0		4	24
3	0 + 0 + 19	15 + 1 + 17	17 + 2 + 15	19 + 3 + 0			0	19
4	0 + 1 + 17	15 + 2 + 15	17 + 3 + 0				0	18

FIGURE 8.8. Dependable Manufacturing Company Model ($n = 2$).

formula (7), the computational process conceptually is no more complex than finding a least-cost route in an acyclic network. You can see this fact by studying the associated network shown in Fig. 8.11. The network is drawn for the cases $n = 1, 2, 3$. Observe that for $n = 2, 3$ there is a set of five nodes for each value of n; each node in the set is associated with one of the possible values for entering

$[C(x) + 1(i + x - 3)] + f_2(i + x - 3)$

Production:

Entering Inventory: i \ x	0	1	2	3	4	5	$x_3(i)$	$f_3(i)$
0				19 + 38	22 + 26	25 + 24	4	48
1			17 + 38	20 + 26	23 + 24	26 + 19	5	45
2		15 + 38	18 + 26	21 + 24	24 + 19	27 + 18	4	43
3	0 + 38	16 + 26	19 + 24	22 + 19	25 + 18		0	38
4	1 + 26	17 + 24	20 + 19	23 + 18			0	27

FIGURE 8.9. Dependable Manufacturing Company Model ($n = 3$).

Entering Inventory	n = 1		n = 2		n = 3		n = 4		n = 5		n = 6	
i	$x_1(i)$	$f_1(i)$	$x_2(i)$	$f_2(i)$	$x_3(i)$	$f_3(i)$	$x_4(i)$	$f_4(i)$	$x_5(i)$	$f_5(i)$	$x_6(i)$	$f_6(i)$
0	3	19	3	38	4	48	3, 4	67	5	79	4	96
1	2	17	5	26	5	45	5	64	5	74	5	93
2	1	15	4	24	4	43	5	54	4	72	4	91
3	0	0	0	19	0	38	0	48	0	67	0	79
4			0	18	0	27	0	46	0	65	0	75

FIGURE 8.10. Dependable Manufacturing Company Model.

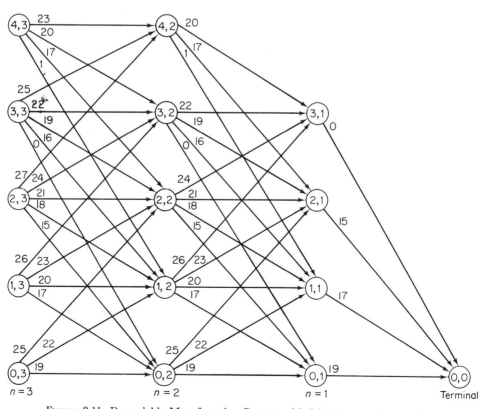

FIGURE 8.11. Dependable Manufacturing Company Model—Network Formulation.

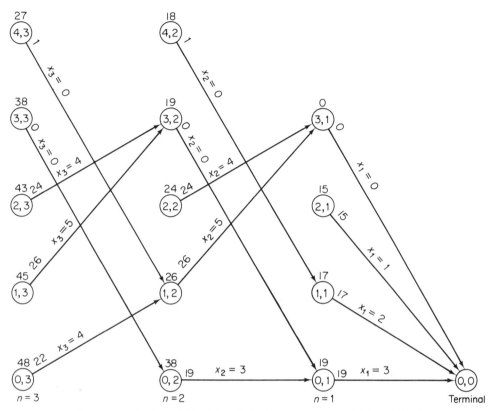

FIGURE 8.12. Dependable Manufacturing Company Model—Optimal Policy.

inventory $i = 0, 1, 2, 3, 4$. To illustrate, the node $(2, 3)$ represents the entering inventory level 2 when 3 stages (periods) remain; similarly, the node $(1, 2)$ represents the entering inventory 1 when 2 stages remain. Thus for each value of n, there is a set of nodes corresponding to the rows in Figs. 8.7, 8.8, and 8.9.

An arc connecting two nodes represents a feasible production decision. For example, the five arcs out of node $(2, 3)$ represent the production decisions $x_3 = 1, 2, 3, 4, 5$; the five arcs out of node $(3, 3)$ represent the production decisions $x_3 = 0, 1, 2, 3, 4$. More specifically, the arc from $(2, 3)$ to $(4, 2)$ corresponds to $x_3 = 5$; when entering inventory is 2 at $n = 3$, and you choose $x_3 = 5$, then entering inventory will be 4 at $n = 2$. For each n and every feasible combination of entering inventory and production in Figs. 8.7, 8.8, and 8.9, a corresponding arc appears in the network of Fig. 8.11, along with its associated production and inventory cost. Thus, the arc from $(2, 3)$ to $(4, 2)$ has the cost 27, which equals production cost $C(5) = 23$ plus holding cost $1 \cdot (2 + 5 - 3) = 4$.

Only those arcs that are optimal are shown in Fig. 8.12; the implied decision x_t

is shown as well. The value of the least-cost route from each node to the terminal node, symbolically $f_n(i)$, appears above the node. Hence, Fig. 8.12 is a network representation of the optimal quantities displayed in Figs. 8.7, 8.8, and 8.9.

8.5 SENSITIVITY ANALYSIS

The tabulated numerical results needed to obtain an optimal production policy also provide considerable information about the sensitivity of the solution to assumed values of the model's parameters, such as the length of the planning horizon and the level of entering inventory. We examine sensitivity questions of this sort using the data for the Dependable Manufacturing Company contained in Figs. 8.7 through 8.10.

Length of the planning horizon. For the sake of definiteness, suppose each period in the model represents a month and that the first period is January. You want to know how the optimal monthly figures change as the horizon N increases, and, in particular, what happens to January production. The results,

Planning Horizon N	Jan	Feb	Mar	Apr	May	Jun	Cost	Cost/Period
1	3						19	19
2	3	3					38	19
3	4	5	0				48	16
4	3 4	4 5	5 0	0 3			67	$16\frac{3}{4}$
5	5	5	0	5	0		79	$15\frac{4}{5}$
6	4	5	0	4	5	0	96	16

FIGURE 8.13. Dependable Manufacturing Company Production Schedule When $i_0 = 0$.

based on Fig. 8.10, are shown in Fig. 8.13, under the assumption that the inventory level at the beginning of January is 0.

Figure 8.13 is constructed as follows. When the planning horizon $N = 1$, January production $x_1(0) = 3$ is found from the first row of Fig. 8.10 under $n = 1$. When the planning horizon $N = 2$, January production $x_2(0) = 3$ is found from the first row in Fig. 8.10 under $n = 2$, since in January there are two periods remaining until the end of the horizon. Then February's entering inventory is 0, and so February production is $x_1(0) = 3$.

Skipping ahead to the case $N = 6$, you first determine January production $x_6(0) = 4$ from the first row of Fig. 8.10 under $n = 6$, since now in January there are six periods remaining until the end of the horizon. Consequently, inventory entering February is $1 (= i + x - d = 0 + 4 - 3)$, and February production is $x_5(1) = 5$, which you find in Fig. 8.10 for $n = 5$ and with the new entering inventory $i = 1$ (in February there are five periods remaining until the end of the horizon).

This in turn means that inventory entering March will be $3 (= i + x - d = 1 + 5 - 3)$, so that March production is $x_4(3) = 0$, as shown in Fig. 8.10. The same line of reasoning establishes that April production is $x_3(0) = 4$, since $n = 3$ with entering inventory of $0 (= i + x - d = 3 + 0 - 3)$. With the April decision given, inventory entering May is $0 + 4 - 3 = 1$, so that May production is $x_2(1) = 5(n = 2)$. Therefore June production $x_1(3) = 0$ is optimal, since entering inventory is $1 + 5 - 3 = 3$ with $n = 1$. Verify that minimum total cost when $N = 6$ is

$$(21 + 1) + (23 + 3) + (0 + 0) + (21 + 1)$$
$$+ (23 + 3) + (0 + 0) = 96$$

which appears as $f_6(0)$ in Fig. 8.10.

The policies in Fig. 8.13 show how the best production amount for January depends on the length of the planning horizon. As the horizon length N increases from 1 to 5, there exist optimal policies such that January production increases. For $N = 6$, however, the best policy calls for January production of 4 as compared to the amount 5 when $N = 5$. Thus initial production can either increase or decrease as the planning horizon lengthens. For $N = 4$, there are two alternative optimal policies. Figure 8.13 also exhibits how the cost per period depends on N. Note that the cost per period does not steadily decrease, but fluctuates as N increases from 2 to 6.

The policy for $N = 5$ deserves special attention. In this case, inventory is increased in January, February, and April. The May demand is thus filled by two units of April production as well as a unit produced in February. In this situation, it turns out to be optimal to bring in inventory to *both* February and April even though a setup cost is incurred in these two months.

Initial inventory. Here we study how an optimal policy depends on the amount of starting inventory. Examine Fig. 8.14 to see how the January production figure varies with different levels of initial inventory. When the horizon length $N = 1$, each additional unit of initial inventory brings about a unit reduction in January production. You can verify this fact quickly by examining the values for $x_1(i)$ in Fig. 8.10. Suppose that the horizon length $N = 2$. Then, as you can see in Fig. 8.10, January production $x_2(i)$ equals 5 units if initial inventory $i_0 = 1$, and equals 4 units if $i_0 = 2$. Suppose instead that $N = 4$. Then from Fig. 8.10, you can conclude that January production $x_4(i)$ equals 5 units if initial inventory i_0 equals either 1 or 2 units. The other optimal January production quantities shown in Fig. 8.14 are derived from the results in Fig. 8.10 analogously. Observe that depending on the horizon length N, the second unit may cause January production to fall (when $N = 2$, production does not fall to the previous level) or remain the same ($N = 4$).

Planning Horizon N	January Production			Incremental Value of Inventory	
	$i_0 = 0$	$i_0 = 1$	$i_0 = 2$	$i_0 = 1$	$i_0 = 2$
1	3	2	1	2	2
2	3	5	4	12	2
3	4	5	4	3	2
4	3,4	5	5	3	10
5	5	5	4	5	2
6	4	5	4	3	2

FIGURE 8.14. Dependable Manufacturing Company Inventory Valuation.

The final two columns of Fig. 8.14 tabulate the reduction in total cost when initial inventory increases. For example, consider the horizon $N = 2$. If initial inventory is 0, the total cost is 38, shown in Fig. 8.10. One unit of initial inventory brings the total cost down to 26 and another unit to 24. Thus the value of the first unit of inventory is 12 and the next 2, as exhibited in Fig. 8.14. Notice that the value of initial inventory depends considerably on the length of the time horizon, and whether the item is the first or second unit. Using the information in Fig. 8.10, trace the optimal policies for horizons $N = 4$ and 6 and initial inventory levels $i_0 = 1$ and 2 to see why the incremental values of inventory differ as they do. (Incidentally, you will find, when $N = 4$ and $i = 2$, that four units of inventory enter February, so that if inventory at the end of each period, i_t, were constrained to be strictly less than four, this solution would be ruled out, and total cost would increase.)

Commentary. Although the particular *numerical* values for the example have been selected with some care, the general description of the situation is reasonable: production expense consists of a setup cost plus a unit cost; inventory holding cost is linear (1 per unit of ending inventory); and simple upper bounds are imposed on production and inventory. Nevertheless, an optimal policy changes drastically with various alterations in the planning horizon. It is impossible to suggest how often you will encounter such extreme planning horizon sensitivity, and how economically serious it is to mistakenly adopt a nonoptimal policy. But you ought to realize from the example that it is difficult to recognize the degree and significance of the sensitivity analysis without undertaking a precise dynamic analysis of the particular application. The operations research approach you have just learned is a fundamental tool for this type of study.

As you know, a mathematical model often is general enough to cover a multitude of real situations; a meaningful evaluation of the model in this chapter must therefore be carried out in terms of what is being assumed rather than in terms of the one particular environment described for the Dependable Manufacturing Company. The crucial assumptions are listed below.

1. *The demand forecast is accurate.* Although a company can rarely forecast several months' demand without error, the margin of error is often small enough for the deterministic model to yield a good approximation. When the forecasting errors are substantial, models of the type described in Chap. 14 must be used.

2. *The manufacturing time is negligible.* The assumption actually required is that manufacturing time can be predetermined with negligible error. To illustrate, suppose it always takes two weeks to produce a batch of items. Then if a schedule found by the recursion formulas in this chapter indicates that February production is to meet February's demand, the batch really would be started two weeks earlier, in the second half of January.

Another facet of this assumption is that manufacturing time can be determined independently of other orders being processed. If several items are each produced on a single piece of equipment having limited capacity, then an agglomeration of schedules, each found independently by a dynamic programming model, may not be feasible.

The models in this chapter are often useful when an item is simply ordered from an outside vendor, who keeps an inventory on hand. The time delay then becomes the delivery lag, and the cost function includes the purchase cost, instead of the production expense.

3. *Each period's cost depends on the amount produced and on the ending inventory; each period's demand is entirely satisfied.* Without much trouble these two assumptions can be altered to cover a much wider variety of situations. We discuss how in the advanced material below.

REVIEW EXERCISES

Exercises 1 through 6 refer to the Stagecoach Problem in Sec. 8.2.

1 (a) Enumerate the 14 distinct routes from the East to the West in Fig. 8.1.
  (b) Explain why it is not necessary to evaluate all of these routes when you employ the principle of optimality.

2 (a) Suppose the stagecoach from State 7 to State 9 does not operate. What is the best routing from the East to the West?
  (b) Suppose a stagecoach service is inaugurated from State 3 to State 8. What is the smallest policy cost for this link such that Mark Off would still prefer the current routing?
  (c) Determine a range for the policy cost of the stagecoach from State 1 to State 3 such that Mark Off prefers the current routing. Do the same for the policy cost from State 3 to State 7. Do the same for the policy cost from State 2 to State 6.

3 Mark Off suspects that it is the *relative* costs at each stage that determine an optimal routing. For example, he suspects that he should select the same routing if the policy costs are $c_{12} = 2 + c$, $c_{13} = 5 + c$, and $c_{14} = 4 + c$, where c can be any constant value. Is Mark Off correct? If not, state why. If so, discuss how his observation may be helpful.

4 Mark Off's father, Pop, lives in State 8. Find an optimal routing from the East to the West that goes through State 8.

5 Mark Off's brother, Buzz, lives in San Francisco and wants to travel East. Assume that the policy cost for each stagecoach remains the same in the easterly direction.

  (a) Explain why an optimal routing for Buzz is the reverse of the one Mark used.
  (b) Carry out the recursive calculations implied by (2) in Sec. 8.2, starting the computations at State 1. (Note here that if $n = 1$ more stage to go, then Buzz is either in State 2, 3, or 4; similarly, if $n = 4$ stages to go, then Buzz is in State 10.)

6 *Stagecoach Problem.* In each part, find an optimal route from the East to the West, where the policy cost from State i to State j equals the c_{ij} shown in Fig. 8.1 plus the modifications specified.

  (a) $c_{ij} + i$ (thus, the cost from State 1 to State 2 is 3, to State 3 is 6, and to State 4 is 2, etc.).
  (b) $c_{ij} + j$ (thus, the cost from State 1 to State 2 is 4, to State 3 is 8, and to State 4 is 5, etc.).
  (c) $c_{ij} + j - i$ (thus, the cost from State 1 to State 2 is 3, to State 3 is 7, and to State 4 is 4, etc.).
  (d) $c_{ij} + i + j$ (thus, the cost from State 1 to State 2 is 5, to State 3 is 9, and to State 4 is 6, etc.).

*7 Compare the algorithm (2) in Sec. 8.2 with the shortest-route algorithm (2) in Sec. 7.4.

Exercises 8 through 19 refer to the production and inventory model in Sec. 8.3.

8 Each part below shows either the production quantity x_t in Period t or the inventory level i_t at the end of Period t; you are to determine the implied levels of the unspecified policy variable, either i_t or x_t. Assume that there are $N = 6$ periods, and that the demand requirements are

$$D_1 = 10 \qquad D_2 = 15 \qquad D_3 = 8 \qquad D_4 = 25 \qquad D_5 = 12 \qquad D_6 = 30.$$

State whether the implied policy is feasible, that is, whether $x_t \geq 0$ and $i_t \geq 0$ for every t. The symbol i_0 denotes initial inventory available at the start of Period 1.

(a) $i_0 = 10$, and $x_t = 15$ every period.
(b) $i_0 = 5$, $x_1 = 20$, and $x_t = 15$ for $t = 2, 3, \ldots, 6$.
(c) $i_0 = 5$, $x_t = 15$ for $t = 1, 2, \ldots, 5$, and $x_6 = 20$.
(d) $i_0 = 1$, $x_t = 10$ for $t = 1, 2, 3$, and $x_t = 23$ for $t = 4, 5, 6$.
(e) $i_0 = 0$, $i_1 = 15$, $i_2 = 20$, $i_3 = 25$, $i_4 = 15$, $i_5 = 5$, $i_6 = 0$.
(f) $i_0 = 10$, $i_1 = 15$, $i_2 = 20$, $i_3 = 25$, $i_4 = 15$, $i_5 = 5$, $i_6 = 0$.
(g) $i_0 = 30$, $i_1 = 15$, $i_2 = 20$, $i_3 = 25$, $i_4 = 15$, $i_5 = 5$, $i_6 = 0$.
(h) $i_0 = 0$, $i_1 = 10$, $i_2 = 10$, $i_3 = 10$, $i_4 = 10$, $i_5 = 10$, $i_6 = 0$.
(i) $i_0 = 35$, $i_1 = 35$, $i_2 = 35$, $i_3 = 35$, $i_4 = 35$, $i_5 = 35$, $i_6 = 0$.
(j) $i_0 = 35$, $i_1 = 35$, $i_2 = 35$, $i_3 = 35$, $i_4 = 35$, $i_5 = 10$, $i_6 = 0$.
(k) How would you revise the plan if $i_6 = 10$ in parts (e), (g), (h), (i), and (j)?

9 Suppose the cost function $C_t(x_t, i_t)$ is described as

$$C_t(x_t, i_t) = C(x_t) + hi_t,$$

where

$$C(x_t) = \begin{cases} 0 & \text{for } x_t = 0 \\ 6 + 10x_t & \text{for } x_t > 0, \end{cases}$$

and $h = 2$. Calculate the total production and inventory cost associated with the plans in exercise 8,

(a) Part (a).   (b) Part (b).
(c) Part (c).   (d) Part (e).
(e) Part (f).   (f) Part (h).
(g) Part (j).

10 Assume you have values for production x_t and inventory i_t that satisfy all the constraints (2) through (5) in Sec. 8.3. Recall that $C_t(x_t, i_t)$ is the production and holding cost function, and that ending inventory $i_N = 0$.

(a) Consider increasing the level of x_2 by 1, decreasing the level of x_3 by 1, and revising inventory levels accordingly. Explain why the new plan is still feasible. Indicate the resultant incremental change in total cost.   (Continued on p. 244.)

(b) Consider increasing the level of x_3 by 1, decreasing the level of x_2 by 1, and revising inventory levels accordingly. Explain why the new plan may not be feasible. Give a condition involving the demand requirements that must be satisfied in order for the new plan to be feasible. Give an equivalent condition involving inventory. Assuming the new plan is feasible, indicate the resultant incremental change in total cost.

(c) Consider increasing the level of x_2 by 1, decreasing the level of x_4 by 1, and revising inventory levels accordingly. Explain why the new plan is still feasible. Indicate the resultant incremental change in total cost.

(d) Consider increasing the level of inventory i_2 by 1, and revising production levels accordingly. Explain why the new plan may not be feasible. Give a condition involving the demand requirements that must be satisfied in order for the new plan to be feasible. Assuming the new plan is feasible, indicate the resultant incremental change in total cost.

(e) Consider decreasing the level of inventory i_2 by 1, and revising production levels accordingly. Explain why the new plan may not be feasible. Give a condition that must be satisfied in order for the new plan to be feasible. Assuming the new plan is feasible, indicate the resultant incremental change in total cost.

*11 Let $N = 6$, and write equations (4) in Sec. 8.3 for $t = 1, 2, \ldots, 6$.

(a) Display the constraints of the model in a technology table.

(b) Derive and draw an associated network structure. [*Hint:* add the six equations in part (a) to form a seventh equation; then rewrite each equation in part (a) after multiplying through by -1.]

(c) Suppose the cost function is linear,

$$C_t(x_t, i_t) = C_t x_t + h i_t,$$

where

$$C_1 = 1 \quad C_2 = 4 \quad C_3 = 3 \quad C_4 = 5 \quad C_5 = 7 \quad C_6 = 4.$$

Let initial inventory $i_0 = 0$, and let the demand requirements be those in exercise 8. Find optimal policies for $h = 0$, $h = \frac{1}{2}$, $h = 1\frac{1}{2}$, and $h = 4$. Indicate alternative optimal policies when they occur.

12 Give a verbal explanation of why the state of the system is completely summarized by the level of entering inventory each period. What are the assumptions about costs and production lags that permit this simple characterization of the state?

13 The recursive calculation process in dynamic programming has been termed a bootstrap approach in Sec. 8.2. Give a verbal explanation of the way the bootstrap approach is applied to obtain a solution to the inventory model in Sec. 8.3.

14 Suppose $N = 6$ and January is Period 1. Let d_n refer to the demand requirement in that period when there are n more periods to go. To what month does d_1 refer? Similarly, d_6? d_5? d_2?

15 Consider the recursion (8) in Sec. 8.3. Suppose that $i = 0$ when n periods remain. What is the smallest feasible value for production, x, in that period? Suppose, instead, that $i = d_1 + d_2 + \cdots + d_n$. What is the value for production in each of the n remaining periods?

16 Consider the recursion (8) in Sec. 8.3. Suppose $c_3(x, j) = 5x + 2j$. Assume that starting inventory $i = 4$ with $n = 3$ more periods to go, and that ending inventory must not exceed 4. Let $d_3 = 10$. Find an optimal level of production and the associated ending inventory level given the following.

(a) $f_2(0) = 100$ $f_2(1) = 90$ $f_2(2) = 82$ $f_2(3) = 76$ $f_2(4) = 75$.
(b) $f_2(0) = 110$ $f_2(1) = 100$ $f_2(2) = 92$ $f_2(3) = 86$ $f_2(4) = 85$.
(c) $f_2(j) = 100 - 6j$.
(d) $f_2(j) = 100 - 9j$.
(e) $f_2(0) = 100$ $f_2(1) = 99$ $f_2(2) = 93$ $f_2(3) = 85$ $f_2(4) = 75$.

17 Recall that $x_n(i)$ is an optimal production level when entering inventory is at level i with n more periods to go. Suppose $d_n = 2$ for every n and that the values for $x_n(i)$ are

$$x_3(0) = 5 \qquad x_2(0) = 4 \qquad x_1(0) = 2$$
$$x_3(1) = 4 \qquad x_2(1) = 3 \qquad x_1(1) = 1$$
$$x_3(2) = 0 \qquad x_2(2) = 0 \qquad x_1(2) = 0.$$
$$x_3(3) = 0 \qquad x_2(3) = 0$$

In parts (a) through (d), indicate an optimal production plan and the associated inventory levels when there are $n = 3$ more periods to go, and entering inventory level i equals

(a) 0.
(b) 1.
(c) 2.
(d) 3.
(e) At $n = 3$ what is the incremental value of $i = 1$ versus $i = 2$? Of $i = 4$ versus $i = 3$? [Use the symbol $c_k(x, j)$ to denote the cost function in the period when there are k more periods to go.]

*18 (a) Modify Fig. 8.6 to treat the case in which demand $d_n = 2$ for $n = 1, 2, 3, 4$.
   (b) Modify Fig. 8.6 to treat the case in which the permissible production values are $x = 0, 2, 4$.
   (c) Explain how Fig. 8.6 is modified when you impose the constraint that inventory at the end of each period cannot exceed the level 1.
   (d) Explain how Fig. 8.6 can be simplified if you know for certain that inventory entering January equals 1.

*19 Explain the connection between finding a shortest route in Fig. 8.6 and the recursive calculations indicated by (8) in Sec. 8.3.

Exercises 20 through 33 refer to the case of the Dependable Manufacturing Company described in Sec. 8.4.

20 In each part below, construct a complete table, laid out like Fig. 8.9, showing $f_n(i)$ and $x_n(i)$ for the indicated value of n. Use the values of $f_{n-1}(i)$ that are given in Fig. 8.10.

(a) $n = 4$.   (b) $n = 5$.   (c) $n = 6$.

21 (a) Verify that the cost function $C(x)$ given as (3) in Sec. 8.4 represents a setup cost of 13 plus a variable unit cost of 2 per item produced.
  (b) Explain why the production level x in a period must be at least $3 - i$, where i is the level of entering inventory.
  (c) Explain why the production level x in a period cannot exceed $7 - i$, given the restriction that ending inventory must be less than or equal to 4.
  (d) Suppose initial inventory is zero. Calculate the average cost per period if the production pattern is to produce three units every period. If the pattern is to produce five units and then one unit. If the pattern is to produce five units, five units, two units, and zero units. If the pattern is to produce five units, five units, zero units, and two units. If the pattern is to produce five units, two units, five units, and zero units. If the pattern is to produce four units and then two units. If the pattern is to produce four units, four units, four units, and zero units. Explain the cost tradeoffs among these different patterns.

22 Construct a table like that in Fig. 8.13, and assume that initial inventory entering January is

(a) $i_0 = 1$.   (b) $i_0 = 2$.
(c) $i_0 = 3$.   (d) $i_0 = 4$.
(e) Given your answers above, verify the incremental values of inventory shown in Fig. 8.14, and extend the table for $i_0 = 3$ and $i_0 = 4$.

23 Construct a table like that in Fig. 8.10 given the constraint on ending inventory as indicated below. (*Hint:* you do not have to repeat all the computations in Fig. 8.10 if you make judicious use of the information contained in Figs. 8.7 through 8.10.)

(a) $i \le 5$.
(b) $i \le 3$.
(c) Given your answers above, what is the smallest limiting value (3, 4, or 5) such that the restriction on the inventory level is *not* binding?

24 Construct tables like those in Figs. 8.10 and 8.13, where the constraint on the production capacity limitation is specified as

(a) Production x in each period cannot exceed four units.
(b) Production x in each period cannot exceed six units and $C(6) = 25$.
(c) Given your answers above, compare the impact of varying the production capacity limit.
(d) What is the form of an optimal policy for this company if it imposes the production level restriction that $x \ge 1$ every period?

25 Construct a table like that in Fig. 8.10 given the constraint that inventory at the end of the horizon equals

(a) One unit.   (b) Two units.
(c) Three units.   (d) Four units.
(e) For each of your answers above, construct a table like that in Fig. 8.13.

26 Construct tables like those in Figs. 8.10, 8.13, and 8.14, given the assumption that demand D_t each period equals

(a) Two units.
(b) Four units.
(c) Explain how the optimal policies differ when stationary demand equals two or four, instead of three.

27 Construct tables like those in Figs. 8.10, 8.13, and 8.14, given the assumption that

(a) The setup cost component in $C(x)$, shown in (3) of Sec. 8.4, is 10, instead of 13.
(b) The holding cost $h = 5$, instead of $h = 1$.
(c) Explain how the optimal policies are affected by a decrease in setup cost or an increase in holding cost.

28 Construct tables like those in Figs. 8.10 and 8.13 given the assumption that demand in the *final* period of the horizon is as specified below, instead of three units. (For example, if $N = 4$, then demand is altered in April.) Compare your results with the policies in Figs. 8.10 and 8.13 and comment on the impact of incorrectly assuming in January that demand at the end of the horizon is three units, instead of the amount indicated below.

(a) Two units.
(b) Four units.

29 Suppose you can increase the limit on production x_t to 6, instead of 5, and $C(6) = 28.5$. Construct a complete table, laid out like Fig. 8.10, showing $f_n(i)$ and $x_n(i)$ for the values of $n = 1, 2, \ldots, N$.

(a) $N = 3$.
(b) $N = 4$.
(c) $N = 6$.
(d) Compare your results with the policies in Fig. 8.10. When is it optimal to schedule $x_t = 6$?
(e) Construct a table laid out like Fig. 8.13 and compare your results with those in Fig. 8.13.
(f) Construct a table laid out like Fig. 8.14 and compare your results with those in Fig. 8.14.

30 Explain your understanding of the following terms:

dynamic programming   bootstrap process (or approach)
principle of optimality   optimal policy
recursion   stage
recursive algorithm   state.

COMPUTATIONAL EXERCISES

31 Mark Off's fame spread world wide. He received an urgent request from the Russian Tsar Kazim to find a route to Rostov from Vladivostok. In this case, the Tsar's wife made the trip, and the expense associated with each leg of the journey is for protection against attacks by Cossacks and local tribesmen. The numbers shown on each arc in Fig. 8.15 are the rubles that must be paid for protection on that route. Find an optimal routing. Display your calculations in tables like those in Figs. 8.2 through 8.5.

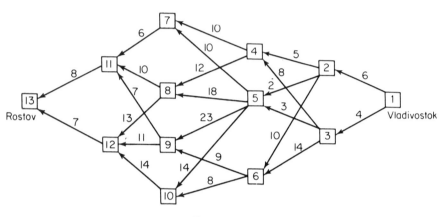

FIGURE 8.15

32 Consider Tsar Kazim's problem in exercise 31. Assume that the same number of rubles must be paid for a journey in the opposite direction. Find an optimal routing starting in Rostov and ending in Vladivostok. Display your calculations in tables like those in Figs. 8.2 through 8.5.

33 Consider Tsar Kazim's problem in exercise 31. The Tsar's wife insists on visiting Territory 5, because she has learned that they have perfected a recipe for caviar pancakes. Find an optimal routing from Vladivostok to Rostov through Territory 5.

Exercises 34 through 39 refer to specific cases of the inventory model described in Sec. 8.3, and characterized by the recursion (8). In each exercise, the production and holding cost function for Period t has the form $C_t(x_t, i_t) = C_t(x_t) + h_t i_t$. (Note if January is the beginning of the horizon, then Period 1 refers to January.) For both the horizon lengths N and $N\text{-}1$, construct a *pair* of tables like that in Fig. 8.10 and insert the implied production policies in a table like that in Fig. 8.13. Be sure to note that the costs change in each period. Consequently, you must perform the recursion (8) *twice*: the first time assume that (7), the end of the horizon, refers to Period N, and the second time that (7) refers to Period N-1. (*Remark*: more efficient algorithms for solving these problems are discussed in Chap. 9.)

34 Let $N = 4$, demand $D_t = 1$, and holding cost $h_t = .1$ for all periods. Assume that

$C_1(0) = 0$ $C_1(1) = 5$ $C_1(2) = 10$ $C_1(3) = 15$ $C_1(4) = 16$

$C_2(0) = 0$ $C_2(1) = 6$ $C_2(2) = 9$ $C_2(3) = 12$

$C_3(0) = 0$ $C_3(1) = 5$ $C_3(2) = 7$

$C_4(0) = 0$ $C_4(1) = 3.$

35 Let $N = 5$. Assume

$$D_1 = 1 \qquad D_2 = 1 \qquad D_3 = 2$$
$$D_4 = 4 \qquad D_5 = 4,$$

and that holding cost $h_t = 1$ for all periods. Suppose the production cost function is

$$C_t(x_t) = \begin{cases} 0 & \text{for } x_t = 0 \\ s_t + c_t x_t & \text{for } x_t = 1, 2, 3, \ldots, \end{cases}$$

where $c_t = 10$ for all periods, and

$$s_1 = 1 \qquad s_2 = 2 \qquad s_3 = 4$$
$$s_4 = 8 \qquad s_5 = 7.$$

36 Let $N = 4$. Assume

$$D_1 = 1 \qquad D_2 = 4$$
$$D_3 = 2 \qquad D_4 = 2,$$

and that $h_t = 0$ for all periods. Suppose the production cost function is the same form as in exercise 35, where

$$s_1 = 1 \qquad s_2 = 12 \qquad s_3 = 1 \qquad s_4 = 2$$
$$c_1 = 3 \qquad c_2 = 1 \qquad c_3 = 2 \qquad c_4 = 1.$$

37 Solve the Bean Pitcher Company case considered in exercises 36 and 51 of Chap. 6.

38 Suppose a firm can produce a limited number of units using its work force at regular-time wage rates and an additional, but limited, number of units using its work force at overtime wage rates. The data are given in Fig. 8.16 on p. 250. Thus, for example,

$$C_1(x_1) = \begin{cases} 2x_1 & \text{for } x_1 = 0, 1, 2, 3 \\ 2 \cdot 3 + 5(x_1 - 3) = 5x_1 - 9 & \text{for } x_1 = 4, 5, \ldots, 9. \end{cases}$$

The fluctuation in costs from period to period is due to special conditions in the company's labor market as well as to varying prices for the product's raw materials. Assume that each unit of inventory stored at the end of a period has a holding cost $h_t = 1$ for all periods.

		Jan.	Feb.	Mar.	Apr.	May	June
Regular Time	cost/unit	2	4	2	5	2	6
	capacity	3	1	4	3	1	3
Overtime	cost/unit	5	6	6	6	3	7
	capacity	6	3	3	2	0	1
Demand Requirements D_t		1	2	7	6	0	2

FIGURE 8.16

39 Assume that the demand requirements are

$$D_1 = 3 \qquad D_2 = 6 \qquad D_3 = 3,$$

and that there are no holding costs. The production costs are described by Fig. 8.17.

January	February	March
Setup cost = 3	Setup cost = 6	Setup cost = 20
Cost/unit for 1 up to 5 units = 1	Cost/unit for 1 up to 5 units = 1	Cost/unit for first item = 1
Cost/unit for each item beyond 5 units and up to 10 units = 5	Cost/unit for each item beyond 5 units = 25	Cost/unit for each item beyond the first = 30
Cost/unit for each item beyond 10 units = 30		

FIGURE 8.17

For $N = 1, 2, 3$, construct tables like those in Figs. 8.10 and 8.13, where $1 \le n \le N$.

FORMULATION EXERCISES

40 Consider the inventory model described in Sec. 8.3. Suppose that $\bar{x}$ represents a "target" production level each period, and that if actual production x deviates from $\bar{x}$, then you must pay the "smoothing cost" $v \cdot |x - \bar{x}|$. Assume $\bar{x}$ is a prespecified constant.

(a) Show how to reformulate the recursion (8) to take this smoothing cost into account. (*Continued on p. 251.*)

*(b) Let $v = 1$, $\bar{x} = 3$, and use the data in Sec. 8.4. Construct tables like those in Figs. 8.10 and 8.13 and indicate the impact of adding a smoothing cost.

*(c) Answer part (b) for $\bar{x} = 2$.

*(d) Discuss the difficulties that arise in the dynamic programming formulation if the smoothing cost is $v \cdot |x_t - x_{t-1}|$. (This case is treated in Chap. 10.)

41 Indicate how you would modify the inventory model in Sec. 8.3 and the recursion (8) to accommodate

(a) Deterioration, that is, inventory at the start of Period t is smaller than inventory at the end of Period $t - 1$.

(b) Spoilage, that is, the production level x yields less than x usable items.

(c) Demand D_t can also be negative, indicating the return of items.

(d) Production x can also be negative, indicating the disposal of items.

*(e) Production cost in Period t also depends on the production level in the previous period.

42 Indicate how to modify the inventory model in Sec. 8.3 and the recursion (8) when $R_t(y_t)$ represents the total revenue from selling y_t units in Period t and y_t is a decision variable. (Assume you cannot sell a unit in Period t unless it actually is available by the end of the period.)

43 Consider the Feedem-Speedem Airline Company case described in exercise 34 of Chap. 2. Formulate (but do not solve) the model in terms of a dynamic programming recursion. Be sure to define all the symbols you use, and answer the five questions at the end of Sec. 8.2. Give the appropriate optimization function when there is a single period remaining, as well as the recursion for Stage n. Explain how to initiate and terminate the calculations.

CONTENTS

CHAPTER 9

Dynamic Optimization of Inventory Scheduling[†]

9.1 EXPLOITING SPECIAL STRUCTURE

The analysis of the deterministic inventory model described in Sec. 8.3 is continued here. You will see that when the cost functions are assumed to have certain shapes, considerably more can be said about the optimal schedules. In particular, you can determine the *form* of an optimal policy, and with such knowledge devise simplified computational procedures to actually find the best policy.

Throughout this chapter we assume the cost functions are

(1) $$C_t(x_t, i_t) = C_t(x_t) + h_t(i_t) \quad \text{for each period,}$$

where

(2) $$C_t(x_t) \geq 0 \qquad C_t(0) = 0 \quad \text{and} \quad h_t(i_t) \geq 0 \qquad h_t(0) = 0.$$

Thus the total cost in each period is the sum of $C_t(x_t)$, which is the cost due to producing x_t, and $h_t(i_t)$, the cost due to having inventory i_t at the end of a period. The inventory balance equations are

(3) $$i_t = i_{t-1} + x_t - D_t \quad \text{for each period,}$$

where we postulate initial inventory $i_0 = 0$ and each demand D_t is a nonnegative integer. An equivalent way of writing (3) is

(4) $$i_t = i_0 + \sum_{k=1}^{t} x_k - \sum_{k=1}^{t} D_k.$$

[†]The focus of this chapter is primarily inventory analysis and secondarily dynamic analysis. Without loss of continuity, you can skip this chapter now if you wish, and return to it when studying Chap. 14.

Finally, we require

(5) x_t and i_t nonnegative integers,

so that all demand is satisfied on time.

9.2 CONVEX AND CONCAVE COST FUNCTIONS

In many real-life production and inventory systems, two important types of cost functions frequently occur, namely, convex and concave. Convex production costs arise when the cost of each incremental unit of production is at least as large as the previous unit of production. For example, direct materials and labor costs may rise at a constant rate (linearly) with output until it is necessary to institute overtime production, at which point the rate of increase in total costs becomes greater because of the higher wages that must be paid for overtime. Convex holding costs may occur analogously. For example, the cost of storing inventory in a public warehouse may rise linearly with the amount kept in storage until a critical warehouse capacity is reached, at which point more costly space elsewhere must be procured.

Concave production costs arise when the cost of each incremental unit of production is no larger than the previous unit of production. This situation may occur when a learning-curve phenomenon reduces the unit cost of production, or when raw materials may be purchased with large-quantity discounts. An example of a concave storage cost function arises when a firm must pay a lump-sum fixed cost for obtaining storage space, which then is sufficiently large to provide all the required room for inventory stocks.

We next provide formal definitions for convex and concave cost functions, and in the subsequent sections show how to take advantage of these special shapes in computing optimal production policies.

A function $g(x)$ defined for integer values of x is said to be **convex** *if*

(1) $g(x + 1) - g(x) \geq g(x) - g(x - 1)$ for all x convex

and **concave** *if*

(2) $g(x + 1) - g(x) \leq g(x) - g(x - 1)$ for all x concave.

Several graphical illustrations of convex and concave functions are shown in Fig. 9.1.

If you view $g(x)$ as a total cost function, then observe in Fig. 9.1 that convex costs occur when each *additional* unit costs at least as much as the previous unit. Analogously, concave costs occur when each *additional* unit costs no more than the previous unit. Sometimes the permissible values of x are constrained to be within a range, such as $x = a, a + 1, \ldots, b - 1, b$ (where $a + 1 \leq b - 1$). Then the definitions are to be applied to $a + 1 \leq x \leq b - 1$.

Convex Cost Functions

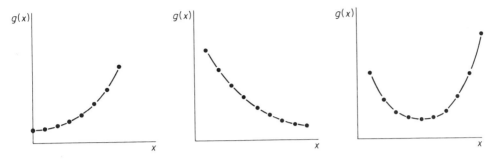

Concave Cost Functions

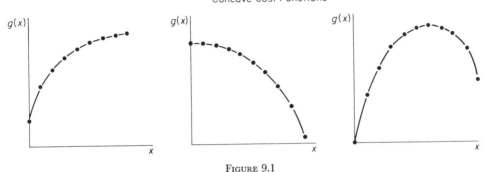

FIGURE 9.1

To examine the forms of particular functions, it is convenient to have the terms in the definitions (1) and (2) rearranged as

(3) $$\frac{g(x + 1) + g(x - 1)}{2} \geq g(x) \quad \text{convex}$$

(4) $$\frac{g(x + 1) + g(x - 1)}{2} \leq g(x) \quad \text{concave.}$$

Consider the following six examples of $g(x)$. You will find it helpful to draw a sketch of each function on scratch paper, and are urged to do so. For this purpose, put $a = 2$, $b = 1$, and $c = 3$ in the first four examples.

Case i. Let $g(x) = ax + b$. Then

(5) $$\frac{[a(x + 1) + b] + [a(x - 1) + b]}{2} = ax + b,$$

so that a linear function $g(x)$ is *both* convex and concave for any values of a and b and all x.

Case ii. Let $g(x) = ax^2 + b$. Then

(6)
$$\frac{[a(x+1)^2 + b] + [a(x-1)^2 + b]}{2}$$
$$= ax^2 + a + b \begin{cases} \geq ax^2 + b & \text{if } a \geq 0 \\ \leq ax^2 + b & \text{if } a \leq 0. \end{cases}$$

Thus for all x, $g(x)$ is convex when a is nonnegative, and concave when a is nonpositive.

Case iii. Let $g(x) = \begin{cases} ax + b & \text{for } x \geq 0 \\ -cx + b & \text{for } x \leq 0 \end{cases}$

with $a \geq 0$ and $c \geq 0$. The test for Case i shows that $g(x)$ is convex (3) for $x < 0$ and $x > 0$. At $x = 0$,

(7)
$$\frac{[a+b] + [c+b]}{2} = \frac{(a+c)}{2} + b \geq b,$$

so that $g(x)$ is convex for all x.

Case iv. Let $g(x) = \begin{cases} 0 & \text{for } x = 0 \\ ax + b & \text{for } x \geq 1 \end{cases}$

with $b \geq 0$. The test for Case i shows that $g(x)$ is concave (4) for $x > 1$. At $x = 1$,

(8)
$$\frac{[2a + b] + [0]}{2} \leq a + b,$$

so that $g(x)$ is concave (for nonnegative x).

Case v. Let $g(x) = \begin{cases} 0 & \text{for } x = 0 \\ 13 + 2x & \text{for } x = 1, 2, 3, 4, 5 \\ 28.5 & \text{for } x = 6. \end{cases}$

The analysis for Case iv shows that (4) is satisfied for $x \leq 4$. At $x = 5$,

(9)
$$\frac{[28.5] + [21]}{2} = 24.75 > 23,$$

so that (3) is satisfied. Consequently, $g(x)$ is neither convex nor concave.

Case vi. As you may verify, the piecewise linear function

(10) $g(x) = \begin{cases} a_1 x + b_1 & \text{for } 0 \leq x \leq w_1 \\ a_1 w_1 + a_2(x - w_1) + b_1 & \text{for } w_1 \leq x \leq w_2 \\ a_1 w_1 + a_2(w_2 - w_1) + a_3(x - w_2) + b_1 & \text{for } w_2 \leq x \end{cases}$

is convex if $a_1 \leq a_2 \leq a_3$ and concave if $a_1 \geq a_2 \geq a_3$. (Make the tests for $x = w_1$ and w_2. Draw the function by letting $a_1 = 2, b_1 = 1, w_1 = 4, a_2 = 3, w_2 = 6, a_3 = 4$.)

Several of the above examples are of special interest. For instance, *Case iii* includes

$$(11) \qquad h_t(i_t) = \begin{cases} h_t i_t & \text{if } i_t \geq 0 \\ -p_t i_t & \text{if } i_t \leq 0, \end{cases}$$

where $h_t \geq 0$ represents a per-unit inventory holding cost and $p_t \geq 0$ a per-unit backlog penalty charge. *Case vi* contains

$$(12) \qquad C_t(x_t) = \begin{cases} r_t x_t & \text{for } 0 \leq x_t \leq u_t \\ r_t u_t + 1.5 r_t(x_t - u_t) & \text{for } u_t \leq x_t \leq v_t \\ r_t u_t + 1.5 r_t(v_t - u_t) + 2 r_t(x_t - v_t) & \text{for } v_t \leq x_t, \end{cases}$$

where x_t is the total labor-hours scheduled in Period t, r_t is the regular-time wage per labor-hour, u_t is a given total amount of regular-time labor-hours available in Period t, $1.5 r_t$ is the "time and a half" wage rate per overtime hour, v_t is a given total amount of overtime hours available in Period t, and $2 r_t$ is the "double-time" wage rate per labor-hour.

9.3 INVENTORY MODEL WITH CONVEX COSTS

In addition to the cost, inventory, and production assumptions already made in Sec. 9.1, assume that

$$(1) \qquad\qquad\qquad C_t(x_t) \text{ is convex } \quad \text{(production cost)}$$

$$(2) \qquad\qquad\qquad h_t(i_t) \text{ is convex } \quad \text{(holding cost).}$$

A convexity assumption is sometimes called a situation of **decreasing incremental returns to scale.** It is also possible to impose, in each period, an upper-bound constraint u_t on x_t as well as a maximum amount b_t on inventory. To keep the explanation simple, suppose you handle these constraints by letting the corresponding values of $C_t(x_t)$ for $x_t > u_t$, and $h_t(i_t)$, for $i_t > b_t$, be infinitely large. This convention preserves the convexity in (1) and (2). Finally, we mention that the analysis can be extended to permit backlogging of demand requirements from a period to later periods.

In brief, the algorithm starting in Period 1 proceeds period by period to fill each unit of demand requirement as cheaply as possible, *given* the production already scheduled and the resultant pattern of inventory. The fact that such a simple algorithm leads to an optimal solution, of course, rests heavily on the convexity assumptions (1) and (2).

The details of the algorithms for this model are as follows.

Step 1. Let p be the earliest period in which the current demand requirement value is $D_p > 0$. For each of the Periods 1, 2, . . . , p, consider increasing production by one unit in the current trial schedule in order that one unit of D_p is filled.

Step 2. For each of the possible p revisions, calculate the entire incremental cost from the increased production *and* inventory holding. Select an alternative with minimum incremental cost and revise the trial schedule accordingly. If there is more than one such alternative, schedule production in as late a period as possible.

Step 3. Reduce the current value of D_p by one unit. Examine whether the current values of *all* D_t have now been reduced to 0. If so, stop; otherwise return to *Step 1.*

The example to follow illustrates the method.

The Highway Rubber Company Problem. This firm is planning its production schedule of tires for six months, January through June. The fluctuating monthly demands D_t are shown on the bottom of Fig. 9.2. Notice they accumulate to 18, so that the *total* demand for the span $N = 6$ is the same as that in the Dependable Manufacturing Company Example of Sec. 8.4.

In each period, there is a capability of producing a given number of tires at regular cost and an additional number at a premium cost. To demonstrate the flexibility of the algorithm, the regular and premium costs, and maximum amounts achievable at these costs, vary from period to period in the illustration. In Fig. 9.2, these costs appear in the pair of boxes on the diagonal, the upper figure being the regular cost. The corresponding maximum capacities are in the next to last column on the right. The far right column accumulates the monthly production capabilities.

For example, in January as many as three units can be produced at a cost of 2 each, and as many as an additional six at a cost of 5 each. In February, one unit can be produced at a cost of 4, and as many as an additional three at a cost of 6. In March, as many as four units can be produced at a cost of 2 each, and as many as an additional three at 6 each, etc. Thus in each period the production cost function is of the form

(3) $C_t(x_t) = r_t x_t$ for $0 \leq x_t \leq u_t$ (regular time)

(4) $C_t(x_t) = r_t u_t + s_t(x_t - u_t)$

           $= s_t x_t + (r_t - s_t)u_t$ for $u_t \leq x_t \leq v_t$ (overtime)

with $r_t < s_t$, so that $C_t(x_t)$ is convex. In (3) and (4), r_t represents the regular cost and s_t the premium cost. The u_t and v_t are the corresponding production capacities. (So for $t = 1$, the values are $r_1 = 2, s_1 = 5, u_1 = 3$, and $v_1 = 3 + 6 = 9$.)

	Jan	Feb	Mar	Apr	May	Jun	Production Capacity	Cumulative Capacity
Jan	2	3	4	5	6	7	3	9
	5	6	7	8	9	10	6	
Feb		4	5	6	7	8	1	13
		6	7	8	9	10	3	
Mar			2	3	4	5	4	20
			6	7	8	9	3	
Apr				5	6	7	3	25
				6	7	8	2	
May					2	3	1	26
					3	4	0	
Jun						6	3	30
						7	1	
Demand D_t	1	2	7	6	0	2		
Cumulative Demand	1	3	10	16	16	18		

FIGURE 9.2. Highway Rubber Company Convex Cost Model.

The rows of Fig. 9.2 refer to production scheduled in each month. The columns refer to the monthly demands. Since no backlogging is allowed, the boxes below the diagonal can be eliminated. Thus the first two rows of the figure indicate that January's *production* can be allocated to the demand in any of the six months, the second two rows indicate that February's *production* can be allocated to demand in February or a subsequent month, etc. Likewise, June's *demand* can be filled by production from any month. In order for a feasible schedule to exist, it is necessary that the cumulative monthly production capability be at least as large as the accumulated demand. Check the right-hand column and the bottom row of Fig. 9.2 to verify that this condition is satisfied in the example.

The computational method about to be described is a slight simplification of the algorithm above and is made possible because of (3), (4), and

(5) $h_t(i_t) = h_t i_t$ (linear holding cost).

To keep the numerical example simple, assume that $h_t = 1$ for all periods. Therefore the cost figures across each row of Fig. 9.2 increase by 1 to indicate the holding cost per item per period. For example, if an item is produced in January at the regular cost of 2 and held until February, the total unit cost becomes $3(= 2 + 1)$, which appears in the first row of the February column. If it is held another month, an additional unit is added, for a total of 4 ($= 3 + 1$), which appears in the first row of the March column. Incidentally, we do not need to *assume* that ending inventory $i_N = 0$, because the cost assumptions (3), (4), and (5) ensure this condition holds in an optimal policy.

To follow the details of the algorithm, copy Fig. 9.2 on a sheet of paper. Notice that the format resembles that of a transportation problem. This is no coincidence, because the linearities in (3), (4), and (5) do yield such a model.

Computation of an optimal policy. Using transportation problem terminology, think of each permissible box in Fig. 9.2 as a route, with the associated unit cost displayed as usual. The idea simply is to fill successive units of demand, starting with January, then February, and so on, by an *available* route having the least cost. Whenever there are ties, production is scheduled as late as possible.

To help you perform the process on your copy of Fig. 9.2, here is a summary of what happens.

  (i) Fill January's demand of 1 at a unit cost of 2.
  (ii) Fill February's demand of 2 at a unit cost of 3.
  (iii) Fill the first four items of March's demand at a unit cost of 2, the next item at a unit cost of 5, and the last two items at a unit cost of 6.
  (iv) Fill the first three items of April's demand at a unit cost of 5, the next two items at a unit cost of 6, and the last item at a unit cost of 7.
  (v) Since there is no demand in May, make no entries in the May column.
  (vi) Fill the first item of June's demand at a unit cost of 3, and the second item at a unit cost of 6.

As you progress from (i) to (vi), reduce the Production Capacity figures in the next to last column of Fig. 9.2. As soon as any such figure becomes 0, do not permit the other routes in that row to be available for the rest of the schedule. Compare your schedule with that shown in Fig. 9.3.

An optimal schedule is then

(6)
$$x_1 = 3 \quad x_2 = 1 \quad x_3 = 7 \quad x_4 = 5 \quad x_5 = 1 \quad x_6 = 1$$
$$i_1 = 2 \quad i_2 = 1 \quad i_3 = 1 \quad i_4 = 0 \quad i_5 = 1 \quad i_6 = 0,$$

	Jan	Feb	Mar	Apr	May	Jun	Production Capacity	Cumulative Capacity
Jan	2 — 1	3 — 2	4	5	6	7	3̶2̶Ø̶	9
	5	6	7	8	9	10	6	
Feb		4	5 — 1	6	7	8	X̶0	13
		6	7	8	9	10	3	
Mar			2 — 4	3	4	5	4̶0	20
			6 — 2	7 — 1	8	9	3̶X̶0	
Apr				5 — 3	6	7	3̶0	25
				6 — 2	7	8	2̶0	
May					2	3 — 1	X̶0	26
					3	4	0	
Jun						6 — 1	3̶2	30
						7 — 1	1	
Demand D_t	X̶0	2̶0	7̶3̶2̶0	6̶3̶X̶0	0	2̶X̶0		
Cumulative Demand	1	3	10	16	16	18		

FIGURE 9.3. Highway Rubber Company Convex Cost Schedule.

which can be obtained by looking at the capacities used (shown in the next to last column of Fig. 9.3) to find x_t, and by summing the amounts in the boxes above and to the right of the diagonal pair in Period $t + 1$ to find i_t.

Obviously, this procedure is much simpler than computing $f_n(i)$, as was done in Chap. 8. It also contains a couple of simplifications in the three-step algorithm above. Specifically, the tabular form makes apparent in *Step 2* the minimum incremental cost alternative with available capacity. And in *Step 3* the current values of demand are reduced as much as possible, given the currently available production capacity for the best alternative.

*9.4 PLANNING HORIZON ANALYSIS
FOR CONVEX COST MODEL

It is clear in the application of the algorithm for the special example above that production in each period may increase, but will never decrease as the planning horizon N lengthens. The conclusion also holds for the general convex cost model of the previous section.

Preparatory to the statement of such a proposition, let cumulative demand and cumulative production for Periods $1, 2, \ldots, p$ be denoted as

$$(1) \qquad\qquad R_p = \sum_{t=1}^{p} D_t \quad \text{and} \quad X_p = \sum_{t=1}^{p} x_t.$$

Suppose you are not entirely certain about the actual demand amounts, but you can state that R_p lies within a specified range

$$(2) \qquad\qquad S_p \le R_p \le T_p \quad \text{for } p = 1, 2, \ldots, N.$$

Let $X_p(S)$ be an optimal production schedule *assuming* that $R_p = S_p$, the minimal forecast, and similarly let $X_p(T)$ be an optimal production schedule *assuming* that $R_p = T_p$, the maximal forecast, for $p = 1, 2, \ldots, N$. Then the following can be said about an optimal schedule.

> CONVEX COST HORIZON THEOREM. (a) An optimal value of x_p will not decrease if any D_t increases. (b) An optimal schedule satisfies $X_p(S) \le X_p \le X_p(T)$ for $p = 1, 2, \ldots, N$.

Part (b) of the theorem is illustrated graphically in Fig. 9.4.

The preceding result is properly called a planning horizon theorem, because you can regard lengthening N to $N + 1$ as being the same as revising the value of D_{N+1} upward from its zero level in the analysis of the N-period horizon problem. Part (a) of the proposition states that you are never required to reduce a previously scheduled amount of production when more demand is encompassed in the plan.

In the Dependable Manufacturing Company Example of Sec. 8.4, both parts (a) and (b) failed to hold. As you can see in Fig. 8.13, when June demand was added into consideration, so that N increased from 5 to 6, January production decreased from 5 to 4, and the combined January and February production decreased from 10 to 9.

An important implication of part (b) is that in particular circumstances, it may be possible to select an optimal production amount x_1 with no more than rough information about demands in later periods. The idea is to find $X_1(S)$ and $X_1(T)$, and see if these differ only a little, if at all. A narrow range implies that x_1 can be set within this interval without much possible loss of optimality. Then in the following period, when more information about demand emerges, the process can be repeated. If the range is large, an examination of the two schedules $X_p(S)$ and $X_p(T)$ will help pinpoint the location where a better demand estimate is required.

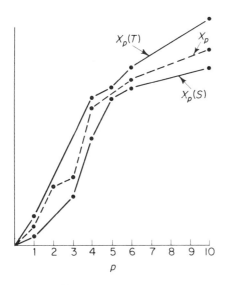

Note: $X_p(S)$ optimal schedule for minimal forecast
$X_p(T)$ optimal schedule for maximal forecast
X_p optimal schedule

Figure 9.4. Bounds on Optimal Schedule for Convex Costs.

9.5 Lot-Size Inventory Model with Concave Costs

The model to be presented here is another special case of the elementary inventory model in Sec. 8.3. It is sometimes referred to as a **dynamic lot-size model** and is noteworthy because it represents a situation of frequent practical importance. Furthermore, it provides a case of complexity intermediate to that of the general model in Sec. 8.3 and the convex cost model in Sec. 9.3.

In addition to the cost, inventory, and production assumptions already made in Sec. 9.1, assume that

(1) $C_t(x_t)$ is concave   (production cost),

(2) $h_t(i_t)$ is concave   (holding cost).

A concave cost assumption is sometimes referred to as a situation of **increasing incremental returns to scale.** In sharp contrast to the convex cost model, upper limits on x_t and i_t are *not* permitted. Recall that an upper bound on production can be viewed as letting $C_t(x_t)$ be infinitely large for x_t beyond the critical value. In such terms, $C_t(x_t)$ would no longer remain concave.

One frequent example of concave production costs occurs when production involves an initial **setup** and then each item incurs a standard unit cost:

$$(3) \qquad C_t(x_t) = \begin{cases} 0 & \text{for } x_t = 0 \\ s_t + c_t x_t & \text{for } x_t \geq 1. \end{cases}$$

Recall that this was the cost function of the Dependable Manufacturing Company Example in Sec. 8.4, with setup cost $s_t = 13$, unit cost $c_t = 2$, for $x_t \leq 5$. Although $C_t(x_t)$ was concave over the range $x_t = 0, 1, \ldots, 5$, that example does *not* fit the assumptions of this section, since upper bounds on x_t are not allowed here.

Another example of concave costs often arises when the model is applied to a situation in which inventory is replenished by purchasing the item from an outside vendor. In these instances, the seller may offer so-called **quantity discounts** for large orders. To illustrate, the schedule of **price breaks** may be given as

(4)
$10 per item for any amount ordered up to a dozen
$ 8 per *additional* item above a dozen and up to a gross
$ 5 per *additional* item beyond a gross.

The mathematical expression corresponding to this schedule is

$$(5) \qquad C_t(x_t) = \begin{cases} 10x_t & \text{for} \quad 0 \leq x_t \leq 12 \\ 120 + 8(x_t - 12) & \text{for} \quad 13 \leq x_t \leq 144 \\ 120 + 1056 + 5(x_t - 144) & \text{for } 145 \leq x_t. \end{cases}$$

The example is of the same form as (10) in Sec. 9.2. Thus $C_t(x_t)$ is concave, since the coefficients of x_t, namely 10, 8, and 5, are progressively smaller. If a setup cost is added to (5), the function remains concave. Hence, in finding an optimal inventory policy for this situation, a firm can add a lump-sum cost attributable to its own paper work and handling associated with its placing and receiving the order.

Structural result. The fundamental insight for the analysis of this model is given in the following proposition.

FORM OF AN OPTIMAL POLICY. There always exists a minimal cost policy with the property that x_t has one of the following values: $0, D_t, D_t + D_{t+1}, \ldots,$ $D_t + D_{t+1} + \cdots + D_N$.

The statement implies that in seeking an optimal policy, you need only consider $[1 + N - (t - 1) = N - t + 2]$ possible values for x_t. Compare this with the general model in Sec. 8.3, where x_t could take on any value between 0 and $D_t + D_{t+1} + \cdots + D_N$. An important algorithmic implication of the proposition is that to compute an optimal policy you need consider only approximately $.5N^2$ different possibilities.

An implication of the proposition is that there always exists an optimal policy with the property that, in each period, if entering inventory is positive, then no production is scheduled. Symbolically, the implication is that there exists an optimal policy for which

(6) $$i_{t-1}x_t = 0 \quad \text{for all } t.$$

Therefore, if D_t is satisfied from inventory $i_{t-1} > 0$, all these items were manu- factured in the latest period in which production occurred. This was certainly not true for optimal policies in the convex cost case.

Whenever an optimal $x_t > 0$, the situation can be referred to as a **regenera- tion event.** The term reflects the notion that, at such a period, entering inventory is zero, so production starts afresh.

What now remains to be discussed is how a dynamic programming recursion can be used to efficiently find an optimum among the schedules satisfying the stated form. In preparation, we illustrate the main ideas with a verbal description.

Suppose January is the first month in the horizon. Then you begin by calculat- ing the cost of producing in January for January's demand requirement. You then lengthen the horizon month by month, using the calculations for the previous months. For example, suppose you have found optimal policies for the planning horizons January; January and February; January, February, and March; and so on, up to January, February, March, April, May, and June. Assume each of these policies has the form stated above. You next want to add July to the horizon.

The form of an optimal policy implies that *all* of July's demand requirement will be produced in either January, February, ..., or July—altogether seven possi- bilities to consider. Further, if it is produced in April, say, then April's production quantity consists of the demand requirements for April, May, June, and July, and an optimal policy for January, February, and March is the three-month horizon policy that you already know. Consequently, an optimal seven-month horizon policy is one that has the smallest total cost of the seven possibilities.

9.6 ALGORITHM FOR CONCAVE COST MODEL

Let

$$e_{kj} = \begin{pmatrix} \text{total cost of producing in Period k to meet the demand requirements} \\ \text{of Periods k, \ldots, j, where } k = 1, 2, \ldots, N \text{ and } k \le j \le N \end{pmatrix}.$$

Thus

(1) $$e_{kj} = \begin{cases} C_k(D_k) & \text{for } j = k \\ C_k(D_k + \cdots + D_j) + h_k(D_{k+1} + \cdots + D_j) \\ \qquad\qquad\qquad\qquad + \cdots + h_{j-1}(D_j) & \text{for } j \ge k + 1. \end{cases}$$

To illustrate, if k is January and j is March, then e_{kj} is the sum of the production cost for all of January, February, and March demand, the holding cost levied at the end of January on the inventory to meet February and March demand, and the holding cost levied at the end of February on the inventory to meet March demand.

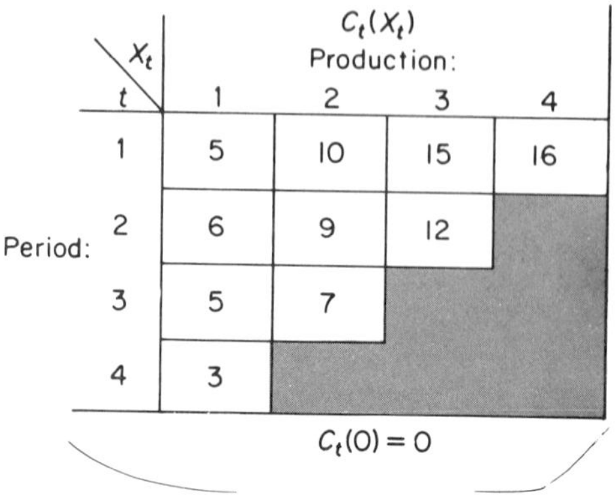

FIGURE 9.5. Selmore Company. Concave Production Cost.

The Selmore Company Problem. The numerical data for this company appear in Fig. 9.5, where the horizon $N = 4$. In addition to the $C_t(x_t)$ displayed, assume that

(2) $$D_t = 1 \quad \text{and} \quad h_t(i_t) = \frac{i_t}{10} \quad \text{for all periods.}$$

(Try to guess the optimal schedules for $N = 1, 2, 3, 4$.)

The following are a few illustrations of (1) using the data in Fig. 9.5:

$$e_{11} = C_1(1) = 5$$

$$e_{12} = C_1(1 + 1) + h_1(1) = 10 + .1 = 10.1$$

$$e_{13} = C_1(1 + 1 + 1) + h_1(1 + 1) + h_2(1) = 15 + .2 + .1 = 15.3$$

$$e_{14} = C_1(1 + 1 + 1 + 1) + h_1(1 + 1 + 1) + h_2(1 + 1) + h_3(1)$$
(3) $$\quad = 16 + .3 + .2 + .1 = 16.6$$

$$e_{22} = C_2(1) = 6$$

$$e_{23} = C_2(1 + 1) + h_2(1) = 9 + .1 = 9.1$$

$$e_{24} = C_2(1 + 1 + 1) + h_2(1 + 1) + h_3(1) = 12 + .2 + .1 = 12.3.$$

Calculate the remaining values e_{33}, e_{34}, and e_{44}, and compare your answers with the amounts shown in Fig. 9.6.
Define

$$f_n = \begin{pmatrix} \text{minimum policy cost for Periods } 1, 2, \dots, n, \text{ given that} \\ \text{the inventory level is zero at the end of Period } n \end{pmatrix}.$$

FIGURE 9.6. Selmore Company. Concave Cost Model.

c_{kj} = cost of producing in period $k+1$ to meet demands in periods $k+1, \ldots, j$

Then the appropriate dynamic programming recursion is

$$(4) \qquad f_n = \underset{k=0,1,\ldots,n-1}{\text{minimum}} \; [f_k + e_{k+1,n}] \quad \text{for } n = 1, 2, \ldots, N,$$

where $f_0 \equiv 0$. Let k_n designate a value of k that yields f_n in (4). What is being sought is the value of f_N.

The bracketed expression on the right of (4) is the sum of two costs. The first cost, f_k, represents all the costs during Periods $1, \ldots, k$, incurred by an optimal policy for this horizon. Such a policy leaves no inventory at the end of Period k. The second cost, $e_{k+1,n}$, represents the additional costs in Periods $k + 1, \ldots, n$ of starting in Period $k + 1$ with no inventory, and producing for all the remaining demand. A value k_n that minimizes these sums provides an optimal policy for a horizon of n periods by specifying Period $k_n + 1$ as the period (in the interval $1, 2, \ldots, n$) at which the last regeneration event occurs. The algorithm can therefore be viewed as a way to determine an optimal sequence of regeneration points. [Because entering inventory is always zero at a regeneration point, we are able to suppress the state variable $i \; (\equiv 0)$ in expression (4).] Observe that the algorithm has been formulated so as to proceed forward in time.

The method is illustrated below for the example appearing in Fig. 9.5:

$$f_0 = 0$$

$$f_1 = \text{minimum } [f_0 + e_{11}] = [0 + 5] = 5 \quad \text{and} \quad k_1 = 0$$

$$f_2 = \text{minimum } [f_0 + e_{12}, f_1 + e_{22}]$$

$$\qquad = \text{minimum } [0 + 10.1, 5 + 6] = 10.1 \quad \text{and} \quad k_2 = 0$$

$$(5) \quad f_3 = \text{minimum } [f_0 + e_{13}, f_1 + e_{23}, f_2 + e_{33}]$$

$$\qquad = \text{minimum } [0 + 15.3, 5 + 9.1, 10.1 + 5] = 14.1 \quad \text{and} \quad k_3 = 1$$

$$f_4 = \text{minimum } [f_0 + e_{14}, f_1 + e_{24}, f_2 + e_{34}, f_3 + e_{44}]$$

$$\qquad = \text{minimum } [0 + 16.6, 5 + 12.3, 10.1 + 7.1, 14.1 + 3]$$

$$\qquad = 16.6 \quad \text{and} \quad k_4 = 0.$$

These calculations show that the optimal schedule for a planning horizon of length N is

(6)
$$
\begin{array}{llll}
x_1 = 1 & & & \text{for } N = 1 \\
x_1 = 2 & x_2 = 0 & & \text{for } N = 2 \\
x_1 = 1 & x_2 = 2 & x_3 = 0 & \text{for } N = 3 \\
x_1 = 4 & x_2 = 0 & x_3 = 0 & x_4 = 0 \quad \text{for } N = 4.
\end{array}
$$

To illustrate how these were found, suppose $N = 3$. Then $k_3 = 1$ in (5) signifies that an optimal policy for Periods 1, 2, 3 is determined by considering Period 1 by itself, and ordering in Period 2 for both Periods 2 and 3. The value $x_2 = 2$ represents the total demand in these periods. The solution to Period 1 considered by itself is given by the schedule for $N = 1$, which indicates that production $x_1 = D_1 = 1$.

Observe that the optimal value of x_1 (January production) fluctuates up and down as the horizon lengthens. As you saw in the horizon theorem of the previous section, this dynamic phenomenon does not occur if the costs are *convex* functions. But in the *concave* cost model, such fluctuations do arise, even in very simple cases, as you can see in Sec. 9.7. Thus, although the algorithm is not much more complicated than that for the convex cost case, the dynamic properties of the model do exhibit more complex behavior.

The motivation for the algorithm above rests on the Form-of-an-Optimal-Policy result in the preceding section, which, in turn, follows from assuming concave costs. But suppose that, irrespective of the actual cost functions, management decrees that its stockage policy is to have that structural form, in other words, the replenishment rule is to schedule a production batch only when the inventory level falls to zero. Then the algorithm in this section provides an optimal schedule from among this restricted class of replenishment policies.

*9.7 PLANNING HORIZON ANALYSIS
FOR CONCAVE COST MODEL

As you already noted, an essential difference between the convex and concave cost models is that for the concave model the optimal value for x_t may decrease as the horizon lengthens. This can happen for the simplest examples.

To illustrate, suppose

(1) $C_t(x_t) = s_t + e_t x_t$ for $x_t > 0$ (setup cost plus linear production cost),

where $s_t \geq 0$ and $c_t \geq 0$. Specifically, let

(2)
$$
\begin{array}{lllll}
s_1 = 1 & s_2 = 2 & s_3 = 4 & s_4 = 8 & s_5 = 7
\end{array}
$$
$$
e_t = 0 \quad \text{and} \quad h_t(i_t) = h_t i_t = i_t \quad (h_t = 1)
$$

and assume

(3) $D_1 = 1$ $D_2 = 1$ $D_3 = 2$ $D_4 = 3$ $D_5 = 4.$

Employ the algorithm to verify that

(4)
$$f_1 = 1 \qquad f_2 = 2 \qquad f_3 = 5 \qquad f_4 = 9 \qquad f_5 = 16$$
$$k_1 = 0 \qquad k_2 = 0 \qquad k_3 = 1 \qquad k_4 = 2 \qquad k_5 = 4,$$

from which it follows that

(5)

$x_1 = 1$					for $N = 1$
$x_1 = 2$	$x_2 = 0$				for $N = 2$
$x_1 = 1$	$x_2 = 3$	$x_3 = 0$			for $N = 3$
$x_1 = 2$	$x_2 = 0$	$x_3 = 5$	$x_4 = 0$		for $N = 4$
$x_1 = 2$	$x_2 = 0$	$x_3 = 5$	$x_3 = 0$	$x_5 = 4$	for $N = 5.$

Once again, to show how (5) follows from (4), consider $N = 4$. Remember $k_n + 1$ represents the latest period in which production occurs when Periods $1, 2, \ldots$, n constitute the entire span of the schedule. Since $k_4 = 2$, Periods 1 and 2 form a horizon, and production is scheduled in Period 3 for Periods 3 and 4. Thus $x_3 = D_3 + D_4 = 2 + 3 = 5$. To determine production in the first two periods, examine the case of $N = 2$. You find $k_2 = 0$, which implies that production occurs in Period 1, and equals the first two periods' demands, namely $x_1 = D_1 + D_2 = 1 + 1 = 2$.

Notice that as the planning horizon increases, both x_1 and x_2 fluctuate up and down; however, the following planning proposition is true.

SETUP COST HORIZON THEOREM. Assume (1) holds and $e_t \geq e_{t+1}$ for $t = 1, 2, \ldots, N - 1$. (a) If $k_n = n - 1$, for $n \geq 2$, then it always is optimal to schedule Periods $1, 2, \ldots$, n $- 1$ as a span by itself. (b) If $t \geq n$, then $k_t \geq k_n$.

To illustrate part (a), suppose when you apply the algorithm to the periods January, February, March, and April, you find $k_4 = 3$. This signifies that for $N \geq 4$, April demand should be met from April production. Then part (a) states that it is correct to adopt the optimal production plan for the three-month span of January, February, and March, irrespective of what demand is beyond April. Of course, if you lengthen the horizon further, you will obtain more information about the correct value x_4 of April production. But in any case, you know $x_4 > 0$, that is, the April production level is positive in an optimal schedule for $N \geq 4$. Notice that part (a) is satisfied for $N = 5$ in the example (4). Thus the values in (5) of x_t, $t = 1, 2, 3, 4$, which are optimal for $N = 4$, are also optimal for $N \geq 5$, regardless of the values of D_t, $t > 5$.

To illustrate the rest of the above proposition, suppose when you apply the algorithm to periods January through April, you find that $k_4 = 2$. This signifies that when $N = 4$, April demand should be satisfied from March production, and the schedule for January and February should be the schedule derived for $N = 2$.

Part (b) states that the demand in any month after April will be filled by production *after* February, that is, in March or a subsequent month. Observe that the example (2) satisfies the hypothesis of the theorem, and accordingly the results in (4) agree with part (b).

The theorem reduces the amount of computation required by the algorithm. When the hypotheses of the proposition apply, the recursion can be written as

$$(6) \qquad f_n = \operatorname*{minimum}_{k = k_{n-1}, \ldots, n-1} \ [f_k + e_{k+1,n}] \quad \text{for } n = 1, 2, \ldots, N,$$

which cuts down on the search for the minimum. To illustrate, in the example (2), f_5 can be found by considering in (6) only $k = 2, 3, 4$, since $k_4 = 2$ in (4). With this approach, not *all* e_{kj}, for $k = 1, 2, \ldots, N$, and $k \le j \le N$, will be needed in executing (6). Therefore it is advantageous to calculate each e_{kj} only if it is required. A helpful recursion for this purpose is

$$(7) \quad e_{k+1,n} = e_{k+1,n-1} + e_{k+1}D_n + h_{k+1}(D_n) + \cdots + h_{n-1}(D_n) \quad \text{for } n > k + 1,$$

where we assume the holding cost function is linear $h_t(i_t) = h_t i_t$.

In contrast with the Convex Cost Horizon Theorem, part (a) here gives a sharper result (it establishes a definite production schedule within a planning horizon), but part (b) is weaker [since as N increases, x_t may fluctuate, as you saw in (5)].

REVIEW EXERCISES

1 Verify the claims in Sec. 9.1 that

   (a) Formulas (3) and (4) are equivalent. Give a verbal interpretation of (4).
   (b) Requiring $i_t \ge 0$, where i_t is given by (4), implies that demand is satisfied on time.

2 (a) Give a verbal interpretation of the definitions (3) and (4) in Sec. 9.2.
   (b) Draw a sketch of the functions described in *Cases i* through *vi* in Sec. 9.2 (let $a = 2$, $b = 1$, and $c = 3$ in the first four cases, and use the parameters given in the text for the last two cases).
   (c) Draw a sketch of the function described in *Case vi*, letting the parameters be $a_1 = 4$, $b_1 = 1$, $w_1 = 4$, $a_2 = 3$, $w_2 = 6$, and $a_3 = 2$.

3 Write the cost functions $C_t(x_t)$ as given by (3) and (4) in Sec. 9.3 for each of the six periods using the data in Fig. 9.2.

Exercises 4 through 7 on p. 271 refer to the case of the Highway Rubber Company shown in Fig. 9.2. Reapply the algorithm to the new data and calculate the incremental effect on total cost. Be sure to indicate total production x_t and ending inventory i_t in each Period t.

4 (a) Assume January demand is 2 instead of 1.
  (b) Assume May demand is 1 instead of 0.
  (c) Suppose demand in every period remains the same, except in Period t. How large
      can D_t be such that there still exists a feasible schedule? (Answer this question
      for $t = 1, 2, \ldots, 6$.)

5 (a) Assume regular-time production capacity in January is 4, instead of 3.
  (b) Assume regular-time production capacity in January is 5, instead of 3.
  (c) Assume overtime production is unavailable in March and April.

6 In each part, explain the impact on the solution in Fig. 9.3 if the cost parameters are
  changed as indicated below.

  (a) Production costs in each period are identical. (For example, two per item at
      regular time, and five per item at overtime.)
  (b) Overtime costs equal regular-time costs. (For example, 2 per item in Period 1,
      with a total capacity of 9 items; 4 per item in Period 2, with a total capacity of
      4 items, etc.)
  (c) Holding cost is $h = 6$ per item.
  (d) Holding cost is $h = .1$ per item.

*7 Suppose the cumulative demands R_p, defined in (1) of Sec. 9.4, satisfy

$$1 \leq R_1 \leq 1 \qquad 1 \leq R_2 \leq 7 \qquad 6 \leq R_3 \leq 14$$

$$10 \leq R_4 \leq 20 \qquad 10 \leq R_5 \leq 25 \qquad 12 \leq R_6 \leq 27.$$

  Find the associated values for $X_p(S)$ and $X_p(T)$, specified in the Convex Cost Horizon
  Theorem. Draw a diagram like that in Fig. 9.4. Can you give an optimal value for
  production in Period 1? Explain why.

8 Suppose a vendor offers the following price-break (quantity-discount) structure: $10
  per item for any amount ordered up to a dozen units; $8 per item (that is, for *every*
  item) for a total amount ordered above a dozen and up to a gross; $5 per item for a
  total amount ordered beyond a gross. Plot the total purchase cost as a function of the
  number of items ordered. Is this a concave cost function? Why? Is the cost function
  concave if a setup cost is added? Why?

9 (a) Explain why the form of an optimal policy given for the lot-size model with
      concave costs in Sec. 9.5 implies that there always exists an optimal policy with
      the property that, in each period, if entering inventory is positive, then no
      production is scheduled.
  (b) Given this form of an optimal policy, calculate exactly how many distinct produc-
      tion schedules need to be considered. For the sake of definiteness, assume that
      every $D_t > 0$ (recall initial inventory $i_0 = 0$).
  (c) Calculate how many different e_{kj}, given by (1) in Sec. 9.6, have to be calculated
      in order to apply the algorithm for the general concave cost model.

10 *Selmore Company* (Sec. 9.6). Consider the example in Fig. 9.5. Find an optimal policy if the holding cost function is $h_t(i_t) = h_t i_t$, where, in all periods,

(a) $h_t = 1$.
(b) $h_t = 2$.

11 In the concave cost model of Secs. 9.5 and 9.6 suppose that demand $D_t = 1$,

$$C_t(x_t) = \begin{cases} 5x_t & \text{for } x_t = 0, 1, 2, 3 \\ 12 + x_t & \text{for } x_t \geq 4, \end{cases}$$

and $h_t(i_t) = h_t i_t$ in all periods. (Note the example resembles the Selmore Company Problem, where the production cost function is the same as that for $t = 1$ in Fig. 9.5.) Find an optimal policy for $h_t = .1$ in all periods, when the horizon length is

(a) $N = 4$.   (b) $N = 5$.
(c) $N = 6$.   (d) $N = 7$.
(e) $N = 8$.   (f) $N = 9$.
(g) Do the same for all $h_t = 1$ (h) Do the same for all $h_t = 2$
    and $N = 9$.   and $N = 9$.

12 Answer the questions in exercise 11 where

$$C_t(x_t) = \begin{cases} 0 & \text{for } x_t = 0 \\ 3 + 2x_t & \text{for } x_t \geq 1. \end{cases}$$

13 Answer the questions in exercise 11 where demand $D_t = 2$ in every period.

14 Answer the questions in exercise 11, except assume demand alternates over the entire horizon as follows:

(a) $D_1 = 1, D_2 = 2, D_3 = 1, D_4 = 2, \ldots$.
(b) $D_1 = 2, D_2 = 1, D_3 = 2, D_4 = 1, \ldots$.

15 Answer the questions in exercise 11, except assume that the holding costs alternate as follows:

(a) $h_1 = 1, h_2 = 2, h_3 = 1, h_4 = 2, \ldots$.
(b) $h_1 = 2, h_2 = 1, h_3 = 2, h_4 = 1, \ldots$.

*16 Consider the example (1) through (3) in Sec. 9.7. Verify the results in (4) and (5).

*17 Compare the planning information given by the Convex Cost Horizon Theorem in Sec. 9.4 and by the Setup Cost Horizon Theorem in Sec. 9.7.

*18 Consider the Setup Cost Horizon Theorem in Sec. 9.7, and assume the first month in the planning horizon is January.

(a) What does $k_6 = 5$ imply about an optimal schedule, according to part (a) of the theorem?

(b) What does $k_6 = 3$ imply about an optimal schedule, according to part (b) of the theorem?

19 Explain your understanding of the following terms:

convex function

concave function

decreasing (increasing) incremental
    returns to scale

*planning horizon analysis

dynamic lot-size model

setup cost (or lump-sum cost)

quantity discounts (or
    price breaks)

regeneration event (point).

COMPUTATIONAL EXERCISES

Exercises 20 through 26 refer to the inventory model with convex costs, as described in Sec. 9.3. (Recall that initial inventory $i_0 = 0$.)

20 Assume the production cost functions are given by Fig. 9.7. For example, the total cost in Period 1 associated with $x_1 = 12$ is 32 $(= 1 \cdot 5 + 3 \cdot 5 + 2 \cdot 6)$. Assume the

Production Cost of Unit k

Production of Unit k	Period 1	Period 2	Period 3	Period 4
$1 \leq k \leq 5$	1	2	1	4
$6 \leq k \leq 10$	3	3	6	4
$11 \leq k \leq 15$	6	5	7	8
$16 \leq k \leq 20$	10	8	12	9

FIGURE 9.7

holding cost functions are $h_t(i_t) = h_t i_t$, where $h_1 = 1$, $h_2 = 2$, and $h_3 = 1$. Suppose the demand requirements are

$$D_1 = 10 \qquad D_2 = 3 \qquad D_3 = 17 \qquad D_4 = 23.$$

(a) Find an optimal production schedule. Be sure to indicate total production x_t and ending inventory i_t in each Period t.
(b) Indicate the impact of requiring an additional unit in Period 1 (that is, let $D_1 = 11$). In Period 2. In Period 3. In Period 4.
(c) Find an optimal production schedule where all $h_t = 0$. Where all $h_t = 5$.
(d) Find an optimal production schedule where the demand requirements are revised such that $D_1 = 3$ and $D_2 = 10$. Such that $D_3 = 23$ and $D_4 = 17$. Such that $D_2 = 17$ and $D_3 = 3$.

*21 Consider the data in exercise 20, part (a). Suppose the cumulative demands R_p, defined in (1) of Sec. 9.4, satisfy

$$\sum_{t=1}^{p} D_t - k \leq R_p \leq \sum_{t=1}^{p} D_t + k.$$

In each part below, find the associated values for $X_p(S)$ and $X_p(T)$, specified in the Convex Cost Horizon Theorem, indicate the associated production levels and ending inventories, and draw a diagram like that in Fig. 9.4. Explain whether or not you can give an optimal value for production in Period 1. Let

(a) $k = 1$.
(b) $k = 2$.
(c) $k = 3$.

*22 Consider the data in exercise 20, part (a). Suppose the cumulative demands R_p, defined in (1) of Sec. 9.4, satisfy

$$\sum_{t=1}^{p} D_t - pk \leq R_p \leq \sum_{t=1}^{p} D_t + pk.$$

In each part below, find the associated values for $X_p(S)$ and $X_p(T)$, specified in the Convex Cost Horizon Theorem, indicate the associated production levels and ending inventories, and draw a diagram like that in Fig. 9.4. Explain whether you can give an optimal value for production in Period 1. Let

(a) $k = 1$.
(b) $k = 2$.
(c) $k = 3$.

23 Assume the planning horizon $N = 3$ periods and that the production and inventory cost functions are $C_t(x_t) = x_t^2$ and $h_t(i_t) = h_t i_t$ for every Period t. In each part below, find an optimal schedule for production and indicate ending inventory for each period.

(a) Assume $h_t = 0$ and the demand requirement is $D_t = 6$ for every Period t.
(b) Assume $h_t = 0$ for every Period t, and $D_1 = 11$, $D_2 = 5$, and $D_3 = 2$.
(c) Assume $h_t = 0$ for every Period t, and $D_1 = 2$, $D_2 = 5$, and $D_3 = 11$.
(d) Assume $h_t = 3$ in every Period t and the same demand data as in part (c). Next, assume $h_t = 11$ in every Period t. Compare the results for $h_t = 0, 3, 11$.
(e) Assume $h_t = 0$ in every Period t, the same demand data as in part (c), and $C_3(x_3) = 1.5x_3^2$. Next assume $h_t = 3$. Finally assume $h_t = 11$. Compare your results with those in part (d).

*24 Assume the production and inventory holding cost functions in exercise 23. Suppose the cumulative demands R_p, defined in (1) of Sec. 9.4, satisfy

$$1 \leq R_1 \leq 3 \qquad 6 \leq R_2 \leq 8 \qquad 23 \leq R_3 \leq 29.$$

Let $h_t = 0$. Find the associated values for $X_p(S)$ and $X_p(T)$, specified in the Convex

Cost Horizon Theorem, indicate the associated production levels and ending inventories, and draw a diagram like that in Fig. 9.4. Explain whether or not you can give an optimal value for production in Period 1. Do the same for $h_t = 3$ and for $h_t = 11$.

25 Assume the planning horizon $N = 8$, and that the production and inventory cost functions are $C_t(x_t) = x_t^2$ and $h_t(i_t) = h_t i_t$ for every Period t. Assume the demand requirements are

$$D_1 = 4 \qquad D_5 = 6$$

$$D_2 = 20 \qquad D_6 = 4$$

$$D_3 = 2 \qquad D_7 = 1$$

$$D_4 = 0 \qquad D_8 = 3.$$

In each part below, find an optimal schedule for production and indicate ending inventory for each period.

(a) Assume $h_t = 0$ for every Period t.
(b) Assume $h_t = 1$ for every Period t. Next assume $h_t = 3$ for every Period t.
(c) Assume $h_t(i_t) = i_t^2$ for every Period t.
(d) Assume $h_t = 0$ for every Period t. Also assume $C_t(x_t) = 1.5x_t^2$ for $t = 2$; then for $t = 4$, instead; then for $t = 7$, instead.
*(e) Assume $h_t = 0$ for every Period t, and the planning horizon $N = 9$. What is the largest value for the demand requirement D_9 such that the optimal production level for x_7 found in part (a) remains unchanged? Answer the same question for x_3. Answer the same question for x_1.
*(f) Assume $h_t = 1$ for every Period t. Answer the same questions as those in part (e).
*(g) Assume $h_t = 3$ for every Period t. Answer the same questions as those in part (e).

*26 Assume the production and inventory holding cost functions in exercise 25. Assume $h_t = 0$ for every Period t. Suppose the cumulative demands R_p, defined in (1) of Sec. 9.4, are as specified in each part below. Find the associated values for $X_p(S)$ and $X_p(T)$, specified in the Convex Cost Horizon Theorem, indicate the associated production levels and ending inventories, and draw a diagram like that in Fig. 9.4. Explain whether you can give an optimal value for production in Period 1.

(a) $\sum_{t=1}^{p} D_t - k \le R_p \le \sum_{t=1}^{p} D_t + k.$

Do for $k = 1$ and $k = 2$.

(b) $\sum_{t=1}^{p} D_t - pk \le R_p \le \sum_{t=1}^{p} D_t + pk.$

Do for $k = 1$ and $k = 2$.

(c) Perform the same analysis with $h_t = 1$ for every Period t.

Exercises 27 through 30 refer to the inventory model with concave costs, as described in Sec. 9.5. (Recall that initial inventory $i_0 = 0$.)

27 Assume the planning horizon $N = 3$, and the production and inventory cost functions are

$$
\left.\begin{array}{l}
C_1(x_1) = 12 + 8x_1 \quad \text{for } x_1 \geq 1 \\
C_2(x_2) = 2 + 9x_2 \quad \text{for } x_2 \geq 1 \\
C_3(x_3) = 5 + 10x_3 \quad \text{for } x_3 \geq 1
\end{array}\right\} \quad \text{and } h_t(i_t) = h_t i_t.
$$

Assume the demand requirements are $D_1 = 0$, $D_2 = 3$, and $D_3 = 20$. In each part, find an optimal production schedule, and indicate ending inventory in each period. Assume all

(a) $h_t = 0$.
(b) $h_t = 1$.
(c) $h_t = 2$.

28 Assume the planning horizon $N = 4$, and the production cost functions are given by Fig. 9.8. For example, the total cost associated with $x_1 = 12$ is 86 ($= 10 \cdot 5 + 6 \cdot 5 +$

Production of Unit k	Production Cost of Unit k			
	Period 1	Period 2	Period 3	Period 4
$1 \leq k \leq 5$	10	8	12	9
$6 \leq k \leq 10$	6	5	7	8
$11 \leq k \leq 15$	3	3	6	4
$16 \leq k$	1	2	1	4

FIGURE 9.8

$2 \cdot 3$). Assume the holding cost functions are $h_t(i_t) = h_t i_t$, where $h_1 = 1$, $h_2 = 2$, and $h_3 = 1$. Suppose the demand requirements are

$$
\begin{array}{ll}
D_1 = 10 & D_2 = 3 \\
D_3 = 17 & D_4 = 23.
\end{array}
$$

(a) Find an optimal production schedule. Be sure to indicate total production x_t and ending inventory i_t in each Period t.
(b) Indicate the impact of requiring an additional unit in Period 1 (that is, let $D_1 = 11$). In Period 2. In Period 3. In Period 4.
(c) Find an optimal schedule where all $h_t = 0$. Where all $h_t = 5$.
(d) Find an optimal production schedule where the demand requirements are revised such that $D_1 = 3$ and $D_2 = 10$. Such that $D_3 = 23$ and $D_4 = 17$. Such that $D_2 = 17$ and $D_3 = 3$.
(e) Find an optimal production schedule where the holding cost function is $h_t(i_t) = \sqrt{i_t}$ for every Period t.

29 Assume the planning horizon $N = 8$, and the production cost function is $C_t(x_t) = \sqrt{x_t}$ for every Period t, and the demand requirements are

$$D_1 = 4 \qquad D_2 = 20 \qquad D_3 = 2 \qquad D_4 = 0$$

$$D_5 = 6 \qquad D_6 = 4 \qquad D_7 = 1 \qquad D_8 = 3.$$

In each part below, find an optimal schedule for production and indicate ending inventory in each period. Assume for every Period t that the holding cost function is

(a) $h_t(i_t) = 0$ for every Period t.
(b) $h_t(i_t) = i_t$ for every Period t.
(c) $h_t(i_t) = \sqrt{i_t}$ for every Period t.

30 In each part, indicate an optimal production schedule and the associated ending inventory level in every Period t for horizon lengths 1, 2, ..., N, where N is specified in each part below. Assume that the production and holding cost functions are of the form

$$C_t(x_t) = \begin{cases} 0 & \text{for } x_t = 0 \\ s_t + e_t x_t & \text{for } x_t \geq 1 \end{cases} \quad \text{and} \quad h_t(i_t) = h_t i_t \quad \text{for every Period t.}$$

(a) Let $N = 10$, $s_t = 36$, $e_t = 5$, $h_t = 1$, and the demand requirements $D_t = 8$ for every Period t.
(b) Assume the data in part (a), except that the demand requirements are $D_t = 20$ for Periods 3, 6, and 9 and $D_t = 2$ for all other periods.
(c) Assume the data in part (a), except that the demand requirements are $D_t = 20$ for Periods 2, 5, and 8 and $D_t = 2$ for all other periods.
(d) Assume the data in part (a), except that the demand requirements are $D_t = 20$ for Periods 1, 4, 7, and 10 and $D_t = 2$ for all other periods.
(e) Let $N = 12$, $e_t = 5$, $h_t = 1$, the demand requirements $D_t = 8$ for every Period t, and $s_t = 100$ for Periods 4, 5, 6, 10, 11, 12 and $s_t = 36$ for all other periods.
*(f) Assume the data in part (a), except that the holding cost function is $h_t(i_t) = \sqrt{i_t}$ for every Period t.
*(g) Assume the data in part (a), and that backlogging is permitted; let the inventory holding and backlog penalty cost function be $h_t(i_t) = |i_t|$ for every Period t.
*(h) In parts (a) through (e), indicate how the computations in the algorithm simplify by employing the Setup Cost Horizon Theorem in Sec. 9.7. Also show how you can use recursion (7).

31 Consider the problem in exercise 39 in Chap. 8. Determine whether you get an optimal schedule if you apply

(a) The algorithm in Sec. 9.3 for the inventory model with convex costs.
(b) The algorithm in Sec. 9.6 for the inventory model with concave costs.
(c) Interpret your results in parts (a) and (b).

FORMULATION EXERCISES

32 Consider the inventory model described in Sec. 9.1. Suppose that production cost in Period t consists of two components: labor cost $L_t(x_t)$ and raw materials cost. The latter arises as follows. In each Period r, the company can purchase an unlimited quantity of raw material at the price p_r per unit (where the units have been selected so that each item of production requires one unit of raw material). Every price p_r is known at the beginning of the planning horizon. If raw materials are purchased in early periods to be stored for use in later periods, then the company incurs a storage cost. Specifically, the charge is H_r per unit of raw material held at the end of Period r. Suggest an efficient way to incorporate the raw materials purchasing decision into the models of Sec. 9.3 and 9.5.

In exercises 33 through 35, you are to formulate a model in terms of a dynamic terms of a dynamic programming recursion. Be sure to define all the symbols you use. Give the appropriate optimization function where there is a single period remaining, as well as the recursion for Stage n. Explain how to initiate and when to terminate the calculations.

33 *Batch Service Problem.* Several food companies send shipments for the Mom-and-Pop Grocery Store to a local public warehouse. Mom-and-Pop pays c dollars per day per hundred cubic feet of storage it utilizes in this warehouse. Suppose Mom-and-Pop forecasts, for each of the next N days, that shipments amounting to D_t hundred cubic feet will arrive on Day t. Suppose each day Mom-and-Pop can arrange to have a truck pick up all the goods stored at the warehouse. Since the cost of this trucking service is s, Mom-and-Pop does not usually order a pickup every day. However, it never lets a shipment remain in the warehouse longer than n days. (Assume that shipments arrive at the start of a day, and that the trucking service picks up the goods at the end of a day; assume that warehousing costs are assessed on the maximum space utilized during a day.) Show how Mom-and-Pop can obtain an optimal schedule for picking up goods at the warehouse.

34 *Site Location Problem.* The Crack Oil Company has a substantial share of the gasoline market in a major population center that is located along a peninsula. The area consists of N cities that are connected by a six-lane highway. Assume the cities are indexed $1, 2, \ldots, N$, and to travel from City j to City k, where $j < k$, you must proceed along the highway passing by Cities $j + 1, j + 2, \ldots, k - 1$. The Crack Oil Company wants to locate distributors in one or more of these cities. The annual fixed cost of operating a distributorship in City j is s_j. The forecasted annual gallonage that must be supplied to City j is D_j. The distance between adjacent Cities j and $j + 1$ is $L_{j,j+1}$. If a distributor in City j serves the requirements in City k, then the annual cost associated with transportation is $h \cdot D_k \cdot$ (distance between City j and City k). The company wants an optimal pattern of locations for its distributors. Formulate a dynamic programming model for this decision problem.

(a) Assume that City k can only be served by a distributor in City j, where $j < k$.

*(b) Assume that City k is served by the closest distributor.

35 *Assortment Problem.* A Japanese industrial firm, Itsa Steel Company, manufactures structural beams of a standard length. The strength of a beam depends on its weight, and Itsa Steel indexes the various strengths it can make as $j = 1, 2, \ldots, N$, where $j = 1$ is the heaviest beam and $j = N$ the lightest. Assume that if a customer requests Strength k, then Itsa Steel may, if it chooses, supply the demand by a beam of possibly greater Strength j, where $j < k$. Itsa Steel must solve the following assortment problem. The demand requirement for Strength j is D_j beams; all demand must be satisfied. If Itsa Steel decides to manufacture Strength j, then it incurs an expensive setup cost s_j. If the company meets the demand requirement D_j by shipping beams of Strength k, where $k \leq j$, then the company incurs a loss of $h \cdot (w_k - w_j) \cdot D_j$, where w_k and w_j are the respective weights of the beams and h is the cost per unit of weight. Formulate a dynamic programming model that will enable Itsa Steel to decide an optimal assortment of strengths to manufacture and the corresponding amounts of each.

CONTENTS

CHAPTER 10

Other Examples of
Dynamic Programming

10.1 REMINDER

Formulating a model in terms of a dynamic programming recurrence relation is partially an art. Hence a variety of examples are illustrated in Secs. 10.2 through 10.8 so that you can acquire a better feeling for such formulations. Our words of guidance from Chap. 8 still apply —be patient and give yourself plenty of time to study the sections. Plan to read each section at least twice. And to keep check on your understanding, for each of the models answer the questions:

1. What are the policy or decision variables?
2. What is the criterion or objective function for determining an optimal policy?
3. How is the problem characterized and then analyzed in terms of stages?
4. What characterizes the state of the problem at each stage?
5. How do the constraints influence the states of the problem and the feasible values of the policy variables?

At the end of this chapter, in Secs. 10.9 through 10.12, we give an overall assessment of dynamic programming. Specifically, we discuss the ingredients that are common to all dynamic programming model formulations, and summarize how this kind of analysis yields insightful information for managerial decision-making. Some perspective is given on what makes the difference between a theoretical exercise and a practical application of dynamic analysis. Finally, we point out in brief the kinds of industrial applications that have proved profitable, and the reasons for their success.

10.2 DISTRIBUTION OF EFFORT—
ONE CONSTRAINT

The following is a hypothetical, but suggestive, example of the so-called *distribution of effort model*. Mr. Chick N. Little, owner of Shopping Basket Markets, has a week's supply of eggs to distribute among his stores. From past experience Little knows for each of the stores how much profit he makes by allocating any specific number of eggs to a store. Little suspects that in order to maximize his overall profit, he should not put all his eggs in one Shopping Basket! Little wants to find an optimal distribution of eggs.

Number of Crates, y	Net Profit Store 1 $R_1(y)$	Store 2 $R_2(y)$	Store 3 $R_3(y)$	Store 4 $R_4(y)$
0	0	0	0	0
1	6	3	2	5
2	10	10	6	9
3	14	15	14	13
4	16	19	20	17
5	18	21	22	21
6	20	22	24	25

FIGURE 10.1. Shopping Basket Markets Example.

To make clear the appropriate model structure, we pose an obviously simplified numerical example, and afterwards we summarize the approach with more general mathematical notation. Suppose that Little has $N = 6$ crates of eggs to distribute to $s = 4$ stores (assume that he cannot split up a crate to ship the contents to more than one store). The net profit associated with distributing from none to all six crates to each store is displayed in Fig. 10.1. These profit figures differ from store to store because of the different demand and breakage experience and the varying costs of shipping and handling at each store.

Let y_j denote the number of crates shipped to Store j and $R_j(y)$ the resulting net profit for Store j when $y_j = y$. Observe in Fig. 10.1 that if all the crates are shipped to Store 1, that is, $y_1 = 6$, total profit is $R_1(6) = 20$. As you can see, if Little ships all the crates to one single store, he should select Store 4, since $R_4(6) = 25$. But clearly he can do better by distributing the crates to more than one store, for example, by letting $y_1 = y_2 = 3$, his total profit equals $29 [= R_1(3) + R_2(3) = 14 + 15]$.

In general notation, then, Little's decision problem can be formulated as

(1) $$\text{maximize} \sum_{j=1}^{s} R_j(y_j)$$

subject to

(2) $$\sum_{j=1}^{s} y_j = N \quad \text{(available number of egg crates)}$$

(3) $\quad y_j = 0, 1, 2, \ldots$ for each j (distribute only whole crates).

To motivate the dynamic programming recursive relationship that will be convenient for computing an optimal solution, we explain how the optimization example in Fig. 10.1 can be viewed as finding a best-profit route in an acyclic network. Although this distribution decision problem is not really dynamic—all the decision variables relate to a single time period—you may view Little as deciding the quantities y_j sequentially, starting with Store 4, then Store 3, Store 2, and, finally, Store 1. Thus, consider that he makes his decisions in stages. To illustrate, after deciding the distribution to Stores 4 and 3, Little then has a certain number of crates left to allocate to Stores 2 and 1, and he makes his Store 2 decision accordingly. Given (1) and (2), that decision ought to depend only on the amount of crates he has left for distribution to Stores 1 and 2, and not on how he specifically allocated the crates between Stores 3 and 4. This multistage characterization makes it possible to draw a network analogous to that for the Dependable Manufacturing Co. problem in Chap. 8.

Specifically, for each decision stage j, at which the Store j allocation is made, the network contains a set of nodes, one for each possible state, namely, the number of crates available to distribute to Stores 1 through j. Therefore, in the network of Fig. 10.2, you see four sets of nodes, one set for each stage $j = 1, 2, 3, 4$,

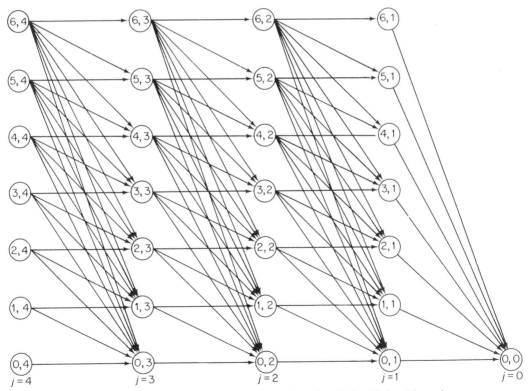

FIGURE 10.2. Shopping Basket Markets Network.

with seven nodes in each set, one for each state possibility $n = 0, 1, \ldots, 6$ crates available for distribution to Stores 1 through j. The node designation (n, j) gives both the state and stage variables. Each arc corresponds to a decision y_j and has an associated net profit taken from Fig. 10.1. To illustrate, the arc between the Nodes $(6, 4)$ and $(6, 3)$ implies that Store 4 received no crates, $y_4 = 0$, and so its arc profit is $R_4(0) = 0$. The arc between the Nodes $(6, 4)$ and $(5, 3)$ implies that Store 4 received one crate, $y_4 = 1$, and so its arc profit is $R_4(1) = 5$. Given that the owner has six crates to distribute, the optimization problem corresponds to finding the best-profit route from Node $(6, 4)$ to the terminal Node $(0, 0)$.

Even in a hypothetical problem such as this, calculating an optimal solution by finding a best route directly on the network diagram would be a clumsy computational process. Hence, it is essential to characterize the computational process of finding a best route through such an acyclic network by means of a recursive formula more amenable to a computerized approach.

To convert the problem statement (1) through (3), and its best route in an acyclic network equivalent, into a dynamic programming version, define

(4)
$$g_j(n) = \begin{pmatrix} \text{profit when } n \text{ crates are distributed optimally} \\ \text{to Store 1, Store 2, \ldots, Store j} \end{pmatrix},$$

$$y_j(n) = \begin{pmatrix} \text{a distribution amount for Store j} \\ \text{that yields } g_j(n) \end{pmatrix}.$$

Watch the notation here. The letter g indicates a value for the company's *goal*, namely profit. The letter n refers to the *number* of crates to be distributed. And the index j denotes *just* a store.

In terms of the network of Fig. 10.2, the quantity $g_j(n)$ is simply the value of the best-profit route from Node (n, j) to the terminal Node $(0, 0)$. Hence, you can apply the underlying logic for finding an optimal route in an acyclic network to determine the values of the $g_j(n)$. By definition, the terminal Node $(0, 0)$ has the value $g_0(0) = 0$. Since only a single arc leads out of each Node $(n, 1)$ for stage $j = 1$, the value of the best-profit route at each of these nodes is $R_1(n)$. Continuing on to each of the nodes for stage $j = 2$, you now must compare decision alternatives to find a best-profit route. To illustrate, consider the Node $(3, 2)$. The value of the best-profit route is calculated as

(5) $g_2(3) = \text{maximum } [R_2(0) + g_1(2), R_2(1) + g_1(1), R_2(2) + g_1(0)].$

Each of the sums on the right of (5) represents the profit from taking one of the three possible arcs out of Node $(3, 2)$ and then proceeding optimally from a node at stage $j = 1$. A similar selection of a maximum sum is required at the other nodes $(n, 2)$. Having found all the $g_2(n)$ values, you next compute each of the $g_3(n)$ values in a similar fashion, and finally all $g_4(n)$. Such logic, which underlies the computation of an optimal route in an acyclic network, is conveniently displayed by means of a dynamic programming recursive formula:

(6) $g_j(n) = \underset{y}{\text{maximum }} [R_j(y) + g_{j-1}(n - y)]$ for $j = 1, 2, \ldots, s$

(7) $g_0(n) \equiv 0$ for $j = 0$,

where $n = 0, 1, \ldots, N$ and the maximization is over only nonnegative integer values of y that satisfy $y \leq n$. In words, the recursion (6) states that the profit from optimally distributing n crates to Stores 1, 2, . . . , j can be calculated by finding a best Store j decision y taking into account both its immediate profit impact $R_j(y)$ and its profit impact from having $n - y$ crates remaining to distribute optimally to Stores 1, 2, . . . , j − 1. Formulas (6) and (7) are applied below to the Shopping Basket Markets example.

The computations start with the last stage $j = 1$, since given (7), the values for $g_1(n)$ in (6) are trivially easy to find. In particular, the profit of Store 1 increases as more crates are shipped, and so

(8) $$g_1(n) = R_1(n) \quad \text{and} \quad y_1(n) = n \quad \text{for } n = 0, 1, \ldots, 6.$$

For example, if four crates are available for distribution to Store 1, then the optimal allocation is to ship them all, $y_1(4) = 4$ and the ensuing profit is $R_1(4) = 16$, from Fig. 10.1. The information for $j = 1$ is summarized in Fig. 10.3.

	n	$y_1(n)$	$g_1(n)$
Crates Available:	0	0	0
	1	1	6
	2	2	10
	3	3	14
	4	4	16
	5	5	18
	6	6	20

FIGURE 10.3. Shopping Basket Markets Example ($j = 1$).

The function $g_2(n)$ is computed in Fig. 10.4. Note that there are seven rows in the table, one for each possible number of crates available to distribute to Stores 2 and 1. Several of the shipment possibilities are blocked out because $y \leq n$ for feasibility. To illustrate, if $n = 3$, then the distribution y cannot exceed three crates. Within the table, the first entry in each column y is the value of $R_2(y)$ from Fig. 10.1. The second entry is the value of $g_1(n - y)$, taken from Fig. 10.3. Their sum is required by the formula on the right of (6). Thus, for each possible value of available crates, n, the amount $g_2(n)$

$R_2(y) + g_1(n - y)$

Shipment Quantity:

Crates Available: n \ y	0	1	2	3	4	5	6	$y_2(n)$	$g_2(n)$
0	0 + 0							0	0
1	0 + 6	3 + 0						0	6
2	0 + 10	3 + 6	10 + 0					0, 2	10
3	0 + 14	3 + 10	10 + 6	15 + 0				2	16
4	0 + 16	3 + 14	10 + 10	15 + 6	19 + 0			3	21
5	0 + 18	3 + 16	10 + 14	15 + 10	19 + 6	21 + 0		3, 4	25
6	0 + 20	3 + 18	10 + 16	15 + 14	19 + 10	21 + 6	22 + 0	3, 4	29

FIGURE 10.4. Shopping Basket Markets Example ($j = 2$).

is the maximum sum across the row, and the decision $y_2(n)$ is a corresponding distribution (note the alternative optimal decisions for $n = 2, 5, 6$).

The function $g_3(n)$ is computed using a table with exactly the same format as that of Fig. 10.4. The entries inside the table differ in that the first term in each sum is $R_3(y)$ and the second term is $g_2(n - y)$, employing the results in Fig. 10.4. The analogous remarks are appropriate for constructing a table to calculate $g_4(n)$. All of these computations are summarized in Fig. 10.5.

Observe in Fig. 10.5 that when six crates are available for distribution to Stores 4, 3, 2, and 1, the optimal Store 4 decision is $y_4(6) = 1$. This implies that $n = 6 - 1 = 5$ crates are made available for the first three stores; hence the optimal Store 3 decision is $y_3(5) = 4$ crates. As a result, $n = 5 - 4 = 1$ crate is made available for the first two stores. Therefore, the optimal Store 2 decision is $y_2(1) = 0$, so that the optimal Store 1 decision is $y_1(1) = 1$. The associated total profit is $g_4(6) = 31$ ($= 6 + 0 + 20 + 5$).

Crates Available:	$j = 1$		$j = 2$		$j = 3$		$j = 4$	
n	$y_1(n)$	$g_1(n)$	$y_2(n)$	$g_2(n)$	$y_3(n)$	$g_3(n)$	$y_4(n)$	$g_4(n)$
0	0	0	0	0	0	0	0	0
1	1	6	0	6	0	6	0	6
2	2	10	0,2	10	0	10	2	11
3	3	14	2	16	0	16	0	16
4	4	16	3	21	0	21	0,1	21
5	5	18	3,4	25	4	26	1	26
6	6	20	3,4	29	3,4	30	1	31

FIGURE 10.5. Shopping Basket Markets—Optimal Strategy.

The information in Fig. 10.5 is helpful for sensitivity analysis. For example, suppose that after the crate is dispatched to Store 4, one of the remaining five crates is destroyed, thereby leaving only four crates for distribution to Stores 3, 2, and 1. Verify that the optimal revised distribution is $y_3(4) = 0$, $y_2(4) = 3$, and $y_1(1) = 1$, with a smaller total profit of 26.

To conclude, you employed the recursion (6) to obtain an optimal solution by beginning the computations at the final stage $j = 1$, and finding $g_1(0)$, $g_1(1), \ldots, g_1(N)$. You then continued by finding $g_2(0), g_2(1), \ldots, g_2(N)$. You proceeded in this same fashion for successively larger values of j until you finally found $g_s(N)$. You then discovered an actual optimal allocation by tracing back, beginning with $y_s(N)$, to obtain the values of y_j that together yielded $g_s(N)$.

10.3 CAPITAL BUDGETING PROBLEM

In this section, you study another application of the *distribution of effort model* with one constraint. The new added complication will be a more complex constraint than that in the Shopping Basket Markets example.

The Out-of-Site Realty Corporation annually budgets several million dollars for land development and for building shopping centers, apartment complexes, and industrial parks. The corporation is now planning to invest up to $10 million on one or more of three large projects. The data for these projects are contained in Fig. 10.6. Observe that each of the three projects can be developed at any of five different investment levels. For instance, the corporation can choose to invest $3 million, $5 million, $7 million, $8 million, or $9 million in Project 2. If the investment choice is Level 1, namely, $3 million for Project 2, then the present value of future earnings is estimated to be $R_2(1) = \$.8$ million; if, instead, the investment choice is Level 5, namely, $9 million, then the value of future earnings rises to $R_2(5) = \$2.1$ million. A similar interpretation applies for the other two projects.

Investment Level: y	Project 2		Project 3		Project 4	
	Cost $I_2(y)$	Value $R_2(y)$	Cost $I_3(y)$	Value $R_3(y)$	Cost $I_4(y)$	Value $R_4(y)$
0	0	0	0	0	0	0
1	3	8	4	9	6	17
2	5	13	5	13	7	18
3	7	18	8	18	8	21
4	8	19	9	19	9	22
5	9	21	10	23	10	24

FIGURE 10.6. Out-of-Site Realty Corporation Problem. (Investment costs in units of $1,000,000 and present values in units of $100,000.)

The corporation also has the option of investing its resources in short-term securities. For expository convenience, let this option be designated as Project 1 and assume that the commensurate economic returns of investing y million dollars is $R_1(y) = 2y$ hundred thousand dollars. A short-term security investment can be at any quantity $y = 0, 1, \ldots, 10$.

For notational purposes, let $I_j(y)$ represent the investment cost of Project j when the investment level is y. To illustrate, Fig. 10.6 indicates that a choice of investment level $y = 2$ for Project 4 requires an expenditure cost $I_4(2) = \$7$ million. You can use the same notation for Project 1 by defining $I_1(y) = y$. Then the mathematical formulation of the Out-of-Site Realty Corporation problem is

(1) $$\text{maximize } \sum_{j=1}^{s} R_j(y_j)$$

subject to

(2) $$\sum_{j=1}^{s} I_j(y_j) = K \quad \text{(available capital)}$$

(3) $$y_j = 0, 1, \ldots,$$

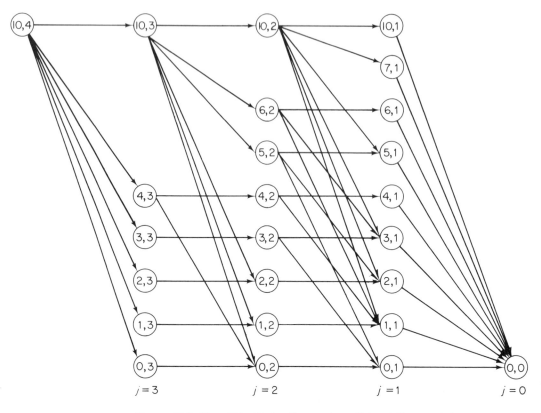

FIGURE 10.7. Out-of-Site Realty Corporation—Network Representation.

where y_j denotes the investment level for each project, $s = 4$ is the number of projects, and $K = 10$ is the amount of available capital for investment. (As you will see, it is not necessary to add the restrictions $y_j \leq 5$ for $j = 2, 3, 4$, and so these upper bounds are left unstated.)

Observe that the primary difference between this and the Shopping Basket Markets problem is that the constraint (2) here is the sum of nonlinear functions of the y_j, whereas previously it was simply the sum of the y_j. Such nonlinearities do not wreak much havoc in the dynamic programming treatment of the optimization problem. The essential point of difference shows up clearly in the representation of the model as a best-route problem in the acyclic network given in Fig. 10.7.

The network is constructed as follows. One column of nodes appears for each project. The node designation is (k, j), where j refers to the project, and the value of k signifies an amount of capital available for possible investment in Projects $1, 2, \ldots, j$. Each arc leading out of Node (k, j) represents a specific decision about Project j. For example, the arc from Node $(6, 2)$ to Node $(3, 1)$ represents the decision to invest $y_2 = 6 - 3 = \$3$ million in Project 2 when capital available to spend on Projects 2 and 1 is $6 million; the result of the decision is to leave $3 million to spend on Project 1. Hence according to Fig. 10.6, the value associated with this arc is $R_2(3) = 18$.

Now you can see the effect of the nonlinear functions $I_j(y)$. Consider Node (10, 4). Only six arcs emanate, since there are only six possible levels of investment. The same observation holds for Nodes (10, 3) and (10, 2). Only level 0 investment arcs emanate from Nodes (k, 3), with $k = 0, 1, 2, 3$, because any positive levels of investment require an expenditure of at least \$4 million, which is not feasible from these nodes. Similarly, only three arcs leave Node (6, 2) because only investment levels 0, 1, 2 are feasible for Project 2 when the available capital is 6. To summarize, given a Node (k, j), the only outward arcs permitted are those for values of y such that $I_j(y) \leq k$.

Finding an optimal investment plan is tantamount in Fig. 10.7 to solving for a route from Node (10, 4) to the terminal Node (0, 0) that gives maximum present value. This idea can be captured by means of a dynamic programming recursive formula. Specifically, define

(4)
$$g_j(k) = \begin{pmatrix} \text{present value when capital, } k, \text{ is available to invest} \\ \text{optimally on Project 1, Project 2, ..., Project j} \end{pmatrix},$$

$$y_j(k) = \begin{pmatrix} \text{an investment level for Project j} \\ \text{that yields } g_J(k) \end{pmatrix}.$$

In terms of the network of Fig. 10.7, the quantity $g_j(k)$ is the present value of an optimal route from Node (k, j) to Node (0, 0).

The procedure for finding a best route assigns the value $g_0(0) = 0$, then puts $g_1(k) = R_1(k)$, and for each stage $j > 1$, determines an arc that maximizes the sum of the immediate profit impact $R_j(y)$ and the profit from continuing optimally from the appropriate node at the next stage. To illustrate, at stage $j = 2$, the present value of a best route to the terminal from Node (5, 2) is calculated by

(5) $g_2(5) = \text{maximum } [R_2(0) + g_1(5), R_2(1) + g_1(2), R_2(2) + g_1(0)].$

Each of the sums on the right of (5) is associated with an arc leading out of Node (5, 2) and into either Node (5, 1), Node (2, 1), or Node (0, 1). The general dynamic programming recursion is

(6) $g_j(k) = \underset{y}{\text{maximum }} \{R_j(y) + g_{j-1}[k - I_j(y)]\}$ for $j = 1, 2, \ldots, s$

(7) $g_0(k) \equiv 0$ for $j = 0,$

where $k = 0, 1, \ldots, K$, and the maximization is over only nonnegative integer values of y that satisfy $I_j(y) \leq k$.

An optimal plan for the data in Fig. 10.6 will now be derived using the recursion (6) to demonstrate the dynamic programming approach. If you start with the last stage, $j = 1$, the computation of $g_1(k)$ is straightforward, because the corporation invests in Project 1 all the capital k that remains after its investments in the other projects:

(8) $g_1(k) = 2k$ and $y_1(k) = k$ for $k = 0, 1, \ldots, 10.$

We omit tabulating these values because they are so readily computed.

You continue with $j = 2$ to derive the computational scheme shown in Fig. 10.8. Observe that there is a row in the table for each possible state, that is, for each amount of capital available. Rows for the values of $k = 7, 8, 9$ have been omitted because they could never arise, as is shown graphically in the network in Fig. 10.7. If the calculations were performed inside an electronic calculator, however, it probably would be simpler to compute these values of k even though they would not be needed to find an optimal solution. In Fig. 10.8, entries in which $I_2(y) \leq k$ fails to hold have been shaded because these combinations of y and k are not feasible.

$$R_2(y) - g_1[k - I_2(y)]$$

Investment Level:

k \ y	0	1	2	3	4	5	$y_2(k)$	$g_2(k)$
0	0 + 0						0	0
1	0 + 2						0	2
2	0 + 4						0	4
3	0 + 6	8 + 0					1	8
4	0 + 8	8 + 2					1	10
5	0 + 10	8 + 4	13+0				2	13
6	0 + 12	8 + 6	13+2				2	15
10	0 + 20	8 + 8	13+10	18 + 6	19 + 4	20 + 0	3	24

(Available Capital: k)

FIGURE 10.8. Out-of-Site Realty Corporation ($j = 2$).

The first number of each entry inside the table is the value of $R_2(y)$, taken from Fig. 10.6. The second number requires a little explanation. Consider the entry for $k = 5$ and $y = 1$. At investment level $y = 1$, Fig. 10.6 shows that the investment cost is $I_2(1) = 3$, which must be netted out of the available capital 5, thus leaving the amount $k = 2$ for investment in Project 1. According to (8), $g_1(2) = 2 \cdot 2 = 4$, and so 4 appears as the second number in the table. In short, the second number is the quantity $g_1[k - I_2(y)]$, which is found by first calculating $k - I_2(y)$ from the quantities k, y, and the information in Fig. 10.6, and then using the formula in (8). For each k, the value of $g_2(k)$ is the maximum sum in the row and $y_2(k)$ is a corresponding investment level.

A similar table in Fig. 10.9 is constructed for $j = 3$. To illustrate the entries, consider the case $k = 10$ and $y = 1$. The first number is $R_3(1) = 9$. Now $k - I_3(1) = 10 - 4 = 6$ is the capital available for stage $j = 2$, and hence the second number is $g_2(6) = 15$, from Fig. 10.8. The value of $g_3(k)$ is the largest sum in the row.

$$R_3(y) + g_2[k - I_3(y)]$$

Investment Level:

y \ k	0	1	2	3	4	5	$y_3(k)$	$g_3(k)$
0	0 + 0						0	0
1	0 + 2						0	2
2	0 + 4						0	4
3	0 + 8						0	8
4	0 + 10	9 + 0					0	10
10	0 + 24	9 + 15	13 + 13	18 + 4	19 + 2	23 + 0	3	26

(left axis label: Available Capital)

FIGURE 10.9. Out-of-Site Realty Corporation ($j = 3$).

$$R_4(y) + g_3[k - I_4(y)]$$

Investment Level:

y \ k	0	1	2	3	4	5	$y_4(k)$	$g_4(k)$
Available Capital: 10	0 + 26	17 + 10	18 + 8	21 + 4	22 + 2	24 + 0	1	27

FIGURE 10.10. Out-of-Site Realty Corporation ($j = 4$).

The stage $j = 4$ is shown in Fig. 10.10. There you see that the optimal investment plan has a present value of 27. The plan itself is found by starting in Fig. 10.10 with the decision $y_4(10) = 1$ for Project 4; that is, the corporation undertakes Level 1 investment for Project 4 at a cost of $6 million. This leaves $4 million to be allocated to Projects 3, 2, and 1. Going to Fig. 10.9 where $j = 3$, you find that $y_3(4) = 0$, so that Project 3 is bypassed. Next refer to Fig. 10.8 where $j = 2$. The corporation still has $4 million to allocate, and you ascertain that $y_2(4) = 1$; this Level 1 investment in Project 2 requires an outlay of $3 million, leaving only $1 million for Project 1. As a check on the recursive computations, note that the total present value from these decisions is $(17 + 0 + 8 + 2 = 27)$, which agrees with $g_4(10)$.

10.4 KNAPSACK PROBLEM

A distribution of effort problem that has a linear objective function and a single linear constraint represents an important class of applications. The following descriptive example suggests why this model is often referred to as a **knapsack problem.**

Ben Dover, an exuberant mountain climber, is preparing for a lengthy hike up a dangerous slope. He can manage up to W pounds in his knapsack that he carries on his back. He has N different types of items that he can include in his pack, and each unit of Item j weighs w_j pounds. For every Item j, he has calculated a numerical value R_j representing the survival value of each unit of the item. To illustrate, if he packs five units of Item 3 and seven units of Item 9, the "value" to him of this knapsack selection is $5R_3 + 7R_9$. Ben Dover's optimization problem is to select the number of each type item to include in his knapsack. The appropriate mathematical formulation is

$$(1) \qquad\qquad \text{maximize } \sum_{j=1}^{N} R_j y_j$$

subject to

$$(2) \qquad\qquad \sum_{j=1}^{N} w_j y_j \leq W \quad \text{(weight constraint)}$$

$$(3) \qquad\qquad y_j = 0, 1, 2, \ldots \quad \text{for each } j,$$

where y_j represents the number of units of Item j to be packed.

You can apply the logic developed in the preceding section to interpret (1) through (3) as a problem of finding an optimum route through an acyclic network. This view leads to the dynamic programming recursion

$$(4) \qquad g_j(w) = \underset{y}{\text{maximum}} \; [R_j y + g_{j-1}(w - w_j y)] \quad \text{for } j = 1, 2, \ldots, N$$

$$(5) \qquad\qquad g_0(w) \equiv 0 \quad \text{for } j = 0,$$

where $w = 0, 1, \ldots, W$, and the maximization is over only nonnegative integer values of y that satisfy $w_j y \leq w$. We do not provide further analysis of this approach or give a numerical example because you can improve on the above recursion by taking an alternative view of the optimization. Another application of this model will serve to explain the idea.

Batch Size: j	Profit R_j
1	4
2	11
3	17
4	24
5	28
6	36

FIGURE 10.11. Why Pout Spot Remover Co. Problem. (Batch sizes are in units of one month's supply —which is 1,000 cases. Profit is in thousands of dollars.)

The Why Pout Spot Remover Co. Problem. The factory manager for the Why Pout Company must schedule plant production of cans of spot remover for each of the next $N = 9$ months. It is company policy to wait until inventory is depleted before producing new cans of product; when inventory falls to zero, the manager then decides the batch size (number of months' supply) to manufacture. (You can find in Sec. 9.5 an extended discussion of when such a policy is optimal.) Assume that the monthly demand for the product is sufficiently stable so that monthly demand over the planning horizon can be treated as a constant for the purpose of production scheduling. For the sake of definiteness, let the demand be 1,000 cases per month. Suppose further that plant production and storage capacity limitations restrict the feasible batch sizes to be between one and six months' supply. The profit R_j associated with the decision to produce a batch size of j months' supply is given in Fig. 10.11. For example, a batch size of three months' supply, namely, 3,000 cases, yields a profit of $17 thousand.

Over the nine months' horizon, a production schedule must produce nine months' supply. Let y_j denote the number of times the factory manager schedules a batch of j months' supply, $j = 1, 2, \ldots, 6$. Then Why Pout's optimization problem is given by

(6)   maximize $\sum_{j=1}^{6} R_j y_j$

subject to

(7) $\sum_{j=1}^{6} j \cdot y_j = N$ (schedule N months' supply)

(8) $y_j = 0, 1, 2, \ldots$ for each j.

In this example, $N = 9$ and constraint (7) is

(9) $y_1 + 2y_2 + 3y_3 + 4y_4 + 5y_5 + 6y_6 = 9.$

Thus, one feasible schedule is to produce a single month's supply every month, $y_1 = 9$. Another is to produce three months' supply every three months, $y_3 = 3$. Still another schedule is to produce four months' supply once and five months' supply once, $y_4 = 1$ and $y_5 = 1$; in this case, total profit $(24 + 28)$ would be the same irrespective of which of the two batch sizes is produced first. Of course, there are further possibilities to consider. The acyclic network in Fig. 10.12 should help you visualize all the possibilities.

Each Node n represents the requirement of producing n months' supply. At Node 9, then, the immediate production decision is drawn from the six feasible batch-size options. The immediate choice of a single month's supply corresponds to the arc into Node 8, since this option implies that eight more months of supply are needed; the profit associated with the arc from Node 9 to Node 8 is $R_1 = 4$. The immediate choice of five months' supply corresponds to the arc into Node 4, since this option implies that four more months' supply is needed; the profit for

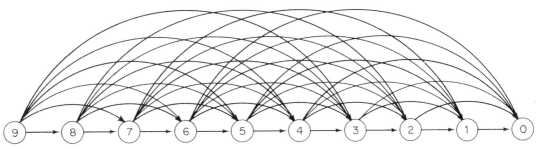

FIGURE 10.12. Why Pout Spot Remover Co.—Network Representation.

the arc from Node 9 to Node 4 is $R_5 = 28$. Similar interpretations hold for the arcs out of the other nodes. Observe that fewer than six arcs emanate from any Node n where $n < 6$, since batch sizes larger than n are not feasible.

The optimization problem (6) through (8) can be viewed as a matter of finding a best-profit route through a network such as Fig. 10.12. The best-route computational logic for the network is conveyed by the dynamic programming recursion

(10) $$G(n) = \underset{j}{\text{maximum}}\ [R_j + G(n-j)]\quad \text{for } n = 1, 2, \ldots, N$$

(11) $$G(0) \equiv 0\quad \text{for } n = 0,$$

where the maximization is over positive integer values of $j \le n$, and in the example, also $j \le 6$. The value of $G(n)$ is the profit of a best route from Node n to the terminal Node 0. The calculations find $G(1), G(2), \ldots$, and finally $G(N)$.

The recursion (10) is illustrated below for the example in Fig. 10.11:

$$G(0) = 0$$

$$G(1) = \text{maximum}\ [R_1 + G(0)] = [4 + 0] = 4\quad \text{and}\quad j = 1$$

$$G(2) = \text{maximum}\ [R_1 + G(1), R_2 + G(0)]$$
$$= \text{maximum}\ [4 + 4, 11 + 0] = 11\quad \text{and}\quad j = 2$$

$$G(3) = \text{maximum}\ [R_1 + G(2), R_2 + G(1), R_3 + G(0)]$$
$$= \text{maximum}\ [4 + 11, 11 + 4, 17 + 0] = 17\quad \text{and}\quad j = 3$$

$$G(4) = \text{maximum}\ [R_1 + G(3), R_2 + G(2), R_3 + G(1), R_4 + G(0)]$$
$$= \text{maximum}\ [4 + 17, 11 + 11, 17 + 4, 24 + 0] = 24\quad \text{and}\quad j = 4$$

$$G(5) = \text{maximum}\ [R_1 + G(4), R_2 + G(3), R_3 + G(2), R_4 + G(1),$$
$$R_5 + G(0)]$$
$$= \text{maximum}\ [4 + 24, 11 + 17, 17 + 11, 24 + 4, 28 + 0] = 28$$
$$\text{for any } j \le 5$$

(12) $$G(6) = \text{maximum}\ [R_1 + G(5), R_2 + G(4), R_3 + G(3), R_4 + G(2),$$
$$R_5 + G(1), R_6 + G(0)]$$
$$= \text{maximum}\ [4 + 28, 11 + 24, 17 + 17, 24 + 11,$$
$$28 + 4, 36 + 0] = 36\quad \text{for } j = 6$$

$$G(7) = \text{maximum}\ [R_1 + G(6), R_2 + G(5), R_3 + G(4), R_4 + G(3),$$
$$R_5 + G(2), R_6 + G(1)]$$
$$= \text{maximum}\ [4 + 36, 11 + 28, 17 + 24, 24 + 17, 28 + 11, 36 + 4]$$
$$= 41\quad \text{for } j = 3, 4$$

$$G(8) = \text{maximum}\ [4 + 41, 11 + 36, 17 + 28, 24 + 24, 28 + 17, 36 + 11]$$
$$= 48\quad \text{for } j = 4$$

$$G(9) = \text{maximum}\ [4 + 48, 11 + 41, 17 + 36, 24 + 28, 28 + 24, 36 + 17]$$
$$= 53\quad \text{for } j = 3, 6.$$

You determine an optimal schedule by first choosing a decision, j, that yields $G(N)$. In the example, $j = 3$ and 6 are optimal for $G(9)$. The decision $j = 3$ implies that the first batch size is three months' supply. This means that six months' supply remains to be scheduled. Examining $G(6)$ you find that $j = 6$ is optimal; in other words, the optimal choice for the second batch size is six month's supply. [Verify that if you select the first batch size to be six months' supply, and then examine $G(3)$, you find that $j = 3$ is optimal for the second batch.]

*Ben Dover and Why Pout Again.** For the knapsack problem optimization (1) through (3), the recursion analogous to (10) is

(13) $$G(w) = \underset{j}{\text{maximum}} \, [R_j + G(w - w_j)] \quad \text{for } w = 1, 2, \ldots, W;$$

since the constraint (2) is an inequality, it is convenient to introduce the decision $j = 0$, with $R_0 = 0$ and $w_0 = 1$, and let the maximization in (13) be over values of $j = 0, 1, \ldots, N$ that also satisfy $w_j \le w$. The computational procedure of (13) can be streamlined even further by means of more advanced analysis.

Regrettably, the simplification (13) is not valid when the variables in the knapsack problem are constrained by upper bounds (for example, each $y_j \le L_j$, where L_j is a positive integer). In such cases, you should apply (4), adding the upper-bound restriction on each y_j during the maximization. To illustrate, in the Why Pout Co. example suppose that no given batch size can be manufactured more than once during the horizon; thus $L_j = 1$ so that each $y_j = 0, 1$. For a nine months' horizon, an optimal schedule does not violate these upper-bound restrictions. But if the horizon is eight months, the previous solution in (12) calls for letting $y_4 = 2$, that is, for manufacturing *two* batches of four months' supply. The appropriate recursion that recognizes the upper-bound restrictions is

(14) $$g_j(n) = \underset{y=0,1}{\text{maximum}} \, [R_j y + g_{j-1}(n - j \cdot y)] \quad \text{for } j = 1, 2, \ldots, 6,$$

(15) $$g_0(n) \equiv 0 \quad \text{for } j = 0.$$

10.5 EQUIPMENT REPLACEMENT MODEL

The application in this section seems far removed from the batch production example in the preceding section yet it gives rise to the same network structure.

The Goode-O'Toole Company runs a machine shop containing an expensive drill press that must be replaced periodically as it wears out. The vice-president of manufacturing has just authorized installing a new computerized tape-driven model, but she has asked the foreman to devise an optimal replacement plan for the next five years, after which the drill press will no longer be needed.

The relevant economic data are shown in Fig. 10.13. The value of p_t represents the purchase price of a new machine. Thus, the new press that must be purchased immediately costs $p_1 = 100$; if another press is purchased four years from now, the price paid will be $p_4 = 115$. The amount v_t represents the scrap value of a press

Time t	Purchase Price p_t	Scrap Value v_t	Operation cost r_t
1	100	50	30
2	105	25	40
3	110	10	50
4	115	5	75
5	120	2	90

FIGURE 10.13. Goode O'Toole Company Example.

that is sold at the end of t periods of use. Thus, if the machine to be purchased immediately is replaced after one year's use, the company receives as revenue the salvage value 50; if it is replaced after two year's use, the revenue is only 25; if it is kept all five years and then scrapped, the revenue falls to 2. For simplicity of exposition, assume that these scrap values do not depend on the year a machine is purchased; hence, even if prices rise and a new machine is bought three years from now, the salvage value of the machine after one year's use will still be 50. The costs of operating and maintaining a machine also depend on the machine's age. The value r_t represents the operating cost of a piece of equipment in its tth consecutive year of use. Hence, if a machine is kept only a single year, its operating and maintenance cost is 30; if it is kept two years, its operating cost over this time span is 70 ($= 30 + 40$).

Let

$$c_{ij} = \begin{pmatrix} \text{sum of the purchase price and operating costs less scrap value} \\ \text{of a new press bought in Year i and retained until the start of} \\ \text{Year j, when it is salvaged} \end{pmatrix}.$$

To illustrate,

$$
\begin{aligned}
c_{12} &= p_1 + r_1 - v_1 = 100 + 30 - 50 = 80 \\
c_{13} &= p_1 + (r_1 + r_2) - v_2 = 100 + (30 + 40) - 25 = 145 \\
c_{35} &= p_3 + (r_1 + r_2) - v_2 = 110 + 70 - 25 = 155 \\
c_{36} &= p_3 + (r_1 + r_2 + r_3) - v_3 = 110 + 120 - 10 = 220.
\end{aligned}
$$

(1)

All the values of c_{ij}, where $i = 1, 2, \ldots, 5$ and $j = i + 1, \ldots, 6$, are shown in Fig. 10.14.

Purchase price and operating costs less scrap value if press bought in Year i and retained until start of Year j

i \ j	2	3	4	5	6
1	80	145	210	290	373
2		85	150	215	295
3			90	155	220
4				95	160
5					100

FIGURE 10.14. Goode O'Toole Company Example—c_{ij}.

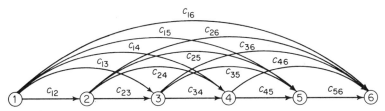

FIGURE 10.15. Equipment Replacement Network.

The appropriate network for the equivalent replacement problem is displayed in Fig. 10.15. Each Node n represents the event that a new drill press is purchased at the start of Year n. Thus, the initial position is Node 1, since a new machine is needed immediately. The decision to keep that press throughout the horizon of five years (and scrap it at the start of Year 6) corresponds to the arc from Node 1 to Node 6, and it has the associated cost c_{16}. The decision to keep that press only a single year and then replace it corresponds to the arc from Node 1 to Node 2 with cost c_{12}; at Node 2, a new machine is to be purchased, and each arc out of Node 2 represents the decision to keep that machine from one to four years. An optimal replacement policy over the entire horizon is tantamount to finding a minimum-cost route from Node 1 to Node 6, and the appropriate dynamic programming recursion is

$$(2) \qquad G(n) = \underset{k=n+1,\ldots,N}{\operatorname{minimum}} \; [c_{nk} + G(k)] \quad \text{for } n = N - 1, N - 2, \ldots, 1$$

$$(3) \qquad G(N) \equiv 0,$$

where $N = 6$ in this example, and $G(n)$ represents the cost of a best route from Node n to Node 6. In other words, $G(n)$ is the minimum replacement-policy cost from Year n until the start of Year N, assuming that a new machine is purchased at the start of Year n. You apply (2) by calculating, in turn, $G(N), G(N-1), \ldots,$ and finally $G(1)$.

An optimal replacement policy for the Goode-O'Toole Co. is found as follows:

$G(6) = 0$

$G(5) = \text{minimum } [c_{56} + G(6)] = 100 + 0 = 100 \quad \text{for } k = 6$

$G(4) = \text{minimum } [c_{45} + G(5), c_{46} + G(6)]$

$\qquad = \text{minimum } [95 + 100, 160 + 0] = 160 \quad \text{for } k = 6$

$G(3) = \text{minimum } [c_{34} + G(4), c_{35} + G(5), c_{36} + G(6)]$

$\qquad = \text{minimum } [90 + 160, 155 + 100, 220 + 0] = 220 \quad \text{for } k = 6$

$G(2) = \text{minimum } [c_{23} + G(3), c_{24} + G(4), c_{25} + G(5), c_{26} + G(6)]$

$\qquad = \text{minimum } [85 + 222, 150 + 160, 215 + 100, 295 + 0] = 295 \quad \text{for } k = 6$

$G(1) = \text{minimum } [c_{12} + G(2), c_{13} + G(3), c_{14} + G(4), c_{15} + G(5), c_{16} + G(6)]$

$\qquad = \text{minimum } [80 + 295, 145 + 220, 210 + 160, 290 + 100, 373 + 0] = 365$

$\qquad \qquad \qquad \qquad \qquad \qquad \qquad \qquad \qquad \qquad \qquad \text{for } k = 3.$

Thus, the immediate optimal decision at Node 1 ($n = 1$) is to purchase a new drill press and keep it until the start of Year 3 ($k = 3$). Three years from now, diagrammatically at Node 3 ($n = 3$), the optimal decision is to purchase a machine and keep it until the start of Year 6, the end of the horizon ($k = 6$). The total cost over the horizon is $G(1) = 365 (= c_{13} + c_{36} = 145 + 220)$. Years 1 and 3 are termed **regeneration points,** implying that the decision process starts afresh at these times. (If an optimal policy called for replacing every year, then all five years would be regeneration points.)

*10.6 INVENTORY MODEL
WITH PRODUCTION SMOOTHING

The elementary inventory model that you studied in Chap. 8 only balanced off manufacturing with inventory holding costs. The economic cost of *varying* production levels from one period to the next was ignored. Suppose that this factor is so important that the firm must assign an explicit **smoothing cost** incurred by changing production.

For expository convenience, we assume the same data as in the Dependable Manufacturing Company's problem, which is repeated below. For each Period t, the cost incurred depends on the production quantity x_t, the ending inventory level i_t, and the *previous* period's production quantity x_{t-1}:

(1) $$C_t(x_t, i_t, x_{t-1}) = C(x_t) + 1 \cdot i_t + 1 \cdot (x_t - x_{t-1})^2,$$

where

(2) $$\begin{aligned} C(0) &= 0 & C(1) &= 15 & C(2) &= 17 \\ C(3) &= 19 & C(4) &= 21 & C(5) &= 23 \end{aligned}$$

for all periods. Note that the third function on the right of (1) represents the smoothing cost, which is given by the square of the fluctuation in production levels over two successive periods. In this illustration, the cost impact of a variation in production is quadratic, and an upward fluctuation of a given magnitude is as costly as a downward fluctuation of the same magnitude. The required demand and the feasible production and inventory levels are

(3) $$D_t = 3 \quad \text{(stationary demand)},$$

(4) $$x_t = 0, 1, \ldots, 5 \quad i_t = 0, 1, \ldots, 4 \quad \text{and no ending inventory.}$$

What changes are required in the dynamic programming recursion to accommodate this new smoothing cost factor? Recall that the relation previously used in Chap. 8 was written as

(5) $$f_n(i) = \underset{x}{\text{minimum}} [c(x) + 1 \cdot (i + x - 3) + f_{n-1}(i + x - 3)]$$

$$\text{for } n = 2, 3, \ldots,$$

where $i = 0, 1, 2, 3, 4$ and the minimization is over only nonnegative integer values of x in the range $3 - i \le x \le \text{minimum} (5, 7 - i)$, assuming inventory is 0 at the end of the horizon. Now, knowledge of entering inventory is not sufficient to characterize the state of the system at the beginning of a period. You also need to know the production level in the previous period because this quantity affects the costs incurred in the current period. Hence, the state variable for this model must contain *both* the levels of entering inventory and the previous period's production.

Even though the situation has become more complex because of the additional information required to characterize the state of the system at each stage, the problem still can be characterized as the finding of a least-cost route through an acyclic network. In the simpler model of Chap. 8, the required network, shown in Fig. 8.12, consists of a set of nodes for each stage, and each node within a set represents a possible value for entering inventory. The node designation (i, n) conveyed the inventory level and stage number. Here, the network also consists of a set of nodes for each stage, but each node within a set represents possible values for *both* entering inventory and the previous period's production level. The appropriate node designation is (i, y, n), where y is the production level in the previous period. An arc out of Node (i, y, n) represents a feasible decision for current production x, has the associated cost $C(x) + 1 \cdot (i + x - 3) + 1 \cdot (x - y)^2$, and leads into Node (i + x - 3, x, n - 1).

In the simpler model of Chap. 8, at the stage $n = 1$ the network contains four nodes corresponding to entering inventory $i = 0, 1, 2, 3$ ($i = 4$ is not feasible, since inventory at the end of the horizon must be 0), and at each stage $n \geq 2$, the network contains five nodes corresponding to $i = 0, 1, 2, 3, 4$. In the present network, the network contains 18 nodes for $n = 1$ and 21 nodes for $n \geq 2$. This expansion occurs because of the added production variable in the state description, and it arises as follows. The possible values for the previous production level are $y = 0, 1, 2, 3, 4, 5$. Since $i_t = i_{t-1} + y - 3$, you can rearrange terms to give $i_{t-1} = i_t - y + 3$. The restrictions on i_{t-1} are $0 \leq i_{t-1} \leq 4$, which implies that $y - 3 \leq i_t \leq 1 + y$; also $0 \leq i_t \leq 4$, for $n \geq 2$, and $0 \leq i_t \leq 3$ for $n = 1$. Therefore, the feasible values for entering inventory i, given y, are maximum $(0, y - 3) \leq i \leq$ minimum $(4, 1 + y)$ for $n \geq 2$ and maximum $(0, y - 3) \leq i \leq$ minimum $(3, 1 + y)$ for $n = 1$.

If the planning horizon is N periods, the inventory level entering the initial period is i_0, and the production level immediately prior to the initial period is x_0, then the network optimization problem is to find a least-cost path from Node (i_0, x_0, N) to the terminal Node $(0, 0, 0)$. The familiar logic underlying a best-route computation can be characterized by a recursive formula. Toward that end, let

$$f_n(i, y) = \begin{pmatrix} \text{minimum policy cost when entering inventory is at level } i \text{ and} \\ \text{previous production at level } y \text{ with } n \text{ more periods to go} \end{pmatrix}$$

$$x_n(i, y) = \text{a production level yielding } f_n(i, y).$$

The appropriate recursion can be written as

$$f_n(i, y) = \underset{x}{\text{minimum }} [C(x) + 1 \cdot (i + x - 3) + 1 \cdot (x - y)^2$$

(6)
$$+ f_{n-1}(i + x - 3, x)] \quad \text{for } n = 1, 2, \ldots, N,$$

where $y = 0, 1, \ldots, 5$, i is a nonnegative integer in the range $y - 3 \leq i \leq$ minimum $(4, 1 + y)$ for $n \geq 2$, and the minimization is over only nonnegative integer values in the range $3 - i \leq x \leq$ minimum $(5, 7 - i)$. The computations are initiated with the values of

(7)
$$f_1(i, y) = C(3 - i) + 1 \cdot (3 - i - y)^2 \quad \text{for } y = 0, 1, 2, 3, 4, 5$$
$$x_1(i, y) = 3 - i$$

and i a nonnegative integer in the range $y - 3 \leq i \leq$ minimum $(3, 1 + y)$.

The calculations for $n = 1$ in (7) are displayed in Fig. 10.16. Since ending inventory is 0 by assumption, the optimal production $x_1(i, y)$ depends only on i and is independent of y. As you will observe next, $x_n(i, y)$ does depend on y for $n > 1$.

$$f_1(i, y) = C(3 - i) + \left[(3 - i) - y\right]^2$$

Previous Production:

Entering Inventory	$y = 0$		$y = 1$		$y = 2$		$y = 3$		$y = 4$		$y = 5$	
i	$x_1(i,0)$	$f_1(i,0)$	$x_1(i,1)$	$f_1(i,1)$	$x_1(i,2)$	$f_1(i,2)$	$x_1(i,3)$	$f_1(i,3)$	$x_1(i,4)$	$f_1(i,4)$	$x_1(i,5)$	$f_1(i,5)$
0	3	28	3	23	3	20	3	19				
1	2	21	2	18	2	17	2	18	2	21		
2			1	15	1	16	1	19	1	24	1	31
3					0	4	0	9	0	16	0	25

Figure 10.16. Dependable Manufacturing Company Production Smoothing Model ($n = 1$).

The computations for $n = 2$ are exhibited in Fig. 10.17. Study the entries in the table to see how they are derived from the dynamic programming recursion (6). In particular, notice that the third entry in each box of the main part of the table comes from Fig. 10.16. For example, if $y = 0$, $i = 1$, and $x = 3$, then the amount 18 is the value of $f_1(i + x - 3, x) = f_1(1, 3)$ contained in the $i = 1$ row and $y = 3$ right column of Fig. 10.16.

The calculations for $n = 3$ are shown in Fig. 10.18. The format for this table also applies to larger values of n. The first number in each sum in the table represents the production, inventory, and smoothing costs; these numbers will not change in tables for larger n. The second number in each sum is the cost of an optimal policy for the remaining stages; these numbers will change in tables for larger n.

Several illustrative optimal schedules for the planning horizon $N = 3$ are given in Fig. 10.19. Suppose the first month of the horizon is January, the previous

$$\left[C(x) + 1\cdot(i+x-3)\right] + \left[1\cdot(x-y)^2 + f_1(i+x-3, x)\right]$$

Production: x

Previous Production: y	Entering Inventory: i	0	1	2	3	4	5	$x_2(i,y)$	$f_2(i,y)$
0	0				19 + 9 + 19	22 + 16 + 21	25 + 25 + 31	3	47
	1			17 + 4 + 20	20 + 9 + 18	23 + 16 + 24	26 + 25 + 25	2	41
1	0				19 + 4 + 19	22 + 9 + 21	25 + 16 + 31	3	42
	1			17 + 1 + 20	20 + 4 + 18	23 + 9 + 24	26 + 16 + 25	2	38
	2		15 + 0 + 23	18 + 1 + 17	21 + 4 + 19	24 + 9 + 16		2	36
2	0				19 + 1 + 19	22 + 4 + 21	25 + 9 + 31	3	39
	1			17 + 0 + 20	20 + 1 + 18	23 + 4 + 24	26 + 9 + 25	2	37
	2		15 + 1 + 23	18 + 0 + 17	21 + 1 + 19	24 + 4 + 16		2	35
	3	0 + 4 + 28	16 + 1 + 18	19 + 0 + 16	22 + 1 + 9			0, 3	32
3	0				19 + 0 + 19	22 + 1 + 21	25 + 4 + 31	3	38
	1			17 + 1 + 20	20 + 0 + 18	23 + 1 + 24	26 + 4 + 25	2, 3	38
	2		15 + 4 + 23	18 + 1 + 17	21 + 0 + 19	24 + 1 + 16		2	36
	3	0 + 9 + 28	16 + 4 + 18	19 + 1 + 16	22 + 0 + 9			3	31
	4	1 + 9 + 21	17 + 4 + 15	20 + 1 + 4				2	25
4	1			17 + 4 + 20	20 + 1 + 18	23 + 0 + 24	26 + 1 + 25	3	39
	2		15 + 9 + 23	18 + 4 + 17	21 + 1 + 19	24 + 0 + 16		2	39
	3	0 + 16 + 28	16 + 9 + 18	19 + 4 + 16	22 + 1 + 9			3	32
	4	1 + 16 + 21	17 + 9 + 15	20 + 4 + 4				2	28
5	2		15 + 16 + 23	18 + 9 + 17	21 + 4 + 19	24 + 1 + 16		4	41
	3	0 + 25 + 28	16 + 16 + 18	19 + 9 + 16	22 + 4 + 9			3	35
	4	1 + 25 + 21	17 + 1 + 15	20 + 9 + 4				1, 2	33

FIGURE 10.17. Dependable Manufacturing Company Production Smoothing Model ($n = 2$).

month's production level is $x_0 = 0$, and entering inventory is $i_0 = 1$. Then, referring to the second row of Fig. 10.18 for ($n = 3, y = 0, i = 1$), you find that an optimal production decision is $x_3(1, 0) = 2$. Consequently, inventory entering February (stage $n = 2$) is 0 ($= i_0 + x - d = 1 + 2 - 3$), and the optimal February production decision is $x_2(0, 2) = 3$ from the sixth row of Fig. 10.17.

$$[C(x) + 1\cdot(i+x-3)] + [1\cdot(x-y)^2 + f_2(i+x-3, x)]$$

Production: x

Previous Production: y	Entering Inventory: i	0	1	2	3	4	5	$x_3(i,y)$	$f_3(i,y)$
0	0				28 + 38	38 + 39	50 + 41	3	66
	1			21 + 39	29 + 38	39 + 39	51 + 35	2	60
1	0				23 + 38	31 + 39	41 + 41	3	61
	1			18 + 39	24 + 38	32 + 39	42 + 35	2	57
	2		15 + 38	19 + 37	25 + 36	33 + 32	43 + 33	1	53
2	0				20 + 38	26 + 39	34 + 41	3	58
	1			17 + 39	21 + 38	27 + 39	35 + 35	2	56
	2		16 + 42	18 + 37	22 + 36	28 + 32	36 + 33	2	55
	3	4 + 41	17 + 38	19 + 35	23 + 31	29 + 25		0	45
3	0				19 + 38	23 + 39	29 + 41	3	57
	1			18 + 39	20 + 38	24 + 39	30 + 35	2	57
	2		19 + 42	19 + 37	21 + 36	25 + 32	31 + 33	2	56
	3	9 + 47	20 + 38	20 + 35	22 + 31	26 + 28		3	53
	4	10 + 41	21 + 36	21 + 32	23 + 25			3	48
4	1			21 + 39	21 + 38	23 + 39	27 + 35	3	59
	2		24 + 42	22 + 37	22 + 36	24 + 32	28 + 33	4	56
	3	16 + 47	25 + 38	23 + 35	23 + 31	25 + 28		4	53
	4	17 + 41	26 + 36	24 + 32	24 + 25			3	49
5	2		31 + 42	27 + 37	25 + 36	25 + 32	29 + 33	2	57
	3	25 + 47	32 + 38	28 + 35	26 + 31	26 + 28		4	54
	4	26 + 41	33 + 36	29 + 32	27 + 25			3	52

FIGURE 10.18. Dependable Manufacturing Company Production Smoothing Model ($n = 3$).

This decision implies that March's entering inventory is 0, so that March's production level is $x_1(0, 3) = 3$ from Fig. 10.16. The total cost over the horizon is $f_3(1, 0) = 50$.

Suppose, instead, that the previous month's production level is $x_0 = 4$ and entering inventory is $i_0 = 3$. Then $x_3(3, 4) = 4$ in Fig. 10.18 gives an optimal January decision. As a result, February's entering inventory is 4 ($= 3 + 4 - 3$),

Initial Inventory i_0	With Smoothing— Previous Production						Without Smoothing		
	$x_0 = 0$			$x_0 = 4$					
	Jan.	Feb.	Mar.	Jan.	Feb.	Mar.	Jan.	Feb.	Mar.
0	3	3	3				4	5	0
1	2	3	3	3	3	2	5	0	3
2				4	3	0	4	0	3
3				4	2	0	0	3	3
4				3	2	0	0	5	0

FIGURE 10.19. Dependable Manufacturing Company Production Smoothing Model for Planning Horizon $N = 3$.

and hence, the optimal production level in February is $x_2(4, 4) = 2$ from Fig. 10.17, and in March it is $x_1(3, 2) = 0$ from Fig. 10.16. The total cost over the horizon is $f_3(3, 4) = 53$.

Observe the impact of the smoothing cost on the production schedules of Fig. 10.19. For comparison, the analogous optimal schedules when the Dependable Manufacturing Co. does not pay a smoothing cost are also known in Fig. 10.19; these schedules are derived from the information in Fig. 8.11. As you would expect, the smoothing cost reduces the amount of fluctuation in production levels from one period to the next. Observe that a peak production of $x = 5$ is never optimal. Note that in the case $i_0 = 2$ and $x_0 = 4$, the production quantities are the same with and without smoothing costs, but the impact of the smoothing factor causes production to take place in two consecutive months, January and February, instead of in January and March.

10.7 DISTRIBUTION OF EFFORT— TWO CONSTRAINTS

The advertising agency of Hooke, Lyon, and Cinquer is planning a radio promotion campaign for Genghis Motor Company automobiles in a large metropolitan area. The spot commercials will introduce the firm's new models, and will be aired over a two-week period. The area has S radio stations. The ad agency has *estimated* for Radio Station j a sales response relation indicating the net return (sales less advertising costs) $R_j(y_j)$ due to allocating y_j dollars to commercials played on that station. The total promotional budget is N dollars. The ad agency also wants only a limited number M of announcements during the daytime hours. Radio Station j has indicated that $K_j(y_j)$ is the number of daytime spots it would schedule, given that the agency purchases a total of y_j dollars of advertising.

The optimization model can be written as

(1) $$\text{maximize } \sum_{j=1}^{S} R_j(y_j)$$

subject to

(2) $$\sum_{j=1}^{S} y_j \leq N \quad \text{(promotional budget)}$$

(3) $$\sum_{j=1}^{S} K_j(y_j) \leq M \quad \text{(daytime announcements)}$$

(4) $$y_j = 0, 1, 2, \ldots \quad \text{for each } j.$$

Assume that N, M, and $K_j(y_j)$ are all nonnegative integers.

Since previously, in Sec. 10.2, you needed a one-dimensional state variable to represent one constraint, such as (2), now you might reasonably, and correctly, guess that a two-dimensional state variable is required. In the appropriate acyclic network diagram of the problem, each node is designated as (n, m, j), where n represents the amount of budget available and m the upper limit on the number of daytime announcements for Radio Stations $1, 2, \ldots, j$. At the Node (n, m, j), a decision to allocate y_j dollars to Radio Station j is represented by an arc leading into Node $[n - y_j, m - K_j(y_j), j - 1]$ and has the associated profit $R_j(y_j)$. [Also, to be feasible, the decision y_j must be a nonnegative integer such that $y_j \leq n$ and $K_j(y_j) \leq m$.] Finding an optimal allocation corresponds to obtaining a best route from Node (N, M, S) to the terminal Node $(0, 0, 0)$. In terms of a dynamic programming recursion, the computational logic for finding a best route is, for $j = 1, 2, \ldots, S$,

(5) $$g_j(n, m) = \underset{y_j}{\text{maximum}} \{R_j(y_j) + g_{j-1}[n - y_j, m - K_j(y_j)]\}$$

where $n = 0, 1, \ldots, N$, and $m = 0, 1, \ldots, M$, and the maximization is over only nonnegative integer values of y_j such that $y_j \leq n$ and $K_j(y_j) \leq m$. Tables designed to make convenient the computations indicated in (5) resemble those utilized in the preceding section in which the state variable was also two-dimensional. The computations are initiated at the $j = 1$ stage, where $g_0(n, m) \equiv 0$, and terminated at the $j = S$ stage with the value of $g_S(N, M)$.

*10.8 DISTRIBUTION OF EFFORT—NESTED PROBLEM

The Giant Electrical Company, which is divisionally organized, annually allocates funds for research and development (R & D) projects. Each of the s divisions submits information in three categories. The first pertains to research activities of an exploratory and highly speculative nature. If v_j thousand dollars are allocated to such projects in Division j, the long-term expected return is $P_j(v_j)$ million dollars. The second category refers to products that have been researched and are ready for development and field testing. In these cases, an outlay of w_j thousand dollars is expected to return $Q_j(w_j)$ million dollars over the long run. The final category is development work to improve existing manufactured products. An expenditure of x_j thousand dollars is forecasted to yield a total of $R_j(x_j)$ million dollars additional revenue.

The board of directors authorizes a total budget of N thousand dollars for all R & D projects, and the chief executive places an upper limit L_j on the amount that Division j can receive. The vice-president responsible for R & D management is to allocate the funds so as to maximize the company's total return subject to the several budget restrictions.

The mathematical model of the vice-president's problem is

(1) $$\text{maximize } \sum_{j=1}^{s} [P_j(v_j) + Q_j(w_j) + R_j(x_j)]$$

subject to

(2) $$\sum_{j=1}^{s} (v_j + w_j + x_j) \leq N \quad \text{(company R \& D budget)}$$

(3) $$v_j + w_j + x_j \leq L_j \quad \text{for } j = 1, 2, \ldots, s \quad \text{(division budget limit)}$$

(4) $$v_j, w_j, x_j \text{ nonnegative integers for each } j.$$

Since there is only one budget constraint (2) imposed on all the policy variables, and the other budget and integer-value constraints (3) and (4) pertain to Division j, you can expect the distribution of effort problem for one constraint to apply here. Pursuing this line of reasoning, you obtain the recursion

(5) $$g_j(n) = \text{maximum } [P_j(v_j) + Q_j(w_j) + R_j(x_j) + g_{j-1}(n - v_j - w_j - x_j)]$$
$$\text{for } j = 1, 2, \ldots, s,$$

where $n = 0, 1, \ldots, N$, the maximization is over only nonnegative integer values of v_j, w_j, and x_j that satisfy $v_j + w_j + x_j \leq \text{minimum } (L_j, n)$, and $g_0(n) = 0$.

Notice a new difficulty appears in (5). Whereas in the previous distribution of effort examples you had only one variable y_j to vary in the search for a maximum at each stage, now you must solve an optimization problem involving three variables. Of course, you could try to enumerate all possibilities, but that is not necessary. In this particular illustration, *at each stage* you are able to use the distribution of effort technique to solve the maximum problem, which can be stated as

(6) $$\text{maximize } P_j(v_j) + Q_j(w_j) + R_j(x_j)$$

subject to

(7) $$v_j + w_j + x_j \leq y,$$

where v_j, w_j, and x_j must be nonnegative integers. You need the solution for each value $y = 0, 1, \ldots, L_j$.

The recursive approach for (6) and (7) is to let

(8) $$p_j(y) = P_j(y) \quad \text{for } y = 0, 1, \ldots, L_j,$$

(9) $$q_j(y) = \text{maximum }_{w_j} [Q_j(w_j) + p_j(y - w_j)] \quad \text{for } y = 0, 1, \ldots, L_j,$$

where the maximization is over only nonnegative integer values of $w_j \leq y$, and

(10) $$r_j(y) = \text{maximum }_{x_j} [R_j(x_j) + q_j(y - x_j)] \quad \text{for } y = 0, 1, \ldots, L_j,$$

where the maximization is over only nonnegative integer values of $x_j \leq y$.

In summary, for each j you use $p_j(y)$, from (8), and (9) to find $q_j(y)$, and use $q_j(y)$ and (10) to find $r_j(y)$, for $y = 0, 1, \ldots, L_j$. Then you restate and solve (5) by the relation

(11) $g_j(n) = \underset{y}{\text{maximum}}\ [r_j(y) + g_{j-1}(n - y)]$ for $j = 1, 2, \ldots, s$,

where $n = 0, 1, \ldots, N$, the maximization is over only nonnegative integer values of y that satisfy $y \leq$ minimum (L_j, n), and $g_0(n) = 0$. Thus this problem requires **nesting** s distribution of effort calculations within an overall distribution of effort model.

10.9 STRUCTURE OF MULTISTAGE ANALYSIS

Having seen a variety of dynamic programming applications and explored a few in depth, you may find it helpful to summarize the essential features in the approach. The remaining sections provide an overview of dynamic programming models.

The dynamic programming approach attacks an optimization problem with multifold constraints and many variables by splitting the problem into a sequence of stages in which lower-dimension optimization takes place. In contrast, most linear and other nonlinear programming approaches attempt to solve such problems by considering all the constraints simultaneously.

The dynamic programming approach casts a problem into the following structure:

(i) The decision variables with their associated constraints are grouped according to stages, and the stages are considered sequentially.

(ii) The only information about previous stages relevant to selecting optimal values for the current decision variables is summarized by a so-called state variable, which may be n-dimensional.

(iii) The current decision, given the present state of the system, has a forecastable influence on the state at the next stage.

(iv) The optimality of the current decision is judged in terms of its forecasted economic impact on the present stage and on all subsequent stages.

▶ There is a canonical form that conveniently illustrates the structure of points (i) through (iv) above. Let the symbol s stand for a state of the system and S_n the collection or set of all possible states at Stage n. Define d_n as the decision made at Stage n, and let $D_n(s)$ designate all the *feasible* values for d_n given that the system is in State s. Finally, given that the system is in State s, let $R_n(s, d_n)$ denote the immediate economic return of decision d_n, and $T_n(s, d_n)$ the transformed state of the system at Stage n $-$ 1. Then a common form for a dynamic programming recursion is

(DPR) $f_n(s) = \underset{d_n \text{ in } D_n(s)}{\text{optimum}} \{R_n(s, d_n) + f_{n-1}[T_n(s, d_n)]\}$ for every s in S_n,

where *optimum* means maximum or minimum, depending on the particular context.

You should keep in mind an important feature of (DPR). The optimization at Stage n does *not* require the values of the *decision* variables which bring about the return

$f_{n-1}[T_n(s, d_n)]$. The "bootstrapping" nature of the recursion means that at each stage you only optimize with respect to a limited number of decision variables, and you retain for further calculation only the *objective-function* values. This essential simplicity is what makes the method attractive. Employing linear programming terminology, you can think of the dynamic programming process as sequentially obtaining values for the dual variables. Such an analogy is exact in the examples of this chapter for the reasons to follow.

In all of the illustrations, the stage, state, and decision variables were represented by integer numbers. (The term **discrete variable problem** is applied to such situations.) In addition, the decision processes extended over a finite time span or number of stages. Finally, no probabilistic elements influenced the outcomes and transitions from state to state.

All these assumptions made it possible to analyze (DPR) in terms of finding a best route in an acyclic network, such as you studied in Chap. 7. To construct the network, you establish a Node [s, n] for every possible value of s and n in the dynamic programming recursion (DPR). Each d_n in $D_n(s)$ results in an arc from Node [s, n] to Node $[T_n(s, d_n), n - 1]$ with arc cost $R_n(s, d_n)$. The State s at the final stage is specified (for example, as "ending inventory must equal zero"). Therefore, this node is taken as the terminal of the network, and $f_n(s)$ represents the length of a best route to the terminal from Node [s, n].

In the linear programming characterization of the network problem, $f_n(s)$ represents the value of the dual variable for the conservation of flow equation at Node [s, n]. Of course, to solve (DPR) you never need to *draw* the acyclic network. You are facilitated in comparing the relative computational merits of alternative dynamic programming formulations by analyzing the complexity of the implied acyclic networks. A rough but usually adequate rule is that the network with the fewest arcs is to be preferred. (This guide is qualified because some formulations require substantial "side calculations" to determine the arc traversal costs *prior* to applying the best-route algorithm.)   ◀

10.10 INSIGHTS TO DYNAMIC PHENOMENA

The dynamic programming approach by its very nature is conducive to studying questions of time horizon sensitivity. The various inventory models in Chaps. 8 and 9 demonstrated that an optimal policy can depend essentially on the length of the planning horizon. Several important ideas emerged from the analysis.

One is the notion of a **strategy.** By solving a dynamic programming recursion, you are in effect determining an optimal policy for every possible value of the state variable at each stage. Thus you obtain a prescription of what to do in every eventuality. To observe the consequences of this, consider a production scheduling model as an example. Suppose you act *as if* demand and the cost functions do not change over time, and you repeatedly consider your horizon to be N periods ahead. Then all you need is the optimal production schedule for each State s when N periods are left to the end of the horizon. Each period you ascertain State s and schedule accordingly. Another impact is that the only thing that matters, when n periods remain, is the current State s and not how you arrived there. So if your decision does not turn out the way you expect, you can let bygones be bygones in your *next* decision. In Chaps. 11 and 12 the notion of a strategy will play a central role, except there you will learn how to find an optimal policy when an unbounded time horizon assumption is built right into the analysis.

Another concept of significance is determining the *form* of an optimal policy. By an auspicious characterization of a dynamic process into a sequence of stages, you sometimes can exploit the special properties of the constraints and economic functions to discover an optimal type of policy. One illustration is regeneration type processes, such as the equipment replacement example in Sec. 10.5. Whenever a regeneration point occurred, you effectively could split the span of optimization into "before" and "after," and handle each part separately.

10.11 COMPUTATIONAL FEASIBILITY

For the problems illustrated in Chaps. 8 through 10, dynamic programming offers a vast improvement over complete enumeration of all possibilities. The feasibility of the technique depends critically on the dimension of the state variable, and this is one reason why skill in formulation is necessary. The difference between a clumsy and a clever characterization can be the deciding factor in whether the approach is workable.

As the examples of this chapter show, the approach can be applied to small-scale nonlinear and integer-valued problems. Because no satisfactory canonical form exists for all of these (not even for finite, discrete, deterministic models), there is no single *efficient* computer program to handle *all* dynamic programming problems. But the form of the dynamic programming recursion is usually simple enough so that it is not much trouble to write a computer program for the particular model to be solved. A number of technical difficulties must be overcome in such programs, but they mainly concern the specialist and will not be discussed here. It suffices to say that in most practical problems with a state variable of one or two dimensions, designing a computer program offers no insurmountable obstacles. Except in rare cases (such as the convex cost inventory model of Sec. 9.3, where the algorithm is quite simple), a computer approach is required—if for no other reason than to eliminate the tedium of the calculations.

Again due to the variation in types of models solved by dynamic programming, it has not been possible to provide any universally applicable technique of sensitivity analysis. Most sensitivity questions that are raised in dynamic programming models tend to affect several costs or constraints simultaneously. Then the formulas required for the analysis need to be worked out for the specific problem.

10.12 APPLICABILITY OF DYNAMIC PROGRAMMING

The results of Chaps. 8 through 10 can be put into two categories. Much of the analysis deepened your understanding of phenomena in dynamic optimization models. The remainder concerned applications of dynamic programming to important industrial problems. By far the most frequent applications of the technique deal with inventory replenishment, production scheduling, and certain regeneration type processes, including equipment replacement. Because a number of dynamic programming problems involve probabilistic elements and unbounded horizons, you should consider the examples you have seen as just an introduction to the subject.

The statement made at the beginning of the chapter warrants repeating in these closing remarks. The practical limitation on the dimension of the state variable in dynamic programming tends to narrow the focus of problems solved by the technique. Only infrequently can all the salient factors in an economic problem of any magnitude be boiled down in such a way as to make feasible the numerical solution to a dynamic programming formulation. This realization does not detract from the value of dynamic programming; rather, it puts into focus certain features that distinguish typical applications of dynamic programming from those of linear programming.

Specifically, many real applications of dynamic programming deal with operating decisions—when to reorder, when to make a machine setup, when to replace a piece of equipment, etc. Many of these decisions are ordinarily delegated by top management to lower echelons. Therefore, implementation of a dynamic programming model involves either using a computer to assist in routine decision-making or providing lower echelons with rules or tables based on an optimal strategy calculation. The limited impact of a single decision found by the usual dynamic programming applications, and the ease with which this decision can be determined, are the very reasons for the technique's success. The approach relieves top management of the burden of reviewing a multitude of individual actions, each having minor import. However, the senior executive is able to exercise policy-making responsibilities effectively by selecting an appropriate model containing what the executive feels are the significant economic and technological considerations.

REVIEW EXERCISES

1 Suppose the restriction (2) in Sec. 10.2 is generalized to the linear constraint $\sum_{j=1}^{s} H_j y_j = N$ (where $H_1 = 1$). Revise (6) accordingly, and indicate the largest value of y_j that needs to be considered in the maximization process at Stage j.

2 Suppose you have a solution to the problem (1) through (3) in Sec. 10.2 for a specified value of N, and now you want to find the solution for the value $N + 1$. Indicate the additional computation required, assuming you use recursion (6) to obtain the answer.

3 *Shopping Basket Markets Problem* (Sec. 10.2). Suppose when egg crates are shipped to Store j that a fraction f_j $(0 < f_j < 1)$ breaks in transit. Revise recursion (6) accordingly.

4 *Shopping Basket Markets Problem* (Sec. 10.2). Suppose the owner has found from past experience that the profit function $R_j(y_j)$ increases as y_j increases up to a point, and then decreases for larger values of y_j (too many eggs in a store create costly handling and storage problems). Indicate how (if at all) you would modify the formulation and resultant dynamic programming recursion to permit shipping less than N crates to all the stores.

5 (a) Verify the calculations in Fig. 10.5 for $j = 3$ and $n = 4, 5, 6$, and for $j = 4$ and $n = 0, 1, \ldots, 6$.
  (b) Indicate all optimal solutions for $N = 3, 4, 5, 6$.

6 In Fig. 10.1, interchange the data for Stores 1 and 4 and for Stores 2 and 3. Apply recursion (6) in Sec. 10.2. How does the optimal strategy compare with that in Fig. 10.5?

7 In Fig. 10.6, add 3 to each $R_3(y)$ for $y \geq 1$. Apply recursion (6) in Sec. 10.3 and find an optimal investment strategy.

8 In Fig. 10.11, add 2 to each R_j. Apply recursion (10) and find an optimal strategy.

9 In each part below, alter the data in Fig. 10.13, recalculate the costs in Fig. 10.14, and find an optimal replacement policy using recursion (2) in Sec. 10.5.

  (a) Add 5 to each p_t.
  (b) Add 10 to each v_t.
  (c) Subtract 5 from each r_t.
  (d) Make all the revisions given in parts (a), (b), and (c).

*10 *Dependable Manufacturing Company Example* (Sec. 10.6). Suppose that the smoothing cost function in (1) is $|x_t - x_{t-1}|$ instead of the quadratic term on the right. Calculate tables like those in Figs. 10.16, 10.17, and 10.18. How does an optimal plan differ from that indicated in Fig. 10.19?

*11 Suggest at least two smoothing cost functions that are reasonable alternatives to that used in Sec. 10.6.

*12 (a) Explain how to modify the recursion (6) in Sec. 10.6 for the case where the cost function (1) also contains the term $(x_t - x_{t-2})^2$.
  (b) Indicate how the number of computations will increase as compared to those required in Figs. 10.16, 10.17, and 10.18.

13 In describing the distribution of effort problem with two constraints in Sec. 10.7, we assumed, for simplicity, that the constraints (2) and (3) are inequalities, and that each $K_j(y_j)$ is nonnegative and integer-valued. Explain what complications arise if each of these assumptions is dropped, and what is the resultant impact on computing a solution with recursion (5).

14 (a) Suppose the restriction (2) in Sec. 10.7 is replaced by

$$\sum_{j=1}^{s} H_j(y_j) \leq N,$$

where the value of $H_j(y_j)$ is a nonnegative integer for $y_j = 0, 1, \ldots$. Indicate how the recursion (5) and the computational process must be modified.

(b) Suppose the restriction

$$\sum_{j=1}^{s} H_j(y_j) \leq P$$

is added to (1) through (4) in Sec. 10.7, where the value of $H_j(y_j)$ is a nonnegative integer for $y_j = 0, 1, \ldots$, and P is a positive integer. Indicate how the recursion (5) must be modified. Discuss the resultant increase in computational effort.

*15 *Giant Electrical Company Example* (Sec. 10.8). Imagine that the board of directors has elected a new president who feels it is important to encourage the pursuit of *basic* research. Let y_j thousand dollars denote an allocation by Division j for such basic research, and $T_j(y_j)$ million dollars be the best estimate the division has on the ultimate return to the company from this expenditure on basic research. The total allocation to basic research is drawn from the company's overall R & D budget, and the amount y_j is drawn from the division's budget. Show how the formulation (1) through (4) must be modified to include the allocations for basic research. Indicate the necessary changes in the recursion (5), and the maximization process (6) and (7). Show how to appropriately modify the approach given by (8) through (11). (Be sure to define your notation and symbols.)

*16 *Giant Electrical Company Example* (Sec. 10.8). Imagine that there is a conservative member of the board of directors who insists that the total amount of money the company allocates to exploratory and speculative projects does not exceed V thousand dollars. Show how the formulation (1) through (4) must be modified. Indicate the appropriate recursion, the corresponding minimization process in (6) and (7), and how to modify the approach given by (8) through (11). (Be sure to define your notation and symbols.)

*17 Consider the recursion (DPR) in the special material of Sec. 10.9.

(a) Indicate how each of the points (i) through (iv) affects the appearance of (DPR).
(b) Show the correspondence between each symbol in (DPR) and the appropriate symbol in the recursion (6) of Sec. 10.2. In the recursion (6) of Sec. 10.3. In the recursion (6) of Sec. 10.6. In the recursion (5) of Sec. 10.7.

18 Explain your understanding of the following terms:

distribution of effort problem   *nested problem
knapsack problem   multistage analysis
regeneration point   *discrete variable problem
batch ordering   strategy.
smoothing cost

FORMULATION AND COMPUTATIONAL EXERCISES

In many of the exercises below, you are asked to formulate a model in terms of a dynamic programming recursion. Be sure to define all the symbols you use, and answer the five questions at the end of Sec. 10.1. Give the appropriate optimization function when there is a single period remaining as well as the recursion for Stage n. Explain how to initiate and when to terminate the calculations.

19 *Knapsack Problem.* Suppose Dover wants to select the lightest knapsack that has a value to him of at least R. Show how to revise the formulation in Sec. 10.4.

20 Howie Kramms is a graduating senior and needs to do as well as possible on the final examinations in order to receive his degree. He divides his available weekend study time into 10 periods of equal length. He is taking four courses, two of which he judges are easy and two difficult. He estimates that for each "gut" course, he will earn no grade points if he does not study at all, four grade points if he studies either one or two periods, seven grade points if he studies three periods, and eight grade points if he studies four periods. Similarly, he estimates that for each difficult course, he will earn no grade points if he does not study, only two grade points if he studies either one or two periods, four grade points for studying three periods, six grade points for studying four periods, and nine grade points if he studies five periods. Disregarding the consideration of whether he is overoptimistic in his assessments, how would you advise him to allocate his time to maximize the total grade points he receives? Formulate an appropriate dynamic programming model and find an optimal solution. How much would an extra study period be worth? What harm will be done if he goofs off for one study period?

21 Libby Doe, a girl friend of Howie Kramms, whom you advised in exercise 20, has just arrived in town and has called Howie for a date. He reassesses his situation and decides that all he really needs are 18 grade points to graduate. Now he wants to allocate his time so that he spends the fewest number of study periods necessary to guarantee his receiving at least 18 grade points. Formulate this decision problem as a dynamic programming model, and find an optimal solution. (If there is more than one optimal allocation, indicate the alternative solutions.)

22 The United Fund wants to assign 10 of its volunteers to solicit contributions from the companies having offices in three large downtown buildings. The executive director estimates that if y_j volunteers are assigned to Building j, then total contribution pledges will be $R_j(y_j)$ hundred dollars, where $R_j(0) = 0$ and

$$
\begin{array}{lll}
R_1(1) = 5 & R_2(1) = 3 & R_3(1) = 20 \\
R_1(2) = 10 & R_2(2) = 6 & R_3(2) = 35 \\
R_1(3) = 15 & R_2(3) = 12 & R_3(3) = 45 \\
R_1(4) = 25 & R_2(4) = 18 & R_3(4) = 55 \\
R_1(5) = 35 & R_2(5) = 30 & R_3(5) = 60 \\
R_1(6) = 50 & & R_3(6) = 65. \\
R_1(7) = 55 & &
\end{array}
$$

(No additional pledges would be received by sending more than seven volunteers to Building 1, more than five to Building 2, and six to Building 3.) How many volunteers should be allocated to each of the buildings? Formulate an appropriate dynamic programming model and find an optimal solution. Show how the solution changes if there are eight volunteers. How does it change with 9, 11, or 12 volunteers?

23 Consider the case of the United Fund described in exercise 22. Suppose the executive director is in short supply of volunteers and restates the allocation problem as follows. The executive wants to use as few volunteers as possible provided that they raise at least R hundred dollars in the three buildings. Formulate this problem in terms of a dynamic programming model, and find an optimal solution for

(a) $R = 80$.
(b) $R = 90$.
(c) $R = 100$.

24 Carrie A. Bowt wishes to give her young niece a birthday present of C cents to be put in the child's piggy bank. Assume that Carrie has available coins of all U.S. denominations (pennies, nickels, dimes, quarters, and half-dollars). She wants to bring her niece the minimum number of coins having a total value of C cents.

(a) Formulate the coin selection problem in terms of a dynamic programming recursion.
*(b) A *greedy* solution to Carrie's problem is defined to be one in which, starting with the largest denomination, she sequentially uses the maximum number of each coin. For example, if $C = 66$, a greedy solution is one half-dollar, one dime, one nickel, and one penny. Demonstrate that a *greedy* solution is optimal for *any* C given the U.S. coin denominations. Suppose that there is a twenty-cent piece; show that then a *greedy* solution is not always optimal.

25 Consider the problem

$$\text{maximize} \quad R_1(y_1) + R_2(y_2) + R_3(y_3)$$

subject to

$$2y_1 + 3y_2 + 4y_3 \leq W$$

$$\text{each } y_j = 0, 1, 2, 3,$$

where each $R_j(0) = 0$ and

$$R_1(1) = 3 \quad\quad R_1(2) = 2 \quad\quad R_1(3) = 8$$

$$R_2(1) = 5 \quad\quad R_2(2) = 11 \quad\quad R_2(3) = 9$$

$$R_3(1) = 9 \quad\quad R_3(2) = 14 \quad\quad R_3(3) = 15.$$

(a) Find an optimal solution for $W = 8$. Also, indicate solutions for $W = 6$ and $W = 7$. Indicate any alternative optimal solutions.
*(b) Draw an acyclic network associated with the recursion that you employ. Label the nodes and arc values appropriately.

26 Consider the Economic Order Quantity Problem for the case of a single item, as described in Sec. 1.6. Suppose that the firm has N items, and is going to replenish each one by means of a lot-size rule. Specifically, for each Item j, let M_j be the number of units the company consumes per week, K_j the fixed setup cost of placing an order, c_j the purchase cost per unit ordered, and h_j the holding cost per unit per week. Similarly, let Q_j be the replenishment lot size for Item j. The average cost per week for *all* items is the summation of N expressions, each of the form (12) in Sec. 1.6. Suppose the company places an upper limit L on the average value of *all* inventory on hand, where each Item j contributes $c_j Q_j/2$ to this average. Show how a dynamic programming formulation can be used to find optimal values for each lot size Q_j.

*27 *Goode-O'Toole Company Example* (Sec. 10.5). An alternative characterization of the dynamic equipment replacement process is to consider that during each period a decision is made to either keep the machine that was available at the start of the period for at least one more period, or to scrap it and purchase a new machine.

(a) Formulate the dynamic programming recursion appropriate to this viewpoint.
(b) Draw the network implied by the recursion in part (a), using the data in Fig. 10.13, and compare the result to that obtained in Figs. 10.14 and 10.15. Assume that a new machine *must* be purchased at the beginning of the horizon.

28 At the start of each day, the plant manager, Topper Hightower, of the Mal O'Dorous Chemical Company decides whether to regenerate the catalyst in one of the large reactors. Assume that Hightower's planning horizon is N days. The cost of regenerating the catalyst is R. If the catalyst at the start of the day is t days old and is not regenerated, then the profit for that day's production is p_t, where $t = 0, 1, 2, \ldots$; the value p_0 represents the profit on a day when the catalyst has been regenerated. At the end of the horizon, a catalyst that is t days old is worth v_t. Formulate a dynamic programming recursion that indicates when Hightower should regenerate the catalyst; assume the catalyst is T days old at the beginning of the horizon.

*29 *Dependable Manufacturing Company Example* (Sec. 10.6). Suppose that the smoothing cost on the right of (1) is dropped and, instead, the production quantity x_t is constrained to lie within the interval

$$ax_{t-1} \leq x_t \leq bx_{t-1}, \quad \text{for } t = 2, 3, \ldots, \quad \text{where } 0 < a < b.$$

Write the appropriate dynamic programming recursion to find an optimal solution.

30 The directors of an old-line Connecticut manufacturer of wire cable, Buono Conn. Tension, Inc., have asked their New Products Manager, Rhea Lee Gross, to investigate s independent ventures, each of which requires a large capital investment. Assume that Venture j calls for a total outlay of K_j dollars from a fixed budget of M dollars that has been allocated for all such ventures in the current year. The expected return on each Venture j is R_j dollars, and the company seeks to maximize its overall return. The corporate directors also have realized that due to the limited availability of supervisory management, no more than N ventures should be approved for the coming year. Each proposal is unique and requires a decision by the firm as to whether

to pursue or drop the venture for the year. Show how Gross can find an optimal selection of ventures.

31 Consider the Buono Conn. Tension Company described in exercise 30. Suppose

$$s = 8 \quad K_j = j \quad \text{for } j = 1,2,\ldots, 8,$$

and

$$R_1 = 16 \quad R_2 = 28 \quad R_3 = 45 \quad R_4 = 48$$
$$R_5 = 65 \quad R_6 = 66 \quad R_7 = 79 \quad R_8 = 80.$$

Find an optimal selection of projects for

(a) The project number limit $N = 4$ and the budget limit $M = 10$. Indicate a solution for $N = 2$ and for $N = 3$. Also indicate a solution for $N = 3$ and $M = 9$.
(b) $N = 3$ and $M = 11$.

32 A responsibility of Tanya Hyde, the Vice President of Marketing for the Get it Altogether Bathing Suit Company, is to decide the color mix of suits to pack in a standard-sized shipping carton. Each carton contains 144 suits. The company can manufacture up to 15 different colors. From accounting data, Hyde has determined that if she includes Color j in a standard-mix carton, she incurs a fixed cost of K_j plus a variable cost of $c_j x_j$, where x_j is the number of suits packed in the carton. (If she decides not to use Color j at all, then she does not incur K_j.) Her marketing experience has taught her that she should include at least six different colors in a standard pack; she also knows that her customers will complain if she ships more than U_j suits of Color j in a carton. Formulate an appropriate dynamic programming model to determine an optimum color mix.

*33 Consider the case of the Giant Electrical Company described in Sec. 10.8. Let $s = 4$, each $L_j = 5$, $N = 10$, and

$$P_j(v_j) = a_j P(v_j) \qquad \text{where } P(0) = P(1) = P(2) = 0$$
$$P(3) = 1 \qquad P(4) = 8 \qquad P(5) = 17$$
$$Q_j(w_j) = b_j Q(w_j) \qquad \text{where } Q(0) = 0 \qquad Q(w) = 3 + w \quad \text{for } w \geq 1$$
$$R_j(x_j) = c_j R(x_j) \qquad \text{where } R(0) = 0 \qquad R(1) = 8 \qquad R(2) = 9$$
$$R(3) = 9.5 \qquad R(4) = 9.75 \qquad R(5) = 10.$$

Find an optimal budget allocation when

(a) All $a_j = b_j = c_j = 1$.
(b) $a_1 = b_1 = c_1 = 1$, $a_2 = b_2 = c_2 = 2$, $a_3 = b_3 = c_3 = 3$.
(c) $a_1 = b_2 = c_3 = 1$, $b_1 = c_2 = a_3 = 2$, $c_1 = a_2 = b_3 = 3$.
(d) Indicate the effect of letting $N = 7, 8, 9$ in each of the above parts.
(e) Indicate the effect of letting $N = 11$ in part (a).
(f) Indicate the effect of letting each $L_j = 4$ in part (a). In part (b). In part (c).

*34 The store manager, Walter Wall, of the Lay It On The Line Carpet Company, must place advance orders for six months of sales requirements. Suppose Walter expects to sell S_t yards of carpet in Month t. He can order any quantity he wishes from three different manufacturers; the cost of purchasing x_{jt} yards of carpet from Manufacturer j in Month t is $C_{jt}(x_{jt})$; the order, x_{jt}, is delivered at the beginning of the month. Because purchase costs do vary over time, Walter is prepared to have some carpet delivered early (that is, in advance of sales requirements). He incurs a holding cost of h per yard of carpet stored at the end of each month; his warehouse capacity limits him to storing no more than Y yards of carpet at the end of each month. Assume at the beginning of Month 1, Walter has y yards of carpets in his warehouse. Show how dynamic programming can be used to determine optimum timing and quantities of purchase from each of the suppliers. (*Hint:* formulate the optimization as a nested problem.)

35 The personnel manager, Hiram Fyram, of the company O Tempura, O Morays, a manufacturer of Japanese style canned foods, each month determines the size of the company's labor force. The Vice President of Manufacturing, R. B. Treary, has given Fyram the work force requirements R_k (in numbers of full-time workers) for each Month k, where $k = 1, 2, \ldots, 5$. Fyram estimates that the wage cost for x_k workers in Month k is $C_k(x_k)$. If the employment level changes, the company also incurs an additional cost of $v_k(x_k - x_{k-1})$, and hence sometimes Fyram maintains a work force in excess of the months' requirements so as to avoid the expense of employment level fluctuations. Assume at the start of Month 1, the initial work force size is x_0 workers, and at the start of Month 6, the company wants at least L workers but no more than U workers.

(a) Formulate the optimization problem by an appropriate dynamic programming recursion.

*(b) In what essential ways does the model in this exercise differ from that in Sec. 7.6?

36 Three brothers operate their father's cattle ranch in Arizona called "Where the Sun's Rays Meet." At the beginning of a planning horizon of N years, the ranchers own S hundred cattle. The expense of caring and feeding for s head of cattle during Year n is $c_n(s)$. If the ranchers decide to send y_n cattle to market at the end of Year n, they receive $R_n(y_n)$ dollars of revenue. The herd not sent to market increases in size by 1.6-fold in the following year. (Thus, if none of the S cattle are sent to market at the end of Year 1, then the herd size is $1.6S$ in Year 2.) Formulate a dynamic programming recursion to determine how many cattle to send to market in each of the N periods.

37 *Capacity Expansion Problem.* The Bill Deplant Company is planning an expansion program over the next N years. At the beginning of Period 1, the firm has a capacity of c_0 units. The company estimates that it should have at least a capacity of R_t units in Period t, for $t = 1, 2, \ldots, N$. If it expands its capacity by x_t units in Period t, the associated cost is $K_t(c, x_t)$, where c represents the capacity at the *start* of the period, and x_t is integer-valued. [If certain levels of x_t are impossible to build, then the corresponding value for $K_t(c, x_t)$ can be defined as arbitrarily large.] Assume that new capacity becomes available early enough in a period that it can be used to meet the requirement R_t. Suppose the company also incurs the cost $H_t(C, R)$ in Period t of operating a plant at the level R, when capacity at the *end* of the period is C units,

where $R \leq C$. Finally, assume that if C units of capacity are available by the *end* of a period, then only $D(C)$ units are available in the beginning of the next period, due to depreciation of the equipment in the plant. Formulate the expansion model in terms of a dynamic programming recursion.

38 The ARKA Mutual Fund is unmatched in its ability to perform well on the stock exchange, because the fund is able to perfectly forecast the price of a given security. Despite this uncanny talent, ARKA must still resort to operations research to derive an optimal strategy for buying and selling. Specifically, assume that p_t is the price of the security in Period t, and that ARKA knows these prices over a horizon of T periods. Let x_t be the number of shares held by ARKA at the end of Period t, where $x_t \geq 0$. Assume that at the start of Period 1, ARKA does not own any shares of the stock. ARKA must pay a transaction cost $C(p_t, x_t - x_{t-1})$ for purchases and sales, where $C(0) = 0$. The fund is also prohibited from speculating in that it cannot make a purchase of shares that exceeds its cash on hand (where M is the cash on hand at the start of Period 1), and it cannot sell short (that is, it cannot sell any shares it does not own at the start of a period).

Formulate the problem in terms of a dynamic programming recursion, assuming that

(a) ARKA wants to maximize the total amount of cash it can accumulate by the end of the horizon.

(b) ARKA places a value $v_t(d_t)$ on withdrawing the amount of cash d_t in Period t for distribution as dividend payments, and wants to maximize the sum of the $v_t(d_t)$ over the entire span of the horizon. Dividends are paid after Period t share transactions.

39 A mid-west farm cooperative, Oat Cuisine, Inc., supplies grain feeds to meat growers, and as a service, advises the growers on an optimum plan for feeding livestock. If an animal that now is t months old and weighs w_t pounds is fed x_t bushels of grain during the month, then next month the animal's weight will be $w_{t+1} \equiv g_t(w_t, x_t)$. The cost to the livestock grower of x_t bushels of grain is $c_t(x_t)$. The grower sells the livestock as soon as it is T months old, and receives a market price of R per pound. Show how Oat Cuisine can calculate a feed plan that maximizes the meat grower's profit per animal.

*40 A production foreman, C. Quince Wright, must schedule N jobs to be performed in the fixed order $1, 2, \ldots, N$. Only one job can be performed at a time, but Wright can schedule either of two work procedures for each job: the first procedure requires a_i hours, whereas the second requires b_i hours, where a_i and b_i are positive integers. If the first procedure is used and Job i is completed by Time t, the company earns a profit of $P_i(t)$; if the second procedure is used, the corresponding profit is $Q_i(t)$. Assume that the entire time horizon available is T hours, which is sufficiently long to ensure that all jobs are performed. Formulate a dynamic programming recursion that indicates which procedure Wright should employ for each job.

*41 Consider foreman Wright in exercise 40. Suppose that each of the N jobs has a deadline and that the penalty for missing the deadline on Job i is p_i. In this case, assume that there is only a single work procedure for performing each job, but that Wright can decide whether or not to meet the job's deadline. The processing time for Job i is a_i. Wright wants to minimize the total penalties. Show how to alter your answer in exercise 40 for this situation. (*Hint:* order the jobs by their deadlines, where Job 1 has the earliest deadline. Let the second procedure in exercise 40 represent deciding that the job misses its deadline, where $b_i = 0$ and the associated cost is p_i.)

42 Van Fuller, the local dispatcher for a moving and storage firm, must arrange to pick up x_1 different shipments that require s_1 units of space each, and x_2 different shipments that require s_2 units of space each. (Thus the total space requirements for the day are $s_1 x_1 + s_2 x_2$.) He has available N different trucks. Truck i has a capacity of C_i units of space, and incurs an operating cost of E_i. (Assume that $C_1 + \cdots + C_N > s_1 x_1 + s_2 x_2$ and that there is a feasible solution.) Fuller wants a minimum cost selection of trucks for picking up all the loads. Formulate the decision problem as a dynamic programming model, and indicate how the recursion optimally selects truck sizes and allocates shipments to the trucks.

43 Consider the case of the Spartan army, described in exercise 32 of Chap. 2. Formulate the optimization problem in terms of a dynamic programming recursion.

44 Consider the case of the Haut Dam Water System described in exercise 33 of Chap. 2. Formulate the optimization problem in terms of a dynamic programming recursion.

45 Consider the case of the Monty Zooma Company, described in exercise 38 of Chap. 2. Formulate the optimization problem in terms of a dynamic programming recursion.

46 Consider the case of the Expando Manufacturing Company, described in exercise 41 of Chap. 2. Formulate the optimization problem in terms of a dynamic programming recursion.

47 *Minimax Route in a Network.* An exchange student from England, Red Bricker, has purchased a not-so-new automobile and plans to spend his summer motoring from New York to San Francisco. To keep the exposition simple, suppose he can choose a route from the same map as did Mark Off, in Fig. 8.1. Red is concerned that if he travels along a route between two cities where the temperature is very hot, the engine in his automobile may explode. He estimates that c_{ij} is the highest temperature he will encounter enroute from State i to State j. He wants a routing that minimizes the maximum temperature along the way.

(a) Formulate a dynamic programming approach, and apply it to the c_{ij} given in Fig. 8.1.
(b) State the recursion in sufficient generality to apply to acyclic networks like those considered in Sec. 7.4 [that is, express the recursion in a form analogous to (1) and (2) in Sec. 7.4].

*48 Consider the problem

$$\text{maximize } \sum_{j=1}^{s} c_j y_j$$

subject to

$$\sum_{j=1}^{s} a_{ij} y_j = b_i \qquad \text{for } i = 1, 2, \ldots, k$$

$$y_j = 0, 1, \ldots \quad \text{for each } j,$$

where each a_{ij} and b_i is a nonnegative integer.

(a) Formulate a dynamic programming recursion that appropriately generalizes (4) in Sec. 10.4.

(b) Explain how the optimization problem can also be characterized by the recursion

$$F(n_1, n_2, \ldots, n_k) = \operatorname*{maximum}_{j} [c_j + F(n_1 - a_{1j}, n_2 - a_{2j}, \ldots, n_k - a_{kj})],$$

where the maximization is over each value of $j = 1, 2, \ldots, s$ that satisfies $a_{ij} \leq n_i$ for every $i = 1, 2, \ldots, k$.

(c) Comment on the computational burden of applying the recursions in parts (a) and (b) to problems of moderate size.

*49 (a) Use the formulation in part (b) of exercise 56 to solve the problem

$$\text{maximize } 3y_1 + 4y_2 + 6y_3 + 8y_4 + 6y_5$$

subject to

$$1y_1 + 2y_2 + 2y_3 + 3y_4 + 1y_5 \leq 3$$

$$2y_1 + 1y_2 + 2y_3 + 1y_4 + 3y_5 \leq 4$$

every y_j a nonnegative integer.

(b) By how much does the objective function decrease when the right-hand-side constant in the first constraint is 2, instead of 3? When the right-hand-side constant in the second constraint is 3, instead of 4? When the right-hand-side constants in both the first and second constraints are decreased by 1?

(c) By how much does the objective function increase when the right-hand-side constant in the first constraint is 4, instead of 3? When the right-hand-side constant in the second constraint is 5, instead of 4? When the right-hand-side constants in both the first and second constraints are increased by 1?

*50 *Equipment Replacement and Overhaul.* Consider the model in Sec. 10.5. Suppose you have the decision opportunities of overhauling as well as replacing the equipment each period after the initial procurement in Period 1 and prior to the salvage of the machine at the beginning of Period N. Assume that the length of time required to overhaul the machine is negligible in comparison with the length of the period; hence, a machine that is overhauled at the beginning of a period is still available for use during the period. Consider a machine is bought at the beginning of Period n, overhauled at the beginning of Periods $t_1 < t_2 < \cdots < t_p$ where $n < t_1$, and is replaced at the beginning of Period k, where $k > t_p$. Assume the associated cost is

$$a_n(n, t_1) + a_n(t_1, t_2) + \cdots + a_n(t_{p-1}, t_p) + b_{nk}(t_p).$$

The quantity $a_n(h, j)$, where $n \leq h < j$, represents the cost of operating a machine during the Periods h through j, plus the expense of overhauling it at the beginning of Period j, given that the machine was initially purchased in Period n and was last overhauled in Period h (or was bought if $h = n$). The quantity $b_{nk}(t_p)$ represents the net total cost resulting from acquiring the machine in Period n, from salvaging it in Period k, and from operating it during Periods t_p through k between final overhaul and sale. The quantity $b_{nk}(n)$ represents the cost of providing the machine during Periods n through k when there are no overhauls.

Show how to use a dynamic programming recursion to calculate values for c_{nk} that then can be appropriately employed in the recursion (2) of Sec. 10.5.

*51 *Caterer Problem.* Consider the case of the Cole Food Company, described in exercise 28 of Chap. 7. Formulate the optimization problem in terms of a dynamic programming recursion.

*52 Consider the problem

$$\text{maximize} \sum_{j=1}^{s} R(x_j)$$

subject to

$$\sum_{j=1}^{s} x_j = N \quad \text{and} \quad \text{each } x_j \text{ nonnegative integer.}$$

Notice that all the functions in the objective function are identical.

(a) Suppose s is a power of 2 (such as 4, 8, 16, 32, ...). Devise a way to compute an optimal solution using dynamic programming that does *not* require you to calculate $g_j(n)$ for *all* $j = 1, 2, \ldots, s$.

*(b) How would you modify your approach in part (a) to accommodate *any* value for s?

53 Suppose a state's legislature has R representatives. The state is sectioned into s districts, where District j has a population p_j and $s < R$. Under strictly proportional representation, District j would receive $R/p_j \equiv r_j$ representatives; this allocation is not feasible, however, because r_j may not be integer-valued. The objective is to allocate y_j representatives to District j, for $j = 1, 2, \ldots, s$, so as to minimize, over all of the districts, the maximum absolute difference between y_j and r_j, that is, minimize [maximum $(|y_1 - r_1|, \ldots, |y_s - r_s|)$].

(a) Formulate the model in terms of a dynamic programming recursion.
(b) Apply your method to the data $R = 4, s = 3$ and $r_1 = .4, r_2 = 2.4$, and $r_3 = 1.2$. Discuss whether the solution seems reasonable, given the context of the problem.

54 *Second-Best Route in Network.* Consider the problem of finding a shortest route from a source node to the terminal node, as discussed in Secs. 7.3 and 7.4. Devise a dynamic programming formulation to find the second shortest route from the source to the terminal. To keep the task unencumbered with details, assume that the network is

acyclic and the shortest route is unique. If you can think of more than one approach, then indicate the alternatives. (*Hint:* a second shortest route must differ from the shortest route in at least one arc. Alternatively, establish the validity and implication of the observation that the second shortest route from Node j to the terminal must consist of traveling along some arc (j, k) and then along either the shortest or second shortest route from Node k to the terminal.) What complications arise in a cyclic network?

55 Consider the problem of finding a shortest route from a source node to the terminal node, as discussed in Secs. 7.3 and 7.4. Devise a dynamic programming formulation to find a shortest route from the source to the terminal that involves exactly K arcs, assuming that at least one such route exists. (Might such a route involve traveling around a loop of arcs?)

*56 Consider the problem

$$\text{maximize} \sum_{j=1}^{n} c_j x_j$$

subject to

$$a_0 \leq x_1 \leq b_0$$

$$a_j x_{j-1} \leq x_j \leq b_j x_{j-1} \quad \text{for } j = 2, 3, \ldots, n$$

where not all the c_j are necessarily positive, and each $a_j \leq b_j$.

(a) Develop a dynamic programming recursion to solve the problem.
(b) Show how to modify your approach in part (a) if the solution must also satisfy the constraint

$$\sum_{j=1}^{n} r_j x_j \leq R.$$

(c) Show how to modify your approach in part (a) if the function to be maximized is

$$\sum_{j=1}^{n} [c_j x_j + d_j (x_j - x_{j-1})^2],$$

where $x_0 = 0$.

(d) Show how to modify your approach in part (a) if both alterations in parts (b) and (c) are postulated.

CONTENTS

CHAPTER 11

Integer Programming and Combinatorial Models

11.1 QUEST FOR A PHILOSOPHER'S STONE

This chapter investigates programming models in which the two assumptions called *divisibility* and *additivity* (Sec. 2.2) are weakened. Recall that these postulates in combination implied linearity in both the objective function and the constraints, and also allowed the variables to take on fractional values, such as 2.5 or $\frac{10}{3}$. Here we drop the **divisibility assumption** and treat problems in which some, or all, of the variables are permitted to take on only integer values (or whole numbers).

Consider the model

$$(1) \qquad\qquad \text{optimize} \sum_{j=1}^{n} c_j x_j,$$

subject to

$$(2) \qquad\qquad \sum_{j=1}^{n} a_{ij} x_j \leq b_i \quad \text{for } i = 1, 2, \ldots, m$$

$$(3) \qquad\qquad x_j \geq 0 \quad \text{for } j = 1, 2, \ldots, n$$

$$(4) \qquad\qquad x_j \text{ integer-valued} \quad \text{for } j = 1, 2, \ldots, p \ (\leq n).$$

This type of optimization model is referred to as an **integer** (or **diophantine,** or **discrete**) **programming problem.** When $p = n$, so that every variable must be integer-valued, the model is called a **pure** integer programming problem; otherwise, it is called a **mixed** integer programming problem.

Depending on the particular application, the sense of optimization in the objective function (1) may be either maximization or minimization. (We will indicate the appropriate sense for each illustration and algorithm below.) Further, an integer programming problem may include ($\geq$) inequalities and equalities. [You can view the linear constraints (2) as a canonical form, however, by applying the procedures given in Chap. 3 whenever the constraints in their original version do not appear as in (2).]

The discreteness stipulations (4) are what distinguish an integer from a linear programming problem. In general, imposing (4) is restrictive, so that the maximum value of an objective function for an integer programming problem usually is smaller than for the corresponding linear programming problem.

Importance of integer programming problems. We indicated earlier that most industrial applications of large-scale programming models are oriented toward planning decisions in the face of complex situations. There are several, frequently occurring circumstances that lead to planning models containing integer-valued variables.

1. *Equipment Utilization.* You may define a variable x_j to be the pieces of equipment that are to operate during the model's planning horizon. If each piece of equipment provides a large capacity and is expensive—for example, an automatic screw machine, an oceangoing oil tanker, or a 150-inch double-knife paper corrugator machine—then a fractional value for x_j, like $\frac{10}{3}$, may be meaningless (nonrealizable) in the context of the actual decision problem. In this event, you would have to restrict x_j to be integer-valued.

2. *Setup Costs.* You may want to consider an activity that incurs a so-called fixed cost (or *setup cost*) C_j whenever the corresponding level $x_j > 0$, where C_j is independent of the actual level of x_j. For example, if x_j represents the hourly utilization of a blast furnace in a steel plant, then C_j represents the cost of starting up the furnace and heating it to the required temperature. You will see in Sec. 11.2 how to encompass setup costs in a programming model by introducing integer-valued variables.

3. *Batch Sizes.* In some production planning situations, you may want to restrict the level of x_j to be either $x_j = 0$ or $x_j \geq L_j$. For example, x_j may be the amount of a special product to be manufactured during Period t, and L_j may represent the minimum possible production batch size for the item. This stipulation is an example of an "either-or" restriction and can be formulated by introducing integer variables, as you will learn in Sec. 11.2.

4. *"Go-No-Go" Decisions.* You may wish to specify other types of "either-or" situations. To do this you can restrict the levels of x_j to either $x_j = 1$ or $x_j = 0$, representing the decisions "go" or "no go," and "yes" or "no." To illustrate, you may let $x_j = 1$ correspond to building a new factory, or to opening up a sales territory, or to acquiring another business, or to selling a currently owned asset. Frequently, these sorts of alternatives are categorized as *capital budgeting* decisions, because they require large expenditures of capital and resources. This is the main

reason why integer programming is so important for managerial decisions. An optimal solution to a capital budgeting problem may yield considerably more profit to a firm than will an approximate or guessed-at solution. For example, a cement manufacturing firm with 25 plants may be able to substantially increase profits by cutting back to 20 plants or less, *provided* this reduction is planned optimally. The decreased overhead with fewer plants can easily outweigh any consequent increase in transportation costs, if the new plant configuration is optimal.

*Combinatorial optimization. Many other decision problems can necessitate integer programming models. One group of problems deal with sequencing, scheduling, and routing decisions. An example is the *Traveling Salesman Problem*. It aims at finding a least-distance route for a salesman who must visit each of n cities, starting and ending his journey at City 1. Another example is the *Machine Scheduling Problem*. A simple illustration is when n items to be manufactured must be sequenced through each of k machines. Suppose an item cannot proceed to Machine j until it finishes being processed on Machine j − 1. Assume the processing time of each item on each machine is determinate. An optimal sequence of items is then defined as a schedule that minimizes total elapsed time to complete all jobs on all machines. Further examples of scheduling, sequencing, and routing problems include *line-balancing, critical path scheduling* (see Sec. 7.5) *with resource constraints, preventive maintenance scheduling with constraints on labor availability*, and *truck dispatching*.

Despite the considerable attention given in operations research journals to such integer programming models for sequencing, scheduling, and routing problems, so far these models have been of only limited practical importance. One reason why is that the integer programming models frequently ignore some of the critical considerations that arise in actual scheduling environments. Another reason is that the computational burden of solving these models has been so great that the cost of obtaining a solution exceeds any improvements resulting from the approach.

Sequencing, scheduling, and routing problems are special cases of what are called *combinatorial* models. A **combinatorial optimization problem** consists of finding, from among a finite set of alternatives, one that optimizes the value of an objective function. For example, the finite set for the Traveling Salesman Problem with n cities consists of $(n − 1)!$ different possible tours starting and ending in City 1. In the simple illustration of the Machine Scheduling Problem, the finite set consists of $(n!)^k$ possible sequences of the n items on the k machines.

With sufficient ingenuity, you can always devise a nontrivial integer programming representation of a combinatorial optimization problem. Frequently, such integer programming problems are very large (that is, there are an enormous number of constraints and variables), and therefore the formulation is of negligible computational interest. But several of the algorithmic techniques for integer programming problems can be applied directly to combinatorial models without first having to transform them into integer programming models.

The search of a lifetime. Would your guess be that integer programming problems are harder or easier to solve than linear programming models of the same size? Most students would answer that integer programming problems are probably easier. To support this opinion, they observe that a dichotomy, say, such as $x_j = 0$ or $x_j = 1$ contains considerably fewer alternatives than does the continuum $0 \le x_j \le 1$. And from this comparison they reason that the search for an optimum ought to be simpler. Regrettably, just the opposite is true—in a programming model, computation is easier with a continuum than with discrete alternatives. The following illustration shows why.

Consider the model

(5)   maximize $21x_1 + 11x_2$

subject to

(6) $7x_1 + 4x_2 \le 13$

(7) x_1 and x_2 nonnegative integers.

After a few moments inspection, you will find that the unique optimal solution is $x_1 = 0$ and $x_2 = 3$. Of course, since this problem is so small, you can think of many ways to discover and verify the solution. But since our goal here is to understand the relative difficulty of solving medium- to large-scale integer programming problems, let us rule out any solution schemes that are ad hoc to a particular problem as well as those systematic algorithms that are practical only for small-scale problems.

There is one approach for finding an integer-valued solution that is frequently suggested by beginners. The procedure is, first, ignore the integer stipulations, and solve for an optimal linear programming solution. If this answer satisfies the integer restrictions, then you have in fact found an optimal solution for the original problem. Otherwise, obtain an integer solution by rounding the linear programming answer to whole numbers.

Now suppose you try this approach on the example in (5), (6), and (7). The optimal fractional solution is $x_1 = \frac{13}{7}$ and $x_2 = 0$. The obvious rounded solution is $x_1 = 2$ and $x_2 = 0$, which is infeasible. A "rounded-down" solution $x_1 = 1$ and $x_2 = 0$ is feasible, but far from optimal. It is hard to think of any general systematic procedure that is practical for rounding a nonintegral solution for a medium- to large-scale model, and that yields the optimal integer solution when applied to this toy problem.

If some of the coefficients a_{ij} in the linear constraints (2) are negative for a particular model, the problem of rounding a linear programming answer to a *feasible* integer-valued solution can be a difficult task in itself. Hence, although rounding may succeed for some applications, you cannot expect such an approach to succeed in general.

An even more serious difficulty inherent in integer programming problems is that there is no easy way to verify whether a given feasible solution is actually optimal. This represents an important distinguishing difference between integer and linear programming problems. To illustrate, suppose in the above problem (5), (6), and (7) that you want to test whether $x_1 = x_2 = 1$ is optimal. To do this, you might examine whether the solution represents a local optimum, in that the objective function does not improve at any neighboring feasible integer (or **lattice**) point $x_1 = 1 + d$ and $x_2 = 1 + e$, where $d, e = -1, 0, 1$. The feasible neighboring points in this case are ($x_1 = x_2 = 0$; $x_1 = 0$ and $x_2 = 1$; $x_1 = 0$ and $x_2 = 2$; $x_1 = 1$ and $x_2 = 0$). The solution $x_1 = x_2 = 1$ is indeed better than *all* of these, and yet is *not* optimal. Thus a point can be locally optimal among neighboring lattice points and still not be globally optimal. (Incidentally, this enumerative test for a local optimum is really not practical for large-scale problems, since there can be a vast number of neighboring points. In fact, if the model is a pure integer programming problem and each x_j is restricted to be either 0 or 1, then searching all the neighboring points of a feasible solution is equivalent to enumerating all the solutions to the original problem.)

By now you may be sufficiently exasperated to wonder whether the best general approach is merely to enumerate all the feasible solutions, and then pick the best. Actually, if there are only a few possible solutions, such an exhaustive procedure may well be easier to implement than any of the algorithms explained later in the chapter. In some real applications, this has been the very approach used (frequently, a number of possible solutions are ruled out immediately as "obviously" nonoptimal). Most often, however, an exhaustive approach proves unworkable, and the reason, simply, is that the number of feasible solutions is not always finite, and even when it is, the magnitude is usually stupendous. For example, consider finding an optimal solution to an integer programming problem consisting of 100 variables, each restricted to equal either 0 or 1. Then the time to enumerate all 2^{100} possibilities on the fastest computer in existence far exceeds a lifetime.

Practical algorithms. It is apparent from the foregoing discussion that in order for an algorithm to be of general use in solving integer programming problems, it must avoid *explicitly* enumerating all possibilities. What we want are techniques that *partially* enumerate a manageable number of possibilities and *implicitly* enumerate all the rest. Recall that the simplex method is just such a technique for solving ordinary linear programming problems—it systematically examines only a small number of all the possible basic solutions. By the same token, dynamic programming recursions exploit the *principle of optimality* to circumvent enumerating all feasible solutions. The success of these partially enumerative optimization methods motivates the quest for finding similar approaches to solve integer programming problems.

Devising such integer programming algorithms is currently a lively area of research among technical specialists. Encouraging evidence of progress in solving real integer programming problems is rapidly accumulating. As such algorithms become perfected, operations research analysts, equipped with high-speed computers, should indeed be credited with having created a philosopher's stone.

11.2 INTEGER PROGRAMMING FORMULATIONS

If you review the various planning models in Chap. 2, you can easily envisage situations in which certain of the variables must be integer-valued. There are a myriad of other examples. These include assigning transportation vehicles to satisfy delivery requirements: scheduling paper-making or steel-rolling machines to meet customer demand commitments; and allocating customer orders to a company's several manufacturing plants that differ in capacities, efficiencies, and costs. It would be misleading, however, to give you the impression that these situations constitute the main focus of interest in managerial decision-oriented applications.

By far, the most significant applications deal with setup costs, dichotomous choices, and complex capital budgeting decisions. Constructing integer programming formulations to handle such considerations is partly an art; hence, we explain below some of the standard devices that are useful.

Capital budgeting —an example with interdependent alternatives. "Go-no-go" alternatives are probably the most important managerial decisions that lead to integer programming problems. These choices frequently arise in the context of an annual or multiperiod strategic planning model and are illustrated in the example below.

The Dewey B. Ginn Company manufactures three products, each of which requires units of two types of capacity, Machinery Y and Machinery Z. The full technology and current input restrictions are given in Fig. 11.1. For example, each 1000 tons of Product 1 requires 7 units of Machinery Y and 2 units of Machinery Z, and yields a corresponding profit of p_1; the production level x_1 represents the annual output in thousands of tons for Product 1. A similar interpretation holds for the other products and their coefficients in Fig. 11.1. At the beginning of the year, only 28 units of Machinery Y capacity and 19 units of Machinery Z capacity are available.

The Dewey B. Ginn Company is considering new equipment additions. If its management decides to expand Machinery Y capacity, it must choose between

Capacity	Products (thousands of tons)			Available Capacity
	1	2	3	
Machinery Y	7	3	1	≤ 28
Machinery Z	2	4	6	≤ 19
Unit profit	p_1	p_2	p_3	Maximize
Production level	x_1	x_2	x_3	

FIGURE 11.1 Dewey B. Ginn Example.

adding either 5 or 15 new units of capacity, with an associated investment expense of 50 or 80, respectively. Similarly, if the management expands Machinery Z capacity, the choices are 12 and 32 additional units of capacity, with investment costs of 30 and 90, respectively. Assume that the annual total investment expense must not exceed 150.

For each of the capacity expansion options, define a zero-one variable that indicates whether or not that option is selected. Let

$$y_1 = \begin{cases} 1 & \text{if 5 units of Machinery Y capacity are added} \\ 0 & \text{otherwise,} \end{cases}$$

$$y_2 = \begin{cases} 1 & \text{if 15 units of Machinery Y capacity are added} \\ 0 & \text{otherwise,} \end{cases}$$

and, similarly, z_1 and z_2 for additions of 12 and 32 units, respectively, of Machinery Z capacity.

Then the optimization problem described so far can be written as

(1) $$\text{maximize} \quad (p_1 x_1 + p_2 x_2 + p_3 x_3)$$

subject to the constraints

$$
\begin{aligned}
7x_1 + 3x_2 + 1x_3 - 5y_1 - 15y_2 &\leq 28 \\
2x_1 + 4x_2 + 6x_3 \quad\quad\quad\quad - 12z_1 - 32z_2 &\leq 19 \\
50y_1 + 80y_2 + 30z_1 + 90z_2 &\leq 150 \\
x_j \geq 0 \quad \text{for } j = 1, 2, 3, 4 & \\
y_1 = 0, 1 \quad\quad y_2 = 0, 1 \quad\quad z_1 = 0, 1 \quad\quad z_2 = 0, 1, &
\end{aligned}
$$

(2)

and thus is a mixed integer programming model. The formulation is not complete, however. Since for each type of machinery a choice has to be made between one of two available alternatives, the integer-valued variables must be further constrained by

(3) $$y_1 + y_2 \leq 1 \quad \text{and} \quad z_1 + z_2 \leq 1.$$

The restrictions in (3) allow for no capacity additions, but force a selection between the mutually exclusive choices if capacity is added. Because three possible investment choices exist for each type of equipment, nine investment programs are conceivable (including the decision not to expand at all). The investment cost restriction in (2) eliminates the possibility of making maximum capacity additions to *both* machinery types during the ensuing year, and so only eight of the programs are feasible in (2).

To see the flexibility of integer programming formulations, consider some other possible side conditions that can arise in a real application. Suppose that the company only wants to add at most a single type of capacity for the coming year. Then, in lieu of the constraints in (3), restrict the "go-no-go" variables by

(4) $$y_1 + y_2 + z_1 + z_2 \leq 1.$$

[In this particular example, (4) makes the investment expenditure constraint in (2) unnecessary. Here five investment programs are feasible.] When you make (4) an equality (=) rather than an inequality (≤), you ensure that exactly one investment must be made. When you make (4) an equality with (2) on the right-hand side and you retain (3), you guarantee expansion of both types of capacity.

Suppose, instead, that the company does not want to add capacity of Machinery Z unless it also decides to add capacity of Machinery Y. Then in addition to (3), append the constraint

$$(5) \qquad y_1 + y_2 - z_1 - z_2 \geq 0;$$

now there are six feasible investment programs. By making (5) an equality (=), the company adds to Machinery Z if it adds to Machinery Y; here four investment programs are feasible. Alternatively, if the company does not want to add Machinery Z capacity unless it decides to add 15 units of Machinery Y capacity, then delete y_1 from (5).

Suppose that if Machinery Y capacity is expanded, the installation process is so disruptive that total annual output cannot exceed 9000 tons. Let U be a sufficiently large number such that total tonnage output does not exceed U if no extra Machinery Y capacity is installed. Then along with (3), add the restriction

$$(6) \qquad x_1 + x_2 + x_3 \leq 9(y_1 + y_2) + U(1 - y_1 - y_2),$$

or, on rearranging terms and letting $U = 20$ to illustrate,

$$(7) \qquad x_1 + x_2 + x_3 + 11y_1 + 11y_2 \leq 20.$$

By now you can see that, with sufficient ingenuity, a host of combinatorial interdependences among the projects can be represented by means of linear stipulations on zero-one variables.

Batch sizes — an example with alternative constraints. Consider a manufacturing model, such as the Dewey B. Ginn Example above, in which x_j is the amount of an item to be produced over the planning horizon. Suppose that the manufacturing economics dictate that either $x_j \geq L_j$, where L_j represents the smallest feasible lot size, or that $x_j = 0$. Assume that you can specify a large enough number U_j, such that the constraint $(x_j \leq U_j)$ is certainly satisfied by an optimal solution. Then the dichotomy $(x_j = 0$ or $x_j \geq L_j)$ can be formulated by adding a zero-one variable $(v_j = 0$ or $1)$ and two linear constraints:

$$(8) \qquad x_j - U_j v_j \leq 0$$

$$(9) \qquad x_j - L_j v_j \geq 0.$$

For $v_j = 0$, the constraints (8) and (9) imply that there is no production $(x_j = 0)$. For $v_j = 1$, the constraint (8) becomes ineffective, and the constraint (9) imposes the required lot-size restriction.

To illustrate with the Dewey B. Ginn Company example, suppose that either $x_1 \geq 2$ or $x_1 = 0$. Inspection of the feasible possibilities shows that under no circumstances can x_1 exceed 7 ($= U_1$). Thus the batch-size constraints can be written as

(10) $x_1 - 7v_1 \leq 0$ and $x_1 - 2v_1 \geq 0$,

where $v_1 = 0, 1$.

Another possibility is that a variable x_j is permitted to take only certain values, say, $X_{j1}, X_{j2}, \ldots, X_{jq}$. You can impose this stipulation by removing x_j and appropriately introducing q zero-one variables w_k. Specifically, replace x_j everywhere in the model by the expression

(11) $X_{j1}w_1 + X_{j2}w_2 + \cdots + X_{jq}w_q$

and then restrict the w_k by the constraints

(12) $w_1 + w_2 + \cdots + w_q = 1$

(13)   all w_k nonnegative integer-valued.

In the case of the Dewey B. Ginn Company, suppose that x_2 must equal either 0, 1, 4, or 7. Then expression (11) becomes

(14) $0w_1 + 1w_2 + 4w_3 + 7w_4$,

and the first constraint in (2) is rewritten as

(15) $7(0w_1 + 1w_2 + 4w_3 + 7w_4) + 3x_2 + 1x_3 - 5y_1 - 15y_2 \leq 28$;

the second constraint and the objective function must be rewritten similarly. The restrictions (12) with $q = 4$ and (13) are added to the rewritten version of (1) and (2).

Plant location—an example with setup costs. In Chap. 6 you studied the classical transportation problem:

(16)   minimize $\sum_{i=1}^{m} \sum_{j=1}^{n} c_{ij}x_{ij}$

subject to

(17) $\sum_{j=1}^{n} x_{ij} \leq S_i$ for $i = 1, 2, \ldots, m$ (supply)

(18 $\sum_{i=1}^{m} x_{ij} \geq D_j$ for $j = 1, 2, \ldots, n$ (demand)

(19) $x_{ij} \geq 0$ for all i and j.

Recall that one interpretation of the problem is that there are m supply points with items available to be shipped to the n demand points. Supply Point i can ship at most S_i items, and Demand Point j requires at least D_j items. The cost of shipping a unit from Supply Point i to Demand Point j is c_{ij}. The objective is to select a routing plan that minimizes total transportation costs.

In some transportation planning applications, part of the problem is to establish which of m possible supply points should actually be in operation. The supply points usually represent plants, and incur overhead expenses that must be combined with the transportation costs in determining company profit. The typical cost tradeoff is between reduced overhead cost from fewer plants and increased transportation costs.

For example, consider the Cummings and Goings Manufacturing Company which intends to expand its business by serving customers in states west of the Rocky Mountains. To accommodate this extension of its marketing area, C and G plans to open several new assembly plants. Suppose that Plant Site i represents a potential location. Assume the plant will have capacity S_i and incur a fixed overhead cost $F_i \geq 0$, independent of the amount it produces. There are m possible sites for these new plants, but the overhead expenses are so significant that it is too costly to open plants on all the sites. Let $c_{ij} \geq 0$ be manufacturing and transportation expenses for shipping an item from Plant Site i to Marketing Area j. Assume, in addition, that there is a setup cost $F_{ij} \geq 0$ associated with maintaining a shipping route from Plant Site i to Marketing Area j; this amount F_{ij} is independent of the magnitude of $x_{ij} > 0$, but is not incurred when $x_{ij} = 0$.

Accordingly, to formulate the problem as a mathematical model introduce the integer-valued decision variables

$$y_i = \begin{cases} 1 & \text{if Plant Site i is selected} \\ 0 & \text{otherwise} \end{cases} \quad \text{for } i = 1, 2, \ldots, m,$$

and

$$z_{ij} = \begin{cases} 1 & \text{if route from Plant Site i to Area j is used} \\ 0 & \text{otherwise} \end{cases} \quad \text{for all } i \text{ and } j.$$

Then, instead of the usual objective function (16), the objective function becomes

$$(20) \qquad \text{minimize} \left[\sum_{i=1}^{m} F_i y_i + \sum_{i=1}^{m} \sum_{j=1}^{n} c_{ij} x_{ij} + \sum_{i=1}^{m} \sum_{j=1}^{n} F_{ij} z_{ij} \right].$$

Instead of imposing the supply constraints (17), you state the capacity restrictions as

$$(21) \qquad \sum_{j=1}^{n} x_{ij} - S_i y_i \leq 0 \quad \text{for } i = 1, 2, \ldots, m \quad \text{(supply)}.$$

If Plant Site i is not opened, so that $y_i = 0$, then (21) ensures that $x_{ij} > 0$ is not allowed. The demand constraints (18) and nonnegativity constraints (19) remain unchanged. For certain integer programming algorithms, it is sufficient to state in addition that the y_i and z_{ij} must be either 0 or 1. But for other algorithms, these same restrictions must be expressed in the expanded form.

$$(22) \qquad y_i \leq 1 \quad \text{and} \quad z_{ij} \leq 1 \quad \text{for all } i \text{ and } j$$

$$(23) \qquad y_i \text{ and } z_{ij} \text{ nonnegative integers} \quad \text{for all } i \text{ and } j.$$

The model formulation is not yet complete, because we have not related the value of z_{ij} to the value of x_{ij}. We want to ensure that $x_{ij} > 0$ only if $z_{ij} = 1$;

this can be achieved by including the linear restrictions

$$(24) \qquad\qquad x_{ij} - U_{ij}z_{ij} \leq 0 \quad \text{for all } i \text{ and } j,$$

where U_{ij} is a sufficiently large coefficient—for example, let $U_{ij} =$ minimum (S_i, D_j). If $z_{ij} = 0$, then the nonnegativity condition (19) and (24) imply that x_{ij} must be equal to zero; and if $z_{ij} = 1$, then (24) is superfluous, given the new supply constraint (21) and the demand restriction (18). (Note that it is never essential for optimality to have $z_{ij} = 1$ and $x_{ij} = 0$.)

It is easy to construct examples in which an ordinary linear programming problem given by (20), (21), (22), and (24) has an optimal solution with fractional values for the variables. Hence the restriction (23), requiring that the y_i and z_{ij} be integer-valued, is essential. As in the ordinary transportation problem, it is only necessary to stipulate that each x_{ij} must be nonnegative, since the integrality property of the usual transportation model continues to hold provided that y_i and z_{ij} are integer-valued.

*Warehouse location—an example with scale economies.

Another common site selection problem involves the location of distribution centers that serve as transshipment points. These centers are used to store stocks that are supplied from a company's factories and are eventually shipped to customers. In addition to the setup or fixed costs for operating the centers, the model must include the transportation costs that depend on the particular routings of items from a plant through a distribution center and then to a customer. Typically, such freight costs are *not* simply the sum of the transportation cost from a plant to a distribution center and the transportation cost from a distribution center to a customer; the freight tariffs are set so that a company gets the benefit of a long-distance rate between a plant and a customer, even if the company uses a distribution center as an intermediate storage (in-transit) point en route. The example below illustrates the model.

The Polly Esther Cosmetics Company has m manufacturing plants, where S_i is the annual productive capacity of Plant i. To simplify the exposition, we assume that the company makes a single product; the model below easily expands to include multiple products. Polly Esther must supply D_j units of product to its jth customer (or demand area), and has n such end-demand points. The company is investigating p possible locations for distribution centers, and it requires that each demand point be served from only one distribution center.

The decision variables are

$$x_{ikj} = \text{amount shipped from Plant i to Demand Area j}$$
$$\text{through Distribution Center k}$$

$$y_k = \begin{cases} 1 & \text{if Distribution Center k is selected} \\ 0 & \text{otherwise} \end{cases}$$

$$z_{kj} = \begin{cases} 1 & \text{if Demand Area j is served by Distribution Center k} \\ 0 & \text{otherwise.} \end{cases}$$

The associated costs are

c_{ikj} = shipping cost per unit sent from Plant i to
Demand Area j through Distribution Center k

F_k = fixed operating cost for Distribution Center k, if selected

f_k = variable cost per unit shipped through Distribution Center k.

The optimization model can be expressed, in part, as

$$(25) \quad \text{minimize} \quad \left[\sum_{k=1}^{p} F_k y_k + \sum_{i=1}^{m} \sum_{k=1}^{p} \sum_{j=1}^{n} c_{ikj} x_{ikj} + \sum_{k=1}^{p} f_k \left(\sum_{j=1}^{n} D_j z_{kj} \right) \right]$$

subject to

$$(26) \quad \sum_{k=1}^{p} \sum_{j=1}^{n} x_{ikj} \leq S_i \quad \text{for } i = 1, 2, \ldots, m$$

$$(27) \quad \sum_{i=1}^{m} x_{ikj} - D_j z_{kj} = 0 \quad \text{for } k = 1, 2, \ldots, p \quad \text{and} \quad j = 1, 2, \ldots, n$$

$$(28) \quad \sum_{k=1}^{p} z_{kj} = 1 \quad \text{for } j = 1, 2, \ldots, n$$

$$(29) \quad \text{each } x_{ikj} \geq 0 \quad \text{each } y_k = 0, 1 \quad \text{each } z_{kj} = 0, 1.$$

The constraints (26) guarantee that no more than the available supply at Plant i is shipped out. Observe that the zero-one conditions on the z_{kj} and the constraints (28) ensure that each Demand Area j is served by a unique distribution center. Hence in (27), for each j there is an associated k such that $z_{kj} = 1$, and for that (k, j) combination, (27) guarantees that the demand requirement D_j is met, that is, all the plants ship sufficient units through Distribution Center k en route to Demand Area j. The objective function is the sum of the fixed costs of operating distribution centers, the transportation costs, and the variable throughput costs.

In any application, additional constraints linking the y_k and z_{kj} are required. For instance, suppose that in a particular city it is possible to choose from among several distribution center sites, each having a different range of feasible throughput capacity and associated fixed and variable costs. Then for each possible site choice, the model also would contain a distribution center option with a lower and upper bound on the throughput if the site is selected. To illustrate, suppose that $k = 1$ and $k = 2$ are a pair of options in a single city, with L_k and U_k being the associated lower and upper throughput bounds. The additional constraints in this case are

$$(30) \quad \sum_{j=1}^{n} D_j z_{kj} - L_k y_k \geq 0 \quad \text{and} \quad \sum_{j=1}^{n} D_j z_{kj} - U_k y_k \leq 0 \quad \text{for } k = 1, 2.$$

(The model can be expressly prohibited from selecting both sites by adding the restriction $y_1 + y_2 \leq 1$.)

If the company desires to open *exactly* r distribution centers, then add the constraint

$$(31) \qquad\qquad \sum_{k=1}^{p} y_k = r.$$

If only one distribution center is to be opened in a particular geographical region, then the sum of y_k for the sites that are in that region can be constrained equal to 1.

If the company incurs a capital investment b_k to build the warehouse at the kth site, and if it must select a plan that prohibits total investment exceeding B, then impose the requirement

$$(32) \qquad \sum_{k=1}^{p} b_k y_k \leq B.$$

Matching and covering. A franchise of Chinese restaurants called Suey Generous intends to open several new establishments in a large metropolitan area. The company's manager of marketing, Kim Ono, has asked her operations research staff to suggest a plan for selecting among six possible sites.

Area	Site					
	1	2	3	4	5	6
1	1	1		1		
2		1		1		
3	1		1			
4	1			1		
5			1		1	
6			1		1	1
7		1		1		1
8		1			1	1
Profit	p_1	p_2	p_3	p_4	p_5	p_6
Rental	r_1	r_2	r_3	r_4	r_5	r_6

FIGURE 11.2. Suey Generous Example.

The staff considers the city as being comprised of eight areas. For each site, the staff estimates on the basis of distance of the eight areas to the site, the associated traffic time, parking availability, and competitive factors, whether or not the site will draw customers from each of the areas and the annual profit that the site may generate. A tabular representation of the forecasts is shown in Fig. 11.2. To illustrate, Areas 1, 3, and 4 will be served by a restaurant at Site 1; Area 7 can be served by a restaurant at either Site 2, 4, or 6. The annual profit p_j at Site j is calculated on the assumption that an area is served only by a single restaurant in the chain. This assumption implies that if Site 3 is selected, for example, then Site 1 should not be chosen in order to avoid covering Area 3 with more than one restaurant; similarly, Site 5 also should not be chosen in order to avoid intrachain competition in Areas 5 and 6.

For $j = 1, 2, \ldots, 6$, define a zero-one variable x_j to designate whether or not Site j is selected. The optimization problem is

$$(33) \qquad \text{maximize} \sum_{j=1}^{6} p_j x_j$$

subject to

(34)
$$\sum_{j=1}^{6} a_{ij}x_j \leq 1 \quad \text{for } i = 1, 2, \ldots, 8$$

(35)
$$\text{each } x_j = 0, 1,$$

where the coefficient a_{ij} taken from Fig. 11.2 equals 1 if Area i is covered by Site j, and it equals 0 otherwise. (For example, the constraint for Area 8 is $x_2 + x_5 + x_6 \leq 1$.) This model is a pure integer programming problem, and, given its special structure with coefficients of only 0 and 1, inequalities ($\leq$), and right-hand sides of 1, it is called a **weighted matching problem** (the weights being the p_j).

On examining this formulation, Ms. Ono felt that the approach was too conservative. In particular, the resulting plan may not select sites so that *every* area is covered. She reasoned that if an area is covered by more than one restaurant site, then the business will be split between the locations, but that each restaurant still will be profitable. She asked the staff to reformulate the model so that each area is covered by at least one restaurant site. For an optimization criterion, she suggested finding a plan that minimizes the total rental costs for all the restaurants combined. These instructions lead to the alternative formulation

(36)
$$\text{minimize } \sum_{j=1}^{6} r_j x_j$$

subject to

(37)
$$\sum_{j=1}^{6} a_{ij}x_j \geq 1 \quad \text{for } i = 1, 2, \ldots, 8$$

(38)
$$\text{each } x_j = 0, 1,$$

where r_j is the annual rental of Site j. This model also is a pure integer programming problem, and because of its special structure it is called a **weighted covering problem** (the weights being the r_j).

*Other formulation devices. Suppose that the decision variables x_j must satisfy at least k out of the q constraints

(39)
$$\sum_{j=1}^{n} a_{ij}x_j \leq b_i \quad \text{for } i = 1, 2, \ldots, q.$$

Then introduce the q zero-one variables ($y_i = 0$ or 1), for $i = 1, 2, \ldots, q$, and impose the $1 + q$ linear constraints

(40)
$$\sum_{i=1}^{q} y_i \geq k$$

(41)
$$\sum_{j=1}^{n} a_{ij}x_j \leq b_i y_i + U_i(1 - y_i) \quad \text{or}$$
$$\sum_{j=1}^{n} a_{ij}x_j - (b_i - U_i)y_i \leq U_i \quad \text{for } i = 1, 2, \ldots, q,$$

where U_i is chosen so large that $(\sum_{j=1}^{n} a_{ij}x_j \leq U_i)$ is certainly satisfied by an optimal solution. [Actually, (40) can just as well be stated as an equality.]

Suppose, instead, that the decision variables x_j must satisfy either the set of constraints (39) or the set of constraints

$$(42) \qquad \sum_{j=1}^{n} A_{ij}x_j \leq B_i \quad \text{for } i = 1, 2, \ldots, r.$$

The approach used for the batch-size example generalizes to imposing the $(q + r)$ constraints

$$
\begin{aligned}
\sum_{j=1}^{n} a_{ij}x_j &\leq b_i + U_i y & \text{for } i = 1, 2, \ldots, q \\
\sum_{j=1}^{n} A_{ij}x_j &\leq B_i + V_i(1 - y) & \text{for } i = 1, 2, \ldots, r,
\end{aligned}
$$

(43)

where $y = 0, 1$, and each of the constants U_i and V_i is sufficiently large so that the corresponding constraint is not binding when this value is added to the right-hand side. In problems in which the alternative sets of constraints contain equalities, first replace each equality by a pair of equivalent inequalities in the manner of Chap. 2; then apply (43).

If a model contains an integer-valued variable x_j, where $x_j = 0, 1, \ldots, U$, then the problem can be reformulated to contain zero-one variables instead. Replace x_j everywhere in the model by the expression

$$(44) \qquad w_1 + w_2 + \cdots + w_U,$$

where each $w_k = 0, 1$. Instead of (44), you can employ a **binary representation** for x_j

$$(45) \qquad 1w_1 + 2w_2 + 4w_3 + \cdots + 2^{t-2}w_{t-1} + aw_t,$$

where t is the smallest integer such that $2^t - 1 \geq U$, and

$$(46) \qquad a = U - (1 + 2 + 4 + \cdots + 2^{t-2}).$$

Suppose that the model contains a polynomial expression in several of the zero-one variables, such as $x_1^3 x_2^4 x_5$. Then it is possible to substitute a single variable for the expression provided that the variable be appropriately restricted. Using the illustration $x_1^3 x_2^4 x_5$, first observe that this term can be rewritten as $x_1 x_2 x_5$ because each of the component variables can only have the value 0 or 1. Let y be substituted for $x_1 x_2 x_5$ wherever this term appears in the model. Then add the constraints

$$(47) \qquad x_1 + x_2 + x_5 - y \leq 3 - 1 = 2$$

$$(48) \qquad x_1 + x_2 + x_5 - 3y \geq 0$$

and require that $y = 0$ or 1. Or, instead of (48), add the constraints

$$(49) \qquad y \leq x_1 \qquad y \leq x_2 \qquad y \leq x_5,$$

and here treat y as a continuous variable. A general approach for handling a polynomial term comprised of q zero-one variables is to define a single variable for the term, add the constraint that the sum of the q variables minus the new variable is less than or equal to $q - 1$, and add either a single second constraint that the sum of the q variables minus q times the new variable is nonnegative, where the new variable is zero-one, or a set of constraints of the form that the new variable cannot exceed each of the q variables, where the new variable is continuous.

11.3 BRANCH-AND-BOUND ALGORITHM

The most widely adopted approach for solving integer programming problems uses a method of tree search, sometimes referred to as a *backtrack algorithm*. Several versions of the approach are available for large-scale computers and have been applied successfully on real decision models. The exposition below explains the fundamental ideas underlying the approach; existing computer programs differ one from another in how the details of the steps are executed.

The method can be applied to mixed, as well as pure, integer programming problems. For definiteness, suppose the model is stated as

$$(1) \qquad\qquad \text{maximize} \sum_{j=1}^{n} c_j x_j$$

subject to

$$(2) \qquad\qquad \sum_{j=1}^{n} a_{ij} x_j \le b_i \quad \text{for } i = 1, 2, \ldots, m$$

$$(3) \qquad\qquad x_j \text{ integer-valued} \quad \text{for } j = 1, 2, \ldots, p \; (\le n)$$

$$(4) \qquad\qquad x_j \ge 0 \quad \text{for } j = p + 1, \ldots, n.$$

In addition, assume that, for each integer-valued variable, you can provide lower and upper bounds that surely include the optimal values

$$(5) \qquad\qquad L_j \le x_j \le U_j \quad \text{for } j = 1, 2, \ldots, p.$$

Usually $L_j = 0$, but it need not. (As you know from Sec. 3.3, no essential generality is lost by assuming that all $L_j = 0$. The algorithm is more simply described, however, by employing the general symbol L_j.)

The idea of the Branch-and-Bound Algorithm stems from the following elementary observation. Consider any variable x_j, and let I be some integer value, where $L_j \le I \le U_j - 1$. Then an optimal solution to (1) through (5) will also satisfy either the linear constraint

$$(6) \qquad\qquad x_j \ge I + 1$$

or the linear constraint

$$(7) \qquad\qquad x_j \le I.$$

To illustrate how this dichotomy can be used, suppose you ignore the integer restriction (3) and find that an optimal linear programming solution to (1), (2), (4), and (5) indicates that $x_1 = 1\frac{2}{3}$. Then formulate and solve two more linear programs. Each of these still contains (1), (2), and (4). But (5) for $j = 1$ is modified in one problem to be $2 \leq x_1 \leq U_1$, and in the other to be $L_1 \leq x_1 \leq 1$. Suppose further that each of these two problems has an optimal solution that satisfies the integer restrictions (3). Then the solution that has the larger value for the objective function is indeed optimal for the original integer programming problem. Usually, one (or both) of these problems has no optimal solution that satisfies (3); hence, additional computations may be required. The algorithm below specifies how to apply the dichotomy (6) and (7) in a systematic manner to eventually obtain an optimal solution.

The method. At any iteration t, you have available a lower bound, say, x_0^1, for the optimal value of the objective function. To keep the exposition simple, assume that at the first iteration, x_0^1 either is *strictly* less than the optimal value, or equals the value of the objective function for a feasible solution that you have recorded. If worse comes to worst, you can let $x_0^1 = -\infty$ if you have no information at all about the problem. In addition to a lower bound, you have a master list of linear programming problems that must be solved; the only differences among these comprise revisions in the bounds (5). At iteration 1, the master list contains a single problem consisting of (1), (2), (4), and (5).

The procedure at iteration t is:

Step 1. Terminate the computations if the master list is empty. Otherwise, remove a linear programming problem from the master list.

Step 2. Solve the chosen problem. If it has no feasible solution, or if the resultant optimal value of the objective function x_0 is less than or equal to x_0^t, then let $x_0^{t+1} = x_0^t$, and return to *Step 1*. Otherwise, proceed to *Step 3*.

Step 3. If the obtained optimal solution to the linear programming problem satisfies the integer constraints, then record it, let x_0^{t+1} be the associated optimal value of the objective function x_0, and return to *Step 1*. Otherwise, proceed to *Step 4*.

Step 4. Select any variable x_j, for $j = 1, 2, \ldots, p$, that does not have an integer value in the obtained optimal solution to the chosen linear programming problem. Let b_j denote this value, and $[b_j]$ signify the largest integer less than or equal to b_j. Add two linear programming problems to the master list. These two problems are identical with the problem chosen in S*tep 1*, except that in one, the lower bound on x_j is replaced by $[b_j] + 1$, and in the other, the upper bound on x_j is replaced by $[b_j]$. Let $x_0^{t+1} = x_0^t$, and return to *Step 1*.

At termination, if you have recorded a feasible solution yielding x_0', it is optimal; otherwise, no feasible solution exists. As the example below demonstrates, you may obtain an integer-valued solution prior to the last iteration. You do not know that it *is* optimal, however, until the final iteration.

The process at *Step 1* is called **branching** because it involves the selection of a linear programming problem for further consideration. The process at *Step 2* is known as **relaxation;** here you solve a linear programming problem ignoring (relaxing) the integer-value constraints Since such a problem is less constrained than the same problem with the integer stipulations in force, the linear programming objective function value is at least as large as that for the corresponding integer problem. Thus, if the linear programming solution does not yield an objective function value larger than the current lower bound, you need not consider the problem further. In this event, the problem is said to have been **fathomed.** (The problem also is fathomed at *Step 3* in the event that the solution satisfies the integer constraints.)

The process at *Step 4* is known as **separation.** Here a "parent" linear programming problem with an optimal objective function larger than the current lower bound gives rise to two **descendants.** If you augment the procedure in *Step 4* to record on the master list with each descendant the optimal value of the objective function for the parent linear programming problem, then the largest of these values for all problems currently on the master list is an *upper* bound on the optimal objective function value for the integer problem. Thus, if you terminate the algorithm before the master list is empty, you can assess the improvement potential from the linear programming problems that remain on the list as compared to the best feasible solution that you have obtained so far.

Illustration. An example will clarify the details of the procedure. Consider

(8) $$\text{maximize}\quad 3x_1 + 3x_2 + 13x_3$$

subject to

(9)
$$-3x_1 + 6x_2 + 7x_3 \leq 8$$
$$6x_1 - 3x_2 + 7x_3 \leq 8,$$

where each x_j must be a nonnegative integer. Suppose we specify the bounds on each variable as

(10) $$0 \leq x_j \leq 5 \quad \text{for } j = 1, 2, 3.$$

As usual, let x_0 denote the value of the objective function. Find the optimal solution by inspection.

At iteration 1, let the lower bound be $x_0^1 = 0$, since all $x_j = 0$ is feasible. The master list contains only the linear programming problem (8), (9), and (10), which is designated as Problem 1. Remove it in *Step 1*, and in *Step 2* find the optimal solution

$$(11) \qquad x_0 = 16 \qquad x_1 = x_2 = 2\tfrac{2}{3} \qquad x_3 = 0 \qquad \text{(Problem 1)}.$$

Since the solution is not integer-valued, proceed from *Step 3* to *Step 4*, and select x_1. Then since $[b_1] = [2\tfrac{2}{3}] = 2$, place on the master list

$$\text{Problem 2:} \quad \text{constraints (9)} \quad \text{and}$$

$$(12) \qquad 3 \le x_1 \le 5 \qquad 0 \le x_2 \le 5 \qquad 0 \le x_3 \le 5$$

$$\text{Problem 3:} \quad \text{constraints (9)} \quad \text{and}$$

$$0 \le x_1 \le 2 \qquad 0 \le x_2 \le 5 \qquad 0 \le x_3 \le 5.$$

Returning to *Step 1* with $x_0^2 = x_0^1 = 0$, remove Problem 2. *Step 2* establishes that Problem 2 has no feasible solution. Hence, put $x_0^3 = x_0^2 = 0$, and return to *Step 1*.

Now remove Problem 3, and obtain in *Step 2* the optimal solution

$$(13) \qquad x_0 = 15\tfrac{5}{7} \qquad x_1 = x_2 = 2 \qquad x_3 = \tfrac{2}{7} \qquad \text{(Problem 3)},$$

which is not integer-valued. Therefore, go from *Step 3* to *Step 4*, where x_3 is selected. Since $[b_3] = [\tfrac{2}{7}] = 0$, place on the master list:

$$\text{Problem 4:} \quad \text{constraints (9)} \quad \text{and}$$

$$(14) \qquad 0 \le x_1 \le 2 \qquad 0 \le x_2 \le 5 \qquad 1 \le x_3 \le 5$$

$$\text{Problem 5:} \quad \text{constraints (9)} \quad \text{and}$$

$$0 \le x_1 \le 2 \qquad 0 \le x_2 \le 5 \qquad 0 \le x_3 \le 0.$$

Observe that Problems 4 and 5 differ from Problem 3 only in the bounds on x_3.

Returning to *Step 1* with $x_0^4 = 0$, remove Problem 4. The optimal solution is

$$(15) \qquad x_0 = 15 \qquad x_1 = x_2 = \tfrac{1}{3} \qquad x_3 = 1 \qquad \text{(Problem 4)}.$$

This leads to *Step 4*; suppose you select x_2, yielding, as a consequence,

$$\text{Problem 6:} \quad \text{constraints (9)} \quad \text{and}$$

$$(16) \qquad 0 \le x_1 \le 2 \qquad 1 \le x_2 \le 5 \qquad 1 \le x_3 \le 5$$

$$\text{Problem 7:} \quad \text{constraints (9)} \quad \text{and}$$

$$0 \le x_1 \le 2 \qquad 0 \le x_2 \le 0 \qquad 1 \le x_3 \le 5.$$

Note that Problems 6 and 7 differ from Problem 4 only in the bounds on x_2.

Returning to *Step 1* with $x_0^5 = 0$, remove Problem 6 so that Problems 5 and 7 remain on the master list. You will discover in *Step 2* that Problem 6 has no feasible solution, so return to *Step 1* with $x_0^6 = 0$. Now remove Problem 7, giving the optimal solution

$$(17) \qquad x_0 = 14\tfrac{6}{7} \qquad x_1 = x_2 = 0 \qquad x_3 = 1\tfrac{1}{7} \qquad \text{(Problem 7)}.$$

Because x_3 is fractional and $[1\frac{1}{7}] = 1$, this creates, in *Step 4*,

$$\text{Problem 8:} \quad \text{constraints (9)} \quad \text{and}$$

(18)
$$0 \le x_1 \le 2 \quad 0 \le x_2 \le 0 \quad 2 \le x_3 \le 5$$

$$\text{Problem 9:} \quad \text{constraints (9)} \quad \text{and}$$

$$0 \le x_1 \le 2 \quad 0 \le x_2 \le 0 \quad 1 \le x_3 \le 1.$$

Removing Problem 8 at iteration 7 gives an indication of no feasible solution in *Step 2*. Remove Problem 9 at iteration 8 and observe that only the value of x_1 can still vary. So for *Step 2* find the optimal *integer* solution, which is

(19)
$$x_0 = 13 \quad x_1 = x_2 = 0 \quad x_3 = 1 \qquad \text{(Problem 9).}$$

Therefore at *Step 3*, you record (19) and let $x_0^9 = 13$.

Returning to *Step 1*, you find that only Problem 5 remains on the master list. The optimal linear programming solution is

(20)
$$x_0 = 13 \quad x_1 = 2 \quad x_2 = 2\frac{1}{3} \quad x_3 = 0 \qquad \text{(Problem 5).}$$

Since x_0 in (20) equals x_0^9, you return to *Step 1* and terminate the computations, as the master list is now empty. The optimal solution to the integer programming problem is (19), which was recorded at iteration 8.

Recapitulation. The history of the iterations can be displayed by means of a tree-like diagram, shown in Fig. 11.3. Notice each node in the tree diagram represents a problem on the master list; each branch leads to one of the problems added to the master list in *Step 4*. The pertinence of this graphical analogy explains why the word "branch" is used in the algorithm's name, "Branch-and-Bound." The word "bound" is suggested by the test in *Step 2*. (The technique might alternatively be designated **Branch-and-Prune.**) Note that for Problem 5 the branch is terminated, even though the optimal solution is not integer-valued. The reason is that when you reach Problem 5 at $t = 9$, you already have a feasible solution with an objective function value 13. Therefore, branching further by imposing stronger restrictions can never improve on the previously obtained feasible solution.

Now you can see why the algorithm is called a **tree search** or **backtrack** method. When you terminate certain branches—as at Problems 2, 6, 8, and 9 in the example—you must go back up the branch in search of any unsolved problem that remains on the tree.

Algorithm design. As you review the method, observe that usually you have choice options to make in two of the steps. At *Step 1*, if more than one linear program is on the master list, you must choose which problem to remove. At *Step 4*, if more than one of the p discrete variables is fractional, then you must select for which of these you will alter the lower and upper bounds, and thereby create the two additional linear programming problems to place on the master list.

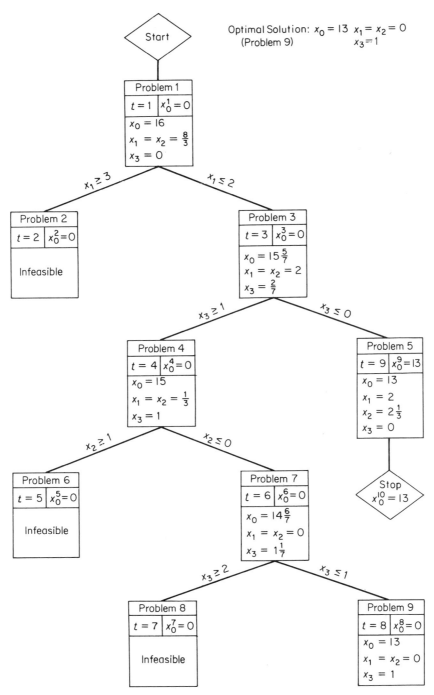

FIGURE 11.3. Branch-and-Bound Example.

In any computerized version of the branch-and-bound method, the choices are made according to rules that must be prescribed in the computer code. The amount of computer resources (computational time and storage space) required to solve realistically sized problems depend critically on such rules. For example, a simple selection rule at *Step 1* is to pick the linear programming problem that was most recently added to the master list. The advantages of this simple LIFO (last-in, first-out) rule must be weighed against the possible increase in the speed of convergence that would occur from selecting a linear programming problem on the master list that has a larger optimal objective function value. Also at *Step 4*, you can improve the rate of convergence by performing additional calculations that indicate on which variable to branch.

Operations research specialists are still experimenting with different ways of implementing branch-and-bound algorithms so that someday you will be able to solve large-scale problems at a reasonable expense.

Computational experience. Several versions of branch-and-bound computer programs are available for commercial use. Although these programs continue to undergo further development and improvement, practical applications of moderate size problems are feasible. Without great danger you can attempt to solve a mixed integer programming model with fewer than 100 zero-one variables. But you must be prepared to terminate the calculations when the algorithm has obtained a feasible solution that is within a reasonable tolerance of optimum. Real problems containing actual data often solve more rapidly than you might predict on theoretical grounds.

11.4 KNAPSACK PROBLEM

The team of astronauts Sonny Day and Renny Knight are preparing for an extended flight around the Earth in an orbital space laboratory. They may take along for their personal reading b pounds of books, and they will select from among n books. The weight of Book j is a_j, and the team jointly assesses the reading pleasure of Book j to be c_j, where the number c_j specifies their relative index of satisfaction. Day and Knight make their choice by solving

(1) $$\text{maximize} \sum_{j=1}^{n} c_j x_j$$

subject to

(2) $$\sum_{j=1}^{n} a_j x_j \leq b$$

(3) $$x_j = 0, 1 \quad \text{for } j = 1, 2, \ldots, n.$$

In this so-called **0–1 knapsack problem** (1), (2), and (3), each decision variable x_j is zero-one, corresponding to rejecting or taking Book j. The objective function (1) is simply the sum of the individual satisfaction values for the books chosen and constraint (2) is the total weight stipulation.

Algorithmic solution. The 0–1 knapsack model is a pure integer programming problem and immediately meets the assumptions for the branch-and-bound algorithm in the preceding section. But since the initial lower and upper bounds for each variable are 0 and 1, respectively, and the model has only a single linear constraint, you can simplify the steps considerably, and in particular, you can easily solve the relaxed linear programs optimized at *Step 2.* (You also could solve the problem by dynamic programming, using the formulation at the beginning of Sec. 10.4.)

In the discussion to follow, assume that b and all a_j are positive integers and that all $c_j > 0$. [If a_k is negative, then let $x_k \equiv 1 - x'_k$, and eliminate x_k from the model; the resulting coefficient of x'_k is $(-a_k)$, which is positive, and since x'_k must be a zero-one variable, the altered problem remains a knapsack model. If $a_k > 0$ and $c_k < 0$, then $x_k = 0$ is optimal, and the variable may be eliminated from the problem statement.] Also assume that the variables have been arranged so that $c_1/a_1 \geq c_2/a_2 \geq \cdots \geq c_n/a_n$.

It can be shown that if (3) is relaxed and replaced by

$$(4) \qquad\qquad 0 \leq x_j \leq 1 \quad \text{for } j = 1, 2, \ldots, n,$$

then an optimal solution to the linear program (1), (2), and (4) is

$$(5) \qquad x_j = \begin{cases} 1 & \text{for } j = 1, 2, \ldots, k - 1 \\ \dfrac{b - \sum_{h=1}^{k-1} a_h}{a_k} & \text{for } j = k \\ 0 & \text{for } j = k + 1, \ldots, n, \end{cases}$$

where $(k - 1)$ is the largest integer such that $(b - \sum_{h=1}^{k-1} a_h \geq 0)$.

Usually x_k is fractional-valued in (5), because typically the numerator is positive; but if $x_k = 0$, then (5) is an optimal solution to the knapsack problem.

At *Step 2* of the branch-and-bound algorithm, if the linear program has some variables constrained at their lower bound 0 and others at their upper bound 1, then you reinterpret (5) to apply only to those variables not yet so constrained, and where the numerator in (5) for $j = k$ reflects all variables at their upper bound. To illustrate, consider the constraint

$$(6) \qquad 4x_1 + 6x_2 + 5x_3 + 2x_4 + 3x_5 + 7x_6 \leq 14.$$

From (5) you have that $x_1 = x_2 = 1$, $x_3 = (14 - 4 - 6)/5 = \frac{4}{5}$, and $x_4 = x_5 = x_6 = 0$. Now suppose that the constraints $x_1 = 0$ and $x_4 = 1$ are imposed. Then rewrite (6) as

$$(7) \qquad 6x_2 + 5x_3 + 3x_5 + 7x_6 \leq 14 - 4 \cdot 0 - 2 \cdot 1 = 12,$$

the solution values for the variables on the left of (7) are $x_2 = x_3 = 1$, $x_5 = (12 - 6 - 5)/3 = \frac{1}{3}$, and $x_6 = 0$.

*11.5 EXTENSIONS OF BRANCH-AND-BOUND

The logic underlying the branch-and-bound algorithm in Sec. 11.3 can be applied to many combinatorial optimization problems with only slight modification of the computational steps. We present a few such examples below.

Transportation model with unique sources. Recall from Chap. 6 the classical transportation problem

$$\text{(1)} \qquad \text{minimize} \sum_{i=1}^{m} \sum_{j=1}^{n} c_{ij} x_{ij}$$

subject to

$$\text{(2)} \qquad \sum_{j=1}^{n} x_{ij} \leq S_i \quad \text{for } i = 1, 2, \ldots, m \quad \text{(supply)}$$

$$\text{(3)} \qquad \sum_{i=1}^{m} x_{ij} \geq D_j \quad \text{for } j = 1, 2, \ldots, n \quad \text{(demand)}$$

$$\text{(4)} \qquad x_{ij} \geq 0 \quad \text{for all } i \text{ and } j.$$

Usually in an optimal basic solution, some demand points will receive shipments from more than one supply point. In a real application, you may want each demand point to be served entirely by a unique supply point. You can formulate such a stipulation employing zero-one variables in a manner analogous to that used in Sec. 11.2 for the warehouse location problem. Alternatively, you can slightly modify the branch-and-bound algorithm and thereby avoid introducing new variables. The procedure is as follows.

At iteration 1, the master list contains only the problem (1) through (4). You leave unchanged *Step 1* and *Step 2* of the branch-and-bound algorithm. In *Step 3* you test whether the linear programming problem satisfies (1) through (4) *and* the unique-source stipulation. You modify the fourth step to read:

Step 4. Select any Demand Point j that does not have a unique source of supply in the obtained optimal solution to the chosen linear programming problem, and choose one of the associated shipments $x_{kj} > 0$. Add two linear programming problems to the master list. These two problems are identical with the problem chosen in *Step 1* except that in one, $x_{kj} = 0$, and in the other, $x_{kj} = D_j$. Let $x_0^{t+1} = x_0^t$, and return to *Step 1*.

You have some flexibility in executing the details of *Step 4*. For example, you can enforce the added stipulation in each of the descendant linear programs by modifying the costs to rule out the inadmissible shipping routes. But the important fact is that since each descendant linear program optimized at *Step 2* remains a classical transportation problem, you can employ a very efficient computational method.

Alternative separations. The separation procedure at *Step 4* of the branch-and-bound algorithm creates two descendants from each parent linear program, based on the current fractional value of an integer variable. This procedure can be modified to create a greater number of descendants, each presumably more tightly constrained and based on other criteria. To illustrate, if an integer variable x_j currently has a fractional-value, and the model stipulates that $x_j = 0, 1, \ldots, H$, then at *Step 4* you can add $(H + 1)$ descendants, each of which restricts x_j to one of the feasible integer values. Or you can add, say, three descendants, where x_j is restricted in each to lie in a specified interval; for example, the three descendants can correspond to the intervals $(0, 4)$, $(5, 10)$, and $(10, H)$, which partition the feasible possibilities.

Many combinatorial problems contain **multiple choice** constraints of the form

$$(5) \qquad\qquad x_1 + x_2 + \cdots + x_p = 1,$$

where each x_j must be zero-one. Thus (5) and the integer stipulations force a choice of a single variable from among the p variables. Suppose in the obtained optimal linear programming solution of the parent problem that both integer variables x_j and x_k, where $j < k$, are at positive levels. Then at *Step 4*, instead of creating two descendant problems with the bounds on x_j or x_k altered, you can create one descendant problem in which $x_1 + \cdots + x_j = 1$, and another in which $x_{j+1} + \cdots + x_p = 1$. Or you can add three descendants, with $x_1 + \cdots + x_j = 1$, $x_{j+1} + \cdots + x_k = 1$, $x_{k+1} + \cdots + x_p = 1$, respectively.

Next-best solutions. When you solve a pure integer programming problem by the branch-and-bound algorithm in Sec. 11.3, that method provides only a single optimal solution. Suppose that you want to examine alternative optimal solutions if they exist and perhaps even solutions that are nearly optimal. The goal, then, is an algorithm that provides the K best solutions, where you specify K in advance of the computations. For example, if you let K equal 3, the method will find the three best solutions. (Hence, if the model has a unique optimum, the method produces that solution and two others with next-best values; if the model has two alternative optima, then both are found along with one other next-best solution; if the model has more than three alternative optima, then only three of these are found.) The required modification of the branch-and-bound algorithm is as follows.

At iteration 1, the master list contains the original pure integer programming problem. Assume that you also have available K lower bounds, say, $x_{01}^1, x_{02}^1, \ldots, x_{0K}^1$, on the K best values for the objective function; these values are revised at subsequent iterations. For simplicity, postulate that at iteration 1, each x_{0k}^1 either is strictly less than the kth best value for the objective function, or that you have K distinct feasible solutions and that x_{0k}^1 is the kth best value for the objective function from among these solutions. If worse comes to worst, you can let each $x_{0k}^1 = -\infty$. The procedure at iteration t is:

Step 1. Terminate the computations if the master list is empty. Otherwise, remove a linear programming problem from the master list.

Step 2. Solve the chosen problem. If it has no feasible solution, or if the resultant value of the objective function $x_0 \leq x_{0k}^t$, then let each $x_{0k}^{t+1} = x_{0k}^t$, and return to *Step 1.* Otherwise, proceed to *Step 3.*

Step 3. If the obtained optimal solution to the linear programming problem *does not* satisfy all the integer constraints, then let each $x_{0k}^{t+1} = x_{0k}^t$. If the solution *does* satisfy all the integer constraints, then record it, and set the bounds x_{0k}^{t+1} accordingly to reflect this new feasible solution. Return to *Step 1* if every $L_j = U_j$. Otherwise proceed to *Step 4.*

Step 4. Select any variable x_j that does not have an integer value in the obtained optimal solution to the chosen linear programming problem; let b_j denote this value. If no such variable exists, proceed to *Step 5.* Add two descendant linear programming problems to the master list, where in one the lower bound is replaced by $[b_j] + 1$, and in the other, the upper bound is replaced by $[b_j]$. Return to *Step 1.*

Step 5. Select any variable x_j for which $L_j < U_j$; let b_j denote its current value. Add two descendant linear programming problems to the master list, where in one the lower bound is replaced by $b_j + 1$ if $b_j < U_j$, and by b_j, otherwise, and in the other, the upper bound is replaced by b_j if $b_j < U_j$, and by $b_j - 1$, otherwise. Return to *Step 1.*

In this procedure, a problem is fathomed in *Step 2* if it is infeasible or cannot be any better than the already obtained Kth best solution, and in *Step 3* if each variable is exactly constrained because its lower and upper bounds are identical. To illustrate the procedure at *Step 3*, suppose that $K = 5$ and that you currently have five feasible solutions with objective function values $(10, 8, 8, 6, 6)$; if the solution recorded at *Step 3* has objective function value 9, then the $(K = 5)$ bounds at the next iteration are $(10, 9, 8, 8, 6)$. *Step 4* is virtually unchanged, but an additional fifth step is necessary. The reason is that the parent problem (in which at least one $L_j < U_j$) cannot be considered fathomed even though all the variables in the linear programming solution are integer-valued. A further constrained descendant problem may have a solution that is better than one of the current candidates for the K best solutions. The algorithm can be improved further by taking account of the observation that at *Step 5* one of the two descendant problems in each case has the same optimal solution as its parent, and therefore need not be reoptimized.

REVIEW EXERCISES

1 (a) Consider a one-period product-mix selection model with activities x_j, $j = 1$, $2, \ldots, n$, each of which incurs a setup cost K_j. Calculate how many different patterns of setups there are (assume all $x_j = 0$ is one of the possibilities).
(Continued on p. 349.)

(b) Consider the constraint $x_1 + x_2 + x_3 + \cdots + x_n = N$, where each x_j must be a nonnegative integer. Calculate the number of different feasible solutions if $n = 6$ and $N = 1$. If $n = 7$ and $N = 1$. If $n = 6$ and $N = 2$. If $n = 6$ and $N = 6$. If $n = 7$ and $N = 6$. If $n = 6$ and $N = 6$ and the restriction is stated as an inequality ($\leq$). If $n = 6$ and $N = 1$, and the restriction is stated as an inequality ($\leq$). If $n = 6$ and $N = 2$, and the restriction is stated as an inequality ($\leq$).

(c) Consider a capital budgeting problem in which there are three categories of projects. Category 1 contains eight projects, and two are to be selected. Category 2 contains ten projects, and four are to be selected. Category 3 contains seven projects and five are to be selected. Calculate the total number of distinct selection combinations that are possible. Show how this number changes if the specified number for each category is only an upper limit on the number that can be selected.

(d) A corporation is working out a strategy for introducing three new products into four marketing areas. The strategy is strictly "sequential" in that the company first selects one area, then selects the sequence in which to introduce the products (one every two weeks), then afterwards selects the next area, followed by a chosen sequence, etc. Calculate the number of different strategies for introducing the new products.

(e) A company plans to build six new plants on sites that have already been selected. It wishes to accomplish this expansion over the next five years. Conceivably, it could build all the plants in Year 1 or wait to build all the plants in Year 5. More likely, it will build some plants each year. Determine the number of different patterns for building these plants. The company is also concerned with the *number* of plants it builds each year (in addition to which plants it builds each year). Determine all the possible patterns for the numbers of plants built over the five years (such as six in Year 1 and none in any other year, or six in Year 5 and none in any other year, etc.).

(f) A firm performs preventive maintenance on four major pieces of equipment. Such work can start during any one of three weeks on Machine 1, during any one of six weeks on Machine 2, during any one of two weeks on Machine 3, and in any one of five weeks on Machine 4. Calculate the total number of distinctly different maintenance schedules (that is, "starting weeks" for each of the four machines).

(g) A company wants to schedule three trucks to visit eight stores. Each truck is able to stop at one or more stores, but there is no store that can be visited by more than one truck. Calculate the number of different ways to assign the trucks to the stores.

*(h) Calculate the number of routes in a Traveling Salesman Problem for 3 cities. For 5 cities.

*(i) Consider a traveling salesman problem with five cities, but assume that the salesman must return to City 1 after visiting two cities and that he must then set out again for the remaining two cities. Calculate the number of possible sequences.

*(j) Calculate the number of possible sequences in the Machine Scheduling Problem with three items and one machine. With three items and two machines. With two items and three machines. With two items and four machines. Show how your

answers change if the items must be processed in the same sequence on each machine.

2 Consider the problem

$$\text{maximize} \quad 3x_1 + 6x_2 + x_3$$

subject to

$$x_1 + 2x_2 + 2x_3 \leq 2\tfrac{2}{3}$$
$$x_1 + 2x_2 + 3x_3 \geq 2\tfrac{1}{3}$$

every x_j a nonnegative integer.

(a) What is an optimal solution if the integer-value stipulation on every x_j is dropped? Is there more than one optimal solution?

(b) Determine by inspection an optimal integer-valued solution. Does your answer in part (a) round to this solution?

(c) Draw a solution space representation of the problem, letting $x_3 = 0$ (that is, draw the implied constraints on x_1 and x_2). Indicate all the feasible integer-valued solutions.

3 Suppose a company has five manufacturing plants that ship to 100 warehouses. If the company continues to operate all of its plants and warehouses, it faces a cost minimization problem that can be characterized by a standard transportation problem, like that described in the beginning of Chap. 6.

(a) Suppose, however, that the total plant capacity is considerably more than is required at the warehouses, and each Plant i incurs a large yearly overhead cost P_i. Suggest a *practical* way to determine which plants, if any, ought to be shut down to minimize the sum of annual overhead and transportation costs.

(b) Suppose, instead, that the company wants to shut down some warehouses (the associated demand requirements would be reallocated to the warehouses that remain open). The company thereby saves overhead costs of operating some of the warehouses, but increases transportation costs as a result. Would your suggestion in part (a) be practical for this problem? Explain.

4 *Cummins and Goings Manufacturing Company* (Sec. 11.2). Consider the following data:

$$m = 3 \qquad n = 4 \qquad S_1 = 40 \qquad S_2 = 50 \qquad S_3 = 60$$
$$D_1 = 10 \qquad D_2 = 15 \qquad D_3 = 20 \qquad D_4 = 25.$$

(a) Write in full detail all the linear constraints in the problem.

(b) Explain why (22) and (23) together ensure that y_i and z_{ij} are each either 0 or 1.

(c) Explain why it is never essential for optimality to have $z_{ij} = 1$ and $x_{ij} = 0$.

*(d) Suppose all $F_i = 100$, $c_{ij} = 1$, $F_{ij} = 0$. What is an optimal solution if the integer-value stipulations are dropped? Are there alternative optimal solutions?

(e) Explain why $U_{ij} = \text{minimum } (S_i, D_j)$ is sufficiently large in (24).

5 Consider the plant location model described in Sec. 11.2.

(a) If every $F_i = 0$, would it be optimal to let every $y_i = 1$? Explain.

(b) Assume every $y_i = 1$ and moreover that the sum of the supplies S_i equals the sum of the demands D_j. Will an optimal solution necessarily use $m + n - 1$ routes? If every $F_{ij} = F$ (a constant), is an optimal solution the same as the one for the standard transportation problem in which the F_{ij} are not present ($F = 0$)? (If you answer "yes" to a question, provide a supporting argument; if your answer is "no," provide a small example showing why.)

6 *Fixed Charge Problem.* Consider the model

$$\text{minimize } \sum_{j=1}^{n} c_j(x_j)$$

subject to

$$\sum_{j=1}^{n} a_{ij}x_j \le b_i \quad \text{for } i = 1, 2, \ldots, m$$

$$\text{every } x_j \ge 0,$$

where

$$c_j(x_j) = \begin{cases} 0 & \text{for } x_j = 0 \\ K_j + c_j x_j & \text{for } x_j > 0, \end{cases}$$

and each $K_j \ge 0$. The K_j are called fixed charges.

(a) Show how to formulate this problem as a mixed integer programming model.

*(b) Discuss the difficulty that can arise if the objective is to maximize instead of minimize (or if not all $K_j \ge 0$). (*Hint:* how small can x_j be, given that it is positive?)

(c) Suppose all $K_j = K > 0$. Give a sufficient condition such that an optimal solution is the same as one for the linear programming problem in which the K_j are not present (all $K_j = 0$).

(d) Show how to alter your formulation if the constraints are of the form

$$\sum_{j=1}^{n} a_{ij}(x_j) \le b_i \quad \text{for } i = 1, 2, \ldots, m,$$

where

$$a_{ij}(x_j) = \begin{cases} 0 & \text{for } x_j = 0 \\ A_{ij} + a_{ij}x_j & \text{for } x_j > 0, \end{cases}$$

with every $A_{ij} \ge 0$.

*(e) Discuss the difficulty that can arise in part (d) if an $A_{ij} < 0$, or if an inequality for a linear constraint is $(\ge)$.

*7 *Warehouse Location—Polly Esther Cosmetics Co.* (Sec. 11.2). Let $m = 3$, $n = 5$, and $p = 4$. Construct a technology table of appropriate dimensions for (25) through (29).

8 *Suey Generous Example* (Sec. 11.2). For the example in Fig. 11.2, write the complete matching problem (33), (34), and (35), and the complete covering problem (36), (37), and (38). Exhibit a feasible solution to the matching problem that is infeasible in the covering problem, and vice versa.

*9 Consider the Knox Mix example in Sec. 2.2. Formulate the model if only one of the three constraints must hold. If only two of the three constraints must hold.

*10 Consider the integer-valued variable x_j, where $x_j = 0, 1, \ldots, U$. In each part below, exhibit a binary representation, such as (45) in Sec. 11.2.

(a) $U = 32$.
(b) $U = 40$.
(c) $U = 100$.
(d) $U = 111$.

*11 Suppose a model contains the expression $x_2^4 x_3^5 x_8^7$, where each variable is zero-one. Show two ways of converting the model into a linear problem.

12 Consider a product-mix selection problem, which is of the form

$$\text{maximize} \sum_{j=1}^{n} c_j x_j$$

subject to

$$\sum_{j=1}^{n} a_{ij} x_j \le b_i \quad \text{for } i = 1, 2, \ldots, m$$

$$\text{every } x_j \ge 0,$$

where every $c_j > 0$ and $n \ge m$.

(a) Suppose the firm wants to produce no more than k out of the n different products. Show how this stipulation can be formulated in terms of integer-valued variables.

(b) What difficulties can arise if the firm wants to produce at least k different products. (*Hint:* how small can x_j be if it is positive?)

*13 *Solution Space Representation.* In each part below, graph the region of feasible solutions for the set of alternative constraints. Assume $x_1 \ge 0$ and $x_2 \ge 0$.

(a) Either $x_1 + 2x_2 \le 1$, or $2x_1 + x_2 \le 1$, or both.

(b) Either $x_1 + x_2 \le 1$, or $x_1 + x_2 \ge 2$, or both.

(c) Either the pair of constraints $x_1 \le 1$ and $x_2 \le 1$ holds, or the pair $x_1 \ge 1$ and $x_2 \ge 1$ holds, or both pairs hold.

(d) At least one of the following constraints must be satisfied: $x_1 \le 1$, $x_2 \le 1$, and $x_1 + x_2 \le 2$. At least two must hold. All three must hold.

*14 Consider the approach for representing alternative constraints as described by (39), (40), and (41) in Sec. 11.2. In each part below, write in full detail the representation (40) and (41). (*Hint:* calculate a value for U_i by examining the constraints; let U_i be the smallest value that will work.)

(a) $x_1 + 2x_2 + x_3 \le 8$
    $4x_1 + x_2 + x_3 \le 20$
    $x_1 + x_2 + 3x_3 \le 15.$
Show the formulation for $k = 1$ and $k = 2$.

(b) Same constraints as in part (a) augmented by $x_2 - x_4 \le 0$. Show the formulation for $k = 3$.

(c) In parts (a) and (b) explain in detail why the representation and the stipulation that each y_i be either 0 or 1 solve the problem (that is, ensure that at least k out of the p constraints are satisfied).

(d) Explain why (40) can just as well be stated as an equality.

*(e) Discuss the difficulty in ensuring that *exactly* k out of p linear constraints (39) are satisfied.

*15 In each part, show how to formulate the problem in terms of an integer program-ming model.

(a) maximize $\sum_{j=1}^{n} c_j x_j$ subject to

$$\sum_{j=1}^{n} a_{ij} x_j \leq b_i \quad \text{for } i = 1, 2, \ldots, m$$

$$\text{every } x_j \geq 0$$

and either the three constraints $x_1 \leq 1$, $x_2 \leq 1$, and $x_1 + x_2 \leq 1.5$ hold, or the three constraints $x_1 \geq 1$, $x_2 \geq 1$, and $x_1 + x_2 \geq 2.5$ hold.

(b) maximize [maximum $(x_1 + x_2, 2x_1 + x_2, x_1 + 2x_2)$] subject to

$$\sum_{j=1}^{n} a_{ij} x_j \geq b_i \quad \text{for } i = 1, 2, \ldots, m$$

$$\text{every } x_j \geq 0$$

(that is, find values for x_j that satisfy the constraints and make as large as possible the maximum value for the three designated linear functions).

(c) How would you go about finding numerical solutions to the problems in parts (a) and (b)?

16 Exercise 1, part (e), describes a company that plans to start building six new plants on sites that have already been selected, and wishes to complete construction within five years.

(a) Characterize the selection problem in terms of linear constraints involving integer-valued variables. (Be sure to define your symbols and explain the meaning of each restriction.) In each part below, show how the stated stipulation can be encompassed by an integer programming formulation. Consider each of the parts separately.

(b) Plants 1, 2, and 3 must be started no later than Year 3.

(c) No more than two plants can be started in any year.

(d) No more than three plants can be started in the first two years, and no more than five plants in the first four years.

(e) Exactly three plants must be started in the first two years, and five plants in the first four years.

(f) Plant 2 cannot be started before Plant 1 (they can be started in the same year).

(g) Plants 4, 5, and 6 cannot be started before Plants 1, 2, and 3 are started (all six plants can be started in the same year).

*(h) Either Plants 1, 2, 3 must be started before Plants 4, 5, 6, or vice versa (all six plants cannot be started in the same year).

(i) Plants 1 and 2 must be started in the same year. Similarly, Plants 3, 4, and 5 must be started in the same year.

(j) If Plants 1 and 2 are started in the same year, then no other plants can be started in that year.

(k) In Year 1, the company starts either Plants 1 and 2 or Plants 3 and 4. (Assume one of these two possibilities must occur.)

(l) In the first two years, the company starts either Plants 1 and 2 or Plants 3 and 4. (Assume one of these two possibilities must occur.)

(m) Plant 1 can be started in Year 1 only if either Plant 2 or Plant 3 is started, but not if both Plants 2 and 3 are started.

(n) Suppose the company has two possible sites for Plant 1 (instead of a single site already selected). Show how to modify your previous formulations to account for this site selection problem. (*Continued on p. 354.*)

(o) Suppose the company has only five sites, instead of six, and Plants 1 and 3 compete for the same site; that is, the company plans to build only Plant 1 or Plant 3 on a specified site. Show how to modify your previous formulations to account for this site selection problem. (You may find it necessary to reinterpret the assumptions in some of the parts to preserve consistency; make explicit mention when this happens.)

*17 Consider the problem

$$\text{maximize} \quad 3x + 7y$$

subject to

$$2x + y \leq 25$$

$$x + 2y \leq 6,$$

where $y \geq 0$, and x can equal only the values 0, 1, 4, and 6.
(a) Formulate the problem in terms of an equivalent integer programming model.
(b) Suppose the objective function contained the terms $3x^2$, instead of $3x$. Revise your answer to part (a) accordingly.

18 Study the application of the Branch-and-Bound Algorithm to the example (8) and (9) in Sec. 11.3. Trace in detail the calculations at each iteration. Specifically, verify optimal solutions in (11), (13), (15), (17), (19), and (20). Check how the constraints in each of the nine problems are generated. Verify that Problems 2, 6, and 8 have no feasible solution. Explain in detail the rationale permitting the calculations to stop with Problem 5 and the logic behind asserting that (19) is the optimal solution.

19 Consider the example in Sec. 11.3. Suppose at iteration 4 you select Problem 5 instead of Problem 4. Complete the steps of the Branch-and-Bound Algorithm with this choice. Construct a tree analogous to that in Fig. 11.3 to show the progress of the iterations.

20 Consider the example in Sec. 11.3, where the right-hand-side constants in (9) are both 22, instead of 8. Apply the Branch-and-Bound Algorithm. Construct a tree analogous to that in Fig. 11.3 to show the progress of the iterations.

21 Explain your understanding of the following terms:

divisibility assumption	backtrack algorithm
integer (diophantine, discrete) programming problem	tree search
	Branch-and-Bound Algorithm
pure integer programming problem	(Branch-and-Prune)
mixed integer programming problem	branching
*combinatorial optimization problem	relaxation
lattice point	fathomed
zero-one variable	separation
alternative constraints	descendant problem
"go-no-go" alternatives	LIFO rule
(weighted) matching problem	0–1 knapsack problem
(weighted) covering problem	*multiple choice constraints
*binary representation	*next-best solution.

COMPUTATIONAL EXERCISES

22 Apply the Branch-and-Bound Algorithm in Sec. 11.3 to solve each of the following problems, assuming here that all the variables must be nonnegative integers. Construct a tree diagram like that in Fig. 11.1 to show the progress of the algorithm.

(a) One-Potato, Two-Potato Problem in Sec. 1.6.
(b) Knox Mix Company Problem, described in Sec. 2.2 and solved by the simplex method in Sec. 4.4.
(c) Exercise 49, part (a), of Chap. 10.
*(d) Exercise 49 of Chap. 10, with the right-hand-side constant in the first equation equal to 2, instead of 3.
*(e) Exercise 49 of Chap. 10, with the right-hand-side constant in the second equation equal to 3, instead of 4. Equal to 5, instead of 4.
*(f) Exercise 49 of Chap. 10, with the right-hand-side constant in the first equation equal to 2, instead of 3, and in the second equation equal to 3, instead of 4.
(g) Consider the problem

$$\text{maximize } x_1 + 2x_2$$

subject to

$$5x_1 + 7x_2 \leq 21$$

$$-x_1 + 3x_2 \leq 8$$

x_1 and x_2 nonnegative integers.

(h) Exercise 21, part (a), of Chap. 4, where the right-hand side of the second constraint is 13 instead of 14.
(i) Consider the problem

$$\text{maximize } 21x_1 + 11x_2$$

subject to

$$7x_1 + 4x_2 \leq 13$$

x_1 and x_2 nonnegative integers.

*(j) In each part above, find the next-best solution.

23 *Knapsack Problem.* Consider the following illustration of a knapsack problem:

$$\text{maximize } 60x_1 + 60x_2 + 40x_3 + 10x_4 + 20x_5 + 10x_6 + 3x_7$$

subject to

$$3x_1 + 5x_2 + 4x_3 + 1x_4 + 4x_5 + 3x_6 + 1x_7 \leq 10$$

$$\text{every } x_j = 0, 1.$$

(a) Solve by the Branch-and-Bound Algorithm in Sec. 11.4.
*(b) Solve by a dynamic programming recursion.
*(c) Find the next-best solution.
*(d) Find the second and third best solutions.

24 Use a branch-and-bound algorithm to solve the Why Pout Spot Remover Co. problem given in Fig. 10.11.

*25 Consider the transportation problem in Fig. 6.12, and assume that the supplies and demands are

$$S_1 = 5 \qquad S_2 = 2 \qquad S_3 = 5,$$
$$D_1 = 2 \qquad D_2 = 5 \qquad D_3 = 3 \qquad D_4 = 2.$$

Find an optimal solution using a branch-and-bound approach assuming that each demand point must be served from a single supply point.

FORMULATION EXERCISES

In exercises 26 through 58, you are to formulate integer programming models. Be sure to define all the symbols you use, justify each of the constraints, and develop the objective function. When an exercise supplies numerical data, write out the model in full detail.

26 The Rite of Weigh Company, manufacturers of dietetic foods, has requested quotations from each of four suppliers of package labels; the company requires 10,000 labels for its forthcoming sales promotion. Each Supplier j returned a bid stating the minimum quantity, L_j, it would consider supplying; the maximum quantity, U_j, it could deliver; and the total price it would charge $P_j + p_j x_j$, where x_j is the quantity ordered by the company. Formulate a model that selects the suppliers and the quantities to order from each.

27 The Land Development Commissioner, Terry Phurma, for a large southern state has opened for bid T offshore tracks for oil well drilling. Each company that is interested in leasing any of these tracts has been instructed that it may submit as many bids as it chooses for one or more parcels. To illustrate, the Wilde-Katz Company submitted a bid for Tract 3, a bid for Tract 10, a bid for both Tracts 3 and 10, and a bid for Tracts 1, 4, and 10. The bid price for Tracts 3 and 10 combined is larger than the sum of the bids for the two individual tracts, because Wilde-Katz feels that it can realize certain economies if it drills on both of these tracts, which are adjacent.

Suppose that Mr. Phurma has received N bids altogether, where the offer price for Bid j is p_j. Formulate a model that selects bids to maximize the total lease revenue received by the state. Assume that the state is not obliged to lease every tract that was offered.

28 The scholarship and financial aids office at Yankee University is preparing its awards for the coming year. It has selected n students to receive awards, and wants to grant at least M_i dollars to Student i, for $i = 1, 2, \ldots, n$. The office has s different scholarships available; Scholarship j confers the amount a_j on its recipient. The office may have to award several grants to an individual in order to provide the student with at least M_i dollars, but the office cannot reduce the amount of any scholarship award below the designated level a_j. If the office does not award Scholarship j for the year, the amount a_j earns interest and is available for distribution in the following year.

(a) Devise a model for granting scholarships that maximizes the amount of undistributed money, subject to giving each student at least the minimal specified level. (*Continued on p. 357.*)

(b) Show how to modify your answer in part (a) if each Student i is not permitted to receive funds from more than two different scholarships, and may not receive a total award in excess of $1.1M_i$.

29 A state government has asked for bids on n construction projects from each of n firms. No firm will be awarded more than one contract, so the decision problem can be viewed as an assignment model, as described in Sec. 6.4. For policital reasons, the government officials want to award no more than N large contracts to firms that are located outside the state. Let Projects 1, 2, . . . , s, denote the large projects and Firms 1, 2, . . . , t, the companies that are located out of state. The objective is to minimize total cost given the added stipulation.

(a) Formulate this optimization problem.
(b) Show that imposing this added stipulation to the assignment model (3) and (4) in Sec. 6.4 and then finding a linear programming solution (where the integer constraints are ignored) need not produce a feasible assignment. (*Hint:* consider $n = 4$, $s = t = 2$, $N = 1$, $c_{11} = c_{22} = 0$, $c_{14} = c_{23} = c_{31} = c_{33} = c_{42} = c_{44} = 1$, all other c_{ij} large.)

30 *Multi-Index Problem.* The governor of the state in exercise 29, Ray Gunn, is unhappy about the policy of limiting awards to out-of-state firms. He does, however, stipulate that one project must be completed in each three-month period, beginning six months from now, and ending $6 + 3n$ months from now. Accordingly, each contractor has resubmitted a bid stating the cost for each project depending on the designated period of completion. Formulate this optimization problem.

31 Suppose that a state sends R persons to the U.S. House of Representatives. There are D counties in the state $(D > R)$, and the state legislature wants to group these counties into R distinct electoral districts, each of which sends a delegate to Congress. The total population of the state is P, and the legislature wants to form districts that each have an approximate population, p, where $p = P/R$. Suppose that the appropriate legislative committee studying the electoral districting problem generates a long list of $N > R$ districts, each of which contains contiguous counties and a total population p_i, for $i = 1, 2, \ldots, N$, that is acceptably close to p. Let $c_i \equiv |p_i - p|$. The committee must select R out of these N possible districts such that each county is contained in a single district and such that the largest of the associated c_i is as small as possible.

(a) Formulate the optimization model using zero-one variables.
*(b) Show how the model with the "minimax" objective function can be transformed into an ordinary integer linear programming problem.

32 The developers of Dizzy Place, a fantastic amusement park now under construction, have requested a team of architects (Hy Pott, Ann Noos) to lay out the paths and roadways connecting the six separate activity areas (Air Place, Boat Place, Car Place, Drink Place, Eat Place, and Fun Place) comprising the park. As the terrain for Dizzy Place contains hills, streams, rocky ledges, and ponds, the roadway building costs are considerable. The architects and developers agree that it is necessary to build just enough connections between the six activity areas so that a person can walk from any place to another; the person may have to walk through other places along the

way; it is not necessary that all possible roadway pairs $[15 = 6!/(2!\,4!)]$ be constructed. Let c_{ij} denote the cost of a connection between Place i and Place j, where $i, j = A, B, C, D, E, F$, and $i \neq j$. Formulate the construction problem as an optimization model.

33 Consider a classical transportation model, like that described in Sec. 6.2. Impose the restriction that no supply point can serve more than M different demand points, and no demand point can be served by more than N different supply points. Assume that these stipulations permit a feasible solution. Formulate this optimization problem.

34 Fran Frosh, a first-year student at Multy University, has decided to take five courses in her first term; these courses are designated A, B, C, D, and E. Each course has four sections that meet at different times of the day; let A1, for example, denote Section 1 of Course A, and let t_{A1} be the hour at which it meets. For simplicity, assume that every course meets every day, and the starting times of courses are 8 A.M., 9 A.M., . . . , 4 P.M. Fran's preferences for when she takes courses are influenced by the time of day and the reputation of the instructor. For example, let P_{A1} denote Fran's preference rating for Section 1 of Course A. Unfortunately, Fran cannot select her most preferred section of each course due to time conflicts.

(a) Devise a model that selects a feasible course schedule which maximizes the sum of Fran's preference ratings.

(b) Indicate how to alter the formulation in part (a) to ensure that Fran has an hour for lunch at either noon or 1 P.M.

*(c) Indicate how to alter the formulation if Fran's objective function is to maximize the number of consecutive hours she has free either from 8 A.M. until her first class, or at the end of the afternoon.

35 Consider the problem of Van Fuller, described in exercise 42 of Chap. 10. Formulate his optimization problem in terms of an integer programming model.

36 *Multiplant Expansion Problem.* The Manne Agricultural Chemical Corporation operates three plants. At the beginning of Period 1, each plant has capacity 10. By the end of Period 3, Plant 1 must have capacity 11, Plant 2 must have capacity 12, and Plant 3 must have capacity 13; these targets are set so that after three periods each plant has enough capacity to be self-sufficient in its own marketing area. The capacity of a plant can be expanded in unit amounts in any period; for simplicity, assume that capacity that is initiated in a period is also available to meet demand requirements during that period. Also assume that capacity does not deteriorate. Thus, there are three possible ways for Plant 1 to increase its capacity from 10 at the beginning of Period 1 to 11 at the end of Period 3: (i) add 1 unit in Period 1, (ii) add 1 unit in Period 2, or (iii) add 1 unit in Period 3. (Verify that there are six possible ways for Plant 2 to increase its capacity from 10 at the beginning of Period 1 to 12 at the end of Period 3.) Let $K_{it}(p, q)$ denote the cost in Period t of adding p units of capacity to Plant i, when its capacity at the beginning of Period t is q units.

Let D_{it} be the demand requirement during Period t in the marketing region served by Plant i. If Plant i lacks the capacity to fill requirement D_{it}, then the firm must ship items into this region from one or both of the other plants. Let c_{jit} represent the cost of shipping an item from Plant j to Plant i during Period t.

Formulate a model to determine a minimum cost policy for building capacity at each of the plants, and meeting all demands during the planning horizon.

37 Mia Kulper administered a difficult 75-question final examination to her Latin class. A perfect answer to Question j was worth p_j points, and a perfect score on the entire exam was 150 points. Since her students did rather poorly, Mia decided to score each student in the following way. She graded each of the 75 questions; assume that for a particular student, the grade on Question j was s_j. Then for this student, Mia wanted to select a *subset* of questions that maximized the student's total grade score, subject to the restriction that a perfect score on this subset would not exceed 100 points. Exhibit the optimization model that Mia must solve for each of her students.

38 The Phil T. Grimes Company must draw up a preventive maintenance schedule for five of its major pieces of equipment; the schedule extends over the next eight weeks. Assume the pieces of equipment are indexed 1, 2, 3, 4, 5. Maintenance on Piece 1 requires four units of labor (say, man-weeks) during the first week of maintenance, six units in the second week, and three units in the third week. The servicing can begin as early as Week 1 or as late as Week 4. Similar data for the other pieces of equipment are shown in Fig. 11.4.

Equipment	First Week	Second Week	Third Week	Early Start	Late Start
1	4	6	3	1	4
2	3	2	5	1	3
3	7	1	1	2	5
4	1	3	6	2	6
5	8	9	2	3	5

FIGURE 11.4

In each part below, formulate an appropriate optimization model.

(a) Assume that the maximum labor available is L_t in Week t. Find a feasible schedule (that is, determine the starting week for maintenance on each piece of equipment).

*(b) Suppose Grimes wants to minimize the sum of the weekly fluctuations in labor utilization. [If, for example, each project is started as early as possible, the weekly labor utilization is 7, 16, 20, 16, 2, 0, 0, 0, so that the sum of the week-to-week fluctuations is $(16 - 7) + (20 - 16) + (20 - 16) + (16 - 2) + (2 - 0) + (0 - 0) + (0 - 0) = 33$.]

*(c) Suppose Grimes wants to minimize the maximum labor utilized during any of the eight weeks.

*(d) Suppose Grimes wants to minimize the maximum weekly fluctuation. (If each project is started as early as possible, the resultant maximum fluctuation is $16 - 2 = 14$, between the fourth and fifth week.)

(e) Show how to modify your answer in part (a) if maintenance on Piece 3 cannot start before maintenance begins on Piece 1. If maintenance on Piece 4 has to start in the same period as maintenance on Piece 3 (hence, its "late start" week is really 5, instead of 6). If maintenance on Pieces 4 and 5 cannot start in the same week. If maintenance on Piece 5 cannot start until after maintenance on Piece 1 is complete (that is, if service on Piece 1 starts in Week 1, for example, then service on Piece 5 can start no sooner than Week 4.)

39 *Covering Problem.* The Trotter Poll Company keeps a variety of data stored on magnetic tape files. It wishes to compile statistics on m different population characteristics (such as the age distribution, income distribution, size of family dwelling, etc., in eight selected metropolitan areas). Assume that all the required information is recorded within n different files. Suppose T_j, for $j = 1, 2, \ldots, n$, is the computer time required to search File j, and assume this search time is independent of the number of characteristics to be summarized from the file. Several of the m characteristics of interest are recorded in more than one of the n files, that is, the files contain duplicate information. Let $a_{ij} = 1$ if the ith characteristic is recorded in the jth file, and $a_{ij} = 0$, otherwise. Thus, for example, $a_{13} = a_{18} = a_{19} = 1$ indicates that the first characteristic is recorded in Files 3, 8, and 9.

  (a) Formulate an integer programming model to determine which of the n files to search so that data on all of the characteristics are gathered in minimum searching time.
  (b) Explain how to modify your formulation if the search time for File j consists of T_j if File j is searched at all, plus t_{ij} if Characteristic i is obtained during the search.

40 *Delivery Truck Problem (Covering Problem).* The Droppit Parcel Company has five customer deliveries to make today. It must unload a shipment of weight 1 at Customer A, of weight 2 at Customer B, of weight 3 at Customer C, of weight 5 at Customer D, and of weight 8 at Customer E. The company has four different delivery vans available; Truck 1 has weight capacity 2, Truck 2 has weight capacity 6, Truck 3 has weight capacity 8, and Truck 4 has weight capacity 11. The cost of operating Truck j is c_j. Assume that a single truck cannot deliver to both Customers A and C; similarly, a single truck cannot deliver to both Customers B and D.

  (a) Formulate an integer programming model to determine the minimum cost allocation of delivery trucks for making all the shipments.
  (b) Show how to alter your formulation if there is an additional cost c_{ij} when the truck delivers to Customer i.
  (c) Show how to alter your formulation if a truck cannot make more than two deliveries during the day.
  (d) Explain the impact on the model formulation of imposing additional constraints on the truck routes.

41 *Trim Problem.* Consider the model in exercise 25 of Chap. 2. In that description, all customer demands were met and only one size jumbo roll was used.

  (a) Suppose, instead, that the Fine-Webb Paper Company can manufacture its customer orders from jumbo rolls of 50-, 60-, and 68-inch widths. There is a setup cost, however, for using each different jumbo size roll (denote these costs by K_{50}, K_{60}, and K_{68}, where the cost units have been chosen to be commensurate with the value of trim loss). Show how to alter the formulation in exercise 27, Chap. 2, to account for the possibility of using different size jumbo rolls.
  (b) Suppose, instead, that the Fine-Webb Paper Company can ship each customer an amount within 20% of the order quantity; hence, the company need manufacture as few as 88 reels of 22-inch width, but may manufacture as many as 132 reels. The foreman wants a schedule that uses no more than two different combinations (ordinarily, a linear programming solution would select three

different combinations, since there are three linear constraints). Show how to formulate an optimization model satisfying these restrictions.

42 *Trim Problem.* Consider the problem described in exercise 25 of Chap. 2. Assume that each inch of trim waste costs Fine-Webb c. Suppose that each different combination schedule also incurs a setup cost K. The company is permitted to ship within $\pm 10\%$ of the customers' orders (for example, the company can supply at least 99 but no more than 121 reels of 22-inch width). Formulate a model that selects combinations and the quantity to be run from each selected combination to minimize total cost.

43 The Mini Manufacturing Company produces four kinds of items. Let D_{kt} be the demand requirement in Period t for Item k, where $k = 1, 2, 3, 4$, and $t = 1, 2, \ldots, T$; assume each D_{kt} is integer-valued. Let x_{kt} denote the production level of Item k in Period t. Assume that all demand must be met each period, but it is possible to produce for inventory in one period to meet demand requirements in subsequent periods. Let $c_{kt}x_{kt}$ be the production cost associated with x_{kt}, and h_k be the inventory holding cost per unit of Item k held at the end of a period. (Assume inventory at the beginning of Period 1 is $I > 0$.) So far, the situation for each product resembles the production and inventory model in Sec. 8.3. There is an additional constraint, however, that at most only one type of item can be produced during each period.

(a) Formulate an optimization model taking account of this production limitation.
*(b) Formulate an appropriate dynamic programming recursion.

*44 Show how the variable cost structure in the inventory and production scheduling model of exercise 39, Chap. 8, can be characterized within an integer programming version of the problem.

*45 Show how the variable cost structure in the inventory model of exercise 8, Chap. 9, can be characterized within an integer programming version of the problem.

*46 *Quadratic Assignment Problem.* The Ireson Engineering Company serves its industrial clients by advising on the layout of plants and office buildings. A typical problem of this sort involves a new plant that has been zoned into n different work areas. Each area is to be the location of one of n different production facilities. If Facility 1 is assigned, for example, to Work Area 3, and Facility 2 is assigned, for example, to Work Area 5, the arrangement gives rise to the cost $c_{13;25}$. The cost is due to the amount of "traffic" in materials and personnel flowing between Facilities 1 and 2 and the distance between Work Areas 3 and 5. (Since there are n^2 *pairings* of facilities to work areas, there are altogether n^4 cost coefficients $c_{ij;kl}$). Formulate a cost minimization model that assigns facilities to locations. (*Hint:* the objective function is quadratic.)

47 A shop supervisor, Hugo Furst, has to schedule N jobs to be processed on a single machine. Job j requires processing time p_j, and has been promised for delivery by date d_j. (The jobs have been ordered so that $d_1 \le d_2 \le \cdots \le d_N$.) If Job j is not manufactured by its due date, then Hugo's company suffers a loss of u_j, irrespective of how late the job is completed. Formulate an optimization model indicating how Hugo should sequence the jobs on the machine to minimize the total loss to his

company. (*Hint:* define a decision variable for each job that indicates whether or not the job is scheduled to be completed by its due date; assume that those jobs that are completed on time are sequenced in the order of their due date.)

48 Ms. Ann Thrope, the personnel director for the Cal. Amity Insurance Company, a West Coast firm, has been asked to recommend five employees who will comprise a nucleus staff that will manage a new branch office in Oregon. She has selected from her files ten possible candidates. Each of the five jobs to be staffed has three different requirements relating to experience, accounting skill and sales ability. Let r_{ij} be the desired minimal level of competence for Skill i, where $i = 1, 2, 3$, and Job j, where $j = 1, 2, \ldots, 5$. Assume that the supervisors of the ten candidates have provided Ms. Thrope with rating scores s_{ik} for each Skill i and each Candidate k. She realizes that it may not be possible for her to make a selection that will provide the desired minimum level of competence for every skill in every job. Hence she is willing to settle for a selection that comes as close as possible to the desired skill levels.

(a) Formulate an optimization model that selects five of the candidates such that for all jobs and all skills the maximum *deficiency* between any desired skill level and the skill level of the assigned individual is as small as possible.

(b) Formulate a model to select five of the candidates so as to minimize the sum of the *deficiencies* between the desired skill levels and the skill levels of the assigned individuals, where the sum is taken over all jobs and all skills. Show how to modify your formulation if the deficiency between the desired skill level and the attained skill level for Skill i and Job j is weighted by $c_{ij} > 0$ per unit of deficiency, where $i = 1, 2, 3$, and $j = 1, 2, \ldots, 5$.

*49 *Critical Path Scheduling.* Consider the Swift Building Company case described in Sec. 7.5 and displayed in Fig. 7.10. Suppose each job requires a specified amount of a scarce resource, such as labor time, per period the job is in process. For example, given that it takes t_A units of time to complete Job A, assume that r_A units of labor are required each week that Job A is being completed. Assume that R_p is the maximum amount of labor available in Week p for all jobs in process.

(a) Formulate the problem as a mathematical optimization model. Use the data in Fig. 7.10. The objective is still to complete the entire project as early as possible. [*Hint:* introduce zero-one variables that indicate the week a job starts. Express the time a job starts in terms of these variables, and rewrite the precedence ordering constraints (2) through (6) in Sec. 7.5 accordingly.] Explain how to modify your formulation if the labor time needed for a job differed from one week to the next while it was being completed.

(b) Show how to modify your formulation in part (a) if there also is a second resource restriction. For example, assume that s_A units of this other resource are required each week that Job A is being completed, and that S_p is the maximum amount of this resource available in Week p for all jobs in process.

*50 *Critical Path Scheduling.* Consider the Swift Building Company case described in Sec. 7.5 and displayed in Fig. 7.10. Suppose there are several alternative ways to construct the entire project. Specifically, instead of Job D, the company can use either Job G or Job H. If it uses Job G, the immediate precedessors for Job C are A and G, for Job D is B, and for Job E is B. The other data in Fig. 7.10 are unchanged. If the company uses Job H, there is no immediate predecessor for Job H, the immediate predecessor for Job E is B, and for Job F is C, E, and H. The other data in Fig. 7.10 are unchanged. Revise the formulation (1) through (6) to account for the choice possibility between Jobs D, G, and H. The objective is still to complete the entire project as early as possible.

51 Consider a discrete programming problem in which x_1 and x_2 are integer-valued variables (not necessarily nonnegative). Let $M > 0$ be a sufficiently large integer such that in any feasible solution, $|x_1| < M$ and $|x_2| < M$. Show how to formulate the model containing the stipulation that either $x_1 \geq 0$ or $x_2 \geq 0$ *but not both*. (*Hint:* if $x_1 \geq 0$, then $x_2 \leq -1$, and vice versa.)

52 Consider a discrete programming problem in which x_1, x_2, and x_3 are integer-valued variables (not necessarily nonnegative). Let M be a sufficiently large integer such that $|x_1| < M$, $|x_2| < M$, and $|x_3| < M$ in any feasible solution. Show how to formulate the model containing the stipulation that if either $x_1 \geq 0$ or $x_2 \geq 0$, or both, then $x_3 \geq 0$.

*53 *Machine (Job-Shop) Scheduling Problem.* Suppose that three items are to be sequenced through n machines. Each item must be processed first on Machine 1, then on Machine 2, ..., and finally on Machine n. The sequence of jobs may be different for each machine. Let t_{ij} be the time required to perform the work on Item i by Machine j; assume each t_{ij} is an integer. The objective is to minimize the total work span to complete all the items.

   (a) Formulate the problem as an integer programming model. Write the model in detail for $n = 4$. (*Hint:* one approach is to let x_{ij} represent the time at which Item i begins processing by Machine j. In this formulation, you must make sure that no two items occupy the same machine at the same time, and that an item does not start processing on Machine j + 1 until the work is completed on Machine j. Another approach is to let a zero-one variable x_{ijk} correspond to assigning Item i to the kth position of the sequence on Machine j.)
   (b) Indicate the simplifications, if any, that are possible when you stipulate that the items are to be processed in the same sequence on each machine. (This can be shown to be an optimal policy if there are two or three machines; in the case of two machines, there is a simple algorithm for finding an optimal solution.)

*54 *Machine (Job-Shop) Scheduling Problem.* In exercise 53, stipulate that the items are to be processed in the same sequence on each of the n machines. Devise a branch-and-bound technique of solution. (*Hint:* given a partial assignment of items to Position 1, 2, ..., k of the sequence, a lower bound on the total time span to complete all the jobs can be found in terms of when the kth job is completed on each machine, and of the sum of the processing times on each machine required by the jobs remaining to be scheduled.)

*55 *Traveling Salesman Problem.* A salesman Rollin D. Haye wants to visit each of n cities, starting and ending at City 1. He visits no other city twice. Let $c_{ij} > 0$ designate the distance between City i and City j. Let $x_{ij} = 1$ if Haye's route includes traveling from City i to City j, and let $x_{ij} = 0$ otherwise. Show that a feasible routing is equivalent to satisfying all the constraints of an assignment problem as well as the constraints

$$u_i - u_j + n x_{ij} \le n - 1 \begin{cases} \text{for} & i = 2, 3, \ldots, n \\ \text{and} & j = 2, 3, \ldots, n \end{cases} \quad (i \ne j)$$

where each u_k is a nonnegative integer. How many integer variables and linear constraints are required by this formulation? Write the model in full for $n = 4$, and exhibit the appropriate objective function.

*56 Devise a branch-and-bound algorithm for the traveling salesman problem as described in exercise 55. Use the assignment problem as the initial relaxation, and devise appropriate descendant relaxations that restrict the assignment problem, motivated by the stipulation that a solution must be a feasible route.

57 *Fixed Charge Problem.* Consider the model described in exercise 6. Devise a branch-and-bound algorithm for solving such problems.

58 Consider the piecewise linear function $c(x)$ in Fig. 11.5, and suppose that $c(x)$ appears in the objective function of an optimizing model; assume $x \le 6$.

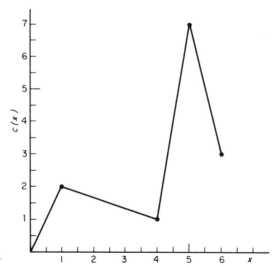

FIGURE 11.5

(a) Explain why the model can be transformed into an equivalent problem by substituting for $c(x)$ the summation

$$0y_1 + 2y_2 + 1y_3 + 7y_4 + 3y_5,$$

and for x the summation

$$0y_1 + 1y_2 + 4y_3 + 5y_4 + 6y_5,$$

where $0 \le y_j \le 1$, for $j = 1, 2, \ldots, 5$, and stipulating that either only one

$y_k = 1$ or at most two adjacent variables y_k and y_{k+1} are positive, where $y_k + y_{k+1} = 1$.

(b) Formulate a branch-and-bound approach where the partitioning in *Step 4* recognizes the restriction that one, or at most, two adjacent weights sum to 1. (*Hint:* consider the alternatives

$$\sum_{j=1}^{h} y_j = 1 \quad \text{or} \quad \sum_{j=h}^{5} y_j = 1 \quad \text{for } 1 \le h \le 5.)$$

CONTENTS

CHAPTER 12

Introduction to Stochastic Programming Models

12.1 IMPACT OF UNCERTAINTY

All the previous examples in this book have assumed that the data required by a model are known exactly. But in real life, since you never know *all* these values with perfect certainty, you may ask distrustfully, "Are the preceding deterministic models and techniques really practical?" Rest assured that they are. But the more important and harder question is, "When?" The discussion below will help you learn *when* to apply what model.

In applying operations research to a real managerial decision-making problem, you always should ascertain

(i) *What uncertainties must be faced, and how they may influence the selection of an optimal decision.*
(ii) *Whether a given mathematical model takes suitable account of these uncertainties.*

Below are two simplified case studies that clarify how you proceed in answering (i) and (ii) in actual situations.

New plant expansion. The Flake Out Company, a breakfast food processor, is deciding whether to expand its present plant or build a new plant. The firm's president, Gaston Booz, believes that an important factor in this decision is his firm's share of the market during the next ten years. Assume that Flake Out's planning staff is fairly confident about the other pertinent data, and finds that the structure of the production and marketing processes can be mathematically represented by a linear model resembling those found in Chap. 2. Booz wants to be sure that the economic analysis of the decision explicitly reflects the element of uncertainty about the company's future market share.

Bear in mind that the critical management decision is *where* to add productive capacity. The values of the other variables calculated by the model, such as the sales quantities of individual products, the average and peak levels of inventory, and the required amounts of raw food supplies, are *assumed* to be of less interest, although they are used in the analysis of the major decision. Consequently, it is quite reasonable for the economic study to proceed as follows.

With a deterministic linear model, find the best expansion alternative for each of several possible and reasonable values for Flake Out's future market share. If the results show that the optimal decision is insensitive to the market-share parameter, the linear model has *adequately* dealt with the impact of uncertainty. If, on the contrary, the decision proves to be highly sensitive to market share, then further study is required. In particular, for each major decision, evaluate the resultant profit for several possible market shares. This may indicate that although the optimal expansion decision is sensitive to market share, the actual profit level is not. If profit also varies significantly with market share, however, then it will be necessary for the analysis to include, in one way or another, a judgment of the relative likelihood (probability) of each possible market share. The company may choose to embark on further market research to narrow the range of this uncertainty prior to making a final expansion decision.

New computer facility. Now we turn to the second case study, which on the surface resembles the first one. The Hard Rock Company, a major producer of iron ore, has several dozen plants scattered throughout the United States. At its central headquarters the firm has four relatively small-scale computers that are used 70% of the time to prepare standard corporate accounting reports, and the rest of the time to perform calculations for special studies conducted by staff groups, such as the Operations Research Department. Although these special studies consume a significant fraction of time on an annual basis, their demands for computer time vary considerably from day to day and frequently occur in bunches. A number of small-scale computers are also located at the different plants; these machines produce plant accounting reports about 50% of the time, and the rest of the time service the needs of resident technical groups, such as the Industrial Engineering staff. Here, too, there is considerable day-to-day variation in work load.

The company's vice-president, Ken U. Diggit, who has corporate responsibility for all these computers, has observed that at least four or five days a month, and sometimes up to ten days, the computers seem overloaded both at headquarters and at the plants. Feeling sure this congestion results in costly and irritating delays in getting jobs processed, he wants to install at corporate headquarters, either a medium-scale computer to replace only the four small ones, or a large-scale computer to replace, in addition, several of the plants' machines.

Diggit realizes that his decision must recognize certain intangible factors, such as the relative merits of decentralized operations, but he wants to weigh these considerations against the possible advantages of a larger and economically more efficient piece of computing equipment. Further, he wants the new configuration of computers to eliminate, or at least drastically reduce, the problem of over-loading with all its ensuing delays and disruptions.

Several years ago, Diggit anticipated he would someday want to make this computer equipment decision, and started collecting data on all the jobs processed by the company's computers. Thus he knew, for example, how many hours of computer time were being spent at each location on processing payroll, keeping inventories, billing accounts receivable, etc. The computer manufacturers supplied him with the comparable amount of time required to process these same jobs on their medium- and large-scale computers.

Diggit asked the Operations Research Department whether it could help him analyze the situation. In fact, he had a rough description of a linear model. He thought the variables would be the annual frequency with which Job Type i is placed on Computer Type j; the coefficients of these variables would show the relative speed of each computer for each job; the constraints would indicate the total annual frequency for each Job Type i and the time available of each Computer Type j; and the objective function would contain the cost of processing Job Type i on Computer Type j.

Do you think Hard Rock's computer capacity expansion decision can be analyzed in the same way as Flake Out's plant capacity question? Is the impact of uncertainty the same? To both questions, the correct answer is "no." Here are the reasons why.

In the Flake Out example, annualized figures appropriately measure profit, because the company's market share, by definition, indicates the overall basis for the year's entire operations. In Hard Rock's situation, the same annualized approach would obscure the very *essence* of the congestion problem: the day-to-day variation in requirements for computer time. After all, under the current computer configuration all jobs are processed *eventually*—the extra capacity is needed to reduce the delays due to daily fluctuations. Thus, for an analytic model to be useful in this case, it *must* indicate the impact of the random elements in the operating environment. In other words, the approach must take daily phenomena into account to show how many jobs will be seriously delayed during a year's operation.

Introducing probabilities. The cases above referred to two approaches for dealing with uncertainty: testing solution sensitivity in deterministic models, and designing models containing probabilistic elements. The underlying theme for the rest of the book is how to introduce probability analysis into optimization models. Now uncertainties will be viewed as imperfect predictions to be charac-terized by probability distributions for the different possible events. Frequently, the resultant models will merely be more complicated versions of deterministic models and can be solved by the same numerical techniques. But this will not always be so. Sometimes you will be justified in substituting a single expected value in the deterministic version; but more often, in order to calculate solutions you will have to exploit the form of an *optimal* strategy, if this is not too difficult to find, or otherwise you will have to use an arbitrary, but reasonable form.

No matter what, you will see that probabilistic models are *inherently* harder to use than deterministic versions. First, there are new conceptual difficulties, such as the interpretation of the probabilities themselves and the meaning of optimality; these are discussed in Sec. 12.2. Second, there are new technical difficulties relating to the mathematics of optimization. To illustrate, even when a stochastic model is a straightforward generalization of a deterministic version, the computational burden increases, since you must consider each possible event instead of only a single estimate. Further, in stochastic models the criterion functions are typically nonlinear, so that the task of optimization is more complex. And third, there are increased data requirements for the specification of the probability distributions. For example, a manager may see that the price of his competitor's product fluctuates, but he may find it difficult to state a meaningful probability distribution for this variation.

Thus, aside from the intellectual curiosity engendered by stochastic phenomena, there would be limited interest in these probabilistic models were it not for their practical necessity in certain real decision-making situations.

The art of management science once more. Here we return to the question, "How do you select the right model for a particular application?" Regrettably, no textbook can furnish you with an infallible set of rules—you will have to rely on experience, mature judgment, and continuing analysis.

In real applications, of course, you can often get expert advice from other people based on their own past experience and mature judgment. There is some solace in that thought. But if you have managerial responsibility, then never forget that you—not your advisors—must bear the ultimate responsibility for your decisions, good or bad. Consequently, if you want to make effective managerial use of the powerful analytic tools in this book, there is no good substitute for educating your own judgment.

Study guide. The remainder of this chapter and the next will show you how to generalize many of the examples in earlier chapters to include random elements. At the same time, you will see a few important general propositions about optimal solutions to stochastic models. Finally, the material will demonstrate the applicability of techniques such as linear and dynamic programming for finding numerical solutions. These two chapters, then, link the first part of the book with what is to come. It is important for you to realize, however, that many of the models in these introductory chapters are really too general. They do not sufficiently exploit a model's special structure or take advantage of the form of an optimal solution. Consequently, they often obscure the fundamental nature of an optimal solution and are computationally inefficient. For these reasons, you will want to study the models in subsequent chapters, where special structure is exploited.

As you continue your reading, you will find it helpful to answer two questions about each stochastic model:

1. What is an optimal policy for a deterministic version of the model?
2. How much information about the probability distributions is required to state an optimal solution?

Conscientious effort to answer these two questions for each example will greatly assist you in gaining the fundamental insights to be had from stochastic models.

12.2 DECISION-MAKING IN
AN UNCERTAIN ENVIRONMENT

From the earlier chapters of this book, you have become fairly well acquainted with model building and optimizing techniques for deterministic problems. In particular, you understand that when you solve deterministic linear and dynamic programming problems, you know exactly what your decisions will be and precisely what future effect they will have. For example, in a deterministic planning model, if you decide to process 10 units of raw material, then you know exactly how many items will be produced for sale. Or, in a deterministic inventory model, if you choose to purchase five dozen units for the next six months and two dozen units for the following six months, then as a result, you can forecast precisely what the inventory levels will be for the 12-month horizon.

But suppose instead that if you decide to process 10 units of raw material, the yield may be any one of several possible numbers of items. Or if you purchase dozens of units as specified above, then the future inventory levels depend on the amounts of demand that actually materialize. In other words, consider the impact on your immediate and future decision choices if you cannot know for certain what will happen as a result of your actions.

When uncertainties do impinge on your choice, you first must resolve the question of what is an *optimal* decision. We elaborate on the question in this section.

If some decisions have to be made now but others can be deferred until several of the *uncertainties* disappear, you also must consider the possibility of employing a **contingency plan** or **strategy.** In the purchasing example above, you may want to decide to order five dozen units this period, and then devise a "set of ordering instructions" to be used over the remaining periods. These rules would state how much to purchase given the *observed* demands and the orders in previous periods. Thus, you do not know exactly how much will be ordered after this period, but only what you will purchase conditional on the actual ordering and demand history when the future purchase decisions must be made. In the paragraphs below, we elaborate further on the notion of a decision strategy.

Expected value. If you have had an opportunity to apply any of the models in the first half of this book to an actual planning situation, you will have discovered that stating a single objective function to be optimized is merely a convenient way to select a solution when there are a myriad of feasible possibilities.

Executives experienced in applying operations research know quite well that such a solution is rarely optimal in any absolute, "all things considered" sense. In fact, almost always such a solution is manually adjusted to provide a better fit to reality, or the model specifications themselves are altered and a new "optimal" solution is found.

In solving decision models containing uncertainties, we continue in the same spirit and state only a single objective function to be optimized. But we caution here at the outset that in an actual application, you should investigate various operating characteristics of a solution that is selected by a single optimization criterion. You may have to adjust this solution or modify the model before being able to successfully implement the result.

For most of the models that you will study, uncertainty will affect the actual or realized value of the economic criterion. We will consistently employ the *expected value* of the economic criterion as the objective function to be optimized. In recent years, scholars of decision-theory have devised several ways of justifying the use of the expected value as the sole criterion for an optimal choice. Many recent texts in statistical analysis present these arguments. As fascinating as the subject is, we do not pursue the topic here, because regardless of whether or not you find these justifications convincing, we still are going to use expected value as the objective function in the optimization models. (We do, however, temper this intransigent attitude by showing in several chapters how you can calculate other operating characteristics of a selected policy.)

Calculating the types of expected values that are used in this text is really not much more complicated than finding the mean of a probability distribution. To demonstrate this claim, we review the ideas below to familiarize you with the process for when you read the subsequent examples.

Suppose X is a random variable that can have any of the values $n = 0, 1, 2, \ldots, N$. Let $P[X = n]$ designate the probability that X takes the value n. Then the expected value of the random variable X is

$$(1) \qquad E[X] \equiv \sum_{n=0}^{N} n \cdot P[X = n] \quad \text{(expected value of } X\text{)}.$$

If X can equal *any* nonnegative integer with positive probability, then we will use the symbol ∞ instead of N in (1); in this case (as well as for all summations over an infinite number of terms), we postulate that the expected value is a finite number.

Next, suppose we want to compute the expected value of the random variable X^2. This is simply

$$(2) \qquad E[X^2] \equiv \sum_{n=0}^{N} n^2 \cdot P[X = n] \quad \text{(expected value of } X^2\text{)}.$$

In general, if we wish to calculate the expected value of a function of X, which we denote as $f(X)$, then we will compute

$$(3) \qquad E[f(X)] \equiv \sum_{n=0}^{N} f(n) \cdot P[X = n] \quad \text{[expected value of } f(X)\text{]}.$$

Hopefully, you remember this much from your previous training in probability theory.

Now let us apply (3) to an example containing an economic criterion function. A simple, but instructive, illustration is the expected cost associated with an inventory stockage rule for a one-period horizon. Let D denote a random variable representing the amount of customer demand in a single period. Assume the possible values for D are $d = 0, 1, 2, \ldots, N$, and the associated probabilities are $P[D = d]$. Suppose that you purchase y items to stock for customer demand, where each item costs c dollars. If any of these items are left over at the end of the period, you incur a holding cost of h per unit. (Assume there is no salvage value for items left over.) But if demand D exceeds the amount you order y, then you incur a penalty cost p per item short. Thus, the actual cost in a period depends on not only how much you order but also what value of demand really occurs. Since you have to order y before knowing demand D, it is reasonable to assess the effect of your decision in terms of *expected* cost.

Specifically, let $f(d \mid y)$ represent the actual cost when demand $D = d$, given that you order y. Then

$$(4) \quad f(d \mid y) = \begin{cases} cy + h \cdot (y - d) & \text{if } d \leq y \quad \text{(demand is less than amount ordered)} \\ cy + p \cdot (d - y) & \text{if } d > y \quad \text{(demand exceeds amount ordered).} \end{cases}$$

Hence the expected cost, given that you order y and $y < N$, is

$$(5) \quad E[f(D \mid y)] = \sum_{d=0}^{N} f(d \mid y) \cdot P[D = d]$$

$$(6) \quad = \sum_{d=0}^{y} f(d \mid y) \cdot P[D = d] + \sum_{d=y+1}^{N} f(d \mid y) \cdot P[D = d]$$

$$= \sum_{d=0}^{y} [cy + h \cdot (y - d)] \cdot P[D = d]$$

$$(7) \quad + \sum_{d=y+1}^{N} [cy + p \cdot (d - y)] \cdot P[D = d].$$

The equation in (5) is simply the definition of expected value; the equation (6) follows by breaking the summation in (5) into two parts, one for demand less than the amount ordered, and one for demand exceeding the amount ordered; the third equality (7) is simply a substitution of the formulas in (4) for $f(d \mid y)$.

You can carry the algebra further. Notice in (7) that the term cy appears inside both summations. Therefore, the amount cy is multiplied by the probability $P[D = d]$ for every possible value d; since the sum of the probabilities $P[D = d]$ over *every* d equals 1, you can write

$$(8) \quad \left. \begin{array}{l} E[f(D \mid y)] = cy + \sum_{d=0}^{y} h \cdot (y - d) \cdot P[D = d] \\[1em] + \sum_{d=y+1}^{N} p \cdot (d - y) \cdot P[D = d] \end{array} \right\} \text{(expected cost, given } y\text{).}$$

The formula in (8) has an important direct interpretation: given that you stock y, the expected cost equals the sum of the purchase cost, the expected holding cost, and the expected penalty cost.

We have derived (8) in a straightforward fashion using only "first principles" of expectations. But in building decision-making models such as this, it is far more convenient to start immediately with the statement in (8). Consequently, we will adopt the practice of initially writing the objective function as a sum of the component expected costs (and revenues). When you are in doubt as to whether the objective function has been written correctly, then make an analysis parallel to the one above. Start with the value of the economic criterion exhibited as a function of the random variables, for given levels of the decision variables. Then take the expected value of this function over the possible values for the random variables, and simplify the results.

Now we analyze a specific decision problem using an expected value criterion to see the impact of uncertainty on making an optimal choice.

Optimal decisions. Consider once again the plant expansion problem of the Flake Out Company discussed in the previous section. The two alternatives are to expand the present facility or build a new plant. For either decision, the resultant profit depends on the firm's future share of the market. Suppose Booz, the president, assesses the probability of his firm's maintaining its present 35% market share as $\frac{1}{2}$, and the probabilities of 30% and 40% shares as $\frac{1}{8}$ and $\frac{3}{8}$, respectively. The corresponding annual profit values are shown in Fig. 12.1.

Share of Market	President's Assessed Probability of Share	Annual Profit ($ Millions)	
		Expand Facility	Build New Plant
30%	$\frac{1}{8}$	90	50
35%	$\frac{1}{2}$	100	100
40%	$\frac{3}{8}$	130	150

FIGURE 12.1. Flake-Out Company.

If you were this company's president, how would you decide between the two alternatives? How calamitous would it be if you built a new plant and the market share then fell to 30%, so that the company made only $50 million instead of $90 million? How embarrassing would it be if you expanded the facility and then the market share increased to 40%, so that the firm made $130 million but could otherwise have made $150 million?

In situations like this, when there are only a few alternative actions, it is feasible to calculate the probability distribution of the possible objective-function values and then examine the relative merits of each action. But in most problems we will at least initially recommend an action that optimizes the expected value of the economic criterion. For the two alternatives in Fig. 12.1, the expected values are:

(9)
Expand facility: expected profit $= (90)\frac{1}{8} + (100)\frac{1}{2} + (130)\frac{3}{8} = 110$

Build new plant: expected profit $= (50)\frac{1}{8} + (100)\frac{1}{2} + (150)\frac{3}{8} = 112.5.$

In terms of expected profit, building a new plant is slightly better.

You well may conclude that the small difference between the expected values in (9) does not really convey the true qualitative difference between the probable economic effects of the two decisions. If that is your feeling, then let this example serve as a lesson. Whenever you employ an objective function that for the purpose of comparison reduces an entire probability distribution of economic outcomes to a single number, at least examine other characteristics of the solution to test the reasonableness of the recommendation.

Uncertain actions. In the various dynamic deterministic models treated in previous chapters, you can predict with perfect certainty the precise sequence of decisions that is implied by any given policy. For example, in a production scheduling model, where demands are known exactly over the horizon, you can trace the precise production levels period by period. But if, instead, the demands can be described only by means of a probability distribution, then ordinarily you cannot say for certain what the production levels are beyond the current decision.

Suppose in this production example that you employ a dynamic policy that specifies the amount to be produced for *each* level of entering inventory at any period. Then such a policy actually induces a probability distribution on the future production decisions.

To illustrate, let $i = 0, 1, 2, 3$ be the possible levels of entering inventory at any period. Let $x(i)$ be the current production decision given i, where

(10) $x(0) = x(1) = x(2) = 3$ $x(3) = 0.$

Hence, each period you produce 3 unless entering inventory equals 3. Suppose in any period the amount demanded is described by the probability distribution

(11) $D_t = 2$ with probability $\frac{1}{2}$ $D_t = 3$ with probability $\frac{1}{2}$.

If entering inventory in the current period is 2, then current production is 3, and production in the next period will be either 0, with probability $\frac{1}{2}$ (if the current demand is 2), or 3, with probability $\frac{1}{2}$ (if the current demand is 3).

Continuing the analysis in the same fashion, production in the period *after* next will be either 0, with probability $\frac{1}{4}$ (if the current and next period's demands are 3 and 2, respectively), or 3, with probability $(1 - \frac{1}{4} = \frac{3}{4})$.

This line of reasoning leads to the important insight that even though the component decisions implied by the strategy (10) are deterministic, they actually will occur over time in a random fashion because of the uncertain elements (11) in the structure of the model. As a result, the associated costs over the horizon are described by a complex joint probability distribution.

In most dynamic models containing probabilistic elements, you will need to treat future decisions so as to reflect their future uncertainty. With this in mind, you should always carefully examine any such model for the specific assumptions as to what information about previous values of the random variables is available each time a decision is to be made. In constructing a mathematical model it is easy to make an error in describing what is typically an intertwined time sequence of random events and the subsequent decisions that are based, in part, on the actual outcome of the earlier events.

▶ Occasionally, the optimal policy for a model calls for the decision-maker himself to introduce randomness as part of his strategy. Of course, issue can be taken about the particular structural details in models giving rise to this type of solution, but there hardly is reason to object to such **randomized strategies** per se, since, as you have just seen, there already is randomness in the actions induced by the uncertain elements.

The following hypothetical example shows how a randomized strategy can be optimal. The manager of the *Toute de Suite* Bakery has found that the daily demand for one of his specialty cakes is described by the probability distribution

(i) $P[\text{no cakes}] = \dfrac{1}{6}$ $P[\text{one cake}] = \dfrac{1}{6}$ $P[\text{two cakes}] = \dfrac{2}{3}$.

Assume that the demand on any day is independent of demands on previous days. Each cake costs c to bake and must be thrown away if it is not sold at the end of the day. The manager does not want to make too many cakes as c is large; but still he wants to satisfy a reasonable level of demand. Accordingly, he formulates his decision problem as: minimize expected baking cost subject to the constraint that the probability of meeting the total daily demand is at least $\frac{1}{3}$.

It might appear that the optimal solution is to bake one cake at a cost of $1c$, for then total demand is met with probability $(\frac{1}{6} + \frac{1}{6} = \frac{1}{3})$. However, suppose the manager uses the following **randomized decision rule:** bake no cakes with probability $\frac{4}{5}$ and bake two cakes with probability $\frac{1}{5}$. He then still meets total demand with probability $[(\frac{4}{5})\frac{1}{6} + (\frac{1}{5})1 = \frac{1}{3}]$, and what is more, his expected cost is $[(\frac{4}{5})0c + (\frac{1}{5})2c = .4c]$, which is less than the cost of $1c$ for the nonrandomized strategy. This randomized rule is optimal.

Suppose that, instead of imposing a probability constraint, he formulates his decision problem as: minimize baking cost subject to satisfying, on the average, at least $\frac{1}{3}$ of expected daily demand. From (i), expected daily demand is $\frac{3}{2}$, so that the constraint is to sell at least $\frac{1}{2}$ a cake a day, on the average. Once again, if he uses a deterministic strategy of baking one cake, on the average he sells $[(\frac{1}{6})0 + (\frac{1}{6})1 + (\frac{2}{3})1 = \frac{5}{6}]$ cakes per day, which is in excess of the minimal constraint, $\frac{1}{2}$. His optimal strategy is to randomize: bake no cakes with probability $\frac{2}{5}$ and bake one cake with probability $\frac{3}{5}$. Then he sells $[(\frac{2}{5})0 + (\frac{3}{5})\frac{5}{6} = \frac{1}{2}]$ cakes per day, on the average, and the expected cost is $[(\frac{2}{5})0c + (\frac{3}{5})1c = .6c]$, which is less than $1c$.

Generally, whenever an optimization model contains constraints on the probabilities of events or their expected values, an optimal solution may indicate randomization.   ◀

Multiperiod objective function. In a dynamic model, where you have to evaluate a stream of returns, each component of which is random, the objective function will be the expected value analogue to the approaches in the first half of this book.

To illustrate, let R_t designate the return in Period t of a dynamic model. When there are uncertain events, a decision strategy followed over the planning horizon gives rise to a joint probability distribution on the elements of the returns stream $(R_1, R_2, R_3, \ldots, R_N)$. Suppose we postulate that the objective function is the expected value of the stream:

(12) $$E[\text{return}] \equiv E[R_1 + R_2 + R_3 + \ldots + R_N].$$

We assume that the value in (12) is finite.

The expected value in (12) is taken over the *joint* probability distribution of $(R_1, R_2, R_3, \ldots, R_N)$. We can simplify the expression by employing a Fundamental Theorem of Random Variables: *the expected value of a sum always equals the sum of the expected values.* Consequently

(13) $$E[\text{return}] = E[R_1] + E[R_2] + E[R_3] + \ldots + E[R_N].$$

In (13), each expectation is taken over the *marginal* probability distribution of the displayed random variable.

Specifying probability distributions. The stochastic models in this book assume that the decision-maker can state probability distributions to describe the elements of uncertainty in the model. Loosely put, the decision-maker must be able to assign nonnegative numerical weights to each possible event such that: (i) If an event is certain, its associated weight equals 1. (ii) If two events A and B are mutually exclusive, the weight of the event "either A or B" equals the sum of the weights for each of the events A and B. Since most elementary texts on probability theory discuss how to characterize a probability distribution in this way, we give no further elucidation here. What is more, for the purpose of this book, nothing else really *has* to be said, as the models to be treated merely apply the weights, employing the type of elementary probability calculations you find in an introductory text. Nevertheless, we do add a few comments on the interpretation of the weights and how a decision-maker might go about assigning specific numerical values, so that you have a better appreciation of these models' intended meaning.

Over the years, probability theory scholars have suggested a variety of interpretations for the weights. The most widespread notion is the *relative frequency* interpretation. In optimization-oriented models, a more insightful view, however, is that probability assessments reflect the decision-maker's state of mind. To illustrate what this means, recall the market-share probabilities in Fig. 12.1 that were specified by the president of the Flake Out Company. These weights are really a quantification of the president's current judgment about the future, and guide him in making an immediate decision (on whether to expand an existing plant or build a new one). For another illustration, consider the Hard Rock Financial V.P. who was evaluating whether to install a new large-scale computer. The historical data he collected, showing congestion, are of decision-making relevance only if he feels that they embody his judgments about future conditions.

Much has been written recently on the issues and techniques of deriving probability weights that reflect the decision-maker's personal prognosis. The topic is usually referred to as *statistical decision theory*, and sometimes by the more restricted term *Bayesian analysis*. Despite the subject's importance and relevance, delving into the details here would only be too distracting from the main task of analyzing optimizing models. But as a pragmatic matter, essentially, you can utilize four approaches to obtain these probability distributions:

1. *Use introspection.*
2. *Employ historical data.*
3. *Find convenient approximations.*
4. *State descriptive axioms.*

Most often, you would apply two or more of these approaches in combination.

To illustrate these, consider the Ryton Company, a wholesale jobber of ball-point pens, that wants to install a computerized scientific inventory control system for stocking about 1500 products. In particular, once a week the computer is to update the inventory status of each item, and if the stock is too low, to indicate that Ryton should send a replenishment order to a manufacturer. Since there is considerable weekly variation in customer demand for each item, the scientific replenishment rules are to be derived from probabilistic inventory models like those you will study in Chap. 14. These models require specifying the probability distributions of weekly demand for each item.

To begin, suppose Ryton has little or no historical demand data. This situation sometimes arises because of insufficient records, and frequently because an item to be stocked is a new product that has no demand history. Then Ryton's inventory manager has no recourse other than to use Approach 1, applying whatever experience she can bring to bear in quantifying her judgments. As the inventory system operates for a while and demand data are accumulated, she can then apply the numerical techniques of Bayesian analysis to update her probability assessments.

Now assume, instead, that this company has customer demand data for 6 to 18 months back, depending on whether an item has a fast or slow turnover. These quantities have been manually posted on makeshift record cards. Then Ryton can combine Approaches 1 and 2 by summarizing between one and two years' weekly demand data into an historical distribution for each item and by applying judgmental corrections to reflect the management's future assessment of demand. You should realize, however, that in most actual situations, using historical data to compute empirical distributions is ordinarily not feasible; usually not enough data are available, and even when they are, the expense of computing so many individual demand distributions is prohibitive.

Hence, Approach 3 is added as a modification to Approaches 1 and 2. To illustrate, the inventory manager may have calculated the empirical mean, and perhaps the variance of each item's weekly demands, making whatever judgmental corrections she deems necessary. Then in a computerized stochastic inventory control model, she may employ, as an approximation, a Normal distribution having such a mean and variance. These values would be systematically updated by the computer as new demand experience accumulates.

Approach 4 is a more sophisticated version of Approach 3. The inventory manager first chooses a model describing the *process* by which demands are generated. For example, the model may include the total number of Ryton's customers, the chance that any one of these will want an item during a week, the pattern of order sizes for a customer, etc. Obviously, this method is more complicated than Approach 3, but it can be effective when the resultant analysis provides an explicit form for the probability distribution of demand, such as a Poisson or a binomial distribution. Then the historical data and judgmental corrections are used to obtain the few parameters needed to describe the derived probability law.

In conclusion, uncertainty influences stochastic models in two ways. The first way is the direct effect stemming from the random phenomena explicitly accounted for by the model. The second is the indirect impact coming from the process of specifying the probability weights to describe the phenomena. For the most part, the rest of this book concentrates only on the direct effect.

Where do we go from here? In the next section, we show how, in a complex dynamic decision process, you can go astray should you try to ignore randomness by using an expected value in lieu of the random variable itself. We dub this mistake the *Fallacy of Averages*. It implies that in a linear programming planning model, for example, you usually are not justified in simply substituting expected values for the problem's coefficients when they really are random. The rest of the chapter explores what you can do in linear programming problems when some of the coefficients are characterized by probability distributions.

12.3 FALLACY OF AVERAGES

The following case is a simplified example of an actual decision problem dealing with uncertain elements. It demonstrates how you can be dangerously misled by using average values in a model appropriate for a deterministic situation.

The Galactic Reaper Company, which manufactures farm machinery, is planning to construct a new plant to build its latest equipment, a combine for harvesting, threshing, and cleaning grain. Five major tasks must be completed in order to put the plant into full operation:

A. Erect plant building.
B. Complete final design of combine model.
C. Expand nucleus labor force to full-scale production size.
D. Install manufacturing equipment.
E. Debug prototype models.

Let $t_A, t_B, \ldots, t_E$ be the number of periods required for Tasks A, B, ..., E. A period consists of three months. Assume that these tasks must be performed in the sequence indicated by Fig. 12.2. For example, both Tasks A and B can be started immediately. Both Tasks C and D can be started as soon as Task A is completed. Task E can start when *both* Tasks B and D are finished. The plant is in full-scale production as soon as *both* Tasks C and E are completed. (The network diagram is identical to Fig. 7.13, p. 202, used to illustrate critical path scheduling. Although the explanation of the case here is complete, you may find it helpful to review Sec. 7.5.)

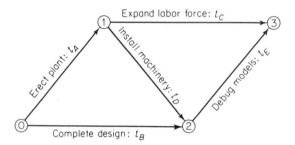

FIGURE 12.2. Galactic Reaper Company Example.

If the values of t_A, t_B, ..., t_E were known with perfect certainty, then the total span of time required to put the plant into operation could be determined by finding the length of a longest route from Node 0 to Node 3 in the network of Fig. 12.2. Several of these values are uncertain, however. Relying in part on past experience in constructing plants, Galactic Reaper's president, Justin Tyme, has estimated the probability of each possible value, as shown in Fig. 12.3. Thus, it is equally likely that t_B be either 2, 3, or 4 periods (that is, 6, 9, or 12 months); similar statements hold for t_C and t_E. The times for t_A and t_D are known exactly. The president believes that there is complete independence among the random events.

When each random event takes its smallest value, the total time span is 4 periods; and when each takes its largest value, the span is 7 periods. Thus the range of completion times is between 12 and 21 months. If each random event takes its average value ($t_B = 3$, $t_C = 3$, $t_E = 2$), then the time span is 5 periods (15 months).

Justin Tyme feels that there is a significant competitive advantage to having the plant in operation as soon as possible. His estimates of the incremental profit impact for different completion times of less than 7 periods are shown in Fig. 16.4. Being concerned about the drop in profit that occurs if the completion time stretches out to 6 or 7 periods, he considers the possibility of hiring an experienced manager, Miles Stone, to act as special assistant to supervise the construction project. He believes that the extra attention such a person could provide would reduce the *total* time span by 1 period in *any* event. That is, even if the span would have been 4 periods, Stone would cut the time to 3 periods, and likewise for any other possible total span between 5 and 7 periods. The total cost of hiring this manager is $20,000. If the president knew for certain that the total span would be 4 or 5 periods, then he would decide against adding Stone, since the gain of $10,000 would not offset the additional cost of $20,000. The opposite would be true if Tyme knew for certain that the span would be 6 or 7 periods. Given the factual information in Figs. 12.2 through 12.4, would you hire the new manager if you were president of Galactic Reaper?

Task	Possible Number of Periods	President's Assessed Probability
A	2	perfect certainty
B	2, 3, 4	$\frac{1}{3}$ each
C	2, 3, 4	$\frac{1}{3}$ each
D	1	perfect certainty
E	1, 2, 3	$\frac{1}{3}$ each

Total Time Span (Periods)	Incremental Profit ($ 1000)
3	120
4	110
5	100
6	50
7	0

FIGURE 12.3. Galactic Reaper Company. Possible Time Requirements (One Period = 3 Months).

FIGURE 12.4. Galactic Reaper Company. Competitive Advantage of Early Completion.

Analysis. If you were to base your analysis on the total span of 5 periods, calculated by using the *average* time for each task, then you would not hire Miles Stone. The reason is that a reduction from 5 to 4 periods implies the profit gain would be $10,000 (= $110,000 − $100,000) and this is less than the additional cost of $20,000. As you will see, this analysis is quite faulty.

Such an approach makes two mistakes: first it assumes that the total time span calculated by looking at individual averages is a useful approximation to the expected total time span. Second, it overlooks the fact that the relevant criterion is expected incremental profit, and not incremental profit for the expected time span.

By evaluating all the different possible events and their probabilities of occurrence, it can be shown that

(1)
$$P[T = 4] = \frac{2}{27} \quad P[T = 5] = \frac{8}{27}$$
$$P[T = 6] = \frac{14}{27} \quad P[T = 7] = \frac{3}{27},$$

where T denotes the total time span. Therefore,

(2)
$$E\begin{bmatrix}\text{incremental profit} \\ \text{without new manager}\end{bmatrix} = (110)\tfrac{2}{27} + (100)\tfrac{8}{27} + (50)\tfrac{14}{27} + (0)\tfrac{3}{27}$$
$$= 64,$$

and

(3)
$$E\begin{bmatrix}\text{incremental profit} \\ \text{with new manager}\end{bmatrix} = (120)\tfrac{2}{27} + (110)\tfrac{8}{27} + (100)\tfrac{14}{27} + (50)\tfrac{3}{27}$$
$$= 99.$$

To keep the arithmetic uncluttered, we have rounded the computations to the nearest thousand dollars. Thus the gain in expected incremental profit from the new manager is $35,000 (= $99,000 − $64,000), which exceeds the additional cost of $20,000. Notice that the faulty analysis using the time average went astray because it was considerably overoptimistic in assessing the *economic* outcome when the new assistant was not hired.

The faulty analysis exhibited the following fallacy.

FALLACY OF AVERAGES. Given an arbitrary nonlinear function $f(x_1, \ldots, x_n)$ of random variables $x_1, \ldots, x_n$, it is usually *erroneous* to assume

$$E[f(x_1, \ldots, x_n)] = f(E[x_1], \ldots, E[x_n]).$$

Although mathematical analysis of a particular nonlinear function *may* establish that its expected value is well approximated by the same function of the expected values, you should never blindly assume that it does.

Uncertainty and information. What is the **economic impact of uncertainty** in the foregoing example? A way to give a quantified answer to this question is to evaluate the gain in expected profit that would occur if Galactic Reaper's president were able to obtain a perfect prediction of the uncertain elements. In other words, the impact of uncertainty can be measured as the maximum amount Tyme would be willing to pay if, *after* the payment, he were able to learn the exact values of the random elements and consequently decide without error whether to hire Stone. This figure is easily computed.

Recall that the decision to hire Stone is better only when $T = 6$ and 7, and the net profit will be $80,000 (= $100,000 − $20,000) and $30,000 (= $50,000 − $20,000), respectively. Then the expected net profit when the values of the random elements are known prior to the decision is

(4)
$$E\begin{bmatrix} \text{net profit with} \\ \text{perfect information} \end{bmatrix} = (110)\tfrac{2}{27} + (100)\tfrac{8}{27} + (80)\tfrac{14}{27} + (30)\tfrac{3}{27}$$

$$= 83.$$

Given the expectation in (3), the expected net profit with uncertainty is $79,000 (= $99,000 − $20,000). Therefore the **gain from perfect information** is $4000 (= $83,000 − $79,000), taking account of the added cost of the new manager. This figure may be interpreted as measuring the impact or loss from uncertainty, for Tyme would not pay over $4000 to have perfect foresight.

12.4 TWO-STAGE LINEAR MODEL

In this section we begin consideration of how to account for probabilistic uncertainty in the coefficients of a linear programming problem. As you know by now, linear programming has a multitude of applications. You may easily have gotten the impression after reading Chap. 2 that linear programming is a "model for all seasons." For this reason alone, trying to extend the linear programming problem to encompass chance elements is a worthwhile goal.

Our task is to devise ways of formulating a so-called **stochastic linear programming model** that yields ordinary linear programming problems as a result. Because of the great diversity of applications mentioned above, we cannot hope to succeed in this task unless we add some specific postulates about the underlying structure of the decision process. In particular, we have to formalize the evolution of "which decisions have to be made when what information is known about the previous decisions and the random variables."

You will learn two things from investigating the two-stage model. First, you will see how to formulate a simple stochastic programming model to yield an equivalent ordinary linear programming problem. Second, you will see that such a formulation magnifies the size of the problem. You will be justified in concluding that a more general situation for several periods is likely to be beyond practicality for most real linear programming applications.

In Sec. 12.5, you will study a chance-constrained model, which is an alternative formulation for a stochastic programming problem. The approach avoids some of the drawbacks in the two-stage formulation below, but, as you will see, it gives rise to some limitations of its own.

An easy case. Before presenting an example of a two-stage model, we acknowledge a fundamental result for what might be termed a simple one-stage problem. To ease the exposition, suppose a *deterministic* version of the model is written in the canonical form:

$$(1) \qquad\qquad \text{maximize} \sum_{j=1}^{n} c_j x_j$$

subject to

$$(2) \qquad\qquad \sum_{j=1}^{n} a_{ij} x_j = b_i \quad \text{for } i = 1, 2, \ldots, m$$

$$(3) \qquad\qquad x_j \geq 0 \quad \text{for } j = 1, 2, \ldots, n.$$

Now assume that the coefficients in the objective function really are random, and that all the levels of the variables have to be determined prior to learning the actual values for the random c_j. Such a situation might arise in a planning model where future market prices and labor costs are not known exactly at the time the plan is being developed. Since all the structural coefficients a_{ij} and the right-hand-side coefficients b_i are known with certainty, no difficulty arises in selecting feasible levels for the x_j.

Postulating that the appropriate objective function is to maximize the expected value of the summation in (1), it is easy to establish the following theorem.

LINEAR CERTAINTY-EQUIVALENCE THEOREM. Assume that all the a_{ij} and b_i in
(2) are known exactly, but c_j in (1) are random variables independent of all
x_j. If the levels of x_j, for $j = 1, \ldots, n$, must be set prior to knowing the exact
values of c_j, then a solution to

(4)
$$\text{maximize } E\left[\sum_{j=1}^{n} c_j x_j\right]$$

subject to (2) and (3), is given by levels for x_j that

(5)
$$\text{maximize } \sum_{j=1}^{n} E[c_j]x_j$$

subject to (2) and (3).

Thus if the only random variables are the objective-function coefficients, and
these are independent of the specific activity levels, then an optimal solution can
be found from an equivalent deterministic linear program, where the corresponding expected values are used in the objective function. As you will see next, a
linear problem with uncertainty is not solved so simply when there are other
random elements, or when there are some x_j that are set after learning the exact
values for several of the random elements.

Example. Each month, the Big Board Company, a wood-products manufacturer
processes a given tonnage supply of timber, T, into lumber and plywood. To keep
the example simple, suppose that Big Board makes only one high-grade quality of
each of the two timber products. At the start of a month, the company must
decide the levels of

x_1 = the tons of timber supply allocated to lumber manufacturing

x_2 = the tons of timber supply allocated to plywood manufacturing.

Assume that by the end of the month, x_1 yields $a_1 x_1$ hundred board-feet of
lumber, and x_2 yields $a_2 x_2$ thousand sheets of plywood. The associated cost of
production is $e_1 x_1$ and $e_2 x_2$ for lumber and plywood, respectively. At the end of the
month, Big Board can sell up to D_1 hundred board-feet of lumber at a premium
price f_1 per hundred board-feet, and any additional amount at a discounted price
g_1 per hundred board-feet; let s_1 and t_1 be the amounts sold at these prices.
Similarly, the company can sell up to D_2 thousand sheets of plywood at a premium
price f_2 per thousand sheets, and it can sell any additional quantity at a lower
price g_2 per thousand sheets; let s_2 and t_2 be the amounts sold at these prices.
Big Board receives f_0 per ton of timber that it sells on the open commodity market;
let s_0 be the tonnage sold. Even if all the company's timber is sold on the market,
the value of f_0 will not be affected.

If the values of a_j, f_j, g_j, and D_i are all known with certainty, the decision
problem can be characterized as an ordinary linear programming problem:

(6)   maximize $-e_1x_1 - e_2x_2 + f_0s_0 + f_1s_1 + g_1t_1 + f_2s_2 + g_2t_2$

subject to

$$x_1 + x_2 + s_0 \qquad\qquad = T \quad \text{(total supply)}$$

(7)

$$-a_1x_1 \qquad\quad + s_1 + t_1 = 0 \quad \text{(lumber production)}$$

$$- a_2x_2 \qquad + s_2 + t_2 = 0 \quad \text{(plywood production)}$$

$$s_1 \le D_1 \quad \text{and} \quad s_2 \le D_2 \qquad\qquad \text{(premium demand limits)}$$

(8)   all x_j, s_i, and t_i nonnegative.

In a typical situation, the market prices for the products vary during a month, depending on the supply and demand conditions. Therefore the Big Board Company cannot know the exact values of the prices f_i and g_i until several weeks *after* the company decides the levels of x_1 and x_2. Actually, the company also does not have precise values for the manufacturing costs e_j; these figures are recovered from accounting data processed at the end of each quarter. Furthermore, both the yields a_1 and a_2 as well as the potential levels for premium demand D_1 and D_2 are subject to random variation. Therefore the s_i and t_i, for $i = 1, 2$, are determined *after* the values of a_j and D_i become known. Observe that s_0 is determined at the same time as x_1 and x_2, since the total supply T of timber is specified at the start of the planning horizon.

To summarize the approach, note that the timing sequence is:

   (i) *First Stage.* The company selects the levels of x_1, x_2, and s_0.
  (ii) *Random Event.* The specific values of the random elements e_j, f_i, g_i, a_j, and D_i become known and are independent of the levels of x_1, x_2, and s_0.
 (iii) *Second Stage.* The company establishes the levels of s_1, s_2, t_1, and t_2.

Given this information structure, Big Board selects those levels for x_1, x_2, and s_0 that maximize expected profit.

Without any further simplifying assumptions, even this small-scale example would be difficult to solve. Hence, we postulate that there are only a finite number Q of different possible sets of values for the random variables (e_j, f_i, g_i, a_j, and D_i). To illustrate with the above example, suppose $Q = 3$. That is, assume that only three sets of values can occur:

$$(e_{11}, e_{12}, f_{10}, f_{11}, f_{12}, g_{11}, g_{12}, a_{11}, a_{12}, D_{11}, D_{12}) \quad \text{with probability } p_1,$$

(9) $\quad (e_{21}, e_{22}, f_{20}, f_{21}, f_{22}, g_{21}, g_{22}, a_{21}, a_{22}, D_{21}, D_{22}) \quad \text{with probability } p_2,$

$$(e_{31}, e_{32}, f_{30}, f_{31}, f_{32}, g_{31}, g_{32}, a_{31}, a_{32}, D_{31}, D_{32}) \quad \text{with probability } p_3,$$

where $p_1 + p_2 + p_3 = 1$.

Since x_1, x_2, and s_0 are determined prior to the outcome of the random phenomena, these variables also appear in the stochastic programming formulation. The remaining decision variables, however, must now reflect the fact that they are determined after the random event. Hence, let s_{qi} and t_{qi}, for $q = 1, 2, 3$ and

$i = 1, 2$, be the corresponding second-stage variables when the qth set of random values occurs. Then the objective function is

(10)
$$\text{maximize} \quad \sum_{q=1}^{3} p_q(-e_{q1}x_1 - e_{q2}x_2 \\ + f_{q0}s_0 + f_{q1}s_{q1} + f_{q2}s_{q2} + g_{q1}t_{q1} + g_{q2}t_{q2}).$$

Observe that since the first-stage variables do not depend on the qth outcome, the expression can be written as

(11)
$$\text{maximize} \quad -E(e_1)x_1 - E(e_2)x_2 + E(f_0)s_0 \\ + p_1(f_{11}s_{11} + f_{12}s_{12} + g_{11}t_{11} + g_{12}t_{12}) \\ + p_2(f_{21}s_{21} + f_{22}s_{22} + g_{21}t_{21} + g_{22}t_{22}) \\ + p_3(f_{31}s_{31} + f_{32}s_{32} + g_{31}t_{31} + g_{32}t_{32}),$$

where $E(e_1) = p_1 e_{11} + p_2 e_{21} + p_3 e_{31}$, and similar expressions hold for the expectations $E(e_2)$ and $E(f_0)$. The appropriate constraints are

(12)
$$x_1 + \quad x_2 + s_0 \quad\quad = T$$

(13)
$$\left.\begin{array}{l} -a_{q1}x_1 \quad\quad\quad + s_{q1} + t_{q1} = 0 \\ \quad\quad - a_{q2}x_2 + s_{q2} + t_{q2} = 0 \\ s_{q1} \le D_{q1} \quad \text{and} \quad s_{q2} \le D_{q2} \end{array}\right\} \quad \text{for } q = 1, 2, 3.$$

(14)
$$\text{all } x_j, s_0, s_{qi}, \text{ and } t_{qi} \text{ nonnegative.}$$

Thus the stochastic programming version of this problem has 13 $[= 1 + (Q \cdot 4)]$ linear restrictions in (12) and (13) as compared with the deterministic version which has only 5 $(= 1 + 4)$ such restrictions in (7); by the same token, the number of decision variables has increased from 7 $(= 3 + 4)$ in the deterministic model to 15 $[= 3 + (Q \cdot 4)]$ in the stochastic version.

Note in (11) through (14) that:

(i) The deterministic timber supply constraint restricting the first-stage variables is included as (12).

(ii) There are $Q = 3$ groups of constraints, one group for each possible set of values for the random elements.

(iii) The first-stage variables appear in each of the three groups of constraints given in (ii). The coefficients of these variables are the specific values of the random elements corresponding to the index q, where $q = 1, 2, 3$.

(iv) There is a set of second-stage variables (s_{q1}, t_{q1}) and (s_{q2}, t_{q2}) associated with each of the three groups of constraints given in (ii). Their levels are relevant and to be implemented if and when the corresponding values for the random elements actually do occur.

(v) The objective function contains the unconditional expected values for the first-stage variables.

(vi) The objective function weights the coefficients for the second-stage variables by the probability p_q that the associated set of second-stage variables
will be relevant.

It is important that you perceive the true nature of the solution. You must
decide right now the levels of the first-stage variables, and the model (11) through
(14) provides the optimal levels. You do not need to set the levels of the second-
stage variables until the uncertainties are resolved. Consequently, what you find
now for the second-stage variables are optimal **decision rules,** that is, a strategy
that indicates what levels you will choose for each and every possible outcome of
the uncertain events, given the values you already selected for the first-stage
variables. The fact that you *have* to determine *rules* for your future actions is what
distinguishes a stochastic from a deterministic dynamic optimization model and
is what makes the computational task much more difficult.

Summary. We give here a general formulation of the so-called **two-stage
linear model.** Using the notation of the deterministic version (1) through (3),
assume that in the stochastic version:

1. The value of each random element is independent of the levels of all x_j.
2. The levels of x_j, for $j = 1, 2, \ldots, k \le n$, must be fixed at the first stage
   before any exact values of the random elements are known.
3. The constraints $i = 1, 2, \ldots, g$ contain only the first-stage variables, and
   the associated a_{ij} and b_i are known with certainty.
4. There always exist feasible levels for the remaining second-stage variables
   x_j, for $j = k + 1, \ldots, n$. These are to be established after all the random
   values are known.
5. There are a finite number Q of possible sets of values for the c_j, where
   $j = k + 1, \ldots, n$, and for a_{ij} and b_i, where $i = g + 1, \ldots, m$ and where
   $j = 1, \ldots, n$. Denote these sets by $(c_{qj}, a_{qij}, b_{qi})$ and the associated probability of occurrence by p_q, for $q = 1, 2, \ldots, Q$.

Then an optimal decision rule can be found by solving the linear program

$$(15) \qquad \text{maximize} \quad \sum_{j=1}^{k} E[c_j]x_j + \sum_{q=1}^{Q} p_q \left[\sum_{j=k+1}^{n} c_{qj}x_{qj} \right]$$

subject to

$$(16) \qquad \sum_{j=1}^{k} a_{ij}x_j = b_i \quad \text{for } i = 1, 2, \ldots, g \quad \text{(first stage)}$$

$$(17) \quad \sum_{j=1}^{k} a_{qij}x_j + \sum_{j=k+1}^{n} a_{qij}x_{qj} = b_{qj} \quad \text{(second-stage decision rules)}$$

$$\text{for } i = g + 1, \ldots, m \quad \text{and} \quad q = 1, 2, \ldots, Q$$

$$(18) \qquad \text{all } x_j \ge 0 \quad \text{and} \quad \text{all } x_{qj} \ge 0.$$

[If any c_j is known exactly, then use this value in (15). If any b_i for $i = g + 1, \ldots,$
m is known, then let b_{qi} equal this value in (17), and do the same for any a_{ij} that

is known.] Notice that (17) contains $(m - g)Q$ equations. In real applications where $(m - g)$ can easily be between 25 and 50, the approach is impractical if Q is large.

12.5 CHANCE-CONSTRAINED MODEL

As you reflect on the solution technique for the two-stage stochastic linear programming model given in the preceding section, you will conclude that one of its major drawbacks is the resultant size of the equivalent standard linear program. The expanded dimensions are due to the explicit provision for complete decision rules to be applied at the second stage. If you make a few more simplifying assumptions, then you can employ another linear programming formulation that has the same number of constraints as the original stochastic model. The approach is called **chance-constrained programming** (named by Professors A. Charnes and W. W. Cooper, who have pioneered the technique). We motivate the approach by re-examining the illustration in the preceding section.

Example. Reconsider the case of the timber products manufacturer, the Big Board Company. We further simplify the problem by assuming that the two yield coefficients a_1 and a_2 are known exactly. Suppose that we no longer specify that each product, lumber and plywood, must be sold at a discount price for quantities exceeding a particular demand level (D_1 and D_2, respectively). Instead, we formulate the model so that all the production has a reasonable chance of being sold at the premium price. The random elements, then, are the production costs e_j, the open market price for timber f_0, and the maximum demand levels D_i at which premium product prices can be obtained.

The objective function can be written as

(1)   maximize $-E(e_1)x_1 - E(e_2)x_2 + E(f_0)s_0 + E(f_1)s_1 + E(f_2)s_2.$

The model contains supply, production, and nonnegativity constraints

$$x_1 + \quad x_2 + s_0 = T \quad \text{(total supply)}$$

(2) $$-a_1x_1 \qquad\quad + s_1 \leq 0 \quad \text{(lumber production)}$$

$$- a_2x_2 + s_2 \leq 0 \quad \text{(plywood production)}$$

(3)   all x_j and s_i nonnegative.

Finally, we must place restrictions to limit production, because otherwise the model, in maximizing expected profit, is likely to indicate a solution that will exceed actual demand. Suppose, then, that the President of Big Board stipulates that with a probability of at least β_i, he wants to be able to sell *all* the output produced. His goal can be expressed mathematically as

(4) $P[s_1 \leq D_1] \geq \beta_1$ (lumber demand)

(5) $P[s_2 \leq D_2] \geq \beta_2$ (plywood demand).

Restrictions (4) and (5) are called **chance-constraints,** because they impose restrictions on probabilities. These restrictions imply an equivalent pair of ordinary linear inequalities:

(6) $s_1 \leq B_1$ (deterministic equivalent for lumber)

(7) $s_2 \leq B_2$ (deterministic equivalent for plywood).

In other words, the linear programming model comprised of the objective function (1), the supply production, and nonnegativity constraints (2) and (3), and the **deterministic equivalent constraints** (6) and (7) yields an optimal solution to the chance-constrained problem. [Based on the assumption that both $E(f_1)$ and $E(f_2)$ are positive, equality will hold in the production constraints of (2) at an optimal solution. Hence, when these constraints are viewed as definitions, s_1 and s_2 can be eliminated, thereby resulting in a model that contains only non-negative variables x_1, x_2, and s_0, the objective function (1) appropriately revised, the total supply constraint, and (6) and (7), in which $a_1 x_1$ and $a_2 x_2$ appear, respectively. With this version of the model, an optimal solution can be found by inspection.]

The appropriate values for each B_i in the deterministic equivalent is the largest number such that $P[D_i \geq B_i] \geq \beta_i$; the number B_i is called the $(1 - \beta_i)$ *fractile* of the probability distribution of D_i. Note that the probability distribution is the *marginal* distribution for D_i. This means that if you start with a joint probability distribution for D_1 and D_2, you must, as a side calculation, derive the two marginal distributions.

A numerical example will illustrate how to determine the B_i from a marginal distribution. Suppose that the marginal probability distribution for D_i is

(8)
$$P[D_1 = 1] = .2 \qquad P[D_1 = 3] = .4$$
$$P[D_1 = 8] = .3 \qquad P[D_1 = 10] = .1,$$

giving the graph of $P[D_1 \geq B_1]$ shown in Fig. 12.5. Then $B_1 = 1$ if $.8 < \beta_1 \leq 1.0$, and $B_1 = 3$ if $.4 < \beta_1 \leq .8$, etc.

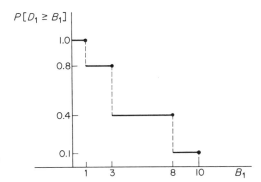

FIGURE 12.5. Big Board Company Example.

The approach. With the Big Board Company Example as background, we give a general statement of the technique. Let x_j for $j = 1, 2, \ldots, k$ refer to the first-stage variables. We do not explicitly represent the second-stage variables. Assume that all the coefficients a_{ij} are known exactly. And, finally, postulate that each random element is statistically independent of the levels for the first-stage variables.

The chance-constrained model is to find levels x_j that satisfy

$$(9) \qquad\qquad\qquad \text{maximize} \sum_{j=1}^{k} E[c_j] x_j$$

subject to

$$(10) \qquad\qquad \sum_{j=1}^{k} a_{ij} x_j = b_i \quad \text{for } i = 1, 2, \ldots, g \quad \text{(first stage)}$$

$$(11) \quad P\left[\sum_{j=1}^{k} a_{ij} x_j \leq b_i \right] \geq \beta_i \quad \text{for } i = g + 1, \ldots, m \quad \text{(chance-constraints)}$$

$$(12) \qquad\qquad\qquad\qquad \text{all } x_j \geq 0.$$

You interpret (11) as constraining the unconditional probability to be no smaller than β_i, where $0 \leq \beta_i \leq 1$, that the actual value for b_i is at least as large as $\sum_{j=1}^{k} a_{ij} x_j$.

Assuming there are levels x_j satisfying (10) through (12), the above formulation can be solved as a standard linear program with objective function (9), constraints (10), (12), and instead of the chance-constraints (11), the linear constraints:

$$(13) \qquad \sum_{j=1}^{k} a_{ij} x_j \leq B_i \quad \text{for } i = g + 1, \ldots, m \quad \text{(deterministic equivalents)},$$

where B_i is the largest number satisfying

$$(14) \qquad\qquad\qquad\qquad P[b_i \geq B_i] \geq \beta_i$$

or, equivalently,

$$(15) \qquad\qquad P[b_i < B_i] \leq 1 - \beta_i \qquad [B_i: (1 - \beta_i) \text{ fractile}].$$

Discussion. You can compare the chance-constrained approach with the earlier two-stage approach. The chance-constrained model has two desirable properties. First, it leads to an equivalent linear program that has the same size and structure as a deterministic version of the model. Consequently, the computational burden of the stochastic version is no greater after the proper right-hand-side values have been determined. Second, the only information required about each uncertain element b_i is the $(1 - \beta_i)$ fractile for the unconditional distribution of the right-hand-side coefficient. These properties compare favorably with the larger size of the linear program of the previous section and the restrictive assumption that there are only Q possible sets of values for the random elements.

The principal weakness of the chance-constrained model is that it only indirectly evaluates the economic consequence of violating a constraint. In the example of the Big Board Company, the chance-constrained approach indicates no differential penalty between a small and large amount of production in excess of the maximum premium demand levels. Put somewhat differently, in most situations, specifying the correct values for β_i should be *part* of the optimization problem. (An additional conceptual limitation is that the approach arbitrarily excludes randomized strategies that could be better, as was pointed out in the advanced material in Sec. 12.2. Also, a particular optimal solution for one formulation may never be optimal in an analogous formulation of the other. So you cannot be assured that there exist probabilities β_i that in a chance-constrained model would yield a given solution that is optimal for a two-stage formulation.)

Therefore, when faced with a choice between the two approaches for modeling a two-stage decision process, you will have to compare the serious limitation on the problem size imposed by the two-stage model of the previous section against the restricted meaning of optimality implied by the chance-constrained version. When you come to a multistage model, you will find the conceptual difficulties in a chance-constrained approach compound tremendously.

REVIEW EXERCISES

1 In each case below, state what you think might be both the sources and the impact of uncertainty on the management decisions at issue. Also discuss whether performing sensitivity analysis on a deterministic model is likely to uncover the impact of uncertainty.

(a) Selecting sites for new warehouses that will serve existing retail outlets.
(b) Eliminating a product.
(c) Introducing a new product.
(d) Choosing the number of elevators to install in a new office building.
(e) Designing delivery routes for postmen.
(f) Determining the number of emergency operating rooms in a hospital.
(g) Floating a new bond issue. (Discuss the situation for a corporation and for a municipal government.)
(h) Determining the frequency of scheduling truck deliveries of gasoline to a major oil company's gas stations.
(i) Determining the size of a corporation's bank balance.
(j) Choosing the number of crews of telephone repairmen.
(k) Selecting the capacity of a dam.
(l) Determining the seating capacity of a supersonic airplane.

2 In each part below, calculate the expected value of the random variable D, the expected value of D^2, the expected value of $f(D) \equiv (-1)^D \cdot D/(D + 1)$, and $E[f(D \mid y)]$ in (8) of Sec. 12.2, where $c = 1$, $h = 2$, $p = 5$, and $y = 0, 1, \ldots, 6$.

(a) $P[D = d] = \frac{1}{7}$ for $d = 0, 1, \ldots, 6$.
(b) $P[D = d] = \frac{1}{6}$ for $d = 1, 2, \ldots, 6$. (*Continued on p. 392.*)

(c) $P[D = d] = \frac{1}{6}$ for $d = 0, 1, \ldots, 5$.

(d) $P[D = d] = \frac{1}{4}$ for $d = 0, 2, 4, 6$.

(e) $P[D = d] = \frac{1}{3}$ for $d = 1, 3, 5$.

(f) $P[D = d] = \binom{3}{d-1}(.5)^{d-1}(.5)^{3-d+1}$ for $d = 1, 2, 3, 4$.

(g) $P[D = d] = \binom{3}{d-2}(.5)^{d-2}(.5)^{3-d+2}$ for $d = 2, 3, 4, 5$.

(h) $P[D = 2j] = \binom{3}{j}(.5)^j(.5)^{3-j}$ for $j = 0, 1, 2, 3$.

(i) $P[D = 2j] = \binom{3}{j}(\frac{3}{4})^j(\frac{1}{4})^{3-j}$ for $j = 0, 1, 2, 3$.

(j) $P[D = 2j] = \binom{3}{j}(\frac{1}{4})^j(\frac{3}{4})^{3-j}$ for $j = 0, 1, 2, 3$.

3 In each of the three parts below, derive an expression analogous to (8) of Sec. 12.2 for the indicated function $f(D \mid y)$.

(a)
$$f(D \mid y) = \begin{cases} cy^2 + h \cdot (y - d)^2 & \text{if } d \le y \\ cy^2 + p \cdot (d - y)^2 & \text{if } d > y. \end{cases}$$

(b)
$$f(D \mid y) = \begin{cases} c(y) + H - v \cdot (y - d) & \text{if } d \le y \\ c(y) + P & \text{if } d > y, \end{cases}$$

where
$$c(y) = \begin{cases} 0 & \text{for } y = 0 \\ K + cy & \text{for } y > 0. \end{cases}$$

(c)
$$f(D \mid y) = c(y) + h(y - d) + p(y, d),$$

where
$$c(y) = \begin{cases} 0 & \text{for } y = 0 \\ K + cy & \text{for } y > 0, \end{cases}$$

$$h(y - d) = \begin{cases} h_1 \cdot (y - d) & \text{if } 0 < y - d \le I \\ H + h_2 \cdot (y - d) & \text{if } y - d > I \\ 0 & \text{otherwise}, \end{cases}$$

$$p(y, d) = \begin{cases} p_1 \cdot \left(\dfrac{d - y}{d}\right) & \text{if } 0 < d - y \le S \\ P & \text{if } d - y > S \\ 0 & \text{otherwise}. \end{cases}$$

4 *Flake Out Company* (Sec. 12.2)

(a) Suppose the annual profit from expanding the present facility when the share of market equals 30% is 90 + e, where $e > 0$. What is the largest value of e such that building a new plant remains the optimal decision? Make the same sensitivity analysis for the profit associated with a 35% market share. With a 40% market share.

(b) Suppose the annual profit from building a new plant when the share of market equals 30% is 50 − e, where $e > 0$. What is the largest value of e such that building a new plant remains the optimal decision? Make the same sensitivity analysis for the profit associated with a 35% market share. With a 40% market share.

(c) Let p_1 be the assessed probability that the market share is 30% and p_2 that it is 35%, where $p_1 + p_2 = \frac{5}{8}$. How large can p_1 be such that building a new plant remains the optimal decision?

*(d) Let p_1, p_2, p_3 be the assessed probabilities that the market share equals 30%, 35%, and 40%, respectively. Note $p_3 = 1 - p_1 - p_2$. Construct a diagram showing all the values for p_1 and p_2 such that building a new plant is the optimal decision. (*Hint:* write an inequality between the expected profits for the two decisions that expresses building a new plant is optimal and then simplify. Draw the resultant solutions space diagram for p_1 and p_2.)

(e) Suppose the assessed probabilities are realistic but, by paying the amount K, the President can learn the actual share of market. In other words, he can find out what the share of market will be *before* having to make his decision. What is the largest value of K that still makes such perfect information worth purchasing?

5 Consider the production policy (10) and the demand distribution (11) in Sec. 12.2.

(a) Assuming entering inventory in the current period is 2, explain why production in the next period will be 0 with probability $\frac{1}{2}$. Explain why production will be 0 with probability $\frac{1}{4}$ in the period after next. What is the probability that production will be 0 three periods from now?

(b) Suppose, instead, that $D_t = 2$ with probability $\frac{1}{4}$ and $D_t = 3$ with probability $\frac{3}{4}$. Revise the probabilities in part (a) accordingly.

(c) Suppose, instead, that the policy is revised such that

$$x(i) = \begin{cases} 5 - i & \text{for } i = 0, 1, 2 \\ 0 & \text{otherwise} \end{cases}$$

and $D_t = 2$ with probability $\frac{3}{4}$ and $D_i = 3$ with probability $\frac{1}{4}$. Determine the probabilities that production will be 0 in the next period, the period after next, and three periods from now, assuming entering inventory in the current period is 2.

*6 Consider the *Toute de Suite* Bakery case, described in the special material in Sec. 12.2.

(a) What is an optimal solution if the manager wants the probability of meeting the total daily demand to be at least $\frac{1}{4}$? At least $\frac{1}{2}$? (*Continued on p. 394.*)

(b) What is the optimal solution if he wants to sell at least $\frac{1}{3}$ cake a day, on the average? If he wants to sell at least one cake a day, on the average?

7 Consider a three-period revenue stream (R_1, R_2, R_3), and assume that each R_t equals either 0 or 1. Let the possibility $(1, 0, 0)$ occur with probability 0, $(0, 1, 0)$ with probability $\frac{1}{4}$, $(0, 1, 1)$ with probability $\frac{3}{16}$, $(1, 1, 0)$ with probability $\frac{1}{16}$, and each other possibility with probability $\frac{1}{8}$.

(a) Determine the expected return of the stream using the joint probability distribution for (R_1, R_2, R_3), that is, calculate the value $R_1 + R_2 + R_3$ for each possible (R_1, R_2, R_3), weight the value by the associated probability, and sum over all possibilities.

(b) Determine $E[R_t]$ for $t = 1, 2, 3$. Calculate (13) in Sec. 12.2 and compare your answer with that in part (a).

8 Consider each example in exercise 1. Suggest how you might obtain the required probability distributions; refer to the four approaches listed in Sec. 12.2.

9 *Galactic Reaper Company* (Sec. 12.3). Consider the data in Figs. 12.2 and 12.3.

(a) Verify the probabilities shown in (1).
(b) Check that the time span is 5 periods if each random event takes its average value. Calculate the actual expected time span.
(c) Should the new manager be hired if there is only a $\frac{3}{4}$ probability of his reducing the total time span by 1 period? Show the calculations justifying your answer.
(d) Suppose the manager has a fifty-fifty chance of either reducing the total time span by 2 periods or not reducing it at all. Assume the incremental profit from a total time span of 2 periods is 130. Should the manager be hired?
(e) Suppose the President decides not to hire the new manager, but considers the option of paying a fee F to ensure that Task B takes exactly 3 periods. What is the largest value for F that makes this option worthwhile?
(f) Perform the analysis in part (e), but assume that the fee F ensures that Task C takes 3 periods.
(g) Perform the analysis in part (e), but assume that the fee F ensures that Task E takes 2 periods.
(h) Perform the analysis in part (e), but assume that both Tasks B and C each take exactly 3 periods.
(i) What are the largest values for the fees in parts (e), (f), (g), and (h) if the President decides to hire the new manager?
*(j) Suppose Task A can take 1 or 2 periods with a fifty-fifty chance, and similarly, Task B can take 3 or 4 periods, Task C can take 3 or 4 periods, and Task E can take 2 or 3 periods; Task D still requires 1 period. Analyze whether the new manager should be hired. Given the optimal decision, calculate the gain from perfect information.

10 Devise an argument establishing the Linear Certainty–Equivalence Theorem in Sec. 12.4. (Illustrate your argument with the problem maximize $c_1 x_1 + c_2 x_2$ subject to $2x_1 + 3x_2 \leq 6$, where there is a fifty-fifty chance that c_1 equals 0 or 1, and similarly, there is an independent fifty-fifty chance that c_2 equals 0 or 1.)

11 *Big Board Company* (Sec. 12.4)

(a) Explain why the structure (6) through (8) is so simple that a numerical solution is trivial once you are given values for a_j, f_j, g_j, D_i, and T. (Illustrate your answer using $T = 275$, $a_1 = 3$, $a_2 = 5$, $D_1 = 10$, $D_2 = 50$, $e_1 = 20$, $e_2 = 23, f_0 = 4$, $f_1 = 30, f_2 = 38, g_1 = 27, g_2 = 35$.)

(b) Show how (11) through (14) are altered if $Q = 4$. Give a formula showing how the numbers of equations and variables depend on Q.

(c) Show how (11) through (14) are altered if there is a constraint on s_0, namely, $s_0 \leq K$, where K is a given constant. How does your answer change if K is a random variable to be included in the characterization (9)? Assume that if s_0 exceeds K, there is a penalty charge $f_3(K - s_0)$.

(d) Show how (11) through (14) are simplified if the values for a_1, a_2, and D_2 are not random (do not allow an excess of Product 2).

12 *Big Board Company* (Sec. 12.4). Suppose the President of Big Board can pay a fee F to learn which of the Q possible values for the random variables will actually occur.

(a) Suggest how to calculate the largest value for F that still makes it worthwhile for the President to purchase this perfect information.

*(b) Suppose the fee F purchases only perfect information about the yield a_1, and that a_1 is statistically independent of the other random variables (knowledge of a_1 is of no help in predicting the values of the other random factors). Explain how to modify your answer in part (a)?

13 Consider the general two-stage linear model in Sec. 12.4. In each part below, explain how the stated assumption is embodied in the formulation (15) through (18).

(a) The value of each random element is independent of the levels of x_j.

(b) The levels of x_j, for $j = 1, 2, \ldots, k$, must be fixed at the first stage before any exact values of the random elements are known.

(c) The levels of the second-stage variables are established after all the random values are known. Is assuming that there always exist feasible levels for the second-stage variables equivalent to assuming that (16), (17), and (18), have a feasible solution? Explain.

(d) There is a finite number Q of possible sets of values for the random variables. Does the formulation imply the assumption that the random variables are mutually independent? Explain. If not, does such an assumption simplify the formulation? Explain.

(e) State why it is permissible to use an exact value that is known for any c_j, b_i, or a_{ij} in (15) through (18). What simplifications occur if any b_i or a_{ij} is known, where $i = g + 1, \ldots, m$? (Be specific.)

*14 (a) Write the dual linear program to (11) through (14) in Sec. 12.4.

(b) Write the dual linear program to (15) through (18) in Sec. 12.4.

15 Consider the two-stage problem: maximize $6x_1 + 8x_2 - 12x_3 - 10x_4$ subject to $a_1x_1 + a_2x_2 + x_3 - x_4 = D$, where every $x_j \geq 0$, where the random quantities are

(a_1, a_2, D) and x_3 and x_4 are the second-stage variables. Suppose the only two possible sets of values for the random variables are $(1, 2, 4)$, occurring with probability $\frac{1}{3}$, and $(2, 1, 10)$ with probability $\frac{2}{3}$. Formulate this two-stage problem in an equivalent linear programming model and find the optimal decision rule. Give an economic interpretation to your answer.

16 *Big Board Company* (Sec. 12.5). Consider the chance-constrained version (1) through (5). Suppose $T = 275$, $a_1 = 3$, $a_2 = 5$, $E(e_1) = 20$, $E(e_2) = 23$, $E(f_0) = 4$, $E(f_1) = 30, E(f_2) = 38$. Assume that D_1 and D_2 each have the marginal probability distribution given in (8). What is an optimal solution if

(a) $\beta_1 = \beta_2 = .9$?   (b) $\beta_1 = \beta_2 = .95$?

(c) $\beta_1 = \beta_2 = .5$?   (d) $\beta_1 = .9, \beta_2 = .5$?

(e) $\beta_1 = .5, \beta_2 = .9$?   (f) $\beta_1 = \beta_2 = .3$?

(g) $\beta_1 = \beta_2 = 0$?

17 *Big Board Company* (Sec. 12.5). Answer the questions in exercise 16, except let the marginal probability distribution for each of the products be $P[D = d] = \frac{1}{10}$ for $d = 1, 2, \ldots, 10$.

18 Explain your understanding of the following terms:

impact of uncertainty

contingency plan, strategy, decision rule

expected value

uncertain actions

induced randomness

*randomized strategies (or decision rules)

Fallacy of Averages

gain from (or value of) perfect information, cost of uncertainty

stochastic linear programming model

two-stage linear model

Linear Certainty–Equivalence Theorem

chance-constrained programming

deterministic equivalent constraint.

FORMULATION AND COMPUTATIONAL EXERCISES

19 *Galactic Reaper Company* (Sec. 12.3). Suppose in Fig. 12.2 that the arc between Nodes 1 and 2 is drawn in the opposite direction. Analyze the same decision problem, assuming that the incremental profit is equal to 0 from a total time span of seven or more periods. (Be sure to indicate the optimal decision and also compute the gain from perfect information, as defined at the end of the section.)

*20 *Critical Path Scheduling.* Consider the example in Sec. 7.5 and its linear programming characterization (1) through (6). Assume that several of the completion times are random, as given by the data in Fig. 12.3. Suppose you want to determine job starting-time values y_{CD}, y_E, and y_F such that the probability is at least $.5$ that each of the inequalities (2) through (6) is satisfied (for example, you want $P[y_F \geq t_C + y_{CD}] \geq .5$). These starting-time values are to be determined prior to knowing the exact values of any of the random completion times. Give a verbal interpretation of the chance-constraints. (*Continued on p. 397.*)

(a) Formulate an equivalent linear programming model. Also exhibit the corresponding dual problem.

(b) Solve the primal and dual problems in part (a). Indicate how the solution varies if the stated probability is .25, instead of .5. Is .75, instead of .5.

21 *One-Potato, Two-Potato Problem* (Sec. 1.6). Typically the actual yields of agricultural raw materials are subject to random variation. Assume that the yields for Source 1 are either (.2, .2, .3), as shown in Fig. 1.1, or (.25, .25, .35), or (.18, .15, .29), where each of these possibilities occurs with equal likelihood. Also assume that the yields for Source 2 are either (.3, .1, .3), as shown in Fig. 1.1, or (.35, .1, .25), where the first possibility occurs with probability $\frac{2}{3}$ and the second with probability $\frac{1}{3}$. Assume that French fries manufactured *in excess* of the stated sales limitation must be sold directly to the institutional buyers and *reduce* profit by F per unit weight, and similarly, *excess* hash browns by H and flakes by L per unit weight.

(a) Write a two-stage linear model that selects purchase quantities to maximize expected profit.

*(b) Write the corresponding dual linear program.

22 *Knox Mix Company* (Sec. 2.2)

(a) Suppose the unit profit of each activity is comprised of a revenue factor less a cost component, where cost is partly random. Specifically, let the unit revenue for Processes 1 and 2 be 15, and for Processes 3 and 4 be 20. Assume that the cost components are

Process 1: $8 + c$ Process 2: $8 + 2c$

where $P[c = 0] = \frac{1}{3}$ $P[c = 1] = \frac{2}{3}$

Process 3: $6 + d$ Process 4: $6 + 3d$

where $P[d = 0] = \frac{1}{6}$ $P[d = 1] = \frac{1}{2}$ $P[d = 2] = \frac{1}{3}$.

Display a model for selecting the production levels to maximize expected profit.

(b) Suppose the availability of labor W is random, where

$$P[W = 10] = \frac{1}{8} \qquad P[W = 12] = \frac{1}{2} \qquad P[W = 15] = \frac{3}{8}.$$

Assume that if the production schedule requires more man-weeks than are available, then the additional requirement is met by scheduling overtime, which costs c per man-week required. (The production levels are established at the start of the week and any overtime is incurred at the end of the week.) Display a model for selecting production levels to maximize expected profit.

(c) Consider the situation in part (b), except suppose that the company seeks a schedule that stays within the available amount of labor with probability of at least .8. (The dollar cost of overtime is not *explicitly* taken into account.) Display an appropriate linear optimization model. Show how to alter the formulation if the probability is .9, instead of .8.

23 *Knox Mix Company* (Sec. 2.2). Consider a two-period version of the model, in which any excess of Material Y and Material Z at the end of the first period can be stored and

used in the second period. Suppose in addition to such stored excesses, a supply S_Y and S_Z of Materials Y and Z, respectively, is made available for production in the second period. The actual values for these supplies are not known until the start of the second period; there are Q possible pairs of supplies (S_{Yq}, S_{Zq}), occurring with probability p_q, for $q = 1, 2, \ldots, Q$. All other parameters in the problem are identical in both periods, and are given in Fig. 2.3. Assume that $Q = 3$, and write a two-stage linear model that selects optimal production levels at each period so as to maximize expected profit.

24 *Hion Hog Farm Problem* (Sec. 2.3). After reading a recent research report issued by the Department of Agriculture, the production manager feels that the minimal amount r of Nutritional Ingredient B is either 225, with probability $\frac{1}{5}$, or 250, with probability $\frac{3}{10}$, or 300, with probability $\frac{1}{2}$. Formulate the appropriate linear optimization model that ensures the hogs receive at least the minimal required amount of B with probability of at least .25. With probability of at least .50. With probability of at least .75.

25 *Trim Problem* (exercise 25 of Chap. 2). Suppose that Fine-Webb produces in anticipation of customer orders for 22-inch width rolls. Assume that such demand turns out to be $100 + D$, where D has the probability distribution $P[D = d] = d/190$ for $d = 1, 2, \ldots, 19$. Formulate a linear programming model that minimizes trim costs subject to the previous demand constraints on the rolls of 20-inch and 12-inch widths, and the restriction that all demand for 22-inch width rolls be satisfied with probability of at least .5. At least .8. At least .9.

26 *Short Circuitry Problem* (Sec. 6.4). Suppose the manufacturer is concerned about the ability of certain subcontractors to meet the required specifications for the electronic components. Let p_{ij} be the manufacturer's probability estimate that each Component i produced by Subcontractor j will meet standards, and let K_i be the loss incurred by the manufacturer when any units of Component i are produced below standard. Formulate an optimization model that minimizes expected total cost. Indicate whether the formulation is still a standard assignment problem.

27 *Shortest-Route Model* (Sec. 7.2). Consider the example in Fig. 7.1. Suppose that the arc costs are random and that traversing each arc requires one period. Assume that during each of the first three periods of the horizon the arc cost from Node i to Node j is either c_{ij}, with probability p_{ij}, or d_{ij}, with probability $1 - p_{ij}$. After the third period, the arc cost is either e_{ij}, with probability q_{ij}, or f_{ij}, with probability $1 - q_{ij}$. Assume that each arc cost for each period is completely independent of every other arc cost. (Thus, for example, one possible sequence of arc costs from Node 3 to Node 4 over seven periods is $c_{34}, d_{34}, c_{34}, f_{34}, f_{34}, e_{34}, f_{34}$.) A complete route must be selected prior to knowing the exact values of any of the arc costs, and the objective is to minimize expected cost in going from Node 8 (source) to Node 1 (sink). Show how to formulate the problem as an equivalent deterministic shortest-route model. (Draw the network diagram and indicate the arc costs.)

28 Consider a linear programming model containing the constraint

$$P\left[\sum_{j=1}^{n} a_{1j}x_j \le b\right] \ge .25,$$

where a_{11} is the random variable and has the probability distribution $P[a_{11} = a] = .1$ for $a = 1, 2, \ldots, 10$.

(a) Show how to convert this chance-constraint into an ordinary linear inequality.

(b) Answer part (a), except let the probability limit be .75, instead of .25. Be .8, instead of .25.

(c) Rework part (a), letting $P[a_{11} = a] = .1$ for $a = 6, 7, \ldots, 15$. For $a = -4$, $-3, \ldots, 5$.

29 *Stochastic Transportation Problem.* Consider the example in Fig. 6.12. Suppose that the demands D_3 and D_4 are not known exactly when the shipments x_{ij} are determined. Assume that the probabilities for these demands are

$$P[D_3 = 1] = P[D_3 = 3] = P[D_3 = 5] = \frac{1}{3},$$

and

$$P[D_4 = 0] = P[D_4 = 1] = P[D_4 = 3] = P[D_4 = 4] = \frac{1}{4}.$$

If demand exceeds the total amount shipped to these locations, then the firm incurs penalties of f_3 and f_4 per unit short at Demand Points 3 and 4, respectively. These penalties are to be added to the firm's costs.

(a) Formulate the appropriate two-stage model.

*(b) Explain how the appropriate optimization can be solved by a linear program. (*Hint:* show how the two-stage model can be treated as an enlarged transportation problem.)

*(c) Let $f_3 = 9$ and $f_4 = 3$. Find an optimal solution.

*(d) Suppose that no penalty cost is levied when demand exceeds the amount shipped, but that the company wants to establish at least a $\frac{1}{3}$ probability that all demand is met at Demand Point 3 and at least a $\frac{3}{4}$ probability that all demand is met at Demand Point 4. Formulate the appropriate chance-constrained model. Find an optimal solution. How does your solution compare to that in part (c)?

*30 Consider the two-stage linear model in Sec. 12.4, as characterized by the linear program (15) through (18). Suppose the objective function is altered so that the criterion is to maximize the minimum profit over the Q possible random outcomes. Show how to revise the formulation accordingly, and exhibit the appropriate linear program. Comment on the merits or limitations of this approach.

CONTENTS

CHAPTER 13

Probabilistic Dynamic Programming Models

13.1 INTRODUCTION

As you saw in the preceding chapter, proper structuring of a model containing random elements must take into account the intermingled sequence of decisions and emergent information about the exact values of the random elements. You learned that stochastic generalizations of linear programming models frequently lead to problems that are too large to solve in practice.

In this chapter, each model is a specific application of probabilistic dynamic programming. The examples will show that stochastic versions of many dynamic programming models are *not* much more difficult to solve than their deterministic counterparts. We assume that you are already familiar with formulating deterministic dynamic programming problems, and suggest that you take a few minutes to review Chaps. 8 and 10 to refresh your memory on the concepts used in dynamic programming, and in particular, on the notions of state and stage variables, the appearance of a recursion formula, and the numerical procedures for computing solutions from such recursions.

To keep perspective on assessing the impact of uncertainty while reading the material below, be sure you answer these questions:

1. What is an optimal policy for a deterministic version of the model?
2. How much information about the probability distribution does an optimal solution require?
3. How does the dynamic programming algorithm for the stochastic model differ from that for the deterministic version?

13.2 DISTRIBUTION OF EFFORT EXAMPLE

We begin with an example in which the introduction of probabilistic elements has an almost trivial impact on the way the appropriate dynamic recursion is formulated. The model is a stochastic version of what was called the Distribution of Effort Problem in Chap. 10. To save you from flipping back to Sec. 10.2 where the particular example was first discussed, we repeat the statement of the deterministic problem here.

Mr. Chick N. Little, owner of Shopping Basket Markets, has N crates of eggs to distribute among his s stores. From past experience he knows that if he allocates y_j crates to Store j, his profit will be $R_j(y_j)$. He wants to find a distribution of crates among his Shopping Basket stores that maximizes overall profit.

The mathematical characterization of the problem is given as

$$(1) \qquad\qquad \text{maximize} \sum_{j=1}^{s} R_j(y_j)$$

subject to

$$(2) \qquad\qquad \sum_{j=1}^{s} y_j = N \quad \text{(available number of egg crates)}$$

$$(3) \qquad y_j = 0, 1, \dots \quad \text{for each } j \quad \text{(distribute only whole crates)}.$$

In Sec. 10.2, we let

(4) $g_j(n) = $ profit when n crates are distributed optimally to Store 1, Store 2, ..., Store j.

You saw that (1) through (3) could be solved as a multistage problem by employing the dynamic programming recursion

$$(5) \qquad g_j(n) = \underset{y}{\text{maximum}} \left[R_j(y) + g_{j-1}(n - y) \right] \quad \text{for } j = 1, 2, \dots, s$$

$$(6) \qquad\qquad g_0(n) \equiv 0 \quad \text{for } j = 0,$$

where $n = 0, 1, \dots, N$ and the maximization is over only nonnegative integer values of y that satisfy $y \leq n$. The optimal value of (1) is given by $g_s(N)$.

The above formulation proceeded under the assumption that the profit from distributing y_j crates to Store j is known with certainty. Suppose, however, that profit depends not only on y_j but also on the actual demand at Store j, which can be described as a random variable independent of the levels of all y_j, and known exactly only *after* y_j are all set. Assume that demand d is measured in dozens of eggs, and that each crate contains Q dozen eggs. Then let

$$(7) \quad r_j(d \mid y) = \binom{\text{profit at Store j when demand actually equals } d,}{\text{given that Store j has been allocated } y \text{ crates}}$$

$$(8) \quad p_j(d) = \binom{\text{probability that demand}}{\text{actually equals } d \text{ at Store } j}.$$

For example, the profit function in (7) might be described by

$$(9) \qquad r_j(d \mid y) = \begin{cases} r_j d & \text{for } d \leq Qy \quad \text{(supply satisfies demand)} \\ r_j Qy & \text{for } d > Qy \quad \text{(demand exceeds supply)}. \end{cases}$$

In this case, the number r_j represents the profit at Store j for each dozen eggs sold. When the supply Qy is large enough to satisfy all demand d, the total profit is $r_j d$; but when actual demand exceeds supply, then only the Qy eggs are sold, so total profit is $r_j Qy$.

The *expected profit* from distributing y_j crates to Store j is

$$R_j(y_j) \equiv \sum_d r_j(d \mid y_j) p_j(d), \tag{10}$$

where the letter d underneath the summation sign designates that the sum is to be taken over every possible value of demand. Using the above definition for $R_j(y_j)$, a solution to (1) through (3) represents an optimal allocation given the criterion of maximizing *expected* total profit, and an optimal solution can still be obtained by employing (4) through (6). Therefore, once the expected profit functions in (10) have been calculated, the stochastic model is no more complicated to solve than the deterministic version.

The following example illustrates the computation for (10). Suppose that $Q = 5, r_j = .1$, and the probability distribution for demand is

$$p_j(d) = 0 \quad \text{for } 0 \leq d \leq 7 \quad \text{and} \quad d \geq 13$$

$$p_j(8) = \frac{7}{32} \quad p_j(9) = \frac{10}{32} \quad p_j(10) = \frac{8}{32} \quad p_j(11) = \frac{4}{32} \quad p_j(12) = \frac{3}{32}. \tag{11}$$

If $y_j = 0$, then no eggs are sold, and expected profit is $R_j(0) = 0$. If $y_j = 1$, then the profit function (9) is

$$r_j(d \mid 1) = \begin{cases} (.1)d & \text{for } d \leq 5 \cdot 1 = 5 \\ (.1)5 \cdot 1 & \text{for } d > 5, \end{cases} \tag{12}$$

and expected profit (10) is

$$R_j(1) = \sum_{d=0}^{5} (.1)d p_j(d) + \sum_{d>5} (.1)5 \cdot 1 p_j(d) \tag{13}$$

$$= 0 + (.1)5 \cdot 1 \cdot 1 = .5.$$

If $y_j = 2$, then the profit function (9) is

$$r_j(d \mid 2) = \begin{cases} (.1)d & \text{for } d \leq 5 \cdot 2 = 10 \\ (.1)5 \cdot 2 & \text{for } d > 10, \end{cases} \tag{14}$$

and expected profit (10) is

$$R_j(2) = \sum_{d=0}^{10} (.1)d p_j(d) + \sum_{d>10} (.1)5 \cdot 2 p_j(d)$$

$$= (.1) \left\{ \left[8 \left(\frac{7}{32} \right) + 9 \left(\frac{10}{32} \right) + 10 \left(\frac{8}{32} \right) \right] + \left[5 \cdot 2 \left(\frac{4}{32} + \frac{3}{32} \right) \right] \right\} \tag{15}$$

$$= .925.$$

If $y_j = 3$, then the profit function (9) is

$$
(16) \qquad r_j(d \mid 3) = \begin{cases} (.1)d & \text{for } d \le 5 \cdot 3 = 15 \\ (.1)5 \cdot 3 & \text{for } d > 15, \end{cases}
$$

and expected profit (10) is

$$
R_j(3) = \sum_{d=0}^{15} (.1)d p_j(d) + \sum_{d>15} (.1)5 \cdot 3 p_j(d)
$$

$$
(17) \qquad = (.1) \left\{ \left[8\left(\frac{7}{32}\right) + 9\left(\frac{10}{32}\right) + 10\left(\frac{8}{32}\right) + 11\left(\frac{4}{32}\right) + 12\left(\frac{3}{32}\right) \right] + 0 \right\}
$$

$$
= .956.
$$

13.3 NEW PRODUCT INTRODUCTION— A DECISION TREE

The "Cool It" Baby Air Conditioner Company is developing a major design improvement for its miniaturized models. The design is far enough along for the change to be made right away. The company prefers to wait, however, until additional research and testing have been completed, because some minor difficulties still beset the manufacturing process. On the other hand, Kenny B. Shure, the president of Cool It, knows that if he delays too long, one or more of his competitors will surely announce a similar product improvement and his share of sales will consequently be smaller. What he must do, then, is balance the profit improvement from waiting until the "bugs" in his production process are worked out against the possible loss of sales to his competitors.

Consider the following mathematical representation of this situation. Suppose Shure wants to decide the optimal month in which to announce the new improvement. Assume that he considers the latest possible month to be T, and that he definitely will introduce the change at any time his competition advertises a similar improvement. Let

$$
r_t = \begin{pmatrix} \text{profit when, in Month t, Cool It announces} \\ \text{the improvement in advance of competition} \end{pmatrix}
$$

$$
g_t = \begin{pmatrix} \text{profit when, in Month t, Cool It and any} \\ \text{competitor simultaneously introduce the change} \end{pmatrix}
$$

$$
h_t = \begin{pmatrix} \text{profit when, in Month t, Cool It announces the} \\ \text{improvement after competition has already done so} \end{pmatrix},
$$

where it is plausible (although not really essential) to postulate that $r_t > g_t > h_t$, and r_t, g_t, and h_t increase as time goes on, that is, with larger values of t.

Assume that if no improvement is announced before Month t, then Cool It and its competitors make their Month t decisions independently, without knowledge of each other's current decisions. Accordingly, suppose that Shure believes p_t represents the probability that his competition will announce an improvement in Month t, *given* that no one of his competitors has introduced the change up to that time, where he feels that $p_T = 1$. By assumption, then, Shure postulates that these values for the conditional probabilities p_t do *not* depend on the particular strategy he decides to use. The president predicts, however, that if Cool It introduces the improvement in Month t in advance of competition, then the competitors assuredly will make a similar introduction in the next period. Consequently, Shure calculates the values for r_t to reflect such competitive reaction.

The underlying decision process can be described by a **decision tree** as shown in Fig. 13.1, where we let $T = 3$. The labels M and C at each node refer to the action taken by Shure and his competitors. The tree terminates at Month t unless *both* Shure and his competitors decide to delay the introduction.

Study the tree to see how it graphically displays the multiperiod decision process. The bottom of the tree represents the first-stage or immediate decision the manufacturer must make. If Shure chooses to introduce the improvement, his decision

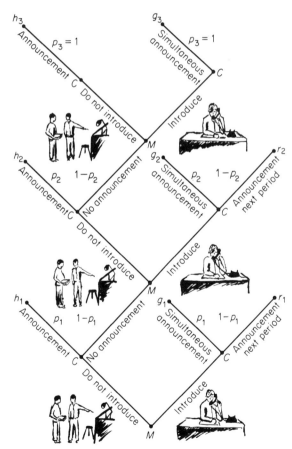

FIGURE 13.1. Cool It Company's Decision Tree for New Product Introduction ($T = 3$).

Note: M = manufacturer's decision (Cool It Company)
C = competitors' decisions

process terminates. But if he decides to delay, then he may or may not have an opportunity to delay again at Period 2, depending on the outcome of the probabilistic element representing the competitors' behavior. Similar remarks hold for his other decision points on the tree.

Assume that Shure wants a strategy that maximizes expected profit. As usual in a dynamic programming problem, you can easily find the optimal decision in case the process continues to the final period, Period T. At that time, you need only compare the expected profit of his introducing the improvement with the expected profit of a further delay. These two quantities are $p_T g_T$ and $p_T h_T$, respectively. Since by assumption $p_T = 1$ and $g_T > h_T$, the better decision is to introduce the improvement if the decision process lasts until the final period. The foregoing computations can be written as

$$(1) \qquad f_T = \text{maximum} \begin{Bmatrix} p_T g_T: & \text{introduce} \\ p_T h_T: & \text{do not introduce} \end{Bmatrix} = g_T,$$

where we have let f_T denote the expected profit of an optimal decision at Period T.

Next consider what happens at an earlier period, Period t. If the president of Cool It chooses to introduce the improvement, his expected profit consists of g_t, weighted by the probability p_t that his competition also makes the same announcement, plus r_t, weighted by the probability $(1 - p_t)$ that Cool It "jumps the gun" on its competition. But if Shure chooses not to introduce the improvement, then his expected profit consists of h_t, weighted by the probability p_t that his competition makes the announcement, plus the value of delaying, weighted by the probability $(1 - p_t)$ that his competition also delays. What is the value of delaying? It is simply the expected profit from an optimal policy given that the decision process lasts until at least Period $t + 1$; let f_{t+1} denote this quantity. Then f_t is the larger of the expected profits for the two possible decisions at Period t. This is all nicely summarized by the recursive calculation, for $t = T - 1, \ldots, 1$,

$$(2) \qquad f_t = \text{maximum} \begin{Bmatrix} p_t g_t + (1 - p_t)r_t: & \text{introduce} \\ p_t h_t + (1 - p_t)f_{t+1}: & \text{do not introduce} \end{Bmatrix}.$$

To compute an optimal decision rule for future periods and the optimal action at Period 1, start the calculations at (1), and perform the arithmetic indicated in (2). This process is called **backward induction.**

The decision yielding f_1 is optimal for Month 1. If it is "do not introduce" *and* the competitors actually make no announcement, then the decision yielding f_2 is optimal in Period 2. The decisions in subsequent months are found in a similar manner, and depend on the specific behavior of the competition. Thus the backward induction process yields a decision rule indicating the decision to make based on the actual history of the system at the time the particular choice is made.

Consider the following numerical example; suppose that the data are

$$(3) \qquad \begin{array}{cccc} h_1 = 40 & g_1 = 50 & r_1 = 60 & p_1 = .2 \\ h_2 = 65 & g_2 = 70 & r_2 = 100 & p_2 = .4 \\ h_3 = 75 & g_3 = 90 & - & p_3 = 1. \end{array}$$

For Period 3, the calculations in (1) are

$$(4) \qquad f_3 = \text{maximum} \begin{Bmatrix} 1 \cdot 90: & \text{introduce} \\ 1 \cdot 75: & \text{do not introduce} \end{Bmatrix} = 90,$$

so that *if* the decision process continues until the final period, Shure should introduce the product at that time. For Period 2, the calculations in (2) are

$$(5) \quad f_2 = \text{maximum} \begin{Bmatrix} (.4)70 + (.6)100 = 88: & \text{introduce} \\ (.4)65 + (.6)90 \;\;= 80: & \text{do not introduce} \end{Bmatrix} = 88,$$

so that *if* the decision process continues until the second period, Shure should introduce the product at that time. Observe that the calculations show that Cool It's introduction will never occur in Period 3, since a Period 2 introduction has a higher *expected* profit. For Period 1, the calculations in (2) are

$$(6) \quad f_1 = \text{maximum} \begin{Bmatrix} (.2)50 + (.8)60 = 58: & \text{introduce} \\ (.2)40 + (.8)88 = 78.4: & \text{do not introduce} \end{Bmatrix} = 78.4,$$

so that Shure's optimal decision for Period 1 is not to introduce the product at that time. There is a .2 probability that his competition will introduce a similar product during Period 1, and in that case he will be forced to do so; but otherwise he will wait until Period 2 and definitely announce the product then.

13.4 ELEMENTARY INVENTORY MODEL

The Cool It Company Example was fairly simple because the state of the system at any Period t was really an indication of whether the decision process had lasted that long, in other words, whether either the manufacturer or his competitors had announced the improvement in prior periods. The state variable in this next illustration accords with what we have presented in deterministic problems.

The illustration is a probabilistic version of the Dependable Manufacturing Company production and inventory example contained in Sec. 8.4. (An extensive treatment of inventory models with stochastic demands will be given in Chap. 14. The emphasis there will be on deriving the *form* of an optimal policy, and then exploiting this knowledge to calculate numerical answers.)

In the previous deterministic case, we made the following assumptions about the data for Dependable Manufacturing Company's problem:

$$(1) \qquad \text{demand } D = 3 \qquad \text{production } x \le 5 \qquad \text{ending inventory } j \le 4$$

$$(2) \qquad \text{production and inventory costs } C(x, j) = C(x) + hj,$$

where x and j are nonnegative integers and

$$(3) \qquad \begin{aligned} & C(0) = 0 \qquad C(1) = 15 \qquad C(2) = 17 \\ & C(3) = 19 \qquad C(4) = 21 \qquad C(5) = 23 \quad \text{and} \quad h = 1, \end{aligned}$$

for all periods. Thus the model's parameters are stationary over time.

The state variable is *entering* inventory, designated by the symbol i, where $i = 0, 1, \ldots, 4$. The appropriate recursion is

(4)
$$f_n(i) = \underset{x}{\text{minimum}} \; [C(x) + 1(i + x - 3) + f_{n-1}(i + x - 3)]$$

for $n = 2, 3, \ldots,$

with

(5)
$$f_1(i) = C(3 - i) \quad \text{for } i = 0, 1, 2, 3,$$

where in (4), $i = 0, 1, \ldots, 4$, and the minimization is over only nonnegative integer values in the range $3 - i \leq x \leq \text{minimum } (5, 7 - i)$.

Suppose now that the demands are independently and identically distributed random variables, where

(6) $\quad P[D = 2] = \dfrac{1}{2} \quad P[D = 4] = \dfrac{1}{2} \quad$ so that $E[D] = 3 \quad$ for all periods.

To make the analysis of this stochastic version comparable to the deterministic model, a few additional assumptions need to be specified. First, assume that inventory at the end of the horizon has no salvage value and incurs no holding cost (in the deterministic case the final inventory level equalled 0). Second, assume that production x is made large enough so that a stockout never occurs, implying the restriction

(7)
$$\text{entering inventory} + \text{production} \geq 4.$$

Since demand may be as small as 2 and ending inventory cannot be larger than 4, the constraint

(8)
$$\text{entering inventory} + \text{production} \leq 6$$

must also be satisfied.

The most important observation is that the state variable in this stochastic version continues to be the level of entering inventory. Think about why. Since the random demands are completely independent, the only thing that matters about the previous history when there are n periods remaining is the level of inventory currently available. Assuming that the objective function is to minimize expected cost over the horizon, the symbol $f_n(i)$ can now be interpreted as the *expected* cost of operating an optimal policy when entering inventory is at level i and there are n periods remaining in the horizon.

The case of $n = 1$ is easy to compute:

(9)
$$f_1(i) = C(4 - i) \quad \text{for } i = 0, 1, \ldots, 4,$$

because the assumptions imply that the optimal production level x is $4 - i$ when $n = 1$.

For larger values of n, the expected cost of an optimal policy, given the level i, can be reasoned as follows. First, you have to add in the production cost $C(x)$ for producing x. Second, you have to include the *expected* holding cost on inventory at the end of the period, which is the quantity $(i + x - D)$. And finally, you have to account for the cost that will be incurred in later periods. But this last amount is simply the expected value $E[f_{n-1}(i + x - D)]$, where D has the probability distribution in (6). Thus the appropriate dynamic programming recursion for the stochastic model is, for $n = 2, 3, \ldots,$

$$f_n(i) = \text{minimum}_x \left\{ C(x) + 1[\tfrac{1}{2}(i + x - 2) + \tfrac{1}{2}(i + x - 4)] \right.$$
$$+ \tfrac{1}{2}f_{n-1}(i + x - 2) + \tfrac{1}{2}f_{n-1}(i + x - 4)\}$$
(10)
$$= \text{minimum}_x \left\{ C(x) + 1[i + x - 3] \right.$$
$$+ \tfrac{1}{2}[f_{n-1}(i + x - 2) + f_{n-1}(i + x - 4)]\}$$

where $i = 0, 1, \ldots, 4$, and the minimization is over only nonnegative integer values in the range $4 - i \leq x \leq$ minimum $(5, 6 - i)$.

Note that the major difference between the recursion for the deterministic problem (4) and for the stochastic problem (10) is that in the latter an extra amount of arithmetic must be performed to compute $E[f_{n-1}(i + x - D)]$.

In Fig. 13.2 optimal production decisions $x_n(i)$ for $n = 1, 2, \ldots, 5$ are shown along with $f_n(i)$. It can be proved that the optimal policy for $n = 3$ is also optimal for all $n \geq 3$. The values for the case $n = 1$ follow from (9) and the data (3). The detailed calculations for the case $n = 2$ are displayed in Fig. 13.3. This table is analogous to the corresponding table for the deterministic case, Fig. 8.8 (p. 235). There is one row for each possible level of entering inventory and one column for each feasible production level. Given the restrictions in (7) and (8), several combinations of i and x are eliminated from consideration. The entries in the table

Entering Inventory	n = 1		n = 2		n = 3		n = 4		n = 5		Unbounded Horizon
i	$x_1(i)$	$f_1(i)$	$x_2(i)$	$f_2(i)$	$x_3(i)$	$f_3(i)$	$x_4(i)$	$f_4(i)$	$x_5(i)$	$f_5(i)$	$x_\infty(i)$
0	4	21	4	41	5	57.5	5	75.25	5	93	5
1	3	19	5	34.5	5	52.25	5	70.00	5	87.43	5
2	2	17	4	32.5	4	50.25	4	68.00	4	85.43	4
3	1	15	3	30.5	3	48.25	3	66.00	3	83.43	3
4	0	0	0	20	0	37.75	0	54.87	0	72.62	0

FIGURE 13.2. Dependable Manufacturing Company Example. Stochastic Version of Inventory Model.

are the sums of production, expected holding, and expected future costs. For each row, the minimum of the sums and the associated production level are indicated at the right.

A comparison of the results in Fig. 13.2 with those for the deterministic version in Fig. 8.10 (p. 236) indicates:

1. For any initial inventory, i, and horizon, n, the expected cost from an optimal policy is higher when demands are stochastic.
2. Given i, the optimal decision $x_n(i)$ never decreases as n gets larger when demands are stochastic.
3. The optimal policy for an extended horizon is obtained as soon as $n = 3$ when demands are stochastic, as compared to $n = 18$ in the deterministic version.

Of course, these conclusions arise from the numerical values of the specific example, but the illustration is evidence of the general observation that the **solution characteristics** for deterministic and stochastic versions of a model can be quite disparate.

$$C(x) + 1[i + x - 3] + .5[f_1(i + x - 2) + f_1(i + x - 4)]$$

Production x :

i\x	0	1	2	3	4	5	$x_2(i)$	$f_2(i)$
0					21 + 1 + .5[38]	23 + 2 + .5[34]	4	41
1				19 + 1 + .5[38]	21 + 2 + .5[34]	23 + 3 + .5[17]	5	34.5
2			17 + 1 + .5[38]	19 + 2 + .5[34]	21 + 3 + .5[17]		4	32.5
3		15 + 1 + .5[38]	17 + 2 + .5[34]	19 + 3 + .5[17]			3	30.5
4	0 + 1 + .5[38]	15 + 2 + .5[34]	17 + 3 + .5[17]				0	20

(Entering Inventory : i)

FIGURE 13.3. Dependable Manufacturing Company. Stochastic Demand Model ($n = 2$).

13.5 OPTIMAL BATCH SIZE MODEL

The Voltex Company, a manufacturer of industrial tape recorders, purchases from a supplier some very expensive and specially made electronic components. The company does not maintain an inventory of these components, since Voltex produces only to customer order and the specifications vary widely from customer to customer. Because of the exceptionally high quality standards required for the tape recording equipment, components often fail from a short circuit during the performance inspection phase. In this event, Voltex can return the components to the supplier for a full refund. In order to avoid the expense and inconvenience of having to delay production until more components arrive from the supplier,

Voltex initially orders a larger batch than it actually needs. But if Voltex orders too large a batch and consequently has excess components, it has to pay a cost penalty. (In some instances, the supplier will repurchase the excess items at a lower price than Voltex paid. But in other instances, the supplier will not buy back the component because it is so special that it is worthless to anyone else.)

The manufacturer's decision problem is to choose an optimum batch size. If Patsy Cotto, the production manager at Voltex, knew *exactly* how many components would fail for each batch size, her decision problem would be simple. But she does not—and that makes the analysis nontrivial.

Let

$$c = \begin{pmatrix} \text{cost per electronic component} \\ \text{purchased from the supplier} \end{pmatrix}$$

$$v = \begin{pmatrix} \text{salvage value per component in excess of} \\ \text{required amount (where } 0 \le v \le c) \end{pmatrix}$$

$$K = \begin{pmatrix} \text{expense of } \textit{reordering if additional} \\ \text{components are required} \end{pmatrix}$$

$$p_x(j) = \begin{pmatrix} \text{probability that } j \text{ out of a batch of } x \text{ components} \\ \text{pass the inspection process [where } p_x(0) < 1] \end{pmatrix}.$$

As you think about the way an actual decision process of this sort would evolve over time, you will discover how to formulate the problem as a multistage optimization model. Suppose N undamaged components are required, and you place an order for $x \ge N$. If j pass inspection and $j \ge n$, then you have met your requirement, and $j - n$ good components are left over as salvage. But if $j < N$, then you still need $N - j$ more. [For example, if to receive 10 good components, you order 15 and 9 work, then you still need 1 ($= 10 - 9$) more component.]

So when $j < N$, you have to reorder. Your decision problem at this point will be of the same character as before, except now you need fewer components (unless all that you ordered before turned out to be defective). In any event, the only information you need to have about the outcome of the previous batch is how many good components you still require. Thus, the appropriate state variable is the number of undamaged components required.

Assume that an optimal policy is one that minimizes the expected total cost to meet the requirements. Let n denote the amount required, and consider what the total expected cost is if you order x. First, you must add in the actual purchase cost times the expected number of components that pass inspection—since components that fail are returned for full credit, you need not include the cost of such items. Second, in case you have some good components left over after meeting your requirements, you must reduce the overall expected cost by the expected salvage value. Third, in case the number of components that pass inspection is smaller than your requirements, you must also add in the reorder cost K, weighted by the probability of having to reorder, and likewise the expected cost because you need more components.

Consequently, letting $f(n)$ denote the minimum expected cost when n working components are required, the value for $f(n)$ must satisfy

(1)
$$f(n) = \underset{x \geq n}{\text{minimum}} \left\{ c \sum_{j=0}^{x} j p_x(j) - v \sum_{j=n}^{x} (j - n) p_x(j) \right.$$
$$\left. + \sum_{j=0}^{n-1} [K + f(n - j)] p_x(j) \right\} \quad \text{for } n = 1, 2, 3, \dots.$$

An $x(n)$ that yields $f(n)$ is an optimal batch size. The set of $x(n)$, for $n = 1, 2, 3, \dots$ is an optimal decision rule.

If N components are required, then $f(n)$ is successively computed for $n = 1, 2, \dots, N$. But note that (1) has to be manipulated slightly because the term $f(n)$ also appears on the right-hand side of (1) for $j = 0$ in the third summation. Accordingly, (1) must be simplified to yield a form suited for computational solution.

The algebra is straightforward and leads to the formula

(2)
$$f(n) = \underset{x \geq n}{\text{minimum}} \; [1 - p_x(0)]^{-1} \left\{ c \sum_{j=0}^{x} j p_x(j) - v \sum_{j=n}^{x} (j - n) p_x(j) \right.$$
$$\left. + K \sum_{j=0}^{n-1} p_x(j) + \sum_{j=1}^{n-1} f(n - j) p_x(j) \right\},$$

where you ignore the final summation on the right for $n = 1$. The minimization in (2) indicates only a lower limit on x; in an actual computation, you must also impose a reasonable upper limit so that the calculations are finite.

Numerical example. To illustrate (2), suppose

(3) $c = 10 \qquad v = 10$

and $p_x(j)$ is described by a binomial probability law

(4) $$p_x(j) = \frac{x!}{j! \, (x - j)!} p^j (1 - p)^{x-j} \quad \text{for } j = 0, 1, \dots, x,$$

where p is the probability of a single component passing inspection. Then Fig. 13.4 shows the optimal batch size amounts $x(n)$, when n components are required, and when the probability of passing inspection $p = \frac{3}{4}, \frac{1}{2}$, and $\frac{1}{4}$, and the reorder cost $K = 50$ and 1000. In the next paragraphs we exhibit several of the computations that underly the results summarized in Fig. 13.4.

Consider the case $c = 10$, $v = 0$, $K = 50$, and $p = \frac{3}{4}$. The binomial probabilities $p_x(j)$, for $x = 1, \dots, 5$, are displayed in Fig. 13.5. Observe that the first summation on the right of (2) is simply the expected number of components passing inspection when x are tested. Hence, this expectation $E(j)$ is also tabulated in Fig. 13.5.

$$(c = 10, v = 0)$$

K	n	$p = \frac{3}{4}$			$p = \frac{1}{2}$			$p = \frac{1}{4}$		
		$x(n)$	$f(n)$	$f(n)-cn$	$x(n)$	$f(n)$	$f(n)-cn$	$x(n)$	$f(n)$	$f(n)-cn$
50	1	2	19.3	9.3	3	24.3	14.3	8	27.8	17.8
	2	3	33.5	13.5	6	38.3	18.3	13	42.7	22.7
	3	5	44.9	14.9	8	51.3	21.3	17	56.1	26.1
	5	8	68.3	18.3	12	75.7	25.7	26	80.9	30.9
	10	15	123.8	23.8	23	132.4	32.4	46	138.8	38.8
1000	1	4	34.0	24.0	7	43.1	33.1	17	50.4	40.4
	2	6	49.8	29.8	11	61.1	41.1	24	69.5	49.5
	3	8	64.4	34.4	13	76.7	46.7	30	86.2	56.2
	5	11	90.3	40.3	19	105.1	55.1	41	116.5	66.5
	10	19	151.7	51.7	31	170.5	70.5	67	184.5	84.5

Note: K = reorder cost
c = purchase cost
v = salvage value
p = passing probability
n = number required

FIGURE 13.4. Voltex Company Batch Ordering Example.

$$p_x(j) = \frac{x!}{j!(x-j)!} \left(\tfrac{3}{4}\right)^j \left(\tfrac{1}{4}\right)^{x-j}$$

x \ j	0	1	2	3	4	5	E(j)
1	.2500	.7500					0.75
2	.0625	.3750	.5625				1.50
3	.0156	.1406	.4219	.4219			2.25
4	.0039	.0469	.2109	.4219	.3164		3.00
5	.0010	.0146	.0879	.2637	.3955	.2373	3.75

FIGURE 13.5. Binomial Probabilities for j Passing Inspection ($p = \frac{3}{4}$).

To begin, let $n = 1$, and consider values $x = 1, 2, 3$. Then (2) implies

$$(5) \quad f(1) = \text{minimum} \begin{cases} [1 - .2500]^{-1}[10(0.75) + 50(.2500)] \\ \qquad\qquad\qquad\qquad\qquad = 26.67 \quad \text{for } x = 1 \\ [1 - .0625]^{-1}[10(1.50) + 50(.0625)] \\ \qquad\qquad\qquad\qquad\qquad = 19.33 \quad \text{for } x = 2 \\ [1 - .0156]^{-1}[10(2.25) + 50(.0156)] \\ \qquad\qquad\qquad\qquad\qquad = 24.26 \quad \text{for } x = 3 \end{cases} = 19.33,$$

so that $x(1) = 2$.

Next, let $n = 2$, and suppose we consider values $x = 2, 3, 4, 5$. Then (2) gives

$$(6) \quad f(2) = \text{minimum} \begin{cases} [1 - .0625]^{-1}[10(1.50) + 50(.0625 + .3750) \\ \qquad + 19.33(.3750)] = 47.07 \quad \text{for } x = 2 \\ [1 - .0156]^{-1}[10(2.25) + 50(.0156 + .1406) \\ \qquad + 19.33(.1406)] = 33.55 \quad \text{for } x = 3 \\ [1 - .0039]^{-1}[10(3.00) + 50(.0039 + .0469) \\ \qquad + 19.33(.0469)] = 33.58 \quad \text{for } x = 4 \\ [1 - .0010]^{-1}[10(3.75) + 50(.0010 + .0146) \\ \qquad + 19.33(.0146)] = 38.60 \quad \text{for } x = 5 \end{cases} = 33.55,$$

so that $x(2) = 3$.

As a final illustration of the calculations in (2), consider $n = 3$ and $x = 5$. Then the associated expected cost is

$$(7) \quad \begin{aligned} &[1 - .0010]^{-1}[10(3.75) + 50(.0010 + .0146 + .0879) \\ &\qquad\qquad + 33.55(.0146) + 19.33(.0879)] = 44.91. \end{aligned}$$

Observe in Fig. 13.4 that $x(n)$ increases as the values of n, $1 - p$, and K increase. Additional information on the way $x(n)$ varies with N and K is given in Fig. 13.6, where $p = \frac{1}{2}$.

If the batch order size is $\bar{x}$, then the expected number of usable components is $p\bar{x}$. Therefore when $\bar{x} = n/p$, the expected number of usable components equals the requirement n. In the example, the value $x(n)$ is always larger than $\bar{x}$. The difference between these two values, which can be termed the **safety component**, is tabulated in Fig. 13.7. Notice that the difference increases with n; however, the *ratio* of the difference to $\bar{x}$ decreases with n.

One way to assess the economic impact of uncertainty is to compare the value of $f(n)$ with cn, which is the minimum cost (to Voltex) of obtaining n usable components. The difference $[f(n) - cn]$ can be interpreted as the most the manufacturer should be willing to pay if the supplier can provide components that always work. This quantity is evaluated in Fig. 13.4 for the numerical example. Note that $[f(n) - cn]$ increases with larger values for n, the reorder cost K, and the failure probability $1 - p$, but the value $[f(n) - cn]/n$ decreases with n.

$(c = 10, v = 0)$

$(c = 10, v = 0, p = \frac{1}{2})$

n	K			
	50	500	5000	50,000
1	3	6	9	13
2	6	9	13	17
3	8	12	16	20
5	12	17	22	27
10	23	30	36	41

Note: K = reorder cost
  c = purchase cost
  v = salvage value
  p = passing probability
  n = number required

FIGURE 13.6. Voltex Company Optimal Batch Size $x(n)$.

K	n	$p = \frac{3}{4}$		$p = \frac{1}{2}$		$p = \frac{1}{4}$	
		$\bar{x}$	$x(n) - \bar{x}$	$\bar{x}$	$x(n) - \bar{x}$	$\bar{x}$	$x(n) - \bar{x}$
50	1	1.33	.66	2	1	4	4
	5	6.66	1.33	10	2	20	6
	10	13.33	1.66	20	3	40	6
1000	1	1.33	2.66	2	5	4	13
	5	6.66	4.33	10	9	20	21
	10	13.33	5.66	20	11	40	27

Note: $\bar{x} = \dfrac{n}{p}$

  K = reorder cost
  c = purchase cost
  v = salvage value
  p = passing probability
  n = number required

FIGURE 13.7. The Voltex Company. Safety Component of Optimal Batch Size.

13.6 STOCHASTIC REGENERATION MODEL—EQUIPMENT REPLACEMENT

The finite horizon deterministic regeneration model can be stated succinctly as follows: over the next n periods, starting with the current period, the decision-maker must choose from among N alternatives, which are indexed $k = 1, 2, \ldots,$ N. If Alternative k is selected at any period, then the next decision opportunity or regeneration occurs k periods later, when a choice must be made again. (When $n < N$, then the choice is limited to $k = 1, 2, \ldots, n$.) Assume that the cost of each alternative depends only on k and not on the period at which the alternative is selected; let

$$(1) \qquad R_k = \begin{pmatrix} \text{cost of Alternative k valued at the start} \\ \text{of a regeneration period} \end{pmatrix}.$$

An optimal regeneration policy is one that yields the smallest possible total cost over the entire horizon.

Define

$$(2) \qquad f_n = \begin{pmatrix} \text{cost of an optimal regeneration policy in which an} \\ \text{alternative must be chosen when } n \text{ periods remain} \\ \text{until the end of the planning horizon} \end{pmatrix}.$$

Then the values for f_n can be computed by the recursion

(3) $$f_n = \underset{k=1,2,\ldots,N}{\text{minimum}} [R_k + f_{n-k}] \qquad f_0 \equiv 0,$$

where $n \geq N$; for $n < N$, the minimum is taken over $k = 1, 2, \ldots, n$.

An important illustration of this model is a simple equipment replacement problem. Suppose that a new piece of equipment is purchased at the current period, and suppose that selecting Alternative k implies that the new machinery is retained for k periods, after which time it is scrapped and replaced with another piece of equipment. In this context, the regeneration problem is to determine the periods at which to replace the machinery. (A more elaborate version of this problem was treated in Sec. 10.5, where the cost of Alternative k was also permitted to depend on the regeneration period.)

For a stochastic version of the simple equipment replacement problem, suppose that the machinery may break down *before* the planned replacement. If, at a regeneration period, the planned replacement decision is k but the machine actually fails during the jth period of usage, then assume that the equipment must be replaced at the start of the subsequent period. Let

$$k = \begin{pmatrix} \text{planned replacement} \\ \text{interval} \end{pmatrix}$$

$$p_j = \begin{pmatrix} \text{probability that the equipment breaks down for} \\ \text{the first time during the } j\text{th period of usage} \end{pmatrix}$$

$$r_j \equiv \begin{pmatrix} \text{cost of operating the equipment during the } j\text{th period} \\ \text{of usage if the equipment does not break down} \end{pmatrix}$$

$$r_j + s_j \equiv \begin{pmatrix} \text{cost of operating the equipment if it does break down} \\ \text{during the } j\text{th period of usage when } j < k \text{ (where } s_j > 0) \end{pmatrix},$$

and where $\sum p_j = 1$, r_1 includes the initial purchase cost of the equipment, and for expositional simplicity, the equipment is assumed to have no salvage value. You can interpret s_j as a penalty cost for early breakdown.

It is notationally convenient to define

(4) $$q_k \equiv 1 - \sum_{j=1}^{k-1} p_j \quad \text{for } k > 1 \quad \text{and} \quad q_1 = 1,$$

so that q_k represents the probability that the equipment breaks down for the first time after the $(k-1)$st period of usage.

Assume that an optimal policy is one that minimizes expected cost over the horizon. If you are at a regeneration period and your planned replacement decision is k, then expected cost is comprised of the following. First, you must add the expected operating cost between this and the next (randomly determined) regeneration point. Second, you must include the expected cost at the next regeneration point and beyond in the event that the equipment does not break down before the planned replacement period. And, finally, you must add the expected cost incurred at the next regeneration point and beyond in the event that the equipment breaks down before the planned replacement period.

Accordingly, the appropriate generalization of (3) for $n \geq N$ is

$$(5) \qquad f_n = \underset{k=1,\,2\,\ldots,\,N}{\text{minimum}} \left[R_k + f_{n-k}q_k + \sum_{j=1}^{k-1} f_{n-j}p_j \right] \qquad f_0 \equiv 0,$$

where now

$$(6) \qquad\qquad R_k = \sum_{j=1}^{k} r_j q_j + \sum_{j=1}^{k-1} s_j p_j.$$

Ignore the last summation on the right of (5) and (6) whenever $k = 1$. For $n < N$, the minimum in (5) is taken over $k = 1, 2, \ldots, n$. [Observe that if a machine never breaks (hence all $p_j = 0$ and every $q_k = 1$), then (5) reduces to (3).] Let $k(n)$ denote an optimal decision found in (5).

In a situation in which the expected cost of Alternative k depends on the period at which the decision is made, the appropriate expected cost R_{nk} is substituted for R_k in (5).

To illustrate the calculations, consider the example in Fig. 13.8, where $N = 5$ (We have arbitrarily let the probabilities p_2 and p_4 equal 0 in order to reduce the amount of arithmetic required by the example.) The implied values for R_k are also displayed in Fig. 13.8.

k	p_k	q_k	r_k	s_k	R_k	$E[j \mid k]$	$\dfrac{R_k}{E[j \mid k]}$
1	$\frac{1}{4}$	1	100	20	100	1	100
2	0	$\frac{3}{4}$	$6\frac{2}{3}$	0^*	110	$1\frac{3}{4}$	$62\frac{6}{7}$
3	$\frac{1}{4}$	$\frac{3}{4}$	20	180	125	$2\frac{1}{2}$	50
4	0	$\frac{2}{4}$	20	0^*	180	3	60
5	0^*	$\frac{2}{4}$	56	0^*	208	$3\frac{1}{2}$	$59\frac{3}{7}$

*Each optimal policy is unchanged
even if these entries are made positive

FIGURE 13.8. Stochastic Replacement Model Example.

For $n = 1$, (5) is simply

$$(7) \qquad f_1 = R_1 + f_0 q_1 + 0 = 100 + 0(1) + 0 = 100 \quad \text{for } k = 1,$$

so that $k(1) = 1$. For $n = 2$, (5) is

$$(8) \qquad f_2 = \text{minimum} \left\{ \begin{aligned} & R_1 + f_1 q_1 + 0 && = 100 + 100(1) + 0 \\ & && = 200 \quad \text{for } k = 1 \\ & R_2 + f_0 q_2 + f_1 p_1 && = 110 + 0(\tfrac{3}{4}) + 100(\tfrac{1}{4}) \\ & && = 135 \quad \text{for } k = 2 \end{aligned} \right\}$$

$$= 135,$$

so that $k(2) = 2$. The computations for $n = 3$ and 4 yield $f_3 = 158.75$ with $k(3) = 3$, and $f_4 = 239.69$ with $k(4) = 3$.

For $n = 5$, the recursion (5) implies

$$(9) \quad f_5 = \text{minimum} \begin{cases} R_1 + f_4 q_1 + 0 \\ \qquad = 100 + 239.69(1) + 0 \qquad\qquad = 339.69 \ \text{for } k = 1 \\ R_2 + f_3 q_2 + f_4 p_1 \\ \qquad = 110 + 158.75(\tfrac{3}{4}) + 239.69(\tfrac{1}{4}) = 288.98 \ \text{for } k = 2 \\ R_3 + f_2 q_3 + f_4 p_1 + f_3 p_2 \\ \qquad = 125 + 135.00(\tfrac{3}{4}) \\ \qquad\quad + 239.69(\tfrac{1}{4}) + 0 \qquad\qquad = 286.17 \ \text{for } k = 3 \\ R_4 + f_1 q_4 + f_4 p_1 + f_3 p_2 + f_2 p_3 \\ \qquad = 180 + 100.00(\tfrac{2}{4}) + 239.69(\tfrac{1}{4}) \\ \qquad\quad + 0 + 135(\tfrac{1}{4}) \qquad\qquad = 323.67 \ \text{for } k = 4 \\ R_5 + f_0 q_5 + f_4 p_1 + f_3 p_2 \\ \qquad\quad + f_2 p_3 + f_1 p_4 \\ \qquad = 208 + 0 + 239.69(\tfrac{1}{4}) \\ \qquad\quad + 0 + 135(\tfrac{1}{4}) + 0 \qquad\quad = 301.67 \ \text{for } k = 5 \end{cases}$$

$$= 286.17,$$

so that $k(5) = 3$. Continuing in the same fashion, you would find that $f_6 = 315.61$ with $k(6) = 3$, and $f_7 = 383.67$ with $k(7) = 3$. The computation for $n = 7$ with $k = 3$ is

$$(10) \quad R_3 + f_4 q_3 + f_6 p_1 + f_5 p_2 = 125 + 239.69(\tfrac{3}{4}) + 315.61(\tfrac{1}{4}) + 0 = 383.67.$$

The decision $k(n) = 3$ is optimal for all $n \geq 3$. Thus, if the planning horizon is at least 3 periods, the initial planned replacement decision is for 3 periods, and remains so at every regeneration point until the horizon is less than 3 periods. (When $n = 1$ or 2, the planned replacement is for n periods.)

*13.7 SALES FORECASTING PROBLEM

Each example so far had a one-dimensional state variable, and the random elements were completely independent. In the illustration below, we show how correlated random variables can be introduced at the expense of enlarging the dimension of the state variable.

Consider the following simplified version of an actual situation. During the first N weeks of a season, the Buss-Stout Company, a manufacturer of lady's sweaters, has some flexibility in adjusting the level of total production for each item in its line. In the fashion-wear industry, as in many another, a manufacturer cannot predict with certainty the total amount of orders it will receive for each item. Since the company's sales staff call on the retail trade throughout the N weeks, new bookings arrive continually during the season.

The manufacturing expenses include not only labor and materials costs but also costs due to adjusting the level of total production. The latter expense arises from the disruptions associated with substantially varying the size of the production line at the factory; it is particularly costly to increase the total production level late in the season. If the Buss-Stout Company sets the level for an item too high, it accordingly has goods left over at the end of the season, and must dispose of them at a loss. If the company schedules the level too low, it may lose potential sales revenue. And the company incurs a penalty cost if it tries to adjust the production schedule upward too much as it receives better information each week about the amount of total orders. In addition to the impact of the penalty cost, the variation in production level is also constrained to be within certain bounds, depending on the production level in the previous period as well as on how many periods in the season have elapsed.

The manufacturer's own season runs several months ahead of its customers' season. Buss-Stout produces the Fall line early in the year, for example. In general, the company completes its production before the retailers' season begins, and sales revenue depends only on how many orders *in total* the company is able to fill by the time it ceases production. Consequently, Buss-Stout's scheduling problem is essentially due to the *uncertain* elements, because if it could know the amount of total orders exactly, the company would produce at an even rate throughout its season.

This scheduling problem for each item can be formulated by an optimization model. Let

$$D_t = \textit{accumulated} \text{ bookings of the item at the beginning of Week t.}$$

Since there are cancellations as well as new orders each week, D_{t+1} may be smaller than D_t. Assume that D_{t+1} depends only on D_t and is independent of earlier bookings and the production level. Let

$$p_t(D \mid d) = \begin{pmatrix} \text{conditional probability that accumulated bookings } D_{t+1} \text{ will equal} \\ D, \textit{given} \text{ that accumulated bookings } D_t \text{ equal } d, \text{ for } t = 1, 2, \ldots, \\ N-1 \end{pmatrix}$$

$$p_N(D \mid d) = \begin{pmatrix} \text{conditional probability that } \textit{total bookings} \text{ for the season will be } D, \\ \text{given that accumulated bookings } D_N \text{ equal } d \end{pmatrix}.$$

The manufacturer bases the values of these probabilities on booking statistics from previous seasons.

Also let

$$r = \begin{pmatrix} \text{dollar return from an item} \\ \text{sold during the season} \end{pmatrix}$$

$$s = \begin{pmatrix} \text{dollar return from an item} \\ \text{disposed after the end of the season} \end{pmatrix}$$

$$c_t(X \mid x) = \begin{pmatrix} \text{cost of setting the } \textit{total} \text{ production level at } X \text{ in Week t,} \\ \text{given that the level was set at } x \text{ in the previous week} \end{pmatrix},$$

where r and s *include* the direct labor and materials cost of manufacturing a unit, and $s < 0$. Assume that $L_t(x)$ and $U_t(x)$ are the lower and upper limits on X, representing the range of feasible levels given that x is the scheduled level just prior to Week t.

A decision rule then consists of a strategy indicating a level for current production X given values for previous production x and D_t; assume an optimal rule is one that maximizes expected return. An optimal strategy may be found by solving the dynamic programming recursion:

$$(1) \qquad f_N(x, d) = \max_{L_N(x) \le X \le U_N(x)} \left\{ \sum_{D=0}^{X} [rD + s(X - D)] p_N(D \mid d) \right.$$

$$\left. + rX \sum_{D > X} p_N(D \mid d) - c_N(X \mid x) \right\}$$

$$(2) \qquad f_t(x, d) = \max_{L_t(x) \le X \le U_t(x)} \left\{ -c_t(X \mid x) + \sum_D f_{t+1}(X, D) p_t(D \mid d) \right\}$$

$$\text{for } t = N - 1, \ldots, 1.$$

where the inequality $D > X$ under the second summation sign in (1) indicates that the sum is over every possible value of end-of-the-season accumulated bookings that is greater than X, and the D under the summation sign in (2) indicates that the sum is over every possible value for accumulated bookings D_{t+1}.

The value of $f_1(X^*, D^*)$ represents the maximum expected return, assuming that the preseason production level is set at X^* and bookings-to-date at the start of Week 1 are D^*. Notice that the state variable in (2) is two-dimensional; the first component reflects the previous decision and the second indicates the realized value of a random event.

13.8 APPLICABILITY AND
COMPUTATIONAL FEASIBILITY

You will find it helpful to review the summary remarks about dynamic programming in Secs. 10.11 and 10.12, since they are equally pertinent to models with stochastic elements. The most important applications of these models are in special contexts, such as finding optimal inventory replenishment rules, minimal cost maintenance and replacement policies, efficient waiting line disciplines, etc. In sharp contrast to the situation pertaining to the application of linear programming, no general purpose dynamic programming computer codes are widely available. This does not represent any real drawback to the use of the technique, however, since the computational formulas for any specific problem are simple enough to be coded for computer solution on an ad hoc basis with only a modest effort.

Using advanced analytic methods, it is possible to solve stochastic dynamic programming models with less restrictive assumptions than those made in this chapter. For example, you sometimes can analyze situations in which time is treated as a continuous variable, where the states and decisions are not necessarily discrete or finite, and where the horizon is unbounded. And in many of these cases, the approaches in this chapter are generalized in a straightforward fashion. But such extensions are not pursued in this text.

REVIEW EXERCISES

1 Consider the Distribution of Effort Model in Sec. 13.2. Assume the demand distribution at Store j is $p_j(d) = \frac{1}{5}$, for $d = 6, 7, \ldots, 10$. In each part below, calculate the expected profit $R_j(y_j)$, for $y_j = 0, 1, 2, 3$, given by (10), employing the specified profit function $r_j(d \mid y)$, as defined by (7). Assume $Q = 4$.

(a)
$$r_j(d \mid y) = \begin{cases} 10d & \text{for } d \le Qy \\ 10Qy & \text{for } d > Qy. \end{cases}$$

(b)
$$r_j(d \mid y) = \begin{cases} 10d & \text{for } d \le Qy \\ 10Qy + 8(d - Qy) & \text{for } d > Qy. \end{cases}$$

(c) Rework part (b), using the coefficient 6, instead of 8.

(d)
$$r_j(d \mid y) = \begin{cases} 10d & \text{for } d \le Qy \\ 10d - 2 & \text{for } d > Qy. \end{cases}$$

(e) Rework part (d), using the constant 4, instead of 2.

*(f) Suggest situations that might give rise to the profit functions in parts (b) and (d). (*Hint*: consider the possibilities of the customer purchasing another brand or the store manager expediting a resupply.)

2 Answer the questions in exercise 1, parts (a) through (e), except let the demand distributions be

(a) $p_j(d) = \dfrac{d + 1}{15}$ for $d = 6, 7, \ldots, 10$.

(b) $p_j(d) = \dfrac{5 - d}{15}$ for $d = 6, 7, \ldots, 10$.

(c) $p_j(6) = p_j(10) = \frac{1}{9}, p_j(7) = p_j(9) = \frac{2}{9}, p_j(8) = \frac{3}{9}$.

(d) $p_j(6) = p_j(10) = \frac{3}{11}, p_j(7) = p_j(9) = \frac{2}{11}, p_j(8) = \frac{1}{11}$.

*3 *Shopping Basket Markets* (Sec. 13.2). Suppose the demand at the s stores are correlated. In particular, assume there are R possible sets of values for the demands $(D_1, D_2, \ldots, D_s)$ at Stores $1, 2, \ldots, s$, and p_r is the probability of the rth set of values. Show how to determine the cost of uncertainty. (That is, indicate how to calculate the maximum value to the owner of having a perfect prediction of demand before he allocates the eggs.)

4 *Cool It Company* (Sec. 13.3). Suppose the data pertinent to the decision tree in Fig. 13.1 are

$$h_1 = 40 \qquad g_1 = 50 \qquad r_1 = 60 \qquad p_1 = .2$$

$$h_2 = 60 \qquad g_2 = 70 \qquad r_2 = 90 \qquad p_2 = .5$$

$$h_3 = 70 \qquad g_3 = 80 \qquad \text{—} \qquad p_3 = 1.$$

(a) Calculate f_3, f_2, f_1 and exhibit the optimal strategy.
(b) Give the probability distribution for the decision process terminating in Period t, for $t = 1, 2, 3$.
(c) Explain why the expected profit is different at the beginning of Period 1 from what it is at the beginning of Period 2, *given* that the decision process continues beyond the first period.
(d) What is the largest value for r_1 such that the Period 1 decision remains optimal? Similarly, what is the smallest value for h_1? Similarly, what is the smallest value for r_2?
(e) Assuming that the decision process lasts beyond the first period, what is the smallest value for r_2 such that the Period 2 decision remains optimal? Similarly, what is the largest value for h_2? Similarly, what is the largest value for g_3?
(f) What is the largest value for p_1 such that the Period 1 decision remains optimal? Similarly, what is the largest value for p_2?
(g) Assuming that the decision process lasts beyond the first period, what is the smallest value for p_2 such that the Period 2 decision remains optimal?
*(h) Suppose that the p_t are accurate probabilities for the competitors' decisions, but that the President can purchase information indicating whether the competitors will introduce before he has to make his own decision. If the decision process lasts beyond the first period, the President can again find out whether the competitors will introduce in Period 2, etc. How much is such perfect information worth?

*5 *Cool It Company* (Sec. 13.3). Show how the value of f_1 in (2) can be obtained from a linear programming formulation. (Show all the constraints for $t = 1, 2, \ldots, T$ and each decision; display the objective function). Exhibit the model in detail for $T = 3$. Write the dual problem and interpret the variables and constraints. (*Hint:* the variables in the dual problem can be viewed as probabilities.)

Exercises 6 through 12 refer to the stochastic inventory model described in Sec. 13.4.

6 (a) Justify in detail the constraints (7) and (8).
 (b) Explain why the optimal production level x is $4 - i$ when $n = 1$.
 (c) Justify in detail each term after the first equality in (10). (*Continued on p. 423.*)

(d) Suppose the holding cost function is $h \cdot (i + x - D)^2$ for $i + x > D$, and 0 otherwise. How is (10) modified?

(e) Verify the entries in Fig. 13.2 for $n = 3$. For $n = 4$.

(f) Suppose there are three periods remaining in the horizon and entering inventory is 1. What is the probability distribution for the optimal production quantity in the next period? In the final period?

7 Suppose the demand distribution is $P[D = 1] = \frac{1}{3}$ and $P[D = 4] = \frac{2}{3}$.

(a) Write the appropriate recursion analogous to (10).

(b) Calculate $f_n(i)$ and $x_n(i)$, analogous to the entries in Fig. 13.2, for $n = 1$ and 2. For $n = 3$.

8 Suppose the demand distribution is $P[D = d] = \frac{1}{3}$ for $d = 2, 3, 4$.

(a) Write the appropriate recursion analogous to (10).

(b) Calculate $f_n(i)$ and $x_n(i)$, analogous to the entries in Fig. 13.2, for $n = 1$ and 2. For $n = 3$.

9 Give a plausible argument explaining why the optimal policy "settles down" so much faster (at $n = 3$) than it did in the deterministic version (at $n = 18$).

10 Suppose you drop the assumption that a stockout never occurs, so that the restriction in (7) is eliminated; whenever demand exceeds entering inventory plus production, the excess is lost. Suppose, however, the company earns revenue r per item of demand filled. Let the symbol $p(q)$ denote the probability that demand is q, where $q = 0, 1, 2, \ldots$. Show how to alter the recursion (10) accordingly. (*Note:* the objective is to maximize expected profit.)

11 (a) Suppose the minimization criterion is expected *discounted cost*, where the one-period discount factor is α, $0 \le \alpha \le 1$. Show how to alter the recursion (10) accordingly.

(b) Suppose there is a probability q, $0 \le q \le 1$, representing at each period the chance that the items will not be needed anymore in future periods. In other words, q is the probability that the horizon does not last beyond the current period; if, however, the items *are* demanded in the next period, then again probability q is the chance that the horizon does not extend beyond the second period, etc. Show how to alter the recursion (10) accordingly.

12 Suppose the company can obtain a perfect forecast of each period's demand. That is, prior to choosing production x, suppose the company can learn the actual level of demand. [This amount still varies from period to period according to the probability distribution in (6).]

(a) Formulate a dynamic programming recursion to find an optimal policy. (*Hint:* you can let the state variable be entering inventory minus current demand.)

(b) Calculate optimal policies for $n = 1, 2, 3, 4$.

(c) What is the maximum worth to the company of having such a perfect forecast if the horizon $n = 1$? If $n = 2$? If $n = 3$? Assume initial inventory at the start of the horizon equals 0.

13 *Voltex Company* (Sec. 13.5)

(a) Give a verbal interpretation of each term in the recursion (1).
*(b) Give the detailed algebraic justification for transforming (1) into (2).
(c) Consider the data in Fig. 13.4. Suppose you require three items, $K = 50$, and $p = \frac{3}{4}$. Explain the optimal strategy in detail. What is the maximum number of items that may be ordered? (Be careful!) Is it possible that you would ever place an order for three items more than once?
*(d) What is the expected number of items ordered in part (c)?
(e) How do your answers to the questions in part (c) change if $p = \frac{1}{2}$?

14 *Voltex Company* (Sec. 13.5). Consider the policies in Fig. 13.4. Verify the values of $x(n)$ and $f(n)$ for

(a) $K = 50$, $n = 1, 2, 3$, and $p = \frac{3}{4}$.
(b) $K = 50$, $n = 1$, $p = \frac{1}{2}$.
(c) $K = 1000$, $n = 1$, $p = \frac{3}{4}$.

15 *Voltex Company* (Sec. 13.5). Suppose the salvage value $v > 0$. How are $x(n)$ and $f(n)$ in Fig. 13.4 affected? Corroborate your economic intuition by letting $v = 5$, $K = 50$, $p = \frac{3}{4}$, and finding $x(n)$ and $f(n)$ for $n = 1, 2, 3$.

16 *Voltex Company* (Sec. 13.5)

(a) Consider the tabulation of the safety components in Fig. 13.7. Give a plausible explanation of why the ratio of the safety component to $\bar{x} = n/p$ decreases with n.
(b) Give a plausible explanation of why the ratio $[f(n) - cn]/n$ decreases with n, where the bracketed quantity is tabulated in Fig. 13.4.

17 Consider the Optimal Batch Size Model in Sec. 13.5. Suppose N working items are required. Show how the value of $f(N)$ can be obtained from a linear programming formulation. (Show all the constraints for $n = 1, 2, \ldots, N$, and each x; assume that you have an upper bound X_n on x when n items are required.) Write the entire problem in detail for $N = 3$, $X_1 = 3$, $X_2 = 4$, and $X_3 = 5$. Also write the dual problem and interpret the variables and constraints. (*Hint:* the variables in the dual problem can be viewed as probabilities.)

Exercises 18 through 23 refer to the Stochastic Replacement Model described in Sec. 13.6.

18 Consider the finite horizon problem.

(a) Explain each term in the recursion (5).
(b) Derive the formula (6) for R_k. (Start with the conceptualization that the equipment may break down in either the first, second, third, ..., kth period of usage, or not at all during the planned replacement interval.)

*19 Consider the finite horizon problem. Let the horizon length be 6 and $N = 3$. Show how f_6 also can be found by a linear programming formulation. Write the dual problem and interpret the variables and restrictions.

20 (a) Verify all the entries in the examples shown in Fig. 13.8.

   (b) Show why the policy $k = 3$ remains optimal even if the entries marked 0* are made positive.

21 Consider the example in Fig. 13.8. Suppose the horizon is finite and let $N = 5$. Apply the recursion (5) to find an optimal policy for $n = 1, 2, \ldots, 6$.

22 (a) Suppose there is a probability q, where $0 \leq q \leq 1$, that the equipment will not have to be *replaced* again (because it will not be needed). Show how to alter the formulation for the finite horizon model.

   (b) Given that the equipment *is* needed in any Period t, suppose there is a probability q, where $0 \leq q \leq 1$, that the equipment will *not* be required in any future periods. Show how to alter the formulation for the finite horizon model.

*23 Suppose that when a new piece of equipment is purchased, the probability that the equipment breaks down during the jth period of usage is still p_j, but that you can know with certainty in which period a failure actually occurs. Hence you may decide to keep the equipment anywhere from 1 to j periods.

   (a) Formulate a dynamic programming recursion for the finite horizon problem.

   (b) Given your answer to part (a), apply the recursion to the data in Fig. 13.8; let $N = 5$. Find an optimal policy for $n = 1, 2, \ldots, 7$.

*24 *Buss-Stout Company* (Sec. 13.7)

   (a) Explain each term in the dynamic programming recursions (1) and (2). (Specifically, state how the formulation includes the expenses of labor and materials, as well as the costs of adjusting the level of total production. Indicate how disposal loss is accounted for, and how the formulation implies that there is a revenue loss if the production level is too low.) Write a definition for $f_N(x, d)$ and $f_t(x, d)$.

   (b) Explain what factors influence the values for the lower and upper limits on accumulated production in Week t, namely, $L_t(x)$ and $U_t(x)$. (Explain why these limits ordinarily depend both on the scheduled level x in the previous week and on the week itself.) Do the same for the cost function $c_t(X \mid x)$.

   (c) Explain what decision rules emerge from the solution of the recursions. Does the analysis yield a production quantity for each week? If not, suggest how to determine the weekly production level from the analysis.

   *(d) How does the formulation (1) and (2) differ if D_{t+1} depends on both D_t and D_{t-1}? (Be sure to define any new symbols you introduce.)

   (e) Suppose that the disposal value $s > 0$. How, if at all, does this affect the recursion (1) and an optimal policy?

   (f) Many companies like this one use statistical demand forecasting techniques. Is the information conveyed by the probability distributions $p_t(D \mid d)$ and $p_N(D \mid d)$ the same as a demand forecast? Explain. Why would you expect these probabilities to depend on both the accumulated bookings in Week t as well as Week t itself?

25 Explain your understanding of the following terms:

decision rules
decision tree
backward induction
solution characteristics
safety component (in the batch size model).

FORMULATION AND COMPUTATIONAL EXERCISES

In the exercises below, you are asked to formulate models in terms of dynamic programming recursions. Be sure to define all the symbols you use, and give the appropriate optimization function when there is a single period (stage) remaining. Explain how to initiate and when to terminate the calculations.

26 The Ball Sapphire Company is planning its annual budget for the exploration of sites at which to mine rare gems. The company has N potential locations. The President and Chief Geologist, Mr. Ball, estimates that if d_j dollars are spent in digging at Location j, then there is a probability $p_j(d_j)$ of finding gem stones, and *if* there is a successful finding, the return or value of the site will be v_j, where v_j is a random variable with probability distribution $q_j(v_j)$. Formulate a dynamic programming model to determine an exploration budget not to exceed D dollars that maximizes expected total return.

27 Golda Price, who was about to be married, wanted to buy her fiance, Sam Dammerung, a wedding present. One Wednesday morning, she went into downtown Boston to shop at the basement of Filene's Department Store, which is world famous for its sales and bargains. She saw a beautiful walking stick with a fancy filigree metal handle on sale for $30. It is Filene's marketing policy to reduce the price of its sale items each day, so if Golda waited until Thursday and the walking stick hadn't been sold in the meantime, she could purchase it for $25. And if Golda waited until Friday and the walking stick still hadn't been sold, she then could purchase it for $10. She estimated that if she didn't buy the walking stick on Wednesday, there was a .7 probability that it would be available on Thursday, and if it were available on Thursday but she delayed another day, there was a .6 probability it would be available on Friday. She knew that it would be sold by Saturday for sure. If she postponed buying the present until Thursday or Friday and then found it had been sold to someone else, she planned to buy her fiance a tennis racket for $40.

(a) Draw a decision tree and determine Golda's optimal strategy.
(b) If Golda uses her optimal strategy, what is the expected cost of the gift? What is the probability that the gift will be the walking stick?

28 *Ghengis Motor Company* (Sec. 10.7). The previous objective function for this example was to maximize net return from a radio advertising budget. Suppose, instead, that

the company wants most to reach a certain type of customer with its ads. It estimates that each daytime spot announcement on Station j has a probability p_j of reaching the desired type of customer, where p_j is assumed independent of the total number of spots on that station; recall $K_j(y_j)$ is the number of daytime spots aired on Station j from an allocation of y_j dollars. Similarly, let q_j denote the probability of reaching this type of customer in a prime time, and let $H_j(y_j)$ denote the number of such prime-time spots obtained on Station j with an allocation of y_j dollars. Define an optimal allocation to be one that minimizes the probability that the desired type of customer misses all of the commercials.

(a) Formulate the problem as a mathematical model, and show how a dynamic programming approach, analogous to that in Sec. 10.7, can be used to find an optimal solution.
(b) Show how to alter the formulation in part (a) if the objective is to maximize the expected number of times such a customer hears the company's ads.

29 The Saki Tumi Company is a Japanese manufacturer of portable television sets. It is designing a high-priced model and wants to ensure maximum reliability. The set contains N circuits in series, so that a failure in any one of the circuits causes the set to malfunction. Therefore, the design will include redundant parallel circuitry. Specifically, let x_n denote the number of parallel elements placed in the nth circuit, let $p_n(x)$ denote the probability that the nth circuit operates properly during the first year of usage, given a redundancy level x, and let $c_n(x)$ be the corresponding manu-facturing cost.

(a) Formulate an optimization model that maximizes the first-year reliability of the set, subject to the constraint that total manufacturing cost cannot exceed C.
(b) Show how the model can be solved by dynamic programming.
(c) Use your answer to part (b) to find an optimal solution for $N = 3$, where $c_n(x) = nx^2$, $C = 15$, and $p_n(x) \equiv 1 - p_n^x$, where $p_1 = .08$, $p_2 = .05$, $p_3 = .1$.
(d) Formulate an optimization model that minimizes cost subject to the constraint that first-year reliability of the set be at least R. Show the model can be solved by dynamic programming.

30 The D. P. Poole Company must sign a one- or two-month contract with its local electrical utility, the New Clear Power Company. One provision of the contract deals with the charge Poole must pay for the utility to provide a specified *peak* level of power during each month. The peak level is defined as the maximum number of megawatts used during any one-hour period within a month. Poole estimates the probabilities for the peak usage it requires in each of the next two months to be:

1 MW	2 MW	3 MW	4 MW	5 MW
.1	.3	.3	.1	.2

The peak usages for the next month and the month after are identical. If Poole contracts for a smaller peak load than it actually uses in a month, the excess is charged to Poole at a penalty rate of $100 per megawatt. For example, if Poole contracts for 3 MW and its actual peak usage in a month is 5, then it pays the utility a monthly penalty of $100 \times (5 - 3) = \$200$. The monthly cost of contracting for each level of peak usage is shown below:

1 MW	2 MW	3 MW	4 MW	5 MW
$2	$5	$10	$25	$50

These costs are applicable in each of the next two months.

The power company has offered Poole the options of either two one-month contracts (the second contract will be for the actual peak usage figure which becomes known at the end of next month), or a two-month contract at a discount of $k\%$ for each month. (For example, if the discount is 8% and if Poole makes a two-month contract for 3 megawatts peak usage, the contractual cost is

$$(1 - .08) \times 2 \times (\$10) = \$18.40.$$

If the peak usage is 5, then Poole pays an added penalty of $2 \times \$200 = \$400$.)

Use a decision tree to find the smallest value of k such that a two-month contract is preferred, and also determine the optimal amount of power to D. P. Poole.

31 Rock Kitt and his crew are planning a space mission to a distant planet. They must carry N different types of electronic gear, which, even in this day and age, are prone to failure. Each unit of Equipment i weighs w_i pounds, and there is a total weight restriction W. The value of W is large enough to permit taking along a limited number of spares to be put into operation when a piece of equipment fails. Let $p_i(t)$ be the probability distribution of the number of periods t that a unit of Equipment i operates before it breaks down (and must be discarded), and let x_i be the number of spares of Equipment i that Kitt takes along. When the supply of *any* of the types of equipment is exhausted (that is, when, for any Equipment i, all x_i have broken down) the mission has to return to Earth.

(a) Devise a dynamic programming model for selecting the quantities x_i to maximize the probability that the mission stays on the planet at least T periods. (*Note:* all N types of equipment are operated continuously on the mission.)

*(b) Devise a model for selecting the quantities x_i to maximize the expected time the mission stays on the planet. Can your model be solved using dynamic programming?

(c) Let $T_i(x_i)$ be the total expected number of periods that x_i units of Equipment i operate, *irrespective* of the other types of equipment. Devise a dynamic programming model that maximizes minimum $[T_1(x_1), \ldots, T_N(x_N)]$.

32 Newton Dewing has to solve a difficult homework problem for his operations research course. He knows from past experience that if he works too long on a problem, he goes "stale." Hence, he realizes that he may have to make several tries. Let $p_q(t)$ denote the probability that he solves the problem if he allocates t hours on the qth trial. He wants to minimize the probability of his failing to solve the problem.

(a) Formulate a dynamic programming model to give him an optimal strategy assuming that he will spend no more than T hours in total trying to solve the problem. (*Note:* he may take as many as T trials, each one lasting one hour.

Also, at the qth trial he can not have more than $T - q + 1$ hours left, since each trial must take at least one hour.)

(b) Show how the formulation simplifies if $p_q(t)$ does *not* depend on q, that is, if the probability of solution at each trial depends only on the number of hours t that is spent and not on how many previous trials there have been.

*(c) Show how the formulation becomes more complicated if the probability of success at the qth trial also depends on the total number of hours previously allocated to solving the problem.

33 Toulouse Maupentz is considering the purchase of a property that he hopes will appreciate in value. He feels that the value will either increase, thereby yielding a net *profit* of $100,000, or decrease, thereby yielding a net *loss* of $100,000. Maupentz can get an appraisal from his banker Flo Talone, whose predictive accuracy is summarized as follows. For properties that actually have increased in value, Talone has given a high appraisal 70% of the time, and a low appraisal 30% of the time. For properties that have decreased in value, Talone has given a high appraisal only 20% of the time, and a low appraisal 80% of the time.

(a) Suppose that Maupentz estimates that the probability of the property increasing in value is $p = .6$, and that *if* he seeks Talone's advice, he has to pay a fee of $10,000. What is Maupentz's optimal strategy? Draw a decision tree to illustrate your analysis.

(b) What is the largest fee that Maupentz should be willing to pay for Talone' appraisal? (*Continued on p. 732.*)

(c) Over what range of values for p will Maupentz want to use Talone's advice, which costs $10,000? Over what range of values for p will Maupentz forego obtaining Talone's advice?

34 Professor Frank N. Stein is notorious for his monstrous examinations. This term he is offering his students the opportunity to take a treacherously planned oral exam. He will ask a series of questions, each question being progressively more difficult. If the student correctly answers Question k, where $k = 1, 2, \ldots, K$, he can exercise the option of going on to the next (more difficult) question or terminating the exam and receiving the grade G_k, where $G_k < G_{k+1}$. If he misses Question k, Professor Stein flunks him. Suppose you are a student in this class, and you estimate p_k to be the probability of your correctly answering Question k.

(a) Formulate a dynamic programming model that gives you a rule for when to voluntarily terminate the examination if you have not already flunked—your objective is to maximize the expected grade you receive.

(b) Alter your formulation in part (a) if Professor Stein looks kindly upon you and allows you to make one error before flunking. (*Note:* if you decline Question k and missed Question k-1, your grade is G_{k-2}.)

35 The Chuckles Ice Cream Company operates a fleet of small trucks that cruise through residential districts and sell products directly to consumers. Assume that there are I products, where $i = 1, 2, \ldots, I$, and each unit of Product i requires c_i cubic inches of space in a truck. The total cubic space available on a truck is C. Consider the route

of a particular truck and assume that the demand q_i for Product i is described by a continuous uniform distribution, having the density function

$$p_i(q_i) = \begin{cases} \dfrac{1}{b_i} & \text{for } 0 \le q_i \le b_i \\ 0 & \text{otherwise.} \end{cases}$$

Let x_i be the number of units of Product i loaded into the truck; for simplicity, assume x_i is a continuous nonnegative variable. Since all the products sell for the same price, the company sets as its objective to minimize the expected number of unsatisfied demands per trip. Formulate the optimization problem for loading the truck. Explain how it can be solved by dynamic programming.

36 Selma Penny Stox owns shares in a large company whose securities are traded on the American Stock Exchange. The current price of her shares is $8. She intends to sell her shares within the next four weeks, and so must decide whether to make the sale now, wait a week, wait two weeks, or wait three weeks before selling. The stock market is in a state of wide fluctuation, and Selma believes that each week she waits, the share price may go down or up $2.

Thus, next week the price might be $6 or $10. The week after, the price might be $4 or $8 if next week the price is $6, or the price might be $8 or $12 if next week the price is $10, etc. Selma's estimates of the probabilities of the price going up or down are shown in Fig. 13.9. Thus, if she waits 1 week, then the probability is p that next week the price is $10 and the probability is $1 - p$ that the price is $6. Similarly, if after three weeks the price is $4, then the probability is .8 that the price in the following week will be $6 and the probability is .2 that the price in the following week will be $2.

(a) If $p = .3$, what is her optimal strategy?
(b) If p is sufficiently small, then Selma should sell immediately. At what value of p is she indifferent between selling immediately and waiting?
(c) Suppose that she alters her probabilistic beliefs, and states that under no circumstances does she believe the share price will ever go above $10. What is her optimal strategy for $p = .3$? What is the smallest value for p that would make her willing to wait at least one week before selling?
*(d) Suppose that Selma is vacillating in her assessment of the proper value for p, and is willing to give even odds that either $p = .1$ or $p = .5$. She can seek advice from her brokerage firm Byer, Lowe, Celler, Hye. How much would it be worth to her if this firm could give her perfect advice? (*Hint:* assume that the scenario is that Selma pays the firm a fee F, and after the payment learns whether $p = .1$ or $p = .5$; assume that the firm will reveal either of these values with equal probability.)

Week	Probability of Price Increase	Probability of Price Decrease
1	p	$1 - p$
2	.5	.5
3	.8	.2

FIGURE 13.9

37 Ivan Tew is a salesman for the Suburban Life Insurance Company. This week he will make as many as T telephone calls during the evening hours in trying to reach n potential clients. He estimates that Individual j may buy a policy worth v_j. To keep matters simple, suppose that he decides to allocate up to x_j calls in order to reach Individual j, where the sum of the x_j cannot exceed T. If he reaches Individual j before making x_j calls, assume he does *not* reallocate the unused calls to other potential clients. Let the probability that he can reach Individual j be p_j for each call he makes to Individual j, and assume this probability is independent of the previous (unsuccessful) calls he has made. He wants to select the x_j to minimize the expectation of the estimated policy values for all those individuals he fails to reach during the week.

(a) Formulate the problem as a mathematical optimization model. Show how a solution can be found using dynamic programming.

*(b) Show how to formulate the problem if Tew does not select the x_j at the beginning of the week, but makes his calling decisions one by one (depending on which potential clients he has not yet reached). Will this formulation yield a lower expected value than that in part (a)? Explain.

38 The Dolittle Washing Machine Company has been approached by Slips, a large chain of retail department stores, to manufacture a specially branded line of washing machines for sole distribution by Slips. Dolittle's annual profit is currently $1 million, and Slips' proposition will bring about an annual contribution to profit of $250 thousand. But the promotion of these machines by Slips will cut into Dolittle's own sales in such a way that the profit on its current business will drop by 25% with probability .1, 30% with probability .6, and 35% with probability .3.

If Dolittle turns Slips down, then there is a .4 chance that a competitor will accept Slips' offer. In that case, Dolittle stands to lose profit, as already described, unless it undertakes a costly advertising campaign or lowers its price. The advertising budget will reduce profit by $100 thousand; as a result, the profit on current business will only decline by 10% with probability .2, 15% with probability .7, and 20% with probability .1. The price cut has the combined effect of keeping the profit-reduction to 10% with probability .1, 15% with probability .8, and 20% with probability .1, *provided* that competition does not also reduce price. But there is a probability .5 that competition meets the price cut, in which case profit will decline by 10% with probability .1, 15% with probability .6, and 20% with probability .3. Construct a decision tree showing the structure of the problem, and determine an optimal strategy.

39 The Trans-Send Television Network has an elaborate approach for developing and selecting programs to be viewed over its affiliate TV stations. Each possible program goes through one or more stages of idea review, script development, pilot testing, and audience preview. (Actually some of these stages are subdivided into component stages.) Suppose there are at most T stages, and let c_t denote the cost of making the tth review. A program is judged a hit if the audience reaction is high, as determined by the Neil Downe TV Rating Service; the network stands to gain r dollars in revenue from a hit. The probability of a hit is p. But if a program turns out to be a bomb, the network earns only s dollars, where $s < r$. Since Trans-Send can always show old movies which earn v dollars, where $s < v < r$, it does not want to air a bomb.

If the program *is* going to be a hit, then p_t is the probability that the tth stage of review judges it so; *if* the program *is* going to bomb, then q_t is the probability that the

tth review judges it so. Assume that after the tth review, you can safely ignore the review test information from the previous stages. Thus, given the tth review outcome, you can calculate the probability of a hit using p_t or q_t along with p. After each review, Trans-Send can choose to drop the program from further development (and show a movie in the time slot), or to go on to the next review stage, or to air the show without any further reviewing stages.

(a) Let $T = 4$, and draw a decision tree for the review process.
(b) Devise a dynamic programming formulation for determining a review strategy that maximizes expected net return (that is, earnings less total reviewing costs).
(c) Compute an optimal strategy for $s = 50$, $v = 100$, $r = 200$, $p = \frac{1}{4}$, and

$$p_1 = \frac{1}{3} \qquad p_2 = \frac{1}{2} \qquad p_3 = \frac{2}{3} \qquad p_4 = \frac{3}{4}$$

$$q_1 = \frac{9}{10} \qquad q_2 = \frac{3}{4} \qquad q_3 = \frac{1}{2} \qquad q_4 = \frac{5}{6}$$

$$c_1 = 1 \qquad c_2 = 10 \qquad c_3 = 30 \qquad c_4 = 5.$$

40 Polly C. Holder has a theft coverage clause in her protection contract with the Sure-lock Homes Insurance Company. Polly estimates that each year there is a .1 probability that her home will be burglarized. This year, her insurance policy premium is $1000. Polly's insurance agent Izzy Fareel has advised her that if she has a theft during a year and makes a claim, her policy cost will rise 20% in the following year. (The insurance company never reduces the premium once it has been raised.) Assume that Polly's planning horizon is four years beyond the current year—that is, she expects to pay four more annual premiums.

(a) For the current and each of the next four years, determine the smallest theft amounts that are worthwhile for her to claim if her home is burglarized. In other words, for each of these years, determine the corresponding critical amount below which she is better off to absorb the loss than report it and thereby incur a higher premium in subsequent years.
*(b) Suppose that each year the insurance company reduces the premium by 5% if Polly has made no claim for the previous two years. Answer part (a) for this assumption.

41 The Eurohne Bag Company has made considerable profits on the sale of its major product due to a lack of any direct competition. The President of the company believes that in all likelihood the Micks Bag Company will announce a highly competitive product. To ward off a significant drop in his share of market, the President is going to allocate D dollars for advertising during the next T months. He estimates that the probability is p_t that Micks Bag will enter the market in Month t, if it has not already done so by then (assume $p_T = 1$ and that each p_t is unaffected by Eurohne's advertising strategy). If the President allocates d dollars in Period t to advertising, he can purchase $m_t(d)$ "messages." He feels that if his competitor enters the market at the end of Period t and if he has accumulated M advertising messages over the first t periods, then his company has a probability $q_t(M)$ of maintaining most of its present

share. Formulate an advertising expenditure strategy that maximizes the probability of the Eurohne Bag Company retaining its market position.

42 Consider the *deterministic* inventory model, summarized by (1) through (3) in Sec. 13.4. Suppose that the production cost function is random

$$
C(x) = \begin{cases} 0 & \text{for } x = 0 \\ 13 + cx & \text{for } x = 1, 2, \ldots, 5, \end{cases}
$$

where $P[c = 1] = P[c = 3] = \frac{1}{2}$.

(a) Assume that the production quantity x must be decided each period *prior* to knowing the value of c. Formulate the appropriate dynamic programming recursion, and indicate how it differs from (4) and (5).

(b) Assume that the production quantity x is decided after learning the value of c. Formulate the appropriate dynamic programming recursion.

(c) Find optimal policies in part (b) for $n = 1, 2, \ldots, 5$.

43 Consider the stochastic inventory model in Sec. 13.4, characterized by the recursion (10). Suppose that when one or more units of inventory exist at the end of a period, there is a probability $\frac{1}{5}$ that one of these units is damaged beyond use.

(a) Show how to alter the recursion (10) accordingly.

*(b) Find an optimal policy for $n = 1, 2, 3$.

44 Consider the stochastic inventory model described in Sec. 13.4. Suppose that $\bar{x}$ represents a "target" production level each period, and that if actual production x deviates from $\bar{x}$, a "smoothing cost" $v \cdot |x - \bar{x}|$ is incurred, where $\bar{x}$ is a prespecified constant.

(a) Show how to reformulate (10) to take account of this smoothing cost.

*(b) Let $v = 1$ and $\bar{x} = 3$. Find an optimal solution for $n = 1, 2, \ldots, 5$.

45 Consider the example of the Elementary Inventory Model with stochastic demands in Sec. 13.4. Suppose that the value of demand in Period t influences the value in Period t + 1. Specifically, assume that

$$
P[D_{t+1} = 2 \mid D_t = 2] = \frac{4}{5}
$$

$$
P[D_{t+1} = 4 \mid D_t = 2] = \frac{1}{5}
$$

$$
P[D_{t+1} = 2 \mid D_t = 4] = \frac{1}{5}
$$

$$
P[D_{t+1} = 4 \mid D_t = 4] = \frac{4}{5}.
$$

(a) Write a dynamic programming recursion analogous to (10).

(b) Find an optimal policy for $n = 1, 2, \ldots, 5$, and compare the results to those in Fig. 13.2. Assume $D_0 = 2$. *(Continued on p. 434.)*

(c) Rework part (b), assuming that

$$P[D_{t+1} = 2 \mid D_t = 2] = \frac{1}{5} \qquad P[D_{t+1} = 4 \mid D_t = 2] = \frac{4}{5}$$

$$P[D_{t+1} = 2 \mid D_t = 4] = \frac{4}{5} \qquad P[D_{t+1} = 4 \mid D_t = 4] = \frac{1}{5}.$$

Also compare the results with those in part (b).

46 The Waite and Cee Co. operates a printing shop that specializes in textbooks. The company's ambitious sales executive, Wanda Mae Kitt, has the responsibility of deciding what jobs to accept from the various publishers that utilize the services of Waite and Cee. Assume that each week, Kitt receives an offer from a publisher to print a book of p pages, where the range for p is $501 \leq p \leq 800$, and each value of p in this range is equally probable. The associated profit is given by the function $r(p)$, and the number of weeks to produce the book by the function $w(p)$; Waite and Cee, however, can only produce one book at a time. If a job arrives when the shop is engaged in the printing of another book, this job has to be refused and the customer goes elsewhere. If the shop is idle for a week, Waite and Cee incurs a cost K. When a job is completed, Kitt's decision problem is determining when to accept the next job. Observe that if p is too small, Kitt may prefer to keep the shop uncommitted for the following week, and if p is very large, Kitt may wish to forego the job because it will commit the shop for too long. Assume that Kitt's planning horizon is N weeks.

(a) Show how Kitt can determine whether to accept or refuse a job of size p.
(b) Alter your formulation in part (a) if Waite and Cee receives three different and independent offers each week.
*(c) Alter your answer to part (a) if Waite and Cee receives with equal probability either one, two, or three different and independent orders each week.
*(d) Alter your answer to part (a) if Waite and Cee can produce as many as two different books, provided that the total number of pages under commitment during a week does not exceed 1200.

47 *Equipment Replacement with Uncertain Costs.* Consider the example of the Rhode-Bloch Trucking Company in Sec. 7.2. Suppose the cost of a new piece of equipment leased at the start of Year i and replaced at the start of Year j is a random variable. Specifically, let r be a random variable having probability distribution $p_i(r)$ in Year i, and assume that the cost of initiating rental in Year i and replacing in Year j is given by a function $c_{ij}(r)$. Also assume that when a replacement occurs in Year i, the value of r in Year i is known before the decision is made to next replace at Year j.

(a) Formulate an appropriate dynamic programming model.
(b) Suppose that the probability distribution of r in Year i depends on the value of r in the previous year; let $p_i(r \mid r_{i-1})$ designate this probability distribution, where at $i = 1$, the value of r_0 is known exactly. Show how to alter the formulation in part (a) accordingly.

48 *Shortest-Route Model* (Sec. 7.2). Consider the example in Fig. 7.1. Suppose that the arc costs are random and that traversing each arc requires one period. Assume that

during Period t, the arc cost c_{ij}, where $c_{ij} = 0, 1, 2, \ldots$, occurs with probability $p_{ij,t}(c_{ij})$. Assume that each arc cost each period is completely independent of all the other random events. Suppose you can learn the actual value of c_{ij} only when the system arrives at Node i. The objective is to select a route from Node 8 (source) to Node 1 (sink) that minimizes expected total cost; the route must end no later than Period T. (*Note:* the *entire* route is *not* selected at the beginning of the horizon; each period you select an arc, depending on the current node and the arc costs.)

(a) Formulate a dynamic programming model to find an optimal strategy.

*(b) Suppose the number of periods to traverse arc (i, j) is random. Specifically, assume that during Period t, the arc time d_{ij}, where $d_{ij} = 1, 2, \ldots$, occurs with probability $q_{ij,t}(d_{ij})$. Suppose you can learn the actual value of d_{ij} only after you have selected arc (i, j). Show how to alter your formulation in part (a) accordingly.

49 *Stagecoach Problem* (Sec. 8.2). Consider the data in Fig. 8.1 and let $c_{ij}/20$ represent the probability that Mark Off does not survive the journey from State i to State j; for example, the probability of mortal danger in traveling from State 2 to State 6 is $c_{26}/20 = \frac{3}{5}$. Find a route that maximizes Mark Off's probability of survival. If you were Mark Off, would you take the trip? Explain.

*50 *Assortment Problem* (exercise 35 of Chap. 9). Suppose Itsa Steel does not know the exact amounts for the demand requirements D_j when it has to select the assortment of strengths. The company does, however, learn the demand quantities prior to the actual manufacturing of the beams. Let $P[D_j = D] \equiv p_j(D)$ be the demand distribution for Beam j. Show how to formulate the problem as a dynamic programming model.

51 Consider the study-time allocation problem of Howie Kramms, described in exercises 20 and 21 of Chap. 10. Suppose the grade point assessments given in those exercises occur only with probability $\frac{3}{4}$, and that the actual outcomes are one grade point lower with probability $\frac{1}{4}$. For example, if Howie studies a "gut" course for three periods, he receives seven grade points with probability $\frac{3}{4}$ and six grade points with probability $\frac{1}{4}$. Assume each random event is completely independent of the others.

(a) Formulate a dynamic programming model and find a solution; assume that Howie's objective is to maximize the expected number of grade points he receives.

(b) Assume instead, that Howie's objective is to maximize the probability that he receives at least 18 grade points. Revise your formulation in part (a) accordingly.

52 Consider the cattle ranching problem in exercise 36 of Chap. 10. Suppose that the revenue received in Year n is $R_n(y_n \mid p)$, where p is a random variable representing a general price level, and $q_n(p)$ designates the probability distribution of p in Year n. Also assume that the herd not sent to market increases in size by f-fold by the beginning of the following year, where $q(f)$ denotes the associated probability distribution for f. Formulate a dynamic programming recursion to determine how many cattle to send to market in each of the N periods; assume that

(a) The value of p is *not* known until after y_n is chosen.

(b) The value of p *is* known prior to choosing y_n.

53 *Capacity Expansion Problem* (exercise 37 of Chap. 10). Suppose each capacity requirement R_t is random, with probability distribution $p_t(R)$. Assume that $H_t(C, R)$ is also defined for $R > C$, and in that case includes a penalty cost for having too little capacity. Formulate the expansion model in terms of a dynamic programming recursion; assume that

   (a) The value of R_t is *not* known until after x_t is chosen.
   (b) The value of R_t *is* known before x_t is chosen.

54 *ARKA Mutual Fund Problem* (exercise 38 of Chap. 10). Suppose ARKA's gift of perfect prophecy is nullified, and instead, ARKA knows only the probability distribution $q_t(p)$ for the security price in a future Period t. Assume that when Period t occurs, the actual value of p_t becomes known before x_t is chosen.

   (a) Formulate the problem in terms of a dynamic programming recursion, and assume that ARKA wants to maximize the expected total amount of cash it can accumulate by the end of the horizon.
   *(b) Show how to alter the formulation in part (a) if the price in Period t depends on the price in the previous period, and the associated probability distribution is denoted by $q_t(p \mid p_{t-1})$.

55 Consider the case of the Feedem-Speedem Airline Company, described in exercise 34 of Chap. 2. Let the flight service requirement in Month t be D_t, where D_t has a probability distribution $p_t(D_t)$. Assume that D_t becomes known at the beginning of each month, and that the company must pay a penalty cost C for each stewardess-flight-hour that is required in excess of the time actually available for flight service during that month. Show how to find an optimal hiring and training schedule by means of dynamic programming.

56 Ina Rush is a busy lawyer with a passion for peanut brittle. Each day she passes a crowded candy store and faces the "moment of truth" as to whether to enter. Addicted to rationality as well as sweets, she estimates that each minute of her time is worth c; so if she waits w minutes in line, the associated waiting cost is cw. The candy, however, is worth r (measured in the same units as cw). She has carefully observed that if there are n customers in the store ahead of her, then there is a probability $p_n(s)$ that s of them will be served each minute (for the sake of simplicity, assume the random events take place in intervals of a minute and are independent in successive minutes). She limits the time she is willing to wait until being served to T minutes, and is psychologically prepared to leave the store if she finds the service is too slow.

   (a) Formulate a dynamic programming model to find an optimal policy for entering or leaving the store that maximizes Ms. Rush's expected value.
   (b) Explain whether the formulation changes if Ms. Rush only leaves the store after she is served or when the T minutes have elapsed.

57 Each year Willie B. Poore allocates funds between personal consumption and investment in either common stocks or bonds. Let $U_t(c)$ represent the value, or utility, to Poore in Year t of spending c dollars on consumption. Let r_s denote the return per dollar invested in stocks (that is, a dollar put into stocks at the beginning of the year yields r_s dollars at the beginning of the next year). Similarly, let r_b denote the return

per dollar invested in bonds. Let $p_t(r_s)$ and $q_t(r_b)$ be the associated probability distributions of the returns in Period t. (Assume these distributions are discrete, and $r_s \geq 0$ and $r_b \geq 0$.) Suppose Poore's horizon is T years and he starts with M dollars. He wants to maximize the expected sum of his consumption utilities over the entire planning horizon; assume cash after Period T is of no value to him.

(a) Exhibit a dynamic programming model that finds an optimal consumption and investment policy.

(b) Discuss how the formulation is changed if he revises his probability estimates each year on the basis of the previous year's return performance in stocks and bonds.

(c) Show how to alter the formulation if Poore does not have a fixed horizon T, but instead estimates that if he is still living in Year t, he will survive another year with probability l_t, where $l_t = 0$ for $t > T$. [Make the beneficent assumption that if Poore dies during Period t, he will have already enjoyed $U_t(c)$.]

58 James Stock, Agent 0007, is assigned to make photocopies of documents in the secret files of The Unfriendly Country. There are two such files, situated in separate locations. File X has M documents to be copied and File Y has N documents. Agent 0007 figures that he can make at most T tries at photographing the documents. For each picture-taking session, he believes the probability is p_X that he will be caught when rifling through File X, and similarly p_Y for File Y. Assume that if Stock gets caught, it means the demise of his life and camera. If he selects File X on his tth trial and it contains m documents remaining to be copied, he estimates that he can photograph $g(m)$; similarly, if he selects File Y and it has n documents remaining, he can photograph $h(n)$.

(a) Construct a dynamic programming model to devise a strategy that maximizes the expected number of documents photographed.

*(b) Suppose the probability is q_X for File X and q_Y for File Y that he hears a guard approaching while he is rifling a file. When this happens, he is able to slip away but must forego taking photographs during this attempt. Show how to revise your formulation in part (a) accordingly. (Assume that hearing a guard and being caught are mutually exclusive events and $p_X + q_X < 1$, and $p_Y + q_Y < 1$.)

59 Hedda Gambler is a bettin' woman and unlucky only in love. On each of the next N days, she has the opportunity to wager money on probabilistic outcomes. Assume she begins with I dollars and each day can bet any sum up to the amount she has at the start of the day. If she bets y_n dollars on Day n, the probability is p_n of increasing her capital by the same amount and the probability is $1 - p_n$ of losing that amount. She wants to maximize the probability that she has S dollars at the end of the N days.

(a) Formulate a dynamic programming recursion to find an optimal betting level each day, given the amount of cash at the start of the day.

(b) Suppose the situation is altered so that if she bets y_n dollars on Day n, she has probability $\frac{1}{4}$ of increasing her capital by $(8p_n - 1)y_n$, where p_n is the same *quantity* as above, and probability $\frac{3}{4}$ of losing y_n. Show how to revise the formulation in part (a) accordingly.

(c) Assume $N = 3$, $I = 1$, $p_1 = \frac{3}{8}$, $p_2 = \frac{5}{8}$, and $p_3 = \frac{1}{2}$. Find optimal policies in parts (a) and (b) for $S = 3$. For $S = 6$. Draw the corresponding decision trees. (Continued on p. 438.)

(d) Given the probabilistic assumptions in parts (a) and (b), show formulations appropriate to the objective of maximizing the expected amount of cash at the end of Day N.

(e) Apply the formulations in part (d) to the data in part (c) and find optimal policies.

60 *Cash Management Problem.* New York bankers always look forward to meeting their friends at the Bankers Tryst, a long established annual convention in the Poconos. This year members of the Chaste National Bank have proposed the following service-charge structure for corporate bank accounts. Each time a corporation makes a direct deposit or withdrawal of cash from its account, the bank will charge D or W, respectively. These cash transactions must occur at the start of the day. During the day, the balance of the corporation's account fluctuates due to deposited checks from creditors and due to other companies cashing the checks the corporation has written. If the balance falls below 0, the bank will automatically lend the customer the additional amount at the interest charge of r per dollar per day.

Suppose you are a Chaste customer and assess that your "opportunity cost" is s per dollar per day (that is, you can earn s on each dollar invested elsewhere). Assume that s, like r, is assessed on the bank balance at the end of the day. Let q be the amount by which the level of your account fluctuates during a day, and let $p_t(q)$ be the probability distribution of q on the tth day. Note that q may be either positive or negative.

(a) Formulate a finite dynamic programming model to determine the optimal amount of cash to deposit or withdraw at the start of each day.

(b) Show how your formulation changes if the transaction service and interest charges are deducted from your account.

61 An end-of-the-year sale on late model automobiles is being held by the Wheeler Dealer Agency. The firm has N autos it wants to sell in the next T days. The agency owner estimates that if he has n autos on Day t and sets the price at r, he can sell s autos that day with probability $p_t(s \mid r, n)$, where $s = 0, 1, \ldots, n$. If he has any cars left at the end of Day T, he realizes a value v on each. Formulate a dynamic programming model that sets price each day so as to maximize Wheeler's expected return on the N autos.

62 The Plutocratic Party, a national political organization, is trying to gain support for its Presidential candidate. It intends to spend as much as S dollars in newspaper advertisements over the next T weeks to raise campaign funds. If it has raised r dollars by the beginning of Week t, then $p_t(r_t \mid r, s_t)$ is the probability that it will raise r_t dollars during the tth week, given that it spends s_t on advertising. The Party wants to advertise in such a way as to maximize the expected number of dollars raised (inclusive of unspent advertising funds).

(a) Show how an optimal strategy for the amount of advertising to be done each week can be found using dynamic programming.

(b) Show how to alter the formulation in part (a) if S dollars are available at the beginning of Week 1 and the Party is willing to spend any additional funds it raises during the ensuing weeks to finance further advertising.

63 The Buy-and-Bye Food Store gives its customers excellent service by keeping open sufficient checkout stands to take care of the afternoon rush hour surge of customers.

The manager has gathered data on the number of customers that enter the store in each period (15 minutes) as well as on the number of customers m served during a period, which depends on both the number of customers in the store and the number of checkers s. Let $p_t(e)$ denote the probability that e customers enter the store at Period t (for simplicity, assume they enter at the start of the period). Let $q_t(m \mid n, s)$ be the probability that m customers are served during Period t, given that n are in the store at the beginning of the period and s checkout stands are open. Let w be the cost per period per checkout stand open. The manager makes a rough estimate of a com- / mensurate cost due to customers waiting for checkout. Assume that this cost is h_t per customer remaining in the store at the end of Period t.

(a) Formulate a dynamic programming model to determine an optimal policy during the rush hours, which consist of T periods.
(b) Show how to alter your formulation in part (a) if there is an added cost K each time a checkout stand is opened up (hence, the cost is pK if p stands are opened up in a period).

64 A beverage manufacturer is planning to introduce a new instant drink called Nicetea. He estimates that if the product is successful, then the company will make a profit of R (this figure actually represents a present value over a horizon of several years). He currently assesses the likelihood of this event to be p. If the product fails, the company stands to *lose* L, due to expenditures on equipment, packaging, and initial advertising. The manufacturer can do some preliminary market testing before spending L, and thereby get a better idea as to whether to introduce the product. Assume, for simplicity, that there are at most two market areas in which to test Nicetea, and that he does not have to decide to make a test in the second market area until he sees the outcome in the first. If Nicetea is going to be successful, the probability is p_1 that the first market deems it such, and q_1 that the first market deems it a failure. Similarly, if the product is going to be successful, the probability is p_{s2} that both the first and second markets deem it such, and p_{f2} that only the second market deems it such. If the product is going to fail, the probability is q_{f2} that the first and second markets deem it such, and q_{s2} that only the second market deems it such. Let the first market test cost C_1 and the second market test cost C_2 (you can assume that these amounts do not depend on test outcomes).

(a) Draw a decision tree for this problem. (*Note:* the manufacturer can decide to introduce or drop Nicetea at any point, and he only incurs L when he introduces the product.)
(b) Explain how to find an optimal strategy. Use the following data to illustrate your procedure: $R = 100$, $L = 50$, $C_1 = 5$, $C_2 = 10$, $p_1 = .5$, $q_1 = .75$, $p_{s2} = .8$, $p_{f2} = .5$, $q_{f2} = .9$, $q_{s2} = .6$.
(c) How does the procedure in part (b) simplify (if at all) when $p_{s2} = p_{f2}$ and $q_{f2} = q_{s2}$? Give a verbal interpretation of this assumption. Illustrate your answers using the data in part (b), except let $p_{f2} = .8$, and $q_{s2} = .9$.

65 *Secretary Problem* (Sec. 1.6). Formulate this example in terms of a dynamic programming recursion. Assume that the executive Kay Sera wishes to see no more than n secretaries (in Sec. 1.6, we let $n = 3$). Show how to alter the formulation if there is a cost c per interview.

*66 *Parking-Place Problem.* You are driving with your date to a movie and want to decide on an optimal strategy for parking your car (prior to seeing the movie). You can always put your car in a parking lot that charges B, which represents a lot of "bread" to you. Or you can try to park on the street. But if you park too far away from the movie, your date will think you are a piker, and probably inept in solving other parking problems. Suppose there are N parking slots on the street on each side of the movie house; for purposes of analysis, assume these are numbered $-N$, $-N+1$, $-N+2, \ldots, -1, 0, 1, \ldots, N-2, N-1, N$. (Place 0 is in front of the movie and not available for parking.) You estimate that the "piker factor" loss is $|n|$, where n is the number of the slot where you decide to park. Let p_n, for $n = -N, \ldots, -1$, $1, \ldots, N$, be the probability that slot n is vacant.

(a) Formulate a dynamic programming model that yields an optimal strategy. For simplicity, assume you only see one place at a time. (*Hint:* let the states of the system refer to the parking slot number and whether or not it is empty.)

(b) Write in detail primal and dual linear programming characterizations of your answer in part (a). Assume $N = 3$.

*67 Consider the inventory model with perfect forecasts of fluctuating demand that is described in exercise 12. Suppose that the forecasting procedure yields perfect knowledge of the amounts for both the present and following periods' demands. What is the most the company would be willing to pay for such a perfect forecast if the horizon $n = 2$? If $n = 3$? Assume initial inventory at the start of the horizon equals 0.

*68 *Astronaut Problem.* Not wanting to make mercurial decisions, an astronaut, C. U. Rowan, has turned to operations research for guidance. His mission plan calls for N orbits around the Moon. At the beginning of each orbit, he must judge his spacecraft to be in States 1, 2, or 3, corresponding to AOK (all systems "go"), minor malfunctioning, and major malfunctioning. In State 1, Rowan always elects to make another orbit if he has not completed his mission, and in State 3, Rowan must terminate the mission. In State 2, he can elect to go another orbit or to terminate. Let $P_n(j \mid i)$ denote the probability that if the astronaut makes the nth orbit and the state of his craft is i, where $i = 1, 2$, then the state of his craft at the next orbit is j, where $j \geq i$. Let $j = 4$ refer to the disastrous event that the mission has to be terminated immediately due to an emergency condition, and let $P_n(4 \mid i)$, for $i = 1, 2$, be the associated probability. If the astronaut terminates the mission after completing n orbits successfully, the value of the mission is v_n, where $v_n > v_{n-1}$. But if he must terminate during the nth orbit because of an emergency condition, the value is only w_n, where $w_n < v_n$.

(a) Formulate a dynamic programming model that yields an optimal strategy.

(b) Write in detail primal and dual linear programming characterizations of your answer in part (a). Assume $N = 4$.

*69 Each month the Bank of Hong Kong determines the amounts of funds it needs to borrow on the world money markets in order to finance the loan demands of its own customers. For simplicity, assume that the total requirements for Month t are D_t. Let the actual value for D_t be given according to a probability distribution $p_t(D_t)$, but suppose that the value of D_t is known at the start of Period t, prior to making any decisions in that period. Each month the Bank may decide to borrow funds for one, two, or three months, and denote these quantities as x_1, x_2, x_3. Since D_t is to be interpreted as a "capacity" requirement, the amount $x_1 + x_2 + x_3$ can be used, in part, to meet the requirement for D_t, and similarly, $x_2 + x_3$ for D_{t+2}, and x_3 for D_{t+2}. Suppose that the cost of borrowing x_j in Period t depends on a parameter r and is given by the function $c_{tj}(x_j \mid r)$, where r has a probability distribution $q_t(r)$, and the exact value of r is known at the start of Period t, prior to making any decisions in that period. Assume that all the random elements are completely independent of each other.

(a) Formulate a dynamic programming model that yields a minimum total expected discounted cost subject to the stipulation that all loan requirements are met. (Write a dynamic programming recursion for a general Period t, letting α denote the one-month discount factor.)

(b) Show how the formulation in part (a) simplifies (if at all) when the requirement D_t is known after making the Period t decisions; assume that if D_t exceeds the supply of available funds, there is a loss of c per unit.

*70 *Optimal Batch Size Problem.* The example of the Voltex Company in Sec. 13.5 can be described as a single-stage production process. Batch size problems frequently arise in multistage processes. Consider, for example, a manufacturing sequence comprised of four stages. The first stage is like that in Sec. 13.5, namely, a decision must be made to select the initial batch size x in an attempt to produce n good items by the end of the final stage. Some items that are produced at this stage do not meet standards and are scrapped. Assume every good item is then transmitted to the second stage. Here the production quantity cannot exceed the number of good items entering, but it can be less and the resultant excess can be sold. (If the number of good items entering is less than n, all of them are processed at this stage.) Again, some of the items processed at the second stage may not meet standards and are scrapped; the rest are transmitted to the third stage. A similar decision structure exists at the third and fourth stages. If fewer than n good items have been manufactured at the end of the fourth stage, the process starts all over again in an effort to fill the remaining requirement (which typically is smaller than n).

For Stage t, where $t = 1, 2, 3, 4$, let $c_t(x)$ denote the cost of processing x units, let $p_{tx}(j)$ denote the probability that j out of a batch of x components fail to meet standards, let s_t be the scrap value of an item below standard, and v_t the disposal value of an item sold.

(a) Write a dynamic programming formulation of the model. (*Hint:* let the state variable at the first stage be the number of good items required, and at subsequent stages be the number of good items required along with the number of items that met the standards from the previous stage.)

(b) Let the requirement $n = 2$ and assume that a batch size at Stage 1 cannot exceed 3. Write in detail the formulation in part (a). Then exhibit equivalent primal and dual linear programming models for finding an optimal policy. Also state the numbers of equations and variables in these models when the limit at Stage 1 is 4. When the requirement $n = 3$ and the limit at Stage 1 is 4.

CONTENTS

CHAPTER 14

Probabilistic
Inventory Models

14.1 NEW ORIENTATION

Previous chapters have focused on the development of widely applicable mathematical models and algorithms. Throughout, the mathematical models and the algorithms were illustrated by specific examples suggestive of real managerial applications of operations research.

In Chaps. 14 and 15, the orientation of "models first, applications later" is reversed. These chapters deal with particular decision areas in which operations research has proved beneficial, namely the management of inventories and the design of waiting line systems. The resulting mathematical models and algorithms are designed to fit the particular context of the problem. The solutions commonly yield optimal decision rules to be applied in an operating environment, and not merely guidelines to be used for planning purposes.

Of course, in a strictly formal sense, each model and algorithm can be classified as a special case of the models and algorithms you have already studied. But the new insights you will experience come from analyzing the particular nature of the models, *not* from recognizing that the models can be viewed as linear or dynamic programming problems. Now you will fully exploit the specific structure of these models.

The change in emphasis requires that you make a corresponding change in *your* study orientation. You should seek the fundamental concepts that are critical to the analysis of most problems in the particular area of application. Since there are infinite variations in the circumstances describing a particular application, it is impossible for any book, let alone an introductory text, to provide enough models to cover every eventuality. You can, however, learn the ideas that make

443

up the basic building blocks of such models, and these fundamentals are contained in the next two chapters.

In studying the material, remember to answer the following questions:

1. What decisions are to be made? What managerial problem is being solved?
2. What causes the real decision environment to be so complex as to require the use of operations research models? What elements of this complexity are embodied in the models? How do these elements affect the solution? What elements are ignored?
3. What distinguishes a good decision from a poor one?
4. If you were a manager, how would you employ the results of the analysis? In what ways might you want, or need, to temper the results because of factors not explicitly considered in the models?

Keep in mind that the answers should reflect the day-to-day nature of the decision problems in these areas.

14.2 SCIENTIFIC APPROACH
TO INVENTORY MANAGEMENT

Seeing inventories everywhere, every day, may have dulled your awareness that they are the direct result of managerial decisions. Your awareness is likely to be sharpened only when you find some item you want is out of stock in a grocery store, a hi-fi shop, or a bookstore. Irritated, you may say, "Somebody slipped up!" If the item is a Valentine's Day greeting card and the date is February 13, that "somebody" may be *you*. A shopkeeper can hardly be expected to have a large inventory of stock when his forecast of future demand is negligible.

Of course, the sheer pervasiveness of inventory decisions in business enterprises is not enough to justify an operations research approach. At least one additional condition must be present to warrant a company's applying this point of view: both the likelihood and economic impact of incorrect inventory decisions must be substantial enough to outweigh the cost of scientific analysis. To illustrate, a large stationery store may well find it profitable to derive an optimal inventory policy for stocking its supply of pencils, whereas you would find it silly to derive such a policy for the supply of pencils in your desk drawer.

So that you are not misled by the frequent reference to retail firms we mention that applications of inventory models are more widespread in manufacturing and wholesale companies, although this historical pattern is rapidly changing. For example, you will commonly find scientifically based inventory replenishment rules employed in large manufacturing plants to control hundreds, and often thousands, of items of raw materials, intermediate goods, and finished products. Typically, in these situations, only a very few persons are responsible for all the inventory replenishment decisions. You may wonder how mathematically derived rules can be an improvement over the experienced judgment of these individuals. The answer is given below.

Systemwide economics. Often a manager *does* outperform a mathematical formula in the replenishment of any given item. But to do so, the manager must carefully forecast the demand for the item and keep tab on the exact length of time required to obtain a resupply. If the item is important to the firm—because of its high cost or essentiality to the production process—then continual managerial review may well be the best policy. But there is a limit to the number of items that an individual can closely scrutinize. Since most companies inventory a myriad of items, it is inevitable that many of them will be stocked according to some routine or rule-of-thumb approach. Operations research can provide a cost-saving means of management for this large segment of the inventory system.

By establishing methodical procedures for replenishing most inventoried items, the scientific approach frees the decision-maker to concentrate talents on discretionary and exceptional situations, where experience is of greatest benefit. Thus an effective scientific inventory system really requires a harmonious combination of human judgment and mathematical formulas.

Operational simplicity. Inventory models are among the few instances in which the resultant optimal solutions of operations research models are implementable on a day-to-day basis. The reason is that in most inventory situations, the essence of the solution is simply

(i) A rule indicating *when* to replenish.
(ii) A rule indicating the *amount* to replenish.

In other words, an inventory policy signals the timing and magnitude of the resupply decision. No matter how complex the mathematical model or algorithm underlying the replenishment rules, the description of the policy in terms of (i) and (ii) is always easy to understand. Sometimes the rules are given by tables and only require the manager to state data, such as the item's price and average demand. But frequently the entire system is computerized, in which case the computer keeps an up-to-date record of the inventory level, and at the appropriate time prints out a replenishment order showing the correct amount. — Computerized

Even though inventory models are widely accepted, there are still many environments in which replenishment decisions are made according to arbitrary rules and judgment, despite the substantial losses that mistakes can inflict. A major contributing factor for the persistence of such rules-of-thumb is that these situations have not yet been studied intensively by operations research specialists. Further, the few solutions derived so far are much more complicated than (i) and (ii), so that implementation is correspondingly more difficult. Typically, these highly complex environments include situations in which there are significant interrelationships between the demands for the different items (for example, when several of the items can be substituted for each other) and when a firm stocks an item at more than one location (for example, at a regional warehouse as well as at several retail outlets). In time, operations research will deal successfully with these difficult problems.

Study objective. In the remainder of this chapter you will see several formulations of inventory models. Each is a prototype of a class of models that has been studied by operations research theorists. By understanding these basic approaches, you will become familiar with the main principles of inventory theory. Consequently, you will have the mastery required of a manager to comprehend the objectives, strengths, and limitations of a scientific inventory system. What is more, you will be equipped to study an in-depth text devoted to operations research inventory models, if you wish to learn more within this area.

14.3 GROUND WORK FOR INVENTORY ANALYSIS

What considerations are important for a firm's decision of when and how much to inventory of an item? The significant elements fall into three major categories. These factors are discussed below in general terms, and in the subsequent sections, they are made precise by the particular mathematical formulations of the models. For clarity of exposition, consider the case of the Les Luster Company, a wholesaler of fabricated metal supplies, such as aluminum wire, rods, coils, sheets, and plates, etc., which it buys from a vendor aluminum company. You should have no trouble in relating this wholesaler's decision considerations to those of other firms carrying inventory.

Demand and supply. Certainly the wholesaler needs to forecast, in one way or another, its own local customers' future demand for the item. Such a forecast directly influences the order quantity, and most frequently is represented by a probability distribution. This chapter assumes throughout that different item-demands are independent of each other. Even when this assumption does not strictly hold, it is often an adequate approximation on which to base an inventory rule. Further, the demand distribution is assumed to be independent of the selection of a replenishment rule or any other managerial action. By using advanced mathematical analysis, one can find optimal policies in which these approximating assumptions are omitted.

Employing a probability distribution to describe future demand is a useful way of combining partial knowledge with partial ignorance. By stating the *form* and parameters of the distribution—such as the mean of a Poisson distribution, or the mean and variance of a negative binomial distribution—you can express what you know about the relative *likelihoods* of demand values. Thus the probabilities summarize your uncertainty about the precise demand value that will occur.

The wholesaler also needs to know the so-called **lead time** or **delivery lag** between the moment the replenishment action is initiated and the moment the items ordered are available to meet its customers' demands. The interval obviously encompasses all the time required by the vendor to process the wholesaler's order, including shipping time; but it also encompasses any delays on Les Luster's own premises due to placing the order as well as receiving and unpacking it on arrival.

The lead time may be specified deterministically or stochastically, depending on the situation.

Occasionally, there may be variations between the amounts ordered and actually received—for example, scrap losses are significant in some manufacturing processes, and the vendor may have some leeway in the amount that is shipped. Such situations will not be considered in this chapter; however, they can be treated by using more advanced analysis.

Replenishment economics. If you examine most large-scale inventory systems, you will quickly find that for items frequently demanded, the replenishment quantity is usually sizeable, and certainly greater than 1. There are several reasons why. The most important is that very small orders would result in frequent reordering and thereby incur a considerable expense associated with processing and receiving the order; this expense is referred to as the **setup** or **reorder cost.** A second and less obvious reason is that a large order protects the company against running out too often. Other reasons that are sometimes significant (but not treated by the models in this chapter) include quantity discounts or minimal order sizes stipulated by the vendor, or the firm's forecast of rising vendor prices.

What limits the order quantity? The principal factor is the **inventory holding cost.** Keeping items in stock is costly because inventories tie up capital that might otherwise be profitably employed, and also they incur the expenses of storage, maintenance, insurance, etc. Other limiting reasons that arise in real situations (but will not be embodied in the models of subsequent sections) include spoilage, obsolescence, budgetary and space restrictions, etc.

So far we have not discussed *which* items the wholesaler should try to keep in inventory. After all, even a supermarket or department store does not stock *everything* that its customers might want. Presumably there is a **penalty cost** or **profit loss** whenever the wholesaler is out of stock of an item a customer requests. Obviously, a lost sale means less revenue. But there is a penalty even if the customer is willing to have the order backlogged, for then the wholesaler must incur some extra expense from keeping backlog records and filling the order in a later shipment. As a consequence, the firm will inventory an item if the out-of-stock cost is high; this qualitative statement is made precise for each of the inventory models in this chapter.

The optimality criterion for inventory models is stated traditionally in terms of expected cost rather than expected profit. Since most models consider the item's selling price to be fixed, this cost convention is legitimate, provided sufficient care is exercised in defining the penalty cost to include lost or delayed revenue when a sale is lost or backlogged. Another reason for this cost convention is that frequently such inventory models are applied to items used by a firm's own personnel; consequently, the items are not really being "sold" at a profit.

Assuming an item is to be stocked, an optimal inventory policy is one that strikes the proper balance among the reorder, holding, and penalty costs. As you will see, all *three* cost elements influence how much and when to reorder. The timing decision usually amounts to a specification of a reorder point: whenever the inventory position falls below the reorder level, a replenishment action is taken. The higher the reorder point, the more protection there is against stockouts. Thus in changing the reorder level, there is a direct tradeoff between stockout and holding costs. Incidentally, if the order quantity is so large as to give considerable protection against stockouts, and if customers are willing to have their demands backlogged, the company may find it is optimal to allow a backlog to build up before placing a replenishment order. You will see how this happens in Sec. 14.5.

It is important for you to realize that in real applications of inventory models, the task of estimating reordering, holding, and penalty costs can be quite difficult. Nevertheless, the problem is not insurmountable, as demonstrated by the widespread adoption of these models. What you seek are approximate and reasonable cost estimates. More will be said about such matters of implementation in Sec. 14.7.

Systems specifications. The third category of elements influencing the selection of an inventory policy deals with a disparate variety of environmental factors, only some of which are under the control of the decision-maker.

One such specification relates to whether the inventory level is continuously or only periodically reviewed. In the continuous case, a replenishment order is initiated as soon as the inventory level drops below the reorder point. In the periodic or discrete review case, the inventory status is checked only at specified intervals—for example, each Monday. In this system, replenishment occurs only at the interval point—even when inventory drops below the reorder point at an early moment in the interval. Section 14.6 analyzes a continuous review model with probabilistic demand; Sec. 14.7 treats the periodic review case.

A related specification concerns restrictions on the order quantity. Sometimes it is required or convenient to order only in multiples of a standard amount, such as a dozen. (Note that, in this case, it is not generally permissible merely to change the scale of measurement—to dozens, say—since *customer* demand may not occur in the same transformed units.) Sometimes the order quantity is limited because the company has limited warehouse space available for inventory. These kinds of restrictions have been successfully treated in the operations research literature, but they will not be considered in this book.

Finally, the replenishment rule may be affected by interactive factors. For example, Les Luster Company, the metals-supply wholesaler, may be constrained to ordering a freight-car load at a time from the fabricating mill. Therefore, its order quantities for individual items must reflect this overall constraint. Or an item may be stocked at several different warehouse locations, so that more than one inventory level must be examined in determining a replenishment action. Again, for the sake of simplicity, this text will not treat inventory optimization models with interactive constraints, although such models have been solved by operations research technicians.

Summary and a look ahead. In brief, the models in this chapter separately consider each different type of item inventoried. They take as given the environmental factors of continuous or periodic review, the planning horizon, the lead time, future demand, purchase cost, setup cost, holding cost, penalty cost, and the discount factor. Then each model finds an optimal rule for when and how much to order. No additional system constraints are imposed. In studying these models, be sure to ask yourself how each of the environmental factors affects the optimal policy.

Although the goal of this chapter is to analyze models in which demand is treated as being probabilistic and the inventory decision problem is recurring, that is, dynamic, you will find it helpful to consider each of these two elements in isolation. Specifically, Sec. 14.4 discusses finding an optimal inventory policy when demand is probabilistic but the ordering decision is made only once. Section 14.5 treats the situation where the decision problem is dynamic but demands are perfectly forecastable (in terms of an average rate). Sections 14.6 and 14.7 then, will combine the two elements so as to highlight the interaction between them.

In each case analyzed, the aim is to completely characterize an *optimal* policy in terms of merely two numbers: the reorder point and the order quantity. The resultant algorithmic problem of calculating the optimal values becomes one of optimizing a nonlinear objective function of only two variables. As you will see, knowing the form of an optimal solution and having so few decision variables make the algorithmic task fairly easy and also allow you to use simple, yet very effective, numerical approximations.

14.4 STATIC (SINGLE DECISION) MODEL

This section treats the so-called static, or one-period, model in which only a single inventory decision is made in anticipation of demand, which is viewed as a random variable.

The model is important for two reasons. First, occasionally the model does fit a real situation, as exemplified by the example in the next paragraph. Second, the optimization analysis provides a useful starting point for considering the subsequent dynamic models.

The following illustration, based on an actual application, suggests how a static model can be employed. (The discussion overlooks several details that influenced the exact policy implemented, but that are unimportant here.) The *Daily Defender*, a large newspaper in a major metropolitan area, has been concerned with controlling the number of papers to be distributed to individual newsstands. Unsold papers are returned to the publisher, and as a result the total out-of-pocket costs attributable to these returns amounts to over $1 million annually. Better stockage rules would therefore promise sizeable savings.

Although the daily decision as to the total number of papers to put on each stand is a recurring one, the *decision problem* can be treated by a static model. Each day's newspaper is unsalable by the following day, so there is only one inventory decision to be made about these papers. The daily demand for newspapers can be viewed as a random process that is only partly predictable by such factors as the day of the week and the importance of the headline story. Also, the unit cost of the papers differs daily; for example, the Sunday edition, being larger, costs more to print than the other daily editions. Consequently, the *Daily Defender* applied an operations research model such as that given below by the *linear holding and penalty cost* case. (For the obvious reason, this model is sometimes referred to as the **newsboy problem.**) On any particular day, the appropriate costs are used in the model and the probability distribution for demand employed depends on the predictable factors for that day.

Can you think of any other commercial situations in which a one-period inventory model is applicable? Under what circumstances would it be profitable to use an operations research approach for these situations?

Form of replenishment policy. To begin the discussion, we define the symbols

$$i = \text{level of inventory } prior \text{ to the ordering decision}$$
$$x = \text{amount ordered } (x \geq 0)$$
$$y = i + x = \text{total inventory available to meet future demand}$$
$$q = \text{actual demand quantity (a random variable, where } q \geq 0)$$
$$p(q) = \text{probability that demand equals } q.$$

For expository convenience, we assume i, x, y, and q are integer-valued. Typically, optimal values for x and y will depend on the level of starting inventory i, and so the symbols $x(i)$ and $y(i)$ will be used to denote an optimal policy.

It is easy to construct plausible-looking examples that have surprising-looking optimal policies. Commonly, however, managers use the following simple type of replenishment rule:

(1)
$$x(i) = 0 \qquad \text{and} \quad y(i) = i \quad \text{for } i \geq s \quad \text{(do not order)}$$
$$x(i) = S - i \quad \text{and} \quad y(i) = S \quad \text{for } i < s \quad \text{(place an order)}.$$

According to (1), no order is placed if initial inventory $i \geq s$; but if i is small enough $(i < s)$, then an order is placed so that the *total* inventory available for future demand is S. The rule in (1) is referred to as an **(s, S) policy,** where s denotes the **reorder point** and S the **reorder level.**

Linear holding and penalty cost. Suppose that the expected cost for the entire period is the sum of the purchase cost and the expected holding and penalty cost. Specifically, let the cost of ordering the amount x be

(2)   order cost $$c(x) = \begin{cases} 0 & \text{for } x = 0 \\ K + cx & \text{for } x > 0, \end{cases}$$

where $K \geq 0$ represents the setup cost and $c \geq 0$ the unit purchasing cost.

Assume that the expected holding and penalty cost during the period depends only on the *total* amount of inventory available to meet demand, namely, the level y, which equals initial inventory i plus the order amount x. Let $L(y)$ denote this expected cost function, and in particular, assume that $L(y)$ is calculated from the formula

$$(3) \qquad L(y) = \sum_{q=0}^{y} h \cdot (y - q) p(q) + \sum_{q>y} \pi \cdot (q - y) p(q) \quad \text{for } y \geq 0,$$

where $h \geq 0$ is the unit holding cost per item left over at the end of the period, and $\pi \geq 0$ is the unit penalty cost per item short at the end of the period. Thus the first summation is the *expected* holding cost and the second summation is the *expected* penalty cost. We also make the reasonable assumptions that $c + h > 0$ and $\pi > c$, implying that $h + \pi > 0$.

To illustrate, let

$$(4) \qquad p(q) = \frac{1}{5} \quad \text{for } q = 0, 1, \ldots, 4 \quad \text{so that } E[q] = 2.$$

Then

$$(5) \qquad L(y) = \begin{cases} h \cdot (y - 2) & \text{for } y \geq 4 \\ \dfrac{h}{5} \sum_{q=0}^{y} (y - q) + \dfrac{\pi}{5} \sum_{q=y+1}^{4} (q - y) & \text{for } 0 \leq y \leq 3. \end{cases}$$

The values of $L(y)$ for holding cost $h = 5$ and penalty cost $\pi = 0, 5, 10, 20, 25$ are shown in Fig. 14.1. [For $h = 5$ and $\pi = 10$, plot $L(y)$ to see its convex shape.] Note that the value of y that minimizes $L(y)$ increases as the penalty cost π increases.

When there is a salvage value v (where $0 < v \leq c$) for each item remaining at the end of the horizon, this value can be subtracted from the unit holding cost. Consequently, h in (3) really represents the *net* holding cost ($h = h' - v$), and can be negative. By the same token, if the item is being stocked for sale, and demand in excess of inventory on hand is lost, then π includes the sales price r ($\pi = \pi' + r$).

It is easy to show that an (s, S) rule is the optimal form of policy for this special case. We now explain how to find optimal values for s and S. Let

$$(6) \qquad R \equiv \frac{\pi - c}{\pi + h},$$

and denote the value of R as the **critical ratio.** Observe that $0 < R < 1$ because we assumed that $\pi > c$ and $\pi + h > 0$. Then it can be shown that an optimal reorder level $S \geq 0$ is the *smallest* integer such that

$$(7) \qquad P(S) \equiv \sum_{q=0}^{S} p(q) \geq R \quad \text{(determination of reorder level S)}.$$

Since $P(S)$ is simply the *cumulative* distribution function at $q = S$, an optimal

y	Penalty Cost π				
	0	5	10	20	25
0	0	10	20	40	50
1	1	7	13	25	31
2	3	6	9	15	18
3	6	7	8	10	11
4	10	10	10	10	10
5	15	15	15	15	15
$y \geq 6$	$5(y-2)$	$5(y-2)$	$5(y-2)$	$5(y-2)$	$5(y-2)$

FIGURE 14.1. $L(y)$ for $h = 5$.

reorder level S is set such that there is at least a probability R of satisfying all demand.

Observe from (6) that

(i) R increases as π increases, so that the reorder level S is a nondecreasing function of the penalty cost π.

(ii) R decreases either as the holding cost h or purchase cost c increases, so that the reorder level S is a nonincreasing function of h and c.

(iii) If $\pi \geq 2c + h$, then $R \geq \frac{1}{2}$ and S is at least as large as the median of the demand distribution.

To illustrate, consider the example in (4) and (5). The graph of the cumulative distribution

(8) $$P(y) = \sum_{q=0}^{y} p(q) = \frac{y + 1}{5} \text{ for } y = 0, 1, \ldots, 4$$

appears in Fig. 14.2. The graph is drawn as a staircase to assist in the exposition. Suppose the holding cost $h = 5$, the penalty cost $\pi = 10$, and the purchase cost $c = 0$ so that $R = \frac{2}{3}$. Then according to (7) and (8), S in this special example is the smallest integer such that

(9) $$\frac{S + 1}{5} \geq \frac{2}{3},$$

and therefore,

(10)   reorder level $S = 3$.

For *any* probability distribution of demand, an optimal S can always be read off

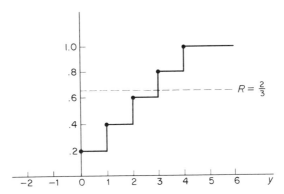

FIGURE 14.2. Cumulative
Distribution $P(y)$.

immediately from a graph of the cumulative distribution function such as Fig. 14.2. You merely locate the value of the ratio R on the vertical axis, extend a horizontal line over until it intersects the cumulative function $P(y)$, and the reorder level S is the associated value of y. [If R coincides with a horizontal segment of $P(y)$, then S is the smallest value of y associated with that segment.]

To summarize, an optimal reorder level S can be found by first calculating the critical ratio R in (6) and then using the cumulative function $P(y)$. Note it is not necessary to calculate the expected holding and penalty cost function $L(y)$ to obtain S.

Suppose the setup cost $K = 0$. Then, as we demonstrate later in this section, it is optimal to let $s = S$. This means that if initial inventory i is *any* amount less than S, you order the quantity $x = S - i$. And if initial inventory is larger than S, you order nothing.

Consider the more challenging case where the setup cost $K > 0$. Now an optimal value for the reorder point s may be strictly less than S. The reason is that if the setup cost K is relatively large and initial inventory i ($\leq S$) is sufficiently close to S, then the additional expense of the setup and purchase costs may not be offset by the reduction in expected holding and penalty costs. For simplicity of exposition we will assume that an optimal $s \geq 0$.

The (s, S) rule states that you do *not* order when initial inventory *equals* s. Hence, the expected holding and penalty cost of letting $y = s$ (that is, amount ordered $x = 0$), which is $L(s)$, must be no greater than the ordering cost plus expected holding and penalty cost of letting $y = S$ (that is, amount ordered $x = S - s$), which is $K + c(S - s) + L(S)$. But since you *do* order when initial inventory is less than s, the preceding cost advantage must go the other way for $y = s - 1$.

We can summarize the reasoning so far by stating that you choose s to be the smallest number such that

(11) $L(s) \leq K + c(S - s) + L(S)$ (determination of reorder point s).

Thus, when $K > 0$, you calculate the reorder point s by computing and comparing the expected holding and penalty cost function $L(y)$ with the sum $[K + c(S - y) + L(S)]$, for successively smaller trial values of y, starting at $y = S$, and then continuing until $y = s$ is the smallest trial value for which (11) holds. [In performing the calculations, you may find it easier to make the equivalent comparison between $L(y) + cy$ and $K + cS + L(S)$, since then the latter value is a constant.]

In the example (8) with $h = 5$, $\pi = 10$ and $c = .1$, the inequality (11) yields

$$(12) \qquad L(s) \leq K + .1(3 - s) + 8 = 8.3 + K - .1s.$$

Suppose $K = 4$. Then $s = 2$, since

$$(13) \qquad \begin{aligned} L(2) &= 9 \leq 8.3 + 4 - .1(2) = 12.1 \\ L(1) &= 13 > 8.3 + 4 - .1(1) = 12.2, \end{aligned}$$

where the values of $L(s)$ are found in the $\pi = 10$ column of Fig. 14.1.

14.5 ECONOMIC-ORDER-QUANTITY MODELS

The assumptions to be made here depart substantially from those employed in the model of the preceding section. Now consider the situation in which the horizon is unbounded so that an infinite number of replenishments will occur. Having complicated the analysis by introducing a dynamic factor, let us make an offsetting simplifying assumption that demand is perfectly forecastable at a stationary *rate*:

$$M = \text{number of items demanded per unit of time.}$$

The particulars of any actual application will dictate a convenient unit of time to use; but for the sake of definiteness in the discussion to follow, let the unit be a week. Then if $M = 30$, the demand assumption is that exactly 30 units are demanded in one week, 60 in two weeks, 15 in a half a week, etc.

We pause momentarily to mention that most textbooks treat the model below in chapters on deterministic inventory models, like Chap. 9. But we have waited until now to discuss this model in detail because *in practice* it almost always is modified to take account of uncertainties in demand. So you should look upon this section as establishing the groundwork for the modified versions that are presented in the next section.

In the lost-size models below, both time itself and the inventory level are treated as continuous variables. Note that this approach is in sharp contrast to most of the dynamic models you have studied in previous chapters. The impact of the continuity postulates is easily conveyed by a diagram. Suppose again that $M = 30$ items a week and the replenishment rule is to order 45 whenever the inventory reaches the 0 level. Assume for this illustration that there is no lead time, so that the items arrive immediately after an order is placed. Then the pattern showing inventory on hand at any moment in time appears in Fig. 14.3. Notice three features of this sawtooth pattern:

(i) The inventory repeatedly drops from the level 45 continuously to the level 0 as time moves forward continuously.

(ii) The downward slope of the sawtooth is -30, representing the rate of withdrawal due to demand M.

(iii) A replenishment occurs every $\frac{45}{30} = 1.5$ weeks.

Clearly, you can rarely be certain that demand behaves in so precise a manner. Both the stationarity and perfect predictability of demand are severe postulates. Nevertheless, many industrial firms have been able to employ these models and have thereby realized substantial inventory cost savings. To do so, however, the

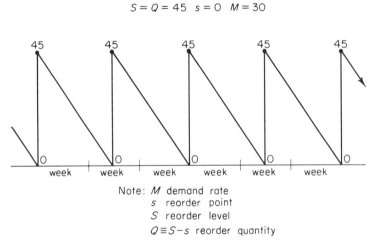

$$S = Q = 45 \quad s = 0 \quad M = 30$$

Note: M demand rate
s reorder point
S reorder level
$Q \equiv S - s$ reorder quantity

FIGURE 14.3. Sawtooth Pattern of Inventory.

models below are usually modified so that demand is treated probabilistically. The generalization required to handle uncertain demand is explained in the next section. You will find it helpful in preparing for that section to first study how an optimal inventory policy can be obtained when demand is perfectly predictable.

Let the ordering cost for items consist of a setup cost $K \geq 0$ plus a unit purchase cost $c \geq 0$ times the amount ordered x:

(1) $$c(x) = \begin{cases} 0 & \text{for } x = 0 \\ K + cx & \text{for } x > 0, \end{cases}$$

and let the holding cost be linear, where

(2) $$h = \text{cost for each item per unit of time (a week)},$$

and $h \geq 0$. Observe that the costs in (1) and (2) are stationary (unchanging over time). Also note that (2) implies it is equally costly to hold five items in inventory for one week, or one item for five weeks, or 2.5 items for two weeks, or two items for 2.5 weeks, etc. Ordinarily, h is a function of the purchase cost c, such as $(h = h' \cdot c)$, but to keep the notation simple, only the symbol h will be used. As you study the formulas, remember that a change in c will typically imply a corresponding change in the value of h. Without much difficulty, you can analyze models with more complicated cost assumptions—for example, the ordering cost function can exhibit quantity discounts. But such cases will not be treated in this chapter. (See exercise 50.)

Assuming repeated replenishments *are* to occur, suppose next that all demand must be met. (The formulas to follow actually indicate when it is preferable not to stock an item.) You can allow a backlog to build up, however, before placing a replenishment order; in such a case, the entering inventory would be immediately allocated to the backlogged demand, and the remainder then used for future demand. A backlog condition is represented by a negative value for i. For many reasonable stationary functions representing the penalty cost of a backlog, an optimal policy will be of the (s, S) form:

(3)   when inventory level $i = s$,   order $Q \equiv S - s$.

The form in (3) has been written more succinctly than the description of an (s, S) policy in the preceding section. The reason is that if, at any instant, the inventory level equals the reorder level S, then Q/M weeks later, it will *exactly* equal the reorder point s, because of the continuity and demand rate assumptions.

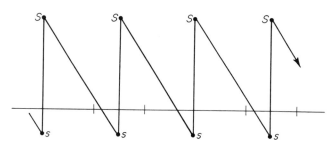

FIGURE 14.4. General Sawtooth Pattern.

After a few moments thought, you can see that a *strictly* positive value of s is not optimal, for then there would always be at least $s > 0$ units of inventory on hand that incur a holding cost and serve no function in meeting demand. By the same token, given that repeated replenishments *are* to occur, you can conclude that, for a reasonable penalty cost function, a strictly negative value of S is not optimal. Consequently, the search for optimal values of s and S can usually be restricted to $s \le 0$ and $S \ge 0$.

Assuming that lead time is 0, so that a replenishment occurs as soon as the reorder decision is made, the resultant **sawtooth cyclic pattern** for a general (s, S) policy is shown in Fig. 14.4. (Actually, the essential lead-time assumption underlying the pattern in Fig. 14.4 is that lead time is a known constant value. If you know that lead time is L, and you want the order to arrive at the moment when inventory equals s, then you would place the order L weeks earlier. So if $LM < Q$, the reorder point is simply LM plus the value of s as determined for $L = 0$.) Note that when the reorder point $s < 0$, demand continues at the rate M

per unit of time, so that the slope of the inventory function in Fig. 14.4 remains $-M$ throughout each cycle.

Finally, assume that the optimality criterion is minimum cost per unit of time. Provided the item is to be stocked, the purchasing and holding cost contribution to the average cost per unit of time is

$$(4) \qquad \frac{KM}{Q} + cM + \frac{hS^2}{2Q}.$$

Each term in (4) can be derived as follows:

(i) Since M/Q is the average number of setups per unit of time, KM/Q is the average setup cost per unit of time.

(ii) Since all demand must be met, cM is the average purchase cost per unit of time.

(iii) Given the sawtooth pattern in Fig. 14.4, inventory is positive for a fraction of time equal to S/Q. The *average* level of inventory, during the interval when inventory *is* positive, is $S/2$. Consequently, $(S/Q) \cdot (S/2)$ represents the average level of inventory per unit of time, and $hS^2/2Q$ is the corresponding holding cost.

If the reorder point $s < 0$ so that a backlog builds up before a replenishment occurs, then an average penalty cost should be added to (4) to give the overall average cost per unit of time. Since in this model any backlogged demand is filled by the next replenishment, no sales are lost and the penalty cost will not include a factor representing lost profit. But a backlog condition frequently does require extra paper work to maintain the records of which customers are awaiting delivery. Further, there may be a loss in good will if a customer has to wait at all for delivery. In these situations you would expect that the penalty cost contains a factor proportional to the size of the backlog right before a replenishment, namely, the amount $(-s)$. In contrast, if the item is being used by personnel within the company, then frequently the penalty cost includes a component that is not only proportional to the size of the backlog but also to the length of time the backlog condition is present. The implications of each of these two types of penalty costs are explored below. In order not to obscure their effect on the selection of an optimal policy and also to keep the mathematical manipulations simple, the two types of penalty costs will be handled separately. They can, of course, be combined into a single model, but we will not do so in this text.

Size-of-backlog penalty cost. Suppose here that each time a backlog occurs the associated cost is π times the maximum amount short $(-s)$, where $\pi > 0$ and $s \leq 0$. Then the cost $\pi(-s)$ is incurred once during each cycle, and so the average shortage cost per unit of time is

$$(5) \qquad \pi(-s)\,\frac{M}{Q}.$$

Since $Q = S - s$, you can substitute $(Q - S)$ for $(-s)$ in (5); doing so and adding the result to (4) yields

$$(6) \quad \left(\begin{array}{c}\text{average cost per}\\ \text{unit of time}\end{array}\right) \equiv \text{AC} = \frac{KM}{Q} + cM + \frac{hS^2}{2Q} + \pi M - \frac{\pi MS}{Q}.$$

The discussion below is considerably simplified if you assume further that the backlog cost factor $\pi > \sqrt{2Kh/M}$; this postulate is not very restrictive, since a backlog cost factor is usually large.

Given that the item is to be stocked, it can be shown that the optimal value for S is Q, and therefore $s = 0$. But it may not be optimal to keep the item in inventory at all.

To begin, suppose $S = Q$ is optimal. Then (6) simplifies to

$$(7) \quad \text{AC} = \frac{KM}{Q} + cM + \frac{hQ}{2}.$$

The optimal Q is found by differentiating AC with respect to Q, setting the derivative equal to 0, and solving for Q, giving

$$(8) \quad \text{optimal } Q = \sqrt{\frac{2KM}{h}} \quad \text{minimal AC} = cM + \sqrt{2KhM}.$$

The formula for the optimal Q is frequently called the **economic order quantity, or EOQ.** (Sometimes you will find it referred to as the **lot-size formula,** or the **Wilson lot size.**)

If the item is not stocked, then there is a cost associated with *not* meeting the demand of M per unit of time. For simplicity, suppose that cost is represented by $\bar{\pi}M$. In this instance, you would ordinarily include in $\bar{\pi}$ a factor indicating lost profit, so that $\bar{\pi}$ need not equal π. The economic test is

$$(9) \quad \text{if } \bar{\pi}M \leq cM + \sqrt{2KhM}, \text{ do not stock,}$$

and otherwise order according to (8).

The following example illustrates how to find an *EOQ*. Suppose that

$$(10) \quad K = 32 \quad h = 4 \quad M = 9.$$

Then from (8),

$$\text{optimal } Q = \sqrt{\frac{2 \cdot 32 \cdot 9}{4}} = 12$$
$$(11)$$
$$\text{minimal AC} = c9 + \sqrt{2 \cdot 32 \cdot 4 \cdot 9} = c9 + 48.$$

The policy $S = Q$ and $s = 0$ is optimal provided that the backlog cost factor $\pi > \sqrt{(2 \cdot 32 \cdot 4)/9} = \frac{16}{3}$, and the product ought to be stocked provided that $\bar{\pi} > c + \left(\frac{16}{3}\right)$.

Sensitivity analysis of EOQ. Notice that the EOQ increases *less* than proportionately with increases in the setup cost K and the demand rate M, and decreases in the holding cost h. For example, if the rate M quadruples, then the EOQ only doubles. Analogously, if the value of h quadruples, then the EOQ only decreases by a half. Observe that the time interval between orders is

$$(12) \qquad \text{optimal } T = \frac{\text{EOQ}}{M} = \sqrt{\frac{2K}{hM}}.$$

Thus as the demand rate M gets larger, not only does the optimal Q get larger but the optimal time interval between orders T gets smaller so that ordering occurs more frequently.

In many situations the vendor requires that the amount ordered be a "convenient" number. To illustrate, if the optimal $Q = 53$, you may have to place an order for either 50 or 60. You should note that there is very little impact on average cost when only a *near*-optimal Q is employed. Let

$$(13) \qquad \text{actual } Q = r \cdot \text{optimal } Q = r \cdot \sqrt{\frac{2KM}{h}},$$

where $r > 0$, and let the *variable* cost be written as

$$(14) \qquad \text{VC}(r) = \frac{KM}{\text{actual } Q} + \frac{h \cdot \text{actual } Q}{2} = \frac{KM}{r\sqrt{2KM/h}} + \frac{h \cdot r\sqrt{2KM/h}}{2},$$

so that the *fixed* purchase cost component cM is omitted. Then from (14) you have that

$$(15) \qquad \frac{\text{VC}(r)}{\text{VC}(1)} = \frac{1}{2}\left(\frac{1}{r} + r\right).$$

As you can see by calculating (15) for trial values of r, the increase in variable cost from a near-optimal Q is slight. For example

$$(16) \qquad \frac{\text{VC}(r)}{\text{VC}(1)} \leq 1.1 \quad \text{for } .64 \leq r \leq 1.56.$$

[Also note in (15) that the ratio has the same value for a given r and its reciprocal $r' = 1/r$.]

Average-backlog penalty cost. Now suppose the penalty cost is assessed against the average level of backlog per unit of time, analogous to the inventory holding charges. Looking again at Fig. 14.4, you will see that a backlog condition exists for a fraction of time $-s/Q$, where the reorder point $s \leq 0$. The average level of backlog, during the interval when inventory is negative, is $-s/2$. Consequently, the average level of backlog per unit of time is $s^2/2Q$, which must be multiplied by the corresponding penalty cost. It is convenient for the purpose of comparison to again let the penalty cost be denoted by the symbol $\pi > 0$. But you should realize that the cost measurement units are different in the previous case than they are here. Specifically, now π represents the cost per item per unit of time the backlog is present, whereas previously π was simply the cost per item backlogged. Using the identity $(S - s \equiv Q)$ to eliminate s, you obtain after simplification,

(17) $\begin{array}{l}\text{average cost per}\\\text{unit of time}\end{array} \equiv \text{AC} = \dfrac{KM}{Q} + cM + \dfrac{(h + \pi)S^2}{2Q} - \pi S + \dfrac{\pi}{2} Q.$

(Here it is not necessary to explicitly assume that π is large relative to the other costs.)

Taking the partial derivative of AC in (17) with respect to S, setting the result equal to 0, and simplifying yields

(18) $$S = \left(\frac{\pi}{h + \pi}\right) Q.$$

Doing the same with respect to Q and using (18) to eliminate S gives

(19)

$$\text{optimal } Q = \sqrt{2KM} \cdot \sqrt{\frac{1}{h} + \frac{1}{\pi}} \qquad \text{optimal } S = \sqrt{\frac{2KM}{h}} \cdot \sqrt{\frac{\pi}{h + \pi}}$$

$$\text{optimal } s = -\sqrt{\frac{2KM}{\pi}} \cdot \sqrt{\frac{h}{h + \pi}} \qquad \text{minimal AC} = cM + \frac{\sqrt{2KM}}{\sqrt{\dfrac{1}{h} + \dfrac{1}{\pi}}}.$$

As in the previous case, the decision of whether to stock at all depends on a comparison of the minimal AC in (19) with the cost of not meeting demand.

As you were already cautioned, the measurement unit for the penalty cost in (19) is not the same as in (8), since here π represents the cost per item per unit of time a backlog is present, whereas previously π represented the cost per item backlogged. Nevertheless, it is instructive to compare the solutions in (19) and (8) assuming that π has the same numerical value in both sets of formulas. Specifically notice in (19) that for a finite value of the penalty cost π, the optimal order quantity Q is larger, the optimal reorder level S is smaller, the optimal reorder point s is smaller (actually negative), and the minimal average cost is smaller. Only when π is infinite do the values in (19) equal the corresponding solution in (8). Also, only when the holding cost factor h is infinite is the optimal $S = 0$; but even then, Q and s are finite.

Study (19) to see how each optimal quantity varies with changes in the values of K, h, π, and M. In particular, note that the optimal order quantity Q decreases as the penalty cost π increases, and the optimal reorder point s decreases as either the setup cost K or the demand rate M increases. Observe from (18) that if $h = \pi$, then there is a backlog condition during the second half of the interval between successive orders.

Consider the following illustrative example. Assume that

(20) $$K = 32 \qquad h = 4 \qquad \pi = 36 \qquad M = 9.$$

Then applying the formulas in (19) yields

$$\text{optimal } Q = \sqrt{2 \cdot 32 \cdot 9} \cdot \sqrt{\frac{1}{4} + \frac{1}{36}} = 4\sqrt{10} = 12.6491$$

$$\text{optimal } S = \sqrt{\frac{2 \cdot 32 \cdot 9}{4}} \cdot \sqrt{\frac{36}{4 + 36}} = \frac{36}{\sqrt{10}} = 11.3842$$

(21)

$$\text{optimal } s = -\sqrt{\frac{2 \cdot 32 \cdot 9}{36}} \cdot \sqrt{\frac{4}{4 + 36}} = -\frac{4}{\sqrt{10}} = -1.2649$$

$$\text{minimal AC} = c9 + \frac{\sqrt{2 \cdot 32 \cdot 9}}{\sqrt{\frac{1}{4} + \frac{1}{36}}} = c9 + \left(\frac{144}{\sqrt{10}}\right) = c9 + 45.5367.$$

*Production lot sizes. So far the discussion of economic order quantity models has been in the context of a company replenishing its inventory by ordering an item from a vendor. Accordingly, the inventory policies indicated *when* and *how much* to reorder. Let us now turn to a related problem of a company that manufactures certain of its items in lot-size quantities. Many of the economic considerations encompassed in the preceding models are just as relevant in this situation: a setup cost, the direct manufacturing costs, and holding and shortage costs. Assuming the stationarity and demand assumptions remain reasonable, can the (s, S) policies derived in (8) and (19) be used here as optimal lot sizes and production trigger points? Sometimes, but not usually.

The significant difference between ordering an item from a vendor and producing it in your own plant is that a production activity requires the use of other limited resources, namely, labor, equipment, and component materials. Most manufacturing plants carefully schedule ahead, taking into account available personnel and equipment capacity limitations, and ensuring that sufficient materials are on hand. Consequently, if an economic lot-size approach is used for all the manufactured items and is based on the above models—or those in the next section—the result may not yield a feasible overall schedule for a production plant. In short, a single-item EOQ model applied to a multitude of internally manufactured items is typically a poor approximation to reality, for it ignores the operating constraints on scarce resources.

What is required in a production setting is a dynamic planning model that combines the cost elements in EOQ models with the constrained multi-item considerations. The component time periods in the model must be short enough so that the plan can be implemented by production decisions. Several breakthroughs have occurred in operations research models capable of handling these situations, but the complexity of the analyses goes beyond the scope of this text.

*Raw materials inventories. A related area of inventory decisions is the stockage of raw materials to support a manufacturing firm's production activities. Here too the economic considerations encompassed in the EOQ models are relevant to storing raw materials. But analogous to the production lot-size situation, the manufacturing activity itself, through a production schedule, also exerts an influence on the inventory policy. Only in the case of continuous and nearly level production would you expect an EOQ approach to be useful. A more widely applicable operations research approach for the stockage of raw materials is a dynamic programming model like one of those in Chap. 9. Such a model employs the production schedule requirements as "demand" data, and while minimizing costs, at the same time ensures that the required raw materials are on hand when needed.

14.6 STOCHASTIC DYNAMIC CONTINUOUS REVIEW MODEL

This section extends the preceding economic lot-size model analysis to include probabilistically described demand. Continue to assume that time is a continuous variable; the ordering and holding costs are stationary

$$(1) \qquad c(x) = \begin{cases} 0 & \text{for } x = 0 \\ K + cx & \text{for } x > 0 \end{cases} \quad \text{(ordering cost)}$$

$$(2) \qquad h = \text{holding cost for each item per unit of time,}$$

where $K \geq 0$, $c \geq 0$, and $h \geq 0$. Suppose that any demand occurring when the inventory level is 0 is backlogged and eventually filled. Assume here that the penalty cost $\pi > 0$ is stationary and proportional to the size of a backlog just before a replenishment order arrives. Now the objective is to minimize *expected* average cost per unit of time. Let

$$M = \begin{pmatrix} \textit{expected } \text{number of items demanded} \\ \text{per unit of time} \end{pmatrix}$$

$$(3) \qquad L = \begin{pmatrix} \text{lead time, the length of the interval between} \\ \text{placing and receiving an order} \end{pmatrix}$$

$$M_L = \begin{pmatrix} \textit{expected } \text{number of items demanded} \\ \text{during an interval of } L \text{ units of time} \end{pmatrix},$$

where L is fixed and known. Since "the expected value of a sum is always equal to the sum of the expected values,"

$$(4) \qquad M_L = ML.$$

If the lead time $L = 0$—an order arrives immediately after it is placed—then the analysis of the averge cost formula (6) in the preceding section needs to be modified only slightly. Provided the items should be stocked, and the optimal reorder point $s = 0$, the optimal order quantity and minimal cost formulas in (8) above apply, where the cost expression now represents an expected value.

The reason is that when $L = 0$, there is never an opportunity for a backlog condition to arise.

If the lead time $L > 0$, however, the situation is quite different. Let

$$q_L = \begin{pmatrix} \text{actual demand during an interval between} \\ \text{placing and receiving an order} \end{pmatrix}.$$

Here the random variable q_L may exceed s, which is the level of inventory at the start of the interval, so that a backlog condition occurs. How then should Q and s be chosen optimally?

A naive approach is to calculate Q according to the economic-order-quantity formula (8) above, and to pick s using the static model analysis in Sec. 14.4, in which the demand probability distribution relates to demand during lead time and the expected holding and penalty cost function $L(y)$ is given by (3) in that section. Then $S = s + Q$.

For example, suppose

(5)　purchase cost: $c = 1$　　setup cost:　$K = 31.25$　　holding cost: $h = 5$

　　　penalty cost: $\pi = 20$　　demand rate: $M = 2$　　　lead time:　$L = 1$.

Then

(6)
$$Q = \sqrt{\frac{2KM}{h}} = 5.$$

Suppose further that the probability distribution of **demand during a lead time** is

(7)　　　　$p_L(q_L) = \dfrac{1}{5}$　for $q = 0, 1, \ldots, 4$　　$E[q_L] = M_L = 2$.

The distribution in (7) is the same as that in (4) of Sec. 14.4, and as the entries in Fig. 14.1 show for penalty cost factor $\pi = 20$,

(8)　　　reorder point $s = 3$　so that　reorder level $S = s + Q = 8$.

Therefore this naive analysis leads to the policy $(s, S) = (3, 8)$.

The logical error in the above approach is that the analysis ignores the cost interaction between the reorder point s and the order quantity Q. Specifically, if you keep s fixed and let Q get larger, then the actual penalty cost component of average cost will decrease. The reason is there are fewer replenishments and corresponding exposures to stockouts per unit of time. Consequently, you can reduce average cost by letting the order quantity Q be larger than indicated by the economic lot-size formula. By the same token, you may obtain further cost savings from an even lower value for the reorder point s.

Having recognized that optimal values for s and Q are interdependent, you are ready to explore a way to calculate them. As usual, the first step is to develop the appropriate expression for the criterion function, and afterwards to optimize the value of the expression with respect to s and Q. Before taking the first step, we will impose a few additional assumptions. Of course, all assumptions, in one way or another, represent approximations to a real situation. But the ones to follow are imposed primarily to keep the exposition simple and the mathematical manipulations tractable. Nevertheless, the model below (and minor variants of it) have proved in practice to be very effective in establishing workable inventory policies.

Assume for the mathematical development of the criterion function that

    (i) The probability distribution of demand during a lead time $p_L(q_L)$ does not depend on when the inventory reaches the reorder point s.

    (ii) The inventory level i can be treated as a continuous variable.

    (iii) After a replenishment order arrives, there exists a future moment in time when the inventory level $i = s$, and a reorder action occurs as a consequence.

    (iv) In an optimal policy, the reorder point $s > 0$ and during any lead time, actual demand does not exceed the order quantity $(q_L \leq Q)$.

The meaning of these assumptions is clear, but you should observe where each is used in developing the criterion function. The postulate that the optimal $Q \geq q_L$ deserves further comment. Note that just before a replenishment order arrives the inventory level is $s - q_L$, and just after it is $s - q_L + Q$, which is at least s given postulate (iv). As a result, there is never more than one replenishment order outstanding at any instant.

Expected cost. The purchase cost component of the objective function is just like the lot-size models:

(9) $$\frac{KM}{Q} + cM \quad \text{(average ordering cost)}.$$

We next obtain the expected holding and penalty cost. You can, if you want, skip this derivation and go directly to the end result in (16) below.

Consider the time interval between two successive reorder actions; two examples of what can happen are shown in Fig. 14.5, one for actual demand during lead time less than the reorder point, $q_L < s$, and one for $q_L > s$. In the case $q_L > s$, taking into account that the inventory level is 0 *before* the replenishment arrives makes the holding cost formulas complicated. Therefore, as a mathematical approximation, assume that when $q_L > s$, inventory becomes 0 just before the replenishment arrives. Then

(10) $$\begin{pmatrix} \text{expected average} \\ \text{inventory level} \\ \text{during lead time} \end{pmatrix} \approx \sum_{q_L=0}^{s} \tfrac{1}{2}[s + (s - q_L)]p_L(q_L) + \sum_{q_L>s} \tfrac{1}{2}[s + 0]p_L(q_L)$$

$$= \frac{1}{2}\left[s + \sum_{q_L=0}^{s} (s - q_L)p_L(q_L) \right],$$

Case $q_L < s$

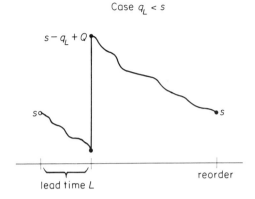

reorder

lead time L

Case $q_L > s$

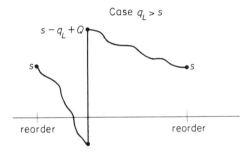

reorder   reorder

Note: q_L demand during lead time L

FIGURE 14.5. Sawtooth Patterns for Probabilistic Demands.

Q reorder quantity
s reorder point

(11) $\left(\begin{array}{l}\text{expected average inventory} \\ \text{level after replenishment} \\ \text{until next reorder}\end{array}\right) \approx \frac{1}{2}[(s - M_L + Q) + s] = \frac{1}{2}(2s - M_L + Q).$

The expression in (10) must be weighted by M_L/Q, the fraction of time the system is waiting for a replenishment, and correspondingly, the expression in (11) must be weighted by $(1 - M_L/Q)$. After applying these weights, adding the results, and rearranging terms, you get

(12) $\left(\begin{array}{l}\text{expected average} \\ \text{inventory per} \\ \text{unit of time}\end{array}\right) \approx \frac{M_L}{2Q}\left[-2s + M_L - Q + s + \sum_{q_L=0}^{s} (s - q_L)p_L(q_L)\right]$

$$+ \frac{1}{2}(2s - M_L + Q).$$

Now

(13) $\sum_{q_L=0}^{s} (s - q_L)p_L(q_L) = s - M_L - \sum_{q_L>s} (s - q_L)p_L(q_L),$

so that the expression in (12) can be written as

(14) $$\frac{Q}{2} - M_L + s + \frac{M_L}{2Q} \sum_{q_L > s} (q_L - s) p_L(q_L).$$

Finally,

(15) $$\begin{pmatrix} \text{expected shortage} \\ \text{during a lead time} \end{pmatrix} = \sum_{q_L > s} (q_L - s) p_L(q_L),$$

which must be weighted by M/Q to obtain the expected shortage per unit of time just as in the economic lot-size model of the previous section.

Combining (9), (14) multiplied by the holding cost h, and (15) multiplied by M/Q times the penalty cost π gives

(16) $$\begin{pmatrix} \text{expected average} \\ \text{cost per unit} \\ \text{of time} \end{pmatrix} \equiv E[AC] = \frac{KM}{Q} + cM + h\left(\frac{Q}{2} - M_L + s\right)$$
$$+ \left(\frac{hM_L}{2Q} + \frac{M\pi}{Q}\right) \sum_{q_L > s} (q_L - s) p_L(q_L).$$

To see the relation between (16) and the formulas derived in the preceding section, observe that if demand is deterministic, then the optimal reorder point $s = M_L$ and the summation on the right of (16) would be 0, since each of the probabilities would be 0; the resulting expression agrees with the average cost formula (7) in Sec. 14.5.

Partially differentiating $E[AC]$ with respect to Q, setting the derivative equal to 0, and solving for Q, gives the formula

(17) $$\text{optimal } Q = \sqrt{\frac{2KM}{h} + \left(M_L + \frac{2M\pi}{h}\right) \sum_{q_L > s} (q_L - s) p_L(q_L)}$$

(determination of order quantity).

Define the cumulative demand distribution as

(18) $$P_L(y) \equiv \sum_{q_L = 0}^{y} p_L(q_L).$$

Then it can be shown that the optimal $s \geq 0$ is the *smallest* integer such that

(19) $$P_L(s) \geq R \quad \text{(determination of reorder point),}$$

where here the critical ratio is

(20) $$R \equiv 1 - \frac{hQ}{\dfrac{hM_L}{2} + M\pi}.$$

More precisely, the order quantity Q and reorder point s are optimal values if they *simultaneously* satisfy (17) and (19). Substituting (17) into (16) yields

$$\text{minimal } E[AC] = cM + \sqrt{2h\left[KM + \left(\frac{hM_L}{2} + M\pi\right) \sum_{q_L > s} (q_L - s)p_L(q_L)\right]}$$

(21)

$$+ h(s - M_L),$$

assuming that s is found according to (19). [To decide whether the item is to be inventoried at all, the value in (21) must be compared to the cost of not stocking.]

Notice the second term under the radical sign in (17) causes the optimal value for Q to be larger than the economic lot size for the case of deterministic demand. Also the smaller the value of s, the larger the value of Q. By the same token, the larger the value of Q in (20), the smaller the value of R and the smaller the value of s satisfying (19). The value of $P_L(s)$ is sometimes referred to as the **service level** and the amount $s - E[q_L]$ as the **buffer** or **safety stock.**

Unless you make additional assumptions about the form of the probability distribution $p_L(q_L)$, you are not able to state much about the sensitivity of the optimal policy to the economic parameters, the mean demand M, and the lead time L. To see why, consider an increase in the penalty cost π. On the one hand, it tends to directly increase the second term under the radical in (17); on the other, it tends to indirectly decrease that term due to its direct effect on R and s in (19) and (20). Several illustrative examples showing policy sensitivity will be given in the discussion of a Normal distribution approximation below.

▶ The formulas developed in (17) and (19) have a wider applicability than simply the model specified by the various assumptions so far. To illustrate, suppose lead time L is random but the assumption that demand during lead time $q_L \leq Q$ still holds. Then $p_L(q_L)$ is defined accordingly to be the probability distribution of demand during a lead time.

As another illustration, suppose the value of s is determined by (19) but R is a probability *prespecified* by the decision-maker; that is, R represents the minimum allowable probability of filling all demand during a lead time. (The value $1 - R$ is the maximum allowable probability of having any shortages.) Postulating that only a policy of the (s, S) form is to be considered, and that expected average purchase and holding cost per unit of time is to be minimized, then the optimal Q is given by (17) with $\pi = 0$.

Finally, with only minor modifications, the approach can be applied to the situation where unfilled demand is not backlogged but is lost. (See exercise 53.)   ◀

Algorithmic solution. The following simple procedure can be used to yield values for Q and s that simultaneously solve (17) and (19):

Step 1. Let the initial trial value of Q be $\sqrt{2KM/h}$.

Step 2. Compute R in (20) using the current trial value for Q, and find a corresponding trial value for s in (19).

Step 3. Stop if the new trial s is the same as the previous trial value. Otherwise calculate a new trial value for Q according to (17), and return to *Step 2*.

Notice, as the iterations progress, the trial values of s get smaller and of Q get larger. The method will always converge in a finite number of iterations provided that the optimal s *is* positive. A sufficient condition ensuring convergence is that

$$(22) \qquad Q_{max} < \frac{\dfrac{hM_L}{2} + M\pi}{h},$$

where Q_{max} is the expression on the right of (17) evaluated for $s = 0$ (so that the summation term is simply M_L). Once again, because no assumptions have been made about the form of $p_L(q_L)$ other than that it is a discrete distribution, the terminating value for s may not be globally optimal; at worst, a neighboring value of s and the associated optimal Q may have a lower expected cost.

Consider the following example, which contains the same data as (5) and (7):

$$(23) \qquad \begin{array}{cccc} c = 1 & K = 31.25 & h = 5 & \pi = 20 \\[2mm] L = 1 & p_L(q_L) = \dfrac{1}{5} \text{ for } q = 0, 1, \ldots, 4 & E[q_L] \equiv M_L = M = 2. \end{array}$$

According to *Step 1*,

$$(24) \qquad \text{initial trial } Q = 5.$$

Then for *Step 2*,

$$(25) \qquad R = 1 - \frac{25}{5 + 40} = .44 \quad \text{and} \quad P(2) \geq .44.$$

Using the trial value $s = 2$, the computation in *Step 3* is

$$(26) \qquad \text{trial } Q = \sqrt{25 + (18)(.6)} = 5.98.$$

Repeating *Steps 2* and *3* gives

$$(27) \quad R = .34 \quad \text{and} \quad P(1) \geq .34 \qquad \text{trial } Q = \sqrt{25 + (18)(1.2)} = 6.83.$$

The final iteration is

$$(28) \qquad \begin{array}{ll} R = .24 \quad \text{and} \quad P(1) \geq .24 & \text{optimal } s = 1 \\[2mm] \text{optimal } Q = 6.83 & \text{optimal } S = s + Q = 7.83 \end{array}$$

and as a consequence,

$$(29) \quad \text{minimal } E[AC] = 2 + \sqrt{10[62.5 + (45)(1.2)]} + 5(1 - 2) = 31.13.$$

Observe how the optimal solution differs from the policy in (6) and (8) obtained by the naive analysis. That approach led to a policy $(s, S) = (3, 8)$; the associated expected cost according to (16) is 33.9, which is 9% larger than the optimal value in (29).

Normal approximation. When applying the model in this section to an inventory system containing a multitude of items, you typically would assume as an approximation that the distribution $p_L(q_L)$ is of a particular type, such as Poisson, negative binomial, uniform, etc. Then you would only need to specify the parameters of the selected distribution. A very convenient approach is to use a Normal distribution (which is continuous), letting the mean and variance be

$$(30) \qquad E[q_L] = M_L \qquad \text{Var}\,[q_L] = \sum_{q_L \geq 0} (q_L - M_L)^2 p_L(q_L) \equiv V_L.$$

From a practical point of view, the approximation method turns out to be very effective, even though the theoretical properties of the Normal distribution (such as symmetry, and the possibility of arbitrarily small and large values of the random variable) may depart considerably from the distribution $p_L(q_L)$. Of course, you should not apply this or any other approximation unless you investigate how well it holds for the range of parameters in which you are interested.

Define

$$(31) \qquad\qquad u_s = \frac{s - M_L}{\sqrt{V_L}},$$

so that

$$(32) \qquad\qquad s = M_L + u_s\sqrt{V_L}.$$

Accordingly, as before, let

$$(33) \qquad\qquad R = 1 - \frac{hQ}{\dfrac{hM_L}{2} + M\pi}.$$

Denote the *cumulative standardized Normal distribution* as

$$(34) \qquad\qquad P_N(u) = \int_{-\infty}^{u} \frac{1}{\sqrt{2\pi}} e^{-.5t^2}\, dt,$$

and the so-called **standardized Normal loss integral** as

$$(35) \qquad\qquad I_N(u) = \int_{u}^{\infty} (t - u)\, \frac{1}{\sqrt{2\pi}} e^{-.5t^2}\, dt.$$

The loss integral is used for the approximation

$$(36) \qquad\qquad \sum_{q_L > s} (q_L - s) p_L(q_L) \approx \sqrt{V_L} \cdot I_N(u_s).$$

The functions $P_N(u)$ and $I_N(u)$ are tabled in Fig. 14.6.

Then, instead of (19), the value u_s is determined by

(37) $$P_N(u_s) = R,$$

and, instead of (17), the value of Q is found by

(38) $$\text{optimal } Q = \sqrt{\frac{2KM}{h} + \left(M_L + \frac{2M\pi}{h}\right)\sqrt{V_L} \cdot I_N(u_s)}.$$

Write down the expression corresponding to (21) for the minimal $E[AC]$.
   The algorithm is

Step 1. Let the initial trial value of Q be $\sqrt{2KM/h}$.

Step 2. Compute R in (33) using the current trial value for Q, and find a corresponding trial value for u_s from (37) and s from (32).

Step 3. Stop if the new trial s is approximately the same as the previous trial value. Otherwise calculate a new trial value for Q according to (38) and return to *Step 2.*

Notice in *Step 3* you must specify a numerical tolerance defining when two trial values for s are approximately the same.
   To illustrate the method, consider the example

(39) $$K = 32 \qquad h = 1 \qquad \pi = 9$$
$$L = 1 \qquad M = M_L = 16 \qquad V_L = 48.$$

From *Step 1*,

(40) $$\text{initial } Q = 32,$$

and for *Step 2*,

(41) $$R = \left(1 - \frac{32}{\frac{16}{2} + 144}\right) = \frac{120}{152} = .789,$$

so that from Fig. 14.6 you have

(42) $$\text{trial } u_s = .8 \quad \text{and} \quad \text{trial } s = 16 + (.8)\sqrt{48} = 21.6.$$

Then in *Step 3*,

(43) $$\text{trial } Q = \sqrt{(32)(32) + (16 + 144)\sqrt{48}(.12)} = 35.71.$$

Returning to *Step 2*,

(44) $$R = \left(1 - \frac{35.71}{\frac{16}{2} + 144}\right) = .765,$$

so that

(45) $$\text{trial } u_s = .72 \quad \text{and} \quad \text{trial } s = 16 + (.72)\sqrt{48} = 21.01.$$

u	$P_N(u)$	$I_N(u)$	$P_N(-u)$	$I_N(-u)$
0	.5000	.3989	.5000	.3989
.1	.5399	.3509	.4601	.4509
.2	.5793	.3068	.4207	.5068
.3	.6180	.2667	.3820	.5667
.4	.6555	.2304	.3445	.6304
.5	.6915	.1977	.3085	.6977
.6	.7258	.1686	.2742	.7686
.7	.7581	.1428	.2419	.8428
.8	.7882	.1202	.2118	.9202
.9	.8160	.1004	.1840	1.0004
1.0	.8414	.0833	.1586	1.0833
1.1	.8644	.0686	.1356	1.1686
1.2	.8850	.0561	.1150	1.2561
1.3	.9032	.0455	.0968	1.3455
1.4	.9193	.0366	.0807	1.4366
1.5	.9332	.0293	.0668	1.5293
1.6	.9453	.0232	.0547	1.6232
1.7	.9555	.0182	.0445	1.7182
1.8	.9641	.0142	.0359	1.8142
1.9	.9713	.0110	.0287	1.9110
2.0	.9773	.0084	.0227	2.0084
2.1	.9822	.0064	.0178	2.1064
2.2	.9861	.0048	.0139	2.2048
2.3	.9893	.0036	.0107	2.3036
2.4	.9919	.0027	.0081	2.4027
2.5	.9938	.0020	.0062	2.5020
2.6	.9954	.0014	.0046	2.6014
2.7	.9966	.0010	.0034	2.7010
2.8	.9975	.0007	.0025	2.8007
2.9	.9982	.0005	.0018	2.9005
3.0	.9987	.0003	.0013	3.0003

FIGURE 14.6. Table of Cumulative and Loss Integral for a Standardized Normal Distribution.

Then in *Step 3*

$$(46) \qquad \text{trial } Q = \sqrt{(32)(32) + (16 + 144)\sqrt{48}(.14)} = 36.24.$$

Further iterations will affect only the decimal parts of s and Q in (45) and (46). The associated expected cost is

$$(47) \qquad E[\text{AC}] = c16 + 41.3.$$

Check your understanding of the method by finding an optimal policy for $M = 16$, $L = 5$, $M_L = 80$, $V_L = 240$, and the other parameter values as given in (39). (The optimal s is about 91.)

Several optimal policies found by the approximation method are shown in Fig. 14.7. Note that an increase in each parameter π, K, M, L, and V_L tends to increase both the optimal s and Q, *except* that an increase in π decreases Q and an increase in K decreases s. This sensitivity pattern holds provided that the probability that q_L is negative is negligible in the Normal approximation to $p_L(q_L)$, as is true when $M_L/\sqrt{V_L}$ is larger than 2. Also observe that the optimal Q can be significantly larger than the deterministic EOQ formula value, but even when this occurs, the values are found in only three or four iterations.

*14.7 STOCHASTIC DYNAMIC PERIODIC
REVIEW MODEL

The model in the preceding section treated time as a continuous variable and assumed that a replenishment order occurred whenever the level of inventory reached the reorder point s. In this section, a reorder decision is permitted to occur only at fixed intervals of time, such as every 10 days or on each Monday. For convenience of exposition, suppose that we let the time period be a week.

Assume that the time sequence of events that occurs within each period is

  (i) ordering decision
  (ii) delivery of any order due in
  (iii) customer demand,

and let

$p(q)$ = probability that demand is q during a period (where $q \geq 0$).

We postulate that demand in each week is statistically independent of all previous demands and that $p(q)$ is stationary over time.

Define T, a nonnegative integer, as the fixed and known **delivery lag** for a replenishment order. When $T = 0$, an order placed in Week t arrives immediately prior to the customer demand for Week t. When $T = 1$, an order placed in Week t arrives in Week t + 1 immediately prior to the customer demand for Week t + 1, and the same sequence applies with larger values of T. Recall in the model of the preceding section that if the lead time $L = 0$, so that delivery is instantaneous, then there is no need to protect against uncertain demand occurring over any interval of time. But in the periodic review model, if $T = 0$, so that delivery is immediate, one period's random demand still occurs prior to the next opportunity to reorder. In general, a value for T in the periodic review models corresponds to a value $L = T + 1$ in the continuous review model.

If customer demand in a period exceeds the stock on hand, assume that all the unfilled demand is backlogged and eventually satisfied by future deliveries. We postulate costs to be the same as in the model of the preceding section, namely, stationary ordering, holding, and penalty costs:

(1)
$$c(x) = \begin{cases} 0 & \text{for } x = 0 \\ K + cx & \text{for } x > 0 \end{cases} \quad \text{(ordering cost)}$$

Case	Varied Parameters	s	Q	E[AC]	EOQ
1	None	11	26	28.0	24
	$\pi = 99$	15	25	31.2	24
	$K = 64$	10	36	37.2	33.9
	$\pi = 99$ $K = 64$	14	35	40.2	33.9
	$L = 5$	49	28	32.5	24
	$V_L = 27$	11	28	29.6	24
2	None	18	16	26.0	16
	$\pi = 49$	16	16	24.2	16
	$K = 32$	18	12	22.2	11
	$\pi = 49$ $K = 32$	17	12	20.5	11
	$M = 6$	39	30	39	28
	$L = 1$	6	17	21.8	16
	$V_L = 10$	14	17	21.8	16

Nonvaried Parameter Values:

Case 1: $h = 1$ $\pi = 9$ $K = 32$ $c = 0$ $M = 9$ $L = 1$ ($M_L = 9$) $V_L = 9$

Case 2: $h = 1$ $\pi = 99$ $K = 64$ $c = 0$ $M = 2$ $L = 5$ ($M_L = 10$) $V_L = 30$

(The values for s and Q have been rounded to the nearest integer)

FIGURE 14.7. Sensitivity Analysis for Normal Approximation.

$$(2) \qquad h = \begin{pmatrix} \text{holding cost for each item remaining in inventory} \\ \text{at the end of a period} \end{pmatrix}$$

$$(3) \qquad \pi = \begin{pmatrix} \text{penalty cost for each item backlogged} \\ \text{at the end of a period} \end{pmatrix},$$

where $K \geq 0$, $c \geq 0$, $h \geq 0$, and $\pi \geq 0$. The optimality criterion is minimum expected cost per period.

By means of advanced analysis, it can be demonstrated that the form of an optimal replenishment policy is (s, S): when the sum of stock on hand plus stock on order at the start of a period is strictly less than s, replenish so that stock on hand plus stock on order equals S, and do not reorder otherwise. The exact computations for an optimal (s, S) policy are sufficiently onerous as to make useful a much simpler approximate approach, which closely resembles the Normal approximation described at the end of the previous section.

Let

(4) $$E[q] = M \qquad \text{Var } [q] = V.$$

Define

(5) $$u_s = \frac{s - (T + 1)M}{\sqrt{(T + 1)V}}$$

so that

(6) $$s = (T + 1)M + u_s\sqrt{(T + 1)V}.$$

Denote the *cumulative standardized Normal distribution* as

(7) $$P_N(u) = \int_{-\infty}^{u} \frac{1}{\sqrt{2\pi}} e^{-.5t^2} \, dt$$

and the *standardized Normal loss integral* as

(8) $$I_N(u) = \int_{u}^{\infty} (t - u) \frac{1}{\sqrt{2\pi}} e^{-.5t^2} \, dt.$$

Both $P_N(u)$ and $I_N(u)$ are tabled in Fig. 14.6.
  The approximation algorithm is as follows.

Step 1. Calculate

(9) $$\text{EOQ} \equiv \sqrt{\frac{2KM}{h}}.$$

Step 2. Compute

(10) $$R_N = \frac{h \cdot \text{EOQ}}{\pi\sqrt{(T + 1)V}}$$

and find the value for u_s such that

(11) $$I_N(u_s) = R_N.$$

Step 3. If $M < .8888 \, K/h$, then let (s, S) be determined by s in (6) and $S = s + \text{EOQ}$. Otherwise go to *Step 4*.

Step 4. Compute

(12) $$R = \frac{\pi}{h + \pi}$$

and find the value for v_s such that

(13) $$P_N(v_s) = R,$$

Define

(14) $$w_s = \text{minimum } (u_s, v_s)$$

and let (s, S) be determined by

Case	Varied Parameters	Normal Approximation			Optimal		
		s	S	$S-s$	s	S	$S-s$
1	None	7	31	24	7	28	21
	$\pi = 99$	12	36	24	13	33	20
	$K = 64$	5	39	34	6	37	31
	$\pi = 99$ $K = 64$	11	45	34	12	42	30
	$M = 16$	13	45	32	14	37	23
	$T = 4$	45	69	24	45	68	23
	$V = 90$ (Neg. Bin.)	11	35	24	10	33	23
2	None	18	34	16	20	37	17
	$\pi = 9$	11	27	16	11	28	17
	$K = 32$	19	30	11	21	33	12
	$\pi = 9$ $K = 32$	13	24	11	12	25	14
	$M = 8$ $V = 24$	56	88	32	58	90	32
	$T = 0$	5	21	16	6	22	16
	$V = 2$	14	30	16	15	30	15

Nonvaried Parameter Values:

Case 1: $h = 1$ $\pi = 9$ $K = 32$ $c = 0$ $T = 0$ Poisson $M = 9$ $V = 9$

Case 2: $h = 1$ $\pi = 99$ $K = 64$ $c = 0$ $T = 4$ Negative Binomial $M = 2$ $V = 6$

FIGURE 14.8. Approximately Optimal (s, S) Policies.

(15) $s = (T + 1)M + w_s\sqrt{(T + 1)V}$

(16) $S = (T + 1)M + \text{minimum } [u_s\sqrt{(T + 1)V} + \text{EOQ}, v_s\sqrt{(T + 1)V}].$

Justification for these steps involves mathematical arguments too advanced for an introductory text. The test in *Step 3* determines whether or not a replenishment order is likely to be placed more frequently than every other period, and if so, computes values for s and S in *Step 4* that reflect an appropriate balance primarily between the holding and penalty costs, since the setup cost K is incurred in most periods.

Several examples using the approximation are given in Fig. 14.8. (The data employed permit you to compare the results with those in Fig. 14.7, which exhibited a Normal approximation method for the continuous review model.) To see how the algorithm works, consider data for Case 1 in Fig. 14.8:

$$(17) \qquad h = 1 \qquad \pi = 9 \qquad K = 32 \qquad T = 0 \qquad M = 9 \qquad V = 0.$$

According to *Step 1*,

$$(18) \qquad \text{EOQ} = \sqrt{\frac{2 \cdot 32 \cdot 9}{1}} = 24.$$

Then in *Step 2*,

$$(19) \qquad R_N = \frac{1 \cdot 24}{9\sqrt{9}} = .889,$$

and so from Fig. 14.6,

$$(20) \qquad u_s = -.75.$$

Since $9 < .8888(32/1)$,

$$(21) \qquad \text{EOQ} = S - s = 24 \qquad s = 9 - .75\sqrt{9} \approx 7 \qquad S = 31.$$

As Fig. 14.8 shows, the optimal policy is (7, 28).
  Now suppose $M = V = 36$. Then

$$(22) \qquad \text{EOQ} = 48 \qquad R_N = .889 \qquad u_s = -.75.$$

Since $36 > .8888(32/1)$, calculate

$$(23) \qquad R = .9 \qquad v_s = 1.3,$$

so that

$$(24) \qquad w_s = \text{minimum} \ (-.75, 1.3) = -.75.$$

Then

$$(25) \qquad \begin{aligned} s &= 36 - .75(6) \approx 33 \\ S &= 36 + \text{minimum} \ [-.75(6) + 48, 1.3(6)] \approx 44, \end{aligned}$$

which is the exactly optimal policy if the demand distribution is Poisson.

14.8 CONCLUDING REMARKS
ON IMPLEMENTATION

  Any detailed discussion of the steps required to implement a scientific inventory management system would go far beyond the intended scope of this chapter. But because the text mentioned that models as simple as those in the preceding sections have proved effective, the paragraphs below briefly indicate how in reality you would handle the approximating assumptions. Remember throughout that the context of the discussion is the employment of a mathematical approach to stocking those items that are to be managed on a *routine* basis.

Stationarity. The foregoing dynamic continuous and periodic review models postulated that the economic parameters as well as the demand distribution are unchanging over time. In an application, each time the policy is calculated for an item, you would use the current economic parameters and a probability distribution estimated by giving greatest weight to the most recent demand data. In many inventory systems, each policy is updated at most every three months, and often not until six months or a year elapses. If the economic parameters and demand distribution are shifting so rapidly as to invalidate the approximations made in the above models, you then will have to resort to a dynamic programming approach.

Form of the economic functions. Ordering and holding cost functions as simple as those exhibited in this chapter are obviously approximations. Nevertheless, as such they are still capable of being estimated within an acceptable degree of accuracy. Ordinarily you would arrive at the setup cost element by looking at cost of the total annual employment and associated costs required to support the reordering function (consisting mainly of placing and receiving replenishment orders) and averaging this cost over the corresponding reorder activity level. Often the principal component of the inventory carrying charge is the firm's cost of working capital. The additional holding costs due to warehousing and insurance are easily calculated in aggregate, and typically are prorated among the different items stocked.

The shortage or penalty cost is the hardest economic factor to estimate. Typically, you would first make a rough guess and then perform a sensitivity analysis to refine your estimate. A little more will be said about this aspect under the topic of "Validation" below.

Form of the demand distribution. In an inventory system with a multitude of items, you necessarily have to develop a routine procedure for estimating the demand distributions using historical data. Standard statistical approaches for estimating means and variances are usually employed. You must apply a certain amount of caution, however, in the data processing step. For example, you must be careful not to use data so old as to be irrelevant for future demand prediction. Similarly, you must be careful to cull out of the data so-called extreme values, which can exert a strong upward bias in the value of a sample mean, and which in fact represent occasions when a demand is so large that it *has* to be treated on a nonroutine basis.

You will ordinarily assume a standard form for the probability distributions. For example, if you use the Normal approximation approach in the preceding sections, then you need to estimate only the mean and variance of demand during lead time. Often, by examining a sample of items, you will find through statistical regression analysis that you can employ an approximating relationship between the mean and variance. To illustrate, you may find there is a reasonably constant ratio between the mean and variance. In such a case, you would estimate the variance indirectly from an estimate of the mean.

Calculation of optimal policies. There is a variety of techniques for computing the specific optimal policies. The primary factor determining the appropriate method is whether an electronic computer is employed to maintain current inventory records. When a company utilizes a computer to keep an up-to-date record of stock on hand, then ordinarily it also has the computer calculate the policies according to formulas such as those in the preceding section. The electronic calculator uses recent demand data to update the policies, and as already mentioned, the policies are revised from one to four times a year. In the most sophisticated computer applications, as soon as the inventory level reaches the reorder point, the electronic calculator prints out a reorder slip to be mailed to the vendor.

The scientific approach to inventory decisions has also been implemented in companies making only minor use of a computer for stock control. In such situations, tables (or nomographs) are constructed so that an inventory manager is not required to perform any complex computations, but only needs to enter a modest amount of economic and demand data to find the optimal policy. The tables themselves are usually calculated by means of an electronic computer.

Validation. By now, having seen a succession of simplifying assumptions piled one on top of another, you must be wondering how it is possible to tell whether the resultant recommended policies will *really* bring about an improvement in an actual inventory system. The real test is how well all of the policies will operate in the aggregate.

The most commonly employed technique for performing this test is computer simulation, and several standard computer programs are available for just this purpose. Since the topic of simulation is taken up in detail in Chap. 16, only a few comments are given here. A simple, yet effective, approach to the validation phase is the following. You take a sample of items, use historical data to estimate the statistical parameters, and thereby determine the recommended policies. Then, employing these policies, you simulate how the inventory system would have operated using more recent data. All of the calculations are done by an electronic computer, so little manual effort is involved in the simulation.

The simulated results are then compared against data showing the historical performance, looking at, for example, average inventory levels, frequency of orders, size of backlogs, etc. Usually you would perform a sensitivity analysis, especially with respect to the stockout parameters. The higher the penalty cost, the higher the average inventory.

In evaluating the simulation sensitivity results, the exercise of managerial judgment is far more important than technical expertise. The reason is that it is operating management who must accept the final responsibility for balancing low purchase and holding costs against maintaining customer service at a competitive level.

REVIEW EXERCISES

1 In each part below, discuss the elements of the situation that may make the inventory decisions nontrivial. Specifically, describe what you think might represent the appropriate considerations relating to supply and demand, the replenishment economics, and the systems specifications, as illustrated in Sec. 14.3.

(a) Refilling an auto's gasoline tank.

(b) Refilling a gasoline station's storage tank.

(c) Maintaining an adequate balance in a personal checking account.

(d) Maintaining an adequate balance in a corporation's checking account.

(e) Determining an adequate level of cash reserves and liquid assets for a bank. For a savings and loan company. For a life insurance company. For a fire insurance company.

(f) Determining the number of cans of tomato juice to keep in your kitchen cupboard. In a restaurant's store room. On a grocer's shelf.

(g) Determining the numbers of new and used automobiles to be stocked by a car dealer.

(h) Determining the number of buses and their replacement dates by a local transit authority.

(i) Determining the number of spare flashlight batteries to keep at home.

(j) Determining the number and size of auxiliary power generators to install in a hospital.

(k) Determining the number of paper clips an executive should keep in the home and office desks.

(l) Determining the number of spare jet engines an airline should keep at its different maintenance bases.

(m) Determining the number of different size scratch pads to stock in a busy office.

(n) Determining the number of different size boards of lumber to stock in a lumber yard. In a lumber mill.

(o) Determining the number of towels a department store should stock at its annual white sale. Determining the number of bathing suits the store should stock at the beginning of the summer season.

(p) Determining the total number of seats in a new movie theater.

(q) Determining the number of first-class seats in a new jet aircraft.

(r) Determining the number of prizes to award in a state-run lottery.

(s) Determining the number of persons to recruit monthly into the armed services.

(t) Determining the amount of ammunition to keep in a field-supply area. In a continental U.S. depot.

(u) Determining the amount of funds to allocate each year to aid so-called *disaster areas*. Determining the amount of funds to put in a Community Chest contingency fund. (*Continued on p. 480.*)

(v) Determining the amount of water to let spill over a dam.

(w) Determining the number of life jackets and life boats on an ocean liner. Determining the number of bottles of champagne to have in store for passengers.

2 Suggest some commercial situations in which a one-period inventory model is applicable. Discuss the circumstances under which it would be profitable to use an operations research approach to derive an inventory policy for these situations.

3 (a) Consider the inventory policy $(s, S) \equiv (3, 10)$. What is the order quantity if entering inventory equals 0? Equals 2? Equals 3? Equals 5? Equals 10? Equals 15? In each of these cases, what is the amount of inventory available to meet demand *after* the order is placed? Assume no delivery lag.

(b) Let $c(x)$ have the form given by (2) in Sec. 14.4, and let $K = 5$ and $c = 2$. Draw a graph of $c(x)$ for $x = 0, 1, 2, \ldots, 5$.

(c) Consider the expected cost function (3) in Sec. 14.4. Explain why it is reasonable to assume that $c + h > 0$ and $\pi > c$. Show that these two inequalities imply $h + \pi > 0$.

(d) Verify that the probability distribution in (4) yields the expression $L(y)$ given in (5) of Sec. 14.4.

(e) Let $h = 5$ and $\pi = 10$ in (5) of Sec. 14.4. Calculate $L(y)$ and check your answers with the values in Fig. 14.1. Also plot $L(y)$.

(f) Rework part (e), except let $\pi = 20$.

(g) Rework part (e), except let $\pi = 5$.

(h) Rework part (e), except let $h = 10$. [*Hint:* make use of your answer in part (f).]

(i) Explain in detail why the holding cost h in (3) of Sec. 14.4 can be interpreted as a *net* cost, where the salvage value has been subtracted out. What would be an optimal policy if the salvage value v were greater than the unit purchasing cost c?

(j) Suppose entering inventory is 0, and optimal $s > 0$. Derive a formula for the "cost of uncertainty" appropriate to (2) and (3) in Sec. 14.4.

4 Consider the critical ratio R, given by (6) in Sec. 14.4.

(a) Assume $c = 0$ and $h = 1$. What value of π yields $R = \frac{1}{2}$? $R = \frac{2}{3}$? $R = \frac{3}{4}$? $R = \frac{9}{10}$? $R = \frac{99}{100}$?

(b) Assume $c = 1$ and $h = 1$, and answer part (a).

(c) Assume $c = 10$ and $h = 1$, and answer part (a).

(d) Assume $c = 10$ and $h = 10$, and answer part (a).

(e) Assume $c = 100$ and $h = 10$, and answer part (a).

(f) Describe the optimal policy when $c = h = 0$.

(g) Describe the optimal policy when $\pi \le c$. Justify your answer.

5 Consider the critical ratio R, given by (6) in Sec. 14.4.

(a) Plot the region of values for π/c and h/c that yields R in the interval $.8 \le R \le .9$.

(b) Plot a region of values for π/h and c/h that yields R in this interval.

(c) Plot a region of values for c/π and h/π that yields R in this interval.

6 Consider the critical ratio R, given by (6) in Sec. 14.4. Suppose $.8 \le R \le .9$, and

find the corresponding interval for π, given that

(a) $c = 0$ and $h = 1$.
(b) $c = 1$ and $h = 1$.
(c) $c = 10$ and $h = 1$.
(d) $c = 10$ and $h = 10$.
(e) $c = 100$ and $h = 10$.
(f) Answer parts (a) through (e) for the interval $.7 \le R \le .8$.
(g) Answer parts (a) through (e) for the interval $.85 \le R \le .95$.

7 (a) Consider the cumulative distribution in Fig. 14.2. Determine an optimal S from (7) in Sec. 14.4 for $h = 5$, $\pi = 10$, and $c = 5$. For $R = .8$. For $R = .6$.
   (b) Plot $cy + L(y)$, where $h = 5$, $\pi = 10$, and $c = 5$, and indicate the optimal S.

8 Consider the critical ratio R, given by (6) in Sec. 14.4. In each part below, find an optimal S for values of R equal to $\frac{1}{2}$, $\frac{3}{4}$, and $\frac{9}{10}$.

(a) $p(q) = (q + 1)/15$, for $q = 0, 1, \ldots, 4$.
(b) $p(0) = p(4) = \frac{1}{9}$, $p(1) = p(3) = \frac{2}{9}$, $p(2) = \frac{3}{9}$.
(c) $p(q) = (5 - q)/15$, for $q = 0, 1, \ldots, 4$.
(d) $p(0) = p(4) = \frac{3}{11}$, $p(1) = p(3) = \frac{2}{11}$, $p(2) = \frac{1}{11}$.

9 Consider the probability distribution (8) in Sec. 14.4 and assume that $h = 5$, $\pi = 10$, and $c = .1$ in (2) and (3).

(a) Verify that the optimal $S = 3$.
(b) Plot $L(y)$ for $y = 0, 1, \ldots, 5$.
(c) Let $K = 4$ and plot $K + c(S - y) + L(S)$, where $S = 3$. Show graphically that the optimal $s = 2$.
(d) Let $K = 12$ and answer part (c).
(e) Find a range of values for K such that $s = 1$ is optimal.

10 Assume $p(q) = \frac{1}{10}$ for $q = 1, 2, \ldots, 10$. Let $h = 5$, $\pi = 10$, and $c = .1$ in the one-period model (2) and (3) of Sec. 14.4.

(a) Find an optimal S.
(b) Find an optimal s for $K = 1$. For $K = 2$. For $K = 5$. For $K = 10$.
(c) Find a range of values for K such that $s = 2$ is optimal.
(d) Let $c = 5$ and answer parts (a) and (b).

11 Consider the economic order quantity examples displayed in Figs. 14.3 and 14.4. Assume $Q = 45$, $s = -10$, $M = 30$.

(a) Calculate S, the average number of setups per week, the average level of inventory during the interval when inventory *is* positive, and the average level of inventory per week.
(b) Suppose lead time $L = 1$ week. When should a replenishment be initiated?
(c) Suppose lead time $L = 2$ weeks. When should a replenishment be initiated?
(d) Answer parts (a), (b), and (c) for $Q = 60$.   (*Continued on p. 482.*)

(e) Answer parts (a), (b), and (c) for $M = 15$.

(f) Answer parts (a), (b), and (c) for $s = -5$.

12 (a) Verify the algebra leading to the formula for average cost per unit of time as given by (6) in Sec. 14.5.

   (b) Show that if $S = Q$, then (6) simplifies to (7).

   (c) Show that if the square root formula for Q as given in (8) is used, then the minimal average cost is that also given in (8).

   *(d) Differentiate AC in (7) with respect to Q, set the derivative equal to 0, and solve for Q; verify that the result is the formula in (8).

13 (a) Consider the lot-size formula (8) in Sec. 14.5. Determine the value for the ratio K/h such that an order is for one week's demand. For two weeks'. For four weeks'. For 12 weeks'. For 26 weeks'.

   (b) Define the *turnover ratio* as the average inventory level divided by the rate of demand per unit of time. Assume that you employ (8), and derive a formula for the turnover ratio. Explain how the ratio varies with the demand rate. With the ratio K/h.

14 (a) Verify from (14) in Sec. 14.5 the sensitivity analysis formula (15).

   (b) Find a range for r in (15) such that $VC(r)/VC(1) \le 1.15$.

   (c) Explain why the ratio in (15) is the same for a given r and its reciprocal $r' = 1/r$.

   (d) Draw a graph of the ratio in (15) for r in the range $.1 \le r \le 10$.

15 Consider the economic order quantity formula given by (8) in Sec. 14.5. Suppose M is the true demand rate, but that you mis-estimate the rate to be $r \cdot M$, where $r > 0$. Let $VC(r)$ be the variable cost, analogous to (14), assuming that $r \cdot M$ is used in (8), instead of M.

   (a) Derive a formula for $VC(r)/VC(1)$.

   (b) Find the interval of values for r such that $VC(r)/VC(1) \le 1.1$.

   (c) Plot $VC(r)/VC(1)$ for r in the range $.1 \le r \le 10$.

16 Perform the analysis in exercise 15, except suppose that the setup cost K is mis-estimated to be $r \cdot K$.

17 Perform the analysis in exercise 15, except suppose that the holding cost is mis-estimated to be $r \cdot h$.

18 Consider the average-backlog penalty cost model expressed by the cost function (17) in Sec. 14.5.

   (a) Verify the formula in (17).

   *(b) Take the partial derivative of AC in (17) with respect to S, set the result equal to 0, and solve for S; verify the formula in (18).

   *(c) Verify the results in (19).

   (d) What is the optimal time interval between successive orders?

   (e) Simplify and interpret the results in (19) for the case $h = \pi$.

   (f) Simplify and interpret the results in (19) for the case $3h = \pi$.

19 Assume $h = 1$, $\pi = 9$, $K = 32$, $c = 0$, $M = 9$.

   (a) Evaluate the formulas in (19) of Sec. 14.5.
   (b) Let $h = 4$ and rework part (a).
   (c) Let $\pi = 36$ and rework part (a).
   (d) Let $M = 36$ and rework part (a).

20 Consider the formulas for an optimal policy, as given by (19) in Sec. 14.5. Suppose that you actually use an order quantity that equals r times the order quantity in (19), where $r > 0$. Let VC(r) be the associated variable cost (exclusive of cM).

   (a) Derive a formula for VC(r)/VC(1).
   (b) Assume $h = 1$, $\pi = 9$, $K = 32$, $M = 9$, and plot VC(r)/VC(1) for r in the range $.1 \le r \le 10$.

21 Consider the formulas for an optimal policy, as given by (19) in Sec. 14.5. Suppose M is the true demand rate, but that you mis-estimate the rate to be $r \cdot M$, where $r > 0$. Let VC(r) be the corresponding variable cost (exclusive of cM), assuming that $r \cdot M$ is used in (19) instead of M.

   (a) Derive a formula for VC(r)/VC(1).
   (b) Assume $h = 1$, $\pi = 9$, $K = 32$, $M = 9$, and find the interval of values for r such that VC(r)/VC(1) ≤ 1.1.
   (c) Plot VC(r)/VC(1) for r in the range $.1 \le r \le 10$.

22 Perform the analysis in exercise 21, except suppose that the setup cost K is mis-estimated to be $r \cdot K$.

23 Perform the analysis in exercise 21, except suppose that the holding cost h is mis-estimated to be $r \cdot h$.

24 Perform the analysis in exercise 21, except suppose that the penalty cost π is mis-estimated to be $r \cdot \pi$.

25 Consider the formulas for an optimal policy, as given by (19) in Sec. 14.5. Assume $h = 1$, $\pi = 9$, $K = 32$, $M = 9$, unless stated otherwise below. Plot each of the optimal quantities in (19), as a function of

   (a) The holding cost h.   (b) The penalty cost π.
   (c) The setup cost K.   (d) The demand rate M.

*26 (a) Exhibit all the intermediate algebraic steps to justify the derivations in (9) through (15), leading to the formula for the expected average cost per unit time, given by (16) in Sec. 14.6.
   (b) Partially differentiate $E[AC]$ with respect to Q, set the derivative equal to 0, and solve for Q; verify that the result is that given by (17).
   *(c) Derive the formula (19) that determines an optimal s.
   (d) Substitute the optimal Q formula given in (17) into the $E[AC]$ formula in (16),

and verify that the result is (21). What terms in (21) indicate the impact of uncertainty?

27 (a) Verify the calculations in the numerical example (23) through (29) of Sec. 14.6.
   (b) Find an optimal policy using the data in (23), except let $\pi = 30$.

28 Assume $p_L(q_L) = \frac{1}{10}$ for $q = 1, 2, \ldots, 10$, where $L = 1$. Let $h = 5$, $\pi = 10$, and $c = .1$. In each part below, find an optimal inventory policy using the algorithm in Sec. 14.6.

   (a) Let $K = 1$.   (b) Let $K = 5$.
   (c) Let $K = 10$.   (d) Let $\pi = 20$ and $K = 10$.
   (e) Let $\pi = 50$ and $K = 10$.

29 Assume $p_L(q_L) = \frac{1}{20}$, for $q = 0, 1, \ldots, 19$, where $L = 1$. In each part below, apply the algorithm in Sec. 14.6 to graph the optimal Q, s, S, and expected cost, as functions of the indicated parameter. (Only consider cases where optimal $s > 0$. *Suggestion:* select a few sample points for the indicated parameter, and, by eye, fit the curves through the optimal policies for these sample points.)

   (a) Let $h = 1$, $\pi = 50$, and let the parameter be K, where $0 < K \le 30$.
   (b) Let $h = 1$, $K = 20$, and let the parameter be π, where $0 < \pi \le 100$.
   (c) Rework parts (a) and (b), assuming that $L = 2$.

*30 Consider the Normal approximation approach described at the end of Sec. 14.6. In each part below, find the approximately optimal Q, s, S, and the associated approximate value for the expected cost.

   (a) $M = 16$, $L = 5$, $M_L = 80$, $V_L = 240$, and all the other parameters are those given by (39).
   (b) Case 1 in Fig. 14.7.
   (c) Case 2 in Fig. 14.7.

*31 Study the sensitivity analysis in Fig. 14.7. Give a plausible explanation of why an increase in each parameter π, K, M, L, and V_L tends to increase both the optimal s and Q, *except* that an increase in π decreases Q and an increase in K decreases s. (Trace the direct impact of the economic parameters on the policy variables and the consequent indirect impact due to the interactive effect among the policy variables.)

*32 Consider the Normal approximation approach in Sec. 14.7. In each part below, find the approximately optimal s, S, and the associated approximate value for the expected cost.

   (a) $M = 16$, $T = 4$, $V = 48$, $K = 32$, $h = 1$, $\pi = 9$.
   (b) Case 1 in Fig. 14.8.
   (c) Case 2 in Fig. 14.8.

*33 Consider the sensitivity analysis in Fig. 14.8. Give a plausible explanation of how s, S, and $S - s$ vary with changes in the parameters π, K, M, V, and T.

*34 Consider the Normal approximation for Case 1 in Fig. 14.8. Plot s, S, and D as a function of

(a) The holding cost h.   (b) The penalty cost π.

(c) The setup cost K.   (d) The mean demand M.

(e) The variance of demand V.   (f) The delivery lag T.

(g) A parameter c such that holding cost is $1c$ and penalty cost is $9c$.

*35 Consider the Normal approximation for Case 2 in Fig. 14.8. Answer the questions given in exercise 34.

36 Explain your understanding of the following terms:

lead time (delivery lag)	backlogged demand
setup (recoder) cost	economic order quantity (lot-size) models
inventory holding cost	sawtooth pattern of inventory
penalty cost (profit loss)	size-of-backlog penalty cost
static (single decision) model	EOQ (lot-size formula, Wilson lot size)
newsboy problem	average-backlog penalty cost
(s, S) policy	demand during lead time
reorder point	service level
reorder level	safety (buffer) stock
linear holding and penalty cost	*standardized Normal loss integral
critical ratio	*delivery lag.

FORMULATION AND COMPUTATIONAL EXERCISES

37 The Sayure Prairie Airlines is ordering a fleet of new jet aircraft. Provisioning engine spare parts in advance is less expensive than waiting until they are needed. Specifically, suppose c_1 is the unit purchase price now, and c_2 the price if ordered subsequently, where $c_1 < c_2$. Assume that any parts left over when the fleet becomes obsolete have a salvage value v per unit. Let $p(d)$ be the probability that d parts will be needed by SPA over the lifetime of the fleet.

(a) Exhibit a formula for the expected total cost associated with purchasing Q spares now.

*(b) Derive a formula for determining an optimal Q. (State any assumptions you are making about the value of v.)

38 The Sayure Prairie Airlines must also decide how many first-class and tourist seats to install in the airplanes. Assume that the total number of rows of seats is R. Let r_1 be the number of rows of first-class seats, and r_2 the number of rows of tourist seats. There are four seats in each first-class row and six seats in each tourist row. Assume that $p_1(d_1)$ is the probability that d_1 customers desire first-class seats on each flight. For simplicity, assume that if all the first-class seats are filled, these customers call another airline. Let v_1 be the profit value from selling a first-class seat. Similarly, let

$p_2(d_2)$ be the probability distribution for tourist-class seats and v_2 the profit value per seat. Write the appropriate expression for expected profit, and explain how you would find an optimal seat allocation.

39 (k, Q) *Inventory Replenishment Policy.* Consider the one-period model with costs given by (2) and (3) in Sec. 14.4; let $K = 0$. Suppose that an order quantity must be an integer multiple of Q, where Q is a prespecified number. (For example, Q may be a dozen.)

*(a) Show that the form of an optimal policy is the following: if entering inventory is less than some number k, the smallest integral multiple of Q is ordered such that inventory after ordering is at least k; if entering inventory is k or greater, no order is placed. For example, suppose the policy is $(k, Q) \equiv (8, 5)$; if entering inventory is 8 or more, then no items are ordered; if entering inventory is 3, 4, ..., 7, then 5 units are ordered; if entering inventory is $-2, -1, \ldots, 2$, then 10 units are ordered, etc.

(b) Given the validity of the policy in part (a), describe how to calculate an optimal k.

(c) Apply your method in part (b) to the numerical example (4) and (5), with $h = 5$, $\pi = 10$, and $c = .1$. Find optimal policies for $Q = 2$ and $Q = 4$.

(d) Assume $p(q) = \frac{1}{10}$ for $q = 1, 2, \ldots, 10$. Let $h = 5$, $\pi = 10$, and $c = .1$. Apply your method in part (b) to find optimal policies for $Q = 2$ and $Q = 4$.

40 In each part below, assume that $h = H \cdot c$ and $\pi = \Pi \cdot c$, where c is the unit purchasing cost. Discuss how the optimal policy depends on the value of c.

(a) The lot-size model given by (7) and (8) in Sec. 14.5.

(b) The lot-size model given by (19) in Sec. 14.5.

(c) The stochastic demand model given by (17) through (20) in Sec. 14.6.

41 Consider the lot-size models in Sec. 14.5 yielding the average cost formulas (6) and (15).

(a) Show how to modify (6) and (17) if the purchase cost of Q is cQ^2, instead of cQ.

*(b) Derive the associated optimal lot-size formulas.

42 Consider the lot-size model yielding formula (7) in Sec. 14.5 for the average cost per unit of time (where optimal $s = 0$). Suppose that the firm can request a fraction f of the order quantity to be delivered right away, and the remainder to be delivered after the quantity fQ is exhausted.

(a) Suppose f is a given fraction. Derive the optimal Q analogous to (8). (*Note:* inventory holding cost is assessed against only the inventory on hand.)

*(b) Suppose both f and Q can be determined by the firm. Find formulas for the optimal values of f and Q. What is the optimal time interval between the arrival of fQ and the remainder of the order?

43 *Optimal Production Lot-Size Model.* Consider a lot-size model like that giving rise to the sawtooth pattern shown in Fig. 14.3. Suppose, however, that the order must be manufactured by the firm itself, and the production rate is N per unit of time, where $N > M$. Hence, the level of inventory no longer exhibits a vertical jump at the arrival

of the lot of Q items. Rather, the inventory level increases at a slope of $N - M$ until the lot Q has been produced, and then decreases at a slope $-M$ (as before).

(a) Suppose $N = 75$ and the rest of the data are as given in Fig. 14.3. Draw the resultant diagram for the inventory level.

(b) Assuming $s = 0$ so that $S = Q$, derive the formula for the average cost per unit of time, analogous to (4) in Sec. 14.5, and determine the corresponding EOQ. Also determine the corresponding minimal average cost and the optimal time interval between successive production startups.

(c) Show how to modify your answer in part (b) where you permit s to be negative and you assume an "average-backlog penalty cost." Derive the formula for the average cost per unit of time, analogous to (15) in Sec. 14.5, and determine the corresponding EOQ, optimal s and S, minimal average cost, and the optimal time interval between successive production startups.

(d) Apply your answers in parts (b) and (c) to the data $h = 1$, $K = 32$, $c = 0$, $M = 9$, $N = 36$, $\pi = 9$.

44 Assume $p_L(q_L) = \frac{1}{10}$, for $q_L = 1, 2, \ldots, 10$, where $L = 1$. Let $h = 5$, $\pi = 10$, and $c = .1$. In each case below, apply the algorithm in Sec. 14.6 to find an optimal policy. (Compare the results with those in exercise 10.)

(a) Let $K = 5$.
(b) Let $K = 10$.

45 Assume $p_L(q_L) = \frac{1}{20}$, for $q = 0, 1, \ldots, 19$, where $L = 1$. Let $h = 1$ and $K = 20$.

(a) Find the values of s corresponding to $P_L(s) = .75, .8, .85, .9, .95$, according to (18), (19), and (20) in Sec. 14.6.

(b) Calculate the corresponding values for Q using (17) and letting $\pi = 0$. Calculate the associated expected average inventory per unit of time using (12).

(c) Summarize the results of the above parts by plotting a graph of expected average inventory as a function of the service level $P_L(s)$. Give an economic interpretation of your results.

46 Assume $p_L(q_L) = \frac{1}{20}$, for $q = 0, 1, \ldots, 19$, where $L = 1$. Let $h = 1$ and $K = 20$.

(a) Find the values of s corresponding to $P_L(s) = .75, .8, .85, .9, .95$, according to (18), (19), and (20) in Sec. 14.6.

(b) For each s in part (a), find a value of π such that using this value and s in (17), the resultant value of R in (20) equals $P_L(s)$.

(c) Employing your answers in part (b), calculate the associated expected average inventory per unit of time using (12).

(d) Summarize the results of the above parts by graphing expected average inventory as a function of the service level $P_L(s)$. Also plot a graph of the service level as a function of π. Give an economic interpretation of your results.

47 Let $p(q)$ represent the probability of demand in a week, where $q = 0, 1, \ldots, D$. Let $t(w)$ represent the probability that lead time is w weeks, where $w = 1, 2, \ldots, W$. Assume weekly demands and lead times are completely independent random variables. (*Continued on p. 488.*)

(a) Derive a computational method for finding $p_L(q_L)$, which represents the probability that demand during lead time is q_L.

(b) Illustrate your method for $p(q) = \frac{1}{4}$, $q = 0, 1, 2, 3$, and $t(w) = \frac{1}{3}$, $w = 1, 2, 3$.

(c) Using the data in part (b), calculate the probability of stockout if the reorder point is 5. Is 8. Is 10.

*48 Consider Case 1 in Fig. 14.7.

(a) Suppose you estimate the demand rate to be 6 and use the corresponding policy, but in fact the actual demand rate is 9. What is the expected average cost increase due to mis-estimation? Answer the same question if you incorrectly assume the demand rate is 12 when in fact it is 9. (*Suggestion:* calculate the actual expected average cost, the expected average cost if you had correctly estimated the parameter, and the expected average cost if the mis-estimated value of the parameter were truly correct.)

(b) Suppose you estimate the variance of demand during lead time to be 6 and use the corresponding policy, but in fact the actual variance is 9. What is the expected average cost increase due to mis-estimation? Answer the same question if you incorrectly assume the variance is 12, but in fact it is 9.

(c) Answer parts (a) and (b) where you mis-estimate *both* the demand rate and variance to be 6. To be 12.

*49 Consider Case 2 in Fig. 14.7. Suppose you estimate the lead time to be 4 and use the corresponding policy, but in fact the actual lead time is 5. What is the expected average cost increase due to mis-estimation? Answer the same question if you incorrectly assume the lead time is 6, but in fact it is 5. (*Suggestion:* calculate the actual expected average cost, the expected average cost if you had correctly estimated the parameter, and the expected average cost if the mis-estimated value of the parameter were truly correct.)

*50 Consider the lot-size model yielding formula (7) in Sec. 14.5 for the average cost per unit of time (where optimal $s = 0$). In each part below, devise a computational technique for finding an optimal order quantity, given that the vendor offers quantity discounts for purchasing large-size lots.

(a) Assume that c_j is the price per item if the order quantity Q satisfies $q_j \leq Q < q_{j+1}$, where $c_j > c_{j-1} \geq 0$. Also assume that $h = H \cdot c_j$, where c_j is the unit cost incurred. Illustrate your procedure with the data $K = 32$, $M = 9$, $H = 1$, and $c_1 = 16$, for $0 \leq Q < 7$; $c_2 = 9$, for $7 \leq Q < 75$; and $c_3 = 1$, for $75 \leq Q$. Determine whether the solution differs if $c_2 = 9$, for $7 \leq Q < 50$; and $c_3 = 1$, for $50 \leq Q$. (*Suggestion:* explain your approach using a graph that contains for each c_j the average cost per unit of time as a function of Q.)

(b) Assume that $C(Q)$ is the total purchase cost and

$$C(Q) = C(q_j) + c_j \cdot (Q - q_j) \quad \text{for } q_j \leq Q < q_{j+1},$$

where $c_j > c_{j-1} \geq 0$, and $C(0) = 0$. Thus the discount is offered on an incremental basis. Illustrate your procedure using the data in part (a) and $h = H \cdot C(Q)/Q$. (*Suggestion:* explain your approach using a graph that contains for each c_j the average cost per unit of time as a function of Q.)

*(c) Determine in parts (a) and (b) whether an optimal Q can ever occur at a price break q_j.

*51 Consider the example (23) in Sec. 14.6. Suppose there are two locations in the firm. Assume these data are applicable at each location, and that the demands at the two locations are completely independent. Suppose the firm has the option of either stocking the item at each location, thereby leading to the policy in (28) and twice the cost in (9), or combining the two sources of demand, and stocking in a single location.

(a) Derive an optimal policy for the combined operation. What is the cost differential between this combined stocking and the independent stocking at two separate locations? [*Hint:* calculate the probability distribution of the sum of two independent random demands during a lead time, where the probability distribution for each demand is given by (23).]

(b) Perform the same analysis as in part (b) except use the data in (39) and the Normal approximation technique. (*Hint:* the variance of the sum of two *independent* random variables is the sum of the variances.)

*52 You can develop as follows a cruder approximate expected average cost per unit of time analogous to (16) in Sec. 14.6. Assume that, on the average, the lowest level of inventory is $s - E[q_L]$ so, as an approximation, the average inventory level is the sum $(Q/2) + s - E[q_L]$.

(a) Derive the cost function analogous to (16).

(b) Find formulas for the optimal order quantity and reorder point, analogous to (17) through (20), and compare the results.

*53 (a) Show how to modify the derivation in (9) through (16) in Sec. 14.6 if excess demand during a lead time is lost. (Hence, the level of inventory never falls below 0, as it does in Fig. 14.5.) Specifically, find the appropriate expected average cost per unit of time, analogous to (16), and derive formulas for the optimal order quantity and reorder point. Compare your results with those in (16) through (20).

(b) Derive a formula for the expected average cost per unit of time in part (a) by taking the ratio of the expected cost between successive reorders and the expected time between successive reorders. (Assume that lead time is constant and that there is never more than one order outstanding at any moment in time.)

CONTENTS

CHAPTER 15

Waiting Line Models [†]

15.1 INTRODUCTION

Waiting lines, like stocks of inventory, are omnipresent. Think back for a moment on the times you waited for service during the past few days—perhaps at a cafeteria, bookstore, library, bank, gasoline station, dean's office, and the like. Less apparent examples occur when you wait for a telephone operator to answer, for a traffic light to change, for the morning mail to be delivered, and for a midterm examination to be corrected and returned. Common to all of these cases are the arrivals of people or objects requiring service and the attendant delays when the service mechanism is busy.

Operations research can very effectively analyze such queuing or congestion phenomena. But, as is true of all practical applications of operations research, the relevant decision problems must be of sufficient economic significance to warrant whatever expenditure of effort is needed to perform the scientific analysis. There are two important situations in which it has proved to be economically advantageous to use waiting line models; as you will quickly recognize, there is no clear line of demarcation between these two situations, and any particular application may fall somewhere in between.

The first relates to a company that must design and operate many similar service facilities. Examples include deciding the number of

- Checkout stands in each store of a large grocery chain.
- Tellers' windows in each local branch of a statewide bank.

†Parts of this chapter require a knowledge of elementary differential and integral calculus. Readers not familiar with the calculus, however, can safely skip over the equations containing integral signs and derivatives and should concentrate on the end-result formulas, all of which are computable by ordinary methods of arithmetic.

- Gasoline pumps and attendants in each station of a major oil company.
- Trunk lines in each local telephone exchange.
- Maintenance staff to service leased photocopy equipment in each city.

Although the environmental data vary from store to store, branch to branch, station to station, and so forth, the same *procedure* can be used to analyze each service facility decision. Consequently, once a company develops the methodology for an operations research approach, the technique can be used repeatedly; for each separate application, the company need only apply the relevant data.

The second category relates to a company that must make a facility decision involving the purchases of very expensive equipment, such as deciding on the number and capacity of automatic elevators to be installed in a large office building, or furnaces in a steel processing plant, or runways at an airport.

To round out the discussion of applications, we mention two examples that combine the characteristics of both categories above: determining the number of check-in counters at an airport, and of fire engines at each local fire station of a metropolitan area.

Once again, reflect on your activities during the past few days, and this time pick out those queuing situations that you think might actually warrant a scientific study. In which of the two categories above do they fall? What are the decisions that might be made as a result of such a study? How would you distinguish a good decision from a poor one? Try to answer these questions for several of the examples you picked.

Perspective. What is said about insects is also true of waiting line models: their variety and number seem infinite. Even a treatise of several hundred pages would be too small for a complete survey of all the mathematical results of queuing models. And then it would have to be significantly enlarged within a year or so to encompass the continual growth in new research findings. Consequently, this chapter cannot possibly provide a survey of all waiting line models; instead this chapter highlights typical and critical insights to be garnered from queuing model analysis, and presents several models that are now fundamental in the literature of waiting line theory.

This chapter deals with many waiting line models that are amenable to *mathematical* analysis. As you will see, the underlying waiting line systems in these models appear considerably simpler than most of the queuing situations you encounter in reality. What we demonstrate in this chapter is that you can sometimes employ these *relatively* simple models to provide qualitative and approximate quantitative information about the behavior of more complex structures. Then later in Chap. 16 you can learn how to apply computer simulation techniques to analyze intricate waiting line situations.

In previous chapters, we have offered at least heuristic proofs of the most fundamental results. When the underlying mathematical intricacies were beyond the intended level of the text, we tried to present verbal arguments that could be made rigorous. Our rationale was that you would reach a better understanding of the results by having a "feel" for the way they are derived. There are some places below where we continue to follow this expository practice. But many mathematical derivations of waiting line results are not, in our opinion, very enlightening to a person intent on applying the theory. (The proofs are important, of course, to technical specialists who may want to apply similar approaches to solving new waiting line models.) Consequently, some of the formulas in this chapter are presented in "cookbook" fashion. Because the calculus is often needed to derive results for queuing models, we have sprinkled a few integrals and derivatives among the equations to suggest to the *cognoscente* the source of the formulas. But you need not be familiar with the calculus to employ the end results; rest assured, the useful formulas presented in this chapter can be calculated with straightforward arithmetic.

We will mostly stress the insights to be gained from performing sensitivity analysis in waiting line models. In reading the material, you should pay special attention to the differing assumptions in the various models, and observe the qualitative effect these differences have on the results. You also should notice the impact of varying the numerical values for the parameters in models. As you will see, the scientific analysis of queuing phenomena can be complex; you will not be able to rely solely on unaided intuition to determine the impact of varying arrival rates, service rates, the number and arrangement of service facilities, etc.

In sharp contrast to the rest of this text, the emphasis in this chapter is on a model's **operating characteristics,** such as the average number of customers in a system, their average waiting time, the probability that all service facilities are busy, and similar measures of operating effectiveness. Once these characteristics have been obtained, you can proceed to construct an appropriate economic framework that encompasses them, and subsequently find optimal decisions.

The optimizing task may be either easy or hard, depending on the complexity of the queuing system and the range of alternatives you wish to consider. For example, if you want to choose between having four versus five checkout stands at a grocery store, you can find the optimal decision by examining the effects of each separate alternative. But if you wish to design an air traffic control system at a busy airport, you may need a more sophisticated optimization technique than "examine each separate alternative"; the number of such alternatives may be unlimited.

At present, there is no unified body of optimization theory for waiting line models. In most applications, the optimizing technique employed is ad hoc. But advanced research is underway in extending dynamic programming techniques to assist in optimizing queuing system design.

15.2 TAXONOMY OF WAITING LINE MODELS

Before examining the solution of specific queuing models, you will find it useful to have an overview of such systems. This section provides a general framework, and also serves the purpose of building your vocabulary of the terms frequently employed in the description of waiting line models. An outline for the rest of the chapter appears at the end of this section.

You can describe a queuing system by its input or arrival process, its queue discipline, and its service mechanism. Several possibilities for each of these are discussed in general terms below. In subsequent sections, more precise mathematical assumptions are specified in treating particular cases.

Input process. The usual description of the pattern of arrivals into the system is given by the probability distribution of time between successive arrival events, and the number of individuals or units that appear at each of these events. For example, an arrival event at, say, a barber shop or a restaurant may occur on the average of once in any 10-minute interval. For the barber shop, each arrival event consists of a *single* customer entering; for the restaurant, a party of *one or more* customers. (When more than one customer can enter the system at an arrival event, the situation is termed **bulk arrivals.**) Often, successive interarrival times are in fact statistically independent and stationary over long intervals of time, but, of course, they need not be in any particular situation. The two extreme assumptions about interarrival times are that they are predetermined or completely random, a notion to be made precise in the next section.

Usually the source population from which the arrivals are drawn is considered as unlimited. To illustrate, such an assumption seems warranted in the case of train passengers seeking help in New York's Grand Central Station.

But in other situations, the source population is more appropriately modeled as being finite. One such example might be the number of drill presses breaking down and requiring service from a factory's regular staff of repairmen.

In some situations, a customer seeing a long line may **balk,** that is, not join the line. Depending on the circumstance, the person may return later for service. Sometimes a customer cannot join the queue because there is no room left for waiting. Thus the input or arrival process may depend in part on the status of the queuing system.

Queue discipline. This characteristic describes the order in which customers entering the *system* are eventually served. Frequently, the discipline is **first come, first served.** Certainly it is the easiest ordering to handle in mathematical models; it is also the ordering applied to customers who have entered a particular *line*. If you reflect on most of the waiting line situations you are familiar with, however, you will realize that many other disciplines are possible. Sometimes it is **last come, first served.** For example, consider what happens when you enter an empty elevator near the top floor of a multistory building, and as the elevator descends, it becomes crowded with additional passengers. The discipline in this situation may well be viewed as last come, first served, if you define "service" to be your exiting from the elevator when it reaches the ground floor.

Sometimes the service order is virtually **random.** For example, teachers often try to use this discipline in calling upon students for recitation. And sometimes the discipline is governed by a priority system, such as "women and children first," when waiting for a seat in a lifeboat on a sinking ship, or "age before beauty," when waiting your turn in a revolving door. Finally, a customer may become **impatient** and decide to leave the system before being served; this behavior is termed **reneging.**

Service mechanism. In common with the arrival process, a specification of the service mechanism includes a description of time to complete a service, and of the number of individuals whose requirements are satisfied at each service event. Referring again to the barber shop and restaurant, a service event is the departure of a single customer or of a party having several patrons. The time needed for service partly depends on the nature of the customer's or patron's requirements. But it may also depend on the state of the system—for example, the servers may hurry if many customers are waiting. Likewise, for each service facility, successive service times may, but need not, be described as independently and identically distributed random variables. Occasionally, it is appropriate to add a probabilistic contingency of a server breaking down over a limited period of time.

The service mechanism also prescribes the number and configuration of **servers** or **channels.** When you arrive at a British airport, for example, you must go through Passport Control. There all passengers wait in a *single* line. When your turn comes, you will be directed to whichever official has just finished processing a passenger. In contrast, when you enter a bank during rush hours, you will find lines in front of each window. There you must select a single line to wait in. If you make a poor choice, you may wait longer to be served than someone who arrived after you did. (If the lines are not too crowded, you may be able to **jockey** into a line that is getting shorter than the one you are in.)

Both the Passport Control and bank counter illustrations are examples of **servers** (or **channels**) **in parallel.** There are also numerous queuing systems in which the servers are arranged **in series (tandem),** and the customer must proceed from one server to the next, possibly waiting in line in front of each channel. One example is a job-shop, in which an order to be manufactured may be delayed at each of several machine facilities. Another example arises in driving an automobile from one end of the main downtown shopping street to the other, if the car has to wait at several stoplights.

Waiting line analysis. Even with as sketchy a description of possibilities as the above, you can quickly appreciate that the number of conceivable waiting line models is enormous. Although it is easy to give precise mathematical formulations for these possibilities, they often do not yield usable mathematical results about the system's characteristics. Consequently, in order to analyze most waiting line systems, you will find it standard practice to combine two approaches. The first is to use simple models, such as those given in this chapter, as rough approximations to the real system. Then, with these results for insight and guidance, you may go on to develop a computer simulation model that takes account of those facets that are important but hard to deal with by mathematical analysis.

Since simulation is treated in Chap. 16, no more will be said about this approach here.

Of course, the context of an application determines the particular system characteristics that are most important for design decisions. But usually you are interested in the probability distributions of the number of customers in the system and their waiting times, or at least in the long-run average values for these random variables. In addition, you sometimes want to know the probability of all the servers being idle or busy, the probability distribution for the length of the idle and busy periods for each server, the probability that the line length will exceed a specified number, and the probability distribution between successive departures. If the queuing model is not too complicated, then explicit and easy-to-compute formulas can be derived for most of the above-mentioned quantities; the results in the present chapter are of this sort.

The preceding section emphasized that an operations research approach to studying congestion systems is used to aid managerial decisions. Review the several examples in this and the previous section, and suggest a variety of managerial options that can be selected for the design of a system. You should find that in practically every instance, the decision-maker can affect all three aspects of the queuing system: the input process, the queue discipline, and the service mechanism. What is more, there are some intricate tradeoffs among the various decision alternatives. For example, the average time a customer spends in the system may be decreased by changing the arrival rate, adding servers, using faster servers, or reducing the variation in service time. The sections below will illustrate the relative effectiveness of each of these possibilities.

A time to be born and a time to die. You can view the rest of this chapter as illustrating **systems synthesis.** We begin in the next section with a description of the **birth** or **arrival process** for customers entering a system. We examine the probabilistic characteristics of perhaps the most important birth process (in waiting line models, that is), namely, *Poisson input.* In Sec. 15.4, we perform a similar study of service times, or as it sometimes is gravely termed, a **death process.** A classic synthesis occurs in Sec. 15.5, which treats a system having a single server. The extension to a multiple-server situation is examined in Sec. 15.6. The advanced material at the end of the chapter presents a fairly general birth-and-death model which can be used to derive many of the earlier results as special cases.

15.3 PROBABILITY DISTRIBUTIONS OF
INTERARRIVAL TIMES

From here on we assume that an arrival event is synonymous with a *single individual* coming to the system. (Bulk arrivals will only be treated in exercise 37.) The most convenient way to describe the arrival mechanism is to specify the probability distribution of interarrival times.

Assume that the lengths of the intervals between arrivals are independently and identically distributed, and described by a continuous density function. This sort of input is an example of what is called a **renewal process,** and the succession of arrivals demonstrates what is termed a sequence of **recurrent events.** Let

$$f(t) \equiv \begin{pmatrix} \text{density function for the time interval } t \\ \text{between any two successive arrivals} \end{pmatrix},$$

where $t \geq 0$, and also *define*

$$\frac{1}{\lambda} \equiv \text{mean time between arrivals,}$$

so that

$$\lambda = \text{arrival rate per unit of time.}$$

Jot down the verbal description of $1/\lambda$ and λ (lambda). You can determine λ from $f(t)$ by taking the mathematical expectation of t:

(1) $$\int_0^\infty tf(t)\, dt \equiv \frac{1}{\lambda} \quad \text{(mean time between arrivals).}$$

For example, if the unit of time is an hour and $(\lambda = 4)$ is the average number of arrivals per hour, then $1/\lambda$ equals one-fourth (.25) of an hour between arrivals (that is, one arrival on the average in any quarter of an hour). Similarly, if one arrival occurs on the average in any 10-minute interval, then the arrival rate λ is one-tenth (.1) per minute.

Random arrivals. The most important example of an interarrival time distribution is that associated with **completely random arrivals.** Complete randomness means that the probability of an arrival occurring in *any* small interval of time $(T, T + h)$ depends only on the length of the interval h and *not* on the interval's starting point T or on the specific history of arrivals prior to T. In other words, the arrival process is both **stationary,** or as it is often called, **homogeneous,** and **memoryless.** The assumption of **completely random arrivals** corresponds to postulating

(2) $f(t) = \lambda e^{-\lambda t}, \quad t \geq 0$ negative exponential distribution,
$$(\text{mean} = 1/\lambda, \text{ variance} = 1/\lambda^2),$$

where $e = 2.71828\dots$. Several examples of the (negative) exponential distributions for different values of λ are given in Fig. 15.1.

To check the *memoryless property* of the exponential distribution, suppose $t = 0$ represents the system's starting point in time. Then the probability that no arrival occurs in the interval $(0, T)$ is the same as the probability that the first arrival occurs after T:

(3) $$P[t \geq T] = \int_T^\infty \lambda e^{-\lambda t}\, dt = e^{-\lambda T}.$$

Now, the *conditional* probability that no arrival occurs in the interval $(0, T + h)$

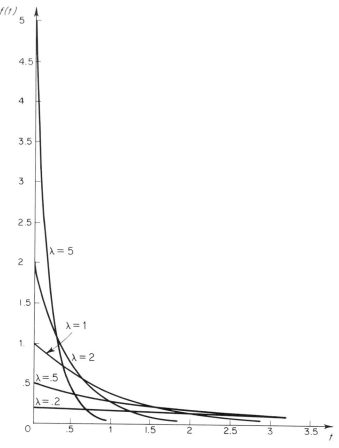

FIGURE 15.1. Exponential Distribution $f(t) = \lambda e^{-\lambda t}$.

given that no arrival occurs in the interval $(0, T)$ is, by definition,

$$(4) \qquad \frac{P[t \geq T + h]}{P[t \geq T]} = \frac{e^{-\lambda(T+h)}}{e^{-\lambda T}} = e^{-\lambda h} = P[t \geq h],$$

which depends *only* on h. According to (4), the probability of no arrival in the interval $(T, T + h)$ is the same *regardless* of whether there is no arrival in $(0, T)$ or whether an arrival occurs at T and thereby "renews" the arrival process.

There is another way of describing the completely random nature of the exponential input process. The idea is given here in rough terms, but can easily be made exact. Suppose there are n arrivals in the interval $(0, T)$. Then if the **interarrival times** are exponentially distributed, the n arrival times are independently and uniformly distributed over the interval $(0, T)$. This observation provides the basis for several statistical tests to determine whether an exponential distribution adequately describes an actual input process.

A complementary insight into the assumption of exponential interarrival times is gained by expressing $e^{-\lambda h}$ in its Taylor series expansion

$$(5) \qquad P \begin{bmatrix} \text{no arrival in} \\ \text{any interval} \\ \text{of length } h \end{bmatrix} = e^{-\lambda h} = 1 - \lambda h + \frac{(-\lambda h)^2}{2!} + \frac{(-\lambda h)^3}{3!} + \cdots.$$

For a very small, but positive, value of h, the term $1 - \lambda h$ in (5) is *relatively* large as compared to the remaining terms in the summation. Therefore, this value can be used to approximate the probability in (5) when h is *very* small. We use the symbol ($\doteq$) to denote such an approximation. So we have, for *very* small $h > 0$,

$$(6) \qquad P \begin{bmatrix} \text{no arrival in} \\ \text{any interval} \\ \text{of length } h \end{bmatrix} \doteq 1 - \lambda h \quad (h \text{ small}).$$

A verbally inexact, but nevertheless helpful, way to explain the mathematical manipulation below is to state that at most only one arrival occurs for a time interval $h \geq 0$ sufficiently small. Since the approximate probability of no arrival occurring in the interval of length h is given by (6), the corresponding approximate probability of one arrival occurring is

$$(7) \qquad P \begin{bmatrix} \text{single arrival} \\ \text{in any interval} \\ \text{of length } h \end{bmatrix} \doteq \lambda h \quad (h \text{ small}).$$

A more precise way of expressing the reasoning would be to display the exact probability of a single arrival, in a manner similar to (5), and then show that for *very* small h, the term λh is *relatively* large as compared to the remaining terms. Throughout this chapter you should always interpret the symbol ($\doteq$) as meaning that a quantity of *relatively* negligible magnitude is being ignored in the approximation.

To illustrate, suppose $\lambda = 4$ arrivals per hour. Then the probability of no arrival occurring in an interval of $h = .01$ hour is exactly .96079 from (5), and approximately $1 - .04 = .96$ from (6); the probability of an arrival is approximately .04 from (7).

Given that the density function for interarrival times is exponential (2), an immediate consequence is that the density function of the *total* arrival time y for any n consecutive arrivals is

$$(8) \qquad g(y) = \frac{\lambda(\lambda y)^{n-1}e^{-\lambda y}}{(n-1)!}, \quad y \geq 0 \quad \text{(gamma distribution)},$$

where n is a positive integer. You may interpret y as the sum of n independent values drawn from the same exponential density (2). Then

(9) $P \begin{bmatrix} \text{total interval for} \\ \text{any } n \text{ consecutive} \\ \text{arrivals } \leq T \end{bmatrix} = \int_0^T g(y) \, dy = 1 - \sum_{j=0}^{n-1} \frac{(\lambda T)^j e^{-\lambda T}}{j!},$

as can be verified by repeatedly applying integration by parts.

Finally, you should note that assuming exponential interarrivals is tantamount to postulating that the probability distribution of the number of arrivals n in *any* interval of length T is Poisson:

(10) $P \begin{bmatrix} n \text{ arrivals in} \\ \text{any interval} \\ \text{of length } T \end{bmatrix} = \frac{(\lambda T)^n e^{-\lambda T}}{n!}$ for $n = 0, 1, 2, \ldots$ (Poisson distribution),

with

(11) $E[n \mid T] = \lambda T$ and $\text{Var}[n \mid T] = \lambda T$

(Poisson—interval of length T).

Hence, if $\lambda = 4$ arrivals per hour, the expected number of arrivals in $T = 2$ hours is 8, and in $T = \frac{3}{4}$ hour (that is, 45 minutes) is 3.

A synonym for the term **exponential arrivals** is **Poisson input.** (Sometimes the term **Markovian** is also used, and abbreviated by the symbol M.)

From (9) and (10), it follows that

(12) $P \begin{bmatrix} \text{total interval for any } n \\ \text{consecutive arrivals } \leq T \end{bmatrix} = P \begin{bmatrix} \text{number of arrivals in} \\ \text{any interval } T \geq n \end{bmatrix}.$

To illustrate, the probability that the total interval for any 7 consecutive arrivals does not exceed $T = 2$ hours is the same value as the probability that the number of arrivals in $T = 2$ hours is at least 7 persons. If $\lambda = 4$ arrivals per hour and $T = 2$ hours, this probability is .687. Actually, (12) is valid for any recurrent input process, not merely the Poisson, if the interval starts right after an arrival.

It is straightforward to apply the foregoing results to a **pure-birth model.** Consider a system that starts at Time 0 with no customers. Assume that customer arrivals obey a Poisson process, and that customers never depart from the system after they have arrived. Then at Time T, the Poisson distribution in (10) gives the probability of n customers in the system. Similarly, (9) gives the density function for the total arrival time of the first n customers.

Taxicab Example. The following illustration indicates both the memoryless property of the exponential distribution and the kind of surprising result that can occur in queuing systems. Consider the illustration of hailing a taxicab on a corner of Times Square in New York City. Assume, on the average, one empty cab goes by the corner in any 30-second interval, that is, the mean time between arrivals is $1/\lambda = 30$ seconds. Suppose that you come to the corner at an arbitrary instant. On the average, how long will you wait until the first empty cab arrives? Most persons reply 15 seconds when asked this question. Did you? As you will see below, that answer is correct *only* if an empty cab arrives at intervals of *exactly*

30 seconds. If there is *any* variability in the interarrival times, the answer is *always* larger than 15 seconds.

It can be shown that if you examine the system at an arbitrary moment, then

$$(13) \qquad \begin{bmatrix} \text{average time} \\ \text{to first arrival} \end{bmatrix} = \frac{1}{2}\left[\frac{1}{\lambda} + \lambda \cdot (\text{variance of interarrival times}) \right].$$

Hence if the term "variance of interarrival times" is positive, then the average time to the first arrival is larger than $\frac{1}{2}(1/\lambda)$. Note that when the interarrival distribution is exponential, its variance is $1/\lambda^2$, so that the average time to the first arrival is $1/\lambda$. And when the variance is larger than $1/\lambda^2$, the average time to the first arrival is actually *larger* than the average interarrival time!

To illustrate (13), suppose that $\lambda = 4$ arrivals per hour, so that the average interarrival time $1/\lambda = .25$ hour (15 minutes). Then if the variance of interarrival times is 0, the average time to the first arrival is $(\frac{1}{2}).25 = .125$ hour (7.5 minutes); if, instead, the variance is $.25^2 = .0625$, then the average time to the first arrival is .25 hour; or if the variance is .25, so that the standard deviation of interarrival times is .5 hour, then the average time to the first arrival is .625 hour (37.5 minutes).

Erlang arrivals. Another important example of an interarrival time distribution is

$$(14) \quad f(t) = \frac{(\lambda n)(\lambda n t)^{n-1} e^{-\lambda n t}}{(n-1)!}, \quad t \geq 0 \quad \text{(Erlang distribution-order } n),$$

where n is a positive integer; the expectation and variance are

$$(15) \qquad\qquad E[t] = \frac{1}{\lambda} \qquad \text{Var } [t] = \frac{1}{n\lambda^2} \quad \text{(Erlang)}.$$

(Frequently, this distribution is denoted by the symbol E_n.) Replacing λn in (14) by λ yields the gamma distribution, shown in (8).

By varying λ and n appropriately, you can use the Erlang distribution to provide good approximations for many different interarrival distributions; several illustrative examples are given in Fig. 15.2. Be sure you notice that when $n = 1$, the Erlang distribution is simply the exponential distribution. What is more, when you let $n \to \infty$, so that Var $[t] \to 0$ as a result, then the Erlang distribution represents the case of **periodic** or **regular** arrival times, that is, a **constant** interarrival interval of $1/\lambda$.

15.4 PROBABILITY DISTRIBUTIONS
OF SERVICE TIMES

The considerations in specifying the probability density for each service time are very similar to those for interarrival times. We assume that each server, or

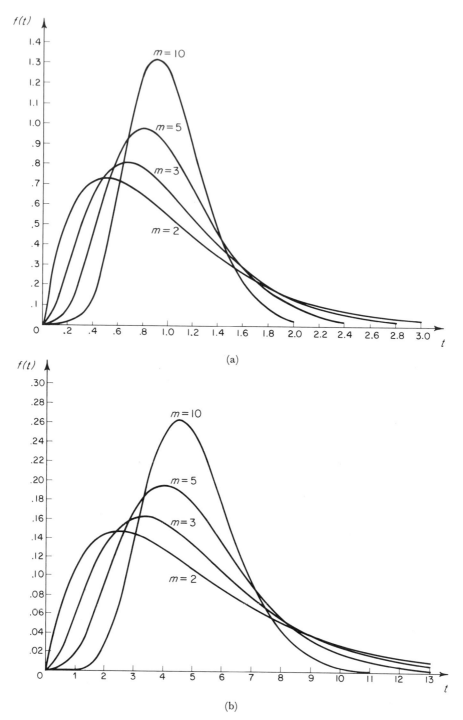

FIGURE 15.2. (a) Erlang Distribution for $\lambda = 1$. (b) Erlang Distribution for $\lambda = .2$.

channel, processes one customer at a time. (We will not consider *bulk service* in this book.) For a specified server, assume that successive serving times are independently and identically distributed, and described by a continuous density function. Let

(1) $g(t) \equiv$ density function for the length of time t to serve any customer,

where $t \geq 0$, and also let

(2)   mean service time $= \displaystyle\int_0^\infty tg(t)\ dt \equiv \dfrac{1}{\mu}$

so that

(3) $\mu =$ service rate per unit of time that the server is busy.

Jot down the definitions in (2) and (3).

To illustrate, if the unit of time is an hour and μ (mu) equals five services per hour while the server remains busy, then the average service time $1/\mu$ is one-fifth (.2) of an hour. Similarly, if a service on the average requires one-half an hour, then the service rate μ is 2 per hour, during an interval when the server remains busy.

Frequently, the service time distribution is assumed to be exponential:

(4) $g(t) = \mu e^{-\mu t}, \quad t \geq 0.$

Mathematical convenience is the usual reason for such an assumption. But the **exponential service** assumption can also provide guiding insight into the operation of any system, since it represents the extreme case of service times that are memoryless. When the service distribution is exponential, the probability of completing a service to a customer in any subsequent interval of length h is independent of how much service time has already elapsed for that customer.

Accordingly, given assumption (4), if a customer is being served at Time t and you observe the system at Time t + h, then

(5) P[service is not completed in interval of length h] $= e^{-\mu h}.$

Consequently, for $h > 0$ *very* small,

(6) P[service is not completed in interval of length h] $\doteq 1 - \mu h$ (*h* small)

and

(7) P[service is completed in interval of length h] $\doteq \mu h$ (*h* small).

Consider the following **pure-death model.** Let $t = 0$ represent the system's starting point in time. Suppose that there are M customers in the system at Time 0, and that no more customers ever arrive. Assume that there is a single server having an exponential time density (4), and let

(8) $P_n(T) =$ probability that n customers are in the system at Time T.

[The dependence of $P_n(T)$ on the value of M has been suppressed in the notation.] The formula for $P_n(T)$ can be derived using an exact approach analogous to the derivation of (10) that we gave in the special material at the end of the preceding section. But the result can also be obtained by employing (6) and (7) above, and the approach is illustrated next because it is so useful for analyzing more complex models.

As in the preceding section, we calculate approximate probabilities by ignoring *relatively* small quantities. And in the same approximative vein, we say that at most only one departure occurs during a *very* small interval of time $h > 0$. Hence, when there are n customers in the system at Time $T + h$, we consider only the possibilities that at Time T either there were n customers and none have departed, or there were $n + 1$ customers and one departed during the very small interval of length h. (Actually, the other possibilities of there being more than $n + 1$ customers and accordingly more than one departure are *relatively* improbable when $h > 0$ is *very* small.) Consequently, for $1 \leq n < M$,

$$(9) \qquad P_n(T + h) \doteq (1 - \mu h)P_n(T) + (\mu h)P_{n+1}(T).$$

The first term on the right is the approximate probability that no service occurred in the interval of length h and that n customers were in the system at Time T, and similarly for the second term on the right of (9). Rearranging terms yields

$$(10) \qquad \frac{P_n(T + h) - P_n(T)}{h} \doteq -\mu P_n(T) + \mu P_{n+1}(T),$$

so that on letting $h \to 0$,

$$(11) \qquad \frac{dP_n}{dT} = -\mu P_n(T) + \mu P_{n+1}(T) \quad \text{for } 1 \leq n < M.$$

The reason equation (11) holds exactly, instead of approximately, is that all the terms of *relatively* small magnitude that were ignored in (10) actually disappear in the process of letting h approach 0 in the limit.

By a similar line of reasoning, you can determine that

$$(12) \qquad \frac{dP_M}{dT} = -\mu P_M(T) \quad \text{for } n = M.$$

The unique solution to the system of linear differential equations (11) and (12) is

$$(13) \qquad P_n(T) = \frac{(\mu'T)^{M-n}e^{-\mu T}}{(M - n)!} \quad \text{for } n = 1, 2, \ldots, M$$

$$(14) \qquad P_0(T) = 1 - \sum_{n=1}^{M} P_n(T) \quad \text{for } n = 0.$$

The distribution in (13) and (14) is sometimes called a *truncated Poisson*.

If the Mth person is the last to be served, then the total time y that the customer spends in the system, including the person's own service time, has the density given by the sum of M exponentially distributed variables

(15) $$h(y) = \frac{\mu(\mu y)^{M-1}e^{-\mu y}}{(M-1)!}, \quad y \geq 0 \quad \text{(gamma distribution)},$$

with

(16) $$E[y] = \frac{M}{\mu} \quad \text{Var}\,[y] = \frac{M}{\mu^2} \quad \text{(gamma)}.$$

Although an exponential service time distribution is by far the most mathematically convenient form to assume, it is possible to derive usable mathematical results for certain simple queuing models when the service distribution is assumed to be Erlangian, as given by (14) in the previous section.

*Self-service model. Now suppose, instead of there being only a single server, that at Time 0 each of the M customers starts self-service. Assume that the service time is the same exponential density for every customer, namely (4). This assumption is reasonable enough in a self-service situation. Consider a very small interval of time $h > 0$. Then because the servers are independent, you can apply binomial probability calculations, using the approximate expression in (6), to obtain

(17) $P[\text{none of } n \text{ customers departs}] \doteq (1 - \mu h)^n \doteq 1 - n\mu h$ (h small)

(18) $P[\text{one of } n \text{ customers departs}] \doteq n\mu h$ (h small).

Once again, the justification for (18) is that when interval $h > 0$ is *very* small, we can restrict attention to the events of no and one departure; the possibilities of more departures have *relatively* negligible probability. Consequently, when there are n customers in the system at Time $T + h$, we consider only the possibilities that at Time T there were n customers and none have departed, or there were $n + 1$ customers and one departed—giving, for $0 \leq n < M$,

(19) $P_n(T + h) \doteq (1 - h\mu n)P_n(T) + (n + 1)\mu h P_{n+1}(T)$ (h small).

Bringing $P_n(T)$ to the left-hand side of (19), dividing by h, and letting $h \to 0$ yields

(20) $$\frac{dP_n}{dT} = -n\mu P_n(T) + (n + 1)\mu P_{n+1}(T) \quad \text{for } 0 \leq n < M.$$

Similar reasoning gives

(21) $$\frac{dP_M}{dT} = -M\mu P_M(T) \quad \text{for } n = M.$$

As can be verified by substitution, the complete solution to (20) and (21) is

(22) $P_n(T) = \binom{M}{n}(e^{-\mu T})^n(1 - e^{-\mu T})^{M-n}$ for $n = 0, 1, 2, \ldots, M$

(binomial distribution),

with

(23) $E[n \mid T] = Me^{-\mu T}$ $\text{Var}[n \mid T] = Me^{-\mu T}(1 - e^{-\mu T}).$

*Queuing model nomenclature. In reading the queuing theory literature, you will find that a standardized terminology is employed. (It is often called
Kendall's notation.) Each model is signified by three symbols: the first
designates the input process; the second, the service distribution; and the third,
the number of servers. The standard symbols for the probability distributions are

$M \equiv$ exponentially distributed interarrival or service time (M is an abbrevia-
   tion for Markovian)

$D \equiv$ deterministic (or constant, regular) interarrival or service time

$E_n \equiv$ Erlangian distribution of order n for interarrival or service time [some
   books also use the symbol K_n, and then employ the formula for a gamma
   distribution (15)]

$GI \equiv$ general independent distribution of interarrival time

$G \equiv$ general distribution of service time.

To illustrate, the model of Poisson input, exponential service, and single server
is denoted by $M/M/1$. If the input were deterministic instead, then the notation
would be $D/M/1$; further, if there were S servers, the notation would be $D/M/S$.

15.5 SINGLE-SERVER MODEL WITH POISSON
INPUT AND EXPONENTIAL SERVICE $(M/M/1)$

Most waiting line systems are comprised of several servers, and more often than
not, the queue *discipline* is quite complex. For example, a shopper choosing a
checkout stand at a supermarket looks at the number of people already in line
and the number of items in their carts. This person also considers which checkout
clerks are the fastest and which lines are closest. Similar considerations are relevant
when someone selects a line in front of a teller's window at a bank, or when a
driver chooses a toll booth on a turnpike. But sometimes the discipline is on a
strict first come, first served basis. One example is a bakery that gives each entering
customer a number, and then serves the customers in numerical order. Other
examples occur at gasoline stations, camera shops, shoeshine stands, and in a
crowded but orderly cafeteria line.

As we have stated earlier, developing an operations research model for an
actual situation inherently involves making approximations. This is so regardless
of whether, in the case of a waiting line model, you analyze the problem using
either mathematics or a computer simulation or both. Often you can obtain approximate information about a complex system's operating characteristics by

examining certain extreme or limiting cases. One such approximate approach is to consider a queuing system with multiple servers as being comprised of a collection of separate and independent single-server systems. For example, suppose the system consists of five servers and the input process indicates that 20 customers arrive per hour. Then *as an approximation*, the system can be viewed as five separate single-server systems, each with an arrival rate of 4 per hour. The approach is approximate for two reasons: a customer is assumed to join each line with equal probability, regardless of the length of the several lines; and once a customer joins a line, the person is assumed to stay there. The expected number of customers that are in each system, summed over all the separate systems, and the average time a customer spends in a system will usually be larger than in most actual multiple-server systems. The reason is that if this queuing system were to operate in real life, then there would be more times than you would expect when one server is idle and yet customers are waiting in line for other servers.

If you also consider the approximation that there is only a *single* line in a multiple-server system and that customers are processed on a first come, first served basis, then you may obtain smaller than actual values for the expected number of customers and the average time each spends in the system.

Fortunately, single-server systems often do yield to mathematical analysis, as do many cases of multiple servers with a single line and a first come, first served discipline. We therefore begin here with a simple single-server queuing system, and treat a simple multiple-server model in Sec. 15.6.

Model description. The simplest single-server model having both input and service processes described probabilistically is one with exponential interarrival and service times (denoted by $M/M/1$). Specifically, assume

(1)
$$\text{exponential interarrival density:} \quad \lambda e^{-\lambda t}$$
$$\text{exponential service time density:} \quad \mu e^{-\mu t}.$$

Define the number of customers n in the system at any point in time as including the persons waiting in line plus those in service. Let $t = 0$ represent the system's starting point in time, and define

(2) $P_n(T) \equiv$ probability that n customers are in the system at Time T.

Actually $P_n(T)$ depends on the number of customers i in the system at Time 0, but this dependence is suppressed in the notation.

Let $h > 0$ be a *very* small interval of time. If there are $n > 0$ customers in the system at Time T + h, then we consider only the possibilities that there were either $n - 1$, n, or $n + 1$ customers at Time T. Any other possibilities are of relatively insignificant probability. Consequently, for $n > 0$

(3)
$$P_n(T + h) \doteq (\lambda h)(1 - \mu h)P_{n-1}(T) + (1 - \lambda h)(1 - \mu h)P_n(T)$$
$$+ (\lambda h)(\mu h)P_n(T) + (1 - \lambda h)(\mu h)P_{n+1}(T) \qquad (h \text{ small}).$$

The first term on the right corresponds to the event of one arrival and no departure when $n - 1$ customers are in the system at Time T. The second and third terms refer to the events of no arrival and no departure, and of one arrival and a departure when n customers are in the system at Time T. And the final term relates to the event of no arrival and one departure when there are $n + 1$ customers in the system at Time T. As the symbol ($\doteq$) indicates, the expression in (3) is approximate; it can be made exact by adding probability terms with coefficients h^k, where $k \geq 2$.

Bringing the term $P_n(T)$ to the left-hand side of (3), dividing by h, and letting $h \to 0$, yields

$$(4) \qquad \frac{dP_n}{dT} = \lambda P_{n-1}(T) - (\lambda + \mu)P_n(T) + \mu P_{n+1}(T) \quad \text{for } n > 0.$$

This expression is exact because the terms neglected in (3) become 0 as $h \to 0$. Similarly, one can show that

$$(5) \qquad \frac{dP_0}{dT} = -\lambda P_0(T) + \mu P_1(T) \quad \text{for } n = 0.$$

With moderately advanced analysis it is possible to solve the system of linear differential equations (4) and (5) for each $P_n(T)$. (To do so, you must also state the number of customers i in the system at Time 0.) The result is called the **transient solution,** since it depends directly on the value of T.

Suppose, however, we examine the values of $P_n(T)$ as $T \to \infty$. If $P_n(T)$ approaches a limiting value, say, P_n, and if $E[n]$ is finite for this limiting distribution, then we will say that the system reaches **statistical equilibrium.** We denote the resulting P_n values as **equilibrium** or **stationary probabilities.** The label "stationary" derives from the property that if the number of customers in the system at any Time t is given according to the probability distribution P_n, then for *any* $h > 0$, P_n is also the probability that n customers are in the system at Time t + h. The value of P_n can also be interpreted as the limiting fraction of an arbitrarily long period of time during which the queue contains n customers.

Provided

$$(6) \qquad \rho \equiv \frac{\lambda}{\mu} < 1 \quad \text{(traffic intensity assumption)},$$

the stationary probabilities P_n always exist; the symbol ρ (rho) in (6) is frequently called the **traffic intensity.**

You can find the equilibrium solution $P_n(T) \equiv P_n$, for all T, by using the consequence that each dP_n/dT must equal 0, if the solution P_n is indeed independent of T. Hence to obtain P_n, all you need to do is set the time derivatives in (4) and (5) equal to 0, yielding

$$(7) \qquad 0 = \lambda P_{n-1} - (\lambda + \mu)P_n + \mu P_{n+1} \quad \text{for } n = 1, 2, 3, \ldots$$

$$(8) \qquad 0 = -\lambda P_0 + \mu P_1 \qquad\qquad \text{for } n = 0.$$

The system of **difference equations** (7) and (8) is easily solved recursively, starting with (8),

(9) $P_1 = P_0 \left(\frac{\lambda}{\mu}\right) = P_0 \rho$

and proceeding to (7) for $n = 1, 2, \ldots$,

(10) $P_n = P_0 \rho^n.$

It is easy to verify that P_n in (10) does satisfy (7). Given (6),

(11) $\sum_{n=0}^{\infty} P_n = P_0 \sum_{n=0}^{\infty} \rho^n = \frac{P_0}{1 - \rho} = 1,$

and it follows that $P_0 = 1 - \rho$, so that

(12) $P_n = (1 - \rho)\rho^n$ for $n = 0, 1, 2, \ldots$ (geometric distribution)

with

(13) $E \begin{bmatrix} \text{number of} \\ \text{customers} \\ \text{in system} \end{bmatrix} \equiv E[n] = \frac{\rho}{1 - \rho} = \frac{\lambda}{\mu - \lambda}$ $\text{Var}[n] = \frac{\rho}{(1 - \rho)^2}$

$$P[n \geq N] = \rho^N.$$

Notice that the probability distribution in (12) depends *only* on the traffic intensity ratio $(\lambda/\mu = \rho)$. Since $\rho(= 1 - P_0)$ is also the fraction of time the server is busy, the quantity ρ is sometimes called the system's **utilization factor.** It is significant that this interpretation of ρ remains valid even when both the interarrival and service time distributions are general (that is, for the model $GI/G/1$).

Operating characteristics. The expected line length can be found by noting that

(14) $\text{line length} = \begin{cases} \text{number in system} & \text{if } n = 0 \\ \text{number in system} - 1 & \text{if } n > 0, \end{cases}$

so that

(15)
$$E[\text{line length}] = 0 \cdot P_0 + \sum_{n=1}^{\infty} (n - 1)P_n = \sum_{n=0}^{\infty} nP_n - \sum_{n=1}^{\infty} P_n$$

$$= E[n] - (1 - P_0) = \frac{\rho^2}{1 - \rho} = \frac{\lambda^2}{\mu(\mu - \lambda)}.$$

Next consider the time intervals when the server is idle. Since these begin when a service terminates and end when a new arrival occurs, the length of the idle periods has the same distribution as the interarrival time, that is, exponential with mean $1/\lambda$. Let the period of length T be so long that we can safely utilize expected values. Then the server is idle for $[TP_0 = T(1 - \rho)]$ units of time, and $[T(1 - \rho)/(1/\lambda) = \lambda T(1 - \rho)]$ is the number of separate idle periods during T. Because idle and busy periods alternate, $\lambda T(1 - \rho)$ is also the number of separate busy periods during T, and ρT is the total duration of all busy periods. Consequently,

$$\text{(16)} \qquad E[\text{length of busy period}] = \frac{\rho T}{\lambda T(1-\rho)} = \frac{1}{\mu - \lambda}$$

and

$$\text{(17)} \qquad E\begin{bmatrix} \text{number of customers} \\ \text{served per busy period} \end{bmatrix} = \mu E\begin{bmatrix} \text{length of} \\ \text{busy period} \end{bmatrix} = \frac{1}{1-\rho}.$$

The relations (16) and (17) are actually valid for any service time distribution (that is, for the model $M/G/1$).

Now turn to the probability density for the time a customer spends in the system, which is defined as the interval a customer waits in line plus the time in service. Suppose the system is in statistical equilibrium, so that when a new customer arrives, he finds n customers in the system ahead of him with probability P_n given by (12). Assume that the queue discipline is first come, first served. Then the total time the customer spends in the system is comprised of the sum of $n + 1$ independent and identically distributed exponential random variables, and has a gamma density

$$\text{(18)} \qquad \frac{\mu(\mu y)^n e^{-\mu y}}{n!} \quad \text{for } y \geq 0,$$

as you already saw in (15) of Sec. 15.4. Hence the density of time that a customer who arrives at an arbitrary instant spends in the system is given by

$$\text{(19)} \qquad \begin{aligned} h(w) &= \sum_{n=0}^{\infty} (1-\rho)\rho^n \left[\frac{\mu(\mu w)^n e^{-\mu w}}{n!} \right] \\ &= \mu(1-\rho)e^{-\mu(1-\rho)w} \quad \text{(exponential distribution)}, \end{aligned}$$

with

$$\text{(20)} \qquad E[\text{time in system}] = E[w] = \frac{1}{\mu(1-\rho)} = \frac{1}{\mu - \lambda},$$

$$\text{(21)} \qquad \begin{aligned} E[\text{time in line}] &= E[\text{time in system}] - E[\text{service time}] \\ &= \frac{1}{\mu}\left(\frac{\rho}{1-\rho}\right) = \frac{\lambda}{\mu(\mu - \lambda)}. \end{aligned}$$

For fixed ρ, the expected times in the system and in line vary inversely with the service rate μ.

▶ Suppose you look at only the time that a customer waits in line, where you exclude the person's service time as well as that of any customers who arrive when the server is idle. Then it can be proved that the *conditional* probability density of the *time spent in line* by those customers who *do* have to wait in line is also given by (19) for any interarrival distribution, that is, for the model $GI/M/1$. Consequently, $E[w]$ in (20) is also the *conditional expected time waiting in line* given that a customer *does* have to wait in line. ◀

Sensitivity analysis. Various operating characteristics of this simple queuing system are displayed in Fig. 15.3 for different values of traffic intensity ρ and service rate μ.

Traffic Intensity ρ	Probability of Server Idle $= 1 - \rho$	Expected Number in System $= \dfrac{\rho}{1-\rho}$	Expected Line Length $= \rho^2/1-\rho$	$\mu = 10$			$\mu = 20$		
				λ	Time in System	Time in Line	λ	Time in System	Time in Line
.1	.9	.11	.01	1	.11	.01	2	.06	.01
.3	.7	.43	.13	3	.14	.04	6	.07	.02
.5	.5	1.00	.50	5	.20	.10	10	.10	.05
.7	.3	2.33	1.63	7	.33	.23	14	.17	.12
.8	.2	4.00	3.20	8	.50	.40	16	.25	.20
.9	.1	9.00	8.10	9	1.00	.90	18	.50	.45
.95	.05	19.00	18.05	9.5	2.00	1.90	19	1.00	.95
.99	.01	99.00	98.01	9.9	10.00	9.90	19.8	5.00	4.95
.999	.001	999.00	998.00	9.99	100.00	99.90	19.98	50.00	49.95

λ = arrival rate per unit of time
μ = service rate per unit of time
$\rho = \lambda/\mu$ traffic intensity

Note: E [Length of Busy Period] $= E$[Time in System]

FIGURE 15.3. Operating Characteristics of $M/M/1$ System.

Notice that as the traffic intensity ρ increases, the expected values of the number of customers, the line length, the time in the system, and the time in line [formulas (13), (15), (20), and (21) above] all increase rapidly. Although these quantities can be made arbitrarily large for sufficiently large $\rho < 1$, the system may take an accordingly long time to reach steady-state equilibrium. For a given service rate μ, when intensity ρ is small, most of the expected time a customer spends in the system is due to the average service time $1/\mu$; but as intensity ρ increases (that is, as the arrival rate λ increases), most of the expected time spent in the system is due to waiting in line.

For the sake of illustration, suppose the unit of time in Fig. 15.3 is an hour (or 60 minutes) and that $\rho = .8$. Then on the average, the server is idle .2 hour (or 12 minutes per hour) and there are four persons in the system. If $\mu = 10$, so that the service rate is 10 per hour (or at the rate of six minutes per customer), then the average time a customer spends in the system is .5 hour (or 30 minutes), and .4 hour (or 24 minutes) of this is due to waiting in line. If ρ remains .8 but both the arrival rate and service rate double, so that $\mu = 20$, then the average times spent in the system and in waiting are cut in half.

Secretaries example. The following hypothetical example will indicate briefly how the model's operating characteristics, such as those shown in Fig. 15.3, can be used to assist decision-making. Noah Peale, the manager of the law offices of Lee, Gall, Eagle, is deciding whether to employ two or four secretaries. To simplify matters, suppose he faces only two alternatives: to hire two experienced legal secretaries who can each type at the rate of 20 documents a day, or four novice secretaries who can each type at the rate of only 10 documents a day. On the average, there are 36 documents to be typed per day. Copy these data on a piece of paper for easy reference, since this example will be used again later in the chapter.

Suppose the manager uses, as an approximation, the simple model above. In the case of the two faster typists, each will be assigned documents at the rate $\lambda = \frac{36}{2} = 18$ per day, and in the case of the four slower typists, at the rate $\lambda = \frac{36}{4} = 9$ per day. In either case, traffic intentity $\rho = .9$.

Then the average number of documents on each secretary's desk is 9, according to (13), so that there are an average of 18 documents in the entire system having two secretaries and 36 in the system having four secretaries. The average time for a document to be in the system is $\frac{1}{2}$ [$= 1/(20 - 18)$] day for the two faster secretaries as compared to 1 [$= 1/(10 - 9)$] day for the four slower secretaries, according to (20). By the same token, each experienced secretary will be busy over intervals that average one-half a day, whereas, each novice secretary will be busy over intervals that average a full day.

In what ways do you think this simple model approximates the real situation? Why would the average delay for a document tend to be smaller than (20) in actuality? If you were the office manager, what else would you take into account in deciding between these two alternatives?

*Finite queue. So far no limitation has been imposed on the total number of customers present in the system at any time. Now suppose that at most M customers are allowed to be in the entire system, and therefore no more than $M - 1$ persons are permitted to wait in line at any instant. (An example is a one-pump gasoline station with a small driveway leading into a busy street.) If a customer arrives when M persons are already in the system, then the customer is restricted from entering, and is said to be lost from the system. (Consequently, this model is sometimes termed a combined **loss-delay system.**) An important difference between the previous model and this **finite-queue model** is that here statistical equilibrium is reached for *any* value of the intensity ratio λ/μ.

The steady-state difference equations (7) and (8) still apply for $n = 0, 1, \ldots,$ $M - 1$, but the equation for $n = M$ is

$$(22) \qquad\qquad 0 = \lambda P_{M-1} - \mu P_M.$$

The corresponding solution for $n = 0, 1, \ldots, M$ is

$$
(23) \qquad P_n =
\begin{cases}
\left(\dfrac{1 - \rho}{1 - \rho^{M+1}}\right) \rho^n & \text{for } \lambda \neq \mu \\[2ex]
\dfrac{1}{M + 1} & \text{for } \lambda = \mu.
\end{cases}
$$

Of course, when $\lambda < \mu$ and $M \to \infty$, P_n in (23) agrees with (12). By elementary calculations it can be shown that for $\lambda \neq \mu$

$$
(24) \qquad E \begin{bmatrix} \text{number of} \\ \text{customers} \\ \text{in system} \end{bmatrix} \equiv E[n] = \frac{\rho}{(1 - \rho)} \left[\frac{1 - (M + 1)\rho^M + M\rho^{M+1}}{1 - \rho^{M+1}} \right]
$$

$$
= \frac{\rho}{1 - \rho} - \frac{(M + 1)\rho^{M+1}}{1 - \rho^{M+1}} \quad \text{for } \lambda \neq \mu.
$$

Observe when $\lambda < \mu$, the expected number of customers in this system is smaller than that for the previous case of an unlimited line length (13). Similarly, it can be proved that for $\lambda = \mu$

$$
(25) \qquad E \begin{bmatrix} \text{number of} \\ \text{customers} \\ \text{in system} \end{bmatrix} \equiv E[n] = \frac{M}{2} \quad \text{for } \lambda = \mu.
$$

A delicate question arises in *defining* the amount of time a customer spends in the system (and waiting in line). If a customer arrives when there are already M persons in the system, the customer does not enter and consequently literally spends no time in the system. Hence average time spent in the system can be defined so as to refer either to all customers who arrive, regardless of whether they enter, or only to those customers who are permitted to enter. We adopt the latter, since in most situations the interest in delay time is only for those who actually do enter the system. So, referring to a customer arriving at an arbitrary moment who *does* join the system, and given that the discipline is first come, first served, it can be shown that

$$
(26) \quad E \begin{bmatrix} \text{time in} \\ \text{system} \end{bmatrix} \equiv E[w] = \frac{\rho}{\mu(1 - \rho)} \left[\frac{1 - \mu\rho^{M-1} + (M - 1)\rho^M}{1 - \rho^M} \right] + \frac{1}{\mu}
$$

$$
= \frac{1}{\mu(1 - \rho)} - \frac{M\rho^M}{\mu(1 - \rho^M)} \quad \text{for } \lambda \neq \mu,
$$

and

$$
(27) \quad E \begin{bmatrix} \text{time in} \\ \text{system} \end{bmatrix} \equiv E[w] = \frac{1}{\mu} \cdot \frac{M + 1}{2} \quad \text{for } \lambda = \mu.
$$

Arbitrary service distribution. It is possible to state in simple terms the expected number of customers in the system and the average time spent in the system for the case in which the interarrival distribution is exponential and the service distribution is arbitrary (that is, for the model $M/G/1$).

Let

(28) $$V \equiv \text{Var [service time]} = \int_0^\infty \left(t - \frac{1}{\mu}\right)^2 g(t)\, dt,$$

where, as before, $1/\mu$ is the mean service time and $g(t)$ is the service time density function. Then

(29) $$E\text{[number of customers in system]} = \rho + \frac{\lambda^2 V + \rho^2}{2(1 - \rho)}$$

(30) $$E\text{[line length]} = \frac{\lambda^2 V + \rho^2}{2(1 - \rho)}$$

(31) $$P\text{[server is idle]} \equiv P_0 = 1 - \rho,$$

where the intensity factor $\rho \equiv \lambda/\mu < 1$, as usual.

Assuming that the system operates on a first come, first served basis, then the average time a customer spends in the system is given by

$$E\text{[time in system]} = E\text{[time in line]} + E\text{[service time]}$$

(32) $$\equiv \frac{\lambda}{\mu^2}\left[\frac{\mu^2 V + 1}{2(1 - \rho)}\right] + \frac{1}{\mu} = \frac{1}{\lambda}\left[\rho + \frac{\lambda^2 V + \rho^2}{2(1 - \rho)}\right].$$

[Frequently, (29) and (32) are referred to as **Pollaczek-Khintchine formulas.**]

When $g(t)$ is exponential, so that $V = 1/\mu^2$, then (29), (30), and (32) reduce to (13), (15), and (20), respectively. The above formulas also give the expectations when service time is constant $1/\mu$, since then $V = 0$ (the resultant model is designated as $M/D/1$). Observe that all the averages vary linearly with V, and depend only on the arrival rate λ, the traffic intensity ρ, and the service variance V, and not on any other parameters of the input and service distributions.

Note further the equilibrium relation

(33) $$E\text{[number of customers in system]} = \lambda E\text{[time in system]}.$$

Actually, (33) holds under much more general conditions, including many multiple-server models. To illustrate, if the expected number of customers in the system is 10 and the arrival rate $\lambda = 25$ customers per hour, then the expected time in the system for a customer is $\frac{10}{25} = .4$ hour (24 minutes). Similarly, if the arrival rate is 12 customers per hour and the expected time a customer spends in the system is .5 hour (30 minutes), then the expected number of customers in the system is 6.

To check your understanding of these formulas, consider once again the above example of hiring either two experienced legal secteraries or four slower novice secretaries. Recall a rapid secretary can complete an average of 20 documents a day, whereas the corresponding figure for a slower secretary is 10. Since an average of 36 documents must be typed each day, the arrival rate for each rapid secretary is 18 as compared to 9 for a slower secretary.

When both the interarrival and service time distributions were assumed to be exponential, there were on the average, 9 documents on each secretary's desk. The average time for a document to be in the system was one-half day for a faster secretary as compared to one day for a slower secretary.

Now suppose instead of exponential service times, the service times are constant $(V = 0)$. Then from (29) there will be an average of only 4.95 documents on each secretary's desk and from (32) the average time for a document to be in the system is .275 of a day for the faster secretary and .55 of a day for the slower one. Hence, elimination of service time variations nearly cuts the averages in half as compared to the exponential case.

In contrast, suppose that the variance of service times is double that of the exponential case—$(\frac{2}{400})$ for a faster typist and $(\frac{2}{100})$ for a slower typist. Then there will be an average of 13.05 documents on each secretary's desk, and the average time for a document to be in the system is .725 of a day for a faster secretary, and 1.45 days for a slower one. Therefore, doubling the service time variability as compared to the exponential case increases these averages by only about 50%.

Priority discipline. In many real situations, the queuing discipline is not according to a first come, first served basis. Consider, for example, a young executive who returns to her office after being away several days on a business trip. She may find a number of telephone messages awaiting her, including an urgent one from her boss. Most likely, she will return her boss's call before any others.

Suppose the input to a queuing system can be classified into r distinct types, and priorities from 1 to r are assigned to these types in decreasing order of importance, so that Type 1 has the highest priority and Type r the lowest. As soon as the server finishes with a customer, the server always goes on to the next customer in line who has the highest priority. (If several individuals in line have the same priority number, then they are served on a first come, first served basis.) In some situations, an additional assumption is made that the service of a customer being waited on is **preempted** whenever a customer with a higher priority enters the system. The results given below, however, are for the *nonpreemptive* discipline.

Assume that each customer Type k arrives according to a Poisson input process with mean rate λ_k. Also suppose that the service distribution for each Type k is arbitrary with density $g_k(t)$ and

(34) $E[\text{service time} \mid \text{Type k}] = \dfrac{1}{\mu_k}$ $V_k \equiv \text{Var} [\text{service time} \mid \text{Type k}].$

Define

$$\sigma_k \equiv \sum_{j=1}^{k} \frac{\lambda_j}{\mu_j}   \sigma_0 \equiv 0$$

and assume $\sigma_r < 1$ to ensure the system reaches statistical equilibrium.

Suppose a Type k customer arrives right after the departure of a customer. Then the expected time the customer waits in line is given by

$$
(35) \qquad E[\text{time in line} \mid \text{Type } k] = \frac{\sum_{j=1}^{r} \lambda_j \left[V_j + \left(\frac{1}{\mu_j} \right)^2 \right]}{2(1 - \sigma_{k-1})(1 - \sigma_k)}.
$$

When $r = 1$, the expression in (35) reduces to that for $E[\text{time in line}]$ in (32). Since $\lambda_k / \sum \lambda_j$ equals the probability that an entering customer *is* of Type k, you can find the expected time in line for an arbitrary customer by calculating

$$
(36) \qquad E[\text{time in line}] = \frac{\sum_{k=1}^{r} \lambda_k E[\text{time in line} \mid \text{Type } k]}{\sum_{k=1}^{r} \lambda_k}.
$$

The following numerical example will illustrate the impact of imposing a priority discipline. Suppose the arrival rate for the system is $\lambda = 18$ and the service rate is $\mu = 20$ without a priority discipline. Then, as you saw in Fig. 15.3 and for the example of the legal office typists, the expected time in line is .45. Suppose instead that the arrivals are classified into Type 1 and Type 2, having the respective arrival rates λ_1 and λ_2, where $\lambda_1 + \lambda_2 = \lambda = 18$. Assume that the service rate μ applies to both types and that the service distribution is exponential. Then according to (35) and (36),

$$
E[\text{time in line} \mid \text{Type 1}] = \frac{18 \left[\dfrac{1}{20^2} + \dfrac{1}{20^2} \right]}{2(1) \left(1 - \dfrac{\lambda_1}{20} \right)} = \frac{.045}{\left(1 - \dfrac{\lambda_1}{20} \right)}
$$

$$
(37) \qquad E[\text{time in line} \mid \text{Type 2}] = \frac{E[\text{time in line} \mid \text{Type 1}]}{\left(1 - \dfrac{\lambda_1}{20} - \dfrac{\lambda_2}{20} \right)}
$$

$$
= \frac{E[\text{time in line} \mid \text{Type 1}]}{.1}
$$

$$
E[\text{time in line}] = .45.
$$

Hence, the average time in line for an arbitrary customer is still .45, but the expected time is always less than .45 for a Type 1 customer and always greater than .45 for a Type 2 customer. Further, the smaller the value of λ_1, the smaller the expected wait in line for *both* Types 1 and 2, even though the average time in line for an arbitrary customer remains unaffected. To illustrate, suppose $\lambda_1 = \lambda_2 = 9$; according to (37) the expected time in line for a Type 1 customer is ($\frac{9}{110} = .0818$) and for a Type 2 customer is .8181.

In some instances, the several types of customers require different lengths of service. Then assigning priorities according to the mean service rates—the highest *rate* having the highest priority—will always reduce the overall average time in line. To illustrate, consider again the above example with $\lambda = 18$ and $\mu = 20$; the associated utilization factor is $(\frac{18}{20} = .9)$, and the expected time in line is .45. Suppose in a two-priority-discipline scheme that $\lambda_1 = \lambda_2 = 9$, and $\mu_1 = 30$ and $\mu_2 = 15$, so that the utilization factor $(\sigma_r = \frac{9}{30} + \frac{9}{15} = .9)$ remains the same. From (35) and (36) the expected time in line for a Type 1 customer is $(\frac{1}{14} = .0714)$ and for a Type 2 customer is $(\frac{10}{14} = .7143)$, which are smaller values than the corresponding averages for $\mu_1 = \mu_2 = \mu = 20$. Now the expected time in line for an arbitrary customer is .3928, which is *smaller* than .45 in the system without priorities or with $\mu_1 = \mu_2 = 20$.

Erlang arrival distribution. Suppose the interarrival time distribution is Erlangian with mean $1/\lambda$, as given by (14) and (and) in Sec. 15.3 (yielding the model $E_m/M/1$). Assume, as usual, that $\rho \equiv \lambda/\mu < 1$. Letting P_n designate the limiting fraction of an arbitrarily long period of time during which the system contains n customers, it can be shown that

(38) $$P_0 = 1 - \rho = P[\text{server is idle}]$$

(39) $$P_n = \rho(1 - s)s^{n-1} \qquad \text{for } n = 1, 2, \ldots$$

(40) $$E[\text{number of customers in system}] = \frac{\rho}{1 - s}$$

(41) $$E[\text{time in system}] = \frac{1}{\mu(1 - s)}$$

where the value of s is a numerical solution to the equation

(42) $$s = \left(\frac{m\rho}{1 + m\rho - s}\right)^m \qquad \text{with } 0 < s < 1.$$

Recall from (15) in Sec. 15.4 that the variance of the interarrival times is $1/m\lambda^2$, so that the case of periodic arrivals $(D/M/1)$ can be obtained by letting $m \to \infty$. Applying this limiting process in (42) yields the equation

(43) $$s = e^{-(1-s)/\rho}.$$

Note that (33) holds for this model. For $m = 1$ (which is simply $M/M/1$), the solution to (42) is $s = \rho$, and (38) through (41) agree with (12), (13), and (20).

15.6 MULTIPLE-SERVER MODEL WITH POISSON INPUT AND EXPONENTIAL SERVICE $(M/M/S)$

Certainly most queuing systems are comprised of several servers, and hence waiting line models with more than one server are important. In this section, we generalize the results in the preceding section. The queuing discipline for this model is relatively simple as compared to most realistic situations. Nevertheless, the results can be used at least as an initial approximation to the behavior characteristics of more complex systems.

Let

(1) $$S \equiv \text{number of servers}$$

and assume that

interarrival density: $\lambda e^{-\lambda t}$

(2)   service time density
                        for each server: $\mu e^{-\mu t}$,

where the individual service times are all mutually independent (that is, for each server as well as among the servers).

The appropriate difference equations [analogous to those for the single-server case (7) and (8) in the preceding section] that determine the stationary probabilities are:

(3)
$$0 = \lambda P_{n-1} - (\lambda + n\mu)P_n + (n + 1)\mu P_{n+1} \quad \text{for } 1 \leq n < S$$
$$0 = \lambda P_{n-1} - (\lambda + S\mu)P_n + S\mu P_{n+1} \qquad \text{for } n \geq S.$$

(These equations are derived in the next section.) The associated solution is

$$P_n = \frac{\rho^n}{n!} \cdot P_0 \qquad \text{for } 0 \leq n < S$$

(4)

$$P_n = \frac{\rho^n}{S! \, S^{n-S}} \cdot P_0 \quad \text{for } n \geq S,$$

where $\rho = \lambda/\mu$ and

(5)
$$P_0 = \frac{1}{\left[\displaystyle\sum_{j=0}^{S-1} \frac{\rho^j}{j!} + \frac{\rho^S}{S! \left(1 - \dfrac{\rho}{S} \right)} \right]}.$$

In order for the system to have the stationary probability distribution given in (4) and (5), you must assume that $\lambda < \mu S$ (or $\rho < S$). [When $S = 1$, (4) and (5) simplify to (12) in Sec. 15.5.]

In the case of an unlimited number of servers—for example, a self-service situation—the first formula for P_n in (4) applies for *all* n. Consequently, P_n is then a Poisson distribution, with $E[n] = \rho$. (This model is designated as $M/M/\infty$. When $S = \infty$, the conclusion that P_n is Poisson actually holds for any general service distribution, that is, for the model $M/G/\infty$.)

▶ The formulas in (4) also apply to the case with a finite limit $M \geq S$ on the total number of customers in the entire system. Then $n \leq M$ and P_0 is determined from

(i)
$$\sum_{n=0}^{M} P_n = 1.$$

Further, the stationary probabilities (4) exist even if $\lambda > \mu S$.   ◀

Operating characteristics. By means of elementary algebraic manipulations involving P_n, you can easily derive most of the system's operating characteristics. A useful quantity for this purpose is the probability that all the servers are busy:

$$
(6) \qquad P[\text{busy period}] \equiv P[n \geq S] = \frac{\rho^S \mu S}{S! \, (\mu S - \lambda)} \cdot P_0 = \frac{\rho^S}{S! \left(1 - \dfrac{\rho}{S}\right)} \cdot P_0.
$$

Some authors call the quantity in (6) the probability of a delay—actually a better term might be **virtual delay.** The value $P[n \geq S + 1]$ represents the fraction of time that customers are actually being delayed in the system.

Define the symbols

$$
(7) \quad \text{Poisson } (x = s \mid \rho) \equiv \frac{\rho^s e^{-\rho}}{s!} \quad \text{and} \quad \text{Poisson } (x < s \mid \rho) \equiv \sum_{x=0}^{s-1} \frac{\rho^x e^{-\rho}}{x!}.
$$

You can compute (6) by the formula

$$
(8) \qquad P[\text{busy period}] = \frac{\text{Poisson } (x = S \mid \rho)}{\text{Poisson } (x = S \mid \rho) + \left(1 - \dfrac{\rho}{S}\right) \text{Poisson } (x < S \mid \rho)}.
$$

The tables on pages 593–595 provide values of $P[\text{busy period}]$ for selected values of $\rho \equiv \lambda/\mu$ and S.

Then

$$
(9) \qquad E[\text{line length}] = P[\text{busy period}] \cdot \frac{\rho}{S - \rho} = \frac{\rho^S \lambda \mu S}{S! \, (\mu S - \lambda)^2} \cdot P_0
$$

$$
(10) \qquad E\begin{bmatrix}\text{number of} \\ \text{customers} \\ \text{in service}\end{bmatrix} = \sum_{n=0}^{S-1} nP_n + S \sum_{n=S}^{\infty} P_n = \rho
$$

$$
(11) \qquad E\begin{bmatrix}\text{number of} \\ \text{customers} \\ \text{in system}\end{bmatrix} \equiv E[n] = E[\text{line length}] + E\begin{bmatrix}\text{number of} \\ \text{customers} \\ \text{in service}\end{bmatrix}.
$$

For this model,

$$
(12) \qquad \lambda E[\text{time in system}] = E[\text{number of customers in system}],
$$

so that dividing (11) by λ yields

$$
(13) \qquad E[\text{time in system}] = \frac{P[\text{busy period}]}{\mu S - \lambda} + \frac{1}{\mu},
$$

the first term on the right of (13) being $E[\text{time in line}]$, and the second being $E[\text{time in service}]$.

A significant property about this system is that the distribution of *departures* over an interval T is Poisson with mean λT per unit of time. Consider, then, a large-scale queuing system comprised of groups of servers in tandem—that is, arranged so that the output of one group becomes the input to the next. If each group can be described by a multiple-server model like that above, the system averages can be easily found by first analyzing each group in isolation, assuming the same input rate λ, and afterwards adding the results.

Sensitivity analysis. Once again, consider the example in Sec. 15.5 of the manager of the legal office, Noah Peale, who is about to hire either two experienced typists or four novice typists. Recall that the arrival rate for documents is 36 per day, and each faster secretary can type 20 documents per day as compared to 10 per day for the newer secretaries. You found in Sec. 15.5 that if each typist operates separately and independently, then there will be an average of 9 documents on each secretary's desk, and a document will spend an average of half a day on the desk of a faster secretary and a full day for a slower secretary. When the service time is a constant (variance $\equiv V = 0$), the average number of documents on each secretary's desk falls to 4.95 and the expected time to .275 of a day for a faster typist, and .55 of a day for a slower one.

Now suppose that the secretaries do *not* operate separately and independently. Instead let the system be comprised of a "typing pool." In this system, a single stack of documents waits to be typed; when any secretary completes one document, the typist goes to the stack and takes the next one in the pile. Accordingly, using the table on page 594, you can find that

$$(14) \quad P[\text{busy period}] = \begin{cases} .7877 & \text{for } S = 4 \text{ and } \mu = 10 \\ .8526 & \text{for } S = 2 \text{ and } \mu = 20 \end{cases} \quad (\lambda = 36).$$

Therefore, from (9), (10), and (11),

$$(15) \quad E \begin{bmatrix} \text{number of} \\ \text{documents} \\ \text{in system} \end{bmatrix} = \begin{cases} 7.0887 + 3.6 = 10.6887 & \text{for } S = 4 \text{ and } \mu = 10 \\ 7.6741 + 1.8 = 9.4741 & \text{for } S = 2 \text{ and } \mu = 20, \end{cases}$$

and from (13),

$$(16) \quad E[\text{time in system}] = \begin{cases} .1969 + .1 = .2969 & \text{for } S = 4 \text{ and } \mu = 10 \\ .2132 + .05 = .2632 & \text{for } S = 2 \text{ and } \mu = 20. \end{cases}$$

Notice that although the probability of a document being delayed before typing is smaller when there are four secretaries, the corresponding slowness of the novice typists is more than offsetting in terms of the average number of documents as well as the average time spent in the system. Pooling the secretaries into a single system substantially reduces the average number of documents in the entire system and the average time each document spends in the system. In fact, the average time is almost that for the constant-service-time case. Also there is not much difference between having two faster or four slower typists, given that their combined service rate in the system is $S\mu = 40$.

The systems you have considered so far are the cases of $S = 2$ or $S = 4$ combined with the possibilities of each secretary operating separately or all S secretaries operating in a typing pool. Turn now to an intermediate possibility having two secretarial pools, each operating independently of the other, and consisting of two novice typists. Then, for each pool, $\lambda = \frac{36}{2} = 18$, and, for $S = 2$, $\mu = 10$.

$$(17) \qquad\qquad P[\text{busy period}] = .8526$$

$$(18) \qquad E[\text{number of documents in each pool}] = 9.4741$$

$$(19) \qquad\qquad E[\text{time in system}] = .4264 + .1 = .5264.$$

Consequently, the probability of a busy period and the average number of documents in each pool are the same as for the case of the two faster secretaries; but the two-pools arrangement results in twice as many documents on the average being in the entire system. Further, the expected time a document spends in the system doubles as compared to the case of $S = 2$ and $\mu = 20$.

The various comparisons in the above illustration are valid for other numerical values of the arrival rate λ, the service rate μ, and the number of servers S. In particular, given values for λ and μS, the $P[\text{busy period}]$ increases for smaller values of S, as does the expected number waiting in line and average time spent waiting. But the expected number in the entire system as well as average time spent in the system decreases for smaller values of S.

Depending on the application, you may be able to affect the values of λ, μ, and S and therefore select them optimally. If the associated objective function is very simple, you may be able to derive an analytic formula or construct tables and nomographs to aid in the optimization search. You may also be able to apply certain advanced algorithmic techniques (not treated in this text).

*Priority discipline. Near the end of Sec. 15.5 we show how imposing a priority discipline affects the average time in line for customers of different types. Recall that Type k arrives according to a Poisson process with rate λ_k, and that the priority numbers are assigned so that $k = 1$ is the highest and $k = r$ the lowest. Here we assume that the service time distribution is exponential with rate μ for *every* type of customer. Define, as before,

$$(20) \qquad\qquad \sigma_k \equiv \sum_{j=1}^{k} \frac{\lambda_j}{\mu_j} = \frac{\sum_{j=1}^{k} \lambda_j}{\mu} \qquad \sigma_0 \equiv 0.$$

Assume $\sigma_r < S$ to ensure the system reaches equilibrium. Then

$$(21) \quad E[\text{time in line} \mid \text{Type k}] = \frac{S/\mu}{(S - \sigma_{k-1})(S - \sigma_k)} \cdot P[\text{busy period}].$$

The average time in the system for an *arbitrary* arrival remains the same as in a system without priorities having an arrival rate $\lambda = \sum \lambda_j$.

To illustrate, consider the example of $\lambda = 36$, $S = 2$, and $\mu = 20$. In a system without any priorities, you saw in (16) that the expected time in line is .2132. Suppose now that there are two priorities with $\lambda_1 = \lambda_2 = 18$. From (21) the expected time in line for Type 1 is $(.8526/22 = .0387)$ and for Type 2 is $(.8526/2.2 = .3875)$. The smaller the value of λ_1, the smaller will be the average wait for both types.

*15.7 BIRTH-AND-DEATH PROCESS

Here we present a unified treatment of the special cases you have seen so far, and, at the same time, develop a model that assists in analyzing other cases as well. This model is termed a **birth-and-death process.**

To begin, assume the probability transition laws for the system do not change over time; that is, postulate the process to be **time-homogeneous.** The system is considered to operate continuously without any specific starting point, and is characterized at Time t by the number of customers n in the system ($n = 0, 1, 2, \ldots$). We will want to designate a particular instant of time, however, to serve as a reference point. It is convenient to let $t = 0$ be this point, and to let i be the number of customers in the system at Time 0.

Define

$$(1) \qquad P_{in}(T) \equiv \begin{pmatrix} \text{probability that the system contains } n \text{ customers at Time T,} \\ \text{given that it contains } i \text{ customers at Time 0} \end{pmatrix}.$$

Because the system *is* time-homogeneous, the value of $P_{in}(h)$ for $h > 0$ not only gives the probability defined in (1) at Time h, but also the probability that the system contains n customers at Time T + h, given that it contains i customers at Time T.

We postulate that the $P_{in}(T)$ satisfy what are known as the **Chapman-Kolmogorov equations** for a **time-homogeneous Markov process:**

$$(2) \qquad P_{in}(T + h) = \sum_m P_{im}(T)P_{mn}(h) \quad (h > 0),$$

for every i and n. You can interpret (2) as stating that the probability of the system having n customers at Time T + h, given that it has i customers at Time 0, can be found by adding, over all possible m, the joint probabilities, that there are m customers in the system at Time T, given the system has i customers at Time 0, and the probability that there are n customers in the system at Time T + h, given that the system has m customers at Time T. The so-called *Markov property* relates simply to the assumption that the only relevant information about the system at Time T is the number of customers in the system, namely, m, and not the detailed history of the process leading up to Time T. In this sense, the system is memoryless, and hence (2) represents a nontrivial assumption. [Think of an example or two in which (2) does not apply.]

The birth-and-death process is a special case of (2). Assume that for a *very* small interval of time, $h > 0$, we need only consider that at most one customer enters or leaves the system, and that

(3)
$$P_{m,m+1}(h) \doteq (\lambda_m h)(1 - \mu_m h) \doteq \lambda_m h \quad \text{for } m = 0, 1, 2, \ldots$$
$$P_{m,m-1}(h) \doteq (1 - \lambda_m h)(\mu_m h) \doteq \mu_m h \quad \text{for } m = 1, 2, \ldots,$$

so that

(4)
$$P_{mm}(h) \doteq 1 - P_{m,m-1}(h) - P_{m,m+1}(h) \doteq 1 - (\lambda_m + \mu_m)h \quad \text{for } m = 1, 2, \ldots,$$
$$P_{00}(h) \doteq 1 - P_{01}(h) \doteq 1 - \lambda_0 h \quad \text{for } m = 0,$$

where $\lambda_m \geq 0$, for all m, and $\mu_m > 0$, for $m \geq 1$; all other $P_{mk}(h) = 0$. In other words, for a very small interval of time, h, the probability that the number of customers increases from m to $m + 1$ is approximately $\lambda_m h$, and that it decreases from m to $m - 1$ is approximately $\mu_m h$. Given our approximation, the probability that the number of customers remains at m can be written as approximately 1 minus these two values. The approximations can be made exact by adding terms that have coefficients h^k, where $k \geq 2$.

The values λ_m and μ_m may be thought of as arrival and departure rates, respectively, when there are m customers in the system. It is important that you realize no assumption has been made about the number of servers or the queue discipline in the system. The postulates refer only to probabilities of an arrival and a departure.

Substituting (3) and (4) into (2) yields for $n \geq 1$

(5)
$$P_{in}(T + h) \doteq P_{i,n-1}(T)P_{n-1,n}(h) + P_{in}(T)P_{n,n}(h) + P_{i,n+1}(T)P_{n+1,n}(h)$$
$$\doteq P_{i,n-1}(T)\lambda_{n-1}h + P_{in}(T)[1 - (\lambda_n + \mu_n)h]$$
$$+ P_{i,n+1}(T)\mu_{n+1}h \quad (h \text{ small}).$$

Bringing the term $P_{in}(T)$ to the left-hand side of (5), dividing by h, and letting $h \to 0$, yields the so-called **forward system of differential equations**

(6)
$$\frac{dP_{in}}{dT} = \lambda_{n-1}P_{i,n-1}(T) - (\lambda_n + \mu_n)P_{in}(T) + \mu_{n+1}P_{i,n+1}(T).$$

The relation (6) is exact because the terms neglected in (5) drop out as $h \to 0$. You can also use (6) to represent the case of $n = 0$ by letting $\lambda_{-1} \equiv 0$ and $\mu_0 \equiv 0$. Thus (6) represents a system of equations corresponding to $n = 0, 1, 2, \ldots$, where i is taken as a given initial condition.

▶ The term "forward" refers to the fact that the equations were derived by looking at the second interval of time $(T, T + h)$ and using (3) and (4) to approximate the transition probabilities in this small interval. You can also derive *backward* equations by interchanging T and h on the right of (2), and then using (3) and (4) to approximate $P_{im}(h)$. In the resulting differential equations for dP_{in}/dT, the value of n at Time T is taken as given, and i at Time 0 is considered as the variable, so that $i = 0, 1, 2, \ldots$.   ◀

Review. Let us pause here to see that (6) really does include queuing models that you have already examined. Consider the pure-birth model with Poisson input, treated in Sec. 15.3. For that situation, $\lambda_n = \lambda$ and $\mu_n = 0$, for all n. Assuming that $i = 0$ at Time 0, (6) becomes

$$(7) \qquad \frac{dP_{0n}}{dT} = \lambda P_{0,n-1}(T) - \lambda P_{0n}(T).$$

The solution for any i is

$$(8) \qquad P_{in}(T) = \frac{(\lambda T)^{(n-i)} e^{-\lambda T}}{(n-i)!} \quad \text{for } n \geq i,$$

which agrees with (10) of Sec. 15.3 for $i = 0$.

Next, consider the pure-death model in Sec. 15.4 having a single-server with exponential service times and M customers in the system at Time 0. For that situation, $\lambda_n = 0$, for all n, and $\mu_n = \mu$, for $1 \leq n \leq M$, so that (6) becomes

$$(9) \qquad \frac{dP_{Mn}}{dT} = -\mu P_{Mn}(T) + \mu P_{M,n+1}(T) \quad \text{for } 1 \leq n < M$$

$$(10) \qquad \frac{dP_{MM}}{dT} = -\mu P_{MM}(T) \qquad\qquad \text{for } n = M,$$

which has the solution $P_{Mn}(T) = P_n(T)$ as given by (13) in Sec. 15.4. Suppose, instead of there being a single server, each of the M customers can start service at Time 0. Then $\mu_n = n\mu$ for $0 \leq n \leq M$; and (6) gives the same results as (20) and (21) in Sec. 15.4.

Finally, consider the single-server model with Poisson input and exponential service treated in Sec. 15.5. For $\lambda_n = \lambda$, for $n \geq 0$, and $\mu_n = \mu$, for $n \geq 1$, the system (6) is the same as (4) and (5) in Sec. 15.5. Recall that the subscript i in (6) designating the number of customers in the system at Time 0 was suppressed in (4) and (5) of Sec. 15.5, since the emphasis there was on obtaining stationary probabilities. [To obtain an explicit transient solution to (6), you must use the fact that $P_{ii}(0) = 1$, and all other $P_{in}(0) = 0$.]

Steady-state solution. The forward equations (6) depend on both i and T. Now suppose that $T \to \infty$, and assume that in the limit the system reaches statistical equilibrium. For the limiting process, the influence of the value of i at Time 0 vanishes, and hence the subscript i can once again be suppressed in the probability notation. As in Sec. 15.5, you can solve for the equilibrium or stationary values of P_n by setting the time derivatives in (6) equal to 0:

(11) $0 = \lambda_{n-1}P_{n-1} - (\lambda_n + \mu_n)P_n + \mu_{n+1}P_{n+1}$ for $n \geq 1$

(12) $0 = -\lambda_0 P_0 + \mu_1 P_1$ for $n = 0$.

Starting with $n = 0$, this system of difference equations can be solved recursively, yielding the general result (assuming all $\mu_n > 0$, for $n \geq 1$)

(13) $P_n = \dfrac{\lambda_{n-1}}{\mu_n} \cdot \dfrac{\lambda_{n-2}}{\mu_{n-1}} \cdots \dfrac{\lambda_0}{\mu_1} \cdot P_0$ for $n \geq 1$.

[If there is a number N such that $\mu_N = 0$ and $\mu_n > 0$ for $n > N$, and if $i > N$ at Time 0, then $P_n = 0$, for $n > N$, and (13) is easily modified by adding N to all the subscripts.]

The value of P_0 is determined from

(14) $1 = P_0 + \displaystyle\sum_{n=1}^{\infty} P_n = P_0\left(1 + \dfrac{\lambda_0}{\mu_1} + \dfrac{\lambda_1}{\mu_2} \cdot \dfrac{\lambda_0}{\mu_1} + \dfrac{\lambda_2}{\mu_3} \cdot \dfrac{\lambda_1}{\mu_2} \cdot \dfrac{\lambda_0}{\mu_1} + \cdots\right),$

where we postulate for all the models to be considered in this text that the infinite series on the right of (14) converges to a finite value. For example, in the single-server, Poisson input, exponential service model of Sec. 15.5,

(15) $1 + \dfrac{\lambda_0}{\mu_1} + \dfrac{\lambda_1}{\mu_2} \cdot \dfrac{\lambda_0}{\mu_1} + \cdots = 1 + \rho + \rho^2 + \cdots = \dfrac{1}{1 - \rho}$ for $\rho < 1$,

so that

(16) $P_0 = 1 - \rho$.

An easily verified sufficient condition ensuring that the series on the right of (14) converges is that for n large enough, say $n \geq N$, all $\lambda_n \leq r\mu_{n+1}$, where $0 < r < 1$.

In the case of a finite limit M on the total number of persons in the system, you can let $\lambda_n = 0$, for $n \geq M$ in (11) and (12), so that $P_n = 0$, for $n > M$ in (13). Consequently, P_0 can always be easily determined from a finite-valued summation analogous to (14).

Examples. We now illustrate the usefulness of the birth-and-death process equations.

Case i. Suppose customers arrive according to a Poisson process with input rate λ, but each customer serves himself, according to an exponential distribution with rate μ. (This situation may be conceived of as a system with an infinite number of servers, and is designated accordingly as $M/M/\infty$.) Then $\lambda_n = \lambda$ and $\mu_n = n\mu$—recall this value for μ_n was established in (17) of Sec. 15.4. Consequently,

(17) $1 + \dfrac{\lambda_0}{\mu_1} + \dfrac{\lambda_1}{\mu_2} \cdot \dfrac{\lambda_0}{\mu_1} + \dfrac{\lambda_2}{\mu_3} \cdot \dfrac{\lambda_1}{\mu_2} \cdot \dfrac{\lambda_0}{\mu_1} + \cdots = 1 + \dfrac{\rho}{1} + \dfrac{\rho^2}{2 \cdot 1} + \cdots = e^{\rho},$

so that

(18) $P_0 = e^{-\rho}$ and $P_n = \dfrac{\rho^n e^{-\rho}}{n!}$ (Poisson distribution).

(Another system in which $\mu_n = n\mu$ consists of a single server that speeds up its service rate proportionately as the number of persons in the system gets larger.)

Case ii. Suppose there is a single exponential server so that $\mu_n = \mu$, for $n \geq 1$. But customers who are about to enter the system are discouraged by a long line in such a way that $\lambda_n = \lambda/(n + 1)$. This assumption also leads to the results given in (17) and (18).

Case iii. Consider the multiple-server model in Sec. 15.6. There

(19) $\lambda_n = \lambda$ for $n \geq 0$.

Applying the result (17) in Sec. 15.4, we may conclude that the departure rate is $n\mu$ when there are $n \leq S$ customers in the system, and $S\mu$ if $n > S$, so that

(20) $\mu_n = \begin{cases} n\mu & \text{for } 1 \leq n \leq S \\ S\mu & \text{for } n > S. \end{cases}$

The difference equations (3) in Sec. 15.6 agree with (11) and (12) above as does the corresponding solution (4) and (5) with the formulas (13) and (14) above.

Case iv. So far, all the examples assumed, in effect, an unlimited population from which arrivals occur. Now consider a model in which the source population is finite, and therefore the rate of arrivals decreases as the number *in* the system grows. An industrial situation of some practical significance that meets this description is a factory containing a group of machines that occasionally break down and require repair. (In queuing theory literature such a problem is sometimes referred to as a **machine interference model.**)
  Let

M = number of machines   and R = number of repairmen.

Assume that if a machine is operative, then the time at which it breaks down is described by an exponential probability distribution that has rate λ and is independent of the operating behavior of the other machines. Suppose further that any nonfunctioning machine requires the attention of only a single repairman, and that the service time probability distribution is exponential with the same rate μ for every repairman and every machine.
  Suppose n machines have broken down, and hence $M - n$ are operative. Then in a *very* small interval of time, $h > 0$, the approximate probability that one of the operative machines breaks down can be calculated as usual:

(21) $P \begin{bmatrix} \text{one out of } M - n \text{ machines} \\ \text{breaks down in an interval } h \end{bmatrix} \doteq (M - n)\lambda h.$

By the same token,

(22) $\qquad P \begin{bmatrix} \text{one out of } n \text{ inoperative} \\ \text{machines completes} \\ \text{service in an interval } h \end{bmatrix} \doteq n\mu h \quad \text{for } 1 \le n \le R,$

and the probability in (22) is $R\mu h$, for $R < n \le M$. Then in terms of a birth-and-death process, you can define

(23)

$$\lambda_n = \begin{cases} (M - n)\lambda & \text{for } 0 \le n \le M \\ 0 & \text{for } n > M \end{cases}$$

$$\mu_n = \begin{cases} n\mu & \text{for } 1 \le n \le R \\ R\mu & \text{for } R < n \le M. \end{cases}$$

Thus the difference equations in (11) and (12) become

$$0 = -M\lambda P_0 + \mu P_1 \qquad\qquad\qquad\qquad \text{for } n = 0$$

$$0 = (M - n + 1)\lambda P_{n-1} - [(M - n)\lambda + n\mu]P_n + (n + 1)\mu P_{n+1}$$

(24) $\qquad\qquad\qquad\qquad\qquad\qquad\qquad\qquad\qquad \text{for } 1 \le n < R$

$$0 = (M - n + 1)\lambda P_{n-1} - [(M - n)\lambda + R\mu]P_n + R\mu P_{n+1}$$

$$\qquad\qquad\qquad\qquad\qquad\qquad\qquad\qquad \text{for } R \le n \le M,$$

and letting $\rho \equiv \lambda/\mu$, (13) can be written as

(25)

$$P_n = \binom{M}{n}\rho^n P_0 \qquad\qquad \text{for } 0 \le n \le R$$

$$P_n = \binom{M}{n}\rho^n \cdot \frac{n!}{R! \, R^{n-R}} \cdot P_0 \quad \text{for } R < n \le M,$$

where $\binom{M}{n} = M!/n!(M - n)!$ is the standard *binomial coefficient* and P_0 is computed from the relation

(26) $\qquad\qquad\qquad\qquad\qquad \sum_{n=0}^{M} P_n = 1.$

There are no simple expressions for the expected number of nonoperative machines, but in any specific case the value of $E[n]$ can easily be computed directly using the values for P_n in (25).

*Model interpretation. The probabilistic structure of each queuing model in the preceding sections was described in terms of interarrival and service time distributions. For the birth-and-death process model, no ambiguity arises in interpreting the corresponding interarrival and service distribution assumptions insofar as the model is applied to situations in which the input *is* a Poisson process, and the service time for each server *is* an exponential distribution. But when λ_n is defined, for example, as in *Case ii* above, there is no simple way of providing a specified form for the interarrival distribution. The reason is that the time between successive arrivals depends on the number of customers in the system, which in turn depends on the service events. A similar remark holds with regard to defining a service time distribution. (For example, such difficulty occurs when μ_n is specified, as at the end of *Case i*, to be the service rate for a single server and dependent on the number of persons in the system.) Therefore only in special cases are you able to interpret the above birth-and-death model as being a combination of Poisson input and exponential service times.

By the same token, it is difficult to work out the probability distribution and expectations of the time a customer spends in the system, even when the discipline is first come, first served.

*15.8 OTHER QUEUING MODELS

Most of the results in this chapter have pertained to queuing models in which arrivals are described by a Poisson input process and the service times for each server are given by an exponential distribution. All of the models have assumed there is a single waiting line, and customers are processed on a first come, first served basis. (The situation of multiple waiting lines was treated approximately as several systems operating side by side and independently of each other.)

It is not too difficult to extend such results to other cases containing minor variations on the assumptions. For example, it is fairly easy to encompass the phenomenon of *balking* (a tendency for a customer not to enter the system as the line gets longer) and *impatience* or *reneging* (a tendency for a customer to leave the system before being served). (The required approach makes only minor modifications in the specification of λ_n and μ_n in the birth-and-death model of Sec. 15.7.) It is also possible to obtain usable formulas to handle different, but simple, queuing disciplines, such as random service or last come, first served. Such variations, however, are not considered in this book.

In any particular industrial application, it is the exception rather than the rule that any of these models precisely represents reality. Therefore you should use these models primarily for general insights and guidance in determining how sensitive a system's operations may be to the relevant decision alternatives. If the resultant approximate analysis shows that the economic impact of a wrong decision may be serious, you should then augment your analysis by applying computer simulation to explore in further detail the specific questions of system design.

REVIEW EXERCISES

1 Suggest two or three queuing situations that you think might warrant a scientific study. State in which of the two categories described at the beginning of Sec. 15.1 your suggested applications might fall. Explain the decisions that might be made after a scientific study, and how you would distinguish a good decision from a poor one.

2 In each part below, suggest one or two queuing situations that illustrate the indicated characteristic. (Be imaginative and do not use the examples already given in the text.)

   (a) Customers arriving singly.
   (b) Bulk arrivals.
   (c) Predetermined arrivals.
   (d) Completely random arrivals.
   (e) Unlimited source population.
   (f) Finite source population.
   (g) Customers that always join the system when they arrive.
   (h) Customers that may balk when they arrive.
   (i) First come, first served discipline.
   (j) Last come, first served discipline.
   (k) Random service discipline.
   (l) Special priority service discipline.
   (m) Customers that always remain in the line after joining it.
   (n) Customers that may renege after joining a line.
   (o) Single waiting line.
   (p) Parallel waiting lines.
   (q) Customers that may jockey for position.
   (r) Servers in parallel.
   (s) Servers in series (tandem).
   (t) Service time mechanism that is independent of the line length.
   (u) Service time mechanism that is influenced by the line length.

3 Consider three or four of the queuing situations that you suggested in exercise 2.

   (a) State what you think are the four or five most important operating characteristics to measure in assessing the performance of these systems.
   (b) Also suggest a variety of managerial options that can be selected in designing these systems to operate efficiently. (Be sure to define what you mean by "efficient.")

4 (a) Consider the negative exponential distribution given by (2) in Sec. 15.3. Show that the mean equals $1/\lambda$ and the variance $1/\lambda^2$.
   (b) Verify the mathematical manipulations that establish in (3) and (4) the memory-less property of the exponential distribution.
   (c) Verify that the sum of n independent values drawn from the same exponential density (2) has a gamma distribution, as given by (8).
   (d) Verify the probability statement in (9) by repeatedly applying integration by parts.
   (e) Use (10) to state the probability of one arrival in an interval of length $T = h$. Then apply a Taylor series expansion and verify the approximation in (7).
   (f) Show that the mean and variance of a Poisson distribution are as given in (11).
   (g) Verify the equality in (12) from (9) and (10). Give a verbal interpretation of (12).
   (h) Show that replacing λn in the Erlang distribution (14) by λ yields the gamma distribution (8).

5 Compare Figs. 15.2a and 15.2b and discuss how the shape and concentration of probability mass shift with variations in n and λ.

6 Consider the pure-death model in Sec. 15.4.

(a) Derive (12) by using reasoning analogous to that employed in obtaining (11).
(b) Show that the probabilities (13) and (14) satisfy the differential equations (11) and (12).
(c) Determine how $P_n(T)$ behaves as T grows without bound, for $n = 1, 2, \ldots, M$. For $n = 0$. [*Suggestion:* use the example $M = 2$ and $\mu = 1$, and draw a graph of each $P_n(T)$.]

*7 Consider the self-service model in Sec. 15.5.

(a) Justify in detail the approximations in (17) and (18).
(b) Justify in detail the approximation in (19), and show how to obtain (20).
(c) Verify that the binomial probability distribution (22) satisfies the differential equations (20) and (21).
(d) Determine how $P_n(T)$ behaves as T grows without bound, for $n = 0, 1, \ldots, M$. [*Suggestion:* use the example $M = 2$ and $\mu = 1$, and draw a graph of each $P_n(T)$.]
(e) Suppose $M = 1$. Compare the probabilities in (13) and (14) with those in (22) for $n = 0, 1$.

8 Consider the single-server model with Poisson input and exponential service, discussed in Sec. 15.5.

(a) Perform the detailed algebraic steps to derive (4) from (3). Also show how to obtain (5).
*(b) Devise a situation in which each $P_n(T)$ approaches a limiting value as $T \to \infty$ but $E[n]$ is not finite. Comment on why the term statistical equilibrium is not applied to such a case. [*Hint:* consider $\lambda > \mu$.]
(c) Give a verbal interpretation of the assumption in (6).
(d) Verify that the stationary probabilities P_n in (10) satisfy the difference equations in (7).
*(e) Perform the detailed algebraic steps to derive the formulas $E[n]$, Var $[n]$, and $P[n \geq N]$ shown in (13) for the geometric distribution.
(f) Provide the detailed justification and show the intermediate algebraic steps for each equality in (15) that gives $E[\text{line length}]$.
(g) Perform the detailed algebraic steps to derive the formula for the waiting time density $h(w)$ in (19).
(h) Perform the detailed algebraic steps to derive the formulas for $E[\text{time in line}]$ in (21).

9 Consider the secretaries example in Sec. 15.5. How does this simple model approximate the real situation? Why would the average delay for a document tend to be

smaller in actuality than the delay given by (20)? If you were the office manager, what else would you take into account in deciding between the two alternatives?

10 Consider the secretaries example in Sec. 15.5. In each part below, determine the average number of documents on each secretary's desk and in the entire system. Calculate the average time for a document to be in the system and the average length of the busy periods.

(a) $S = 1$ and $\mu = 40$.
(b) $S = 10$ and $\mu = 4$.

11 Suppose in the secretaries example in Sec. 15.5, there are an average of 38 documents to be typed per day. For each alternative in the text, determine the average number of documents on each secretary's desk and in the entire system. Calculate the average time for a document to be in the system and the average length of the busy periods.

*12 Consider the finite-queue model discussed in Sec. 15.5.

(a) Give a plausible explanation of why statistical equilibrium is reached for *any* value of the intensity ratio λ/μ.
(b) Verify that when $\lambda < \mu$ and $M \to \infty$, P_n in (23) agrees with (12).
*(c) Derive E[number of customers in system] using the probabilities P_n, for $\lambda \neq \mu$, as given in (23). Do the same for $\lambda = \mu$.
(d) For $\rho = .7, .8, .9, .95$, find the corresponding value of M such that E[number of customers in system] in (24) is within .01 of the same operating characteristic as given by (13).
(e) Determine the limiting value of E[number of customers in system] in (24) as ρ grows arbitrarily large.
(f) Show that (23) is the limiting value of P_n for $\lambda \neq \mu$ for as ρ approaches 1.
(g) Let $M = 3$. Calculate E[number of customers in system] for $\rho = 1, 2, 5, 10$.

13 Consider the single-server model with Poisson input and arbitrary service distribution, as described in Sec. 15.5.

(a) Verify that when the service time is exponential, then (29). (30), and (32) reduce to (13), (15), and (20), respectively.
(b) Assume $\mu = 10$. Calculate the operating characteristics (29), (30), and (32), for $\rho = .7, .8, .9$, and .95 with $V = 0$.
(c) Rework part (b) with $V = .01$.
(d) Rework part (b) with $V = .1$.
(e) Rework part (b) with $V = 1$.
*(f) Assume that arrivals are periodic (constant) and $\mu = 10$. Calculate the operating characteristics (40) and (41) for $\rho = .7, .8$, and .95. Compare your results with part (b).

*14 Consider the single-server model with priority discipline, as discussed near the end of Sec. 15.5. (*Continued on p. 532.*)

(a) Verify that when $r = 1$, (35) reduces to E[time in line] in (32).
(b) Verify the sample calculations in (37).   (*Continued on p. 894.*)
(c) Suppose $\lambda_1 = \lambda_2 = 9$ in (37). Find the expected time in line for Types 1 and 2 customers. Determine what happens when $\lambda_1 = 3$ and when $\lambda_1 = 15$ (remember $\lambda_1 + \lambda_2 = 18$).
(d) Suppose $\lambda_1 = \lambda_2 = 9$, $\mu_1 = 30$, $\mu_2 = 15$, and the service distributions are exponential. Determine the expected time in line for Types 1 and 2 customers.
(e) Suppose $\lambda_1 = \lambda_2 = 9$, $\mu_1 = \mu_2 = 20$, and let $V_1 = 0$ and $V_2 = 1/20^2$. Determine the expected time in line for Types 1 and 2 customers.
(f) Rework part (e), except let $V_1 = 1/20^2$ and $V_2 = 0$.
(g) Suppose $\lambda_1 = \lambda_2 = 9$, $\mu_1 = 30$, $\mu_2 = 15$, and let $V_1 = 0$ and $V_2 = 1/15^2$. Determine the expected time in line for Types 1 and 2 customers.
(h) Rework part (g), except let $V_1 = 1/30^2$ and $V_2 = 0$.   .
(i) Suppose there are three classifications, where $\lambda_1 = \lambda_2 = \lambda_3 = 6$. Assume that the service rate $\mu = 20$ applies to all three types and that the service distributions are exponential. Determine the expected time in line for each of the three types of customers.
(j) Rework part (i), except let $\mu_1 = 33\frac{1}{3}$ and $\mu_2 = \mu_3 = 16\frac{2}{3}$.
(k) Rework part (i), except let $\mu_1 = 40$, $\mu_2 = 20$, and $\mu_3 = 13\frac{1}{3}$.

15 Consider the multiple-server model in Sec. 15.6.

(a) Verify that the probabilities P_n in (4) and (5) satisfy the difference equations (3).
(b) Check that when $S = 1$, the probabilities in (4) and (5) reduce to the formula in (12) of Sec. 15.5.
(c) Give the intermediate algebraic steps to justify the statement that when the number of servers is unlimited (self-service), then P_n in (4) is a Poisson distribution. (*Hint:* use a series expansion for e^x.)

*16 Consider the multiple-server model in Sec. 15.6. In each part below, show the detailed algebraic steps justifying the formula that is cited in the text.

(a) P[busy period] in (6).
(b) P[busy period] in (8).
(c) E[line length] in (9).
(d) E[number of servers] in (10).

17 Consider the secretaries example where they work in a typing pool, as in Sec. 15.6. Suppose the arrival rate is $\lambda = 38$. Calculate the P[busy period], E[number of documents in system], and E[time in system], for each case below.

(a) $S = 4$ and $\mu = 10$.
(b) $S = 2$ and $\mu = 20$.
(c) $S = 1$ and $\mu = 40$.
(d) $S = 10$ and $\mu = 4$.

*18 Consider the multiple-server model with priority discipline discussed at the end of Sec. 15.6. In each part of this exercise, apply (21) to find the expected time in line for each Type k.

(a) Let $k = 2$, $\lambda_1 = \lambda_2 = 18$, $\mu = 10$, and $S = 4$.
(b) Rework part (a), except let $S = 1$ and $\mu = 40$.
(c) Rework part (a), except let $S = 10$ and $\mu = 4$.
(d) Let $k = 3$, $\lambda_1 = \lambda_2 = \lambda_3 = 6$, $\mu = 20$, and $S = 2$.

*19 Consider the birth-and-death process in Sec. 15.7.

(a) Substitute the approximate probabilities in (3) and (4) into the Chapman-Kolmogorov equations (2) and verify the result in (5). Also exhibit the intermediate steps yielding the differential equations (6).
(b) Write the equation in (6) corresponding to $n = 0$.
(c) Examine the pure-birth model for an arbitrary i, and write the exact expression for (6). [For $i = 0$, (6) is given by (7).] Show that (8) satisfies the differential equations.
(d) Show that $P_{Mn}(T) = P_n(T)$, as given by (13) in Sec. 15.4, is the solution to (9) and (10) for the pure-death model with a single server.
(e) Examine the pure-death model where all M customers start service at Time 0. Check that (6) gives the same results as (20) and (21) in Sec. 15.4.
(f) Examine the single-server model with Poisson input and exponential service in Sec. 15.5. Verify that the system (6) is the same as (4) and (5) in Sec. 15.5.
(g) Check that the stationary probabilities P_n in (13) satisfy the difference equations (11) and (12).
(h) Explain why $P_n = 0$ for $n < N$, where N is a number such that $\mu_N = 0$ and $\mu_n > 0$, for $n > N$, assuming that $i > N$ at Time 0.
(i) Verify that if there is an N such that $\lambda_n \leq r\mu_{n+1}$, where $0 < r < 1$, for $n \geq N$, then the series on the right of (14) converges.

*20 Consider the birth-and-death process discussed in Sec. 15.7.

(a) Examine *Case ii* and show that the probabilities P_n are given by (17) and (18).
(b) Examine *Case iii* and show that the difference equations (3) in Sec. 15.6 agree with (11) and (12), as does the solution (4) and (5) with the formulas (13) and (14).
(c) Examine *Case iv*, the machine interference model. Explain why the probability in (22) is $R\mu h$, for $R < n \leq M$. Verify that substituting (23) into the difference equations (11) and (12) yields (24). Also verify that (13) leads to the solution (25).

21 Explain your understanding of the following terms:

operating characteristics
input process
bulk arrivals
balk
reneging (impatience)
queue discipline
first come, first served
last come, first served
random service order
servers (or channels)
jockey

servers in parallel
servers in series (tandem)
systems synthesis
periodic (regular, constant) arrivals
service time
exponential service
pure-death model
service rate μ
*self-service model
*Kendall's notation
single-server model

multiple-server model	pure-birth model
transient solution	arrival rate λ
statistical equilibrium	Erlang arrivals
equilibrium (stationary) probabilities	difference equations
traffic intensity ρ	*finite-queue model
utilization factor ρ	*loss-delay system
birth (arrival) process	Pollaczek-Khintchine formulas
death process	*priority discipline
renewal process	*preemptive priority
recurrent events	busy period
completely random arrivals	virtual delay
stationary (homogeneous) time process	*birth-and-death process
memoryless property	*Chapman-Kolmogorov equations
interarrival time	*time-homogeneous Markov process
exponential arrivals (Poisson input,	*forward system of differential equations
Markovian input)	*machine interference model.

FORMULATION AND COMPUTATIONAL EXERCISES

22 Suppose an item held in inventory is replenished according to the rule "when the inventory level falls *below* 1, order 10 items." Assume that the current level of inventory is 3, that items are demanded one at a time, and that the time between demands is exponentially distributed with a mean rate of two per week.

    (a) What is the probability distribution of the number of items demanded in a two-week period? (Give both the form of the distribution and the values of its parameters.)

    (b) What is the probability that no replenishment will take place during the coming week? During the coming two weeks? (Write the detailed formulas for these probabilities; calculate the numerical values.)

23 Consider a production process with two machines, A and B, in tandem. The output of items from the first machine, A, is Poisson, with the rate of 10 per hour. The second machine, B, processes each item with exponential service time at the rate of 12 per hour. There is a congestion problem when more than two items are waiting to be processed on Machine B.

    (a) Calculate the fraction of time that the system is congested.

  *(b) Suppose Machine A is turned off whenever more than two items are waiting to be processed by Machine B. Explain why your answer in part (a) overestimates the fraction of time that Machine A is turned off. Calculate the correct probability. (Be sure to indicate the specific queuing model you use.)

*24 The P. Kaboo Camera Store tries to keep in stock only one unit of a very expensive lens. When the lens is sold, the store reorders a new one. Assume that, on the average, the store has one customer in four weeks who wants to buy such a lens; if the lens is out of stock, the customer goes elsewhere. What is the probability of the lens being out of stock if the average replenishment time is one week? Two weeks? Four weeks? (Assume the customer interarrival and replenishment time probability distributions are exponential.)

25 Consider a single-server model with Poisson input and a customer arrival rate of 30 per hour. Currently, service is provided by a mechanism that takes *exactly* 1.5 minutes. Suppose the system can instead be served by a mechanism that has an exponential service time distribution. What must be the mean service time for this mechanism in order to ensure the same average time a customer spends in the system? The same average number of customers in the system?

26 Let the value of M denote the "degree of service" offered by a single server. The value $M = 1$ represents a minimal degree of service, and larger values of M represent more thorough and longer-lasting service. Suppose that the form of the service time distribution is gamma, given by (16) in Sec. 15.4, where $u = 1$. Note that both the mean and variance of the service time distribution depend linearly on the "degree of service" parameter M. Suppose the arrival rate is $\lambda = .8$, for $M = 1$, and assume that for $M > 1$, the arrival rate decreases; interarrival times are exponentially distributed. The reason for this effect on the arrival rate is that as the degree of service increases, such service is required less often. In each part below, determine the arrival rate such that the expected number of customers in the system is the same as for $M = 1$ and $\lambda = .8$.

   (a) $M = 2$.
   (b) $M = 4$.
   (c) $M = 8$.

27 The Schmerz Auto Rental Company must choose between operating one of two types of service shops for maintaining its cars. It estimates that cars will arrive at the maintenance facility on the average of one every 40 minutes (assume this rate is virtually independent of which facility is chosen). In the first type of shop, there are dual facilities operating in parallel; each facility can service a car in 30 minutes on the average. In the second type, there is a single facility, but it can service a car in 15 minutes on the average. Assume that each minute a car must spend in the shop reduces contribution to profit by one monetary unit. Let C_1 and C_2 be the cost per minute of operating the first and second type facilities, respectively. Find the value of $C_2 - C_1$ such that Schmerz would be indifferent between operating the two shops.

28 Dusty Page, the Head Librarian of the Free Kowt College, is considering staffing an extra checkout desk in the main library. Up to now, two desks have been in operation. On the average, one student arrived every two minutes, and the total checkout time (that is, time in line plus in service) averaged a minute. The college has just become co-educational, and with the influx of female students, Page expects an increased birth

rate in the system. Determine the value of the arrival rate such that three checkout desks still ensure an average total checkout time of a minute. Assume that the multiple-server model in Sec. 15.6 can be used to yield good approximations.

29 The Gabby Company has leased three WATS ("wide area telephone service") lines to enable its executives to make toll-free long distance calls. Let c be the cost per hour per WATS line. Suppose that the frequency of calls per hour is described by a Poisson distribution with mean 10, and the lengths of the calls are exponentially distributed with mean 15 minutes. Let w denote the cost per hour of executive waiting time (that is, time waiting until one of the lines is free). Let $c = 1$ and determine the range of values for w that will make the decision to lease *three* WATS lines optimal.

30 The manager, Sy K. Dellick, of the Hippon Drug Store is remodeling his facility and is considering three ways of organizing his branded-items business. The first way is to employ a fast clerk to wait on all customers. Assume such a clerk serves customers exponentially at an average rate of two minutes per customer. The second way is to employ two moderately fast clerks to wait on all customers. Assume each serves customers exponentially at an average rate of four minutes per customer. The third way is to use a self-service system in which each customer waits on himself. Self-service, at an average rate of six minutes, is slower than clerk service. The manager wants to calculate the average number of customers in the store, the average time each spends in the store, and the average time each spends waiting for service, under each way of organizing. Assume that customers arrive completely randomly, one at a time, at the rate of 15 per hour. Calculate the operating characteristics of interest to the manager. Also determine these characteristics assuming that the fast clerk could service each customer in *exactly* two minutes time.

31 The Paine N. B. Heind Infirmary of Ye Owl College has noticed that each day two students, on the average, arrive in need of hospital care. Such a student requires, on the average, a three-day confinement to bed. Assume that interarrival times and service times are both exponentially distributed.

(a) What is the probability distribution of the number of students occupying hospital beds? What is the associated average number? (Be sure to indicate which model in the text you are applying to derive your answer.)

(b) Suppose there are five students in the hospital at the start of a day. How many of these students, on the average, will remain in the hospital at the same time tomorrow? Three days from today? Seven days from today?

32 A gasoline station on a throughway operates six pumps. Automobiles arrive at the rate of one every 3 minutes. The average service time is 4 minutes. Assume that the model described in Sec. 15.6 can be applied. In each part below, calculate the probability that there are no cars in the station, the probability that all 6 pumps are in use, the expected number of cars at the station, the expected number of cars waiting to be served, and the expected length of time a car spends at the station.

(a) The system as described.

(b) Suppose, due to a threatened fuel shortage, that cars arrive once every minute, but the service time is reduced to 3 minutes, because each car requires less gasoline. (*Continued on p. 537.*)

(c) Suppose, due to a governmental regulation, that on any day only half the cars on the highway are eligible to purchase gasoline. Consequently, the arrival rate is one every 6 minutes, but the service time is 5 minutes, because each car requires more gasoline.

33 The owner, Toots D. Horne, of the Hackett Cab Company, which operates a large fleet of taxi cabs outfitted with two-way radio communication equipment, has decided to purchase S spare radios that can be used when the installed equipment fails. For example, if a cab's radio is broken, the driver brings the taxi to the company's service garage, and a spare radio is installed rapidly; the malfunctioning equipment is then sent to a factory for repair. Suppose that radios fail at the rate of 3 per week, and the factory repair time averages 2 weeks. When the repaired radio is returned from the factory, it is placed in the inventory of spares at the garage. Assume that the process can be described by the model in Sec. 15.6. For each value of S below, calculate the probability that no spares are available and the expected number of taxis that contain malfunctioning radios (because no spares are available for installation).

(a) $S = 8$.
(b) $S = 10$.

*34 In each part below, apply (13) and (14) in the birth-and-death model in Sec. 15.7 to find the equilibrium probabilities P_n.

(a) $\lambda_0 = 1$, $\lambda_1 = \frac{1}{2}$, $\lambda_2 = \frac{1}{4}$, $\lambda_n = 0$, for $n \geq 3$; $\mu_n = 1$, for all $n \geq 1$.
(b) $\lambda_0 = \frac{1}{4}$, $\lambda_1 = \frac{1}{2}$, $\lambda_2 = 1$, $\lambda_n = 0$, for $n \geq 3$; $\mu_n = 1$, for all $n \geq 1$.
(c) $\lambda_n = 1$, for $n = 0, 1, 2$, and $\lambda_n = 0$, for $n \geq 3$; $\mu_1 = 1$, $\mu_2 = 2$, $\mu_3 = 4$.
(d) $\lambda_n = 1$, for $n = 0, 1, 2$, and $\lambda_n = 0$, for $n \geq 3$; $\mu_1 = 4$, $\mu_2 = 2$, $\mu_3 = 1$.

*35 The Nockov and Weldon Machine Shop operates three delicate pieces of equipment, each of which breaks down on the average of once every 2.5 hours. A single repairman is needed to service a broken machine and requires 45 minutes, on the average, to repair the equipment. Assume the machine interference model (*Case iv*) in Sec. 15.7 applies. In each part below, calculate the equilibrium probability that all the machines are in good working order, and the expected number of machines that are inoperative.

(a) The shop employs only one repairman.
(b) The shop employs two repairmen.
(c) Suggest the various costs that you would measure to determine an optimal choice between one and two repairmen. Indicate the appropriate operating characteristics you would calculate to ascertain the expected cost for each alternative, and display a formula for the expected cost.

*36 A company has 10 machines that break down at the rate of once every 2 hours. The average repair time is 30 minutes. The maintenance manager, Titus A. Topp, must decide whether to split the machines into two groups of five each, and assign one-half of the R repairmen available to each group of machines, or to let all R repairmen service all 10 machines. Assume that the machine interference model (*Case iv*) in Sec. 15.7 applies. For each of the two possible configurations, calculate the total expected number of machines in operation and the equilibrium probability that all machines are in good working order. Assume that the shop employs:

(a) Four repairmen.
(b) Six repairmen.
(c) Two repairmen.

Exercises 37 through 41 refer to the birth-and-death model in Sec. 15.7. In each exercise, define the appropriate values for λ_n and μ_n, and exhibit the linear difference equations that yield the equilibrium probabilities. You will find it necessary in a few of these exercises to adapt the logic used to develop the difference equations in Sec. 15.7. in order to accommodate a more complex description of the states of the system.

*37 Consider a single-server model with exponential interarrival times and exponential service. Suppose, however, that there are bulk arrivals, that is, when an arrival *event* occurs, r customers enter the system with probability q_r, $r = 1, 2, \ldots, R$, where R is the largest group that ever enters.

*38 Consider the following single-server system with Poisson input and exponential service. When a customer arrives at the system and sees n persons present, the customer joins the system with probability r_n, and balks with probability $1 - r_n$. Also, when n persons are in the system, the rate of departure due to reneging is g_n (that is, in a relatively small interval of time, $h > 0$, the probability of one customer in line departing *prior* to service is $g_n h$); note $g_0 = g_1 = 0$.

*39 Consider *Case iv* in Sec. 15.7 and suppose $M = R$.
   (a) Check that the formula for P_n in (25) for $0 \leq n \leq R = M$ is appropriate.
   (b) Show how P_n can be written as a *binomial distribution* with parameter p. Exhibit a formula for the mean number of inoperative machines that explicitly indicates the dependence on the failure and service rates.

*40 Consider a two-server model with Poisson input (rate λ) and exponential output, except let the rate for the first server be μ_1 and for the second server be μ_2, where $\mu_1 \neq \mu_2$. (*Suggestion:* when the number of customers n in the system equals 0 or is greater than 2, let the probability P_n have its usual meaning; when the number of customers equals 1, let P_{01} denote the state that the first server is free but the second is busy, and let P_{10} denote the opposite condition.)

*41 A small city has two fire stations, one for the West Side and one for the East Side. The Fire Chief, Roman Kendall, has observed that fires occur with Poisson input at rate λ_W; similarly, on the East Side the rate is λ_E. A fire is combatted by the station in its district, unless the engines in that station are already out fighting a fire; in that case, if at all possible, the call is answered by the other station in the city. Assume exponential service times with rate μ for fighting a fire. Fires that occur when the engines for both stations are busy are referred to a large neighboring community. What is the probability that both fire stations are busy? What are the probabilities that both stations are free and that each of the stations is busy with its own call?

*42 Consider the following single-server preemptive priority system. Two types of customers arrive at the system: Type 1 at the rate λ_1 and Type 2 at the rate λ_2. Type 1 has complete priority over Type 2. Service will be terminated on a Type 2 customer (implying there are no Type 1 customers waiting in the system) when a Type 1 customer arrives; service will then commence immediately on the Type 1 customer. Service on the "bumped" customer resumes after the system no longer contains any Type 1 customers. Service rates for Types 1 and 2 are μ_1 and μ_2, respectively. (*Hint:* let the state of the system be indicated by both the number of Type 1 and the number of Type 2 customers in the system.)

CONTENTS

CHAPTER 16

Computer Simulation of Management Systems

16.1 WHEN ALL ELSE FAILS . . .

If you have patiently proceeded from one chapter to the next, you have studied a perhaps bewildering variety of operations research models and techniques. Students often ask, in effect, "Is this arsenal of tools powerful enough to encompass all the important managerial decision problems requiring data analysis?" The answer is no, not by a long shot. To see why, reflect on the kinds of problems that you know *can* be effectively analyzed by the operations research tools presented thus far. As you become aware of gaps, you will see more clearly why so many significant types of decision-analysis problems are still not solvable by these approaches, and therefore must be attacked in other ways. In the next few paragraphs we summarize the limitations as well as the strengths of operations research tools including linear and dynamic programming, inventory and queuing theory.

You have already learned that linear programming models are most successful in aiding the planning efforts of corporate enterprises. If the planning horizon is 10 years or longer, a corresponding multiperiod linear programming model typically deals only with annualized data. The effects of the resultant plan on week-to-week and month-to-month operations are left implicit. Analogously, if the planning horizon is much shorter, say three months to a year, the corresponding model usually ignores the day-to-day and week-to-week variations. Thus, for the most part, linear programming analysis falls short of prescribing rules that translate a recommended plan into operating procedures for time spans shorter than the periods in the model.

A second limitation of linear programming analysis relates to uncertainty about the future. Imprecise forecasts to some degree exist in all planning studies. Fre-

541

quently, this uncertainty is not really the *essence* of the planning problem, or it reflects a lack of knowledge about only a *few* parameters in the model. In such cases, sensitivity analysis, as discussed in Chap. 5, suffices to determine the impact of uncertainty. But on other occasions uncertainty pervades the entire model, and standard sensitivity analysis is too clumsy and computationally burdensome for analyzing the impact of uncertainty.

To illustrate, consider a chemical manufacturing company that seeks a long-range strategy for the development and marketing of new products. Substantial research and investment costs are associated with each product, and the actual size of the product's market is uncertain. Furthermore, most of the profits that are generated from a successful product will be used to finance the research and development of new products. A linear programming model that manages to capture the dynamic elements of this situation, but treats the uncertainty aspects by simply using average values, is not likely to yield a good strategy.

In contrast, dynamic programming models can analyze multiperiod planning problems containing uncertainty, and so can be used to determine optimal strategies. But, as compared with linear programming applications, these dynamic programming models in practice can treat only drastically simplified systems. Unless the underlying system is characterized by only a few state variables, the computational task of solving a dynamic programming model is horrendous.

A similar limitation holds for those dynamic probabilistic models that are amenable to mathematical analysis, such as the inventory and queuing phenomena in Chaps. 14 and 15. To solve these models, you not only must restrict yourself to a small-scale system, but you also must simplify the way the system can operate. To illustrate, a *realistic* analysis of waiting lines in a job-shop is intractable using mathematical queuing theory like that presented in Chap. 15. Those models serve only as rough approximations to realistic queuing phenomena.

Thus, despite the great diversity of applications of mathematical programming and probabilisitic models, many important managerial decision-making problems must be analyzed by other kinds of techniques.

Challenge remaining. The expanding scientific literature on operations research bears witness that there is steady progress in finding techniques to over-come the above-mentioned limitations. But for now and the foreseeable future, the approaches given in the preceding chapters cannot be relied on to provide a complete analysis of managerial decision-making problems pertaining to:

(i) *Choice of Investment Policies for Strategic Planning.* A major corporation's invest-ment *policy*, to be comprehensive, should include provisions relating to research and development of new products, expansion into new markets, choice of selection criteria for major projects, measurement and evaluation of risk, means of financing by debt and equity, reinvestment of earnings, disposition of liquid assets, evalua-tion of mergers and acquisitions, and divestment of assets. A full-fledged operations research model for the analysis of alternative *policies* must recognize the impact of the uncertain and dynamic nature of investments, as well as provide a means for screening the enormous variety of investment decisions that face an organization.

(ii) *Selection of Facilities in Operations Planning.* Several examples in this category were already discussed in Sec. 15.1. They included the determination of the number of checkout stands in a supermarket, the number of gasoline pumps at a service station, and the number of elevators in a new office building. There are numerous other examples dealing with personnel staffing, plant layout, and machine capacity decisions. Typical facilities selection questions are of the form: "How many?" "How large?" "Where located?"

(iii) *Design of Information-Feedback Scheduling and Operations Rules.* Illustrations of decision problems in this category are equally numerous, although you may not think of them right away, unless you have had some previous work experience. An important example is the design of scheduling rules for a job-shop manufacturing plant, or an equipment repair facility, or a computer center. Such rules for a manufacturing plant take account of promised due dates to customers, the requirements for, and the availabilities of, machine capacities, the deployment of skilled labor, and the provisioning for raw materials. As information on new orders arrives, and as completed orders leave the system, the shop schedule has to be updated and revised.

Another example of an information-feedback system is a scheduling procedure for routing transport facilities. To illustrate, a freighter shipping company in making a schedule of its ocean going equipment for several months ahead, must take into account cargo demands at various ports, ship capacities and speeds, uncertainties in sailing times due to vagaries in the weather and delays due to port congestion. Many shipping lines that own a large fleet of vessels must re-schedule daily as they receive more accurate information about uncertain events. Similar problems arise in the scheduling of patients into a hospital, and the timing of traffic lights on a major thoroughfare.

What makes the three types of problems described above so difficult to analyze? It is the combined effect of uncertainty, the dynamic interactions between decisions and subsequent events, the complex interdependencies among the variables in the system, and, in some instances, the need to use finely divided time intervals. Such total systems problems are too big and too intricate to handle with linear and dynamic programming models, or standard probabilistic models.

Frequently, actual decisions arising from these three types of problems involve spending at least several hundred thousand dollars, and vitally affect the future operating costs and efficiencies of a company. Thus, management is highly motivated to employ a systematic approach to improve on intuitive, or "seat-of-the-pants," analysis. So far, the best operations research approach available is **digital computer simulation.**

Simulation approach. Our main concern in this chapter will be to describe simulation and the kinds of problems you encounter in employing this technique. We do not show you in detail how to design and run simulations. Such instructions are in texts devoted to simulation and in manuals distributed by computer manufacturers to explain special simulation programming languages.

In brief, the simulation approach starts by building an experimental model of a system. Then various specific alternatives are evaluated with reference to how well they fare in test runs of the model.

If you think about it, you will recall occasions when you have been involved in a simulated environment. For example, an amusement park, like Disneyland, offers you many attractions, such as the jungle boat-ride and the Matterhorn bobsled, that try to simulate actual experience. Less frivolous examples are planetarium shows and the environments in a museum of natural history. You may have learned how to drive an automobile in a mock-up mechanism with a steering wheel and gas and brake pedals. And if you have been in the armed services, you will remember that boot camp or basic training consists mainly of simulated exercises.

It is usually too inconvenient and expensive to solve managerial decision problems by environmental analogue simulations, such as the field combat war games that are used in boot camp and basic training. Rather, it is preferable to represent a complex system by a computerized mathematical model. In a computer, the only thing that can be shot is an electronic circuit.

The uncertainties, dynamic interactions, and complex interdependencies are all characterized by formulas stored in the memory of the high-speed digital electronic computer. The system simulation begins at a specified starting state. The combined effects of decisions, and of controllable and uncontrollable events, some of which may be random, cause the system to move to another state at a future instant in time. The evolutionary process continues in this fashion until the end of the horizon. Frequently, the time intervals are finely divided and extend over a fairly long horizon. As a consequence, the simulation experiments involve a vast number of calculations, rapidly performed by the computer. This feature of years of history evolving in a few minutes on a computer is termed **time compression.**

Computer simulation serves a management scientist in the same way that the laboratory experiment helps a physical scientist. Simulation models are designed and run to provide insights to decision-making and selecting appropriate courses of action. Such analysis facilitates a thorough investigation of both the direct and indirect consequences of random variation within a system. Since the model can be run under many different settings for the parameters and the probabilistic elements, the analyst can identify the prime sources of system fluctuations. Frequently, as a result of computer simulation, management can isolate the principal causes of inefficiencies, bottlenecks, or intermittent functioning, and can thereby substantially improve the system's behavior.

Unlike testing a proposed management system's design in real-time with live participants, a computer simulation of a design proposal has the advantages of allowing easy replication, permitting redesign and retest, recording a completely accurate detailed history, and summarizing and analyzing the emergent data rapidly and immediately. Of course, computer simulation can never provide the absolute realism of an actual system's field test. But since most organizations employ field testing on a very restricted basis, they will find it helpful to use computer simulation analysis to suggest the design of a particular system before that system is implemented on a trial basis.

The only game in town. Most operations research analysts look upon digital computer simulation as a "method of last resort"—hence the title of this section, "When All Else Fails . . . ." There are two reasons for this gloomy attitude.

The first reason is the nature of most simulation results. When the model includes uncertain events, the answers stemming from a particular simulation must be viewed only as estimates subject to statistical error. For example, a simulated queuing model yields only an estimate of a waiting line's average length or the associated probability of a delay. Therefore, when you draw conclusions about the relative merit of different specific trial policies as tested by a simulation model, you must be careful to assess the accompanying random variations.

The second reason for diffidence about simulation involves the nature of the applications themselves. If a system is so complicated that it is beyond the reach of such operations research tools as linear and dynamic programming or standard probability analysis, then the required model-building effort and the subsequent analysis of the simulated results are likely to be difficult. Many unwary analysts have found, to their chagrin, that the simulated world is as unfathomable as the real world they hoped to approximate—they allowed so much to go on in the model that it hampered finding any insightful information.

The above two reasons also suggest why electronic computers are indispensable in performing simulations. To obtain sufficient statistical accuracy for reliable decisions, a considerable number of simulation runs are usually necessary. Each experiment is so complicated that it would be virtually impossible to perform the simulation manually in a reasonable period of time. It is not surprising, then, that computer simulation is often an expensive way to study a complex system.

16.2 SIMULATION IN PERSPECTIVE

Deterministic simulation models have aided management decision-making far more often than simulation models containing random phenomena. Managers often refer to such simulations as their **what-if?** models. A common application of deterministic simulation is an annual or multiyear financial projection of a company's income statement, balance sheet, and cash flow. This sort of financial model is predicated on postulated relationships for market growth and share, price and cost inflation, productivity, and taxation. The model permits varying management policy alternatives regarding new product development, investments, plant expansion, R & D, inventories, acquisitions and divestitures, promotion, dividends, and stock flotation or repurchase. The model must specify the detailed financial impact for each of these policy alternatives. By thorough-going sensitivity analysis of such a model, management often can gain beneficial insights as to potential or real problem areas that require careful attention. Management also can test the likelihood of the company's meeting stated profit and growth objectives.

Another type of deterministic simulation relates to manufacturing process analysis. For example, a company may construct a model of the way materials flow through the various stages of manufacturing, where significant product may be lost because of unacceptable quality performance, or where average production lead times may be long because of capacity limitations. Such a model can pinpoint the most critical quality control problems in the manufacturing process, the leverage potential from improved performance, and suggest where additional investment or training might be warranted to relieve production bottlenecks.

A third sort of deterministic simulation model tests the impact of different operating policies. To illustrate, a company may be investigating several possible warehouse location options and may want to forecast the future pattern of throughputs, peak loads, and associated costs. For this purpose, the company may build a model that uses a file of historical data to simulate how each possible option would have operated in the past; then these **retrospective simulations** are corrected for future trends. Such historical simulations can guide management's choice and may even suggest additional options of greater merit.

We do not pursue the topic of deterministic simulation models any further in this chapter. An analyst with sound training in economics and finance can usually construct these models without much difficulty. From this juncture, the chapter focuses on simulations containing random phenomena. The term **risk analysis** is often applied to such probabilistic models, especially when they pertain to financial outcomes.

Unlike the situation with mathematical programming, there are as yet no underlying principles guiding the formulation of simulation models. Each application is *ad hoc* to a large extent. Computer simulation languages come the closest to providing any general guidelines. (We say more about these languages in Sec. 16.6.]

The absence of a unifying theory of digital simulation is both a boon and a bane. On the positive side, you can build a simulation model containing arbitrarily high-order complexities and a huge number of dynamic interdependencies, as well as nonstationarities and correlated random phenomena. On the negative side, the more complicated the model, the more you will have to rely on embryonically developed statistical theory to perform the data analyses. As mentioned above, the very intricacy of the model can make it difficult to assess the model's validity. If the model is very complicated, you may have to expend a great deal of computer time on replication to obtain trustworthy answers and nearly optimal policies. Given the considerable research interest in simulation techniques, however, many of the current deficiencies in the theory and design of simulation experiments are bound to be eliminated in the years ahead.

Objectives. You would construct a simulation model to assist in analyzing managerial decision problems with one or more of the following purposes in mind:

(i) *To Describe a Current System.* Consider a manufacturing firm that recently has witnessed an increase in its customer orders, and has noticed a consequent marked deterioration in meeting due-dates promised to its customers. This company may want to build a simulation model to study how its current procedures for estimating due-dates, scheduling production, and ordering raw material are giving rise to the observed delays.

(ii) *To Explore a Hypothetical System.* Consider a hospital that is contemplating the installation of a new computerized inventory replenishment system for its medical supplies. It may want to build a simulation model using historical data to test what the average level of inventory investment would be, and how often there would be shortages of various supplies under the proposed plan.

(iii) *To Design an Improved System.* Consider a job shop in which machine capacities are allocated by priorities assigned to each job. The company may want to build a simulation model in order to find an effective way to assign such priorities so that the jobs are completed without long delays and, at the same time, so that equipment utilization is acceptably high.

We turn next to the steps in constructing and applying a simulation model.

So you want to build a simulation. The outline to follow describes the way you would go about constructing a simulation:

Step 1. Formulate the Model. This step is much the same as that for other operations research models. There is an ever-present danger, however, of including too much detail in a simulation model and, as a result, consuming excessive amounts of computer time to perform the experiments. The best guard against this tendency is to keep your specific purpose constantly in mind. For example, if a model is to aid in the choice between two different locations for a new warehouse, it is probably not necessary to simulate activities on an hour-to-hour, or even day-to-day basis; weekly aggregates ought to suffice. If, on the other hand, a model is to aid in the choice between one or two loading docks at a new warehouse, then it may be necessary to simulate activities occurring in intervals as small as 5 to 15 minutes.

Step 2. Design the Experiment. You will reduce the chance of making mistakes and wasting time if you work out the details of the experimental procedures before running the model. This means that you need to think out carefully what operating characteristics of the simulated system you plan to measure. Further, you must consider the statistical tools you intend to apply to take account of the experimental fluctuations in the measurements.

Step 3. Develop the Computer Program. The simulation experiments will be performed entirely by a high-speed electronic calculator. That is, each historical evolution of the model, including the generation of random events, will take place within the computer. If the simulated model has a very simple structure, you may find it easiest to use a standard programming language, such as FORTRAN, PL/1, or ALGOL, to develop the computerized version. Alternatively, you may find it preferable to employ one of the several simulation languages, such as SIMSCRIPT, GPSS, GASP, or SIMULA, that are available on many large-scale electronic computers.

When you undertake an actual application, you will find that the above steps are not completely separate and sequential. For example, if you have already become familiar with, say, the GPSS simulation language, then you may wait to formulate the model, initially, in terms of this language. We give more detail on each of these steps in the sections below.

16.3 STOCK MARKET SIMULATION EXAMPLE

An investor, Wynn Doe, wants to evaluate a particular strategy for buying and selling common stocks. To keep the exposition straightforward, suppose he does all of his trading in a single stock. At present, he holds 100 shares of the stock, which currently has a price of $10 a share. Again for the sake of simplicity, assume that the stock price can change each day by only $1, so that some of the possible stock prices are $8, $9, $10, $11, $12, ... The investor makes, at most, one transaction each day, and pays a commission of 2% of the transaction value whenever he buys or sells; of course, he need not make a transaction every day.

Wynn Doe wants to test the profitability of the following rule for buying and selling that has been suggested by his broker Benton Cherning:

(i) If you own the stock, then sell it whenever the price falls.
(ii) If you do not own the stock, then buy it whenever the price rises.

According to this rule, if Wynn Doe owns the stock he will hold on to it while the price stays the same or rises; if he does not own the stock, he will refrain from buying it as long as the price stays the same or falls.

In order to evaluate this strategy, Wynn Doe must also postulate how he believes the stock price will fluctuate from day to day. After analyzing historical data, he formulates the price-movement model shown in Fig. 16.1. To illustrate, if the share prices on Monday and Tuesday are both $10, then he believes that the price on Wednesday will be $11 with probability $\frac{1}{4}$, $10 with probability $\frac{1}{2}$, and $9 with probability $\frac{1}{4}$, as can be seen in the second row of Fig. 16.1. If, instead Tuesday's price is $9, then he believes that the share price on Wednesday will be $10 with probability $\frac{1}{4}$, $9 with probability $\frac{1}{4}$, and $8 with probability $\frac{1}{2}$, as

Today's Stock Price:

Yesterday's Stock Price:	Increases	Stays the Same	Decreases
Increased	$\frac{1}{2}$	$\frac{1}{4}$	$\frac{1}{4}$
Stayed the Same	$\frac{1}{4}$	$\frac{1}{2}$	$\frac{1}{4}$
Decreased	$\frac{1}{4}$	$\frac{1}{4}$	$\frac{1}{2}$

FIGURE 16.1 Stock Price Movement Probabilities.

can be seen in the third row of Fig. 16.1. Notice that as the stock price increases, the investor thinks there is probability $\frac{1}{2}$ that it will increase again, and analogous statements hold if the price share remains the same or decreases.

To begin testing Cherning's rule by **manual simulation** generate a specific history of price movements according to the probabilities given in Fig. 16.1. A simple mechanism for doing this is to toss a pair of unbiased coins, using the correspondences shown in Fig. 16.2. In Fig. 16.2 the assignments of the outcomes of a toss of two unbiased coins yield the postulated probabilities in Fig. 16.1.

Suppose you simulate 20 days of activity, starting on Day 1 and ending on Day 20. Then you must toss the two coins 20 times; a particular sequence of tosses is recorded in Fig. 16.3. To determine the associated sequence of stock prices, you have to specify the initial conditions, namely, the stock price on Day 0 and whether it represents a fluctuation from the preceding day. In Fig. 16.3, the price on Day 0 is $10, which presents no change from the preceding day. Given these initial conditions and a toss having a head and a tail on Day 1, the stock price for Day 1 is $10, according to the second row of Fig. 16.2. Then on Day 2, since yesterday's price remained the same, the toss of two tails implies that the share price falls to $9, again according to the second row of Fig. 16.2. Proceeding to Day 3, since yesterday's price decreased, the toss of two heads causes the share price to be $10, according to the third row of Fig. 16.2.

You can now determine how well Cherning's suggested rule for buying and selling has performed on this particular simulated 20-day history of price movements. The details are shown in Fig. 16.4; the history of prices from Fig. 16.3 has been copied for easy reference. The entries in the column labeled "Decision" are a direct consequence of the price history and the suggested rule. The entries in the last three columns are determined after some auxiliary calculations.

To illustrate, on Day 2, the investor sells his 100 shares at a price $9; but he must pay a 2% commission, which amounts to (.02 × $9 × 100 = $18); thus he receives only $882 (= $900 − $18) from the sale. On Day 3, he repurchases the stock. Once again he must pay a 2% commission, so effectively the stock price is $10.20 a share. Since he has $882 cash, he can purchase only 86 shares, leaving him $4.80 (= $882 − 86 × $10.20) cash. Notice that at the end of the 20th day, the investor's cash position—$931.90—is worse following the rule than it would have been if he had sold his 100 shares on Day 0 and thereby received $980 cash, after paying the commission.

Given all the model's assumptions, is Cherning's rule profitable? Probably your

Day	Coin Toss	Yesterday's Price Movement	Today's Stock Price
0	– –	– –	10*
1	H/T	Same*	10
2	2T	Same	9
3	2H	Decreased	10
4	2H	Increased	10
5	2H	Same	.11
6	H/T	Increased	12
7	2H	Increased	12
8	2T	Same	11
9	2H	Decreased	12
10	H/T	Increased	13
11	2T	Increased	12
12	H/T	Decreased	11
13	2T	Decreased	11
14	2H	Same	12
15	H/T	Increased	13
16	H/T	Increased	14
17	2T	Increased	13
18	H/T	Decreased	12
19	H/T	Decreased	11
20	2T	Decreased	11

Legend: H/T ≈ A Head and A Tail
2H ≈ Two Heads
2T ≈ Two Tails

*Initial Conditions

FIGURE 16.3. Simulated Price Movements.

Today's Stock Price:

Yesterday's Stock Price:	Increases	Stays the Same	Decreases
Increased	A Head and A Tail	Two Heads	Two Tails
Stayed the Same	Two Heads	A Head and A Tail	Two Tails
Decreased	Two Heads	Two Tails	A Head and A Tail

FIGURE 16.2. Price Movements Generated by Tosses of a Pair of Unbiased Coins.

immediate reaction is, "No." But wait a minute. Suppose instead of arbitrarily selecting 20 days as the length of the simulation, you had picked either 6 or 16 days instead. What would your answer have been then? Or suppose you rerun the simulation with a new history of 20 tosses. Will the rule still look poor at termination? The issue of whether the rule is any good really depends in part on the statistical variability in the result obtained on Day 20, and on the significance of looking at a horizon of 20 versus 200, versus 2000, versus any other number of simulated days.

As you think further about the model, you will realize that the evaluation issue is complicated by the fact that as the horizon lengthens, there is an increase in the possible range of variability in the investor's wealth position at the end of the horizon. Further, even *if* the rule implies an upward drift in the expected wealth

Day	Stock Price	Decision	Shares Held	Value of Stock	Cash
0	10		100	1000	
1	10		100	1000	
2	9	Sell	0	0	882.00
3	10	Buy	86	860	4.80
4	10		86	860	4.80
5	11		86	946	4.80
6	12		86	1032	4.80
7	12		86	1032	4.80
8	11	Sell	0	0	931.88
9	12	Buy	76	912	1.64
10	13		76	988	1.64
11	12	Sell	0	0	895.40
12	11		0	0	895.40
13	11		0	0	895.40
14	12	Buy	73	876	1.88
15	13		73	949	1.88
16	14		73	1022	1.88
17	13	Sell	0	0	931.90
18	12		0	0	931.90
19	11		0	0	931.90
20	11		0	0	931.90

FIGURE 16.4. Twenty-Day Test of Wynn Doe's Trading Rule.

position as the horizon lengthens, there is at least an initial increase in the probability that the investor may go broke along the way.

So as you can see, even this simple-minded simulation gives rise to some difficult questions concerning what to measure and how to design a scientific experiment to test the effectiveness of the rule. What is more, if you take the trouble to run the model by hand for another 20 periods, you will quickly appreciate the desirability of letting an electronic computer do all the coin tossing and arithmetic.

16.4 BUILDING A SIMULATION MODEL

We now return to a more general discussion of the steps involved in using computer simulation. In this section we examine three aspects of model building: specifying the model's components; testing its validity and reliability; determining its parameters and measuring its performance.

Model components. The structure of most simulation models is conveniently described in terms of its **dynamic phenomena** and its **entities.** The dynamic phenomena in the stock market simulation of the preceding section include the investor's activity of buying or selling the stock, according to the stated **decision rule,** and the factors governing the movement of stock prices. The entities on any day include the amount of stock the investor holds, his cash position, and wealth. Typically, the entities in a model have **attributes.** To illustrate, the amount of stock the investor holds has a monetary value, given the associated price of the stock. Further, there are **membership relationships** providing connections between the entities. For example, the investor's wealth on any day includes both his cash and stock positions.

At any instant of a simulation, the model is in a particular **state.** The description of the state not only embodies the current status of the entities but frequently includes some historical information. For example, the state of the system at the beginning of a day in the stock market simulation is described by yesterday's price, how yesterday's price differed from the price on the day before, the number of shares held, and the cash position.

A model also can encompass **exogenous events,** that is changes that are not brought about by the previous history of the simulation. To illustrate, the investor in the stock market simulation may have decided to add $1000 more cash from his savings on Day 21, regardless of how well he has done using the tested strategy.

Knowing the state of the system and the dynamic phenomena, you can then go on to determine the subsequent activities and states. Frequently, simulation models having this evolutionary structure are called **recursive** or **causal.**

Note that in building a causal model, you must resolve the way activities occur *within* a period. For example, on each day of the stock market simulation, first the price is determined, then the decision to buy or sell is exercised. Actually, the price of a stock may change several times during a day, so the model we constructed is only a rough approximation to reality. The model also assumes that if the investor sells the stock, he receives the cash at the end of the day; and analogously, if he purchases the stock, he pays the cash at the end of the day. Such financial transactions do not occur so rapidly in practice.

Model validity and reliability. After building a simulation model, you are bound to be asked, "How realistic is it?" The more pertinent question is, "Does the model yield valid insights and reliable conclusions?" After all, since the model can only approximate reality, it must be evaluated by its power to analyze the particular managerial decisions you are studying.

Once the purpose of the simulation experiment is defined, you construct each piece of the model with a commensurate amount of detail and accuracy. A caveat is in order here. As simulation experts can attest: it is easy for a novice to build a model that, component by component, resembles reality; yet when the pieces are hooked together, the model may not behave like reality. So do not assume blindly that the entire simulated system is sufficiently accurate, merely because each of the component parts seems adequate when considered in isolation. This warning is especially important, because usually the objective of a simulation model is to fathom the behavior of a total system, and not that of the separate parts.

Model parameters and performance measures. It is one thing to describe the pieces of a simulation model abstractly, and it is another to collect sufficient data for a trustworthy representation of these pieces. Limited availability of data may very well influence the way you build a simulation.

You must be particularly cautious when you are dealing with extrapolated data and nonstationary performance measures. (Remember the story of the cracker barrel manufacturer who, not so very long ago, forecasted that he would be selling millions of barrels today. He assumed, unquestioningly, that his sales trend would continue as it had in the past.)

You also must watch out for cyclical or periodic phenomena. When these are present, you must be judicious in selecting the variables to measure in the experiments. If you look only at "ending values," for example, then your conclusions may be very sensitive to the exact length of the horizon that you simulated.

16.5 HOW TO MARK TIME

A dynamic systems simulation model can be structured in different ways. One approach, which is the more obvious, views simulated time as elapsing period by period. The computer routine performs all the transactions occurring in Period t, and then proceeds to Period t + 1. If the events in Period t imply that certain other transactions are to occur in future periods, then the computer stores this information in memory, and recovers it when the future periods arrive. You already saw a simplified illustration of this approach using **fixed-time increments** in the stock market simulation of Sec. 16.4. A more informative example is given below.

In some simulations, the periods have to be relatively short. But there may be many of these periods in which no transactions occur. For such models, there is another approach that lets the simulation advance by **variable-time increments.** This idea is illustrated in the second example below.

Time-step incrementation—inventory model. Suppose that you wish to evaluate the operating characteristics of a proposed inventory replenishment rule. Assume that you can specify the probability distribution for each day's demand, and that daily demand is identically and independently distributed. If demand exceeds the amount of inventory on hand, the excess represents lost sales. Let us postulate that, during a daily time period of the simulation model, the sequence of events is: first, any replenishment order due in arrives; then demand occurs; and finally, the inventory position is reviewed, and a reorder is placed if the replenishment rule indicates it should be. An order placed at the end of Period t arrives at the start of Period t + L, where L is fixed and $L \geq 1$.

To keep the exposition simple, assume that the replenishment rule is to order Q units whenever the amount of inventory on hand plus inventory due in is less than or equal to s, where $Q > s$. The inequality $Q > s$ implies there is never more than one replenishment order outstanding.

A simulation model of this inventory system is easily constructed by stepping time forward in the fixed increment of a day, beginning with Day 1 ($t = 1$).

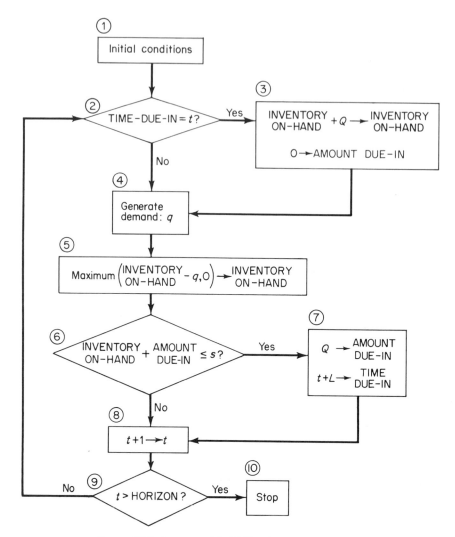

FIGURE 16.5. Inventory Model Simulation Flow Chart.

To start the simulation, you must specify the initial conditions of the level of inventory on hand, the amount due in, and the associated time due in. You must also designate the number of periods that the simulation is to run; let the symbol "HORIZON" denote this value.

A flow chart of the simulation is shown in Fig. 16.5. The initializing is done in Block 1. For example, you can let the amount INVENTORY ON-HAND $= Q$, the AMOUNT DUE-IN $= 0$, the TIME DUE-IN $= 0$, and $t = 1$. When Block 2 is reached, the answer is "No," and you proceed at Block 4 to generate a random value of demand q for Day 1.

At the end of Day 1, INVENTORY ON-HAND is diminished by q, unless q

exceeds the amount available, in which case the amount of INVENTORY ON-HAND becomes 0. This calculation is performed at Block 5.

At Block 6, a test is made to determine whether a replenishment order is to be placed. If so, the AMOUNT DUE-IN becomes Q, and the TIME DUE-IN becomes $1 + L$ (since at the start $t = 1$), as indicated in Block 7. If a replenishment order is not placed, you continue directly to Block 8, where the time step is incremented by 1; that is, the simulation clock is advanced to Day 2.

If Day 2 goes beyond the HORIZON you specified, the simulation terminates. Assuming that you set the HORIZON > 2, the simulation returns from Block 9 to Block 2.

At some day, TIME DUE-IN will equal t, and then the simulation branches from Block 2 to Block 3, where the amount of INVENTORY ON-HAND is augmented by Q, and the AMOUNT DUE-IN is reset to 0.

The flow chart does not indicate where you would collect statistical data on the operating characteristics of the system. In programming the model, you would keep a tally at Block 5 of the level of INVENTORY ON-HAND at the end of a day, as well as of the amount of lost sales and the number of days when a stockout occurs. You would tabulate at Block 7 the number of days an order was placed. Then, before terminating the simulation at Block 10, you would summarize these tallies into frequency distributions, along with their means, standard deviations, and other statistical quantities of interest.

Suppose the item is a "slow mover," that is, there is a high probability that demand $q = 0$ on any day. Then the time-step method may be inefficient, because there will be many consecutive days when the computations in Blocks 2, 5, and 6 will be identical. Such redundancies can be eliminated by using the technique illustrated below on a queuing example.

Event-step incrementation—waiting line model. Suppose that you want to examine the operating characteristics of the following queuing system, which is simple to describe but proves difficult to analyze mathematically. Customers arrive at the system according to a specified probability distribution for interarrival times. The system has two clerks, A and B. When both servers are busy, arriving customers wait in a single line and are processed by a first come, first served discipline. The service times for each clerk can be viewed as independent draws from a specified probability distribution; but each clerk has a different service time distribution. Neither the interarrival nor the service time distributions are exponential.

After thinking about the way this system evolves over time, you will discover that the dynamics can be characterized by three types of events: a customer's arrival, a customer's service begins, and a customer's service ends. Each event gives rise to a subroutine in the computerized version of the system.

A simulation model using variable-time increments also contains a **master program** having an **event list,** which is repeatedly updated as the master program switches from one **event subroutine** to another. At the start of a simulation run, the event list is usually empty; but at a later instant in the run,

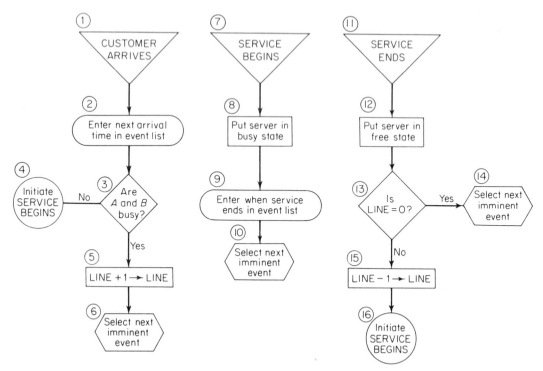

FIGURE 16.6. Waiting Line Model Chart of Events.

it indicates when some of the future events are to occur. The role this event list plays will be clearer as you examine the event flow charts in Fig. 16.6.

Assume that you specify the initial conditions of the simulation as: a customer arrives, say, at Time 0, there are no customers in line, and both the clerks are free. The master program starts with the event subroutine CUSTOMER AR-RIVES, shown as Block 1 in Fig. 16.6. The computer selects a random inter-arrival time at Block 2. The information that this next arrival event occurs at the implied future time is entered into the event list. A determination of whether both clerks are busy is made in Block 3. Since the answer is "No" at the start, the master program switches to the event subroutine SERVICE BEGINS, as indi-cated in Block 4. To keep the flow diagram uncluttered, we have suppressed the details that would specify that the computer must keep track of which clerk serves the customer, an item of information that is needed when the master program switches to the subroutine SERVICE BEGINS in Block 7.

The first instruction in SERVICE BEGINS is at Block 8, which records that the selected clerk is now busy. Then the service time of the customer is determined in Block 9, using the appropriate service time probability distribution for the selected clerk. The information that a service-ends event occurs at the implied future time is entered into the event list. The subroutine then transfers back to the master program with the instruction in Block 10 to find the **next imminent**

event in the event list. So far, this can be either the arrival of the next customer or the completion of service of the first customer. Suppose it is the latter, so that the master program switches to the subroutine SERVICE ENDS in Block 11.

The first instruction in SERVICE ENDS is at Block 12, which records that the server is now free again. Then a test is made at Block 13 to see whether the waiting line designated by the symbol "LINE" is empty. The answer is "Yes." When control switches back in Block 14 to the master program, the next imminent event will be the arrival of the second customer.

Later in the run, the LINE will contain customers, and then the answer is "No" at Block 13. As a result, the length of the LINE is decreased by 1 in Block 15, and control transfers in Block 16 to the subroutine SERVICE BEGINS.

A simulation run progresses as each event subroutine either switches to another event subroutine or instructs the master program to increment time to the next imminent event. As you can imagine, considerable skill is required to write a simulation program that uses event-step incrementation. In particular, expertise is needed to program the updating of the event list efficiently as future events are generated by the subroutines. Many simulation languages of the type discussed in Sec. 16.6 already include a master program that maintains an updated list of events; to employ these languages, you only have to specify the separate event subroutines.

We have glossed over a number of details in describing the queuing simulation model. We briefly mention a few of these before going on to the next section. First, note that the charts in Fig. 16.6 do not show a test for terminating a simulation run. Of course, you must include such a calculation; you might state it by means of a time horizon or limit on the number of customers arriving. Second, observe that tabulating statistics on the operating characteristics is not an easy process because of the variable-time increments between successive events. Care must be taken to measure, for example, not only the frequency with which the waiting line has n customers, but also the associated fraction of the simulated horizon. Finally, recall that the initial conditions were chosen arbitrarily. If the queuing system in fact tends to be congested, then the effect of letting LINE $= 0$ at the start will take a while to wear off. Specifying appropriate initial conditions is part of the tactics of designing a simulation experiment.

The flow chart, Fig. 16.6, illustrates the **event scheduling approach** to simulation models in which time is incremented at the occurrence of events. Other variants have been developed, the most notable being the **process interaction approach.** In this latter method, the simulation model identifies the sequence of operations that must occur for each item or object that flows through the system. For the queuing illustration, the model would be described in terms of what happens when a customer arrives and is processed through the system.

16.6 COMPUTER LANGUAGES

Unless you become both an operations research specialist and a computer programmer, you personally will not have to translate your simulation model into a workable computer program. You should, however, know the major steps involved in this translation.

If your model is fairly simple and is a common application of simulation, then a so-called **canned program** may be available in which all you need do is specify a modest amount of input information. The best examples of this type of program are inventory control simulators. There are a number of canned programs that test the effectiveness of inventory replenishment rules. To employ these routines, you must supply the specific rules, such as "when down to 4, order 10 more," or a formula to calculate the rules, given demand data. You also supply as part of the input either actual historical data on customer demand or a probability distribution for demand. The computer program then simulates the system for whatever number of time periods you designate, and calculates statistics such as the frequency of stockouts, the average inventory level, the number of orders placed, etc.

More typically, your model will require some special computer programming. If the simulation is only moderately complex, is to be used infrequently, and is to be programmed by personnel inexperienced in simulation techniques, then using a general purpose language, such as FORTRAN, PL/1, or ALGOL, is probably the easiest way to accomplish the task. This type of computer language is familiar to all programmers of scientific problems; a programmer requires only the details of your model to translate it into computer language.

There is an important drawback to employing languages like FORTRAN, PL/1, and ALGOL. The programmer has to write, from scratch, subroutines for certain kinds of calculations that are included in almost all simulations. In the vernacular, the programmer has to "reinvent the wheel." For example, since you want to collect statistics on the system's operating characteristics, subroutines have to be written to calculate these statistics, and a fair-sized associated programming effort must be accomplished to format the output of the simulation runs. Even a moderately complex model requires careful attention in organizing the data within the computer memory, writing a master routine for sequencing events in their proper order, and keeping track of simulated time within the computer.

Several computer languages have been developed for the specific purpose of easing the programming task of building a simulation model. These programs require that you specify only the probability distribution functions, and they automatically generate random events according to the distributions you indicate. Several of the languages collect statistics on whatever operating characteristics you want to examine, and report the results on predesigned output forms. These languages also properly sequence events and keep track of time as it elapses in the model.

With such advantages, you may wonder why all simulations are not programmed in one of these languages. At present, there are several good reasons. One is that the languages differ to some extent from FORTRAN, PL/1, or ALGOL, and hence require a programmer to become familiar with a new system.

One of the most powerful simulation languages is SIMSCRIPT; it requires a knowledge of FORTRAN and is fairly complex because of its considerable flexibility. It uses the event scheduling approach described in the previous section. GASP also is based on FORTRAN and uses event scheduling. Another powerful language is SIMULA, which relies on ALGOL and employs the process interaction approach to simulation modeling. At the other extreme of complexity is the General Purpose Systems Simulator (GPSS). It is a self-contained language that is easy to learn by beginners, but, accordingly, is restricted in its scope.

A second reason for not employing a simulation language is that it may not be available on the computer you want to use. This is rarely the determining factor today because SIMSCRIPT and GPSS programs are available for many computers, and there is widespread access to computer service bureaus that have these programs.

A third reason becomes important if the simulation is complex and is to be run frequently. A price you pay in using a simulation language is that if often runs slowly and consumes large amounts of a computer's high-speed memory. As a result, you may find it costly to perform many experiments, and your model may literally not fit into the available memory capacity of the computer.

As further technical improvements in simulation languages continue, and as management scientists gain more experience in employing computer simulation, it seems likely that such languages will be the common mode of solution.

*16.7 design of simulation experiments†

After constructing a simulation model, you face the difficult task of designing a set of runs of the model and analyzing data that emanate from these runs. For example, you must decide the

- Starting conditions of the model.
- Parameter settings to expose different system responses.
- Length of each run (the number of simulated time periods and the amount of elapsed computer time).
- Number of runs with the same parameter settings.
- Variables to measure and how to measure them.

If you are not careful, you can expend an enormous amount of computer time in validating the model to see whether it behaves like a real system, in estimating the system responses of the model to different parameter settings, and in discovering the response relationships among these parameters. Even then, and even after collecting a vast amount of data, you still may not have sufficiently accurate information to guide a managerial decision.

Surprising as it may seem, there has been relatively little development of statistical techniques aimed at constructing efficient designs of simulation experiments. By and large, professional management scientists have tried to "make do" with standard statistical tools to analyze experimental data from simulations.

†This section requires a knowledge of statistical methods.

These techniques at best are only moderately successful, because most of them are not constructed for the analysis of multidimensional time series data. In particular, many (but not all) of the commonly used statistical tools assume that separate observations of the variables being measured are uncorrelated and drawn from a Normal distribution with the same parameters.

We cannot possibly summarize all of the standard statistical techniques that can be applied to analyze simulation data. Instead, we discuss certain design procedures that enable you to employ many techniques ordinarily found in a modern text on experimental statistics. We also give a brief overview of some statistical approaches that are particularly well suited to the design of computer simulations.

In search of Normality. Suppose you have constructed a queuing model to test two different service disciplines. For example, your application may be a model of a job-shop production system, and the two disciplines for processing orders are "first come, first served" and a particular priority scheme. Assume further that the difference in the two disciplines is to be measured solely in terms of the average waiting time (exclusive of service) for orders. How might you ascertain what this difference is?

This question is more difficult than it may appear at first glance. Since your measurements will be random variables, you must consider their statistical variability and be on the watch for certain kinds of complications. In any single simulation run, the waiting times of successive orders will be **serially correlated** (sometimes called **autocorrelated**); that is, there is a greater likelihood that the $(n + 1)$st order will wait if the nth order waits, than if the nth order commences service immediately. The extent of variation in waiting times may itself be affected by the two different disciplines. The model may be unstable and the trend of waiting times may be ever upward. Even if the system does approach equilibrium, which may require a considerably long run, waiting times need not be Normally distributed. To ignore all these considerations and simply compare the average waiting times from a simulated run of each discipline is to court disaster.

Suppose you can demonstrate, on theoretical grounds, that the queuing model is stable, and that the effects of the starting conditions eventually fade away. Then it can be proved that even though the waiting times of successive orders are autocorrelated, the expected value of the sample average of these waiting times, taken over a sufficiently long run, is approximately that implied by the equilibrium distribution.

More precisely, let x_t, for $t = 1, 2, \ldots, q$, represent q successive data observations of the random variable in a given simulation run, and define the **time-integrated average** as

$$(1) \qquad \qquad \bar{x} = \sum_{t=1}^{q} \frac{x_t}{q}.$$

Let μ represent the so-called **ensemble mean** of this random variable, as calculated from the *equilibrium* distribution. Then for q sufficiently large, we have the approximation

$$(2) \qquad\qquad E[\bar{x}] \approx \mu.$$

Furthermore, it can be shown that the sampling distribution of $\bar{x}$ is approximately Normal. You can calculate an estimate of the variance of this distribution as follows. Assuming that the process is **covariance-stationary** (the covariance between x_t and x_{t+k} depends only on k and not on t), and that the associated autocorrelations tend to 0 as k grows large, you first estimate these autocorrelations by:

$$(3) \qquad r_k = \frac{1}{q-k} \sum_{t=1}^{q-k} (x_t - \bar{x})(x_{t+k} - \bar{x}) \quad \text{for } k = 0, 1, 2, \ldots, M-1,$$

where M is chosen to be much smaller than q. (Unfortunately, a discussion of how much smaller M should be is too complicated to be given here, but can be found in the statistics literature under the subject title **autocorrelation** and **spectral analysis.**) The appropriate *estimate* of the variance of $\bar{x}$ is

$$(4) \qquad\qquad V_{\bar{x}} = \frac{1}{q}\left[r_0 + 2 \sum_{k=1}^{M-1} \left(1 - \frac{k}{M}\right) r_k \right].$$

If, in fact, the time series is known to be free of autocorrelation, then the terms r_k, for $k = 1, 2, \ldots, M$, would be eliminated from (4). The presence of positive autocorrelation, however, implies greater statistical variability in $\bar{x}$ as compared with the case of uncorrelated observations.

We now can look at two commonly employed approaches to statistical analyses. For the first method, consider making one very long run of each service discipline; specifically, take T consecutive observations in each run. Then you can apply (1) through (4) with $q = T$. If T is sufficiently large, the statistic $(\bar{x} - \mu)/\sqrt{V_{\bar{x}}}$ is approximately Normally distributed with mean 0 and variance 1. This fact allows you to perform standard statistical procedures for hypothesis testing and constructing confidence intervals for μ, as well as to use modern Bayesian analysis. To compare the effect of the two service disciplines on average waiting time, you can apply standard statistical theory for discerning the difference between the means of two Normally distributed variables that have possibly unequal and estimated variances.

For the second method, consider making n independent replications, that is, n different runs. Suppose you want to have T observations *in toto* from the n replications and that you take T/n observations from each run (assume T/n is an integer). Then for each replication p, calculate a time-integrated average $\bar{x}_p$, for $p = 1, 2, \ldots, n$, using (1) with $q = T/n$. Afterwards compute the grand average

(5)
$$\bar{\bar{x}} = \sum_{p=1}^{n} \frac{\bar{x}_p}{n}.$$

For any T/n, if n is large enough, the sampling distribution of $\bar{\bar{x}}$ is approximately Normal due to the *Central Limit Theorem* for the mean of independently and identically distributed random variables (namely, the $\bar{x}_p$). If you let T/n be large enough, the approximation is improved because of the near-Normality of the sampling distribution for *each* $\bar{x}_p$. What is more, it follows from (2) that when T is sufficiently large,

(6)
$$E[\bar{\bar{x}}] \approx \mu.$$

To determine the accuracy of $\bar{\bar{x}}$, you can *estimate* the variance of the sampling distribution of $\bar{\bar{x}}$ from the variation in $\bar{x}_p$, using

(7)
$$V_{\bar{\bar{x}}} = \frac{1}{n} \left[\frac{\sum_{p=1}^{n} (\bar{x}_p - \bar{\bar{x}})^2}{n-1} \right].$$

Once again, if n and T are large, the quantity $(\bar{\bar{x}} - \mu)/\sqrt{V_{\bar{\bar{x}}}}$ is approximately Normally distributed with mean 0 and variance 1, and so the same sorts of statistical analysis can be performed as in the one-long-replication procedure.

Although the preceding discussion has related to a comparison of two different service displines in a job-shop model, these statistical approaches are generally applicable. In summary, assuming that the simulated system does approach an equilibrium, then under widely applicable conditions, you can legitimately average the successive observations of a simulated time series. As the number of observations grows large, this time-integrated average, in a probabilistic sense, converges to the desired ensemble mean implied by the equilibrium distribution. (You can find the subject of probabilistic convergence treated in detail in texts on stochastic processes under the heading of **ergodic theorems**.) And furthermore, under widely applicable conditions, the time-integrated average is approximately Normally distributed. (The topic of Normal approximations is treated in advanced statistics texts under the heading of the Central Limit Theorem for correlated random variables.)

Therefore, in many situations you can apply Normal-distribution theory if you either replicate simulation runs and then take a grand average of the individual time-integrated averages, or if you take a single time-integrated average from a very long run. A comparison of the relative merits of these two approaches as well as of other methods goes beyond the scope of this text. (The issues involved concern the amount of bias introduced by the starting conditions of the simulation and the stability properties of $V_{\bar{\bar{x}}}$.) Usually, the single-long-run approach is the better procedure.

Sample size. Assume that you take a sufficient number of replications or let the simulation run long enough to justify using the Normal distribution to approximate the sampling distribution of the calculated averages. You still may need even more replications or a longer run to obtain the accuracy you require for decision analysis. The determination of an appropriate sample size for a simulation is no different from sample-size determination in ordinary statistical problems. Therefore, you can find the question discussed in detail in every text on statistical analysis.

We do emphasize, however, the influence of the number of observations on the accuracy of the statistical estimates. Whether you use the single-long-run approach, depicted in (1) through (4), with $q = T$, or the n-replication approach, depicted in (5) through (7), with $q = T/n$, the true variance of the sampling distribution for the calculated mean is inversely proportional to the total number of observations T. Therefore, to reduce the standard deviation of the sampling distribution of either $\bar{x}$ or $\bar{\bar{x}}$ from a value of s, say, to $(.1)s$, you must increase the total number of observations to $100\,T$. More generally, to reduce the standard deviation by a factor of $1/f$, you have to take f^2 as many observations.

Usually, you cannot know how many observations to take at the start of a simulation, because you do not know the factors that multiply $1/T$ in the expressions for the true variances of the sampling distributions of $\bar{x}$ and $\bar{\bar{x}}$. For this reason, a commonly used procedure is to sample in two stages. In the first stage, you take a relatively small number of observations, and thereby calculate an estimate of the factor that multiplies $1/T$. With this estimate, you determine the remaining number of observations to take in the second stage to give the required accuracy.

In actual applications, you may be surprised to find how many observations are needed to yield reasonable accuracy in the estimates. As pointed out above, the root of the difficulty is often the presence of positive autocorrelation. We discuss below a few approaches for coping with inherently large variation in the statistical estimates.

*Variance-reduction techniques. There are a number of ways to improve the accuracy of the estimate of the ensemble average for a given number of data observations. These techniques are explained in texts on simulation under the heading of **Monte Carlo** or **variance-reduction methods.** Their use in management-oriented simulations is not yet widespread, but is growing rapidly. We give only a couple of illustrations to suggest what is involved.

To assist in the exposition, we return to the example above of simulating a job-shop production system. Suppose, for the sake of definiteness, that you are simulating under the "first come, first served" discipline, and that you want to estimate the average waiting time of an order.

The first device we examine is sometimes called the **Method of Control Variates,** or alternatively, the **Method of Concomitant Information.** We present a highly simplified example of the idea. By elementary considerations you know that the interarrival times and the waiting times of each order are negatively correlated—roughly put, the longer the time since the previous order arrived, the shorter the waiting time of the latest order. Therefore, suppose in a particular simulation run that the observed average of interarrival times is greater than the true average. Then you can use this information to add a positive correction to the observed average value of the waiting times. Similarly, suppose the observed average of interarrival times is smaller than the true average. Then you can make a negative correction to the observed average value of the waiting times. The technique explained below calculates either a positive or negative correction, whichever is appropriate.

Specifically, from the input data for the simulation you have the value of the true mean interarrival time, say, $1/\lambda$. Then let x_t represent the waiting time of Order t, and y_t the interarrival time between Orders $t - 1$ and t. Consider the measurement

$$(8) \qquad\qquad z_t \equiv x_t + y_t - \frac{1}{\lambda},$$

and its time-integrated average

$$(9) \qquad \bar{z} = \frac{\displaystyle\sum_{t=1}^{T} z_t}{T} = \frac{\displaystyle\sum_{t=1}^{T}\left(x_t + y_t - \frac{1}{\lambda}\right)}{T} \equiv \bar{x} + \bar{y} - \frac{1}{\lambda}.$$

Note that the expectation of $\bar{z}$ is the same as that of $\bar{x}$, since $\bar{y}$ is an unbiased estimator of $1/\lambda$. So you can use $\bar{z}$ as a consistent estimate of the average waiting time. But if x_t and y_t are sufficiently negatively correlated, then the variance of $\bar{z}$ will be less than the variance of $\bar{x}$. A sample estimate of the variance of $\bar{z}$ can be calculated by assessing the variation in $\bar{z}$ from several replications, or by substituting z_t for x_t in (1), (3), and (4) above.

A more sophisticated method than (8) is to calculate $z_t \equiv x_t + a(y_t - 1/\lambda)$, where now the value of a is specifically chosen to make the variance of $\bar{z}$ small. Under ideal conditions, a can be set such that Var $(\bar{z}) = $ Var $(\bar{x})(1 - \rho^2)$, where ρ is the correlation between $\bar{x}$ and $\bar{y}$.

Before going on, we caution that the preceding example is meant only to be illustrative of the control variate idea. If you actually apply the technique to a queuing model like a job-shop production system, you should select a control variate that would absorb more of the sampling variation than would be accounted for by the interarrival times of orders. In fact, you probably should use several control variates instead of only one.

The second variance-reducing device we examine is called the **Method of Antithetic Variates.** The aim here is to introduce negative correlation between two separate replications of the simulation, so that the variance of the combined averages is less than if the replications were independent. (The idea can also be extended to more than two replications.)

Suppose that in the job-shop production simulation that the random interarrival times equal $(-\log_e u)/\lambda$, where u is a random variable uniformly distributed over the interval $[0, 1]$. (As we explain in the next section, this implies that interarrival times are exponentially distributed with mean $1/\lambda$.) Let u_t, for $t = 1, 2, \ldots, T/2$, be the corresponding uniform random numbers for generating the interarrival times in the first simulation run of the model. Then in the second simulation, by using the values $1 - u_t$, which are also uniform random numbers, the two time-integrated sample averages will be negatively correlated (-0.645).

Notice that the two simulations involve a total of T observations. Whether the mean of the two separate negatively correlated averages has less statistical variation than does the average of T autocorrelated observations from a single run depends on the extent to which the antithetic variates induce negative correlation. Thus, the answer depends on the particular model being simulated, and the specific values of the model's parameters.

The crucial factor in deciding when to use variance-reduction techniques is whether, in fact, a given approach diminishes the variance of the estimates, and if so, whether the reduction is sufficient to warrant the extra computations required.

*Multivariate analysis. The discussion so far has been partly misleading in that we have discussed examples involving the measurement of only a single operating characteristic for a system, such as average waiting time, and the comparison of only two alternatives, such as two different service disciplines. In real applications of simulation models, there are usually several operating characteristics of relevance and a multitude of alternatives to evaluate.

Multivariate analysis is by no means a new subject in statistics literature, but techniques for the analysis and design of experiments involving multivariate time series are just emerging. The reason for this relatively late development is that only recently has the availability of electronic computers made it practical to perform such data analyses.

By employing the approaches previously described to yield measurements that are Normally distributed, you have at least partially opened the storehouse of standard multivariate statistics. But still it is no simple matter to design a simulation experiment that can legitimately apply, say, latin squares, factor analysis, or multivariate regression.

Progress in devising helpful tools for multivariate analysis and complex experimentation is being made on two fronts. One important development, known as *spectral analysis*, aims at exploring the nature of serial correlation and periodicities in time series. The other front seeks methods for finding optimal levels of the decision variables; two such developments are *response surface* and *stochastic approximation techniques*. You can find these developments explained in the technical statistics literature and recent texts on simulation.

*16.8 GENERATING RANDOM PHENOMENA

Frequently, stochastic simulations require thousands, and sometimes hundreds of thousands, of draws from the probability distributions contained in the model. How an electronic computer makes these draws is the subject of this section.

Uniform random numbers. The basic building block for simulating complex random phenomena is the generation of random digits. The following experimental situation is an illuminating description of what we mean by generating a sequence of *uniform random numbers.*

Suppose you take ten squares of paper, number them 0, 1, 2, . . . , 9, and place them in a hat. Shake the hat and thoroughly mix the slips of paper. Without looking, select a slip; then record the number that is on it. Replace the square and, over and over, repeat this procedure. The resultant record of digits is a particular realized sequence of uniform random numbers. Assuming the squares of paper do not become creased or frayed, and that you thoroughly mix the slips before every draw, the nth digit of the sequence has an equal, or uniform, chance of being any of the digits 0, 1, 2, . . . , 9, irrespective of all the preceding digits in the recorded sequence.

In a simulation, you typically use random numbers that are between 0 and 1. So, for example, if you need such numbers with four decimal places, then you can take four at a time from the recorded sequence of random digits, and place a decimal point in front of each group of four. To illustrate, if the sequence of digits is 3, 5, 8, 0, 8, 3, 4, 2, 9, 2, 6, 1, . . . , then the four-decimal-place random numbers are .3580, .8342, .9261, ... In the remainder of this section we use the term "uniform random decimal numbers" to denote random numbers that are uniformly distributed between 0 and 1.

Suppose you have to devise a way for making available inside a computer a sequence of several hundred thousand random numbers. You would probably first suggest this idea: perform something like the "slips-in-a-hat experiment" described above, and then store the recorded sequence in the computer's memory. This is a good suggestion, and it is sometimes employed. The RAND Corporation, using specially designed electronic equipment to perform the experiment, actually did generate a table of a million random digits. The table can be obtained on magnetic tape, so that blocks of the numbers can be read into the high-speed memory of a computer as they are needed. Several years ago, this tabular approach looked disadvantageous, because considerable computer time was expended in the delays of reading numbers into memory from a tape drive. But with recent advances in computer technology and programming skill, these delays have been virtually eliminated.

Experts in computer science have devised mathematical processes for generating digits that yield sequences satisfying many of the statistical properties of a truly random process. To illustrate, if you examine a long sequence of digits produced by these deterministic formulas, each digit will occur with nearly the same frequency, odd numbers will be followed by even numbers about as often as by odd numbers, different pairs of numbers occur with nearly the same frequency, etc. Since such a process is not really random, it is dubbed a **pseudo-random number generator.**

Computer simulation languages, like those discussed in Sec. 16.6, invariably have a built-in pseudo-random number generator. Hence, you will rarely, if ever, need to know specific formulas for these generators. But if you want to strengthen your confidence in the process of obtaining the numbers, then you can study the example of a pseudo-random number generator given below. If not, go on to the discussion of how to generate random variables.

*Congruential method. To begin, we need to review the idea of **modulus arithmetic.** We say that two numbers x and y are **congruent, modulo** m, if the quantity $(x - y)$ is an integral multiple of m. For example, letting $m = 10$, we can write

$$3 \equiv 3 \text{ (modulo 10)}$$

$$13 \equiv 3 \text{ (modulo 10)}$$

$$513 \equiv 3 \text{ (modulo 10)}$$

$$48{,}653 \equiv 3 \text{ (modulo 10)}$$

(1)

$$4 \equiv 4 \text{ (modulo 10)}$$

$$84 \equiv 4 \text{ (modulo 10)}$$

$$124 \equiv 4 \text{ (modulo 10)}$$

$$1{,}000{,}004 \equiv 4 \text{ (modulo 10)}.$$

To find the value of, say, 857 (modulo 10), you calculate the integer *remainder* of 857 divided by 10, which is 7.

One popular approach for generating pseudo-random numbers is the so-called **Multiplicative Congruential Method.** The general formula for producing the random numbers is

(2) $$r_n = ar_{n-1} \text{ (modulo } m),$$

where the parameters a and m, and the **seed** r_0 are specified to give desirable statistical properties of the resultant sequence. Note that because of the modulus arithmetic, each r_n must be one of the numbers $0, 1, 2, 3, \ldots, m - 1$.

Clearly, you must be careful about the choice of a and r_0. For example, if $a = 1$, then $r_n = r_0$, for all n. Or if $r_0 = 0$, then $r_n = 0$, for all n. The values of a and r_0 should be chosen to yield the largest **cycle** or **period,** that is, to give the largest value for n at which $r_n = r_0$ for the first time.

To illustrate the technique, suppose you want to generate ten-decimal-place numbers $u_1, u_2, u_3, \ldots$. It can be shown that if you use $u_n = r_n \times 10^{-1}$, where

(3)

$$r_n = 100{,}003 \, r_{n-1} \text{ (modulo } 10^{10})$$

$$r_0 = \text{any odd number not divisible by 5,}$$

then the period of the sequence will be 5×10^8; that is, $r_n = r_0$ for the first time at $n = 5 \times 10^8$, and the cycle subsequently repeats itself. Given that you want ten-decimal-place numbers, this is the maximum possible length of period using (2). (There are other values for a that also give this maximum period.) The selection of r_0 in (3) eliminates the possibility that $r_n = 0$; so u_n satisfies $0 < u_n < 1$.

Let us look at an example of (3). Suppose $r_0 = 123,456,789$. Then

$$r_1 = (100,003) \cdot (123,456,789)$$

$$(4) \qquad = 12,346,049,270,367$$

$$\equiv 6,049,270,367 \ (\text{modulo } 10^{10}),$$

so that $u_1 = .6049270367$, and

$$r_2 = (100,003) \cdot (6,049,270,367)$$

$$(5) \qquad = 604,945,184,511,101$$

$$\equiv 5,184,511,101 \ (\text{modulo } 10^{10}),$$

so that $u_2 = .5184511101$. The decimals u_n, $n = 1, 2, \ldots, 20$, are shown in Fig. 16.7. Notice that the rightmost digits in this sequence form a short cycle $7, 1, 3, 9, 7, 1, 3, 9, \ldots$. Thus the statistical properties of the digits near the end of the number are far from random.

While (2) works reasonably well for some types of simulation models, it has poor serial correlation properties that make it dangerous to use for dynamic systems. A simple device for rectifying this deficiency is to intermix several sequences, each being generated with a different value for the seed r_0, and possibly a different value for a. For example, you can sequentially rotate among, say, 10 of these generators.

The advantage of using a pseudo-random number generator in lieu of a recorded table of random numbers is that only a few simple computer instructions are required to generate the sequence. Therefore, the approach uses only a small amount of memory space and does not require reading magnetic tape.

n	u_n	
1	.60492	70367
2	.51845	11101
3	.66636	33303
4	.33211	99909
5	.99544	99727
6	.98361	99181
7	.94266	97543
8	.80343	92629
9	.33660	77887
10	.78869	33661
11	.70269	00983
12	.11790	02949
13	.38319	08847
14	.23804	26541
15	.97953	79623
16	.73484	38869
17	.59322	16607
18	.94573	49821
19	.33541	49463
20	.50087	48389

FIGURE 16.7. The Multiplicative Congruential Method:

$$a = 100,003;$$
$$r_0 = 123,456,789.$$

Generating random variables. We turn next to an explanation of how to employ a sequence of uniform random numbers to generate complex probabilistic phenomena. The treatment below suggests several techniques that can be used; but it is by no means exhaustive. Further, the examples that illustrate the techniques are chosen more for expository ease than computational efficiency. In an actual situation, you should seek the advice of a computer science specialist to determine the appropriate technique for your model.

Inverse Transform Method. The following is the simplest and most fundamental technique for simulating random draws from an arbitrary single-variable probability distribution. Let the distribution function for the random variable be denoted by

$$F(x) \equiv \begin{pmatrix} \text{probability that the random variable} \\ \text{has a value less than or equal to } x \end{pmatrix}.$$

For example, suppose the random phenomenon has an exponential density function

(6) $$f(t) = \lambda e^{-\lambda t}, \qquad t \geq 0;$$

then

(7) $$F(x) = \int_0^x \lambda e^{-\lambda t} \, dt = 1 - e^{-\lambda x}.$$

Now $0 \leq F(x) \leq 1$, and suppose $F(x)$ is continuous and strictly increasing. Then given a value u, where $0 < u < 1$, there is a unique value for x such that $F(x) = u$. Symbolically, this value of x is denoted by the inverse function $F^{-1}(u)$. The technique is to generate a sequence of uniform random decimal numbers u_n, $n = 1, 2, \ldots$; that is, the u_n are uniformly distributed between 0 and 1. From these, determine the associated values as $x_n = F^{-1}(u_n)$.

The correctness of this approach can be seen as follows. Consider *any* two numbers u_a and u_b, where $0 < u_a < u_b < 1$. Then the probability that a *uniform* random decimal number u lies in the interval $u_a \leq u \leq u_b$ is $u_b - u_a$. Since $F(x)$ is continuous and strictly increasing, there is a number x_a such that $F(x_a) = u_a$, and a number x_b such that $F(x_b) = u_b$, where $x_a < x_b$. The Inverse Transform Method is valid provided that the *true* probability of the random variable having a value between x_a and x_b equals the generated probability $u_b - u_a$. This true probability is $F(x_b) - F(x_a) = u_b - u_a$ by construction, so that the method is indeed valid.

To see how this method works, return to the exponential distribution (6) and (7). Let v_n denote a uniform random decimal number. Set

(8) $$v_n = 1 - e^{-\lambda x_n},$$

so that

(9) $$x_n = \frac{-\log_e (1 - v_n)}{\lambda} = \frac{-\log_e u_n}{\lambda},$$

where $u_n = 1 - v_n$, and hence is itself a uniform random decimal number. Thus, you generate a sequence of uniform random decimal numbers $u_1, u_2, u_3, \ldots$, and by (9) compute $x_1, x_2, x_3, \ldots$, to obtain a random exponentially distributed variable. A diagrammatic representation of the technique is shown in Fig. 16.8.

The idea can also be applied to a probability mass function $p(j)$. Suppose $j = 0, 1, 2, 3, \ldots$, so that

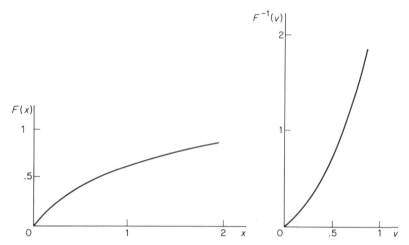

FIGURE. 16.8. Inverse Transform Method for a Continuous and Strictly Increasing $F(x)$. Example:

$$F(x) = 1 - e^{-\lambda x}, \quad F^{-1}(v) = -\log_e (1 - v)/\lambda \quad \text{for} \quad \lambda = 1.$$

(10)
$$F(x) = \sum_{j=0}^{x} p(j).$$

Then the inverse function can be written as

(11)
$$x_n = j \quad \text{for } F(j - 1) < u_n \le F(j),$$

where we let $F(-1) = 0$. For example, suppose the probability mass function is the *binomial distribution*:

(12)
$$p(j) = \binom{k}{j} p^j (1 - p)^{k-j} \quad \text{for } j = 0, 1, \ldots, k,$$

where $0 < p < 1$, and k is a positive integer. In particular, assume $k = 2$ and $p = .5$; then $p(0) = \frac{1}{4}, p(1) = \frac{1}{2}$, and $p(2) = \frac{1}{4}$, so that by (11) you have

(13)
$$x_n = \begin{cases} 0 & \text{for } \ 0 < u_n \le \ .25 \\ 1 & \text{for } .25 < u_n \le \ .75 \\ 2 & \text{for } .75 < u_n \le 1. \end{cases}$$

Since u_n is a uniform random decimal number, there is a $\frac{1}{4}$ probability that u_n lies between 0 and .25, a $\frac{1}{2}$ probability that it lies between .25 and .75, and a $\frac{1}{4}$ probability that it lies between .75 and 1. A diagrammatic representation of the technique is shown in Fig. 16.9.

Of course, many continuous distribution functions $F(x)$ do not have analytic inverse functions as does the exponential distribution. The Inverse Transform Method can still be applied in these instances by employing a discrete approximation to the continuous function, that is, by storing the values of $F(x)$ for only a finite set of x. The accuracy of the approximation can be improved by interpolating between the stored values. In several computer simulation languages (such as GPSS), you need only specify this discrete approximation, and the corresponding random phenomenon will be automatically generated.

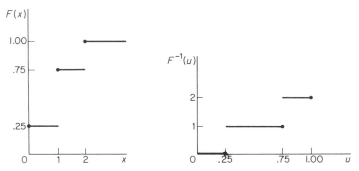

FIGURE 16.9. Inverse Transform Method for a Probability Mass Function. Example: $p(0) = \frac{1}{4}, p(1) = \frac{1}{2}, p(2) = \frac{1}{4}$.

*Tabular Method. The rule in (11) is easily implemented for an electronic computer by means of a few standard programming instructions. But if the range of possible values for j is large, then an excessive amount of time may be consumed in searching for the j that satisfies the inequalities in (11). A faster version of the Inverse Transform Method can be employed at the expense of using part of the computer's internal memory for storing a long table. We illustrate the idea with the binomial example (13). The method is particularly well suited to empirical distributions.

You can store the inverse function in computer memory in the form

$$(14) \qquad G(s) = \begin{cases} 0 & \text{for } s = 1, 2, \ldots, 25, \\ 1 & \text{for } s = 26, 27, \ldots, 75, \\ 2 & \text{for } s = 76, 77, \ldots, 100. \end{cases}$$

Given a value of u_n, let d_n be the number formed from the first two digits of u_n. Set $s_n = d_n + 1$, and let $x_n = G(s_n)$. For example if $u_n = .52896\ldots$, then $s_n = 52 + 1 = 53$, and so $x_n = G(53) = 1$ in (14). Once the function $G(s)$ has been stored in memory, only a few calculations must be performed by the computer to produce x_n.

*Method of Convolutions. Sometimes you can view a random variable as the sum of other independently distributed random variables. When this is so, the probability distribution of the random variable is a convolution of probability distributions, which may be easy to generate. (Occasionally, you can obtain a workable approximation to a complex probability distribution by using a *weighted* sum of independently distributed random variables. For this reason, the approach also has been called the **Method of Composition.**)

To illustrate, consider a random variable having a *gamma density function*

$$(15) \qquad g(y) = \frac{\lambda(\lambda y)^{k-1} e^{-\lambda y}}{(k-1)!}, \qquad y \geq 0, \quad k \text{ a positive integer.}$$

Such a variable can be considered as the sum of k independent random variables, each drawn from the same exponential density specified in (6). Consequently, adding k independent values of x_n, as given by (9), yields a random variable with the distribution in (15). Equivalently, but more efficiently, you would compute the logarithm of the product of k independent values of u_n and then multiply by $(-1/\lambda)$.

Similarly, a binomial random variable, as specified in (12), can be viewed as the sum of k draws of a variable described by

$$(16) \qquad i = \begin{cases} 1 & \text{with probability } p \\ 0 & \text{with probability } 1 - p. \end{cases}$$

You can therefore obtain a binomially distributed variable by adding k values of i. Each of these values for i is determined by the rule

$$(17) \qquad i = \begin{cases} 1 & \text{for } 0 < u \leq p \\ 0 & \text{for } p < u \leq 1, \end{cases}$$

where u is a uniform random decimal number.

*Method of Equivalent Transformations. Sometimes you can generate a random variable by exploiting a correspondence between its probability distribution and that of a related random variable.

For example, consider the Poisson distribution written in the form

$$(18) \qquad p(j) = \frac{(\lambda T)^j e^{-\lambda T}}{j!} \qquad \text{for } j = 0, 1, 2, \ldots,$$

which has mean λT. In terms of the waiting line models in Chap. 15, you can interpret j as the number of customers arriving during a period of length T, where the interarrival times for the customers are independently and identically distributed exponential random variables with the density function specified in (6).

Consequently, you can generate a Poisson distributed random variable by making successive independent draws of an exponentially distributed variable—using (9) to obtain such values. You stop making draws as soon as the sum of $j + 1$ of these variables exceeds T. The distribution of the resultant j is (18). (Equivalently, you stop when the product of $j + 1$ uniform random decimal numbers exceeds $e^{-\lambda T}$.)

Normally distributed random variables. Unfortunately, the distribution function for the Normal density with mean 0 and variance 1,

$$(19) \qquad F(x) = \int_{-\infty}^{x} \frac{1}{\sqrt{2\pi}} e^{-t^2/2} \, dt,$$

does not yield an analytic formula for the inverse function $F^{-1}(u)$. Of course the Inverse Transform Method can be used by employing a discrete approximation, and interpolating between values. But there are other methods for generating a Normally distributed random variable. Only a few are presented here.

One technique requires generating a pair of independent uniform random decimal numbers u and v, and in turn yields a pair of independently distributed Normal random variables x and y having the distribution function in (19). Specifically, compute

$$(20) \qquad \begin{aligned} x &= (-2 \log_e u)^{1/2} \cos 2\pi v \\ y &= (-2 \log_e u)^{1/2} \sin 2\pi v. \end{aligned}$$

Alternatively, you can apply the Method of Convolutions and invoke the *Central Limit Theorem.* This technique employs the sum of k independently and identically distributed uniform random variables. Specifically, let u_i, for $i = 1, 2, \ldots, 12$, be independent draws of a uniform random decimal number; then compute

$$(21) \qquad x = \sum_{i=1}^{12} u_i - 6.$$

The distribution of x will have mean 0 and variance 1, and will be approximately Normal. The approximation is poor for values beyond three standard deviations from the mean.

A third approach is to compute

$$(22) \qquad x = \frac{[(1 - u)^{-1/6.158} - 1]^{-1/4.874} - [u^{-1/6.158} - 1]^{1/4.874}}{.323968}$$

where u is a uniform random decimal number.

Correlated random variables. There are straightforward ways to generate variables from a multivariate Normal distribution, and from other joint probability distributions, as well as random variables having serial correlation. The techniques go beyond the scope of this book, but can be found in most texts on computer simulation.

*16.9 DEUS EX MACHINA

So far we have discussed only simulation models that to some degree represent approximations to real situations. Their orientation has been to provide a simulated environment in which to test the effects of different managerial policies. A related class of simulation models tries to encompass goal-seeking or purposeful behavior. These models display what is termed **artificial intelligence.**

Some of the popular examples of artificial intelligence programs include computer routines for playing such games as chess and checkers. There also have been a few applications to managerial problems. One group of applications focuses on the behavioral patterns of individual decision-makers. A measure of such a model's success is how well it yields decisions agreeing with those of the individual whose behavior is allegedly represented.

Another group of applications deals with complex combinational problems, like those discussed in Chap. 11. They are sometimes referred to as **heuristic programming** methods. For example, several of these models have been designed to derive good schedules for intricate sequencing problems. The following illustration suggests how they work.

Suppose the goal of the model is to schedule orders through a job-shop with maximum equipment efficiency. The computer starts by tentatively scheduling a few orders. It then selects another order to schedule, and examines various feasibility restrictions, due dates, and equipment efficiency. As a consequence, the computer may have to reschedule some of the previous orders. In brief, the computer model uses a number of "look-back" and "look-ahead" rules, and proceeds by educated trial-and-error toward a feasible schedule. If the rules are sufficiently sophisticated, then usually the schedule is good. Frequently, the schedule is nearly optimal according to the specified efficiency criterion, assuming the heuristic rules are promulgated with reference to this criterion.

▶Management scientists have also employed computer models for **operational gaming**. Some of the early applications, known as **management games,** involved several teams of players, each representing a business firm. A team made decisions about pricing, production quantities, advertising, etc. The computer served the two-fold purpose of keeping the accounting records, and of calculating the net impact of the decisions made by the several teams. More recently, such applications have been used to train personnel in administrative procedures, and to explore the system dynamics of an industry in which the competing firms are employing specified strategies. ◀

REVIEW EXERCISES

1 Suggest two or three managerial decision problems that seem to go beyond the capabilities of the mathematical models treated in earlier chapters of this text. Select situations that involve the optimization of an objective function subject, perhaps, to constraints or uncertainties. Explain what makes these problems so complex to solve.

2 Consider the stock market simulation example in Sec. 16.3. Repeat the experiment for another 20 days, starting with the same initial conditions as in Fig. 16.3. Array your calculations and results in tables like Figs. 16.3 and 16.4. Calculate Doe's cash position at the end of Day 20; if he holds stock, compute his cash position by assuming he sells out at the end of Day 20. (*Suggestion:* if you are in a class that is assigned this problem, collect the results from all the students and calculate the mean and standard deviation of Doe's cash position on Days 5, 10, 15, and 20.)

3 Consider the stock market simulation example in Sec. 16.3. Test the rule: (i) if you own the stock, then sell it whenever the price falls two days in a row, and (ii) if you do not own the stock, then buy it whenever the price rises two days in a row.

  (a) Use the same data as in Fig. 16.3, and construct a table like Fig. 16.4. Calculate Doe's cash position at the end of Day 20; if he holds stock, compute his cash position by assuming he sells out at the end of Day 20.

  (b) Extend the length of the simulation run another 20 days, and calculate Doe's cash position at the end of Day 40. (*Suggestion:* if you are in a class that is assigned this problem, collect the results from all the students and calculate the mean and standard deviation of Doe's cash position on Days 30 and 40.)

4 Suggest one or two experimental setups (analogous to the "slips-in-a-hat" approach) for generating uniform random digits. Discuss whether any of these approaches can be modified to generate other discrete probability distributions.

5 Consider the inventory simulation in Sec. 16.5. Assume $Q = 2$, $s = 1$, $L = 2$, and the demand distribution probabilities are $p(1) = p(3) = .5$. Simulate the system for 20 days, letting INVENTORY ON-HAND $= 2$, AMOUNT DUE-IN $= 0$, TIME DUE-IN $= 0$, and $t = 1$ in Block 1. (*Suggestion:* flip a coin to generate the daily demand quantities.)

6 Consider the inventory model simulation in Sec. 16.5.

  (a) Explain how you would modify Fig. 16.5 if lead time L were random.

  (b) Explain what complications arise if $Q \leq s$. If demand in excess of INVENTORY ON-HAND is backlogged.

  *(c) Suppose the probability process for demands can be formulated in terms of a distribution generating interarrival times between successive customers, and a distribution generating the quantity demanded by each customer. Devise an event-step incrementation flow chart for simulating the system.

7 Construct a time-step incrementation flow chart for the stock market example in Sec. 16.3.

8 Explain how to design an event-step incrementation simulation for the stock market example in Sec. 16.3. Try to construct an appropriate flow chart.

9 Consider the waiting line model in Sec. 16.5. Suppose the interarrival time is either 2 or 3, each possibility occurring with probability $\frac{1}{2}$; that service time for Clerk A is either 1 or 2, each occurring with probability $\frac{1}{2}$, and for Clerk B is either 1 or 4, each occurring with probability $\frac{1}{2}$. At $t = 0$, assume that the first customer arrives and that both clerks are free. Simulate an hour's operation of the system. (*Suggestion:* determine the random events by flipping a coin. If you are in a class that is assigned this problem, collect the following statistics for all the students and calculate the associated mean and standard deviation: the number of persons waiting in line at $t = 30$, 45, and 60 minutes; the number of persons that were served during the hour and their average time in the system, in line, and in service.)

10 Consider the OR Airline telephone line simulation, discussed in Sec. 1.6. In each part of this exercise, draw a flow chart indicating how to simulate a two-line system. Also explain what statistics you would tabulate. (*Continued on p. 576.*)

(a) Use a time-step incrementation formulation.

(b) Use an event-step incrementation formulation.

*11 Consider the Multiplicative Congruential Method for generating random digits in Sec. 16.8. In each part below, assume modulo 10 arithmetic and determine the length of the cycle.

(a) Let $a = 2$ and $r_0 = 1$, 3, and 5.

(b) Let $a = 3$, and $r_0 = 1$, 2, and 5.

*12 In each part below, apply the Inverse Transform Method in Sec. 16.8, and devise specific formulas analogous to (9) and (13) that yield the value of the variate x_n, given a random decimal number u_n.

(a)

$$f(t) = \begin{cases} (b - a)^{-1} & \text{for } a \le t \le b \\ 0 & \text{otherwise,} \end{cases}$$

where a and b are real numbers and $a < b$.

(b)

$$f(t) = \begin{cases} t & \text{for } 0 \le t \le 1 \\ 2 - t & \text{for } 1 \le t \le 2 \\ 0 & \text{otherwise.} \end{cases}$$

(c)

$$F(x) = \begin{cases} 0 & \text{for } x < 0 \\ .5x & \text{for } 0 \le x \le .4 \\ x - .2 & \text{for } .4 \le x \le .8 \\ 2x - 1 & \text{for } .8 \le x \le 1 \\ 1 & \text{for } x > 1. \end{cases}$$

(d) Binomial distribution, given by (12), where $k = 2$ and $p = .1$.

(e) Binomial distribution, given by (12), where $k = 3$ and $p = .5$.

*13 Explain how the description of the Inverse Transform Method in Sec. 16.8 needs to be altered to treat the case where $F(x)$ is continuous and nondecreasing (that is, not necessarily *strictly* increasing).

*14 In each part below, explain how you would apply the Tabular Method in Sec. 16.8.

(a) Binomial distribution, given by (12), where $k = 2$ and $p = .1$.

(b) Binomial distribution, given by (12), where $k = 3$ and $p = .5$.

(c) $p(0) = .3$, $p(2) = .25$, $p(5) = .15$, and $p(60) = .3$.

*15 (a) Explain how you can apply the Method of Convolutions in Sec. 16.8 to generate the triangular distribution in exercise 12, part (b). (*Continued on p. 577.*)

(b) Consider the Method of Equivalent Transformations in Sec. 16.8, and explain why the suggested procedure for generating a Poisson random variable is valid.

*16 Consider the approach (21) in Sec. 16.8 for generating Normally distributed random variables. Explain why (21), which involves a sum of 12 uniform random decimals, produces a random variable with a distribution having mean 0 and variance 1.

*17 (a) Suggest one or more methods for generating a geometric distribution $p(j) = p(1 - p)^j$, for $j = 0, 1, 2, \ldots$, where $0 < p < 1$. [*Recall:* let p represent the probability of a head appearing on the toss of a possibly biased coin; then $p(j)$ represents the probability that a head appears for the first time on Toss j.]

(b) Suggest one or more methods for generating a negative binomial distribution $p(j) = \binom{k+j-1}{j} p^k (1 - p)^j$, for $j = 0, 1, 2, \ldots$, where $0 < p < 1$. [*Recall:* let p represent the probability of a head appearing on the toss of a possibly biased coin; then $p(j)$ represents the probability that the kth head appears on Toss k + j.]

18 Explain your understanding of the following terms:

digital computer simulation
retrospective simulation
risk analysis
manual simulation
time compression
dynamic phenomena
entities
decision rule
attributes
membership relationships
state of the simulated
    system
exogenous events
recursive (causal) structure
validity and reliability
performance measure
fixed-time increments
variable-time increments
time-step incrementation
event-step incrementation
master program
event list
event subroutine
next imminent event
process interaction approach
canned program

*19 Explain your understanding of the following terms:

serial correlation
    (autocorrelation)
time-integrated average
ensemble mean (*Continued on p. 578.*)

covariance-stationary
spectral analysis
ergodic convergence
Monte Carlo (variance-reduction)
  methods
Method of Control Variates (Method of
  Concomitant Information)
Method of Antithetic Variates
uniform random numbers
pseudo-random number generator
Multiplicative Congruential Method
modulus arithmetic
congruent, modulo m
seed
cycle (period)
Inverse Transform Method
Tabular Method
Method of Convolutions (Method of
  Composition)
Method of Equivalent
 Transformations
artificial intelligence
heuristic programming
operational gaming (management
  games).

FORMULATION EXERCISES

20 In each part below, describe how you would build a simulation model to represent the system. State explicitly the random phenomena and how you would obtain the probability distributions required as input. Describe the performance measures you would collect, and explain their relevance to the associated managerial decision problem. Try to develop a flow chart describing the simulation of a "toy" version of the system.

(a) Checkout stands in a grocery store. (How would you test the effectiveness of an express counter to serve customers with five or less items?)

(b) Tellers' windows at a bank. (How would you test the effectiveness of having an express window to serve customers requiring only a single transaction?)

(c) Pumps at a gasoline station.

(d) Runways at an airport.

(e) Traffic lights in a configuration of eight city blocks.

(f) Parking lot for a doctors' office building.

(g) Telephone operators at a metropolitan police station.

(h) Restaurant facilities at a World's Fair.

(i) Layout of tables at a posh restaurant.

- (j) Layout of equipment in a job-shop.
- (k) Piers at a harbor facility.
- (l) Allocation of substitute teachers in a school district.
- (m) Layout of rooms and facilities in a new school building.
- (n) Screening methods for evaluating proposed capital investments by a corporation.
- (o) Design of an electronic computer installation at a college or university.
- (p) A decision problem that you suggested in exercise 1.

CONTENTS

CHAPTER **17**

Implementation of
Management Science

17.1 LIKE IT IS

In the past few years, many significant technical breakthroughs have been made in management science. Even greater progress occurred, however, in implementing management science in commercial and governmental enterprises.

In the early 1960s, a practicing operations researcher had to be both a scientific expert and a master of the "art of persuasion." Ethical, but convincing, salesmanship was needed then because relatively few companies firmly believed that management science was a profit-yielding activity. Most executives classified the effort as blue-sky research and development, and, in fact, several major corporations placed their operations research group in an R & D department.

Since then, the picture has changed dramatically. Only rarely now are operations researchers called upon to defend their *raison d'etre*. Today, executives show pride in employing computer models that have been designed to assist them in analyzing complex decision problems. (Many managers guard their computer models as a part of their territorial imperative.) In short, very few executives in leading corporations still ask, "Why do we need operations research?"

The questions that managers do raise are, "What areas of application are the most profitable?" "Is our company spending too little or too much on operations research?" "How can I best use operations research?" In other words, the present interest of businessmen is learning *how* to get the maximum benefit from management science.

The sections below explore the practical implications of this managerial attitude and offer some insights into the implementation process. Although the sections are entitled "How to . . . ," the chapter is not really a comprehensive nuts-and-bolts manual of procedures for guaranteeing implementation. Rather, the chapter

581

provides a few guidelines for making management science work effectually. The orientation of the discussion is toward people, not mathematical techniques.

As you will soon discover, the key to the successful conduct of management science is the joint exercise of good judgment by executives and professional operations researchers. In particular, the managers and technicians must decide in concert what projects to pursue, what goals to sight, what level of effort to expend, and what timetable to follow. These are the subjects analyzed below.

17.2 HOW TO PUT OPERATIONS RESEARCH TO MANAGERIAL USE

What commonly distinguishes executives familiar with employing management science from first-time users is their recognition of the need to exercise responsibility vis-a-vis the conduct of the project. For quite understandable reasons, tyro managers are usually "stand-offish" in their involvement. Such a posture is ill advised and can be expensive to the company, even when the operations research application ultimately succeeds.

In essence, line managers must take responsibility to see that the right problem is analyzed and that adequate controls are exercised to monitor the progress of the application. Experience has shown repeatedly that ignoring this responsibility is detrimental to all and may easily be the root cause of failure, despite the expertise and sincerity of the operations research technical staff. This section suggests some ways for an executive to ensure that a management science effort is well directed and aimed at bettering the entire organization.

What benefits should a manager expect? Operations research can be employed to mount a massive analysis, when warranted, of an important and intricate decision-making problem. As you will readily observe in applying management science, the approach *inherently* requires adhering to systematic procedures and paying careful attention to details. (No other approach for solving complex management problems even comes close in demanding so much discipline in analysis.) The combined utilization of advanced mathematical techniques and enormous computing power permits a thorough exploration of relevant alternatives. A good operations research study will leave no doubt in an executive's mind that all reasonable courses of action have been investigated, and will make crystal clear the relative merits of specific alternative actions and their possible consequences.

A central ingredient to a sound operations research investigation is extensive sensitivity testing. Careful managerial scrutiny of comparative case studies provides the principal means by which executives can confirm their understanding of the underlying model, its assumptions, and its data. Furthermore, the benefits a manager receives from a planning-oriented model stem largely from such insightful sensitivity testing. Rarely, if ever, does an executive seek "numbers" as answers; rather, most decision-makers want a quantitative assessment of what risks are at stake with different actions, what changes in direction are likely to yield profit improvements, and what avenues are promising for further investigation (such as the development of new products, expansion into new markets, location of new plant sites, etc.). Often sensitivity testing reveals that the uncertainty of an allegedly critical factor is actually not very important in making a good decision, whereas another factor, previously thought insignificant, is truly pivotal.

To determine whether a management science project is meeting acceptable standards of quality, some easy items to check are the ready availability of input data and model assumptions in a form understandable to nontechnicians, the summarization of results and the backup detail printed in the format of mangerial reports, and reasonable turnaround times for running additional analyses having slightly modified input data or assumptions. The best way for a manager to make these checks is to ask questions and probe the answers. A competently designed model should provide a manager with comprehensible answers to spontaneous "why does..." and "what if..." questions without requiring a mammoth crash effort. (We hasten to add, however, that it is unfair to expect such rapid service at the initial stages of a study. A line executive should continue to ask questions throughout the duration of the project, and monitor whether the effort required to answer these questions eventually becomes routine and commensurate with the value of the analytic assistance provided.)

Another indicator of project quality is the extent to which the analysis results in a recommended *strategy*, as distinct from a suggested *single decision*. To illustrate, the output from a long-range capacity-expansion study should not be merely a string of recommended equipment purchases and forecasted production levels. Rather, the output should indicate the decisions to take immediately, should include recommendations of when to make the next set of decisions, given the present data, and should establish the circumstances for reviewing, and possibly revising, these future decisions. Even the immediate decision recommendations should be qualified to the point of ascertaining what other alternatives are appropriate if the data are varied within a plausible range of values and any restrictive assumptions are relaxed.

What limitations should a manager recognize? This question was partially answered in Sec. 1.3, and you may want to review that material. Three more cautions are added here.

First, when an operations research model is used to reduce costs, the percentage savings may be *relatively* small. But if this percentage is applied to a large cost base, the absolute savings can pay for the operations research study many times over. Occasionally, a planning model will uncover a costly error in current operating procedures; in such an instance, the savings may be large. Most often, profit improvements stem from executives possessing a deeper understanding of the problem area, and hence developing a keener sense for taking correct actions and maintaining control in an uncertain and competitive environment. It is impossible to assign a precise dollar improvement figure to this type of impact; nevertheless, the benefits are real and are perceived and valued by company management. In a preponderance of successful applications, the beneficial effects are truly manifest in the altered decision behavior of executives and managers at several levels of the corporation.

Second, although an operations research model often uses the mathematics of optimization, the resultant solution should not be viewed as *necessarily* yielding an optimal answer to the real problem. After all, as the text has stressed throughout, a model is *inherently* an approximation to reality, and therefore an optimal solution to this approximation need not be the "final" answer to the actual decision problem. The important issue, however, is not whether a proposed solution is *optimal*, but whether the solution yields a significant enough *improvement* over the alternatives to make it worthy of acceptance.

Third, while providing a solution to one set of problems, the operations research model may create, in turn, another set of problems. For example, the analysis may demonstrate the need for an improved information gathering system or for a restructuring of operating policies. And, ensuring the continued maintenance of an up-to-date model does, itself, pose new managerial problems.

When should a manager initiate an operations research project? It is helpful to distinguish between so-called *one-shot* or infrequent decision problems and *recurring* decision analyses (like devising an annual plan, scheduling personnel and equipment, and replenishing inventories).

In special studies, a decision to apply management science depends on the economic and strategic importance of the decision, the time span available for performing the analysis, and the relevance and availability of data. It is difficult and hazardous to apply operations research under "time pressure." Consequently, a manager should consider employing the approach when the stakes are sizeable, the decision does not *have* to be made next Monday morning, data are available for the analysis, and the choice is not so governed by political and personality considerations within the company that economic analysis is of only minor import.

In planning situations, the decision to apply management science also depends on the economic and strategic stakes of the problem and the available data. But planning applications differ from special studies most critically in the longer time horizon over which the model can be developed and tested. As we point out in later sections, controlling progress in the conduct of a management science study is important; nevertheless, the corporation will not grind to a halt if a couple of weeks' delay postpones the completion of an operations research planning model. (And there always *is* a couple of weeks' delay!)

The decision to develop a computerized model for daily operations usually is more involved. Numerous companies have successfully constructed such models for as diverse applications as inventory control, tanker-fleet routing, and job-shop scheduling. Often the economic benefits are small percentagewise, the systems design effort is staggering, and the implementation process is painful. Hence, this type of application is usually justified in terms of producing economic benefits that will extend over a relatively long term.

Sometimes executives misjudge whether the available data are sufficiently accurate as to warrant using an operations research approach. Applications of statistical techniques to the design of industrial research experiments, to the monitoring of continuous production processes and machinery, and to the auditing of voluminous accounting transactions demonstrate that mathematical techniques can be effective in analyzing sparse data that are subject to variability and measurement errors. Inaccurate or limited data do not *per se* negate the application of a mathematical technique. Even if there are no historical data at all, managers may be able to impart their experience-based knowledge by means of probabilistic statements. Hence, it is inappropriate for an executive to reject using management science solely on the grounds of less than perfect factual information.

Sometimes executives shy away from management science because they feel that their company personnel are not sophisticated enough to use mathematical techniques. This fear may be well founded, but the apprehension also may be based on a limited or even erroneous understanding of the degree of sophistication that is actually required. And all too often, senior managers underestimate the capability of their experienced personnel to learn how to apply operations research.

Many successful applications have been made by personnel who are trained in accounting, engineering, economics, or business, and who have been away from school for years. Their first-hand knowledge of the company more than compensates for their initial unfamiliarity with technicalities of management science. In addition, the widespread availability of easy-to-use canned computer programs has removed much of the burden in going from a model formulation and actual data to a numerical solution and sensitivity analysis. And, finally, although the mathematical methods employed to obtain a numerical solution may be advanced, the solution itself may be easy to interpret and to implement. (A good example of this type of application is inventory control. The computations of a reorder point and replenishment quantity can sometimes be intricate; nevertheless, the resultant ordering policy may simply be of the form "when down to 4, order more" and thus may be easily understood.)

How can managers get what they pay for? Perhaps the most difficult responsibility that an executive faces in controlling the progress of an operations research application is to strike the right balance between conducting the effort as a "research project" and as a "task-force assignment."

Estimating how profitable or beneficial an application will be in a particular company is central to the research aspect. For example, many companies are able to reduce inventory investment by at least 25% by adopting scientific inventory control, but the level of reduction in a specific company can only be estimated *after* the operations research project is begun and some trial tests are completed. Similarly, most medium-sized oil refineries are able to cut costs by $2000 a day when using a linear programming model to make a weekly operating schedule, but an estimate of savings at any particular refinery can only be made after a preliminary model is built and run on a trial basis. Thus, an executive should view the initial phases of an operations research effort as exploratory.

It is erroneous, however, for management to view the *entire* project as research.

Companies with the best record of implementing operations research plan each project from the very beginning as an effort to improve current procedures. The line managers who are involved share a sense of urgency about completing the effort and remain vigilant in keeping the study practical and pertinent to the actual decision problems.

Standard control techniques for managing include formulating a statement of goals, assigning task responsibilities, developing and updating a time schedule for completing various tasks, and planning for managerial reviews. It is the nature of operations research studies to encounter delays and unforseen difficulties. Hence, expect that the unexpected will occur. The inevitability of these contingencies is the very reason why an operations research project needs careful managerial control.

Most operations research efforts require two to three man-years of effort and extend over a period of three to nine months. Naturally, if the project is important and complicated, these figures will be exceeded. The economic benefits of a well-conceived and controlled application should far outweigh the expense of developing and operating the system.

17.3 HOW TO SUCCESSFULLY CONDUCT A MANAGEMENT SCIENCE PROJECT

This section outlines the components of a successful management science application and expands on several of the factors already discussed above; the context here is the conduct of a selected project.

Managerial guidance and participation. Both top management and operating management must recognize their respective roles in the evolution of a project. Since an operations research application typically cuts across different departments, the effort must have the sincere sponsorship of top management and the needed entrees into line activities. Furthermore, top management must watch that the corporation's best interests are held paramount and that the study is not diverted so as to serve the interests of individual groups at the expense of the company.

Operating management must actively participate in the project's goal formulation, administration, and evaluation. It is both difficult and foolish to impose an operations research system on an operating management that has not been a party to the system's design. Anyone with only a modicum of experience knows that the best of plans can be so cleverly sabotaged by a group of unwilling personnel that the promulgator looks like a fool. But more is at issue than just personality conflicts. When operating management has not been actively engaged in the study, there is substantial likelihood that the proposed methods of the system will not be sufficiently comprehensive and flexible to handle the inevitable exigencies. Thus, if operating management has not participated in the evaluation (and, as a result, has little confidence in the worth of the endeavor), trouble looms ahead, even with the most insistent encouragement of top management.

Project planning and control. The need for monitoring the progress of a project has been underscored. Now we highlight several factors in this process that are critical to success.

- The project team should realize at the outset where managerial judgment will be required. Specific plans should be made to obtain this counsel, and these provisions may in turn require some preparatory educational effort. People, not computers, make managerial decisions.

- The technical phase should be executed carefully, because if it is poorly done, the outcome can be disastrous. The team should recognize, however, that the mathematical side of the study will represent probably only a minor part of the total effort of developing and implementing the application.

- The data requirements should be ascertained early, and the information collection indicated soon enough to avoid long delays in the project. Often, this phase is poorly executed in a management science study, even when the project is led by an experienced practitioner.

- Managers and operating personnel should be alerted to any transitional difficulties that may arise in testing and installing a new system. For example, when scientific inventory replenishment rules are implemented, total inventory investment usually rises for the first few months. (Can you imagine why?) Top management is likely to express consternation unless properly forewarned.

- The team should be careful to document the model's components and assumptions, and to record the input data and sources. In a large-scale effort, assumptions made several months earlier are easily forgotten. Furthermore, as test results and new data are examined, the model is inevitably altered. So it is essential that the team systematically catalogues each revision.

Credibility. Just like pregnancy, there is no such thing as a little credibility. Either an executive believes that the operations research representation of the problem is valid or the executive dismisses the results as worthless. The following paragraphs discuss how to develop a model that legitimately earns the trust of managers.

The project team should realize from the very beginning that the economic benefits of an operations research application never prove themselves and are never self-evident. And to make matters worse, a reliable "before and after" comparison is always extremely difficult to perform. There are two reasons why.

First, sufficient data about past operations may not be available, at least not in a form convenient for tabulation and analysis with acceptable accuracy. Hence, in its enthusiasm to design and implement a new approach, the operations research team should not slight the job of installing a data-gathering system to reflect the true economic impact of a change. And when past data are insufficient, the team should start collecting current data long before it institutes new procedures. The team also should recognize the need to design a controlled experiment that focuses the effects to be evaluated. Unless the team heeds these cautions, it will, itself, be unable to prove factually that an improvement has occurred.

Second, only in exceptional circumstances can a team make a completely parallel comparison between two systems operating under different sets of procedures. There is no guarantee that an approach that looks attractive in terms of last year's operations will be just as attractive during this year's activities (or vice versa). Further, because managerial decisions at one point in time may have a specific effect on business conditions later, it may be futile to attempt to show with great precision how anything but an actually operating system behaves over an extensive period of time.

Thus, it is hard to prove precisely how well an operations research approach would have performed historically, or how much better an implemented operations research approach *is* faring as compared to what the previous system *would have done*. Management and the professionals must realize at the outset that they are limited in providing irrefutable evidence that improvements actually result from an operations research approach. But it is important to remember that the same limitations exist in measuring the impact of any competing problem solution!

The above observations mean that by and large credibility ought to be established *during* the course of the project and not relegated to the end. Most executives express the following doubts about an operations research model: "How do I know that it uses the right data? ... makes realistic assumptions? ... computes the economic consequences correctly? ... and encompasses the enormous number of relevant detailed considerations?" If you pause to think, it does stagger the imagination that the essence of a complex decision-making problem can be transferred to the "brain" of an inanimate electronic device. The following analogy may help to explain the psychology of establishing credibility and suggests some ways of allaying those doubts expressed by managers.

Suppose you are handed a telephone book for the first time and told that the volume contains the correct telephone numbers of *everyone* in the city. In a moment, you surely would realize that the claim is an overstatement. After all, telephones are installed and removed every day, so the telephone book is only an approximate representation of *all* the telephone numbers in the city. (In this sense, the volume of listings is a "model.") What really concerns you is whether the approximation is worth using. How would you find out?

Probably you would start by looking up a telephone number that you already know (perhaps, your own). If you find that the listed number is correct, you then might select a person whose number you do not know, look up the number, and place a call to see if the book in fact gives the right listing. After several more tries of this kind, assuming you are successful each time, you would be willing to *start* using the book. And most likely you would continue to use it until you observed an increased frequency of wrong numbers. Then you would complain to the telephone company, or go back to relying upon the Information Operator.

Now consider the telephone company's objectives. It wants to provide a model or system that gives you the right numbers. There are many possible systems (or models, if you like) for providing this service. The telephone company has discovered that the most economical solution is to publish one book containing every listed number and to distribute the volume to you and all other subscribers.

The company knows full well that you will use only a miniscule fraction of all the numbers; even so, you will judge the system's merit on the validity of this small fraction.

The preceding analogy is relevant to the design of an operations research system in several ways. Executives first test the validity of an operations research model by asking questions about data and conclusions; they *know* the right answers to some of the questions and have some intuition about others. Their confidence builds if the forthcoming answers are straightforward, comprehensible, and correct. They will start to rely on the model until their confidence is shaken by some "obvious" mistakes.

The operations research project team should try to anticipate what questions managers *may* ask and what data yield answers. This task is helped by discussing the detailed designs of the data reports and numerical summaries with the executives involved. The computer analysis should include not only summary reports similar to standard management information reports but also detailed backup analyses that clearly show the "how" and "why" of the summary figures. Much of the output may be examined infrequently; but it is there "just in case."

The telephone book analogy should not be pushed too far, because it is impractical and impossible to provide *every* number that an executive might possibly request. But novice operations researchers invariably make the mistake of providing far too little backup information, documentation, and analysis. As a consequence, they are frequently put in a position that is embarrassing to them and annoying to a manager, namely, having to go "back to the drawing board" to obtain the information that executives want in order to understand the model's results.

The above discussion stresses the output requirements of a well-conducted management science analysis. Of course, the team also must employ other means of effective communication. These are familiar to professional task-force leaders and amount to maintaining an open dialogue between the managers, who ultimately have to judge the merit of the results, and the team members. To repeat, managerial guidance and participation is a *sine qua non* for establishing credibility.

Responsive and responsible implementation. Truly effecting change within a corporate organization, whether the change be installing a new computer system or reassigning managerial responsibilities, is usually a difficult job. Aside from any special aversion that personnel may have to computer-based systems analysis, there are few, if any, problems of implementing change that are peculiar to an operations research project. As is true for effecting most significant changes within a company, the support of top management is vital, adequate educational training of operating personnel is necessary, a carefully worked out plan for introducing the changes is essential, and the implementation process must be controlled and monitored to sense and then correct difficulties that may arise. Unfortunately, there is no substitute for experience in knowing how to implement change skillfully.

One problem does deserve additional discussion. The difficulty is reminiscent of that encountered in factory mechanization many years ago. Certain operations research applications, especially those involving daily operations, may drastically change the character of the decision-maker's job. For example, developing a computer scheduling model for the processing of orders in a factory, or the routing of ships between ports, or the purchasing of materials from vendors, may transform a job requiring long familiarity with the decision problem into one of routinely supplying raw data to a computer. An operations research approach may remove the fun, challenge, exercise of judgment, sense of contribution, and mystique in a job. Rarely is top management willing to forego the resultant economic benefits for these reasons. But the project team must face up to the likely reaction of individuals who will be so affected. The team should recognize that the implementation process will arouse hostility; accordingly, they should provide post-implementation procedures to control a situation that might easily deteriorate because of a hostile environment.

Systems design. If the application is to be used again after the initial testing and analysis, then the ultimate success of the project depends upon the model's long-term viability. In the early years of commercial applications of management science, many companies achieved noteworthy success for a while; later they discovered that their efforts had dissipated with the changing of business conditions and the promotion or resignation of management science personnel. Now experienced firms realize the necessity for building systems support to maintain and update a continuing management science application.

This point would not merit special mention except for a commonly observed phenomenon that most executives still find paradoxical. The typical operations researcher, although having expertise in model building and analyzing complex problems, is usually ill equipped and frequently disinterested in the above-mentioned systems requirements. Consequently, experienced companies include systems-oriented personnel in a management science project team to devise procedures for maintaining the model in good working order.

17.4 HOW TO MANAGE AN
OPERATIONS RESEARCH STAFF

In keeping with the tenor of the chapter, this section highlights only a few issues that pertain directly to the profit-making impact of a corporate operations research activity.

Location and size. The proper placement of an operations research group within a large corporation is no longer a subject of much debate among professionals. No standard pattern has evolved, even within an industry, and these technical staffs have successfully operated under the guidance of controllers, chief planners, vice-presidents of manufacturing, as well as chiefs of research and development departments. Today, pragmatic considerations dominate the location decision. And divisionalized companies operating under a policy of decentralized management frequently have operations research activities at both the corporate and division levels.

The size of an operations research staff is an unreliable indicator of the group's productivity; a small staff of six talented professionals may have a much greater profit impact on a corporation than a group of 20 that contains only two or three top-notch scientists. In management science, quantity is a *very* poor substitute for quality.

Corporate responsibilities. Top management expects the operations research staff to exercise a high degree of *intellectual integrity*. This means not only that the group must meet demanding professional standards, but also that the staff must seek truthful conclusions and refrain from organizational partisanship.

The operations research group manager must be careful not to overcommit the staff. In an effort to please, many groups undertake more projects than they can accomplish in a reasonable period of time. As a result, all the users become dissatisfied. An operations research group should have a systematic way to decide what projects to accept and how to allocate its own scarce professional resources to best serve the needs of the entire company.

Cooperation with users. The preceding sections emphasized the importance of working with line managers in the conduct of operations research projects. Here this subject is treated from the technical staff's point of view.

The group should always keep in sight the way an operations research model typically assists managers. In most applications, the model-building effort provides insights into the quantitative implications of specified data and assumptions. Ultimately, it is the managers who make the decisions and are held responsible for the outcomes. Hence these executives must assess the relative likelihood of various assumptions and weigh the risks associated with different courses of action. An operations researcher should avoid the trap of believing that the model is true reality.

When a corporate operations research staff is first establishing its reputation, the group will work under less than ideal cooperative arrangements with its users. The requesting organization may be pleased to see the project completed successfully, and even may pay for the project. Nevertheless, the user organization may not readily provide other necessary kinds of help, which often include the collection of data and careful managerial review of intermediate results; consequently, the effort may get bogged down waiting for essential assistance in the line organization. But when the operations research staff has progressed to where it can pick and choose from among several worthwhile projects, then a major selection criterion should be the willingness of the user organization to commit its *personnel time* to the project team. A good index of user interest and involvement is the extent to which it will allocate the time of its people to assist in the application.

Table of Probability of Delay: P[n≥S] M/M/S Model

	S			
ρ	1	2	3	4
.1	.1000			
.15	.1500	.0104		
.2	.2000	.0181		
.25	.2500	.0277		
.3	.3000	.0391		
.35	.3500	.0521		
.4	.4000	.0666		
.45	.4500	.0826	.0113	
.5	.5000	.1000	.0151	
.55	.5500	.1186	.0195	
.6	.6000	.1384	.0246	
.65	.6500	.1594	.0304	
.7	.7000	.1814	.0369	
.75	.7500	.2045	.0441	
.8	.8000	.2285	.0520	
.85	.8500	.2535	.0606	.0117
.9	.9000	.2793	.0700	.0143
.95	.9500	.3059	.0801	.0171
1.00		.3333	.0909	.0204

Note: $\rho = \lambda/\mu$ traffic intensity

λ = arrival rate

μ = service rate

S = number of servers

ρ	2	3	4	5	6	7	8	9	10
1.0	.3333	.0909	.0204						
1.2	.4499	.1411	.0370						
1.4	.5764	.2033	.0603	.0153					
1.6	.7111	.2737	.0906	.0258					
1.8	.8526	.3547	.1285	.0404	.0111				
2.0		.4444	.1739	.0597	.0180				
2.2		.5421	.2267	.0839	.0274				
2.4		.6471	.2870	.1135	.0399	.0125			
2.6		.7588	.3544	.1486	.0558	.0187			
2.8		.8766	.4286	.1895	.0754	.0270			
3.0			.5094	.2361	.0991	.0376	.0129		
3.2			.5964	.2885	.1271	.0508	.0184		
3.4			.6893	.3466	.1595	.0669	.0256		
3.6			.7877	.4103	.1965	.0862	.0346	.0127	
3.8			.8914	.4795	.2382	.1088	.0456	.0175	
4.0				.5541	.2847	.1351	.0590	.0237	
4.2				.6337	.3359	.1650	.0749	.0313	.0121
4.4				.7183	.3919	.1988	.0935	.0407	.0164
4.6				.8077	.4525	.2365	.1150	.0518	.0217
4.8				.9016	.5177	.2783	.1395	.0650	.0282
5.0					.5875	.3241	.1672	.0805	.0361

Note: $\rho = \lambda/\mu$ traffic intensity

λ = arrival rate

μ = service

S = number of servers

S

ρ	6	7	8	9	10	11	12	13	14	15
5.0	.5875	.3241	.1672	.0805	.0361	.0150				
5.2	.6616	.3740	.1982	.0983	.0455	.0196				
5.4	.7401	.4279	.2827	.1186	.0565	.0252	.0105			
5.6	.8227	.4859	.2706	.1415	.0694	.0319	.0137			
5.8	.9094	.5479	.3120	.1673	.0843	.0398	.0176			
6.0		.6138	.3569	.1959	.1012	.0492	.0224			
6.2		.6836	.4055	.2275	.1204	.0600	.0281	.0124		
6.4		.7572	.4576	.2622	.1420	.0725	.0349	.0158		
6.6		.8345	.5133	.2999	.1660	.0868	.0428	.0199		
6.8		.9155	.5725	.3408	.1925	.1029	.0520	.0248	.0112	
7.0			.6353	.3849	.2217	.1211	.0626	.0306	.0141	
7.2			.7015	.4322	.2536	.1413	.0746	.0373	.0177	
7.4			.7711	.4827	.2882	.1637	.0883	.0451	.0219	.0100
7.6			.8441	.5363	.3256	.1884	.1036	.0541	.0268	.0126
7.8			.9204	.5932	.3659	.2154	.1208	.0644	.0326	.0156
8.0				.6533	.4091	.2449	.1398	.0759	.0392	.0193
8.2				.7165	.4552	.2769	.1608	.0890	.0469	.0235
8.4				.7828	.5042	.3114	.1838	.1036	.0556	.0284
8.6				.8522	.5561	.3484	.2090	.1198	.0655	.0342
8.8				.9246	.6110	.3881	.2364	.1377	.0767	.0407
9.0					.6687	.4304	.2660	.1575	.0891	.0482
9.2					.7293	.4754	.2979	.1790	.1030	.0567
9.4					.7927	.5231	.3322	.2025	.1184	.0662
9.6					.8590	.5734	.3688	.2280	.1353	.0769
9.8					.9281	.6264	.4078	.2556	.1538	.0888
10.0						.6821	.4493	.2852	.1741	.1020

Note: $\rho = \lambda/\mu$ traffic intensity

λ = arrival rate

μ = service rate

S = number of servers

Selected Readings

This section is a modest sampling of books, some now classic references and some recent additions to the literature, devoted to management science. A more complete bibliography (including journal articles) is available in my book *Principles of Operations Research*, Second Edition, Prentice-Hall, 1975. Up-to-date material on the topics in this text can be found in the current issues of *Management Science, Operations Research*, and the *Naval Research Logistics Quarterly*. An excellent reference to journal articles is the quarterly *International Abstracts in Operations Research* (North Holland), published by the International Federation of Operational Research Societies.

· Operations Research ·

Chapters 1 and 17

Ackoff, R. L., *A Concept of Corporate Planning*, Wiley-Interscience, 1970.

Agarwal, R. C., and E. O. Heady, *Operations Research Methods for Agricultural Decisions*, Iowa State University Press, 1973.

Bowman, E. H., and R. B. Fetter, *Analysis for Production and Operations Management*, R. D. Irwin, 1967.

Churchman, C. W., *The Systems Approach*, Delacorte Press, 1968.

Churchman, C. W., R. L. Ackoff, and E. L. Arnoff, *Introduction to Operations Research*, John Wiley & Sons, 1957.

Dantzig, G. B., and T. L. Saaty, *Compact City*, W. H. Freeman, 1973.

Gaver, D. P., and G. L. Thompson, *Programming and Probability Models in Operations Research*, Brooks-Cole, 1973.

Hertz, D. B., *New Power for Management-Computer Systems and Management Science*, McGraw-Hill, 1969.

Hillier, F. S., and G. J. Lieberman, *Introduction to Operations Research*, Holden-Day, Inc., 1967.

Rivett, P., *Principles of Model Building*, John Wiley & Sons, 1973.

Wagner, H. M., *Principles of Operations Research*, Second Edition, Prentice-Hall, 1975.

597

·Mathematical Programming·

Chapter 2 through 7, 11, and 12

Abadie, J., (ed.), *Integer and Nonlinear Programming*, North Holland, 1970.

Beale, E. M. L., *Mathematical Programming in Practice*, Pitman, 1968.

Charnes, A., and W. W. Cooper, *Management Models and Industrial Applications of Linear Programming*, Volumes I and II, John Wiley & Sons, 1961.

Dantzig, G. B., *Linear Programming and Extensions*, Princeton University Press, 1963.

Dorfman, R., P. A. Samuelson, and R. M. Solow, *Linear Programming and Economic Analysis*, McGraw-Hill, 1958.

Fiacco, A. V., and G. P. McCormick, *Nonlinear Programming, Sequential Unconstrained Minimization Techniques*, John Wiley & Sons, 1968.

Ford, L. R., Jr., and D. R. Fulkerson, *Flows in Networks*, Princeton University Press, 1962.

Gale, D., *The Theory of Linear Economic Models*, McGraw-Hill, 1960.

Garfinkel, R. S., and G. L. Nemhauser, *Integer Programming*, John Wiley & Sons, 1972.

Gass, S. I., *Linear Programming: Methods and Applications*, Third Edition, McGraw-Hill, 1969.

Geoffrion, A. M. (ed.), *Perspectives on Optimization*, Addison-Wesley, 1972.

Hu, T. C., *Integer Programming and Network Flows*, Addison-Wesley, 1969.

Karlin, S., *Mathematical Methods and Theory in Games, Programming and Economics*, Vol. I, Addison-Wesley, 1959.

Koopmans, T. C. (ed.), *Activity Analysis of Production and Allocation, Proceeding of a Conference*, John Wiley & Sons, 1951.

Kuhn, H. W., and A. W. Tucker (eds.), *Linear Inequalities and Related Systems*, Princeton University Press, 1956.

Lasdon, L., *Optimization Theory for Large Systems*, MacMillan, 1970.

Mangasarian, O. L., *Nonlinear Programming*, McGraw-Hill, 1969.

Muth, J. F., and G. L. Thompson (eds.), *Industrial Scheduling*, Prentice-Hall, 1963.

Orchard-Hays, W., *Advanced Linear-Programming Computing Techniques*, McGraw-Hill, 1968.

Potts, R. B., and R. M. Oliver, *Flows in Transportation Networks*, Academic Press, 1972.

Pratt, J. W., H. Raiffa, and R. Schlaifer, *Introduction to Statistical Decision Theory*, McGraw-Hill, 1965.

Raiffa, H., *Decision Analysis-Introductory Lectures on Choices Under Uncertainty*, Addison-Wesley, 1968.

Zionts, S., *Linear and Integer Programming*, Prentice-Hall, 1974.

·Dynamic Programming·

Chapters 8, 10, and 13

Beckmann, M. J., *Dynamic Programming of Economic Decisions*, Springer-Verlag, Berlin, 1968.

Bellman, R. E., *Dynamic Programming*, Princeton University Press, 1957.

Bellman, R. E., and S. E. Dreyfus, *Applied Dynamics Programming*, Princeton University Press, 1962.

Denardo, E. V., *Dynamic Programming: Theory and Application*, Prentice-Hall, 1975.

Derman, C., *Finite State Markovian Decision Processes*, Academic Press, 1970.

Howard, R. A., *Dynamic Programming and Markov Processes*, The Massachussets Institute of Technology Press, 1960.

Jorgenson, D. W., J. J. McCall, and R. Radner, *Optimal Replacement Policy*, Rand McNally, 1967.

Kemeny, J. G., and J. L. Snell, *Finite Markov Chains*, D. Van Nostrand, 1960.

Nemhauser, G. L., *Introduction to Dynamic Programming*, John Wiley & Sons, 1966.

Ross, S. M., *Applied Probability Models with Optimization Applications*, Holden-Day, 1970.

· Inventory and Production ·

Chapters 9 and 14

Arrow, K. J., S. Karlin, and H. E. Scarf (eds.), *Studies in the Mathematical Theory of Inventory and Production*, Stanford University Press, 1958.

Arrow, K. J., S. Karlin, and H. E. Scarf (eds.), *Studies in Applied Probability and Management Science*, Stanford University Press, 1962.

Buchan, J., and E. Koenigsberg, *Scientific Inventory Management*, Prentice-Hall, 1963.

Buffa, E. S., *Production-Inventory Systems: Planning and Control*, Irwin, 1968.

Elmaghraby, S. E., *The Design of Production Systems*, Reinhold, 1966.

Hadley, G., and T. M. Whitin, *Analysis of Inventory Systems*, Prentice-Hall, 1963.

Holt, C. C., F. Modigliani, J. F. Muth, and H. A. Simon, *Planning Production, Inventories, and Work Force*, Prentice-Hall, 1960.

Naddor, E., *Inventory Systems*, John Wiley & Sons, 1966.

Starr, M. K., and D. W. Miller, *Inventory Control: Theory and Practice*, Prentice-Hall, 1962.

Tijms, H. C., *Analysis of (s, S) Inventory Models*, Mathematical Centrum, Amsterdam, 1972.

Wagner, H. M., *Statistical Management of Inventory Systems*, John Wiley & Sons, 1962.

Whitin, T. M., *The Theory of Inventory Management*, Second Edition, Princeton University Press, 1957.

· Waiting Lines ·

Chapter 15

Benes, V. E., *General Stochastic Processes in the Theory of Queues*, Addison-Wesley, 1963.

Cohen, J. W., *The Single Server Queue*, North-Holland, 1969.

Cooper, R. B., *Introduction to Queuing Theory*, MacMillan, 1972.

Cox, D. R., and W. L. Smith, *Queues*, John Wiley & Sons, 1961.

Gross, D., and C. M. Harris, *Fundamentals of Queuing Theory*, Wiley-Interscience, 1974.

Jaiswal, N. K., *Priority Queues*, Academic Press, 1968.

Lee, A. M., *Applied Queuing Theory*, St. Martin's Press, 1966.

Morse, P. M., *Queues, Inventories and Maintenance: The Analysis of Operations Systems with Variable Demand and Supply*, John Wiley & Sons, 1958.

Prabhu, N. U., *Queues and Inventories: A Study of Their Basic Stochastic Processes*, John Wiley & Sons, 1965.

Riordan, J., *Stochastic Service Systems*, John Wiley & Sons, 1962.

Syski, R., *Introduction to Congestion Theory in Telephone Systems*, Oliver and Boyd, 1960.

Takács, L., *Introduction to the Theory of Queues*, Oxford University Press, 1962.

· Computer Simulation ·

Chapter 16

Conway, R. W., W. L. Maxwell, and L. W. Miller, *Theory of Scheduling*, Addison-Wesley, 1967.

Cyert, R. M., and J. G. March, *A Behavioral Theory of the Firm*, Prentice-Hall, 1963.

Emshoff, J. R., and R. L. Sisson, *Design and Use of Computer Simulation Models*, MacMillan, 1970.

Fishman, G. S., *Concepts and Methods in Discrete Event Digital Simulation*, John Wiley & Sons, 1973.

Forrest, P. W., *Simulation Modelling: A Guide to Using SIMSCRIPT*, John Wiley & Sons, 1970.

Gordon, G., *Systems Simulation*, Prentice-Hall, 1969.

Hammersley, J. M., and D. C. Handscomb, *Monte Carlo Methods*, John Wiley & Sons, 1964.

Jenkins, G. M., and D. G. Watts, *Spectral Analysis and its Applications*, Holden Day, 1968.

Kiviat, P. J., R. Villanueva, and H. M. Markowitz, *The Simscript II Programming Language*, Prentice-Hall, 1969.

Meier, R. C., W. T. Newell, and H. L. Pazer, *Simulation in Business and Economics*, Prentice-Hall, 1969.

Mize, J. H., and J. G. Cox, *Essentials of Simulation*, Prentice-Hall, 1968.

Naylor, T., *Computer Simulation Experiments with Models of Economic Systems*, John Wiley & Sons, 1971.

Naylor, T. H., J. L. Balintfy, D. S. Burdick, and K. Chu, *Computer Simulation Techniques*, John Wiley & Sons, 1966.

Newell, A., and H. A. Simon, *Human Problem Solving*, Prentice-Hall, 1972.

RAND Corporation, *A Million Random Digits with 100,000 Normal Deviates*, The Free Press, 1955.

Index

601